IGNATIUS

OF LOYOLA

THE PILGRIM SAINT

IGNATIUS
OF LOYOLA
THE PILGRIM SAINT

BY J. IGNACIO TELLECHEA IDÍGORAS
TRANSLATED, EDITED, AND WITH A PREFACE BY
CORNELIUS MICHAEL BUCKLEY, S.J.

A Campion Book
Loyola University Press
Chicago

Loyola University Press
3441 North Ashland Avenue
Chicago, Illinois 60657

Translated from *Ignacio de Loyola: solo y a pie,* 2nd edition. © 1987
Ediciones Cristiandad, S.L., Madrid

Cover and interior design by Nancy Gruenke

Library of Congress Cataloging-in-Publication Data

Tellechea Idígoras, José Ignacio.
  [Ignacio de Loyola. English]
  Ignatius of Loyola : the pilgrim saint / by J. Ignacio Tellechea
Idígoras ; translated, edited, and with a preface by Cornelius
Michael Buckley.
      p. cm.
  Includes index.
  ISBN 0-8294-0779-0 (alk. paper)
  1. Ignatius, of Loyola, Saint, 1491–1556. 2. Christian Saints—
Spain—Biography. I. Title.
BX4700.L7T4513   1994
271'.5302—dc20
[B]   94-11202
                                               CIP

Dedicated to the memory of
Father Pedro Arrupe
First Basque General of the Society of Jesus since Saint Ignatius

Contents

Translator's Preface

In a brilliant essay, Gertrude Himmelfarb took as a point of departure an observation made by the modernist historian William Sloane in the first edition [1895] of the *American Historical Review:* "History will not stay written. Every age demands a history written from its own standpoint—with reference to its own social conditions, its thought, its beliefs, and its acquisitions—and thus comprehensible to the men who live in it." The reason is, Himmelfarb observed, "any work of history is vulnerable on three counts: the fallibility and selectivity of the historical record; the fallibility and selectivity of the historical process; and the fallibility and subjectivity of the historian."[1] What is said of a purely historical study applies *a fortiori* to a historical biography, and Himmelfarb's principles regarding "the frailty, fallibility, and relativity" of historical facts are nowhere more in evidence than in appraising the life of Ignatius of Loyola, particularly when one recalls that shortly before his death, the founder of the Society of Jesus and author of the *Spiritual Exercises* destroyed the greater part of his diary; that some of his autobiographical reflections were later either destroyed or misplaced by his followers; and that even before his death, his early companions deliberately highlighted certain qualities of his character at the expense of others. Moreover, unlike his contemporary, the simple, transparent Saint Philip Neri, Ignatius was an exceptionally private, taciturn man. His first biographer and protégé, Pedro de Ribadeneira, even went so far as to assert that the first Jesuit in history acted in a very jesuitical way by consciously hiding himself behind masks, thereby giving a certain equivocation to his words and actions. None of these facts makes a biographer's undertaking easy, although they have not deterred scholars and hagiographers from trying—no saint has had more written about him. But the chief reason a comprehensive historical biography of Ignatius is difficult to create is not because the historical record of his life presents a mine-field of problems. Ignatius, the man of mystery, is also a saint and a mystic. Such men demand to be accepted on their own terms or not accepted at all. That is why they are who they are, and that is what makes them such difficult subjects for the scholar, who finds them embarrassing obstacles to his methodology. Saints are not partisans to the permissible prejudices and enthusiasms of a given age, and a biographer errs if he tries to fix firmly a meaning of what they said and did in too narrow a historical context.

The challenge saints present is not restricted to historians. Artists, too, find them baffling. Saints are the concrete images of value-oriented ideals, but it is not easy to ground, order, and integrate such ideals convincingly in realistic forms. Moreover, the artist keeps the values of a particular culture in focus by providing it with whatever tangible symbols it endorses and promotes. But, because of what the saints said and did during their lifetime, they challenge the idols of every culture: their message is broader and more universal than any particular art style or than the *dernier cri* of what is fashionable in the world of illustration. The variegated representations of Ignatius stand as a proof that artists share with biographers an enduring impulse to represent him in the self-image of the moment. Late sixteenth-century images of a solemn, static, and exquisitely refined Ignatius, depicted in an ascetic, intro-spective mode, stand in striking contrast to subsequent repre-sentations of him by various biographers, who selected—and rejected—the extant parts of his autobiography and spiritual jottings. As the astringent tone of the Counter-Reformation gave way to the decorative exuberance and visual mystification of the mid-seventeenth and early eighteenth centuries, the earlier carved polychrome effigies of Ignatius, the one-time beggar, were replaced by gilded statues and lavish paintings of Ignatius, the page, courtier, and knight turned reformer. Bio-graphies of the saint, friendly or otherwise, written during the baroque period and the Age of the Enlightenment underwent parallel modifications. During the early nineteenth century, the age of the birth of archetypal romantic heroes, the suppressed Society of Jesus was restored, and painters and sculptors employed their talents in giving Ignatius a new persona. He was no longer portrayed with a visionary aspect, directing his gaze upward, but as the confident, almost defiant, countercultural realist holding aloft in his hand the *Spiritual Exercises* and the *Constitutions,* a study in black and white, his gaze fixed straight ahead on whatever challenges liberalism, nationalism, and socialism might bring. During this same period, hostile writers presented him as a mad genius, intent on conquering the world. It was an interpretation peremptorily denied by his followers, not a few of whom had been soldiers in Napoleon's army. For them, Ignatius was a military man who had bestowed to the Church militant a corps of "light-armed soldiers ready for sudden battles." Such was the image of the founder that influential, novice masters like Jean-Baptiste Gury wove into the fiber of the recruits they trained and dispatched to a network of nineteenth-century missions. But by the last quarter of the twentieth century, military commanders had fallen out of vogue and veterans of the Sexual Revolution appeared, carrying in their baggage the assumptions and modish ideologies of a new culture. They were prepared to denounce all images of Ignatius that were tainted, ever so slightly, with what Sloane termed the social conditions, thoughts, beliefs, and acquisitions of that part of the past that was now held in opprobrium. "'St. Ignatius of Loyola,' whom we were taught to imitate," reflected one twentieth-century successor of Jean-Baptiste Gury, "seemed to have received interior graces of an order and kind altogether different from our own. He came across as a forbidding personality, icily chaste, intellectually certain beyond challenge, preoccupied with obedience and endowed with iron-willed self-control." And he added, "'Iñigo' seems to me almost another person," because his appeal was to a more deconstructionist, multicultural, "laid-back" generation, "'Iñigo' felt at home with every kind of person and spent his time talking—notably with drifters, women, scholars, the rich and powerful."[2]

Simultaneously, it became acceptable to depict the sixteenth-century Basque in late twentieth-century, New Age, pseudo-Byzantine iconography: a guru, stylized with wide brooding eyes, with an intense gaze meant to identify him with assorted exploited groups in their struggles to defend their freedom against the authorities of state and church. And, in a very short time, the historical Ignatius, who was by now used to procrustian beds of the old-fashioned relativistic relativists, settled onto the comfortable Freudian couch, assisted by the agents of psychoanalysis and psychohistory, who endeavored to make him comprehensible to men and women during the final decades of the twentieth century.

J. Ignacio Tellechea Idígoras, the author of this book, is conscious of the inabilities of both biographers and artists to present a composite picture of Ignatius. Certainly no advocate of postmodernism, he has the true scholar's awareness of the limitations of his own discipline, particularly when it comes to analyzing God's dealings with the human soul. As Spain's premier Renaissance historian, Tellechea Idígoras is eminently qualified to provide the setting for early sixteenth-century Europe and to enable the reader to enter the spirits and minds of the men who lived on the cusp of the medieval and modern periods. In this work he endeavors to chip away at the layers of burnish, paint, and plastic that have accumulated over the years on the portrait of Ignatius so that Ignatius himself can make his true self known. His intention is not to intrude, but to reconstruct the age during which Ignatius lived; to supplement this background with a canon of evidence from primary sources and witnesses who knew the saint during his lifetime, and then to step back and let Ignatius tell his own story through his autobiographical and spiritual writings, correspondence, and code of rules. Tellechea Idígoras comes to his task not only as a historian, but also as a humanist, well read in philosophy, theology, psychiatry, the literature of the sociology and psychology of religion, as well as the classics of European and Indian literature. Yet his approach in this biography is not that of the scholar, the humanist. Rather, he comes to his task as a lover of the subject of his biography.

A literal translation of the Spanish title of the book, *Ignacio de Loyola: solo y a pie* (*Ignatius of Loyola: Alone and on Foot*) is awkward; however, it would perhaps be more descriptive for this biography than the English title selected. Central to Ignatius's piety were two interrelated themes: a renunciation of the world so as to be consecrated through Christ to the world, and the experience of total abandonment that comes from being a pilgrim, an exile, an alien (cf. German *Elend* [misery] in an *Ausland* [foreign country]), and the one who was always alone on the way "for souls." The consequence of such renunciation was a lifestyle of radical poverty, and for this reason the author sees a great deal of Francis of Assisi in Ignatius's spirituality. But Ignatius's ascetical life and vision also bear points in common with another equally complex personality, a lesser-known *peregrinus* (the original meaning is "foreign"), an exile, and an outlaw, who traveled the roads of Europe, almost one thousand years before Ignatius set out on his pilgrim way. Like the Basque Ignatius, the Irishman Saint Columban headed a band of *peregrini* whose intent was "to persist in living on the road as wanderers, aliens, strangers on earth" (*Duret igitur apud nos ista definitio, ut sic vivamus in via ut viatores, ut peregrini, ut hospites mundi*). Like the early Jesuits, this band was made up of different nationalities but their commitment to Christ transcended national boundaries and different cultures and sought to bring about a unity of minds and hearts: "We are joint members (*commembra*) of one body, whether Gauls, Britons, Irish, or of any other people." Columban realized that Christ, who effects solidarity between all peoples in every age, was no longer present as he had once been in Jerusalem; yet present he was in the chair of Peter, his vicar, the center of the universal Church. "Rome is only great and famous because of that chair," wrote Columban in the sixth century. That chair is the center, the still point amidst meandering roads and different cultures from which every pilgrim takes his bearings and finds orientation in his *peregrinatio pro Christo*.[3] In the sixteenth century, Ignatius put into operation more concretely this same logic when he and his companions placed themselves at the service of the Roman pontiff and made a special vow of obedience to the vicar of Christ, which became the "principal and foundation" of their *way*.

In the author's preface to this book, Professor Tellechea Idígoras states that it is not his intention to burden the reader with footnotes and other tools of the professional historian. Such a decision will disappoint some readers who regard footnotes as necessary indicators to available sources, especially primary sources that the author is discussing. But the author's decision will delight others who see footnotes and other techniques of reference used by the scholar as pedantic encumbrances, unnecessary distractions that stand in the way of the author's primary purpose, which in this case is to present lovingly the man who eventually became St. Ignatius of Loyola. I have gone along with the author's decision—although not always without a certain hesitancy because my own training has been to treat footnotes with the formal respect owed to proper historical writing—and have refrained from giving references other than those cited by the author himself. These include references to *Don Quixote* and the *Spiritual Exercises,* and I have relied on no particular English translation for either of these two sources. The author cites frequently from the autobiographical account Ignatius dictated to Gonçalves da Câmara, but even without reference it seems the reader should have no difficulty identifying the source.

The Spanish and Latin texts of Gonçalves da Câmara's source, called *Acta P. Ignatii,* and henceforth called the *Autobiography,* can be found in Series IV, *Fontes narrativi de S. Ignatio de Loyola et de Societatis initiis,* vol. 1: *Narrationes scriptae ante annum 1557,* 354–507, of the *Monumenta Historica Societatis Iesu.* A number of English translations have been made of this *Autobiography,* among which are the following: *The Autobiography of St. Ignatius of Loyola with Related Documents.* Edited with an introduction and notes by John C. Olin. Translated by Joseph F. O'Callaghan. New York: Harper and Row, 1974; *A Pilgrim's Journey: The Autobiography of St. Ignatius of Loyola.* Translation and commentary by Joseph N. Tylenda.

Wilmington, Del.: Michael Glazier, 1985; *Inigo: Original Testament: The Autobiography of St. Ignatius of Loyola.* Translated by William Yeomans with introductory material by William Hewett et al. London: Inigo International Centre, 1985; and *St. Ignatius' Own Story: As Told to Luis Gonzalez de Camara, with a Sampling of His Letters.* Translated by William J. Young. Chicago: Loyola University Press, 1980. I have relied on all of these translations as well as my own rendition of the *Autobiography* in the pages that follow.

As far as references to the *Constitutions* in English are concerned, I have relied upon, although not exclusively, *The Constitutions of the Society of Jesus.* Translated with an introduction and commentary by George E. Ganss, S.J. St. Louis: Institute of Jesuit Sources, 1970.

Finally a word about spelling proper names. As a general rule, I have treated people's names according to their linguistic origins, except in cases where common usage or good reason suggests departing from it: for example, Joan (Catalan), not Juan (Castilian), Pascal, but Inéz (Castilian), not Agnès (Catalan), Pascal; Jerónimo (Castilian), not Jerònimi (Catalan), Nadal; Peter Canisius, not Pieter De Hondt or Kanis; Pierre Favre, not Peter Faber; Francis Xavier, not Francisco de Javier.

I am sincerely appreciative and genuinely indebted to three people in my efforts to translate and edit this book: Brother John Moniz, S.J., of Los Gatos, California; Mrs. Carolyn Lemon of San Francisco; and, most particularly, to my dear Basque friend and esteemed colleague, Professor Estanislao Arroyabe of the Department of Philosophy, University of Innsbruck, Austria.

Cornelius Michael Buckley, S.J.
St. Ignatius Institute
University of San Francisco
February 2, 1994

Notes

1. Gertrude Himmelfarb, "Tradition and Creativity in the Writing of History," *First Things* 27 (November 1992): 28–42.
2. Joseph Tetlow, S.J., "The Fundamentum: Creation in the Principle and Foundation," *Studies in the Spirituality of the Jesuits* 21, no.4 (1989): 9–10.
3. Cf. Michael Richter, *Medieval Ireland: The Enduring Tradition* (New York: St. Martin's Press, 1988), 56–64.

Author's Preface

My name is Ignatius. In all the families of my lineage, past and present, and like countless other Basque families, there is an Ignacio, Iñaki, or Íñigo. My ninety-year-old mother tells me that six months before I was born, she took me to Loyola and dedicated me to my patron saint. Eighteen years later, she generously gave her assent to people who assured her that I would become a Jesuit. Saint Ignatius, liberal and magnanimous, accepted that maternal promise and took me under his gentle care, but converted my mother's offering to Ignatian devotion, as opposed to making me a member of his Society. I am indebted to him.

This book, which certainly does not indicate the extent of my admiration for and gratitude to Ignatius of Loyola, has nothing original about it. It was somewhere near my fourteenth birthday when I first read a biography of Ignatius, and shortly afterward I read the one written by my uncle, José de Arteche. When I was twenty or so, I studied the *Spiritual Exercises* for two years in a small group, analyzing the text and reading the many commentaries on it. I also read Saint Ignatius's autobiography, his spiritual diary, the *Constitutions,* along with Pierre Favre's *Memorial,* Saint Francis Xavier's letters, and a number of Ignatian biographies, as well as the writings of Saint Francis Borgia. I literally blew the dust off many volumes of the enormous collection of the *Monumenta Historica Societatis Iesu,* a veritable mine of Jesuit and Ignatian history, which I used while I was at the diocesan seminary at Vitoria. Afterward, I became a student of the Jesuits at the Gregorian University, Rome, and while I was there became an enthusiastic visitor to the Historical Institute and an avid user of the library and archives at the Curia of the Society of Jesus. In one or another of these houses I benefited from the friendship of renowned Ignatian scholars, such as Pedro de Leturia, Ricardo García Villoslada, Cándido de Dalmases, and Ignacio

Iparraguirre. I made the Exercises on a number of occasions and I thanked God and Saint Ignatius for the fruits of this experience. Many times, although never on the feast of Saint Ignatius, I went to Loyola to spend a tranquil afternoon, and there I found a haven of peace and reflection at the *santa casa*. I feel much at home with Saint Ignatius, and my historical research on other subjects of the sixteenth century has made me feel at home with the times in which he lived. The great portrait painter Ignacio Zuloaga y Zaboleta, a Basque like Loyola and myself, never painted a picture of Ignatius. "I can't feel him" was his excuse. As for myself, I cannot give up sketching him because, unlike Zuloaga, I can feel him.

My knowledge, however, is not enough to rid me of fear before a figure as imposing as Ignatius of Loyola, whose greatness, for various reasons, is recognized even by his enemies and by those who have no particular devotion to him. He once correctly observed, "great learning does not satisfy the soul." In my case, to know a little was sufficient to reveal to me the limits of my knowledge and thereby to show even my boldness in putting into print an undertaking on a subject about which the last word remains to be said. When I consider that my mentor, Father Pedro de Leturia, did not even brave a synthesis of his findings, my trepidation increases. Death cheated him from publishing the results of a whole lifetime spent in patient research on Ignatian studies. But there are many reasons—particularly events from Ignatius's own life—that have encouraged me to take on this adventure. Once, when he was in Azpeitia trying his best to plan how to catechize his fellow townsmen, his brother tried to discourage him by telling him that no one would come to listen to him. Ignatius responded that "one would be enough." On another occasion, he said that "if he let himself be carried away by his fervor and desire, he would go everywhere along the streets naked covered with feathers and mud so that he would be taken for a fool." Even if my humility is not as great, I accept the folly of my present project, convinced that there would be at least one person to whom I could make Saint Ignatius known. If I achieve that purpose, Saint Ignatius can always do the rest. An honest and simple effort is all that is needed.

It is not my intention that this work rival the great biographies of Ignatius that exude erudition and are laced with footnotes. My friend, Jean-Robert Armogathe, the notable Sorbonne specialist of the history of seventeenth-century ideas, kindly encouraged me to put down in writing some personal reflections that have come as a result of my years of reading and meditating on Saint Ignatius and his time. This book is a product of my friend's persuasive powers. Greater scholars can fill in whatever it may lack in thorough and detailed erudition.

My own methodology is this: first, I selected what I considered the most important and significant items from a vast amount of available sources, and then I highlighted those facets of Ignatius's personality that are most edifying for today's reader. Historiography shows us how the portrait of Ignatius has been presented in different ways, following the style of a particular period. Indeed, it is difficult to find the real man who was Ignatius of Loyola, particularly after his exaltation in the baroque style of the eighteenth century and his subsequent defamation during the nineteenth. If during his lifetime there were people who were unconditionally attached to him, after he died, suspicions and attacks against him grew in quantity and quality. The skein of the debate has to be unraveled resolutely and honestly before we can approach the historic reality of Ignatius of Loyola, and this is done by refusing to accept the numerous clichés, both positive and negative, that have proliferated over the centuries. The accumulative process of historiography and documentation has both advantages and disadvantages. Among the latter, the worst is a certain sloppiness in verifying cited sources, with the consequent result that errors tend to become repeated.

Father Ignacio Iparraguirre, an authority on the life and times of Ignatius, has used the term *demythification* to describe the result of serious Ignatian studies that have taken place during the past fifty years. This demythologizing process is aimed both at that type of triumphant literature characterized by an overevaluation of Ignatius's attributes or the achievements of the Society, and the literature that depreciates Ignatius and the Society—a kind of literature that has perpetuated itself down to our own times. The demythologist school of Ignatian historians has attacked the caricatures of both hatred and enthusiasm. Positive and negative mythification, of course, is as old as Ignatius himself. At the time of his death, he was defined by Pope Paul IV as "an idol" to his own, that is, to his Jesuit brothers, while a contemporary learned man, Theodore de Beza, included him among the "hideous monsters" (*teterrima monstra*) of his century, in the same company as Michael Servetus and Juan de Valdés. The figure of Saint Ignatius has attracted many historians, writers, psychologists, and essayists, Catholics and Protestants, believers and atheists alike. At times, their information has been partial and defective, and often it has been imbued with a kind of anti-Jesuit sentiment that, lacking scholarly discernment, is dead set against the founder of the Society of Jesus. On the other hand, there are those who have been dazzled by the holiness of the founder and have wanted to antedate his charisma of sanctity and the foundation of the Society to a period long before either one had ever come into existence.

It is true that, from the historical point of view, it is indeed difficult to separate Ignatius from his Society and from the history of the early Jesuits. However, I cannot overstate the point that, in the pages that follow, my intention is to focus exclusively on Ignatius. We tend to view him and his work from where we are in history, from our own perspective. But it is essential for a historian to put aside that perspective so as to keep his attention on a man named Íñigo de Loyola, who became Master Íñigo and then Father Master Ignatius, and finally much later, after his death, Saint Ignatius of Loyola. During his lifetime he was called by very different nicknames. At Manresa, he saw himself as a sinner; the people referred to him as "the sackcloth man" or "Christ's crazy man," and thought of him even as a saint; at Salamanca and Alcalá, he was thought to be a Jew or an *alumbrado,* that is, a member of an illuminist sect. In Paris, Master Diogo Gouveia labeled him a "seducer" of students whereas the seduced students, who called him Íñigo, considered him a veritable father. For a number of years he jealously kept his family name to himself and, as he tells us in his autobiography, he sought to guard his complete anonymity by referring to himself as *the pilgrim.* Later on in history, he was exalted by a triumphalism that was particular to the baroque period, and he was covered with epithets that resounded with a militaristic flavor, such as captain, commander, champion, hero, soldier of Christ, standard-bearer, general of the Loyola militia, patriarch, pillar of the Church, and such similar terms. Baroque imagery presented him as brave and triumphant, and his image was encased in gold, enveloped in a magnificent chasuble, and it took on an altogether splendid air. How far this portrait is from the real picture of the little man who was scarcely five feet three inches tall, poorly dressed, in bad health, and who walked throughout Europe looking positively despicable during so many years of his life! We are going to have to scrape off these numerous coatings of paint in order to get down to the original wood, to the grain of his humanity and spirituality. To do this, as a matter of principle we are going to avoid calling him *Saint* Ignatius. This we are going to do in order that, with greater freedom, we can follow him, Íñigo, the youngest member of the Loyola y Oñaz family, along the roads that he will take. Then, we shall walk along with Master Ignatius during that period of his life when people considered him a father, even though he had not yet been ordained a priest; then we are going to follow him at a time when he was known as Father Master Ignatius; and finally, we are going to be with him during that period of his life when he was "the old saint," as his secretary, Juan Alfonso de Polanco, described him in one of the letters he wrote a few days after his master's death. We must rid him of all the glitter of the military strategist so that, apart from any flurry and excitement, we may follow "the adventure of a poor Christian." Such is the expression I have borrowed from the title of a dramatic piece by the Italian author, Ignazio Silone. The adventure of this poor Christian covered a period of some forty-five years, from the time of his conversion in 1521 until his death in 1556. During these years he let himself be carried along, to where he did not know, and in doing so, he became a founder of a religious order as well as a saint, officially recognized as such by the Church half a century after his death.

Ignatius has been called "a man of the Church." But the term must not be used anachronistically because it has different connotations when applied to the Íñigo who was baptized at Azpeitia; the adolescent, who was a tonsured cleric; and to the young man, who, after his conversion, went off to help souls. The term is not exactly the same when applied to Ignatius the priest, who persisted in his efforts to live and die in the Holy Land, and to him who became a faithful servant of the pope. For many years Ignatius lived as an outsider *within* the Church. He was a solitary, and the great tensions that so affected the life of the Church of his day touched him not at all. The sense of belonging to the Church and the responsibility that this belonging entailed dawned on him gradually and, as a result, took on new aspects at different times of his life. He lived an interior life, and he invited those with whom he came in contact to follow the road that led to the interior of the soul. While Europe was on fire as a result of religious dissensions, Ignatius obstinately dreamed of going to the Holy Land. It was only after this dream became impossible to realize and after he had attached himself to the services of the Roman pontiff that the full dimension of the Church and his consequent plans took on a complete and definitive form.

The challenge of writing a book such as this is that one finds oneself in a thick forest of factual information through which one must search out a path, select some materials and reject others, unmask old stereotypes, demythologize figments of the imagination, be true to the spirit of the age, and, all the while, remain in the company of a close-tongued, guarded Basque who was mysterious and enigmatic. The enigmas and mysteries, however, were not those about which Ignatius's adversaries speak. Rather, they resulted from his determined desire to cover with a veil of silence, which he lifted only on rare occasions, the real secret of his life, namely, God and what that reality meant to him in his life. Loyola added an even deeper silence, a desire of almost chaste reserve to this unutterable reality that all the mystics emphasize as part of their experience. He spoke more readily of contacts with God during the early part of his life and of intimate communications with God during the latter part of his life. He would hint at these communications in disjointed phrases. His followers used to spy on him during his later years, hoping to plumb the depths of his memory and noting down his words and expressions. After his death, his secretary, Juan Polanco, observed that Ignatius was in the habit of hiding the secret graces he had received from God and that the only time he would ever mention them was for the sake of edification. Another privileged observer, Pedro de Ribadeneira, described him as "one who knew how to hide his own virtue." As we shall see, others who were close to him during his life confirmed these observations about his personality, while adding some of their own observations about who he was.

This particular Ignatian trait of studied silence can discourage his most conscientious biographers. Given this fact, how can a biographer burrow his way into the mystery of Ignatius's personality other than *through* those things that he has in some way or another exteriorized? The biographer can only stealthily join the group that spied on Ignatius when he was alive, and then eagerly study everything these spies wrote about him. The biographer can also read between the lines of Ignatius's writings and even analyze his handwriting, but neither practice will enable him to penetrate with facility the depths of Ignatius's personality. The tenacious defender of the citadel of Pamplona's castle defended the citadel of his own soul from the gaze of curious onlookers, opening passages or breaches only to those who are disposed to subject him to a prolonged siege.

Doubts, as much as the boldness of my enterprise, assail me. In a similar situation, Loyola "spurred his horse" and charged on to Pamplona in order to try the impossible. I shall imitate him in the pages that follow, at least in this one exploit of his career. The classical writers always invoked one of the muses before beginning their adventures. How shall I imitate them? What Muse shall I invoke? Calliope, the Muse of epic poetry? Melpomene perhaps? She is the Muse who presides over tragedy, and could therefore relate to my personal situation. I think I shall opt to remain on level ground, imitating Ignatius's realism, and for my protecting mascot I shall take the little beast he left at Azpeitia after his brief sojourn there in 1535. His fellow countrymen showed the respect and veneration they had for him, who had been with them for only a few months, in a rather remarkable way. They tolerated this little pony's wanderings into the fields of grain, leaving it to remain there as long as it pleased. Had this animal belonged to the powerful Loyola family, it would have been a different matter altogether, but the pony had brought back the converted Íñigo to the people of Azpeitia, and so it was given special privileges. In 1552, Father Miguel Ochoa, who is sometimes called Navarro because he was from Navarre, wrote a letter to Ignatius telling him that he had visited the small hospice where Ignatius had stayed for those few months while he was in Azpeitia. "We saw the same pony, Father, that you left at the hospice seventeen years ago. It is now very fat and gentle and it serves the hospice well. It enjoys a privileged role in Azpeitia for whenever it goes into the grain fields, the people look the other way." So, if the veneration given to the saint extended to what he sat on, that is, the humble little horse that brought him from Paris to Azpeitia, he whose intent is to bring the dear image of Saint Ignatius from this corner of the Pyrenees to Paris hopes for a similar consideration!

Ituren (Navarre) July 4, 1980

Contrary to the demands I make on my own students in my courses in Historical Methodology, the preceding introductory pages were written before the book itself. More than a prologue, they are meant as a declaration of intent, which, reread at the end of my work, merit the protocol statement *Vidimus et approbamus,* or as the Roman formula at old law proceedings put it: "and the witness is not able to say more."

Ituren (Navarre) July 31, 1982
Feast of Saint Ignatius of Loyola

Introduction:
Fantasies
and
Sources

Were Saint Ignatius to return today incognito to his native land, as he did in 1535, he would have a hard time recognizing the town where he was born. Where are the winding medieval streets, the city walls, the tower of the parish church that he once knew? At least the restored palace of Emparan would remind him of a name that was associated with his own family. There is also a new building, the convent of the Sisters of the Immaculate Conception, and even though in the town they are referred to as the old nuns, *monja xarrak,* he would be the only one who knew that their original convent had been built at the end of the fifteenth century. The magnificent house of the Anchietas, built in that foreign *mudéjar* style, is there too. It does not go back to his time either, but the name Anchieta would bring back dark memories of antagonisms that had led to bloodshed. If he entered the parish church, he would find the old baptismal font now restored, and near it there is an inscription capable of shaking his soul: *Emenchen batiatuba naiz,* "Here I [Ignatius of Loyola] was baptized." Wandering through the oldest section of the inner city, which today has been enlarged and surrounded by ugly factories, he would come across a street named Calle de San Ignacio. If curiosity should prompt him to ask passersby who the street was named after, some might show a certain enthusiasm and devotion for this countryman of theirs; others might register indifference, dislike, or, what is the strangest of all, disdain because he had been a Basque. That he would be slighted and rejected by strangers would be painful but understandable, but to be despised by his own countrymen . . . !

Disappointed, he would now make his way out of the town and would head toward Loyola, the house where he was born and for centuries the cradle of his ancestors. The valley yet retains the greenery of ages past and above it, immovable and passively defying the centuries, stands Mount Izarraitz. But where is the hermitage of Olatz, before whose shrine of the Virgin Mary he used to pray, and where is the giant oak that once rose from the thick woods marking the location of his manor house tower? What is that huge graystone structure with the magnificent cupola built by Francisco de Ibero y Odriozola rising up before him? He had always been the pilgrim and so once again he would keep secret his name, as pilgrims do, and enter this splendid basilica. Housed high in the niche above the central altar is the statue of Saint Ignatius, his own likeness cast in hundreds of pounds of silver, an eighteenth-century gift from the Guipúzcoan Company of Caracas. He would be bewildered and confused by all of the changes he saw and would fall in line with a crowd of weary tourists. They would cross the portico of the basilica to visit one of the "musts" on the tour. It is called the *santa casa*. Suddenly his heart would begin to beat faster because there they are—the unmistakable walls of his home, the solid rocks, the carved coat of arms, and the brickwork upper stories that his grandfather Juan built after the king had ordered the towers and fortifications razed as a punishment for his grandfather's rebelliousness. Two statues set in a patio, new to him, would also be familiar and immensely suggestive. One portrays a knight standing erect and dressed in heavy armor and the other some soldiers carrying a wounded man on a litter. A dog in this second group is giving the invalid a warm welcome home. Ignatius would remember the dog's name and what company it was to him during his long, lonely hours of seclusion.

Stepping in line with the flow of tourists, he would walk over the threshold of *his own* house where he would stop and listen to the patter of the guides. Everything would be about him, always him. Ignatius and his family would be the center of all their talk, except the guides would not discuss his own flesh-and-blood family even though they had been very prominent. Instead, they would speak of members of his spiritual family. He would see references to them everywhere—in statues, relics, stained glass windows, and in a chapel where the kitchen had been a large number of them are depicted as grouped under the mantle of the Blessed Virgin. The kitchen served as the place for telling stories during the long winter nights as chestnuts crackled on the *tamboril*. But no matter how much information the guides could possibly give, what could they possibly say about Ignatius, his family, and his beloved companions that he did not already know infinitely better? What would interest him now would be those things that he once knew: the lineaments of his old home that lay hidden behind artistic statuary and brocades; the heavy beams under which now stood chapels with magnificent altars; and the chestnut- or oak-carved beds, the heavy chests and armoires that he could still picture in his mind's eye. He would have no difficulty recognizing the delightful painting of the Annunciation that Queen Isabella had given to his dear sister-in-law, Magdalena de Araoz, who had been like a mother to him during his convalescence after the wounds he had received at Pamplona. He would experience a greater surge of emotion if he went up to the upper story of the house that was so full of memories and would look at the statue of the young convalescent with his eyes raised from the book he has been reading to gaze at a little wooden statue of the Blessed Virgin. How poorly it resembled what he had really seen. But the fact was, this was the room where his adventure had begun. Through the small windows he could again contemplate Izarraitz, which remained ever as it was, even with the passage of so many years. The sight of it would bring to mind more vividly his past experiences. It was within these walls that he had been born anew. It had been a slow, difficult birth into a life that would not be directed by a compass of his own making. Up until that moment, everything he had previously experienced, all those many years, had been emptiness, illusion, swirls of smoke that the wind blew away once he resolutely burned what until then he had treasured. The dreams he had nurtured during the long evenings spent in the solitude of this room had marked his life, because from that time on he was free, his life truly became his own. More exactly and closer to reality, after that his life did not belong to himself but to Another, to the One who would take him where he never dreamed of going during those fervent hours when he had been planning so many changes and considering so many projects. After all, where did this man who contemplated entering the Carthusians finally end up? Georges Bernanos summed it up so well when he observed that few men have lived lives like Ignatius of Loyola.

Leaving this room and going down the stairs he would suddenly feel a strange anxiety. Every corner of this place would bring back so many memories, but none would evoke the picture, the hint of his mother. Her face had never been impressed upon him in such a way that he could associate her with any experience. Could it have been that during his wanderings, in an instinctive and almost biological way of desiring to heal this wound caused by maternal absence, he had been really searching for the mother he had never known? He remembered his brother Martín, who became heir of the ancestral house and title of Loyola after the death of their oldest brother, Juan, during the wars in Italy; and he remembered Pedro, the overbearing and loose-living priest, who became the rector of the parish church in Azpeitia; and Hernando, who had been lost in the conquest of America; and Ochoa, who died young within these same walls; and Magdalena, who had welcomed him in Anzuola, where he had been first brought after having been wounded in Pamplona; he also remembered another brother, Beltrán, and his sisters Juaniza, Petronila, and Sancha. Along these same walls fluttered the shadowy images of the bastard children, who were added to the family with unfailing regularity generation after generation. Pride and lust were the family's real armorial bearings. *Loyola* means "bog." He was fashioned out of the same bog mire as the rest, and he would have turned out to be like them had it not been for what had taken place in the house that he had left behind.

And what was to be said of the cottage at Eguibar that was such a short distance from the manor house, the place where Martín de Errazti the blacksmith had lived with his wife, María Garín, who had nursed him as a child? He owed his life to her, and in owing life he owed everything else because, in the last analysis, it is in life where we become what we are. Was the smithy's forge still there, where he had seen for the first time how wrought iron was given form by hammering it out? He too had been shaped by the blows of life, and so it was that he wanted his companions to be likewise trained. On his way to Eguibar, he would be tempted by unexpected curiosity. Right close to his house there is now a center for spirituality, El Centro de Espiritualidad. By chance, he might ask a Jesuit priest what this place was all about and the priest might give him a thorough explanation of the different activities that the center supported. It was, he would say, a house designed to radiate spirituality; a person could make an "updated" version of Saint Ignatius's Spiritual Exercises here, and this was the place where the review with the strange name *Manresa* was published. The priest's presentation might leave the visitor speechless and profoundly touched; as he was reflecting on what he had heard, his mind would race back in time. He would look into the center's library, and the people in charge would leave him alone to browse. Once again he would find himself the object of so much writing, but what could they tell him that he did not already know? His heart would beat faster when he gazed down on some familiar titles of the works before him: the *Spiritual Exercises,* the *Formula of the Institute,* the *Autobiography,* the *Constitutions.* With pensive care he had once chiseled out each word in these publications. Why did people come along and dress them up with strange, bewildering introductions and erudite notes! They seemed determined to fill in gaps; intent on guessing motives and creating some kind of exegesis of the texts. Had what he wrote really been all that complicated! He believed that he had simply followed his way; it is true there had been some unexpectedly rough and roadless places, but this way was as direct and artless as the rivulets that cascaded down from Pagotxeta's summit seeking, without any vacillations, the call of the valley below and its river, the Urola. Oh yes, for many years he had resisted showing others the thread of his life, but with the mellowing that comes with old age, he finally had given in to their pleadings and revealed some bits and pieces of his life, careful however to keep to himself those matters that defied words. Could this wandering life possibly fill three thick volumes that bore the pompous title *Fontes narrativi de S. Ignatio de Loyola et de Societatis Iesu initiis*? Could so much be said about his simple life, and who were these indiscrete and eloquent narrators?

He would thumb through the indexes of these volumes and the familiar names of friends would spring forth. Unwittingly, he would attach descriptive adjectives to several of them. There was the grave Diego Laínez; the gentle, angelic, and therefore scrupulous Savoyard, Pierre Favre, and the patient Juan Polanco, who spent so many years at his beck and call, and like a sturdy Castilian mule was always overburdened. There was also the enthusiast Jerònimi or Jerónimo Nadal, who for so many years resisted the invitation to become one of his companions, and the favored Luis Gonçalves da Câmara, who was his confidant. Strange, even to this day he could not say why he had opened up to this young man and not to one of his old companions who had made up the little Paris group. After the contributions of all of these came the thick volume of Pedro de Ribadeneira written in beautiful Toledo prose. Was it possible! Pedro was a boy "who never left his side," plying him with questions that were not considered offensive, due to his youth and lively temperament. The pilgrim could not resist skimming through the foreword of Pedro's biographical work. He found the introduction stilted and wordy. Certainly, the author had been anything but that when he himself had received him into the Society.

He would skip through a few more paragraphs and it was a good thing he was alone because when he came to this section of what Pedro had written, he would be overwhelmed by emotion. The author stated in the prologue of his work that his effort was "a pious and dutiful appreciation, a delightful memorial, and a sweet recollection of that blessed man and father of mine who begot me in Christ, who fostered and reared me, through whose pious, devout tears and ardent prayers, I confess to have made me the insignificant person I am." He then went on to say that he was in a most advantageous position because he alone could assert: "I can recount what I heard, saw, touched with my own hands about our B[lessed] Father Ignatius, who from my earliest days reared me close to himself . . . inside and outside of the house, within the city and away from it, I was never away from his side, accompanying him, writing for him and serving him on every occasion I could, noticing all his manners, sayings, and actions." To say the least, the subject of Ribadeneira's biography would be deeply grateful to this youngster he had received into the Society, and in the eyes of the pilgrim, gratitude was always the primary quality for a well-bred, proper man and a true Christian. This Ribadeneira was a meticulous and keen observer, otherwise he could never have written what he did in the paragraphs the pilgrim would read here and there in his extensive biography.

The sly Ribadeneira did not stumble where the honest and upright Laínez got all tripped up. Laínez took everything at face value. Our visiting reader would be soundly amused by this definitive judgment his former colleague and companion had made about him. "Ignatius," Laínez wrote, "had many things that made him beloved by his own." Some inquisitive improviser could deduce from this that those venerable fathers, who were examples of discretion, had been spying on him all along; that they had penetrated his privacy, which he had jealously kept to himself, and that already during his lifetime, and even much more after his death, they had fought over how they could rescue with affection and veneration their personal memories of him. After all, love does know better than hate.

As a contrast to such testimonies of esteem and loving admiration, there existed others—cold, distant evaluations that concealed a basic dislike for him. He could verify this as he continued going through the bookshelves that were filled with biographies. There would be many surprises here where he could see at firsthand that, in addition to those who admired him, there were many who were formidable enemies. A good number of these found the secret of Loyola's strength intriguing, and they were determined to set up straw men representing his enigma and mystery so that they could tear them apart. One of these biographers called him a brilliant psychologist who wanted to infiltrate society (Heinrich Boehmer); another categorized him as an integral diplomat who had dreams of controlling the whole of Christendom from his Roman headquarters, a victim of the temptation of power (René Fülöp-Miller). Only a distinguished orator could have praised him as a genius when it came to military organizational techniques, asserting that he was a first-rate general, and then affirm immediately afterward that he wanted to destroy liberty, totally annihilate the human being, and lead mankind to suicide (Emilio Castelar). Another biographer called him "a dictator of souls," a severe man, hypocritical, unsusceptible to human feelings, "not a father who could weep or laugh with his children" (Ludwig Marcuse). He would not understand very well why he could be considered a hero at the service of the Church, a champion and exponent of the Counter-Reformation (Ederhard Gothein), but his astonishment would know no bounds when he saw himself portrayed in other books as a victim of history; a Jewish, anti-German spirit; or an occultist and a closet guru. How could all this be? He would feel much more interest in the ideas of his fellow Basque, Miguel de Unamuno y Jugo, when he compared him (Ignatius) to Don Quixote. What could he do? Should he bring suit against those who had denigrated him? Should he go to the pontifical tribunals or the civil courts to defend his good name or "his rights to his image," as he had done so often during his lifetime? Indeed, human beings for some strange reason did respect that maxim, which he, with a totally different intention in mind, had inserted in his book, the *Spiritual Exercises.* "I should always be intent on seeking what I desire" (p. 76). What kind of mysteries *did they desire* to find in his life?

He would close the books when they came for him. It was time to lock up the library for the day. He would bid his farewell to the friendly Jesuit from the Centro de Espiritualidad and turn away from his native manor house. As he would walk across the broad esplanade that extended out from the house, he would see the statue perched high up on a pedestal: Saint Ignatius of Loyola. A few yards away there might be a crowd of boys playing and running to and fro, shouting out one another's names—Íñigo, Iñaki, Ignacio! Seeing the attention he would be giving to the statue that was so much a part of the landscape, one of the boys might wonder aloud: "What is that guy looking at?" The boy certainly would not recognize who he was. The pilgrim would go on his way, disappearing into the late afternoon sunshine. He had decided that he would climb the lower slopes of Izarraitz. As he did so, the valley, gradually shrinking into the distance, dropped off around him as the horizon expanded beneath the widening sky. A light mist toned down the bluish hue of the afternoon, while Venus was just beginning to shine and the first stars were making their appearance in broad sky. The pilgrim would look up to these heavens and from his heart might come a spontaneous exclamation that in one instant would fuse the centuries together, thereby giving witness to the perduring continuity of the spirit: "How sordid is the earth when I look at the sky."

Through the use of contrasts in a somewhat contrived sort of way, the preceding fantasy has helped us to appreciate better the difficulties anyone encounters whenever he tries to reconstruct the *vera effigies,* the real face of Saint Ignatius, and as he attempts to make sure his efforts do not result in a dithyramb or a pamphlet, for he wants to avoid the consequences that come from both types of these literary models. One has to make an effort to befriend the original image of the pilgrim in order to walk alongside him on his pathway that is full of unexpected bends. In order to do this, one has to choose the firsthand documents, the primary reference works, or simply what historians call in their trade the sources. Afterward, he must have recourse to monographs of recognized quality, and today we are fortunate in having biographies and other excellent studies for our use, some of which are global and synthetic, and others more limited and analytic in scope.

As far as the sources are concerned, we have nowadays the extensive edition of the *Monumenta Historica Societatis Iesu* containing more than one hundred huge volumes, many of which concentrate directly on the figure of Ignatius. No other religious order has made a comparable effort to exhume all the documentation that pertains to its origins, beginning with the first half century of its existence. Begun toward the end of the last century, the publisher of this series, the *Institutum Historicum Societatis Iesu* at Rome, tenaciously carries on its task. The results speak for themselves, not only in the newly published volumes, but also in a number of updated revisions of the earlier volumes in the series. In addition to being of better quality, these revised editions are also more accessible because they are printed in larger quantities.

Many of the published volumes deal with the early companions—Laínez, Favre, Nadal, and Polanco—and also Francisco de Jassu y Javier, known to us today as Saint Francis Xavier, Nicolás Alonso Bobadilla, Francisco Borja, better known as Saint Francis Borgia, Paschase Broët, Claude Jay, Jean Codure, and others. However, no less than twenty-four volumes deal with Ignatius himself: twelve in the series containing the *Epistolae et Instructiones,* or Ignatius's letters and instructions; two on the *Exercitia Spiritualia . . . et eorum Directoria,* or the *Spiritual Exercises* and the *Directories;* four containing the *Constitutiones et Regulae,* or the *Constitutions and Rules;* and one entitled *Scripta de S. Ignatio,* which is dedicated to the writings of Saint Ignatius by his contemporaries. There are also four volumes of the revised *Scripta* entitled *Fontes narrativi de Sancto Ignatio,* which includes Ribadeneira's classic *Vita Ignatii Loyolae* of 1572. The last volume in this revised series is a recent work (1977), edited by Cándido de Dalmases, that covers the research materials on the background of Ignatius's family, country, youth, and early acquaintances.

Within this enormous mass of documentary materials, the actual writings of Ignatius have a special place of importance. They have been edited with the highest scholarly textual standards and this editing is enhanced by vehicles of great illustrative value—literate introductions to the text and erudite footnotes that comment on it. Of course, everything in the text itself does not have the same weight of importance, even though each detail does have some biographical bearing. Paramount among all of Ignatius's biographical texts is what is called the *Autobiography,* or the memoirs Ignatius dictated to Gonçalves da Câmara in 1553. This work is a real milestone for the greater part of Loyola's life. The *Spiritual Exercises,* the tiny volume that is the key to Ignatian spirituality because in it Ignatius has postulated principles and a plan of action that flowed from his own most intimate spiritual and apostolic experience, likewise contains rich autobiographical source materials. His own life illustrates many of his maxims, and these maxims in turn shed light on real situations that took place during his lifetime. In typical legalistic prose, the *Constitutions,* which he patiently worked on until the end of his life, show what Ignatius had in mind for himself and his followers to do, and they show that his overall plan was being continuously modified in terms of living experience. The *Spiritual Journal,* hopelessly concise and ciphered in places and not even edited in its entirety until 1934—a fact that is in itself beyond one's comprehension—deals with a very short span of Ignatius's life (1544–1545), but it presents us with an unexpected observation post from which we can view the saint's high mystical experiences. Without these short pages it would be difficult to guess how intense these experiences were.

Leaving aside shorter writings, which are nevertheless important, such as the *Formula Instituti,* the deliberation on poverty, and others, let us say something about the *Epistolae et Instructiones,* or the Letters of Saint Ignatius, which take up twelve volumes of the first series in the *Monumenta Ignatiana.* Apart from the letters that have been lost, his edited letters number almost seven thousand. They go from the year 1524 down to the year of his death, 1556, and include every type of correspondence, from very short courtesy notes, to letters dealing with specific business matters, to some pieces that are truly remarkable because of their spiritual content. Some letters he addressed to kings and cardinals; others to devout women in Barcelona; and still others to his blood relatives or to his spiritual children. No matter what their form or to whom they were addressed, they reveal to us an Ignatius who vibrated with life, giving his undivided attention to persons and concrete situations; who was sensitive to times and situations; who continuously stated and applied those fundamental principles that were the core of his teachings; and who commented on the spirit of his Spiritual Exercises and his Constitutions. Since he was a man who carefully weighed his words whenever he spoke, and since he very often read, reread, corrected, and rewrote his letters, he may very well have edited them so that we will never be able to find in them some hidden vein of his spirit.

Unfortunately, we must consider lost forever his youthful poem in honor of Saint Peter; the copybook with the excerpts from the *Vita Christi* he wrote out in red and blue ink as he was convalescing at Loyola; his first spiritual notes; the redactions he made on his *Exercises* while he was in Manresa, and some other smaller items. The disappearance of some of these items is understandable, although it is not easy to account for the loss of all of them. In any case, we do have a considerable amount of extant material of his and we must use it as we trace the steps of his spiritual adventure. Saint Ignatius wrote a great deal, but he published nothing. The first edition of the *Spiritual Exercises* (Rome, 1548) appeared without the name of its author and was restricted solely to Jesuits. Since then, this same book has been edited forty-five hundred times in twenty languages.

We also have the accounts written about him that go back to a very early date. These writings sought more to plumb the depths of his being than to criticize his personality; they were written by his friends, and let us never forget it. They were composed by men who, at a particular historic moment in their own lives, had attached themselves to him, committed themselves to take on his way of life, and ultimately consented to form a compact group approved by the Church. Each one of these men regarded Loyola as his own father. Moreover, they looked up to him as being the father to the corporate group. In a loving way they spied on Ignatius, who was not exactly an exhibitionist when it came to his own private life. They wanted to know everything about him, because they considered that everything about him was pertinent and had a bearing on themselves as individuals and on the group.

At Juan Polanco's request, Diego Laínez, one of the companions of the first hour, broke the ice by "faithfully and simply" putting down in a long letter the things he personally remembered "pertaining to our Father Master Ignatius." He was able to write a firsthand witness account about how the Society came into being. Probably Alfonso Salmerón, his old companion at the universities of Alcalá and Paris and an *Iñiguista* of the first hour himself, collaborated with Laínez in the composition of this letter. These two companions had spent many years with Ignatius, and they had had the opportunity to carry on long conversations with him as the three of them traveled together from northern Italy on their way to Rome in 1537. Moreover, Laínez had the privilege of being Ignatius's confidant at the time of the La Storta vision. Laínez's long letter, which today is divided into six chapters that are composed of sixty-two long parargraphs, was well known throughout the Society and was something like the first official Ignatian cliché during the first years after the saint's death. Although it was written in 1547, it remained unedited until 1904. It summarizes the life of Loyola, beginning with his conversion and extending to the date the letter was written.

At a very early period, Juan Polanco showed an interest in collecting information pertaining to Saint Ignatius. Polanco had been Ignatius's secretary for nine years (1547 to 1556, the year of Ignatius's death), and therefore he enjoyed a privileged position. He had to deal with the saint on a day-to-day basis and meet with him regularly to discuss the many documents and papers that crossed his desk. As an attentive secretary and tireless worker, Polanco was determined to take advantage of his unique situation by devoting some of his time to writing the first draft of a sketch that he would later expand in different versions. He entitled this draft, "The Summary of the Most Notable Things Dealing with the Beginnings and Progress of the Society of Jesus." In 1549 he translated his effort into Italian and in 1551 he revised it. Many years later (1574), he gathered new details of Ignatius's life and incorporated them into the *Commentariola* (1564–1573). The result was a life of Saint Ignatius that served as a preface to his voluminous *Chronicon,* or summary of events that had transpired up to 1549. Polanco, who was really more a collector of factual information than a biographer, corrected errors and filled in the missing pieces from the biographical accounts he found in Laínez's letter and in Gonçalves da Câmara's text.

Luis Gonçalves da Câmara has given us the pearl of Ignatian sources, although for some incomprehensible reason it was not even edited and published until 1904. We shall use it frequently in our text because it is called, and not without reason, the *Autobiography,* and has been translated into Latin, and just about every other modern language. The genesis of this work is, in a way, surprising. One should read the author's preface slowly, for it is here that he gives the background of the day he never dreamed would ever dawn, the day when Ignatius decided to give him the details of his life's story. Gonçalves da Câmara was a Jesuit of the second generation. He was born on the island of Madeira, where his father was the governor, and, in 1535, he studied liberal arts in Paris; however, he did not become a Jesuit until 1545, and when he did so he entered the Society in Portugal. Pierre Favre, who had been a fellow student with him at Sainte-Barbe, was the one who encouraged his vocation and when the two met again at the College of Coimbra in Portugal, years after they had left Paris, they became fast friends. Meanwhile, Luis had become a specialist in Latin, Greek, and Hebrew, but despite his academic accomplishments, he filled out his novitiate days in Valencia, attending to the sick and dying at the local hospital.

In the beginning of 1547 he again met Favre, this time in Madrid. On this occasion he wrote that "It seemed to me that there could be no other man in the world who could be so God-filled as he. I was so convinced of this that when later on I heard people speaking of the wonderful experience that came from their dealings with Father Ignatius, I took what they said on faith." In other words, he created a lofty ideal of Ignatius, and the fact that the object of his admiration lived far away only encouraged him to see Ignatius as an even greater pattern of perfection, so much so, in fact, that in a letter he wrote to Saint Ignatius in 1552, he addressed him as "my Father and my God on earth." His burning and deeply rooted desire to meet and to come to know Saint Ignatius was rewarded when he was chosen by the visitor, Father Miguel de Torres, to go to Rome and give an account to the general of the state of the Society in Portugal. Seeing the flesh and blood Ignatius face to face in no way dimmed the idealized image of him that he had created. In fact, it enhanced it; he wrote that from that moment on, Favre seemed to be "a child when compared to our Father." He came to Rome on May 23, 1553, and left the city to return to Spain and Portugal on October 23, 1555. It was to this newcomer, however, that Ignatius revealed the secrets that his old friends had yearned so badly to know.

This miracle did not take place all at once. But first some background: two years earlier, Nadal had surprised Loyola at a time when the latter was apparently wrapped up in some kind of ecstasy or rapture. Loyola said to him, "Just now I was higher than heaven." The meaning was mysterious, and all indiscreet efforts on Nadal's part to find out exactly what such a phrase meant and what was behind Ignatius's experience came to naught because Loyola changed the conversation and proceeded to talk about something else. But Nadal wanted to make a breach in this wall of secrecy erected by the other man, and so later on he confronted him. Ignatius reminded Nadal that God had already granted him the three graces he had asked to be given before he left this world; namely, the approval of the Society, the approbation of the *Spiritual Exercises,* and the completion of the final draft of the *Constitutions.* Under these circumstances, Nadal asked, was it not reasonable for Ignatius to believe that his death was not far off? It was obvious to anyone who looked at Ignatius that his health was definitely showing signs of deterioration. Why could he not be obliging enough "to tell us how the Lord has guided him from the beginning of his conversion"? Such an explanation, he said, could serve as a testament, a paternal instruction to members of the Society. Loyola gave business reasons as his excuse for not cooperating; moreover, he said he had neither the inclination nor the desire to comply. He added that he did not want to oblige what may have been purely human curiosity, but that he would change his mind if he could be persuaded that God was asking him to sacrifice his privacy.

A year later, Nadal asked him if he had done anything about the matter they had discussed. "Nothing," was his reply. It was the laconic answer of a man taken up with other affairs. As the years passed, all of Nadal's insistent solicitations continued to fall on deaf ears. Later on, Nadal seemed to stress the fact that it was his insistence that finally caused Ignatius to open up to Gonçalves da Câmara. But this was a piece of information he learned from Gonçalves da Câmara, not from Ignatius. Before he was aware of this detail, however, Nadal was forced to resign himself to accept the fact that Ignatius had given his young friend the greater measure of trust, and that from that point on, Nadal's role was to encourage the Portuguese to pry out of Ignatius his deepest guarded secrets.

With unabated simplicity Gonçalves da Câmara describes the circumstances surrounding the extraordinary day when Ignatius opened up. He described the event in his preface to the *Autobiography*. Although the accuracy of the document as a whole is a testimony to the recorder's excellent memory, the factual details he gives are enhanced by his affection for the narrator. It all began "one Friday morning, August 4, the vigil of Our Lady of the Snows, in the year 1553, while the Father was in the garden near the house or apartment known as that of the duke," so called because Francis Borgia, while he was still the duke of Gandía, took up lodgings there when he visited Rome during the Holy Year of 1550–1551. It was in this setting that the miracle came about simply, unexpectedly, perhaps because at the time Gonçalves da Câmara was not asking Ignatius for anything, but was giving him an account of some matters pertaining to his own soul. He confided to Ignatius that he constantly had to fight against vainglory. His family's rank, his natural gifts, the studies he had completed, and the reputation he enjoyed at the court in Lisbon—all of these things worked together to make it more difficult for him to have a low opinion of himself. Gonçalves da Câmara did not realize at the time that he was touching a nerve, though now dead, that once had been exceedingly raw for Ignatius himself. The older man gave the younger some advice and encouraged him, and then he made an unexpected revelation about his own past. He confessed that for two years he too had had to struggle against the temptation of vainglory. This is what prompted him to conceal his name when he was about to set sail from Barcelona to Jerusalem in 1523. In other circumstances he had acted in a similar way. The anecdotes he shared with Gonçalves da Câmara on that event were extended and detailed and went back to distant places and to times gone by. Vainglory, Loyola said, was an immature temptation that never again disturbed the peace of his soul. By speaking about such matters, Ignatius was betrayed by his own subconscious, but at the same time, he realized that this totally spontaneous action on his part had done a great deal of good for his confidant. Had not similar small and rare peepholes into his soul been the reason why he was able to attract others, way back in those distant days of Manresa, Alcalá, and Paris? His natural unwillingness to reveal himself to others began to weaken. Perhaps by that time he had come to realize that his life did not belong exclusively to himself.

Two hours after his conversation with the young Jesuit, Ignatius, Polanco, and Gonçalves da Câmara were at the dinner table. On this occasion the normally taciturn Ignatius surprised everyone present by his loquaciousness. He told them about his meeting with Gonçalves da Câmara in the garden. He went on to say that he had later reflected on their conversation in his room where God inspired him to see where his duty lay in this matter. He said that he was now going to honor the special requests Nadal and others had repeatedly made of him. At long last, "he was now determined to do it." Gonçalves da Câmara continued his account of the event, and speaking of Ignatius, he wrote: "He was determined to narrate all that had happened in his soul up to the present time, and he decided that I was to be the one to whom he would reveal these matters." For Loyola, a *determination,* an explicitly stated decision that came from making up one's mind, was always a very serious matter indeed. Eleven times in the *Spiritual Exercises* he used the word *determination* in its different forms to describe decisions that call for a commitment. This new "determined intention" gave him another reason to go on living. He was accustomed to thinking that he had very few days of life left. Moreover, whenever someone would say that he thought a project would take more than two weeks to complete, Ignatius would ask: "What's that? Do you think you will live that long?" Now, on this occasion, he announced to everyone at the table that he expected to live for three or four months in order to complete "this thing."

Oh, Ignatius, what are you doing? You who are such a prudent and reliable man, so resolute in carrying out your promises, you who never leave for tomorrow the promises you can carry out today—what are you doing now? Remember, you tight-lipped Basque, this time it is not a question of performing exploits, doing deeds, or making changes; now it means dealing with words, hard, straight words, and *that thing* you are going to do consists in revealing your inner self! For once, you are going to be slow in carrying out your promise. But your companions have already taken you at your word. Your word—ordinarily that means a project almost already carried out.

Beginning the very next day, the sensitive Portuguese is going to come making his request and Ignatius will have to accept the fact that each day that man is going to remind him of that solemn promise he made. Ignatius will say that he is very busy with other matters, that he wants to be reminded of *this thing* every Sunday. Weeks will pass without his even making a start. Ever since that hour when he gave his word, his friends have been looking at him in an inquisitive, imploring way; they have become living, silent reminders to him of what he announced in that moment of weakness. And they do not disguise their fear. Father Ignatius is in very poor health, in the care of the doctors; he has weakened considerably during the past two months and his friends fear that he is about to leave them forever. Did he not realize that people were conjuring up plans on what they should do, that they were trying to get his old companion, Simão Rodrigues, to come up to Rome as fast as he could so that he might see his sainted friend before he died? Ignatius's silence, which seemed to have lasted an eternity, was at last broken in September. Finally, he called for Gonçalves da Câmara, who reports, "He began to tell me about his entire life."

During the course of a month they met on three or four occasions. Loyola relived and told his past with such astounding clarity that "it seems that the whole past is made present to the listener." Loyola gave a detailed account to the silent Portuguese who admired him so much, of "his youthful escapades clearly and distinctly, in full detail," just as if he were repeating the old general confession that he had written out at Montserrat, the one that had taken him three whole days to recount to the confessor. During this block of time with Gonçalves da Câmara, Ignatius carried his story up to his first days in Manresa. Questions were not necessary because he did not fail to relate whatever was essential in his story.

Gonçalves da Câmara wrote down the points quickly, first in a sketchy manner and afterward, when he had returned to his own room, in greater length. He tried not to write a single word other than those he had heard from Ignatius himself. He felt, however, that in places he was not able to explain the force of some of Ignatius's words. But very shortly, this happy beginning was interrupted, and, with a desperate tenacity, Ignatius turned to other affairs. From then on, all sorts of excuses to postpone future meetings managed to crop up— sickness, various matters of business that demanded immediate attention, the financing of the Roman College, and the Ethiopian affair, to name but a few. Meanwhile, the months followed one another in rapid succession.

Nadal returned to Rome in October 1554, a full year after Ignatius had interrupted his narrative. He was happy that the project had already gotten under way, and he encouraged Gonçalves da Câmara to keep after Ignatius and to gently prod him to continue what he had begun. Nadal told Gonçalves da Câmara that Ignatius was really *founding* the Society by this autobiographical account. Ignatius resumed the narration on March 9, 1555. The death of Julius III, the very short pontificate of Marcellus II, the election of Paul IV, the summer heat, and pressing business matters all had the effect of making the months race by without any advancement in the narrative. On top of all of these delays, Gonçalves da Câmara was told that he was soon going to be sent to Spain. As a result of this contingency, he made an appointment, on September 22, to meet Ignatius in the small red tower, a recently purchased building that acted as the infirmary, where he "strongly urged" him to finish what he had promised to do. A minor incident put an end to that day's dictation. Again, Gonçalves da Câmara put pressure on him and this time his perseverance bore good results. Ignatius dictated his narrative as he paced the floor. He became annoyed when the young recorder got nearer and nearer to him in an effort to capture his facial expressions. Gonçalves da Câmara's point was that whenever he contemplated Ignatius's face, the light of God flooded his soul and lifted up his spirits. Ignatius warned him several times that he should observe the rule in the Society that calls for one to keep a certain modesty of the eyes. On one occasion Ignatius even stopped him short from what he was doing and then walked away.

Ignatius resumed his monologue a short time later and with a certain haste. The hour for Gonçalves da Câmara's leave-taking was drawing near, but on the very eve of his departure from Rome he was still at work on his project. He did not even have time to put his last draft into a finished form. This he did en route and while he was in Genoa; but because there was no secretary available there who could take dictation in Spanish, he had to recompose what he had written and dictate the last part of the *Autobiography* in Italian. This took place in December 1555. Gonçalves da Câmara then sent back the last pages of Ignatius's short tale to Rome and he continued on his journey to Spain. By that time, copies of the first and most extensive part of the *Autobiography* were already in circulation. If we are to believe Ribadeneira, Saint Ignatius knew of their existence because he had ordered a copy be given to Ribadeneira at the time of his departure for Flanders. At that date, Ribadeneira never suspected that he would one day be Ignatius's first important biographer. As for Ignatius, he had but a few months of life left.

It is unbelievable—and one is inclined to be suspicious of the reasons—that not a single page of Gonçalves da Câmara's original manuscript is extant, even though many copies, including the early Latin version of the text that was slated for promulgation throughout the Society, have come down to us. How does one go about explaining the disappearance of such a precious heritage, one that was so coveted and so laboriously put together? In the text that we presently have, there are only two lines dealing with his "youthful escapades," which Ignatius had described so clearly, distinctly, and in such full detail. We know that he told what these escapades were all about. Did Gonçalves da Câmara write them down? Did he respect the candor of Ignatius the man, or was he overwhelmed by his respect for Ignatius the saint? Whatever the case, Ignatius comes across as being distressfully sedate in the first part of the account that we now possess. The first copy made of this version is the so-called copy of Nadal, a man who was excessively bent on theologizing the edifying events in Ignatius's life and on trying to make them the mirror of the newly formed Society. As a result, we lose touch with Ignatius *the man,* who showed more of a proclivity to portray his weaknesses than to describe his gifts. Gonçalves da Câmara went back to his ordinary work, but added a substantial preface and appended some notes to the *Autobiography.*

During his stay in Rome, apart from his task as the conscientious recipient of the intimate details of the founder's life, Gonçalves da Câmara began collecting the sayings of Saint Ignatius and selected anecdotes about him. He gave himself to this task unsparingly. The hundreds of personal notes he made, all of which were associated with the year prior to Saint Ignatius's death, were collected in a *Memoriale* (1573–1574) that is an inexhaustible quarry of remembrances. Later in life, Gonçalves da Câmara became something of a rigorist, and so he could have felt tempted to strengthen his own prejudices by citing selected samples from this compilation for the finished *Memoriale.* Whether this is the case or not, this double manuscript, written in Spanish and Portuguese, offers a number of assorted vignettes of Saint Ignatius that have really not been fully appreciated.

Surely, however, the jewel of greatest value is what is justifiably called the *Autobiography* itself, Ignatius's story that Gonçalves da Câmara recorded, because, as Ribadeneira so rightly observed, "It was written almost out of the mouth of our father." We can detect the living authentic echo of Loyola in its style, and indeed, many expressions in this book are what we might call the *ipsissima verba* of the narrator. At peace with himself and having come to terms fully with his past, with all of its shadows and lights, Ignatius keeps that same distance in his narrative that he recommends in the *Spiritual Exercises* to a person trying to make a decision. He writes, "I should represent to myself a man whom I have never seen or known . . . then I would consider what I would tell him to do" (185). In this case, it would be telling him what to say. Ignatius's intention in the *Autobiography* is really quite simple: he does not want to show off; he seeks, rather, to tell us the story of his life, about how God had rescued him from sin. Gonçalves da Câmara is not a modern-day gossip columnist nor is Ignatius a self-centered braggart. The protagonist in his tale is not himself; it is God. Loyola the pilgrim is the object of God's mysterious governance, which can now be viewed clearly from the very summit of his life's journey, at the time he dictated his story. For this reason, Ignatius has no intention of creating his own persona. He employs the same serenity and even-mindedness to describe his vanities, dreams, desperations, labors, persecutions, and failures that he does to describe his visions, mystical graces, and heroic deeds. With startling confidence, he shows himself to be far less susceptible than his friends to the spirit of times so full of inquisitorial suspicions and threats. In his biography, Ribadeneira will cut out some of the details that illustrate Ignatius's independence from the social and political environment of his age. Loyola also happens to be an extraordinary storyteller, direct and descriptive. When it comes to expressing himself he always uses nouns, very few adjectives, and he seems to have a horror of superlatives. His narrative is a literary challenge. The Swiss historian, Eduard Fueter, considered the *Autobiography* "a model of the realistic and intuitive soul, a marvelous tale which can only be the fruit of an auto-observation that extended over a long stretch of years. . . . There are no loaded expressions nor contrived sentences aimed to edify."

Is this true? Evidently there are no "contrived sentences," but this soul-evacuating process on the part of Saint Ignatius can have no other purpose than the edification of others. It is a song to the mercy of God, emanating from a reserved Basque, not from an ardent African like Augustine, who sows interjections and question marks into the text of his autobiography, nor is his life's story comparable to the prodigious Teresa of Avila, whose words flow so freely. His tale is the story of a pilgrim, a man who peregrinates—*peregre* meaning "far from his native place"—toward the unknown, and guided by a fundamental trust in Him who was leading him, not knowing to what he was being led or to where. As he was giving his account to Gonçalves da Câmara, he was in a position to view his adventures from hindsight, to decipher the enigma of his life, and, by retracing his steps from the goal he had now reached, he was able to grasp the meaning of those sure yet obscure steps in the long labyrinthine passageways of his life. He does not recall everything, only those things that are meaningful. He deliberately caps a filter over his memory, whenever it is not the memory itself that allows the many patches of grass along his pathway to fade away, or when it is not purifying his recollections. The Indian poet Rabindranath Tagore observed in his book *My Reminiscences:*

> I know not who paints the pictures on memory's canvas; but whoever he may be, what he is painting are pictures; by which I mean that he is not there with his brush simply to make a faithful copy of all that is happening. He takes in and leaves out according to his taste. He makes big things small and small things big. He has no compunction in putting into the background that which was to the fore, or bringing to the front that which was behind. In short he is painting pictures, and not writing history. . . . Life's memories are not life's history, but the original work of an unseen Artist. The variegated colors scattered about are not reflections of outside lights, but belong to the painter himself, and come passion-tinged from his heart.

Ignatius remembers at a distance and with distance. He is no longer the same person who lives in his memory. But he does not abhor, as Martin Luther does, his generous efforts of the first hour, his penitential excesses as a convert. He contemplates them in a kindly way, as expressions of pure and ardent fervor. No longer does he have the strength for such exaggerated practices, but most of all, he does not think that they are necessary. In their way and at that time, they were the expression of a burning passion for the absolute that sought, through rough pathways, to discover and conquer God. But from today's summit, that is open very simply to the divine—*patiens divina* or "theopathy"—he sees those distant years as his "primitive church," haloed with the charm of an ingenuous fervor.

Ignatius concluded his story with some allusions to his initial Roman activities. From that date on, there were no more mysteries in his life, at least no more external mysteries. Nadal could tell that part of the story. Gonçalves da Câmara also wanted to know a bit more about Ignatius's editing of the *Exercises* and the *Constitutions.* Ignatius gave him small but valuable secrets; however, his labors were coming to an end. Ignatius had more than kept his promise, although there was still something that he was sorry he had not said. One day, just before the principal meal, he called for Gonçalves da Câmara. His expression was even more grave than usual. With great seriousness he hurried through a kind of final affidavit, explaining his motivation for opening up his private life in such a straightforward manner. This man, whose practice it was to consider and weigh every he word he spoke, wanted to assure Gonçalves da Câmara of one thing: he had not spoken too much about anything. Of course, had he done so he would not have been a Basque. But in a few final broad strokes, he opens for us some privileged spiritual depths that are intimately connected with his interior life. Indeed, he did confess something new. He said that since his conversion he had offended God often, but never by consenting to a mortal sin; that his devotion had grown; that now, as never before, he found God easily; and that he enjoyed visions and graces while saying Mass or when he was working on the Constitutions. For him these were like a final interior move- ment, the ultimate consolation he experienced in his process in making decisions; they confirmed the choices he had made. Finally, Gonçalves da Câmara asked Ignatius if he could see, even take a quick peek at the papers on which he was drafting the Constitutions, but "he did not want it."

We have spent a long time on the *Autobiography,* which is something like an Ignatian testament, because this is the cornerstone upon which we build all of our knowledge of Loyola. Right from the earliest days it was used extensively by Ribadeneira, Giovanni Maffei, and others. Needless to say, it is one of the chief sources we use throughout this book. We shall be more brief in introducing now those sources that date from the time of Ignatius's death.

With the circular letter, dated August 6, 1556, that Polanco sent announcing the death of Loyola, a new phase began. It was initiated by Nadal. What Nadal did was to gather up all the known historical data about Ignatius, and then he attempted to hypostatize this data. He did this through his exhortations and sermons in Rome, Coimbra, Alcalá, and Cologne; in his *Apologia* in defense of the Exercises before the doctors of Paris, and in other examples of his writings. Nadal was much more interested in edifying than in presenting real history, and he was persuaded that the life of the dead founder was a kind of fundament of the Society itself. Nadal assumed the role of interpreter of the Ignatian spirit, and his admiration for the founder knew no limits. He gave the Ignatian profile some cosmetic sprucing up; the stereotype of the saint is made more stylish, more exemplary, and it is given some timely finishing touches. In his role as the Society's official visitor, Nadal spread *his* vision of Ignatius of Loyola throughout Europe, and he also broadcast his loving complacency for the newly founded Society, a complacency that is not altogether devoid of a certain exaggeration of Ignatius's attributes. The image of the Ignatius who dictated and sent out messages, of the Ignatius who was still alive in the memory of those who knew him, and of the Ignatius who lived an ordinary day-to-day life now gave way to the new, official image of Ignatius.

The hour for the publication of this official image comes with Ribadeneira. Jesuits, long since dispersed throughout the world, were asking for a written account of the life of the Society's founder that could fix the oral tradition and could supplement the papers and manuscripts that were already in circulation. In 1567, Laínez formally entrusted Ribadeneira, who had lived the last sixteen years in the company of Ignatius, to write this biography, and at the same time the general gave him access to all circulating papers and manuscripts dealing with Ignatius's life. According to some, Ribadeneira had been collecting research materials since 1549, and according to others, he began in 1553. He was not one of the first companions of the Paris days, but he was a skilled writer, and, ever since his adolescence, he had known Ignatius well and was therefore a first-rate authority on the type of life he had led during his Roman years. He realized the fact that his biography would be the official biography of Saint Ignatius. He was a conscientious worker and relied heavily on the sources, one of which, naturally, was the *Autobiography*. When it came to a firsthand knowledge of Ignatius, he could indeed tell what he had seen, heard, and touched, as he himself descriptively expressed it. There is a sense of gratitude and devotion that permeates everything he wrote in this biography, for he wanted his effort to be a partial payment for whatever he owed Ignatius. At the same time, he was conscientious in his observation of the first rule of the historian, which is to tell the truth.

Ribadeneira's work was examined thoroughly by the surviving founding fathers who had had intimate dealings with

Ignatius. A Latin version was finally authorized and published in Naples in 1572. Five hundred copies were printed, mainly for Jesuit houses. In 1583, the longer and more improved Castilian version was published in Madrid. New editions appeared in 1580 and 1584. Since then, Ribadeneira's biography has become one of the classical, absolutely indispensable sources for Ignatius's life, a valuable reference and a book written in a tasteful style. The author was convinced he had said the definitive word about Ignatius, and he was even pretentious enough to believe—and there were others who shared his opinion—that he had authoritatively critiqued the *Autobiography* in order "to eliminate all diversity." He held Gonçalves da Câmara's work in the highest esteem, considering it to be "basically quite faithful" and written "almost out of the mouth of our father." On the other hand, he took it to be "an imperfect thing" that could confuse the reader and cause him to question the veracity of everything in the text, and he even indicated that the saint, "weakened by his old age," had a faulty memory in regard to chronology. The historian Eduard Fueter, along with some other scholars, has given lavish praise to the quality of Ribadeneira's *Vida,* calling it a historiographical jewel of Spain's *Siglo de Oro.* True, its author tried to be objective and truthful, but the saint overpowered him; his infatuation did not permit him to see the interior change that took place in Loyola over the course of time. As a way of verifying his historical methodology, it is quite useful to refer to his compilation of Saint Ignatius's sayings and deeds that can be found in his *De actis Patris nostri Ignatii,* which he began in 1549 and finished in 1566. The same thing can be said for his extensive collection of the same material in his *Dicta et facta* of 1573.

The official image of Ignatius that Ribadeneira had assumed that he had fixed once and for all was later opened to criticism. Some of his critics among the early Jesuits were Saint Ignatius's cousin, Antonio Araoz, who was the first provincial of Spain; the famous catechist, Saint Peter Canisius, who was subsequently named a Doctor of the Church; Miguel Ferrer, a former disciple of Saint John of Avila; Manoel Teixeira, Saint Francis Xavier's companion and first biographer; and Olivier Mannaerts, the first rector of the Roman College and first provincial of France. Some of this criticism had to do with form, but some also dealt with content and accuracy. The Third General Congregation (1573), which elected the Luxembourger Everard Mercurian superior general of the order, was far from being enthusiastic about Ribadeneira's work and asked the Italian Giovanni Maffei to do a biography. It was inferior to the Toledan's *Vida*, but it was enough to embitter the *Vida's* author. In any case, all the caustic and abusive exchange that resulted has benefited the present-day historian. Finally, we have the account of the origins of the Society by the Portuguese Simão Rodrigues, which this last survivor of the original Parisian group wrote in 1577, shortly before his death in 1579. It is a delightful account, rich in details, particularly when he describes the trip the companions made from Paris to Venice in those far-off days of 1537–38. Benedetto Palmio, who had been accepted as a novice in 1546 by Ignatius himself, also wrote some memoirs at the end of the century. By this time the generation of those who knew Ignatius personally had all but faded. They had relied on their own memories; those who followed them were witnesses of the second tier, and these would have had to depend on the written media for their information.

At the end of the century, the beatification process was set in motion. The result was that the vast operation of rediscovering and stabilizing Ignatius's image was given a new impetus. The initial interviews before the tribunal took place in Azpeitia, Barcelona, Manresa, Montserrat, and Alcalá—places linked to the life of Saint Ignatius so many years before. The ultimate result of the process was that Ignatius was exalted and venerated by the Church, but what is really touching about the testimonials is that he still had a light that warmed the lives of the octogenarians and nonagenarians who tried to dig into their fragile memories in order to bring out innumerable details about how, such a long time ago, this saint had touched their lives. The beatification tribunals were set up in Flanders and Italy, as well. The process was about the same everywhere, but occasionally it is possible to extract a golden nugget from the witnesses' testimonials. These men and women represented the last vestige of the saint's direct influence. Now he would be catapulted to the altars. In 1609 he was beatified, and in 1622 he was canonized along with his dearest friend, Francis Xavier, and Teresa, the extraordinary woman from Avila. The mythification was at last solidified and the results would be spectacular. This was the age of baroque art, triumphant, splendid beyond all measures, heroic, and miraculous. Could anyone standing under the glorious vaults of the Gesù in Rome ever recognize the poor pilgrim who walked shoeless over half of Europe?

To return to the details of Ignatius's life, we still have some more sources, lifeless and dry documents, evidential, factual, sober fragments that establish details of his life. About 150 of these were collected by Father Cándido de Dalmases, who published them in his book *Ignatius of Loyola: Founder of the Jesuits* (1985). These include royal and pontifical privileges granted to the Loyola family, wills, matrimonial contracts, faction settlements, and judicial suits of the saint's ancestors and of the members of his family who were his contemporaries. They also include the statutes of the clergy of Azpeitia, records from the Dominican Confraternity of the Blessed Sacrament in Rome, popularly known as "della Minerva," with which he was affiliated in 1541, and the statutes he was instrumental in writing up for works of beneficence in his native town—all of these documents, and many others besides, help us to create an ambiance and to give us a background for Saint Ignatius's activities. There are other documents that have been discovered that simply mention the name of Íñigo. For instance, there is a very early contract (1505) regarding the purchase of a horse, to which he was a witness, and there are also some fragments of the judicial case against Íñigo and his brother in 1515; the permission Charles V gave him to bear arms in 1518; the testimony of Captain Herrera, the man in charge of the defence of Pamplona, who cited the recently wounded Loyola as a witness to the events; the 1526–27 proceedings of the court at Alcalá; the registration records at the University of Paris that give the titles and the dimissorials of orders; the record of his ordination; his plea of innocence in Paris (1535) and in Venice (1537); the court case in Rome that declared him not guilty of any of the charges made against him (1538); the diets forced upon him by his doctors; and the deferred payment to a doctor who treated him for wounds he had incurred in his youth. All of these documents, written in their various types of bureaucratic jargon, bring to life the image of that flesh-and-blood man who left traces behind him that today have been patiently discovered and treasured.

To sum it all up: anyone wishing to do any research on Saint Ignatius at the present time has an abundance of documentary evidence that is also of great qualitative value. At the same time, one cannot dismiss the impression that he is dealing with an iceberg, the visible tip of which is much smaller than the hidden mass. Despite this fact, it is reasonable for one to think that it is possible to understand the real inner core of the Ignatian personality embodied in the saint's thoughts, deeds, and actions, and to appreciate that inner radiation of his that had such an effect on so many different people. Even his handwriting has become interesting to graphologists.

Obviously, the limitations of space as well as our own literary style forces us to stick to what is essential. This means we have to forgo resorting to the infinite number of minutiae that abound in Ignatian bibliographical research and accept the fact that we cannot deal with every facet of Saint Ignatius's personality. We have decided that it is of relative interest to follow in detail all of Loyola's different itineraries; to discourse upon all of the regulations governing the Parisian colleges; to review the financial arrangements of the various houses in which he lived; and to comment on the the lives and times of the countless persons who crossed his path. The same can be said about all of the things, large and small, that preoccupied his thoughts and about his many-sided skills. What interests us is his basic attitude toward God and life; we want to listen to his voice as if it came from the depths of our own selves; we want to be able to contemplate, with his light, our own life with greater appreciation and more peaceful acceptance.

This is precisely the reason why we have to look at him face-to-face, not seeing him from the hindsight perspective of history. We must rid our memories and imaginations of what the French call clichés, those glorious stereotypes we have of him. We have to go back in time; we have to accompany him along his lengthy itinerary, his extensive pilgrimage, without knowing what is coming next. In other words, we first of all have to forget the saint. As Manuel Machado y Ruiz said in his beautiful sonnet to Loyola:

> A saint, but after not being so much a saint,
> so as to be, later, a better one. . . .

As a symbolic detail, I never call him Saint Ignatius. In pure chronology, he was first Íñigo de Loyola, the youngest of thirteen children, who because he lost his mother early and, with too many brothers older than he to claim the inheritance, could not expect life to give him many gifts, knew he had to fight to find his own way. But which way? He himself did not know which way.

Part I
From Loyola
to Loyola

Pilgrim, pilgrim,
You know not the way.
So where are you going?
Manuel Machado y Ruiz (1874–1947)

1
Land and Times

Ignatius was an Oñaz-Loyola—the names of the two ancestral houses that those of his lineage used as surnames. He adopted the second of these names, and as a result, it became known throughout the world. When he began his adventure, Ignatius's brother Martín tried every way possible to dissuade him, reminding him of his dignity and hinting about the greater honors he could confidently expect. How could Martín ever have imagined that it would be the globe-trotter, the disgrace of the family, who would bring the greatest honor to the family? Íñigo de Loyola was a Basque, the best known of all Basques, the Basque who made his name and the name of his birthplace commonplace throughout the world. Many of his contemporaries would have called him a "Biscayan," according to the custom of the time, but he must have made his origin very clear because as early as 1547 Laínez and Polanco refer to him as a native of Guipúzcoa, or of *The Province,* the province par excellence, as Guipúzcoa was known up until the nineteenth century. As a rule, contemporary non-Spanish biographers stress his origins, but there are some Spanish authors who brush over his earliest life with great rapidity, and, snatching him away from us Basques, they place him at Arévalo and then, following their prejudices, they make him out to be a typical product of the budding Spanish empire. They do this as if the distinctive genetic code, the singular familial mold, and the particular background against which we introduce him were of little importance—as if such factors do not put an indelible mark on the personality of every individual at the very deepest level of his being.

The Land and the Times: this is where the story begins.

Land: The term is singular; it is complex, indefinite. *Times* is plural because it does not fit neatly in the chronological charts found in history textbooks, nor is it homogeneous and uniform. What was the news in those days and how did it get to be news? In the consciousness of the people of the period, what was significant about what was happening around them? They did not even have an exact notion of the year when they were born. Their habitual formula, "more or less," indicated an attempt to be precise about someone's age. On the other hand, the times in which one lived took on a number of very different meanings, according to the familiar windows through which men would view passing events. Finally, leaning out of these windows supposes, particularly for the child and the adolescent, that a good deal of attention, interest, and curiosity would change with the passing years. In this biography we are not so much interested in chronological interaction as we are in the spiritual concurrence of events.

A child lives in the present that envelops him and he must make a great effort to conceive of an immediate past in which he did not exist. He acquires directly the experience of time and of its flow by learning about his family's past, by discovering his place within the family structure, and by his gradual identification with what the family means when they say "ours." The Basques place enormous importance on lineage, and this is so not merely because it charts out a person's noble pedigree. The linear family, comprised of two or three generations, becomes something like a short history of the lineage of the whole family extending over a period of time. The children do not say "my father" or "my house," but rather "our grandfather," "our house," "our trees," and "our sheep." Individualism expands into the consciousness of the family. Over the years what could this "ours" have meant, or have begun to mean to the youngest of the Loyolas?

It was the things that were within reach, those tangible and unchanging things that were associated with where he lived, such as the strong stones in the thick walls of the tower house that resisted the attack of the *gamboínos* in the fifteenth century: "and they could not capture it because there was a strong wall. . . ." There was one stone that stood out more enigmatically than the others; it was the one upon which the ancient coat of arms of the Oñaz and the Loyola families was chiseled: wolves that spoke for themselves of dominion, daring, and greed, and the cauldron that seemed to be making a stock from past generations but never knew what it would cook up for the future. Along with the stones were the arms, well kept and polished; the casks; the farm implements; the clothes; and the utensils that contributed to making the family's inventories grow in importance. All of these were duly cataloged in the various last wills and testaments.

But before we get to the family, let us go back to the land, to this great, multifaceted concrete force we call the landscape. Let us look at Loyola as it appeared during Íñigo's lifetime. It was nestled in the middle of a wide and slightly curved valley through which flowed a small river, the Urola, which could barely inch along because of all the different mills and blacksmith forges along its banks. This valley, like so many others in the region, is lost in a maze of mountains and is boxed in, offering us, the viewers, nothing more than what we see directly before us. A brilliant green is the color that dominates the landscape during the spring and summertime. In the autumn, this verdant appearance takes on a golden hue mixed with the warm shades of oncoming fall, and then when winter comes, all becomes muted violet and rust. During any season of the year, on a day when the sky is overcast, everything turns to charcoal gray flecked with shimmers of blue, and then when the thick fog rolls in from the sea and hovers over the valley, or when some passing storm has exhausted its fury and begins to roll on beyond the mountains, the valley appears to be washed in lead gray.

Hills rise up sheer enough on one side of the Loyola manor house. They are blanketed with thick groves of chestnut, beech, and oak. These are generous trees that copiously share their wood, fruit, and shade, and create a veritable nursery for all types of edible fungi that grow beneath their branches. Each year as the leaves fall they become gentle reminders of the passage of time, change, the shortness of seasons, and the hope the future brings. On the other side of the manor house stands the imposing, limestone Mount Izarraitz. On those days when the sun beats down upon it, its bald, bare dome takes on a pinkish shade and gives the appearance of being under siege by the vegetation that has won a stronghold along its slopes. Anyone who scales its summit gains a reputation for courage and is rewarded by a view of a spectacular panorama stretching before him: innumerable surrounding mountains and the immense expanse of the sea. In stormy weather, rain clouds charge in from the Bay of Biscay to gather around Izarraitz's heights, and then, as furious routed winds rush through the mountainous hollows toward the nearby town of Cestona, they all seem to dash down together from the mountain's slopes like an invading army. On days such as these, the mountain, appearing like a majestic wall, seems to take on a dark and somber aspect that borders on the omi-nous. Izarraitz is at once heartless, magnificent, inhuman, tremendous—and almost bewitching. It is mysterious, magi-cal, and behind it each day the sun goes to hide his rays. On either side of Loyola there are these two faces, these two mir-rors of cosmic reality.

Within this natural framework, how could we ever forget the manor house of Loyola itself? In my opinion, Íñigo was basi-cally always a solitary man. The hunger he once demonstrated for the eremetical life was not some passing fancy. He was a man with a capacity to live by himself, alone. Within the depths of his soul he longed for solitude, a solitude that came from his very nature and from those interior spaces stocked with sadness. How else could a child turn out, who had been born in a lonesome, isolated house, standing cautiously aloof from two nearby towns, Azpeitia and Azcoitia, and, as a finish-ing touch, in a house surrounded by a dense grove? "Completely surrounded by a forest and by trees of many kinds of fruits, so thick that one almost does not see the house until he is at the door." So, full of astonishment, did the Castilian Jesuit Father Pedro Tablares describe what Loyola looked like in 1551. We can see the house, situated on a slight elevation and shaded by a gigantic tree, a signal to those who are approaching where the door could be found. Íñigo, then, was born and lived in a world isolated from urban culture: cut off both by physical space and by the distance his ancestors had imposed upon the world outside. It is for this reason that his family background takes on something more than just ordinary importance.

2

Oñaz-Loyola: The Youngest of Many Children

Íñigo had no grandparents to smother him with affection, to tell him stories, to help him get through his early experiences with life, and to show more tolerance toward him than the authority figures in the household. His father died when he was about sixteen, just shortly after he had left the manor house. And his mother? The most persistent investigator of the Loyola family has to admit with resignation that nothing is known for sure about Íñigo's mother except her name, Doña Marina Sánchez de Licona, and the date, 1467, when she married his father, Beltrán de Oñaz. We do not even know for sure when she was born or the date of her death, which most certainly took place before that of her husband. In the last will and testament of Íñigo's brother, Ochoa de Loyola, mention is made of the already deceased father in the settlement of Ochoa's debts, and then, in the acknowledgment of debts and requests to be granted, there is reference to "a vow that the lady his mother requested that three ducats be sent to Guadalupe," and to a skirt that she had left as a bequest. She brought sixteen hundred gold florins with her in her dowry and was the daughter of Martín García de Licona, a man of eminence at the Court, where he was known as Dr. Ondárroa. In the will of the family's eldest son, Juan, drawn up at Naples in 1496, there is no mention at all of his mother Doña Marina. Strangely enough, we do not find Íñigo making the slightest allusion anywhere to his mother. Did he ever have the opportunity to know her or did she always remain simply a faceless name for him? I strongly suspect the latter, and I believe that the intensity with which the death of his mother affected him during the course of his childhood days must have left its indelible mark on the deepest part of his psyche, on what one of Spain's most eminent physicians, the world-renowned Juan Rof Carballo, calls the affective personality, that area that defines what is fundamentally human in us.

This primordial bonding between Íñigo and his mother, or rather the nonexistence of such a bonding, suggests the absence of the protective, liberating, fostering maternal presence that would have given him early direction, basic confidence, and would have opened up new objectives for him. This absence of affective nurturing during his early years could have even resulted in retarded physical growth. Íñigo was a runt, hardly a representative of the Basques, who are considered the tallest of the Spanish people. The lack of nurturing by a mother engenders habits of depression later in life; it affects the way one reacts to and relates with others; it incites vague feelings of guilt. Again, we cite Rof Carballo, who has written extensively on the relationship between psychoanalysis and religion, on this particular point: "Deep within the recesses of his affectivity, every wandering adventurer is responding to the hidden and irresolvable need to compensate for the lack of that maternal nurturing, whose function is to provide the child with affective perimeters." Could this be the key to explaining why Íñigo was a wandering adventurer during the greater part of his life? Then there is the mysterious figure of "the lady of his thoughts," whose identity for Íñigo, as the convalescing courtier, has so intrigued historians, particularly because this lady's rank was "higher than that of a countess or duchess." Perhaps they have not taken into account the fact that the dream of every inaccessible Dulcinea, who herself is a mother image, betrays a lack of affective development in the dreamer. In Íñigo's affections, his mother was substituted for either by his wet nurse, his sister-in-law, Magdalena de Araoz, the good woman of Manresa, or by his more sophisticated benefactors. He would always have to people his inner, impossible-to-be-filled emptiness with surrogate personalities.

Another fact that has important consequences is that Íñigo was the youngest of thirteen brothers and sisters. His mother and father had been married twenty-four years when he was born. We find a chance reference to this indisputable fact in the 1606 Valencia beatification testimonies by Doña Leonor de Oñaz. This lady, who had been reared at Loyola, wanted to make the birth of Íñigo a miraculous event because, she said, he was born of "a mother of advanced years," and also because he was born "thirty-six years" after his oldest brother. Although the number of years between these two births was great, it was by no means that extensive. He was only seven years old when a new mistress took charge of the house of Loyola. This lady was the wife of Martín, his next to oldest brother and heir to the family estate. The eldest brother had died two years previously, in 1496 at Naples, during the wars of *el Gran Capitán,* Gonzalo Fernández de Córdoba, and his third brother was soon to die under the same circumstances.

Íñigo grew up side by side with his brother's children, strad-dling two generations, and dealing with all the psychological baggage that comes from living under such circumstances— that is, identifying with the adults, before whom he felt small, while distancing himself from his nephews and nieces, before whom he felt older. It was just at this time in his life that Íñigo's father decided his son should have "a change of air," and so when the opportunity presented itself he sent Íñigo to Arévalo. But we should not get ahead of ourselves. For the moment, let us emphasize the fact that, in one's earliest years at least, it is ordinarily a good thing to be one of many broth-ers and sisters and to be the youngest, too, having arrived almost unexpectedly. Twelve siblings preceded him: Juan, Martín, Beltrán, and Ochoa, who, after having served in the army in Flanders and in Castile, died at Loyola about 1510. Then there was Hernando, who disappeared in America with-out leaving a trace; Pedro, the priest; his sisters, Juaniza, Magdalena, Petronila, and Sancha; and finally, the two illegiti-mate children, Juan and María, whose names appear only in wills and testaments and who were known to be adults.

In the broad sense of the term, the family spread out to include genealogical offshoots who bore such illustrious names as Lazcano, Iraeta, Emparan, Licona, and Yarza, and in some ways it even extended to include the house servants, who were always a part of the family. More distantly, there were the tenants and lessees of lands, ironworks, and mills, and, closer by, both because of physical proximity and ties of the heart, there was Íñigo's wet nurse, María Garín. Her husband was a blacksmith and they lived close to Loyola in a house that still bears the same name—Eguibar. Her position in the family had not necessarily come about because of Doña Marina's advanced age at the time of Íñigo's birth. It is interesting to note that Íñigo's oldest brother, who died at Naples in 1496, left a bequest of five thousand Castilian maravedís to a certain Ochanda, "the nurse who reared me"; and Ochoa, who died at Loyola about 1510, left a skirt and a woman's cape to "the mother who suckled me." The familial wet nurse has long since disappeared from our society, but at that time her presence evoked powerful sentiments that were all but boundless. María Garín has entered into history because of the generous physiological role she played as Íñigo's wet nurse, but no one ever speaks of the nurturing psychological role that she must have played in his early life. Did she nurse Íñigo at the same time she was nursing one of her own children? Even though we read in Saint Matthew that it is difficult to serve two masters, perhaps it is possible to suckle two separately related infants. At any event, it is in the face, arms, and breasts of María Garín where are forever hidden those ultimate secrets that researchers seek in vain to find in historical documents.

3

When Was He Born?
His Nurse's Account

Apart from the life-supporting service she rendered him, María Garín (and who would have ever guessed that such would be the case?) was destined to play a vital role in determining the year of Íñigo de Loyola's birth. Ignatius's age had been agreed upon during his own lifetime and in the early written tradition of the Society, a tradition based on what Íñigo himself had declared. When he dictated his autobiography to Luis Gonçalves da Câmara, he confidently began with a chronological fact: "Up to his twenty-sixth year he was a man given over to the vanities of the world." This would mean that he was born between 1495 and 1496. From other statements he made, it would seem that he was born even two years earlier than that. At the time of his death there were some fathers, among whom were scholarly masters of the University of Paris, who had doubts about the commonly held reckoning of his age. Their doubts were put to rest when it was decided that the inscription on his tomb would read that he was sixty-five years old when he died, and not sixty-two, which he claimed to be.

This surprising and last-minute change was due to the fact that María Garín was positive that Íñigo was two years older than he had believed, and she would assure anyone who wanted to listen to her that she knew what she was talking about. With that characteristic self-assurance of women of the common people, the tenacious *nutrix* convinced contemporary Jesuits with her arguments. She has also won over historians of our own times, especially since they are now able to reinforce so charming a source with a notary's document. Íñigo was witness to this contract, dated 1505. Now since the legal age required to serve as a witness was fourteen, we are forced to believe that in 1505 he was fourteen. Only the moral authority of his nurse could have baffled the prodigious memory of Ignatius with arguments stronger than the best of syllogisms. She had never studied in Paris, but standing pat with her hands on her breasts, she proved that the little Loyola was two years older than people had thought. She did not know how to subtract so as to fix the year of his birth, but those who knew how were certainly able to do so. This fact is important because it determines how long Íñigo remained at Loyola. There are some who have placed him at Arévalo at the age of seven. Today, we are all but absolutely positive that he went there when he was about sixteen. By that time, he was already a hardy sapling with roots planted deep in his life-giving native soil.

Meanwhile, among his many pursuits Íñigo had had ample time to survey the properties owned by the Loyolas and to say before the Azpeitia houses, the farm houses, the mills, ironworks, fields, chestnut groves, and woods, "This is ours." But this "ours" was relative, because according to the Basque common law, his brother Martín García de Oñaz was the heir and had been the sole master and lord of Loyola since 1498, and he owed his brothers only a modest share called the *legitima*. To be "more" was to have "more"—such was Íñigo's first lesson. But little by little he began to discover that one can also have nonmaterial possessions, like a past, which transcends the human being while it is thrusting its roots into time. The past makes itself known better to the young child through what he hears than through what he sees. No doubt the adolescent who witnessed the 1505 contract drawn up for purchasing a horse had acquired an almost religious awe for papers and the office of the notary. One of his sisters would marry the notary of Azpeitia and another the notary of Anzuola. Perhaps he would have had the opportunity to hold in his hands and contemplate the venerable house documents, those wordy witnesses of past grandeur. Among these were the 1402 privileges granted to Don Beltrán, giving him the right to the parish tithes. Such documents were very old in the eyes of a child. There was also the bull of Benedict XIII, signed at Perpignan in 1415, which referred to the patronage of the church at Azpeitia and there were also papers confirming this patronage that were issued by Juan I and Juan II of Castile.

It is easy to imagine that Íñigo would have fondled the more recently acquired documents from their Catholic majesties that in his eyes had assumed an almost mythical dimension. These attestations spoke of his father, and they contained words about "his many good and loyal services" and they told about how he had placed his person "in danger and peril." These events had occurred in that grave hour when the throne of Isabella the Catholic was tottering. The Basques, one of whom was Íñigo's father, had played a vital role at three key events: the lifting of the siege at Toro, the lifting of the siege at Burgos, and the final defense of Fuenterrabía against the French (1476). The war cry at Toro, *Erru, erru, daca Rey,* had become a legend not only because of the victory, but also because it had sounded so odd to Castilian ears. The rhythm of this cry shouted out by centurion voices was enough to fire up the imagination of the youngster, who would repeat it in his children's games. There were still more documents, and these contained matters pertaining to tenant farms, family alliances, and truces. It was in these records that Íñigo could have learned something about human nature: "According to the different intentions and conditions of men, one can pass easily from affection to discord."

4

The *Parientes Mayores*

Discord was also at the very heart of his family's heritage—
and what discord it was! More than once Íñigo must have
heard about how his grandfather and some other lords
became a terrible threat to the Guipúzcoan towns in 1456;
how his grandfather had been defeated and exiled by the
king, who had the battlements of his manor pulled down; and
how, after he had been given amnesty, he had the upper stories of the manor, that part which most probably would house
Íñigo's bedroom, rebuilt in brick. With the passing of his
grandfather, there came an end to the turbulent and dominating energy of the Loyola family; it also marked the end of
the important houses of Guipúzcoa, the end of the *parientes
mayores,* who were something like the "chiefs of the clans."
Moreover, the demise of this generation finally put to rest the
bloody family feuds. The Loyolas had been a powerful family
in their particular faction, the *oñacinos,* second only to the
party controlled by the Lazcano family, with whom they were
connected by marriage. On the opposite side were the *gamboínos,* whom they despised. "Those of Oñaz would never walk
the streets of Gamboa nor would those of Gamboa walk the
streets of Oñaz; even their dress and garb were different; and
in wearing the plume, those of Oñaz wore it on the left side,
but those of Gamboa wore it on the right." Íñigo's grandfather, Don Juan Pérez de Oñaz, and the other rebellious
nobles had been exiled to a town in the war zone called
Jimena de la Frontera, where the king encouraged them to

fight against the Moors, the enemies of their faith, as opposed
to the enemies of their blood. During his three years of exile,
Don Juan fathered two children. The mother was called
Hermosa, meaning "Beautiful." Afterward, he married Doña
Sancha, who was a gamboína from the House of Iraeta, and
he thereby showed that love knows no frontiers. She bore him
Beltrán, the future father of Íñigo, and two daughters; besides
these, he fathered an illegitimate child—fathering bastards
was a family pastime. However, there were standards. A few
generations earlier we come across a certain Teresa, who was
formally disinherited because she "had chosen to live an
improper and unchaste" life. The poor creature was a woman
who had stepped beyond the conventional moral limits set by
the Loyola men.

As far as morals are concerned, there is no question the
Loyola family had them, and this fact is borne out in the wills
they drew up. Sin was a part of the legacy of the "ours," about
which we have spoken, but also a part of this legacy was faith,
and even before Íñigo wrote out his meditations on death and
hell, thoughts of death and the fear of hell had already been a
part of his thinking. Did he sometimes read the last wills of his
ancestors and contemporaries that we so delight in today?
How thoroughly had his ancestors already put into practice
what was to be his third rule of the second way of making a
correct and good election: "What norm would I wish to have
followed in the present choice, if I were at the moment of
death?" To the delight of genealogists, the names of legitimate and illegitimate children appear in these last wills and
testaments; to the joy of economists and sociologists, they contain lists of the testators' possessions, what debts they owed,
and the still-outstanding accounts payable they left for their
heirs to regulate; for jurists, there are samples of matrimonial
contracts and inheritance deeds drawn up according to
Basque laws and customs; and for those who are interested in
learning something about the commonly practiced ways,
spirit, and mentality of the people, there is a mine of information about how monies are to be given for redeeming cap-
tives, for hospitals, for the parish church, and for the many
neighboring hermitages. There is not a trace of sorrow for
what came as a result of their ferocious hatreds and terrible
vendettas, but there is evidence enough of their ardent desire

to make up for lost time, to look for penitential atonement for whatever was incompatible with personal responsibility. "Let a man be sent to Santiago [de Compostela] in Gallica for the salvation of my soul," said Lope García de Lazcano in 1441. In 1464, his wife Doña Sancha wrote that two people should be sent to Guadalupe, "one [to pray] for my soul, the other for the soul of Juan Pérez de Oñaz." In 1508, Ochoa de Loyola left provisions for "a good person" to go to Guadalupe "on a pilgrimage for my soul." In those critical times the "protection and salvation of my soul" had become an obsession, and this was long before Íñigo would write his famous phrase, "and by this manner save his soul."

Once all the accounts and balances had been made, once "benefits and favors received" had been compared to sins committed, his forefathers confessed there was nothing else they could do beyond trusting that the "immense divine mercy was greater than the sins of the world"; having confidence that "He who nourished and redeemed our soul would want to save it"; and putting their trust in the intercession of the saints, especially the Virgin Mary. They never improvised so beautiful and so many invocations to Mary as when they faced the fear of death. "Intercede for me and be the advocate and the petitioner of my soul before your precious Son," wrote the powerful Lope García de Lazcano in 1441. In 1464, his wife Doña Sancha, invoked the "holy Virgin Mary, in whom [I place] my hope," confident that Mary's compassion "has never failed nor will fail those who with good will recommend themselves to her." Íñigo's older brother, Juan, who died at Naples and had requested to be buried in Santa Maria Nuova, began his will in that far-off land in the name of the Trinity and "in the name of the most glorious blessed Virgin Mary, mother of my Lord and Savior Jesus Christ, who was my lady, my help, and my advocate in all my undertakings, and before whom I now, with the greatest devotion and with all of my heart, dedicate myself to be her slave and servant." His brother, the priest and great sinner, also invoked Mary as his lady and particular advocate (1527), while his brother, Don Martín, the heir of Loyola, conscious of his "enormous sins" sought help from "the immaculate Queen of the angels" and bequeathed many contributions to her hermitages. Long before he was able to read the delightful verses of Fra, later

Archbishop, Ambrosio de Montesinos, Íñigo had already acquired in his own home and from his earliest days that devotion to Mary that he never lost.

This was also the period when the undeniable Franciscan influence was implanted in the soul of Íñigo. The Franciscans had first come to Guipúzcoa in the fifteenth century. The picture of Our Lady at Aránzazu dates from 1469, and as early as 1501 there was a house there of the Penitential Brothers of the Third Order of Saint Francis. This establishment was raised to a canonical Franciscan convent in 1514. In 1503, Juan Pérez de Licona, a close relative to Íñigo's mother, founded the convent of Sasiola. Geographically closer to Loyola at this period of time were the convents of Poor Clare nuns that sprang up one after another at Oñate, Elgóibar, Mondragón, and Vergara. Special mention should be made of the convent of the Sisters of the Immaculate Conception of Azpeitia, which began as a house of the Franciscan Third Order in 1497 and was raised to a Convential convent in 1497. One of Íñigo's close relatives, María López de Emparan y Loyola, played a very important part in founding this establishment. As the nun in the family, she began by being a member of the hermitage of San Pedro, and Don Beltrán, the patron of the church at Azpeitia, made it a point to be present at her profession. The name *Francis* that he had heard from the lips of his nun cousin would not have meant much to Íñigo as a child. Later, when he was at Arévalo he would meet one of his aunts who was a Franciscan nun. But like a seed, the name of Saint Francis of Assisi had been sown in Íñigo's mind at an early age and the day would come when it would burgeon forth to enlighten his spirit.

5
Here or Far Away

Íñigo would open his eyes to the voice of his loving nurse, who would sing cajolingly and with pride over and over again in her heavy Azpeitian accent an improvised lullaby: "*Loyolako Txikie, Loyolako Txikie,*" that is, "little Loyola, little Loyola." He would have discovered the rhythms of nature in this privileged corner that Father Tablares declared was "the shadow of an earthly paradise." The sensation of the flow of time was born with the flow of nature—day and night and the seasons of the year. There was the sweetness of flowering apple trees during the spring and the toilsome work of brewing cider in the fall. In winter, with its short days and its long nights, one would feast on chestnuts. And then there was the wind—the peaceful afternoon breezes that blew in from the south and the gusty winds that came from the north. Tomatoes, tobacco, chocolate, and those beans that to this day are called *indibabak*—beans from the Indies—had not yet made their appearance from the Americas. Sundays broke the monotony of the week, and Sunday meant that the Loyolas had to make their appearance in town where they had their *jantzi-etxe,* that is, their de rigueur vesting house, the place where they, who were ever conscious of their rights of patronage, would change into their Sunday best in preparation for going to the parish church for services.

The liturgical cycle, with its repetitious rhythm—the solemn sequence of Lent and Easter, the festive joy of Christmas, and the countless feasts in honor of the Blessed

Virgin, the apostles, and the saints—all of this seemed more like an eternal beginning and rebeginning. Ever since 1499, each feast day observed in Azpeitia was officially defined and fixed and every one of these was centered around the celebration of High Mass, but whenever there was a pilgrimage—and pilgrimages took place often during the course of the year—the dignity of the formal parish ceremonies relaxed somewhat and became rustic, with the people walking to the numerous hermitages consecrated to the Blessed Virgin, Saint John, Mary Magdalen, or Saint Peter.

This closed-in, tight environment was happy and to all appearances impenetrable; however, it did present some cracks or fissures, as if to call attention to the fact that the world was not limited to a large valley protected by the mountains of Izarraitz and Araunza on one side, and on the other by the coasts of Oleta, Izaspi, and Pagotxeta. What was on the other side of those mountains? Just more ranges. And where went those sluggish waters of the Urola, whose headlong flow swelled during the wintertime, giving the impression that the agitated river was in a great rush to arrive at its destination? These waters flowed into the sea, the sea that went as far as Flanders and England, and even farther—as far even as the New World. Where was that Moorish frontier where his grandfather had been exiled? Where was that Naples where his oldest brother had died, that faraway place where there were so many Basques on hand to witness his last will and testament? His father had told him about the French and the siege of Fuenterrabía in whose defense he had taken part; about his maternal grandfather, Don Martín García de Licona; about Dr. Ondárroa, a member of the *Consejo Real,* who had purchased the Balda house in Azcoitia; and about his kinsman, Artieta, the one who had gotten a squadron together in 1493 so as to follow up on the discoveries in the New World. Artieta had a ship ready for the expedition, but his plans had to be put on hold because he was ordered to transport Boabdil, the last king of the Moors, to his exile in Africa. During these days, the maritime achievements that began in Guipúzcoan districts like Arriola, Mendaro, Lazcano, and others were still being talked about, and very soon (1522) the Basque Juan Sebastián del Cano, the successor of Ferdinand Magellan, would be the first to circumnavigate the world. The new lady of Loyola, Doña Magdalena de Araoz, would have told him about Queen Isabella, in whose service she had been, and the youngster Íñigo would have watched her as she wept whenever she spoke of the queen's death, holding close to her breast the little picture of the Annunciation that the queen had given her before she had left her service. It was also the queen who had most certainly given her some very beautiful books, including the *Vita Christi* and a *Flos Sanctorum*, both of which were written in Castilian.

The world was growing much wider in Íñigo's adolescent imagination; it was peopled with foreign names, faraway monarchs, and wars. In its shadow, notions of courage and loyalty, of service, honor, and fame were beginning to take shape. All of this growth evolved in his space and time. Chronology is a cold invention of people who write textbooks. "Chronopathy" is a sixth sense, a diffused sentiment that develops and grows firm within the human being, like his bones and teeth, and it blends itself with his blood's flow and with the secretion of mysterious hormones.

Íñigo kept up his reading and writing lessons, but rather than mull over the *Flos Sanctorum,* he went off to visit the blacksmiths of Aranaz and Barrenola, where they smelted the iron that went into swords and cuirasses. He felt right at home in the blacksmith shop closest to him, the one owned by Martín de Errazti, his nurse's husband, and he looked on ecstatically as Martín worked at his small forge. He watched him stir up the fire, lay the red-hot iron flat on the anvil, hammer it with hard, swift, well-aimed blows until it took the shape of either a hoe, a weapon, or a horseshoe. Whatever shape the finished product took depended on the intention of the blacksmith. He alone determined what it was going to be. "See that?" Martín would laconically ask. *Seeing,* knowing how to see, was enough to learn the power of *action* with its hard, resistant, lasting results. This was one veritable lesson that remained imprinted on Íñigo's soul, a lesson that appealed to him more than learning how to trace out letters with a goose quill. "We stay here," continued the blacksmith tersely, "but the iron is to go to England, Flanders . . . to soldiers too . . . to your brothers—far away."

Here or far away? By temperament, Íñigo was hungry for adventure and achievements. This factor, plus the force of necessity due to his status in the household, compelled him to consider the alternatives of remaining at Loyola or seeking his fortune in far-off lands. His brother Martín was already the Lord of Loyola and he had heirs. As long as his father was still alive, no one would force him to leave the house, but his father's advanced years were beginning to show; clearly he was declining. Even though that reassuring "ours" would maintain a certain amount of continuity under his father's protective shadow, the familiar hearth was not as protective as he had believed during his childhood days, and there was no mother around to advise him about what he should do. Before bidding his last farewell to life on earth, Don Beltrán wanted to direct Íñigo's steps along a safe path, and so he considered using the influence of his family's honorable name. At last, a lucky star appeared to quell the worries of his old age. No less a person than the *Gran Contador* of Castile, that is, the Chief Treasurer of the Realm, opened the doors of his home to Íñigo and received him as a son. In the Gran Contador's household he would be educated, and from there it would not be difficult for him to obtain a position at court. The Gran Contador's wife was a relative of the Loyolas. Finally, this new place that was situated right in the middle of the Castilian plain had a name—Arévalo. But there was also a price to be paid for going there: Íñigo had to leave Loyola's green valley. On his last night at home he let his eyes slowly take in the blue slopes of Izarraitz; he rested them long on its hermitages, fixed them hard on Errazti's blacksmith shop, and finally, he let them caress the stones of his manor house. That evening, the bells that rang from Azpeitia's parish church and the bells on the sheep returning to their fold took on a different sound for him. He was steeling himself to make "an oblation of great price and importance." Would he end up in "personal kingly service"? It had never even occurred to him that the word *king* could be used in an adjectival sense. Many years had to pass before he would distinguish between the temporal and eternal king.

Such might have been the thoughts of Íñigo on a certain day in the year 1506. He would have felt the reassuring hand of his father on his shoulder, and at the same time he would have lamented more than ever his mother's absence. His father would go to his rest peacefully on October 23, 1507. Íñigo was then all alone, but he was well situated to take on whatever the future had in store for him.

6

A New Home: Arévalo

During the days before Íñigo departed from Loyola, Doña Magdalena de Araoz, who was both his sister-in-law and the one who had taken the place of his mother, tried to describe for him what the fortress of Arévalo was like. She had come to know it while she was a lady-in-waiting to Queen Isabella. But any attempt to give a description of the Castilian landscape to a young Basque made about as much sense as an endeavor to describe the blue of the sea to a young man from the heartland of Castile. I myself was a bit older than Íñigo had been at this period of his life when I first saw Burgos on a beautiful day in July, and to this day I can vividly remember the impression that the cathedral's high towers made on me. On his way to Valladolid and Arévalo, where the plain begins to grow more and more limitless, Íñigo must have passed through Vitoria and Burgos. For the person who is from a region where the landscape is more kindly, that is, a region of small valleys and close-at-hand mountains, the greatness of this breathtaking plain is overwhelming, making him feel totally insignificant. Between himself and the horizon there is nothing for the eyes to focus on; his vision becomes lost in the infinite. A tree is not a friend nearby; it is merely a pinpoint on the skyline, some kind of mistake of nature interrupting the all-surrounding vastness. And the immense sky is either pure blue, luminous, or ink black, studded with stars. As he continued along his journey, what Íñigo saw stretching out before him were Castilian fields that resembled a sea of gold, making the Loyola holdings seem like small garden plots in comparison; his proud, well-built house stood humble and unassuming against the palaces of Castile's leading families. The general impression this journey made upon him was eloquently reinforced by Velázquez de Cuéllar, and even more so by his wife, Doña María de Velasco, who was related to him. Both welcomed Íñigo into their home as a son.

In this large family that numbered six sons and just as many daughters, Íñigo once again became number thirteen. His insertion into the family circle posed no problem because the difference in ages among his peers was not great. The oldest boy was only seven years his senior, while Miguel, Augustín, Juan, and Arnao were closer to his age. Although he fit easily enough into the daily regime of studies and recreation, the process of adjusting to the level of a new and different kind of life would have been more difficult for him. It must have taken some time for his initial, unsophisticated bewilderment to yield before the routine, before what had at first seemed grandiose became habitual. Today, we know more about the atmosphere Íñigo breathed during those ten long years of his life. It was the worst novitiate imaginable for his future life of poverty, a fact that makes the choice he made so much more praiseworthy. Íñigo freely chose extreme poverty, although he had known a life of sumptuous riches. But what am I saying? Íñigo did not choose anything, much less poverty. Someone else decided his destiny, a destiny that was truly enviable.

The home in which he lived, the habitual residence of the Velázquez-Velasco couple, was in every respect a royal palace, and the life he led within those walls taught him lasting lessons about a number of things. He had become a part of the family at a time when they were basking in dazzling prosperity and glory. He was gradually made aware of this fact by simply keeping his eyes and ears open, as the children of the family told him everything during their long conversations with him. Don Juan Velázquez de Cuéllar was an important man. His children could not have said that he had been a bureaucrat who rose to the highest spheres of influence and from that exalted place was well connected with the nobility. That was for historians to say at a later time. The children would only have recounted that their great-grandfather had fought against the Moors alongside the Infante Don Fernando, later King Ferdinand of Aragon, at the famous battle of Antequera in 1410, and that he had been chancellor of the realm, and three times viceroy in Sicily. No doubt they would have said that their grandfather Don Gutierre had been a member of the *Consejo Real,* that he had served Queen Isabella for thirty years and had become the master of the palace where they were now living, and that their father was the *Contador Mayor* of the Realm. They would *not* have remembered that in 1486 he had begun as a captain in the *contino,* that is, one of the one hundred specially picked personal guards of the king of Spain, and that he had participated in the capture of Málaga in 1478. Probably they would have passed over the fact that he had been the intendant and treasurer to Prince Juan of Asturias, the son and heir of Ferdinand and Isabella, who had died in 1497 at the age of nineteen, and that he now served as the governor and magistrate of Arévalo and the lieutenant of all the royal palaces. The young people only would have recounted those events that were more recent and important, such as the fact that their father was a personal friend of King Ferdinand, that he had the king's confidence, and that he had profited from his many favors. They knew that he had been the executor of the will and testament of the near-mythical Queen Isabella, who had paid some eleven visits to his home so that she might visit her mother, Doña Isabel de Alvís, who died there in 1496.

It would take time, months, and even years for a person to absorb the extent of the royal favors that had been bestowed upon Íñigo's protector. Íñigo could not possibly have known all the offices and benefits his protector enjoyed, among which were salaries, church tithes, and the offices of magistrate and secretary. It was enough for him to have realized that this eminent man of great importance was a friend of his father who had requested "that he would give him one of his sons so that he might receive him in his home and so that he might help him through his favor," and later on might introduce him into the royal antechambers. It was not necessary that Íñigo study the domestic budget to appreciate the sweet luxury of opulence in which the family lived. It was enough merely for him to live where panels, paintings, and precious tapestries were ever before his eyes, and where his body had adjusted comfortably to the rich feel of chambray bed sheets.

On feast days, the house displayed splendors that he had never even dreamed of before. How could one ever forget the elegant banquets Doña María de Velasco gave in honor of King Louis XII of France's sister, Queen Germaine de Foix, who had taken the place of the great Isabella in the heart of her grand-uncle Ferdinand, whom she married in 1506. During Íñigo's stay at this royal mansion the old king would come and spend a few days and even weeks there. To prepare for his stay, the splendid tableware of gold and silver and the jewelry of the mistress of the house were polished, and for the services in the chapel they brought out the fabulous missal set with 219 pearls. These were some of the wonderful things Íñigo saw, and to enhance their enjoyment was added heavenly fragrances of precious perfumes that pleased his sense of smell, and he marveled at what he heard because Doña María was in the habit of repeating over and over again while standing before her treasures and her collection of pearls and precious stones, "This one had belonged to Queen Isabella." In order to honor Isabella's bequests and pay her debts, an incredible auction was held following her death, which had taken place in 1504. At this event many nobles and grandees of Castile had purchased similar treasures, but it was Doña María who had had the good fortune to be on hand at this auction of dreams, because her husband was the manager, appraiser, and liquidator of the queen's treasury, and so she was left with the better and greater part of it.

7
Loyal Vassal, Perfect Knight

There is a passage in the *Autobiography* where Íñigo alludes to these years: "at the time when he served at the court of the Catholic monarchs." He was not a genuine page, although the sons of Don Juan Velázquez were, and his daughters were ladies in waiting. But the court was where the king was and during the course of the years 1508, 1510, 1511, and 1515 King Ferdinand remained for days and even weeks at a time at Arévalo. Moreover, the Infante Don Ferdinando, who would succeed his brother Charles V in 1556 as the Holy Roman Emperor Ferdinand I, was also reared in Don Juan Velázquez's home. On some occasions Velázquez and his family were summoned to serve the king outside of Arévalo, at Burgos, Valladolid, Seville, Segovia, or Medina del Campo. Together with the boys in the family, Íñigo played the role of junior page and would experience the almost charismatic touch of the monarch. His presentation at court was all but a foregone conclusion: "Your Majesty, this is the youngest son of Don Beltrán de Loyola."

"Indeed, what has become of your father, Don Beltrán?"

"He died in October 1507, your Majesty."

"He was a loyal vassal, a great knight, and he conducted himself valiantly before Burgos and Fuenterrabía. And what has become of Doña Magdalena de Araoz?"

"She married my brother Martín, Your Majesty, and is living at my home in Loyola." Those magic terms "loyal vassal" and "perfect knight" that came from the monarch's lips resonated for the first time in Íñigo's ears. They enchanted and dazzled him. It meant more to be called a "vassal" by a great king than to be conscious of being the petty lord among vassals or even "chief of the clan" in Guipúzcoa. What would it mean to hear oneself referred to as "an unworthy knight?" What power these words took on when they came from the lips of kings! The words he had heard King Ferdinand speak later at the banquet resounded even more in his ears: "My will is to conquer all of the lands of the Infidels. The cardinal of Toledo is to be in charge of this enterprise, and the kings of Portugal and England will assist us. We shall conquer the Holy Land, and the cardinal will celebrate Mass before the Holy Sepulcher. My hope is that those who wish to show greater affection and excel in my service will offer their persons to my undertaking and that they will make sacrifices of great worth and merit."

Such were the adventures about which he could dream, as his field of vision merged with the infinite plains. From the heights of this stupendous tower-castle called Arévalo, he contemplated the world, savoring its excitement. More news reached here than had ever come to Loyola and each piece of news was like a tempting challenge. *Italy* was so sweet sounding a word. His brother had died there, but the war continued on and with it strange alliances. Don Juan Velázquez spoke to the family about the Holy League formed by the Catholic king, the pope, the Emperor Maximilian I, Henry VIII, and Venice, and how it had suffered defeat at Ravenna in 1512. King Ferdinand had occupied Navarre—as if Íñigo could ever forget Beotibar, the field in Guipúzcoa where the Loyolas, loyal to the king of Castile, were part of the Basque force that defeated the combined army of the Navarrese and the French in 1321. And there were names of other lands, farther away and even more mysterious-sounding, like the Indies, the name that had seduced his brother Hernando. Don Diego Velázquez had just conquered Cuba (1510), and Ponce de León had done the same in Florida (1511), while Nuñez de Balboa had discovered a broad sea farther to the west of these lands (1513). "My will is to conquer. . . ." Closer to home were Valladolid, and, more significantly, Salamanca with its university, where his companion Don Arnao Velázquez de Cuéllar had been appointed chaplain to Queen Juana and would be going to Salamanca for studies leading to the priesthood.

There was also a great deal of talk about the new University of Alcalá, founded by the cardinal of Toledo, Francisco Jiménez de Cisneros, but the world of letters held no attraction for Íñigo. The old saw that he had heard so often at Loyola summed up what Basques thought essential for the man determined to make his mark on the world: "The Church, the sea, or the court."

So, Íñigo's road was marked out. He, too, in a certain sense would say: "It is my will." These dreams would evaporate whenever his teachers called him back to reality. Íñigo was very talented when it came to handwriting, and so if he were content with less he would make a fine secretary. A Basque who kept his mouth shut and who excelled in copying documents could be a royal secretary. The example of his compatriot Pedro de Zuazola was there to prove it so. Zuazola was a member of a distinguished family of Azcoitia, and had become the personal secretary to Charles V. As a sign of his indebtedness to his secretary, Charles authorized him to add the Hapsburg eagle to his coat of arms. The young Íñigo was also thrilled by the refined court music and wanted to learn how to play musical instruments. Another countryman, and a relative of his, was the court musician and composer of a number of religious scores, Joanes de Ancheta, tutor to the Infante Don Juan. Perhaps even another one of Íñigo's teachers was that true man of the Renaissance, Pedro Mártir de Anghiera, a confidant of Columbus, Magellan, and Vasco de Gama, who never seemed to stop writing letters. But the young pupil did not care at all for Latin. His teacher most probably would have handled the precious books from the house library with reverence, and he would have given them one by one to Íñigo while lecturing him on their contents and informing him of their worth. This same teacher would undoubtedly have preferred these books to all of Doña María's pearls because they taught something that was important for everyday living, including how to pray. This was the purpose of those Books of the Hours. Moreover, to direct one's way along the road of life there were the works of Saint Augustine, and a book such as *Arbor Vitae Crucifixae Iesu* by Ubertinus de Casale, or *Specchio di Croce* by Dominico de Cavalca, O.P., about making a pilgrimage to the Holy Land. Fra Dominico was a poet, an ascetical writer, a contemporary

of Dante, and, like this great poet, one of the creators of the
Italian language. There was also the Revelations of Angela de
Foligno, who had placed such stress on living a life of poverty;
or even the Castilian translation of *The Pilgrimage of the Life
of Man* by Guillaume de Deguillerville, an allegorical work
that contained 13,540 octosyllabic verses. Íñigo had made pilgrimages to the hermitages in his native land, but a pilgrimage of life? A pilgrim? There were also many other books in
the Arévalo library with even stranger titles, such as *On the
Government of the Conscience, The Reform of the Powers of the Soul,*
and an old manuscript about the Holy Land. Íñigo's eyes and
even more so his attention would skim over words that did not
yet mean anything to him. As far as books were concerned, he
was interested only in those dealing with chivalry that his
newly found older brothers would secretly pass on to him.
Battles, tournaments, famous exploits, feats of glory, "to be
more"—the same old themes sung by the *parientes mayores* only
now orchestrated and sung by numerous and powerful voices.
He would identify with the brilliant image he had dreamed up
for himself, one in which he would surpass, be "more" than all
the other valiant knights. (The reader will pardon this antici-
pation, but the word *more* does appear countless times in the
book of the *Spiritual Exercises.*)

And what about the lady fair who was so essential in the life
of every valiant knight, the "woman of his thoughts and mistress of his heart"? At the very least, she had to be "very beautiful, generous, and virtuous," as was Doña María in the eyes
of her contemporaries; moreover, she had to be a countess or
a duchess. And when and how did Íñigo choose this inaccessible woman who would fill that immense subconscious vacuum
created by the absence of his mother? Queen Germaine was a
fat, middle-aged, chronic alcoholic, scarcely the person to
awaken feelings of romance in the heart of a young man. The
Infanta Leonor of Austria, whom he had seen innumerable
times at the feasts in Valladolid, was twenty years old in 1518.
As yet, he had not seen her sister, the Infanta Catalina of
Austria, King Philip the Handsome's posthumous daughter,
who was locked up at Tordesillas with her deranged mother,
Queen Juana *la loca,* and who would one day become the consort of King John III of Portugal. Fra Lope de Hurtado would

say that Catalina was "the most beautiful creature there was in the world."

For Íñigo, the greatest challenge among all of these impossible exploits was becoming a poet and writing verse. Because of his sensitive nature he could be a poet. But a versifier? If only he could compose verses like Fra de Montesinos! Íñigo was used to his own native language and therefore he lacked vocabulary and fluency in Castilian. But he did try. We know that he wrote a verse in honor of Saint Peter, but in reality it was nothing more than a poor imitation of a real poet's style. Ah, but remember, Íñigo, the spiritual life disintegrates when it is reduced to aesthetics. You are no aesthete. But, who are you? Right now, you do not have time to think about that. Wait a bit longer. "I will seek and ask for what I desire . . ."; "to relish. . . ." Right now, your blood is boiling and you are a young man in too much of a hurry. For the moment, what is awaiting you are hunting parties and fiestas with ladies with faces and figures more substantial than those of the lady of your thoughts. Now you are beginning, little by little, to forget your Loyola; you are distancing yourself from your homeland, physically and spiritually. You do not remember María Garín anymore, nor the blacksmith Errazti, who used to call out to you: "We are still here." Every prodigal son that ever was ends up by leaving *in regionem longinquam*, "for a distant country" (Lk 15:13), drunk with the present and casting aside the past like so many tattered garments.

8
A Process: But Not for Beatification

Íñigo, of course, did not remain at Arévalo all of the time during his sojourn there. He returned at least once to Loyola, and on that occasion he left behind him an unpleasant memory of his stay, the result of an incident that he had orchestrated. He was now an outsider, a conceited, arrogant young man who was used to rubbing shoulders with the high and mighty in Arévalo. His caper ended up in court, the first of a number of court appearances that he would experience during his lifetime. This particular process, however, was not exactly designed to forward the cause of his beatification. We have sufficient fragments of the court case to enable us to construct the event that took place during Mardi Gras of the year 1515. We do not know if on that occasion Íñigo had time to visit his cousin, the nun at the monastery of the Immaculate Conception, but we do know that, accompanied by his brother Pedro, who was the priest in the family, he had time to engage in some nocturnal misdemeanors, "certain excesses," that the court records testify were "premeditated and enormous . . . crimes." We know something of the nature of these wrongdoings. They took place "at night and deliberately, as a result of a conversation during which ambush and treachery were prearranged." But nowhere do we find a precise definition of what these nocturnal misdeeds entailed. Could it have been a practical joke designed to frighten someone, a prank that went wrong? Or was it a plot to beat up someone? Were there women involved? Whatever it was, it was more than a childish prank, although we should not be taken in by the adjective "enormous." The fact is that whatever the crime, it certainly went beyond conventional limits and it led to the intervention of Don Juan Hernández de la Gama, Guipúzcoa's *corregidor,* that is, the provincial magistrate who exercised administrative and judicial functions.

Íñigo lived through some tense moments as a result of his wrongdoing, during which his future was in the balance. As soon as what he had done was discovered, he left Loyola in a great hurry. For Arévalo? No, for Pamplona where he sought episcopal protection under the pretext that he was a tonsured cleric. Once there, he was arrested and confined to the episcopal prison. The document describing the case was not discovered until the twentieth century, and ever since it has presented historians with problems. Perhaps, like so many other men of that time, Íñigo had received the tonsure at a very young age so as to be able to leave a door open to the future, that is, for a possible ecclesiastical prebend (the Loyolas, it will be remembered, were patrons of the churches at Azpeitia and Azcoitia), or perhaps it was envisaged that one day he might find useful protection provided by canon law. The Church came to his aid in the person of Paul Olivier, vicar of the absentee bishop-administrator of Pamplona, Giovanni Baptiste Costanzi, who also happened to be the archbishop of Cosenza, in Italy. But the corregidor did not back down before the threats of canonical censure and he brought charges against the curia of Pamplona. In his claim, he argued with insistence that Íñigo was a layman, not a true tonsured cleric, and he built his case on external data. Even if he was a bona fide cleric, he argued, his name had never been inscribed in the registers of Pamplona and he had never worn the clerical garb as was prescribed by the synodal constitutions. According to edicts issued by the Catholic monarchs, that fact alone was sufficient to prevent him from having recourse to ecclesiastical jurisdiction. The Crown wanted to put a stop to the abusive practice of those who were not identified as clerics by some religious habit or by other external signs, such as the tonsure, from taking refuge in ecclesiastical courts after they had broken the law of the land. With the obvious intention of emphasizing the lay, even worldly character of Íñigo, the corregidor brilliantly put together a set of notes that throw light on the impression the young Loyola courtier made on the people at the time. The magistrate pointed out that it was well-known that far from wearing ecclesiastical dress, Íñigo had for months, and even years, been carrying arms and wearing a wide-open cape, and that his hair, which was styled shoulder length, gave no outward sign of having been tonsured. In other documented records, the Corregidor excelled the best of painters in depicting for us an Íñigo bedecked in clothing designed with multicolored checked materials, a red cap—the distinctive mark of the Oñaz—a sword fastened to his belt, wearing a metal breastplate and other knightly accoutrements, and clutching onto his cross-bow. Then, dipping his brush in shadier hues, the Corregidor added that the youth was involved in worldly pursuits in a way that belied clerical decorum, both in his dress and even more in his morals.

Even a scrutiny of these several documents does not answer certain questions. For example, it is not altogether clear whether the "said cleric" was really a layman or if he had in fact abandoned the imposed ecclesiastical offices he had assumed. Years later, this same question came up anew. Whether or not the young Loyola with the long blondish hair had told the truth or lied cannot be proven one way or the other, but what is clear is that he had recourse to the Church in order to escape, rather than to face his responsibilities. A fine beginning for a man who one day would be counted among the illustrious congregation of the "men of the Church." During the course of history, there have been many others like him, but they make their entrance into this esteemed assembly only as a muffled counterpoint to those whose virtue was more conspicuous and outstanding. The Corregidor was not successful in the pursuit of his case and was left no happier than his predecessor, the *licenciado* Vela Núñez who had tried to imprison Martín de Loyola and have him banished from Guipúzcoa. Íñigo hurried as fast as he could back to Arévalo where he bragged about his adventures and his escape. This was the first warning signal for this young man so full of self-assurance. At Arévalo there would be more forebodings, specifically the warning that Doña Marina de

Guevara, his good old aunt, the nun, once gave him, "Íñigo, you will not learn nor become wise until someone breaks your leg." It was an ingenious warning, a witticism of sorts. She had no way of knowing that what she spoke was a premonition. But life teaches us by events that happen, not by words spoken, and already there were many circumstances taking place that would cast a shadow over Íñigo's former carefree days.

In 1515, the year of his escapades in Azpeitia, the Archduke Charles (soon to be Charles I of Spain) reached his majority. The question now was: What star would guide the people in the countries to the north in their future endeavors? Charles was the son of Philip I the Handsome and Juana *la loca,* the daughter of Ferdinand and Isabella. In 1506, Philip came to Spain from the Netherlands to claim the throne of Castile in the name of his consort whose mental condition had deteriorated to the point where she could not rule. He was king for less than one month before he died, and during that brief reign his partisans and adversaries had begun feuding, and these factions continued down to 1515. On January 23, 1516, King Ferdinand died and Charles became king of Aragon. Kings are temporal, not eternal. Don Juan Velázquez de Cuéllar presided at the reading of Ferdinand's last will and testament. Although his role at this event was evidence of the great honor bestowed upon him, it was also the last display of confidence and generous protection that the Crown would show him. Ferdinand had lived his final days, as the Protestant divine Peter the Martyr, Pietro Vermigli, would say, "gnawed away by depression." Queen Germaine had prescribed that he be given a good dose of aphrodisiac remedies to cheer him up, and thus he passed his final days on earth. On February 22, 1517, the eldest son of Velázquez de Cuéllar died at Arévalo at the height of his glory. He had been a page first to Prince Juan and later to Ferdinand and Isabella, who had lavished innumerable sinecures and other gifts on him, and after this he was put in charge of collecting the royal rents and excise taxes for Queen Juana. He had married an Enríquez from the house of Don Fadrique Enríquez, the Admiral of Castile, a blood cousin to King Ferdinand, and at the time of the marriage, the king gave him a gift of five hundred thousand maravedís, made him a knight of Santiago and the commander of the city of

Membrilla. The Castilian poet Gómez Manrique was so right when he wrote:

> Our lives are like the rivers
> that flow into the sea,
> which is death.
> Along these rivers are carried also
> the rich and powerful of this world.

9

Left without a Patron

A few months later, on August 12, 1517, to be precise, Don Juan Velázquez de Cuéllar died unexpectedly. But before this physical death he had already undergone another kind of death, one that gravely affected Íñigo and the whole Arévalo family. After the demise of King Ferdinand in 1516, the new monarch, Charles I, gave as a gift all of the revenues and manorial rights from Arévalo, Madrigal, and Olmedo to Ferdinand's widow, Queen Germaine. This transaction did not at all please Cardinal Cisneros, who first went to Velázquez and warned him to be prepared to accept the decision of the sovereign, and then went directly to the young king to protest what he had done. Velázquez was more vexed than Cisneros, and the town of Arévalo judged Charles's decision uncon-scionable. But at this date, 1516, Charles was adamant, although in 1520, as Emperor Charles V, he would revoke the order. Velázquez resisted the king's command, and he went so far as to place the town of Arévalo in a state of defense against the royal troops. At this turn of events, Cisneros removed him from office, and Velázquez had to retire to Madrid to weep over his disgrace, the death of his son, and his huge debts. The Velázquez family was ruined, stripped of their offices, and evicted from their home that was to be turned over to Queen Germaine.

It was not very long before this time that Germaine could not pass a single day parted from the company of Doña María

de Velasco, her retainer and friend. She saw her "more than
was proper," observed the long-time advisor to a number of
Spanish monarchs, Don Lorenzo Galíndez de Caravajal, but
as a result of the recent changes that had taken place, Doña
María "no longer loved" her old friend, and from what had
been love sprang forth the opposite sentiment, hatred. Doña
María passed from opulence to humiliation, from her accustomed royal favor to being the object of disgrace in the eyes of
the new foreign king, and this situation proved disastrous for
Íñigo. A certain Montalvo, one of his companions of
this period, would correctly attest many years later that
Íñigo's protector had died "without having been able to
leave him well-placed." This fact was the cause of a bitter
awakening for him.

Doña María de Velasco was generous, but she did not labor
under any illusions about Íñigo's future prospects, and so she
sought out a new, powerful protector for him, a man also
related to the Loyolas. After giving him two horses and the tidy
sum of five hundred ducats, she sent him off with letters of
introduction to his new prospective patron's household,
because, after the glorious days spent at Arévalo, he was humiliated at the prospect of having to return to Loyola. But he had
to start out all over again. His lucky star had been a shooting
star, like one of the stars he would watch on August 10, Saint
Lawrence's night. This was the night when the annual mete-
orite shower was most visible. He could imagine his star like
one of those shooting stars that sparkled brilliantly for an
instant in the vast Castilian sky before plunging into the inky
void. Fortune was fickle and capricious; it pleased her to store
up calamities. One small event was enough to throw everything
else into confusion. Many years later, Íñigo would recount to
Ribadeneira the following event: Íñigo, the young caballero,
developed a large sore in his nose accompanied by a foul-
smelling psoriasis on his skin. When he found himself shunned
by all because of his misfortune, he was thrown into despair. He
consulted a number of doctors, but none of them was able to
prescribe a remedy. For awhile, he even imagined that he
would have to end his days in a monastery. But he got rid of his
terrible afflictions by soaking his sores with ordinary water, and
he carried on his life as before. "You will never learn. . . ." his

old aunt the nun had told him at a time when she was so close to her own death.

Íñigo left Arévalo with his two horses and a few écus, and that is all he had. His ambitions to be a courtier had been dashed to pieces. There was nothing else open to him but the life of a professional military man in the service of another, even though his soul and body had been stamped with the fine polished manners of the court. He would always carry himself with a certain dignity and elegance that he could never conceal, not even in the disguise of a beggar's rags. Toward the end of the century, there were some Catalan women who still could remember the beggar's genteel comportment and his delicate hands. Ever the dreamer, he would always bear within himself a deep-rooted desire *to be more,* and he had the gift of conceiving grandiose ideas. But apart from all of this, now he would have to begin over again by becoming the satellite of another star, the duke of Nájera, Don Antonio Manrique de Lara, who had been viceroy of Navarre since 1516. Cardinal Cisneros had named him to this post, and on June 7 of that same year, King Charles I, who was at the time in Brussels, confirmed his appointment.

10

The Household of the Viceroy of Navarre

There had been authentic kings in Navarre going back to the time of Charlemagne, kings who were completely sovereign in their own right. So the question arises: When and why were Castilian viceroys appointed to Navarre? Surely, a long list of dynasties whose blood was intermingled with the royal families of Aragon, Castile, France, and even with monarchs of the ancient Moorish kingdoms had counted for something. The beginning of the end of Navarre commenced as early as 1511. During the course of the fifteenth century, this small kingdom tucked away in the Pyrenees had been torn apart by agonizing internecine wars between the Agramontese and Beaumontese factions, and most assuredly these feuds found reverberations in the vendettas fought in Guipúzcoa between the *gamboínos* and the *oñacinos* during the same period. But the agony of Navarre did not end in a natural death; rather, it came about through a military occupation force launched by Ferdinand the Catholic, who besides being king of Aragon was, since the death of Philip I, regent of Castile. Ferdinand's plan had been, first, to request the permission of passage for his army that was going off to fight Louis XII of France, who had been recently excommunicated by Pope Julius II. When his proposal was turned down by the Navarrese, he made the claim that the papal censure also applied to the House of Navarre, which was allied to the French cause. Accordingly, on the strength of this papal excommunication, Ferdinand appropriated to himself the title, King of Navarre, but he put the kingdom under the subjection of the crown of Castile, rather than that of Aragon. The troops of the duke of Alba soon had the last word in this dispute when six thousand infantrymen, twenty-five hundred calvary, and twenty cannon persuaded all to see that a display of power took precedence over any papal bull. Navarre's deposed king, Jean d'Albret, sent his children to Béarn, where he would shortly join them in permanent exile. Thus, the sovereignty of Navarre came to an end in 1512. Historians are accustomed to designate this plundering assault with a number of euphemisms, such as the incorporation, annexation, or the union of Navarre with Castile. But no matter what name is used to describe the result, the action was reminiscent of a more recent term: *Anschluss.*

Jean d'Albret attempted to regain his kingdom in October of that same year by fielding an army of some fourteen thousand men—from Navarre, France, and Germany—under the command of the great field marshal Jacques II La Palice. La Palice began a siege of Pamplona, but before midwinter had set in, he suffered losses in both men and artillery on the rock-bound promontories of Valete. He was also subjected to continuous harassment by the joint forces of Guipúzcoans and Beaumontese, in whose ranks Don Martín de Loyola fought. These two reasons explain why the Navarrese and their allies were forced to retreat. La Palice's losses cost him dearly, and seeing that the right of conquest is more persuasive than logical arguments, Navarre was annexed to the crown of Castile on June 14, 1515. By this date, Julius II, who had been responsible for the ominous bull of excommunication, was dead; Louis XII had just died; Jean d'Albret, the last king of Navarre, was soon to follow them both to the grave; and in January following the annexation, Ferdinand the Catholic likewise disappeared from the scene. Men die, but problems remain. On June 10, 1516, Prince Charles, who succeeded his grandfather to the thrones of Aragon and Castile as Charles I of Spain, and who, in 1519, would become the Holy Roman Emperor Charles V, swore that he regarded Navarre "a kingdom entirely separate" from Castile. In May, he appointed the duke of Nájera, the archenemy of the Agramontese, viceroy of Navarre. The following year, Íñigo de

Loyola came to present this same duke with letters from their mutual relative, Doña María de Velasco, in support of his petition to be received and given employment in the service of the newly named viceroy.

Íñigo's request was granted and he was received as a gentleman by the duke, who regarded him as "a member of his household." Although Íñigo did indeed delight in the exercise of arms, and even though he could be adept in handling a sword when necessity called for it, he was not a soldier. He began his new life at Pamplona by taking up residence either in the duke's palace at Nájera or in the town of Navarrete. Like some lovely Capua—that voluptuous spot that had lulled Hannibal into disastrous inactivity—Arévalo was already fading into the shadows. In Navarre, "to serve" meant "to work by day . . . to watch by night" (*Spiritual Exercises,* 93) in the shadow of a military leader who for the most part was hated by the people. It was not a time of outright war, but it was not a time of peace, either; it was simply a time of truce. The duke, after all, was the representative of a foreign king; he was part of the occupation. And there was more. He sought out support and alliances that might give his position a certain allure of normalcy and legitimacy, while at the same time he exercised his power as the foreign invader in hundreds of different ways. For example, there were some antiquated castled fortifications that were no longer of military use that he ordered demolished, and he also handed out command posts to his friends. Thus, Luis de Beaumont succeeded the prestigious Dr. Juan de Jassu to the presidency of the Royal Council of Navarre. Jassu's two older sons had fought with distinction in the ranks of the deposed king, but the doctor died from sheer grief on October 16, 1515, preoccupied with the fate of his third and youngest son, Francis, who lived with his mother in the family castle at Xavier, and who was just about nine years old at the time of his father's death. The following year, the greater part of the Xavier castle would be demolished and reduced to an ordinary dwelling manor. Cardinal Cisneros was instrumental in the dismantlement of Navarre, but he, too, was destined soon to follow the legitimate king, Jean d'Albret, to the grave. Old men were disappearing from the scene, turning over their failures and accomplishments to those who would take their places. The new pope was called Leo X; the new king of

France, Francis I; the new king of Spain, Charles I; and then there was a teenager named Henry, who was intent on reclaiming his crown, the crown of Navarre. Although he would not succeed, he would be known in history as Henry II, king of Navarre, and his grandson, Henry III of Navarre, would become King Henry IV of France.

Each one of these men was watching and waiting for a favorable opportunity to make his move. When Ferdinand died, there was an attempt to reconquer Navarre from France by a charge through the valley of Roncal. It failed, but stringent measures such as cruel retaliations and tearing down houses followed on the heels of this venture. News of Cisneros's death also rekindled hope in the hearts of the victims, and so the duke of Nájera tried to prevent any communication with Prince Henry, now living in Béarn. Moreover, he issued an order strictly forbidding anyone from asserting that Navarre belonged to the Albrets. He could shackle public opinion but not the sentiments of the people, and that is why he tried to make haste in fortifying Pamplona. The old castle was useless for defense, but plans were drawn up to construct a new fortress. However, he first had to tear down a Dominican convent, raze the sepulchre where the lord of Xavier had been recently buried, and then obliterate the Xavier mansion in Pamplona. The solid beams from this house were used in the building of the new castle, which was called the Fortress of Santiago, or Saint James, and a swarm of stonecutters imported from Guipúzcoa were put to work on its construction.

Pamplona was no Arévalo. There were no kings visiting here, no festivals, and no news from the New World. Castilians slept uneasily in their beds and walked with caution down the narrow streets. The eyes of the Navarrese people glared menacingly and tended to make the hands of those they stared at nervous and ready to grasp their weapons. For the Castilians, the very unpredictability of the atmosphere conjured up ominous phantoms on all sides. The amount of resistance and provocation that lay hidden behind the most insignificant motion, the slightest action on the part of the conquered people, became tangible. Many years later, in far-off Ratisbon, the duke's brother would recall with tears in his eyes the day when a crowd of men met Íñigo in a narrow street and pressed him up against a wall. He unsheathed his sword and ran down the street after his unknown attackers. Who had done the provoking, Íñigo or his assailants? The witness to this scene was a friend of Íñigo's, a man who "had known him for a long time at his home," and he continued, "If someone had not stopped him he would have killed one of them, or one of them would have killed him." What is the final judgment that can be made about this incident? Was it the reaction of an infuriated Loyola, or perhaps fear in action and dressed in its most deceptive disguise, or was it an example of sterling courage?

Íñigo spent three years as a gentleman of the viceroy-duke's household, and during most of this time he remained in Pamplona. Since the duke was present, "along with his whole household," at the ceremony in Valladolid when the new monarch, Charles I, took his oath of office, it is certain that Íñigo witnessed this ceremony as well. Charles chose to take possession of his kingdom at Valladolid, Castile's capital, at this particular time because the ceremony would coincide with the meeting of the Castilian *cortes*. On February 7, 1518, a most spectacular procession, headed by drummers, buglers, and heralds, and followed by a number of ambassadors, solemnly marched through the city streets. These participants began to parade at nine o'clock in the morning, although the rain and snow that were falling did manage to dampen the display a bit as the cortege made its way toward the Church of San Pablo. The grand masters, the constable, the admiral, the dukes of Alba, Nájera, Béjar, and Acros; and the many marquises and counts, in whose number was Ureña, were all "sumptuously dressed" as they accompanied King Charles on foot. Meanwhile, Charles's siblings, the Infanta Leonor and the Infante Ferdinand waited at the church with the prelates and members of the city governments. Cardinal Adrian of Utrecht celebrated the Mass, during the course of which members of the royal family, bishops, and important nobles, including Nájera, made their homage to the king. During the weeks that followed there were jousts and tournaments, and therefore it is difficult to state precisely how long Nájera remained in the city. On the eleventh, King Charles, accompanied by six hundred archers and halberdiers, took part in a combat between six gentlemen on horseback and jousters "richly dressed," but it is impossible to know just where so many ceremonial robes, all embroidered with gold and silver, could have come from. This same event was reenacted on the sixteenth. After the twelfth contest, the king furtively left his dais, put on his arms and equipment, and took part in the tilting. The great joust took place on February 26, 1518.

There was one event that occurred on this occasion that we should not overlook. The young Infanta Catalina was present at the tournaments performed on the twelfth and thirteenth. She and her mother had been freed from their prison at Tordesillas for a few hours to witness these events. The mother, Doña Juana, was also the mother of King Charles. The young girl could scarcely believe what she was seeing, for she was used to watching the world from the tiny windows of Tordesillas, to seeing only the people and animals that passed by in front of her limited view. She took special pleasure in watching children, who were poor but free, and whenever she could, she would throw them coins from her window. The children needed no formal summons in writing to appear before the court, for they knew and cared nothing about protocol and so they came joyfully to play in front of the windows of the palace in order to give the little Infanta the opportunity to see them. To men with the habit of reading romantic novels of chivalry, Catalina's tender beauty, enhanced by her rich attire and her condition as a prisoner cut off from the world, made her an object of dreams, an inaccessible lady of singular beauty, and most important of all, a lady held in captivity. Was she "the lady of the thoughts" of that ardent and bold Íñigo de Loyola? His brother Martín, more of a realist than a dreamer, was also in Valladolid at this time, but Martín satisfied himself with less ambitious a prize. Through Nájera's influence, he obtained the royal permission to entail the Loyola estates. Had Íñigo exercised, during these days in Valladolid, that remarkable faculty for sizing up people and situations that in later years became such a distinctive mark of his personality, he most certainly would have come to the conclusion that all the revelry of these days was not able to drown out the unheeded clamor of grievances and dissatisfaction throughout Castile that followed on the heels of the profound changes imposed by the new monarch and his rapacious entourage. Much to the surprise of all, the king had dismissed Cisneros from the see of Toledo and, disgraced, the cardinal died. The king made the young absentee bishop of Cambrai,

Guillaume de Croy, the new archbishop of Toledo. Men with foreign-sounding names—Guillaume, the Lord of Chièvres, who was de Croy's uncle, the all-powerful Jean Sauvage, Adrian Florenszoon Boeyens, the cardinal of Utrecht, who was also the absentee bishop of Tortosa and would later be Pope Adrian VI—were now enjoying the positions of authority while the old nobility was snubbed and pushed aside. Even though the causes were not always the same, discontent was growing both among the high nobility and the lower-class ordinary soldiers. Along with this invasion of foreigners with their new tastes, the cost of living had risen considerably and the former austere ways of life began to disappear. There was concern about the devaluation and recall of the old doubloon stamped with the images of Ferdinand and Isabella, and so the popular saying, "Lucky you, two-faced doubloon, for Chièvres has not as yet put his finger on you." Such a saying was designed to cause alarm, but usually when people are lulled to sleep by comfort, they are loathe to be awakened.

The new, young king left Valladolid on March 22, bound for the kingdom of Aragon in the company of the Infantes Ferdinand and Leonor, and with Queen Germaine at his side. They arrived in Zaragoza on May 9, 1518, where they took up residence until the following January 24. Among the thousands of pieces of correspondence that passed to and from king's chancellory, there is one that interests us in a special way, and not merely because it indicates that Íñigo had also been in Zaragoza. It was just recently discovered, and it reads:

All Powerful Lord: Íñigo López de Loyola declares that he has a difference and disagreement with a Gallician, Francisco de Oya, a man in the service of the countess of Camina. He says that this man wants to kill him and that he is looking for the opportunity to put his resolutions into effect, that he has often pursued him, and that he has never accepted reconciliation, despite the fact that it has been offered to him many times. For this reason the said Íñigo has great need to carry arms to safeguard and defend his person, as he will explain to you if necessary. He begs Your Highness to grant him the right to bear the said arms; on his part, he offers surety that he will not engage nor offend anyone else with these said

arms. He will be the most grateful if Your Highness grant
him his request.

This document, discovered in the Archives de Simancas,
contains two annotations written in another hand: "Zaragoza,
December 20, 1518," and "Let him be given the authorization,
for himself alone." Before commenting on this petition, we
should point out that it was renewed and given new royal
authorization and sent to the *Corregidor* of the city of
Valladolid, dated Zaragoza, November 10, 1519, and a third
permission was granted on March 5, 1520. The texts of these
two later documents are longer and the concessions are more
detailed in respect to the requests made. Thanks to these last
two petitions, we know that the original incident that
prompted this royal concession went back to the time when
Íñigo was living in Arévalo. His adversary, Francisco de Oya or
del Hoyo, was a Gallician in the service of Doña Inés de
Monroy, a resident of Valladolid and, since 1498, the widow of
Alvaro de Sotomayor, count of Camina. This Hoyo wanted to
do harm to Íñigo and, indeed, he had even wounded him on
one occasion and sent him a warning that he intended to kill
him. His hate was not abated after Íñigo left Arévalo. He followed up by making inquiries where his enemy was living and
he promised to pay a woman if she could help him in wound-
ing and killing him. The woman warned Íñigo of the plot and,
understandably, Íñigo believed his enemy would put his evil
purpose into execution. Consequently, he asked again for permission to carry arms, and he even requested an escort of two
armed bodyguards. The seriousness of the case can be verified
by the fact that the king gave him authorization to bear arms
for one year, and this is why he had to renew Íñigo's request in
1520. May Saint Ignatius—but not Íñigo de Loyola—pardon us
if we suspect that this desire for revenge, which was so tenacious and relentless, and that this will to murder, which was so
determined and well planned, makes sense only in the context
of a love affair, of an external triangle in which the woman this
time was not an ethereal, inaccessible Dulcinea, the lady of his
thoughts. Years later, when Father Master Ignatius spoke of the
devil, "the enemy of our human nature," he described him as
the one who can be compared in his manner of acting to a
false lover. He seeks to remain hidden and does not want to be

discovered. If such a lover speaks with evil intention to the daughter of a good father, or to the wife of a good husband, and seeks to seduce them, he wants his words and solicitations kept secret. He is greatly displeased if his evil suggestions and depraved intentions are revealed by the daughter to her father, or by the wife to her husband. Then he readily sees he will not succeed in what he has begun (*Spiritual Exercises*, 326).

Since every analogous example is rooted in some human experience, could it be that in this excerpt from the *Spiritual Exercises* Ignatius is proposing a reconciliation with Francisco del Hoyo, a good husband or a good father, whom Íñigo had offended, and who responded with the incurable hatred of a heart that had been profoundly wounded?

On March 7, 1519, at the meeting of the Barcelona chapter of the Order of the Golden Fleece, the duke of Nájera was given the greatest honor he could possibly have received. Along with the kings of Denmark and Poland, Jacob of Luxembourg, and the dukes of Alba, Escalona, Infantado, Frías, Béjar, and Cardona, and some other dignitaries, he was invested as a member of this most highly esteemed order. Many of the Spanish candidates were distant relatives of Íñigo, and it is very probable that he too was present at this ceremony, a fact that would explain an event that took place later in his life. In August 1522, dressed as a pilgrim and intent on maintaining his anonymity, he went to Manresa without passing through Barcelona, and he did so "in order not to be recognized," because "there were many who would know and honor him" in Barcelona. Who were these "many people" who could have known and received him so warmly if not the very same people who had known him three years previously, on that famous day that marked the triumph of his master and kinsman, the duke of Nájera? Furthermore, we also know that the duke, accompanied by "his relatives," made a trip to Rome, and in the letters of that period, mention is made of a trip to Rome in April 1520 by Pedro de Oñaz, accompanied by one of his relatives who was identified as "the gentleman from Azpeitia." Can we conclude from this that the reference is to Íñigo?

11
Different Men, Different Nightmares

Putting aside conjectures, let us now plant our feet on the solid ground of historical fact. While Íñigo was forced to live entangled in the nightmare that Francisco del Hoyo had woven for him, the duke of Nájera found it impossible to extricate himself from the nightmare of Navarre, and Charles V was struggling with the anxieties and terrors that came from the empire because the death of Emperor Maximilian I, on January 12, 1519, had left the imperial throne empty. Charles's bête noire was not named Francisco de Hoyo; he was called Francis I, king of France. Many years later, Charles would confess that he and his rival were in agreement on one subject: they both coveted the duchy of Milan. In addition to their mutual interest in this area, there was another desire they shared in common; control of the empire. These two monarchs squandered mountains of money and entered into countless diplomatic intrigues in order to carry away this prize. Charles was the winner and was elected emperor on June 23, 1519. But other unresolved problems still remained; for example, each of the rivals had designs on Naples. Yet above all, both of them lusted after the recently conquered Navarre, which Charles was intent on turning into "a peaceful possession" of the Spanish throne. When he drew up his last will and testament, the Emperor Charles V, who was King Charles I in Spain, confessed to having had some scruples about the

peaceful incorporation of Navarre into Castile, and so he left a
door slightly open to future negotiations on this subject. In
1519, there was the young Henry d'Albret, who continued to
make a claim for what he considered was rightfully his. Francis
I was delighted to stand up in support of him, inspired as he
was by the pursuit of justice and the vexation of his powerful
neighbor. The Navarre dispute was put on the agenda at the
Treaty of Noyon in 1516. France protested the implementation
of the treaty and the all-powerful francophile, the duke of
Chièvres, supported by his protégé, the Piemontese-born chancellor of Castile, Mercurino Gattinara, and others sympathetic
to the French cause, arranged the colloquies at Montpellier to
resolve the problem. This turn of events displeased Castile,
which had no intention of giving up Navarre because it considered the kingdom the "key" to Spain in the same way that
Milan was the "key" to Italy. The negotiations dragged on end-
lessly and no solution seemed forthcoming. For this reason,
and because a possible attack on the part of France seemed a
likely contingency, construction on the newly built fortress of
Pamplona was accelerated, and by the beginning of 1518, it
was manned by a permanent garrison and stocked as an
armory. The king also promised to send three companies of
cavalry from Flanders, plus a part of the Galves army and three
thousand German mercenaries to reinforce the regular troops,
although this promise was never kept. In fact, the opposite to a
reinforcement of the army in Navarre was under way. Troops
in Pamplona were being withdrawn to Castile where the situation had become critical as a result of the uprising known as
the *Comunero* movement.

Charles's departure from Spain was disastrous. When he
embarked from La Coruña bound for Germany on May 20,
1520, the rebellious local parliaments or *corteses* in the cities of
Castile rekindled the battle and thereby made the possibility of
civil war a reality. In a few months' time, what had been discontent turned to rebellion and then to revolution. By June 1520,
all of the principal cities and towns in Castile were in revolt.
The various *juntas comuneras,* or provisional governments set
up in the rebellious towns, did not recognize the authority of
either Charles's appointed regent, Cardinal Adrian of Utrecht,
or the *Consejo Real.* During the times of crisis when there was a
vacuum of royal power, a number of the local nobles played a

double game, supporting the Crown at one instance and the *juntas* at another. Although modern historians disagree on the political-social significance of this rebellion, what is clear is that the instability of the situation and the weakness on the part of the government played into the hands of Francis I, and also into the hands of many Navarrese, who looked to the enthronement of their legitimate king and the freedom of their kingdom. So, Castile's crisis augured well for the cause of the French and Navarrese; it became the pretext for their mutual collaboration and even better, it assured the alliance that followed. Even before the actual war broke out in Navarre, the Castilian crisis had a twofold effect on the new life of Íñigo. The political situation was felt in the Rioja country. The town of Haro in southwestern Navarre rose up against its lord, the powerful Pedro Fernández de Velasco, brother of the constable of Castile, and the town of Nájera, reacted in the same way against its duke. The anti-seigneurial tone of both of these rebellions was evident. At Nájera the duke's officials were deposed, his followers persecuted, and one of his retainers hanged. Hoards of peasants went so far as to occupy the town, capture two of the duke's castles, and lay siege to the third. They gave an account of their behavior and the reasons that had impelled them to act in this fashion toward the men who made up the *junta*. "They had been tyrannized," they said, and naturally they asked for help that never arrived. What did arrive after four days of these disturbances was the duke's army, threatening the insurgents with death and the expropriation of their property. Two thousand infantrymen soon occupied the town, but not before having to put up a good fight. The repression was brutal: imprisonment, confiscation of property, the execution of four *comuneros,* and a horrible pillage of the town "according to the practice of war." Íñigo was in the duke's army. He had fought but did not want to participate in the pillaging. "Even though he could have taken a large part of the booty, it seemed to him *of little value,* and he never wanted to take the smallest bit." His was a noble, proud gesture, a gesture of decency—perhaps the only grand and glorious gesture of that whole inglorious day. The events of this day, September 18, 1520, remained deeply ingrained in Íñigo's memory, and, in 1547, Polanco would record for us what Íñigo's feelings were on this subject.

A month and a half after the Nájera affair, another crisis
that was more serious and complex took place in the province
of Guipúzcoa. The regent Adrian of Utrecht had named a
councillor, the *licenciado* Cristóbal Vázquez de Acuña, the new
Corregidor of the province. Acuña, however, encountered considerable difficulty in getting his nomination accepted by the
towns. A few days after this nomination, convoys loaded with
powder, pikes, halberds, and artillery intended for Castile
were detained at two Guipúzcoan towns, Tolosa and Hernani.
Some of the townsmen of Guipúzcoa had been fired up by the
comunero fever and were in league with the Castilian *junta* at
Tordesillas in the province of Valladolid. Once again, throughout Guipúzcoa factions began to take shape. But unlike in
times gone by, these new partisans did not represent the leading families; they were not men under the control of the *parientes mayores*. The new rival groups represented different
towns. There had already been armed attacks followed by
reprisals, and the opposing sides had sent accounts to faraway
King Charles. The province was on the brink of all-out civil
war, and because Guipúzcoa was Castile's first line of defense
for the containment of Navarre, the royal government's control of this province was becoming more and more important.
The viceroy of Navarre paid a visit to San Sebastián in January
1521, with the intention of bringing peace to the wasps' nest
that Guipúzcoa had become. But the province had proved
more difficult to subdue than Nájera. The viceroy was a realist, and so in his report to the *Consejo Real* he informed the
government that violence was rampant throughout Guipúzcoa;
that the province was in terrible shape; that many of its towns
were protected by strong ramparts, and that the rebels could
count on six thousand armed men. He argued that the same
number of royalist troops would be needed to confront the
rebels, but if this step were taken, it would mean troops would
have to be pulled out of Castile and Navarre where they were
absolutely necessary, and it would also mean that an
undreamed-of outlay of money would have to be forthcoming.
Moreover, a "war fought in fire and blood" would destroy
Guipúzcoa and leave Navarre in a more precarious state than
she had ever been before. Under these circumstances, the
duke-viceroy was persuaded to buy peace at whatever price he
could, and he went to extremes in showing remarkable

wisdom, patience, and even leniency. He used every tactic and means he could to appease the bitter factions until at last he was able to arbitrate peace between them on April 12, 1521. As is often the case, those who were the real negotiators of the peace terms remained in the shadows, and in this instance it was Íñigo de Loyola and Ibáñez de Ercilla, the father of the soldier-poet, Alonso Ercilla y Zúñiga, the author of the most celebrated epic poem of the Renaissance, *La Araucana,* whose theme was the Araucanian Indians of Chile. In the recollections that Polanco later put together, we can read about the part Íñigo played in this event. "One day he distinguished himself in a remarkable way in *this*. . . ." The "this" referred to his ability and insight into the workings of the world, his dexterity in discerning "the way of men's thinking," and particularly the gift for resolving differences and disagreements, for becoming a peacemaker. Would not Íñigo have made a good diplomat? He did not have time to think about it, because during this same period there were unnerving rumors circulating everywhere. On April 15, Hernán Pérez, the mayor of the small Guipúzcoan frontier town of Behovia, reported that "King Jean's son was getting together a mighty army with the help of the king of France to march on Navarre, and he was bringing seven thousand Germans and a formidable artillery with him." During the subsequent days, Pérez continued to dispatch messages that were becoming more and more alarming.

12

The War: Invasion
or Liberation

Everyone was aware of what was taking place in the spring of 1521. Spies had reported that significant preparations were afoot on the French side of the border, and this could only mean that war was imminent. The castles of Fuenterrabía and Behovia, as well as the fortress of Pamplona, sent out calls to Castile for help. But the captain general of the three Basque provinces of Guipúzcoa, Álava, and Viscaya, was Pedro López de Ayala, the count of Salvatierra and a choleric partisan of the *comuneros,* and he had made communication between Castile and the North all but impossible. The result was that the cardinal-regent, Adrian of Utrecht, had to flee from Valladolid while troops from Pamplona were deployed to Castile, leaving the fortress there in worse shape than it had ever been. On April 12, these troops were instrumental in dislodging Salvatierra, and a short time afterward, on April 23, the comuneros were crushed at the battle of Villalar. Toledo refused to give in to the royalists and appealed to the French for help. At this critical moment, on May 12 to be exact, Count Andrés de Grailly de Foix-Lautrec, lord of Asparros (Esparros or Lesparre in French), ordered his impressive army of twelve thousand men to begin their march south. This army was equipped with twenty-six pieces of heavy artillery and was made up of Gascons, Germans, Béarnese, and those Navarrese who were faithful to their prince. On the fifteenth, these forces easily overrode Saint-Jean-Pied-de-Port, today a town in France, but at that time an important northern bastion of the kingdom of Navarre. From this point on, events followed one another with great rapidity. Today, we can reconstruct and analyze them in slow motion. For some of the participants, these days were full of dreams; for others, they were full of hope.

Scouts raced down to Pamplona with the news of the fall of Saint-Jean-Pied-de-Port. The Castilians would attempt the impossible, but it was already too late. The reality of the situation, which up until then had been played down or denied, now showed how serious it was. On the sixteenth, the advance guard of the formidable army made its appearance a half a league from Pamplona. Were these the invaders from across the French frontier? That is what the duke considered them to be—invaders—but the fact was that thousands of mountain-dwelling Navarrese Basques rose up in support of Prince Henry, and on that same day a number of cities, among which were Sangüesa and Cáseda, followed suit. This was not going to be simply a conventional war between two armies, as the events of the seventeenth would show and as future events would confirm. Moreover, there was really only one army—the Franco-Navarrese army that had come to capture the city of Pamplona. Before it stood the unfinished fortress with a military garrison that was all but worthless—a handful of underpaid, demoralized, veteran soldiers—and a sullen civilian population in the city, which remained hostile to the Castilian presence. At least this is how the commander of the fortress, Miguel de Herrera, described what Pamplona had been like. (It should be remembered, however, that his description was given after the debacle had taken place, at a time when he was eager to excuse himself from all responsibility.) With the arrival of the army, panic became widespread. The duke of Nájera fled to seek reinforcements—and to save his life. After these events became history, the admiral of Castile came to his defense. "It is better that a captain be free and able to help," he said, "than be chained and thus incapable of doing anything." The contemporary, Miguel de Añués, gave his opinion of the duke's action and what his consequent attitude should be when he wrote, "The duke has fled from Pamplona and he should thank God if he ever reaches Castile." He left his command in the hands of

Pedro de Beaumont, who immediately followed the example of his master by leaving Pamplona for Logroño to the south and taking with him 800 troops from the region of La Rioja and 250 veteran infantrymen. The duke's Guipúzcoan assessor, Bishop Mercado of Zuazola, also ran off. The lords of Góngora and Guendulain departed south for Alfaro "with their goods, wives, and children." Likewise, those Navarrese favorable to the Castilians escaped. With this vacuum of power, "the people of the city rose up so that those who were from Castile departed and ran off in fear of having their throats cut," noted an anonymous reporter in a memorandum, dated Logroño, May 18. At this point, Pamplona was helpless and on the verge of becoming a ghost town.

On the eighteenth, the greater part of the—what was it, liberating or invading?—army entered Pamplona. There was no need for the troops to unbuckle their spurs to take the fortress. The city dwellers immediately began to sack the ducal mansion, to tear down the coat of arms of Spain, and to rise in rebellion against the soldiers who pretended to defend the place. Any defense was impossible and it could even be prejudicial; besides, nobody wanted to put up a fight. It was at that moment that Beaumont, accompanied by his troops, chose to make his slow retreat. In order to prevent a senseless siege, the members of the town council requested the command of the city be turned over to them. At this critical moment, the first Guipúzcoan reinforcements under the command of Don Martín de Loyola, arrived at the scene. They were to defend the town against the French. Did Íñigo have time to go to Guipúzcoa and return with these troops after the flight of the duke and Beaumont in whose service he continued to be? It is impossible to say, but what is certain is that he met his brother on the outskirts of Pamplona. The situation was desperate and each hour that passed was decisive. The Loyolas demanded they be entrusted with the command of the remaining Spanish garrison so that they could carry out their responsibilities, but the city council refused their persistent requests. Don Martín, wild with bitterness and anger, would not even enter the town and retired with his troops, but Íñigo felt that to abandon the task would be shameful. He took leave of his brother, spurred on his horse because there was no time to lose, and, followed by a few knights, galloped into Pamplona. Years later, he must have spoken about this decisive moment on more than one occasion because Nadal and Polanco describe it in detail. Shame—the bosom companion to dignity—had flung Íñigo toward the impossible, and now he had to stretch beyond his own resources. "He judged it disreputable to retreat," said Nadal. Later on, Íñigo came to believe that "shame and fear for his good name in the eyes of the world" will be obstacles for the man who strives to serve God freely, whereas the deep feeling of "shame and confusion" in oneself are gifts from heaven (*Spiritual Exercises*, 9, 48). The firm rock into which this second kind of shame, which is true realization of our dignity, plunges its roots is, perhaps, of a very different nature indeed, from the first type of shame.

13

One Against All

With classic rhetoric, Polanco described Íñigo's rushing down the streets through crowds of deserters and troops fleeing with the stragglers of Beaumont's army, convinced that it was impossible to put up a stand against the enemy, and fearful of remaining in Pamplona because of the hostility of its inhabitants. "Íñigo was ashamed to leave lest it might seem that he too was fleeing, and so he did not want to follow [Martín], and so before the eyes of those who were running away, he entered the fortress to defend it alongside the few men who had remained there." The verb *entered* here almost takes on the meaning of a transitive reflexive (he entered himself into the fortress) because the fact is that it was Íñigo alone who threw himself into his heroic venture. He had crossed the Rubicon of his life. Honor lay on the other side of the fortress's drawbridge. And with honor, awaited agony—in the basic etymological sense of that word so dear to Miguel de Unamuno y Jugo, that is, in honor awaited "a struggle, a contest for a prize."

Íñigo begins his autobiography at this moment and does so with this disconcerting sentence: "Until the twenty-sixth year of his life." Eduard Fueter states that this is the only *lapsus memoriae* in the account. But some scholars, who accept the factual information contained in this sentence at face value and who, at the same time, believe the calculations that establish Íñigo's date of birth to be exact, argue that it was during the unhappy months of his stay at Arévalo in 1517 that he went through the first steps of his conversion, or at least it was then that his attitude underwent a profound change. Whether that is true or not, what is important is that the definitive change did not take place until after his dramatic experience in Pamplona. That is why in 1553, Father Ignatius, by now completely cured of the vanities and the bravado of his youth, keenly recalled the events he lived through at that moment of his life, and he took pleasure in highlighting the impetuosity of his self-giving action in the face of danger. It was an impetuous gesture that was his and his alone. "He was in a fortress that the French were attacking, although *all the others saw clearly* that they could not defend themselves and were of the opinion that they should surrender provided their lives were spared, *he* gave so many reasons to the commander that he *persuaded* him at last to defend it. This was contrary to the views of *all* the knights, but they were energized by his courage and gallantry."

Ignatius, wiser in 1553 because he was older, admitted deep down that his companions-in-arms were right and he was wrong. It was clear that Pamplona could not have been defended. But what he meant was that, however wrong his arguments, he had shown a kind of courage that borders on madness, a madness that for a few hours had been contagious. With reason, Miguel de Unamuno sees a comparison between Loyola and Don Quixote in so many episodes of their respective lives. Just as Cervantes describes the many mad adventures in the life of his character Don Quixote, so too are there many mad incidents in the life of Loyola—none more exquisitely mad than what had just taken place. Sorcerers had tricked Don Quixote, too, taking away from him an adventure. But in depriving him of "valor and courage, never" were they successful (*Don Quixote,* I, ch. 16, 17).

The fact that Íñigo could perform such a heroic act enabled him later to size up different attitudes of men. He was able to describe in his *Spiritual Exercises* how "The Three Classes of Men" go about making a choice. Each type has different ways of being honorable and loyal to the king. The service of the first is external, limited to appearances. Then there is the studied, calculated approach that is characteristic of the second class. Finally, there is the generous service that accepts "being considered worthless and a fool." (*Spiritual Exercises* 113–15, 150–55, 165–67).

Íñigo had made it down the street. He thought he had left the enemy on the other side of the fortress's moat, but the enemy had already infiltrated through the embrasures in the castle's groundworks. Their presence there gave rise to a reasonable and justified fear on the part of the defenders. A meeting was held in one of the castle's rooms at which everyone agreed the garrison should surrender because the castle could not be defended—everyone, that is, except Íñigo, who "gave his opinion that they should not surrender but that they should defend or die." Meanwhile, attempts were being made in Pamplona to use every means possible to avoid what could become a catastrophe for the city, and negotiations were being hammered out to allow the army to attack the surrounding ramparts, which would leave the center part of the city intact. Apart from these negotiations, the general feeling in the city was quite clear, although this opinion was made palatable by the excuse that the city was impossible to defend. Captain Charles de Artieda, a former official of Ferdinand the Catholic, was the president of the town council, and it was he who formally presented himself at the French camp where he surrendered, recognized Prince Henry as the king, made his oath, and in turn received the promise of "the ancient liberty and freedoms" of the city of Pamplona. He then gave the French the keys to the city and on that same day, which was the feast of Pentecost, Pamplona welcomed the two flags of France and Navarre. On the following day, the magnificent army marched into the city. The commander of the fortress, Miguel de Herrera, exhorted the people to expel the enemy from their city and warned them that if they failed to comply they would pay dearly. His words fell on deaf ears.

To prevent a disastrous and irremedial end to this drama, the lord of Asparros called on the fortress citadel to surrender. The citadel was the last place of resistance. A meeting was arranged with leaders from both sides in order to work out an honorable agreement. Herrera came to this meeting with three associates, one of whom was Íñigo. Asparros would certainly have recognized Íñigo; he would have recalled that when he had accompanied Queen Germaine de Foix to Arévalo, he tried to talk him out of his rash and suicidal impatience. Now, the conditions Asparros proposed for surrender seemed "shameful" to Íñigo, who was against any form of compromise. There was only one way out—"to take up arms," to fight and defend the castle. But in order to do so they had go back to the fortress. This was a most lopsided and absurd war; it was the madness of honor and loyalty. But for Íñigo it was "the most dangerous situation of all the ages." One does not have to be Cervantes or to have been at Lepanto to feel that such was the case. After all, a man dies only once and the greatest gift he can offer is his life.

Íñigo "entered" the citadel. Death, hard-pressed to claim him, looked him square in the eye. Unlike the vengeful Gallician Hoyo, who had stalked him from behind, death was there to meet him face to face.

Íñigo also "entered" the citadel of his soul. "When the day arrived on which they expected the bombardment, he confessed his sins to one of his companions-in-arms."

During the Middle Ages the practice of confessing to a layperson at time of danger was not an unknown exercise. Saint Thomas Aquinas takes up the question in Book Four of his *Commentary on the Sentences,* and closer to our own time, Fra Hernando de Talavera poses the question in regard to the practice of confession in a manual he wrote for confessors in 1482. Talavera observed that "whoever administers [confession] without being a priest commits a sin, except in cases of necessity, when one is in danger of death, and not being able to have a priest, he wants to confess to someone who is not ordained. Although such a confession is not necessary, because if a priest is not available, having sorrow for one's sins is enough." The indulgent Talavera, who was the famous first bishop of reconquered Granada, is dealing here with the sacramental, as opposed to the psychological, need to confess. The latter is an almost biological need. By asking pardon a person reassures himself and seeks to unburden himself, not from complexes that arise from guilt—these are a modern invention—but from the sins of his lifetime which, in Íñigo's case, were so heavy that they weighed on his soul like the cuirass that weighed on his shoulders. When a person acknowledges his sins before a third party, especially before a layman, he takes the first real step toward a radical purification. It is a way of asserting his deep desire for forgiveness and the resolution on his part to do all in his power to gain God's mercy. This action of Íñigo's was a kind of photographic negative of an inmost conviction that the weight that could crush one person could be borne better by two. It was an instinctive way of inserting himself into the Communion of Saints. While he nervously awaited the roar of bombards and culverins, Íñigo poured out his conscience to his surprised companion-in-arms, who with some astonishment, learned more about the hidden and unsuspected facets of the personality of his proud confidant than he did about the man's serious, but run-of-the-mill, sins.

14

"Until They Break Your Leg"

The roar of the first cannonade awakened the soldier's primary instincts and put him on the alert. Was Íñigo running to the defense of his post? Or perhaps he had not taken cover under the merlons? At any rate, he was brought down, wounded by a ricochet shell. Tradition has it that he was wounded on May 20, and, without giving any precise dates, the *Autobiography* adds, "shortly after he fell, the defenders of the fortress surrendered to the French." This chain of factual events, fanned by the unique circumstances surrounding them, has contributed to create the myth of Íñigo's part in the defense of Pamplona. His valor and his role as the soul of resistance are sufficiently verified without having further need to make him out to be what he was not. There are some things that could have happened differently in this drama, but at least today we know with certainty that the actual surrender of the citadel did not take place until May 24.

Unquestionably, the artillery duel began on the nineteenth, and because the equipment shelling from the fortress did some damage in the city and on the attackers, we know that this combat was not one-sided. However, the besiegers' formidable heavy artillery did not arrive in place until the twenty-third and the twenty-fourth, the day the castle surrendered. At that time, after a few hours of serious bombardment that succeeded in opening a breach in the thick walls, the battle was over. Recalling these events at a later date, Íñigo was very precise about what had taken place. "After the bombardment had been going on for some time, a cannon ball struck him on one leg, crushing its bones, and because it passed between his legs the other was also seriously wounded. Shortly after he fell, the defenders of the fortress surrendered to the French. . . ." If all of this had taken place during the first artillery exchange on the twentieth, then the words *shortly after* [*luego*] must be interpreted broadly, since the actual surrender did not take place until three or four days later. The description he gives of the projectile that passed between his legs leads us to center our attention on the early part of the assault when shots were being fired high onto the castle's upper stories, rather than during the heavy artillery barrage employed during the last hours of the assault. One can also conjecture that the leg wounds he described could not have resulted from a missile shot through one of the castle's windows or embrasures. Moreover, his body was discovered on the higher, unfinished part of the castle that we know did not as yet have a protecting parapet. If the battery used had been heavy artillery, it would not have wounded Íñigo where he fell, and so, we would have to reject the twentieth as the day on which he had been wounded. The surrender took place a few hours after the heavy batteries were used, six hours to be exact, according to one contemporary. If we accept the first supposition, namely that Íñigo was wounded on the twentieth in the light artillery assault, then we must conclude that he had to remain several days in the castle badly wounded. If we opt for the second possibility, which is that he fell on the twenty-third or twenty-fourth, we come to the same conclusion, which is that he suffered a similar fate because neither those waging the siege nor those being besieged could have left their posts for at least another three days. Representatives from both sides would have had to agree on the terms of the retreat and the conditions of the cease-fire, but even then and in spite of all agreements, the withdrawal would not have taken place without some instances of violence. Those who managed to escape from the castle without paying the price for their involvement with their lives had to be escorted as far as Logroño by Asparros. There were also wounded who remained within the castle, among whom were Alonso de San Pedro, Pedro de Malpaso, the inspector of the works who died the following month, and Íñigo de Loyola.

Many days had already passed since Íñigo was wounded. Defeated physically and morally, he had lain helpless in one of the corners of the castle where he had received inadequate emergency care and had waited feverishly for the victor's arrival. During those hours that seemed like an eternity, he may well have embarked on the road that led within. If the physical pain and the instinct for survival had not gotten the better hand, he would have had to contemplate his whole past, like every prodigal son who must retreat within himself to find himself and to examine the long road that led to his self-estrangement. Perhaps his intuition told him that ever since those intoxicating days of Arévalo, his life could be summed up in two words—running away—words that seemed to him to be filled with ignominy. Running away from himself . . . had he not been, in the words of Saint Augustine, a stubborn "fugitive from his own heart"? He had fled from his interior citadel; he had fled toward an imaginary, uncertain future, which, in the present circumstances, left him alone and empty, a dupe to danger and uncertainty. Would he have felt a new kind of shame—the shame of vain honor, of the emptiness of life, the numbness of his dormant faith? Perhaps we are anticipating the interior processes that came about with greater intensity at a later date; he explicitly places this "first reflection . . . concerning the things of God" at Loyola. If, at this moment, in a corner of Pamplona's castle, he did not reflect on God, he must have remembered the prediction of Doña Marina de Guevara at Arévalo: "Íñigo, you will never learn or become wise until someone breaks your leg."

The arrival of the victors awakened again his hopes and illusions, and he concentrated all his energies on survival. When he recollected the memory of this long-ago event, he extended a mark of chivalrous gratitude to the French when he said, "They treated the wounded man very well, and they conducted themselves in a most courteous and kindly fashion." It is possible that Asparros, who would suffer a fate similar to Íñigo's during the siege of Pamplona in 1527, took care of his valiant and loyal adversary. "They found him lying on the ground," Polanco tells us, "and they brought him into the town (because many knew him there) and his own enemies exerted themselves in taking care of him, providing him with doctors and the rest until it seemed better to send him home so that during his convalescence, which would be long, he would be better off." Íñigo was a privileged wounded casualty of the war. His adversaries visited him and he repaid their civility by presenting them with his buckler, dagger, and cuirass. An old friend of his Arévalo days named Montalvo, who would never forget the courage Íñigo had shown during his painful convalescence, also paid him a visit.

After giving him preliminary care over a two-week period, they put him on a litter and brought him home. Even though the countrymen turned litter-bearers carried him with great care, his journey home was physically and morally painful. He showed unbelievable strength in the face of suffering and to this attribute was added another in his favor. In the midst of all of his pain, "he did not show himself hateful toward anyone and he did not blaspheme God." He showed character.

15
Life in the Balance

Like another Don Quixote, worn out, wasted, and in no mood to enjoy the lush green countryside, Íñigo arrived back at Loyola sometime during the first part of June. Such was his reintroduction to his native land and his family. Don Martín would have upbraided him for the lunacy he had shown at Pamplona. Doña Magdalena would have nursed him in silence and with care. The blacksmith would have reminded him with the same sing-song monotony he used while hammering his anvil, "As I told you before, we are here." Because Íñigo's sufferings were unbearably persistent, which is normally the case with any injury affecting the bones, he did not feel like engaging in the kind of small talk that ordinarily follows the kind of adventure he had been through. His right knee, which had been shattered, began getting worse, either because the bones were not set properly at Pamplona or because they had become dislocated during the journey home. Doctors and surgeons from many places were summoned to his bedside, but we know the name of only one of them and this was Martín de Iztiola who received, in 1539, the last three ducats of the ten owed him for the services he had rendered. All of the medical men were of the same opinion: the bones had to be reset or they would never heal properly. Years afterward, Father Ignatius would talk about this extremely painful operation. "And again he went through this butchery," he wrote, preferring the use of grisly noun to the superlative degree of an adjective. His description of what took place during this operation further shows his incredible courage, "and during it, as in all other operations he had undergone, he uttered no word nor showed any sign of pain other than to clench his fists." Íñigo was indeed a man of incalculable inner strength, but his steel-like character was not forged by a hard life; it was rather part and parcel of his personality; it was a component of his nature.

Despite everything, his condition worsened; he could not eat, and "symptoms that normally presage death" began to appear. The doctors gave him little chance to pull through. June 24 was the feast of Saint John, the day on which the Azpeitians traditionally flocked to the hermitage dedicated to the Baptist, and it was on this day that "he was advised to make his confession." Was it Pedro, the bad priest of the family, who gave him this advice? Whatever else he was, this priest was by no means a fervent Christian. But in the face of death, advice from lips such as his can often verify what is hidden behind a dishonest life, for beneath the sin can be found the embers of faith. Or perhaps it was Magdalena who was his discrete advisor. If so, she showed more courage than the men of the household when it came to fulfilling such a duty. Íñigo received the sacraments and thereby validated the hasty confession of sins he had made at Pamplona. He was once again forced to make an appraisal of his life. But this time it was done peacefully, without pressure. It may have been that many idols crashed noisily to the ground during this hour that he could have considered his last, but we do not know because Íñigo is silent about what actually did take place. If it was not at this exact moment that he looked back on the balance sheet of his first thirty years, he did so very soon afterward because he gives us a glimpse of it in the *Autobiography*, and we can also find references to it in the recollections that were compiled at a later date by his early companions. He uses the present perfect to describe these events that took place so long ago, and occasionally he uses an even more descriptive phrase when speaking to his companions, such as, "I used to have the habit of" doing such and such. We should not be deterred from recreating his past with the aid of his reminiscences because Íñigo seriously scrutinized himself and his motives in these recollections. He was rigorous in judging himself and what caused him to act the way he did; moreover, during this process of self-evaluation, he regarded himself objectively, with a cold eye, and he attempted to set the record straight with utter sincerity. Without a shred of hesitation, he grappled with the past. He loved the truth and so refused to hide it under the kind of false modesty his admirers would find so attractive. And so we ask ourselves: What was the bottom line of his self-evaluation?

In the first line of the *Autobiography*, the prudish Gonçalves da Câmara condenses the details of what he had heard in this manner: "Until the age of twenty-six he was a man given up to the pleasures of the world, and, motivated by a strong and vain desire to win renown, he took special delight in the exercise of arms." Except for the inglorious action in the town of Nájera and the disastrous affair at Pamplona, neither of which was a pleasant adventure, Íñigo never fought as a soldier nor was he ever really a soldier properly speaking. His delight in the vanity of arms was limited to participating in breathtaking tournaments, duels, and challenges of honor. But these were only make-believe battles involving play-acting soldiers, who were spurred on by the kind of vanity and self-importance that came from reading frivolous literature. "He had been much given to reading worldly and fictitious books which are generally known as tales of chivalry. . . ."

As if he were uttering some kind of revelation for us, Ribadeneira confessed that Father Ignatius's mild manner and peaceful gravity were actually cover-ups for a choleric temperament that had been domesticated, but which, when without bridle or check, as was the case during his youth, had given his personality its distinctive trait. Moreover, gifted with a vivid imagination, he had readily identified with the supermen he found in the exciting books of knight-errantry. All who knew him emphasized that his temperament was "impetuous, courageous, and even valiant in grand undertakings." Ribadeneira wrote that he was a vigorous and polished young man who was very much enamored of fineries and loved being well dressed. As Unamuno said about Don Quixote, "He reasoned with his will," but it was a will he put to the service of his own honor. Quixote was a contentious rabble-rouser, although when involved in dangerous situations he would compose verses in honor of Our Lady. It is the honorable Polanco who has sketched the personality of Íñigo with the strongest and boldest strokes. He depicted him as "a man of great and liberal spirit," capable "of giving himself unstintingly to what he was dedicated to doing or undertaking." But what else did this young man with the long, beautiful, fair-colored hair dream about if not fantasies of exploits and adventures? His dreams were always oriented toward the exterior, far from those interior regions deep within himself. In a later account, Polanco makes excuses for him and presents him as a victim of the spirit of the times that dominated the court. He tells us that his life was far from being spiritual and he justifies this assertion by a Latin phrase that says it all: "*Satis liber in mulierum amore, ludis, et concertationibus honoris causa susceptis,*" that is, "He was very free when it came to loving women, gambling, and quarreling about personal honor." It was in these pursuits that he wasted away his youth.

In his written account of Ignatius's early life, however, Polanco uses a phrase that should be read with the greatest attention: "Until that time, even though he had an *affection* for the faith, he did not live it, nor did he avoid sin; rather, he was particularly wayward in gambling, womanizing, quarreling, and in matters of arms. However, all of this was because of the custom of the times." This affection or feeling for the faith, the smoldering embers of what he had received, was infinitely far from the intensity that he would later place on the words *afección* and *afectarse* in his book the *Spiritual Exercises*. But what Polanco meant by his affection for the faith was a pure, superficial conformism, a habitual way of acting that each day became more and more watered-down, notwithstanding the occasional gusts of chivalrous devotion for the Virgin Mary and an attachment to Saint Peter. His faith was neither alive nor operative. "He in no way lived according to his faith." His life was not integrated: "He did not keep himself from sin." Today, when Spanish-speaking people use the word *travieso,* they mean "mischievous" or "naughty," but in Polanco's time it had a much harsher connotation. It meant "restless, rebellious, and it was applied to the person who was dissipated in vices, particularly sensuality." Moreover, Polanco does not conceal how this "mischievousness" manifested itself. Gambling, womanizing, and brawling is his abridgement of the same old refrain. The exploits that peopled Íñigo's fantasies at this time of his life had nothing to do with virtue or self-mastery. They were purely other-directed. His "exploits" in the Spanish picaresque sense of this term should be translated as deliberate moral bankruptcy. Laínez told the story without palliatives when he said that Íñigo was "attacked and defeated by the vices of the flesh," and all of this came about "because of bad customs." Did this mean his own personal habits were depraved or did it mean that the customs or surroundings in which he lived were evil? We do not know, but Laínez does give us an extenuating circumstance that may have diluted Íñigo's moral responsibility; yet from the psychological point of view, it explains how the heavy weight of habit gradually took from him all semblance of compunction, uneasiness, yearnings, and a clear, exacting judgment of personal guilt, rendering him susceptible to surrendering to a kind of invincible fate. Powerful sensuality begins by lulling faith to sleep, and later it smothers it altogether. Is this a subject for ascetical literature? Yes, but there is nothing Manichean or imaginary about it. It is a fact that one can observe in the same way that one can observe that stagnant water breeds mosquitoes.

Nadal describes Íñigo's religious practices as reflecting *populariter christianus,* "an everyday Christian." His choice of words is very modern because today, after so many puritanical and even heretical attacks on popular religious practices, we have begun to rediscover hidden values and depths underneath the foliage of appearances. Even in a person who has led a most dissolute life, the live embers of the faith can exist alongside the intact bastions of his personality, and those hidden resources are capable of regenerating what was once in evidence. There were three things Íñigo held onto during his destructive early life. First, he did not partake in the pillaging of Nájera after that city was fought for and captured because "it seemed to him an undignified thing to do." In this respect he was like Cyrus the Great, king of Persia, who harangued his troops in the sixth century B.C., saying, "If we win, do not indulge in pillaging; to act like this is not proper for a man, but of a lackey." Second, we should remember that although blasphemy was a common vice in those days, never did he blaspheme, not even when he was suffering the greatest pain. Finally, he never hated anyone, neither his rivals in his affairs of honor nor his enemies in times of war. These three "nots" are clues to his interior disposition, which, although at first sight might appear negative was in fact a positive stance indicating that he had said no in three important areas—areas that dealt with his hands, mouth, and his heart and soul—that is, in those areas that represented the last frontier where total moral turpitude was held at bay, in those last bastions of self-respect, dignity, and shame. Whenever a person is able to keep intact those small particles of his real self, nourish them, and then channel their energies into another direction, he redeems himself because redemption means to salvage oneself, and each man does this whenever he restructures the "noes" in his life under the commanding impulse of a new "yes." It is only when the pandemonium of life is stilled that one can hear the voices that are never quiet; or as the physician, biologist, and Nobel Prize winner Alexis Carrel observed, God does not speak to man until man is successful in creating a silence within himself.

Íñigo made his confession and received Communion, but his health did not improve. As a matter of fact, it got worse and his condition became critical. In the opinion of the physicians, "If he did not get better by midnight, he could consider himself as good as dead." Such a stated prognosis has a way of engraving itself into one's memory. Moreover, the day it was said was auspicious, for it was the vigil of the feast of Saint Peter, for whom he had a great devotion. If Íñigo died, he would not leave any greater mark in history than did his brothers—Juan, who had died in Naples; Ochoa, who had gone to Flanders to die; Beltrán, who finished his days in Italy; and Hernando, who disappeared in the Americas. But "that very night" he began to improve noticeably, and a few days later he was out of danger of death. He had come back and—believe it or not!—he returned to his vain illusions. He would soon have learned about the devastating defeat of Asparros's army and would have heard about the thousands of dead lying in the fields of Noain (June 30, 1521), where Ugarte, the captain from Azpeitia, and especially his brother, Don Martín, had distinguished themselves. But, alas, he had not been able to participate in this campaign. The duke of Nájera, however, had been there and made up for his earlier shameful desertion; but this did not keep him from being relieved of his post as viceroy, which was bestowed on Pedro Zúñiga y Avellaneda, the count of Miranda. Thus, for the second time Íñigo saw himself robbed of a protector. A few months later, there was more news: the Navarrese and French had overrun the frontier castles of Behovia and Fuenterrabía. These they would hold onto for several more years. Such avatars of war and fortune so highly praised by Machiavelli spelled opportunities lost for Íñigo de Loyola. And it was the same for the commander Herrera, who had to give an account for his faulty defense of Pamplona. Among the witnesses he quoted during his trial was the gravely wounded Íñigo, but the copy of this statement has not survived. Spanish collaborators in Navarre would also feel the avatars of war as judgments of reprisal, expropriation, and capital punishment were enacted against them. But compensations and indemnifications also came out of the war; however, no one remembered Íñigo when such were bestowed. All he had was his honor. At least he was not declared a rebel like Miguel and Juan, the sons of Dr. Juan de Jassu, the lord of Xavier, and the brothers of Francis. Ever since the capture of Fuenterrabía, they had fought on the side of the French, under the command of Pedro Navarro, the count of Olivetto, that near-mythical soldier in the wars of Italy, who was captured by the French. After lingering three years in prison, forgotten by the Spaniards, he at last won his freedom by entering the service of Francis I against Charles V.

16
"Determined to Follow a Worldly Career"

All of these events could have had repercussions in the life of Íñigo, but his greatest preoccupation at this time was how to repair the poorly set bones in his knee "because the bone protruded so much that it was an ugly sight. He was unable to abide it because he was determined to follow a worldly career and he judged his leg would be unsightly, and so he asked the surgeons if they could cut off the protrusion." Of course they could! But it would be a long operation and the pain would be greater than any other pain he had already suffered. His brother Martín was horrified and said he could never stand for such a terrible operation to be done in cold blood. Íñigo was "determined, nevertheless, to undergo this martyrdom to gratify his own inclinations," and "with his customary patience" he suffered the horrible filing down of the knobbed bone. Once this ugly protuberance was removed, the surgeons tried to avoid making his bad leg shorter than the other by applying ointments and stretching it with weights, "which caused him many days of martyrdom." His physical strength enabled him to endure all of these sufferings. He finally recovered completely, but he could not put any weight on his bad leg, and for this reason "he had to remain in bed." To fill these hours of discomfort and "to pass away the time," he asked for some tales of chivalry "to which he was very much addicted."

There is something rather surprising about his request. Did he want to become absorbed in these books for reasons similar to those of Doña Beatriz Dávila y Ahumada, the mother of Saint Teresa of Avila, "so as," her daughter wrote, "not to think about the troubles she had"? Or was he addicted to these worldly and fictitious books out of a desire to flee from reality, or was this craving to immerse himself in this reading similar to the desire of Saint Thérèse of Lisieux, who confessed in her autobiography that she could not be happy unless she had a new book? Whatever the reason, for months it would be the shadow of *Amadís de Gaula* that would hover over the restless conscience of the converted Íñigo. "Amadís," as Cervantes said through the mouth of Don Quixote, "the most perfect, the chief and prince of all . . . being the Pole star and sun of valorous and amorous knights, it is he we ought to set before our eyes as our great example, all of us that fight under the banner of love and chivalry" (*Don Quixote* I, 25). Such was the mind of Quixote for whom Dulcinea "was the most worthy and esteemed princess of the land." It may well be that Íñigo's sentiments were similar to those of the knight of La Mancha who also confessed, "I imagine everything that I say." This picturesque desire on Íñigo's part, this taste for books of chivalry, can reveal to us deeper areas of his personality. Of course, there is always a danger here of being led far afield; however, we might consider his attraction to tales of chivalry in the light of what Rof Carballo has written concerning Don Quixote's madness. He says that its origin was not so much in his having read fictional books of knight-errantry as it was in his lack of an affective life. Why, he asks, did he take refuge in reading such books, and he answers, "Deprived of a close relationship with his mother, he plunged into books of chivalry. I offer as a proof of this theory the fact that he ascribed great importance to the typical wanderings of the knight. Such is the condition of the errant in pursuit of the ideal, and it is always a sign in a man that he was deprived of basic affectivity during the state I call the affective framing, that is, at that time of a person's development when he is building foundations of loving protection." Could it have been that Íñigo, the future errant was at this time pursuing the shadow of his mother, who had been absent since the earliest days of his life?

17
God's Knight

Íñigo's request for a book about knight-errantry was not met because "none of those books he was accustomed to reading could be found in the house," although this request does open up a crack for us to see into the unconscious part of his psyche at this date. There were other books at hand, "and so they gave him a *Vita Christi* and a book in Castilian on the lives of the saints." These two works, particularly the second, were written in a style typical of medieval literature. Neither of them is listed in the prestigious catalogue of "books that changed the world"; however, both did change Íñigo. The title *Vita Christi,* or *The Life of Christ,* is most generic. At this date, there were many books that bore similar titles written by such authors as the Catalan Franciscan, Francisesch Eximenis, bishop of Elna, Gabriel López de Mendoza, Saint Bonaventure, and a number of others. Some scholars have claimed that the book Íñigo read was *Retablo de la vida de Cristo* by Juan de Padilla, a Carthusian poet from Seville. It was a work that had undergone a number of editions in Spain between 1505 and 1518. If so, Íñigo would have read verses like these:

> There are three things that encourage
> The heart of men to give in to the flesh:
> Great riches and great beauty,
> And the gentle melodies of sweet songs. . . .
> Look at the greatest Divine Clemency

Who, provided you are converted, opens His arms to you.
And so look at who He is, and then who you are:
Dust of the earth, sorrow and infirmities.

Padilla's book was better known in Spain than the four-teenth-century book by Ludolph the Carthusian that bore the same title, *Vita Christi*. But it was perhaps because of Padilla's book that Íñigo later showed interest in the charterhouse of Seville. At any rate, we find an echo of Padilla's sentiments in the *Spiritual Exercises:* "I will consider who I am and . . . who God is" (58–9). However, scholars are almost unanimously inclined to favor the work of Ludolph, which was translated into Castilian at the beginning of the sixteenth century by the Franciscan poet, Archbishop Ambrosio de Montesinos, and published in a deluxe edition of several volumes of fine Gothic type. The rich house of Loyola was poor indeed when it came to all types of books, except perhaps those ledgers in which accounts were kept. It would not be rash to suspect that such a precious book was brought from the court by Magdalena de Araoz. Its prologue contained a panegyric to the Catholic mon-archs, who were more dear in Íñigo's memory than the reign-ing king, Charles I. It spoke of their successes against the Turks and in the Indies and of their passion for Church reform. After this introduction came a lengthy study of the different stages in Christ's life. Scholars who have carefully studied both of the books he was given, in order to see if Íñigo drew any ideas from his readings, are inclined to place greater importance on the second of the two, that is, on the *Flos Sanctorum,* which was a free rendition of the *Legenda Aurea Sanctorum* by the Dominican Jacobus de Varagine (Jacopo da Varazze). By 1500, this work had already been published in almost one hundred editions, both in Latin and in a number of vernacular languages, and by this date there were two different Castilian editions in circula-tion. Pedro de Leturia identifies the edition Íñigo held in his hands as that which contained a prologue written by Fra Gauberto Fabricio de Vagad, a Cistercian historian and poet who had been a soldier before he became a monk, and who later wrote the first history of the kingdom of Aragon (1499). Íñigo, who had dreamed of accomplishing great deeds and who of his own choosing opted for martyrdom in order to correct a physical defect, was now introduced to new types of exploits and different kinds of martyrdom, both of which were also ungrudgingly embraced—even though for reasons completely different from his own. He was now being introduced to flesh and blood saints! These men professed themselves to be followers of "the eternal prince, Jesus Christ," "the gentle captain" of their souls. This was religious chivalry. According to the author, who wrote about the saints, they were "the knights of God." Such a description stealthily resonated in Íñigo's imagination. He began to conjure up images of a different King, of another kingdom, of new banners, of other knights. Such men were not abstract ideals, but flesh and blood role-models with whom he could identify, more real and no less courageous than Amadís. Íñigo was the grandson of the man who had stood up to challenge the towns of Guipúzcoa, and he was a man obsessed with meeting challenges and of "being more," and so now he began to consider this new stimulating interest in terms of a challenge, and he began to become just a bit more involved in what he was reading. Sometimes, "putting his reading aside, *he sometimes stopped to think about the things that he had read.*"

18

"Putting His Reading Aside, He Sometimes Stopped to Think about the Things That He Had Read."

Íñigo had never before put a book down in order to think about what he had just read. He would, however, learn this skill and go on to be the first to put into practice what was later to be an essential prerequisite for making the Spiritual Exercises. Saint Augustine had discovered how important this type of reflection was, thanks to his reading Cicero's *Hortensius* and the writings of the Platonists, and Saint Teresa of Avila did likewise as she read the *Spiritual Alphabet* by Fra Antonio de Osuña. However, no one has ever been converted by a book, only by what the book reveals to him. And what the book reveals is what he had already somehow been yearning to find. The world one perceives, modern psychology tells us, rests on an expectation. Or to formulate this notion schematically—one first perceives whatever he is prepared to receive. Íñigo's ardent soul was dissatisfied by mediocrity and it longed to meet difficult challenges. Within his soul there was a force that pressed him to go beyond himself. Of course, a person can easily be seduced by the illusion of wanting to be a saint, because romanticizing about sanctity is a most pleasing experience; however, a conceptual or aesthetic brand of narcissism does not have the power to change us. As for Íñigo, he was always a man who thought with his will. "Putting his reading aside, he sometimes stopped to think. . . ." This thinking was almost tantamount to action. Almost—because even for him, it was not that easy. But at least his admiration for those he met through his reading grew, and a desire to do something as a result began to flicker: "Suppose I were to do what Saint Francis *did,* or what Saint Dominic *did?*" Or what if I were *to do* what the early anchorite Saint Onuphrius had done for Christ—that is, live a life of complete austerity and total poverty in the desert, a solitary life spent in doing penance. What if I were *to do* this—I? The moment to say yes had not yet come. How difficult it is for every prodigal son to take the first step that will put him on his return trek home from a far-away land (Lk 15, 13). The reason is that the distance is neither geographic nor spatial; it is mental—the pulling away from oneself, from the deepest part one's conscious interior. *Intimior intimo meo,* "more intimate to me than I am to myself." As the French writer Georges Bernanos observed, the first step toward conversion is taken in the silence at the deepest part of one's being, in the silence that youth fears and rejects.

As early as 1553, Father Miguel Ochoa came to Pamplona where he devoutly contemplated the walls of the citadel "where all of us in the Society gained a father." Ochoa is one more example of those who see the facts backward. What the artillery charge of May 1521 produced was a seriously wounded man, or better, a number of wounded men, one of whom died a month later from his injuries. Another, the man in charge of the artillery unit, Alonso de San Pedro, recuperated quickly. He was an old man, so old, the author of a letter written in August of that year observed, "that there [was] not a single black hair on his head and he did not [have] a whisker that was not white. He [would] spend his time shaving, but without any result"—the white whiskers were all but invisible anyway. Yet his advanced age had not deterred him from marrying a twenty-year-old woman. "If the old succumb to the pleasures of the flesh," the correspondent continued, "what kind of danger lurks for us young men!" Merely having been a casualty at Pamplona did not guarantee conversion.

But it would be wrong to say that the Pamplona affair, or better, the painful physical and moral consequences of that affair, did not have an effect on Íñigo. Pamplona had created what psychology sees as a favorable framework for a radical reevaluation of one's life. Death had grazed Íñigo with her wings, but it was physical suffering, relentlessly digging her talons into his flesh over a period of weeks, that produced the deepest impression. The result of the suffering was that he experienced those lasting effects about which the French novelist Léon Bloy writes, "Man has recesses in his heart that were not there until pain came along to create them." Such recesses existed in Íñigo's heart, but they existed there as if they did not exist. Intense pain has the magical power of revealing to us muscles and marrow the existence of which we had never before divined, and this it does as it discloses for us unknown and unchartered regions deep within our heart.

We are going to follow Íñigo at this key moment of his life, the moment of his conversion. This unique experience in the life of a man is much like the experience of being born or of dying, two events with which it has much in common. It is an experience that has been relived so often that a description of what takes place does not seem inappropriate here. There are some conversions that are intellectual—the conclusion of reasoning or the bare-fisted conquest of truth. There are others that are voluntaristic in nature, conversions that come about as the result of appropriating great ideals to one's own self, and there are still others that are the fruit of emotion, of irrepressible enthusiasm, or of a flashing vision of sheer beauty. Rather than being the master of his conversion, man is conquered by it. He is seduced by truth, goodness, or beauty. Every conversion presupposes an integration of dispersed forces within a person, forces that come together and at the same time point him in a new direction, the direction toward which these forces converge (*versus*). This change affects a person at the deepest roots of his personality; it breaks the linchpin of his old way of being. So, every conversion is a *subversion* precisely because it presupposes a rupture, a rearranging, an *ad-version* or the turning away from to something else. Augustine of Hippo, who was the expert par excellence on the critical moments of this twofold direction, spoke of the *adversio a Deo et conversio ad creaturas,* "the turning away from God and the turning to creatures," which became the *conversio in Deum et diversio a creaturis,* "the turning to God and the turning away from creatures." With marvelous psychological strokes he depicted his lost and longed-for interior unity. "I was cut up in pieces the moment I separated myself from your Unity, to become lost in a multitude of things." Even before Saint Augustine, Saint Cyprian of Carthage, another convert, wrote of the conversion process:

> For as I myself was held enlivened by the many errors of my previous life, of which I believe that I could not divest myself, so I was disposed to give in to my clinging vices, and in my despair of better things I indulged my sins as if now proper and belonging to me. But afterward, when the stain of my past life had been washed away by the aid of the water of regeneration, a light from above poured itself upon my chastened and pure heart; afterward when I had drunk of the Spirit from heaven, a second birth restored me into a new man; immediately in a marvelous manner, doubtful matters clarified themselves, the closed opened, the shadowy shone with light, what seemed impossible was able to be accomplished. . . . Our power is of God, I say, all of it is free from God. From Him we have life, from Him we have prosperity; by the vigor received and conceived of Him, while still in this world, we have foreknowledge of what is to be" (*Ad Donat,* chap. 4).

This experience is outside the ken of men like André Gide, another French essayist, novelist, and agnostic critic, who confessed, "I have never been able to renounce anything; I have lived a disjointed life, protecting within myself the best and the worst." Íñigo, who had been concentrating on nothing more than adjusting the bones of his battered knee, ended up by adjusting his disintegrated soul and his disjointed life. In this second repairing operation, the surgeons had to saw away a number of protuberances, while the patient had to nurse his soul and renounce his will. It was a long, delicate process, and he described it for us in a marvelous way in the account he gave in his autobiography. We should linger on what he says, study it as if it were a transparency. His words are just as sober, no less charged with remarkable descriptive worth than those he used in his description of that butchery wherein his flesh was the subject matter. Íñigo lived this first critical moment in perfect and complete solitude, but above all, he wrapped it in absolute silence. He took no one into his confidence. Thirty years later, however, he would describe what had taken place then with a vividness that differed not a bit from what he would have used to describe an experience he was living through at the moment. He could not have acted otherwise, for all converts agree what does take place at that critical moment is an event comparable to a second and definitive birth. Everything that had happened up until then was rejected and seen as insignificant, empty, and worthy only to be relegated to the realm of death or oblivion; before that experience, everything was—vanity.

19

"He Sometimes Stopped to Think"

Before we again have recourse to Íñigo's autobiography, let us recreate the scene during which this great change took place. Íñigo lived nine long months, from June 1521 until February 1522, shut away within the upper story of the Loyola manor house. During the course of these weeks he played host to physical pain, serious reading, peaceful silence, and reflection; to old ambitions and impossible dreams; and to a preoccupation with what he would do in the future. These weeks forced him to take stock of what his life had been up until then and they also had the effect of bringing back to him his childhood days. His reveries were made easier by the almost maternal care of Doña Magdalena, the daily contact with his brothers, nieces, and nephews, and the rediscovery of his forgotten home, with its daily routine, customs, noises, and odors, and also by the weather and landscape of his native land. He looked with new eyes at scenes washed in the autumn light that fell across his window pane, and he watched Izarraitz don variegating colors, going from rose to gray and then to blue, depending on the passing hours of day or the weather's changing moods. With ears different now than before, he heard the familiar bells of sheep returning to their fold, the well-known cry of the *cashero* goading on his lazy oxen and cattle, the rhythmic ring that came from Errazti's anvil, and the distinctive tones of Azpeitia's church bells ringing of an evening as the wind blew up from the south. Landscape is a state of the soul, and Íñigo's interior had begun to change, although ever so slightly. Slow and imperceptible was the Spirit at work liberating his spirit and sensibilities. Areas within his being that had lain dormant since his earliest years began to awaken, causing vague feelings of wistfulness to stir within him. He was beginning to claim possession of his childhood—at this, the sixth hour of his life. He was pulling apart the cloth of life he had so anxiously woven, although he refrained from cutting the knots. These he untied with the patience of a weaver who loves his yarn. Grasping the present, he returned to the past, and retraced his steps down through the labyrinthine corridors of his life's history until he reached the farthest recesses of his recollections—and then going beyond, he forged into those murky zones of his unconscious, into the inmost core of his personality, with all its possibilities and deficiencies, to the very animal roots of his being. From this point he could retrace his thirty years and look at them with all of the differences they had brought. The panorama was fascinating and the task was vital for him in order to fill up his forced hours of inactivity.

But we must ask ourselves this question: At that juncture of his life, was Íñigo a failure? The truth is that with thirty years behind him he had very little to show, as far as lasting and tangible results were concerned. The opportunities life had already offered him and the possibilities he still had before him were, doubtless, far greater than those of most men. So, the answer to our question depends on the norm we use to determine what we mean by a failure. Íñigo himself had rated the Pamplona affair highly, but his action there was more the result of a willful act than a well-thought-out plan. It was a suicidal, noble deed, but one in which he had been true to his own principles and to his temporal king. However, his was an unrequited loyalty, for he was unpaid and unthanked for what he had done. He had received no commendations; his name did not even appear on the list of those singled out for merit during the time of war. His companion Malpaso had received twelve ducats to cover the expenses incurred as a result of his wounds, but Íñigo did not receive such compensation. The reason was, unlike Malpaso, he was not a soldier. The commander Herrera went out of his way to save his own skin during the investigation that was called to determine who was responsible for what had taken place at Pamplona. The master gunner wanted the authorities to cut off Herrera's head as a punishment for what he had done, but Herrera managed to defend his own cause better than he had defended the garrison, and so he continued to enjoy the office of commander; moreover, he was even entrusted with more military duties. As for Íñigo, he had come out of all of this with his honor, and his honor alone—if one makes exception for the credit he had gained in the eyes of his master, the duke of Nájera. The duke, for his part, forfeited his good name and had to give up his position as viceroy. True, Íñigo could always have been assured of a post and a salary in the duke's household, and probably even a position as the overseer of one of his castles. But what would such a poor future mean to someone like himself, who dreamed great dreams and was capable of falling in love with a princess? Now, if we consider the case from the point of view of his own ambitions, we can ask the question: Was Íñigo on the brink of failure?

When all was said and done, life had not turned its back on him nor did he feel any contempt for himself and his life. He was not an embittered man given to resentment or skepticism. He had not given up on his life, and what is more remarkable, he kept unaltered his ability to dream chimerical dreams. He was not yet a convert; he was simply a convalescent whose health, together with his dormant and far-from-dead illusions, was growing stronger each day. In his daydreams he was still given to the things of the world "that he used to think about before." Was he a failure? Certainly, he was not defeated nor dejected. It is difficult to picture this Basque of a poetic bent and enamored of an inaccessible lady, a man given over to fantasizing about fabulous adventures, as a defeated man. It would be even more difficult to visualize someone who fancied reading the tracts and tales of love as a beaten, disheartened man. Whoever could have guessed what his thoughts were at this period of his life unless he himself, as an old man, had revealed them to us in these words that seemed to rekindle the glowing, tender thoughts of the past:

Of the many vain things that came into his mind, one took such hold of his heart that he would spend two or three hours at a time absorbed in thinking about it. He dreamed about what he would do in the service of a certain lady, the means he would take to go to the land where she lived, the clever sayings and words he would speak to her, and the deeds of gallantry he would do in her service. He became so wrapped up in these fantasies that he would not even consider that it would be impossible to put them into effect, for the lady was not of the lesser nobility, nor was she a countess, nor a duchess, but her station was much higher than any of these.

In the eyes of every lover, the object of his love is always "more" than a countess or a duchess, even though her name may be Aldonza Lorenzo, the name of the sweaty peasant girl of Toboso whom Don Quixote idealized under the name of Dulcinea del Toboso. When it appeared to others she was running grains of buckwheat through her farm-girl hands, in Don Quixote's eyes she was actually sifting pearls and gold. However, Ignatius's confession does seem to indicate that the lady of his dreams was not really an abstract ideal, as the Czech Joseph Susta has suggested; much less was she the Virgin Mary, as Georges-Nicolas Des Devises du Desert has argued. Her very high position in the order of nobility forces us to consider her a woman of royal blood. We have already shown that many have suggested Íñigo's Dulcinea was Queen Germaine de Foix, despite the fact that she was the cause of the disgrace of his protector, Velázquez de Cuéllar. But by 1519 Germaine was married for the second time, was quite fat, and was a heavy drinker. Others, we mentioned, have put forth the candidacy of Leonor, whom Íñigo had had the opportunity to see at the festivals following the oath Charles I pronounced before the Castilian *cortes* at Valladolid. At that date she was twenty years old. Leonor was soon cast into the role of a political pawn when preparations were made to have her marry the prince of Navarre; however, she eventually ended up the wife of Manuel I of Portugal, and later of Francis I of France. Father Pedro de Leturia favors Catalina, the young prisoner of Tordesillas and future consort of Manuel's son, John III, who had been snatched from her lonely confinement to attend these Valladolid festivities where Íñigo could have contemplated her, dressed in violet satin bordered in gold, "the sweetest woman . . . the most beautiful creature in all the world." She was younger than Íñigo, but the difference was not as great as the disparity of years between his companion-in-arms, Alonso de San Pedro, and the young girl from Ezpeleta whom he had just married. This strange combination of love and pity for her, so familiar to a devotee of the Amadís adventures, could also have been a subconscious projection stemming from his lack of maternal nurturing.

Whether this lady was real or imaginary, Íñigo was in a delirium because "he became so wrapped up in these fantasies that he would not even consider that it would be impossible for him to put them into effect." He was aware that they had taken complete possession of him, but that fact made no difference to him at all. If his lady were real, all he had to do was open his eyes to concur with reality; if she were the product of his imagination, all he had to do was come to terms with his will. Mad, certainly; but not crazy, because, as Unamuno observed, unlike crazy men, madmen are powerless to control themselves. Poor Íñigo acted with such earnestness that, without being aware of it, he was enraptured by dreams that took up all the hours of his waking days. Íñigo: Who says that you, who were able to be "engrossed for two, three . . . four hours at a time" thinking about her without noticing the time passing, were a rigid man, calculating and cold, a man impervious to love and steeled against any kind of affection? You imagined what you thought, and you thought about what you imagined.

Since his fixation was so firmly set, so doggedly sweet, how was it possible that when his soul came under siege, another idea was able to open a breach into his dream? The answer is that this new idea was empowered by the arm of God, who would shake him "bringing it about that these thoughts were followed by others that arose from the things he had been reading." Since when can a book blur and blot out a woman's face? This new idea was not like a frontal attack, but more like a fortified tunnel or an entrenchment dug under the foundations of the fortress that would undermine it. The result: thoughts clashed against thoughts, and both sets sprang from the same source, from his two-sided, severed self. While reading the life of Christ and the lives of the saints, "he sometimes stopped to think about" such things. To stop and think in this way is to attend and answer, to debate and struggle. And this process, which we conventionally call a monologue, is the deepest of dialogues. It is a dialogue between two parts of oneself and a third part that attempts to act as the deciding arbitrator in a merciless civil war that goes on within, an irreconcilable conflict between Siamese twins that no one can separate. I say two voices, but there were many—they were legion, as numerous as the parts within his person, and their objectives were as diverse as those that tortured Saint Augustine.

20
"I Thought That I Was Two"

Certainly, this was not the first time that Íñigo had stopped to dialogue within himself about something. He had done so before, whenever he read books of chivalry, and now he was doing it as he read the life of Christ and the lives of the saints. He did more than read; he looked into himself. The words written on the pages he read germinated in his soul and became indistinguishable from his own thoughts. It was as if they were forgotten pieces of himself. He had always been susceptible to the fascination exercised by heroic role-models. His growing admiration for them was then transformed into imaginary emulation. Reflecting on what he had been reading, he began to ask himself: "What if I were to do what Saint Francis did, or to do what Saint Dominic did?" In this way he began to reflect on many things he considered good, all the while proposing *to himself* the possibility of doing difficult and serious things, and when he considered them this way, it seemed to him that they would be easy to put into practice. But all of this reasoning was reduced to this proposition: If Saint Dominic did this, I ought to do it and if Saint Francis did that, I ought to do it. This is a wonderful example of what the French philosopher Paul Ricœur called the "semantic of desire," going from the "if I were to do it" to the "I ought to do it." Íñigo got a glimpse of the peaks of sanctity from these two examples that he had chosen from the rich assortment found in the *Flos Sanctorum*. At first sight, sanctity for him consisted in *having to do* something hard and difficult. For

Unamuno, the knight-errant is "the poet of action," irrespective of whether his motivations are of human or divine origin.
We can appreciate Unamuno's definition as we analyze Íñigo's
reflections on these two saints. At first sight, Francis of Assisi
and Dominic de Guzmán performed heroic deeds—they gave
up all material goods, practiced frightful penances, and they
made a complete break with their past. By identifying with
them, Íñigo passed from thought to desire, and then from the
conditional desire to the firm purpose, although all of this
was still in the realm of fantasy. He believed it would be possible, even easy, to put into practice what he fantasized and projected in the dark caverns of desire, and his imaginings and
plans did not seem any less a dream than the ideal inaccessible lady who was the cause of inspiration for other kinds of
exploits. It was his fantasy, not his firm will, that kept him busy
going from one direction to the other. This "succession of
such diverse thoughts," this invading tide with its ebb and
flow, did nothing more than to show him how deeply divided
he was. He could have expressed this interior opposition in
verses similar to those written a century later by the Jesuit,
Juan Bautista Dávila, which were cited by another famous
Jesuit, Baltasar Gracían, the author of the classic volume, *The
Art of Worldly Wisdom:*

> Tell me who I am, my God,
> Because I am one in my being,
> But when I sinned in deed
> and thought, I thought that I was two.
>
> Why, O my soul, in times of danger
> Do you act so differently in your heart,
> From who you are?
> So much so that I believe at the same time
> There is one soul that desires
> And another that acts.

It is important to note that while one soul is set on carrying
out its intention, the other soul resists and erects barriers
against the execution of whatever the first proposes. Today,
there is a tendency to ascribe this and other dualistic interpre-
tations of man's activity to the Hellenistic influence on Christian

anthropology—as if such a simplistic explanation could ever free us from those interior conflicts and agonies that the Greeks relied more on *seeing* than on theorizing when they compiled their *theoreîn*. We should not be surprised to read that this painful tug-of-war between desire and execution, which was definitely described by Saint Paul (Rom 7:15), took place in Íñigo, nor should we be surprised that Íñigo's intermittent enslavement between two contrary desires should have exhausted him to the point of weariness. With a master stroke of phenomenology, he described how he was surprised by something in the very fine anatomy of these projected desires. Worldly daydreams delighted him as long as he entertained them, but when "he grew weary of them," he put them aside only to discover that he "was dry and restless." On the other hand, while he thought of what he would do in pursuit of sanctity—"of going barefoot to Jerusalem, of eating nothing but vegetables, and in imitating the saints in all the rigors that they had undergone"—he found he was consoled as long as these thoughts remained, and even afterward, when he was not thinking about them any longer, "he remained happy and joyful."

This intriguing alternation of ideals was followed by a change of the state of his soul, but Íñigo did not notice the subtle contrast until one day when "his eyes were partially opened and he began to wonder at this difference." How suggestive is this phrase in its laser-like precision. It meant opening his eyes to the flow of his spirit, registering the distinct resonances of contradictory signals, allowing himself to be won over by the surprising discovery of different reverberations that issued from the depths of his being. Out of curiosity and wonder was born the science of nature, and these same parents sired the speleology of the spirit.

Wonder, for Íñigo, was followed by reflection, and from reflection came verification. His experience was clear and precise: "From experience he knew that some thoughts left him sad, while others made him happy." As a consequence of experience, he learned a lesson that he never forgot; he had discovered that "different spirits were moving in him." This phrase has an objective and impersonal connotation. Ribadeneira emphasized this point when he informed us that Íñigo "understood that there were two different spirits, not only different, but completely and totally opposed to one another." He contrasted them as light and darkness, truth and falsehood, Christ and the devil. Perhaps Ribadeneira was running ahead of Íñigo, who at this time was still timidly considering this dualism that was going to demand a choice and a struggle. The two spirits that seemed to entice him from without, and the two tendencies that began to take shape within, were unduly associated with the creations of his fantasies—feats of valor in the service of a lady and feats of valor in competing with the saints. God was not challenging him personally, for God was far off, not as yet personalized or intimate, but separated from him, like that blurred horizon He shared with His saints. Yet, at this point of his laboring reflection, God was indeed raising him onto the first rung of his upward journey and was teaching him a lesson, the consequences of which would be momentous. According to an off-the-record note that Gonçalves da Câmara scribbled on the margin of the autobiographical papers Íñigo was dictating to him thirty years later, Íñigo clearly saw then what were the origins of these contrary tensions. "This was the first reflection he made on the things of God; and later on, when he was composing the Exercises, it was from this experience within himself that he began to draw light on what pertained to the diversity of spirits."

The first reflections on the things of God always implies a duality—God and myself, good and bad, spirit and flesh, substance and feeling, dreams and reality, this desire or that. Wherever there are two, there are always tensions, problems, doubts. Only the monist temptation can produce in us the illusion of simplification, fusion, and artificial absorption, of the reduction of the one before the sacrifice of the other. For a person to imagine that he is a pure spirit is as great a mistake as to allow that he is composed of body alone. To integrate this supreme hope into one harmonious psychological act supposes diversity, a very ordered diversity. The discovery of tensions that came about as a result of the duality of spirits, forces, desires, was a great lesson for Íñigo, and it provided him with "no little light." It was a light that clarified for him the cause of his present waverings, and, at the same time, it illuminated the darkened corners of his past. "He began to think more seriously about his past life, and he realized the great need he had to do penance for it." The simple comma in this sentence is indeed a small mark to differentiate a yawning chasm separating these two concepts. To recognize oneself as a sinner is to enter the antechamber of regeneration. To recognize oneself as a sinner is a far simpler and efficacious formula to do away with guilt than is a false deliberate attempt to efface the feeling of guilt. The long distance between reviewing his life, and being convinced that he had to do penance, was not yet a change or *metanoia* in the etymological, proper sense of that term, but it provided the motivation for him to make satisfaction and compensation for the emptiness and sins he discovered he had committed. This desire grew yet stronger. It was not a presumptuous or vain desire to be as good as the saints, rather it was a humble desire just "to imitate the saints," simply and without considering the circumstances, by imitating what they had done during their lifetimes. This desire was almost reaching the point where it would become a promise, and the promise was already having recourse to a power greater than his own: "Without giving any consideration to his present circumstance, he promised to do, *with God's grace*, what they had done."

Íñigo's determination was taking shape, becoming concrete. All he wanted to do was to go to Jerusalem as soon as he became well, in order, as he said, "to observe all the fasts and to practice all the disciplines any generous soul on fire with God usually wants to do." At the moment of their death, his forbears had been accustomed to ask that someone "make a pilgrimage for their soul" to far-off holy places or the Roman basilicas. Íñigo wanted to make his own pilgrimage himself, and from the very beginning it was the holy city of Jerusalem that appealed to his fancy. What did this word—*Jerusalem*—mean to Íñigo, a word that had such a strong appeal during the whole of his life? The Holy Land was a part of the Guipúzcoan tradition. The people contributed to the maintenance of its churches and went there on pilgrimages. In his songs, the composer Ancheta recounted what he knew or what he had heard tell about pilgrimages to Jerusalem, and Antonio Montesinos did the same in verse. Don Pedro Vélez de Guevara, the nephew of Doña Marina, who had accompanied the Marquis de Tarifa to the Holy Land in 1519, used to talk about what he had seen there. The Catholic monarchs had set up an endowment for the holy places on Mount Zion and created the *Obra Pía* to help them. This foundation carried on for centuries. In his *Vita Christi,* Ludolph the Carthusian declared that there was no "sight more delightful" than seeing with the eyes of the body and contemplating with the powers of the soul the land where Christ earned our redemption, and Ludolph goes on at length in describing the devout who visit the holy places and wash them with their tears of repentance. Moreover, after the conquest of Oran in Algeria (1509–10), a kind of messianism spread throughout the land heralding the imminent conquest of Jerusalem by the Catholic monarchs and predicting that Cisneros would soon offer Mass at the Holy Sepulchre. Íñigo did not dream of conquering anything other than himself, and this by doing penance. Jerusalem was the land of Jesus, the theater of our redemption, the desert wherein he could perform these penances. Because of its great distance, Jerusalem was seen as symbolizing a rupture with the past, and perhaps and most importantly, it represented a quest—an ethereal land, the unconscious call to the faraway place.

Íñigo had already overcome his deep-rooted emptiness, and he had clearly and critically evaluated his past during this lengthy period of recovering his spirits. He began to regroup and sort out his motives. One set of desires gave way to another, and he ended by having one sentiment. In a wonderful understatement he noted that "it seemed that all the fantasies he had previously pictured in his mind gradually faded away before the holy desires he now had. . . ." They began to fade away, becoming more formless and blurred until that moment when an unexpected, but certainly welcomed, event took place. This was an inner support he called a "visitation," and many years later he described it with matter-of-fact frankness and with the same kind of plain-speaking style he would use when telling about his trips to Flanders. He describes it in the *Autobiography* and it would be impossible to improve on his own rendition.

> One night, as he lay sleepless, he clearly saw the likeness of our Lady with the Holy Child Jesus. From this vision he received great consolation for a remarkably long time. He felt so great a disgust for all his past life, especially for the deeds of the flesh, that it seemed to him that all the fantasies that had been previously imprinted on his mind

were now erased. Thus from that hour until August 1553, when this is being written, he never again gave the slightest consent to the feelings of the flesh. For this reason the vision may be considered the work of God, although he did not dare to claim it to be so, nor did he say anything more than to affirm what he had said above.

This page is a marvel of psychological insights, an example of discernment of spirits on the part of the one who would one day give precise rules for discerning spirits. Íñigo related this episode very carefully, but he does not dare say with certainty that it came from God. On the other hand, he positively states the exceptional and lasting effects that resulted from it, and he was convinced that so radical a transformation could not have come about as a result of his own efforts or his natural inclinations. Finally, he "felt so great a disgust for all his past life," and while he considered the question, "Who am I?" all the false, personal honor that had been so much a part of him was peeled away, enabling him to see himself "as an ulcer and abscess from which has issued countless sins and the most offensive poison" (*Spiritual Exercises,* 58). This was the moment in his life when he became a convert, a man in need of profound redemption, a man goaded on to find ways to make up for lost time. Disgust is the corridor that leads to sincerity. Or is it the other way around? It was at this point in his life, at this moment, not before the merlons of the castle of Pamplona, that Íñigo fell wounded and vanquished. But disgust devoid of hope does not make a saint. What it does is weaken the person and brings on depression, defiance, and self-hate. The loathing Íñigo spoke of was not the cause of his transformation, rather, it was the effect of a light that had flooded him from within, enabling him to see the emptiness of the abyss that lay at his feet and, at the same time, marking out the pathway to the Absolute.

21

A Change of Soul:
"Madmen Are Uninhibited"

At that very moment, Íñigo began to become another man, and energies that would generate peace and freedom were beginning to burgeon within him, even to the extent that this interior change became visible to those who saw him. "So his brother and other members of the household recognized from his exterior the changes that had been working inwardly within his soul." Indeed, his grandnephew, Millán, and his grandnieces, Magdalena, Catalina, and Marina, became vaguely aware of the alteration. And was it possible that this change would have gone unnoticed by Doña Magdalena, about whom Íñigo later described as, she "who was ever sensitive to the marvels of God"? The changes that had taken place within him were also reflected in the way Íñigo saw things, for he now regarded everything in a different light. He began to become a person engrossed in thought. To the surprise of his family, he rediscovered his freedom, and a new kind of warm affection had come into being within him. He was "affected" in the special sense he would later give that word. "Without a care in the world, he persevered in his reading," just as he had done before, when he was absorbed in books about knight-errantry. He followed out his good resolutions and spent time talking about the things of God with the members of the household. This was the supreme proof of the change that had taken place in him, especially when we recall that he never divulged anything to anyone about his interior emotional stirrings, not even to his brother, the priest. Now his words produced an effect because they were laden with something that came from within him. It was his first experience as a spiritual guide.

His enthusiasm increased, and with new eyes he eagerly reread those same books that he had read before, because there had been nothing else around to read. He even got the idea of selecting from their pages the most important events in the life of Christ, and these he wrote down in a notebook, soon covering three hundred pages. The psychological effort involved in consigning to the written page a person's favorite thoughts and sentences causes their meaning to sink into one's soul and fix themselves in one's memory. Scholars have been able to trace beyond doubt the reappearance of certain catch phrases from the *Flos Sanctorum* and from Ludolph the Carthusian in the printed version of the *Spiritual Exercises*. The fact that one chooses a particular passage helps fix it in his memory, just as much as if he wrote it himself. The act of choosing a phrase or an idea already indicates a certain interior option and preference for that idea when the meditation is repeated. Ludolph the Carthusian recommended that "each day one should savor, step by step, with ordered discretion" a particular chosen passage, and he offered as an example of this "ordered discretion" the example of Saint Cecilia, who would select a particular passage from the Gospel and would then think about it day and night, and as she did so she "savored it with pleasure." Her example was a lesson for Íñigo. He would later write in the introductory annotations to the *Spiritual Exercises* that "it is not much knowledge that fills and satisfies the soul, but the intimate understanding and relish of the truth" (*Spiritual Exercises,* 2). If Íñigo's choice *sylva rerum* were extant today, it would furnish us with a precious look at the "choice attractions" he had culled from his reading, the particular lights that had awakened and enriched his spirit. This frustrated composer of amorous verses and declarations of love now attempted to transcribe faithfully, and with artistic penmanship, the passages that had moved him and that he had savored interiorly. On "polished and lined paper" he wrote out the words of Christ in red ink, and then he would change ink and pen to copy out the words of our Lady in blue. His precise and detailed account of what he had done at that time still has an unsophisticated freshness about it and does not at all conform to the image of the tough military man that some still insist on seeing in this part-time soldier. A simplicity so genuine and transparent could only have sprung from the fountain of an innocence rediscovered. Unamuno, with an intuition worth tons of erudition, gave us the key to this and Íñigo's other simple excesses when he said, "The hero is always a child within, his heart is always a heart of a child, the hero is nothing more than a child gotten big." Or, as he said in another place, "Madmen"—like children, I would add—"are uninhibited; it is the sensible people of this world who really kid themselves."

How intent was Íñigo in creating his personal anthology of texts! He spent long hours at this task because he had already gotten up and had begun to walk about the house. He also spent some of his time "in prayer." This is the first time we come across this phrase, so fraught with mystery. It is not difficult for a person to pray when he finds his soul overflowing with desires and projects, when he is invaded by feelings of loathing for the life he has been leading, and when he has need of help. It is not important that he use many and precise words to describe how he feels, because words are powerless to express exactly what he feels deep down. Íñigo must have had at hand a Book of Hours, which saved him from the creative effort of using a language to which he was so little accustomed, and in it he must have found the prayer *Anima Christi*, which incorrectly passed for a number of centuries as a prayer he himself had composed. We also know, thanks to a conversation Íñigo had years later with a Jesuit novice who was worried because of the affective attachment he bore for his family, that this book was costly and richly illustrated. To reassure and instruct this young man, Íñigo confided to him that in the early days of his conversion, he had found in a Book of Hours a picture of the Virgin Mary that bore a striking resemblance to his sister-in-law, Doña Magdalena. The face of the Virgin troubled him and stirred up in him human affections, and so his solution was to cover the picture with a piece of paper. With the enthusiasm of the convert, this man, who was more inclined to *ferrera extremositas* (hard-core extremism), had already begun to put in practice his tactic of *oppositum per diametrum* (the opposite of any compromise). He still bore within him a natural tendency toward harshness and excess. A gruff reprimand that he once gave to his attentive sister-in-law, Doña Magdalena, was characteristic of the excessive righteousness of a recent convert. The background to this event was that some relatives who were of the house of Iraeta had asked to borrow a pack of hounds. Doña Magdalena said that the pack was not *in the house,* a statement that was not altogether false. Almost everyone thought that Íñigo would become a bit aggravated by Doña Magdalena's white lie, even though some members of the family saw in her clever mental reservation a refusal to let the hounds go. After all, the Iraeta family were *gamboínos.* But when Íñigo heard about it, his reaction was excessively harsh. "Because of this, he rebuked her harshly and told her she could not sit at the same table with him, and for a few days he even gave her the silent treatment." One wonders if at that time he would have also removed the little piece of paper that covered her look-alike in the Book of Hours!

All of his fierce bark notwithstanding, each day Íñigo's soul was becoming more pliant, more susceptible to the subtle influence of consolation. He frequently spent long periods of time contemplating the heavens and the stars. What would the commander Herrera or Montalvo of Arévalo have said had they known "that his greatest consolation was to gaze upon the heavens and the stars, which he did often and for long stretches of time, because when doing so he felt within himself a powerful urge to be serving our Lord"? Only an exceptional poet like the Bengali mystic, Rabindranath Tagore, can help us understand this deeply personal inspiration of Íñigo's. He observed that when Nature speaks, words are hushed in our hearts as she asks us, in exchange for a response, for music that suggests the unutterable, and he said that at that moment thought arises—or has already risen— beyond thought itself. By the end of his days, Íñigo, who had been so reticent when it came to expressing poetic feelings, would allow other fleeting outbursts of similar emotion to escape from his heart, such as the famous, "How sordid is the earth when I contemplate the heavens!" or when he spoke about contemplating ordinary flowers. Here again Tagore comes to our aid, "As we are tempted by the spell of the insolent spirit of human prosperity . . . we encounter a flower, a messenger from another shore, and it whispers softly into our ear: 'Here I am; He sends me. I am the messenger of the Beautiful, whose soul is the paradise of love. His bridge already touches the beach of this distant island. He has not forgotten you and now He will save you. He will carry you toward Himself and make you His own.'" Íñigo was now seeing things from another point of view, and that is why he was contemplating nature in a way he had never imagined he would. Like Francis of Assisi, whom he admired so much, he let himself be open to an invasion of cosmic feelings. But with him these sentiments were transformed into a dynamic force geared toward action. He would never be a master of the art of expression. He is considered the master of the art of willpower. But his hidden secret was lodged in feelings, in the way he came "to feel interiorly." All his life Íñigo allowed himself to be governed by vague interior waves, which he called "movements," and which the ancient Greek ascetics named *kinesis,* and methodically he would seek out their meaning. The day would come when he would learn that there were periods of dryness bereft of all feelings, times when affective love and love of service would have to depend solely on sheer willpower.

Would this quiet man who gazed intently on the heavens become a contemplative? First, he wanted to achieve a goal that had been burning within him, and "he desired to be entirely well so that he could take to the road." Even though he was passionately attached to living the present moment in all of its riches and depth, he still considered the future and imagined what he would do after he returned from Jerusalem. He was enthralled by the idea of living a life of perpetual penance, hidden away, eating only vegetables, like Saint Onuphrius. To this loathing he had for himself was now joined the desire "to indulge the hatred he had conceived against himself." Íñigo, you are excessive and ardent, and you now dream of entering the famous charterhouse of Seville, "without saying who [you are] so as to be held in scant esteem." You have not yet overcome your pride. The obsession for anonymity besets only those who savor the luster of their own genealogy, the glory of their name, not the vast number of ordinary men who already live simply in their own anonymity. Will you be more hidden in obscurity doing your penances than "by going about the world"?

The charterhouse of Miraflores in Burgos was not far off. One day Íñigo surprised one of the Loyola servants, who was being sent on an errand to this sometime capital city of Castile, by entrusting him with a secret commission. The man was to obtain information on the rule followed by the monks at Miraflores. He fulfilled his mission, and Íñigo was satisfied with the information he had brought him. But first, Íñigo had to go to Jerusalem, and soon, too. By this date he must have been "almost completely healed." To get to Jerusalem he had to cut the ties with his family, to pass once more—and this time for good—beneath the lintel of Loyola's gate, past the cauldron on the Loyola coat-of-arms, while keeping secret the project that was simmering within the cauldron of his heart. Christmas of 1521 had come and gone. It was the last time he celebrated this feast day at home. He probably left Loyola in mid-January 1522. The hour had come, the breaking-away point that had incalculable personal, familial, and social consequences. Íñigo himself felt confident and free, but he was afraid of his family's reaction, and especially did he fear his brother Martín, who was his guardian and the head of the family.

For once, the intrepid Íñigo did not fight face-to-face; he seemed timid and ill at ease, jealously hiding his secret. He sought some pretext to justify his leaving. One day, he hinted to his brother that he thought it would be good if he went to Navarrete. He did not press the subject beyond saying that his benefactor the duke was there and that the duke knew that he was now healed. What he said was true, but he was not telling the whole truth. However, Íñigo was talking face-to-face with another Basque, as reserved as himself, a man just as shrewd as the wolves rampant on the Loyola coat-of-arms. This brother and other members of the household had already suspected that Íñigo wanted to "be up and going," and so Martín was not caught off guard by any of his brother's disguised intentions. The brotherly exhortation Martín delivered was, therefore, not made up on the spur of the moment. Employing the indirect style and using a number of descriptive verbs, Íñigo recreated the family scene beautifully in the *Autobiography*: "His brother took him from one room to another and with many protestations of love begged him not to make a fool of himself, but to consider what hopes people had in him, and to see what he could make of himself, and similar other words all with the purpose of turning him away from his good intentions." Íñigo saw himself "tempted grossly and openly" (*Spiritual Exercises,* 9), confronted by the firm, coherent logic, which up until the time of his conversion had been his own way of thinking, and with a number of arguments that were convincing for the one brother, but crude and weak for the other. Sweet talk was no sedative for a man engaged in spiritual combat, nor did threats have any effect in taking from him the peace and freedom he had gained by the end of the confrontation. It was blood that was speaking to blood in this mélange of pleading and commanding, of praising and appealing, and added to blood, there was the past, present, and even the future in the form of expectations. It was a frontal attack against the dangerous and shameful adventures Íñigo intended to undertake. His family wanted him to be as they were, reminiscent of Søren Kierkegaard's delightful parable about the eagle tamed by ducks.

Íñigo weathered the assault, and withdrew as best he could. Martín's tactics, however inglorious, were also used in war. For once, Íñigo gave up his honor and, for all appearances, retreated. In fact, however, he claimed victory because he had the last word and that was the word that prevailed. "But he answered in such a way that, without departing from the truth about which he was always very scrupulous, he avoided direct issue with his brother." Probably he had not deceived his brother at all. Íñigo was not going to where he was going, but he was going to where he was not going. Any polemicist less perceptive than Pascal would see in this episode the birth of the Jesuit form of mental reservation. However, the Jesuits were not yet born, not even in the mind of the one who would be their father.

22
"Converted Passion"; Self-Integration

Íñigo prepared himself for the journey as if he were going to settle in at the house of his protector, the duke. He packed his bags, dressed in all of his finery, and he did not forget to attach his sword and dagger to his belt. He alone knew his secret plan, but a careful observer would have noticed something about the way he looked at people around him, because whoever says good-bye for an indefinite period of time, and possibly forever, caresses with his eyes the faces and characteristics of those he loves. Once again he crossed under the lintel of Loyola's entrance as if he were someone crossing the frontier to freedom. Fifteen years previously, he had gained uncertain freedom *from* something; this time it was freedom *for* something. But was Íñigo really free? He was not yet a saint; he was only an imitator of saints as far as their external idiosyncrasies were concerned. He paid no attention to abstractions, seeking always the concrete. Now his will was possessed by something stronger than itself. His "converted passion" had pointed him to a new direction in life. The French psychologist of religion, Louis Lavelle, correctly observed that in the saint freedom and necessity are merged, and what he wrote on this subject casts light on this particular moment in Íñigo's life.

> We are always differentiating between the interior and the exterior, truth and opinion, what we want and what

we can do. The realization of one's homogeneity is proper only to the saint. We always imagine that the saint lives a life of continuous sacrifice because we concentrate on the sacrifice, which is really exterior and separate from the person of the saint. What frightens us is the opinion of others, because we think it disdains the truth of who we really are. We have recourse to our weakness, thinking that it makes our deepest desires impossible to realize. The saint does not know such a fear nor does he encounter such an obstacle. Because he is always totally aware of who he is, the saint never calculates losses and gains. And so he never has the impression that he is sacrificing anything. How could he make the sacrifice of the exterior, which for him is nothing more than the interior of a presence that is aware of him?

"So, riding a mule," Íñigo left Loyola in February 1522. He had defiantly thrown himself into the Pamplona adventure mounted on a horse at full gallop; now, gently goading his mule, he began a new adventure, a future that was less defined. Unforeseeable consequences hide themselves behind the small, although deliberately chosen, actions in our lives. Íñigo set out accompanied by two house servants who we know as Andrés de Narbaitz and Juan de Landeta. These were sent along by the family as a precaution, however unnecessary, to guarantee that he would arrive at his destination. His brother Pedro was also part of the group. This was the same Pedro who would become the parish priest in Azpeitia and who had been his companion in the Mardi Gras capers of 1515. He had fathered a daughter a few months before this historic journey. For Íñigo he was the closest and most tangible "man of the Church" that he had known. Along the way, the layman persuaded the priest that they should "make a vigil at the chapel of our Lady of Aránzazu." They climbed up to the little hermitage hidden away in the steep crags. Íñigo made his prayer, gaining added strength for the road. Many years later he would recall the benefits he had received from that vigil in the darkness that was broken only by the dawn. Afterward, they went down to Oñate, and Pedro remained there at the house of one of their sisters whom he had gone to visit. This sister, Magdalena, was the wife of Juan de Gallaiztegui, and it was she who had let Íñigo stay in her house for a few days after he was wounded at Pamplona. Here the brothers bade good-bye to one another. These good-byes solidified the distance that had grown between them and the cool hostility and unfriendliness on the part of Pedro. They would never see each other again. After the assassination of García de Anchieta, Pedro became the rector of the parish church at Azpeitia, and in 1529 he died on the way home from one of his numerous trips to Rome, where he would go on a regular basis to argue his case against the Poor Clare nuns of his native town.

As a result of the generosity that prompted his making a vigil at the shrine, Íñigo not only regained his strength, but he also began to lose that powerful drive he thought was always with him. The French Catholic existentialist Gabriel Marcel observed that having certitude does not mean that our thinking and emotions are immobilized; certitude can exist alongside certain fear—even the fear of oneself. Íñigo now wanted to tie his will with sacred knots. He was not motivated by fanaticism, but by fear—the fear that came over him when he remembered that he had not been fearful during difficult battles in the past. Accordingly, it was probably at Aránzazu, this prelude-place for the new life he was about to embark upon, where he made a vow of chastity. Many years later he admitted that such was the case to Laínez, and Ribadeneira also records it. We are more partial to Laínez's version, which says that "since he was afraid of being overwhelmed in matters regarding chastity more than in any other areas, he made a vow of chastity before Our Lady, to whom he had a special devotion, while he was still en route." He could lose the battle, as he had at Pamplona, but no one could take away from him his generous spirit or, as Laínez would call it, his "pure intention." Laínez vouches for the efficacy of the gesture and of the sought-for protection when he says, "Although up until then he had been attacked and conquered by the vice of the flesh, from that moment until the present time, our Lord gave him the gift of chastity and, as I believe, to a high degree of perfection." Saints are not born but made, and in moments of weakness they drink the elixir of heroes, strengthening their vacillating faith with willpower. "Only the one who attempts the absurd is able to conquer the impossible," observed Unamuno. So that this vow would not remain in the realm of beautiful rhetoric, "from that day when he left his native land, he took the discipline every night."

"And he went on toward Navarrete" probably, if he had no other reason, because he did not want to be involved in telling a lie. He had already decided that the first stop on this journey to Jerusalem was to be at Montserrat, the famous center for pilgrims. It does not seem likely that he saw the duke face-to-face at Navarrete. But, despite the fact that he had already resolved to give up all material possessions, he did request that the duke's treasurer give him the salary that was owed him. At the time, the duke's treasury was seriously strained, but the duke said that "even though he lacked money for all else, he would never be short of money for Loyola"—Loyola is what Íñigo most probably was called among the members of the court—and he was even ready to place him in charge of one of his better pieces of property "in recognition of the reputation he had earned in the past." Íñigo did not care about being an overseer of any property or person; what he wanted was to become the protagonist in his own uncertain personal adventure. He took the money, however, asking that part of it be paid to unspecified persons to whom he was still in debt; the other part was to be used to refurbish a statue of the Blessed Virgin.

Íñigo dismissed the servants who had accompanied him. They could now truthfully report to his brother Martín that he had indeed gone to the duke's palace. Moreover, he confided in them his plan to go to Montserrat "as a poor, penitential pilgrim." This was the last trace his family had of him for a number of years. He was now in a hurry. The reason was not only because of the zeal that consumed his soul, but it was also because he wanted to put distance between himself and Adrian of Utrecht's cortege that was pursuing the same route. Adrian had accepted his election to the papacy at Vitoria on February 10, and on March 15 the duke welcomed him as his guest at the castle in Nájera. Had Íñigo so desired it, he could once more have tested the sweetness of high society and could have had doors opened for him to an unseen promising future. But he followed his own lonesome path: choice before destiny, choice of his own making.

23

"He Set Out Alone Riding His Mule"

"He set out alone riding his mule" toward Montserrat, just as Don Quixote sallied forth one morning before daybreak, alone, and likewise "wonderfully pleased to note with how much ease he had succeeded in the very beginning of his enterprise"(*Don Quixote,* I, ch. 2). But he was not as alone as he had thought. He was a Loyola. His fine clothes cried out for all to see that he was a man of importance, and he knew it. These clothes would be companions of consequence for him. We have no way of knowing whether our knight, still a novice in matters of spiritual adventures, recited aloud the foolishness he had learned through his reading of romantic tales, but we certainly do know that these stupidities were running through his mind. Even though the years had put a certain distance between these days and the recording of their events, they did not tone down the vivid impression they had made on him. He narrated his adventure in one of the most colorful and exciting pages in his autobiography.

On the road there occurred an incident that is worth relating for the better understanding of how our Lord dealt with Íñigo's soul, which, although still blind, had a great desire to serve Him in every way he knew. He had determined *to practice* great penances not so much with an idea of making satisfaction for his sins, as *to make himself agreeable* to God and please Him. Thus whenever he *made up his mind to do* some penance that the saints *had performed,* he was *determined to do* the same, and even more. From such thinking he took all his consolation. He never took a spiritual view of anything, nor did he even know the meaning of humility, charity, or patience, or that discretion was a rule and measure of these virtues. Without having any reason in mind, his sole idea was *to perform* these great, external works, because the saints had done so for God's glory.

He repeats all of these verbs that imply *doing* ad nauseam only to end up with *great* and *even more.* He was thinking about imitating penances, not about repentance for sins. He blithely outlined his future in terms of exterior signs, just like Don Quixote, that is, "all in imitation and in the very style of those that the reading of romances had furnished him with" (*Don Quixote,* I, ch. 2, 33–4). Despite his previous exercises in introspection, he no longer looked into the interior. He had not even begun to learn the very basic facts about humility, charity, patience, nor the day-to-day practice of a number of other virtues. He had no need of these now. He was inflamed with an uncontrollable fire and was confident that God asked him for generosity alone. The other virtues would come simply as frosting on the cake. What Teresa of Avila said about a similar change in her life is much like the change Íñigo was about to make in his. "As a consequence [of advice she was given by her confessor, Saint Francis Borgia], I began to make many changes, and I did so for the love of God and not through constraint . . . in exterior matters the change was apparent" (*Life,* 24, 1).

Íñigo followed the road that very likely was the only one he could have taken, passing through the towns of Logroño, Tudela, Alagón, Zaragoza, Fraga, Lérida, Cervera, and Igualada. There were a number of things that happened to Don Quixote en route that were worth documenting, but for Íñigo, "there was one thing that would be good to record"; as for the others, he passed them over in silence. One day, as he progressed along his way, a Moor riding a mule caught up with him. "They fell into talking, and the conversation turned on our Lady." Íñigo, who was going from Aránzazu to Montserrat, was overjoyed. The conversation turned deeply serious, even ecumenical in tone, because "the Moor admitted that the Virgin had conceived without man's aid, but he could not believe that she had remained a virgin as a result of the birth process." He explained the reasons for his thinking, and the theological arguments proffered by Íñigo did not make him change his mind. The Moor then took his leave, hurried on, and finally passed out of Íñigo's sight, leaving "the pilgrim with his own thoughts on what had taken place." Had he ever read Padilla's *Retablo de la vida de Cristo*, he would have found three verses like these apropos to Mary's virginity:

> Cursed be those who do not believe in [Mary's virginity]
> Basing their arguments on our own nature . . .
> I strongly advise you, O Christian:
> Flee from those who do not believe in this mystery.

As Íñigo reflected on his conversation with the Moor he was caught up in a tide of emotion that he describes magnificently. His "interior movements" carried him on progressively from discontent to sorrow for failing in his duty, to wild indignation against the Moor for his audacity, to an urge to defend the honor of our Lady, to the desire to search out the Moor, not merely to tie him captive to the knight's mule and bring him to our Lady of Montserrat where he would make him kneel at her feet, but with the intent of stabbing him a number of times with his dagger for what he had said. "He struggled with this conflict of desires for a long time, uncertain to the end as to what he ought to do," because, among other things, in order for him to realize his plan, he had to turn off from the Royal Highway to pursue the Moor. "Tired from trying to figure out what would be best to do," he still found no satisfactory solution, and so he decided "to let the mule go with the reins slack" up to where the Royal Highway crossed the village road, along which the Moor had gone, and at that point the mule could make the decision. Despite the fact that the road taken by the Moor was wider than the Royal Highway, Íñigo's mule chose the latter, thereby saving the Moor from death and Íñigo from the galleys and from a broad detour away from the road upon which he had recently embarked. So he was like Don Quixote, whom Cervantes describes in this manner: "And having thus dismissed . . . busy scruples, he very calmly rode on, leaving it to his horse's discretion to go which way he pleased; firmly believing that in this consisted the very being of adventures" (*Don Quixote*, I, ch. 2).

Most probably, the "large town" near Montserrat where Íñigo wanted to buy the clothes that he decided to wear when he went to Jerusalem, was either Lérida or Igualada. He remembered the purchase very distinctly as "some cloth of the type used for making sacks, with a very loose weave and a rough prickly surface." Someone took the material and made him a long garment that went all the way down to his feet. He bought a staff as well as a small gourd, obligatory accouterments in the gear of a pilgrim, and these he attached to the saddletree of his mule. Íñigo also purchased a pair of sandals, but he did not use both. One of his legs was still bandaged and in bad shape, so much so that it was swollen by the end of each day, even during those times when he rode. He decided to wear one sandal on the foot of this bad leg, and he continued his journey toward Montserrat with the kind of fever in his head and in his heart that was typical of the knight-errant in the novels he had read. As the *Autobiography* describes:

> And he continued his way to Montserrat, thinking as always about the great deeds *he was going to do* for the love of God. As his mind was filled with the adventures of *Amadís de Gaula* and similar kind of books, thoughts corresponding to these adventures came to his mind. He determined, therefore, on a vigil of arms through the whole night, without ever sitting or lying down, but standing a while and then kneeling before the altar of our Lady of Montserrat, where he resolved to leave his fine attire and to clothe himself in the armor of Christ.

Scenes from *Amadís de Gaula* flooded Íñigo's imagination. In Book 4, Espladián, an armed knight, spends a vigil before the Blessed Virgin's altar, and the scene described here corresponds exactly with the ritual prescribed in the *Siete Partidas*, the great corpus of constitutional, civil, and criminal law promulgated by Alphonso X the Wise, king of Castile and León. The knight who would make the vigil should be "sometimes kneeling down and sometimes standing rigidly erect . . . for the knights' vigil of arms is not designed for amusement, nor for anything like that, but to beg God to protect them . . . as men who are entering a career of death." And to think that this Íñigo was a contemporary of Machiavelli!

Íñigo finally arrived at Montserrat on March 21, 1522. It was the first stop in his peregrinations. He had long dreamed of coming here, which at first sight may seem strange, but the devotion to the Black Virgin enshrined at Montserrat was fashionable among the courtier milieu—in the household of Queen Isabella and in that of Queen Germaine, and even in the household of the duke of Nájera. The duke's wife, Doña Juana de Cardona, who belonged to the highest Catalan nobility, had a devotion to the Black Virgin, and her father had been educated in the monastery's choir school. Devotion to our Lady of Montserrat was also popular throughout Guipúzcoa, where collections were regularly made in the churches for this distant shrine; where last wills and testaments provided offerings for this same monastery; and where there were many people who made a vow to go there on pilgrimage. At one time, the assembly of Guipúzcoa authorized a collection be taken up to provide the monastery with two priests who could hear confessions in Basque, so that Guipúzcoan pilgrims "would be able to unburden their consciences in their own language." Our elegant knight arrived at the monastery "with expensive, beautiful, and fine clothes . . . in the fashion and style of soldiers," on the morning of March 21, 1522. He was so engrossed in his own thoughts that he did not have the time to contemplate the unusual landscape surrounding the shrine. The first place he went to was the church, lavishly bathed in a candlelight, so that he could pray and then look for a confessor. This was not a difficult task in a monastery that numbered some fifty monks, who, since the beginning of the century, had been inspired by an authentic spirit of reform. García Ximénez de Cisneros, a cousin of the famous cardinal of the same name, had restored the divine office and the practice of contemplation, and made these the center of the monastery's life. He was the first in Spain to introduce method in prayer and the most famous promoter of meditation as it is generally understood. A few years earlier, Íñigo could have met (or perhaps avoided meeting) monks here who were his fellow countrymen, men such as Juan de

San Juan de Luz, who wrote treatises on the Holy Spirit, and Alonzo de Vizcaya, who was the author of another treatise, this one on the spiritual marriage. The monastery was noted for how highly it regarded books and it took pride in its rich library and its own printing press.

Íñigo, however, was not looking for books but for a confessor before whom he could come to terms once and for all with his past. "He made a general confession in writing which lasted three days." He also sought out someone in whom he could confide his future plans, because up until then he had taken no one into his confidence. The first man with whom he shared his jealously guarded secret was Jean Chanon, or Juan Chanones, a saintly French monk who also knew a thing or two about what it meant to give away wealth generously; before being clothed in the Benedictine habit of Montserrat, he had renounced the revenues from his benefice of Mirepoix. Although he was accustomed to confess pilgrims, it was not every day that he encountered a pilgrim like the one who now stood before him—this dashing knight who wanted to make him his accomplice in a chivalrous ritual he wished to go through so that he could devote himself to a life of prayer and penance, a rite of passage to a new life that would culminate in his making a meticulously prepared confession. Chanones, however, was a most competent man for understanding and guiding this newly arrived, intensely zealous pilgrim whose confession was far from being trivial or routine.

The prudent confessor realized that he was dealing with a penitent who was accustomed to acting out the books he had read and who was now disposed to reevaluating his life. Therefore, it would not be surprising that he gave him either a *Confessionario,* a book containing a compilation of sins that he often gave to pilgrims who knew how to read, or the monastery's treasured work, *Ejercitatorio de la vida espiritual,* the legacy of its reformer, García de Cisneros. There was an abridged version of this volume that had gone through a number of editions, the latest of which was published in 1520. It was a kind of handbook of prayers and pious practices designed for pilgrims. These books did not pretend to offer anything original nor were they in the vanguard of a new spiritual movement, but they did contain a rich spiritual heritage, largely cultivated and expressed by authors in far-off lands with strange sounding names, like Jean Mombaer, Gerard Zerbolt of Zutphen, and Thomas à Kempis. These three men were members of the Society of the Brothers of the Common Life that had been founded toward the end of the fourteenth century by Gerard de Groote and Florens Radewyns. Mombaer, a contemporary of Chanones, was particularly indebted to Zerbolt, who was a proponent of the so-called *devotio moderna* spirituality. The striking originality of the three Flemish and Dutch writers consisted in the importance they placed on the methodical steps in the spiritual process, and all three were especially strong in the way that they treated the experience of prayer. Íñigo knew well how important dueling exercises were, and he knew that he had to have a method when it came to breaking a horse, in learning to play music, in firing a crossbow, and in producing artistic penmanship. He was now about to learn that the road he had undertaken was not about extraordinary and disconnected exploits, but that it was made up of phases, or stages—purgation, illumination, and union— and that a general confession was not an end of the process but a beginning; that there were rules and precautions for learning about how to examine one's conscience and control- ling one's thoughts; that there were helps for learning how to pray successfully, such as the invocation at the beginning of the prayer, the control of the imagination, and an ordered reflection by means of points and parts of the prayer; and that the colloquy develops spontaneously. It was not enough that he learn or know all about these things; it was necessary that he perseveringly and patiently *exercise* himself in them. This was veritable revelation, an authentic discovery that made a profound impression on him. The results of this insight will make themselves evident in the first draft of notes he would begin to jot down and that he would afterward call his *Spiritual Exercises.* Scholars would come along at a later date and ferret out the influential sources of these Exercises, but they would leave no doubts about the basic originality of Loyola's creation.

The initial three days he spent at Montserrat were too brief for us to suppose that he had assimilated much of anything, because such assimilation demands time. Íñigo already had enough to do to make a good confession and to put into effect the initial part of his plan with less complicated methods. He would divest himself of all that he had, as a first step in his pilgrimage to Jerusalem. Chanones was his secret accomplice in this affair. He had no difficulty arranging with him that his mule should be given to the monastery, a mule that had indeed seen many years. It was not unusual either that Chanones should hang up as an ex-voto before the statue of the Blessed Virgin the sword and dagger that the knight had entrusted to him in confidence. For many years these arms remained on the grille that separates the church from the alcove where the statue of the Blessed Virgin is placed. Hanging his fine clothes on the grille would have been a bit more dramatic, and it would have been impossible to reconcile it with the complete anonymity with which Íñigo wanted to proceed. But he took heart from the great opportunities he now had at hand and made the decisive step that put an end to the anxieties with which he had been living for so many weeks, anxieties that concluded a long chapter of his life story. With the following gesture, he annihilated his entire past: "On the vigil then of Our Lady's Annunciation, March 24, in the year 1522, he went at night, as secretly as he could, to a poor man and, removing his fine clothes, gave them to him and put on the attire he so wanted to wear," namely, the pilgrim's long, loosely woven, very prickly garment he had purchased on the way to Montserrat. To cast aside his finery meant more than embracing a life of poverty; it meant breaking away from whatever was symbolic of his standing in the eyes of men. He now deliberately cut asunder the bonds that tied him to the past. In his joyful, violent hurry, he got the unfortunate inspiration to offer his clothing to the first street beggar who would accept his ill-suited gift. Íñigo had dreamed of being poor and forgotten, and the beggar had dreamed of being rich and esteemed; the few yards of cloth exchanged between one owner and the other had brought about a simple miracle. Íñigo, dressed in his pilgrim robe, was now disguised as a poor unknown—as if taking off his clothes would strip from him all realization of who he was, who his family was, and what his name and reputation meant. Exteriorly, he had already become a Francis of Assisi who could call only God "Father," and all the people he met along his way, "brother" or "sister." There is something of the "hippie" in this theatrical rupture with the past. He had become a nonconformist, a protester. The real difference was within himself, since he now knew where he was going, or at least, he thought he knew. He had usurped his freedom, but this freedom was not an end in itself.

Dressed in his sackcloth, his new strange badge of knighthood, he was copying the heroes from the books of chivalry, "and he went to kneel before our Lady's altar. Alternating between kneeling and standing, with his pilgrim's staff in his hand, he thus spent the whole night." It was the night of March 24–25, which was interrupted by matins for the feast of the Annunciation. It was a night of promises and prayers crowned by the rapture of the joyful Mass and matins accompanied by music that Íñigo found pleasing indeed. Lost within the crowds of pilgrims and hidden by the friendly shadows of the church, he received Holy Communion. Then "at daybreak he left to avoid being recognized." To shun such a possible discovery, he did not take the road to Barcelona, "where he would meet many who would recognize him and honor him," but he made a detour to a town that turned out to be Manresa, and here he decided to spend a few days in a hospice "and to make a few notes in his book that he carried very carefully with him and that was a source of great consolation for him." He had experienced too many things in too short a time and therefore he had a need to stop and pour out his emotions in writing on the pages of the only treasure he kept in his knapsack: his notebook.

Without realizing it, he had left a storm behind. All of his disguises and precautions were of no avail. Someone had followed him from Montserrat, caught up with him, recognized him, and anxiously asked him if he had indeed given his clothes to a poor man, as the individual had asserted. The beggar had been in as much a hurry to pass himself off as a rich man as Loyola had been in passing himself off as a poor man! Íñigo told the plain truth. He did not feel he had to say who he really was, where he had come from, nor what his family name was—not even to free the innocent beggar. Why would the simple truth not be enough? Now in his pilgrim robe he found himself identified with the poor and it was then that he came to see the personal, human drama of the situation, and for the first time he understood the cruelty of blind, human justice before the innocence of a poor man dressed as a rich man. "I gave him the clothes," Íñigo answered dryly while "tears of compassion started from his eyes," as he himself recorded in his autobiography that he felt "compassion for the poor man to whom he had given his clothing, sympathy for him because he realized that the poor man was being harassed since they had presumed he had stolen the clothes." In his first hour of his lonely anonymity and profound meditation, he had discovered a nameless neighbor caught up in the most grotesque and deplorable helplessness. He who was able to have his bones sawed off without uttering a whimper, doing nothing more than tightening his fists, now wept with compassion. Although his weeping was most probably in variance with the tenants of orthodox chivalry, it is nevertheless rich in significance. To weep for oneself or for another, according to the world-renowned Spanish psychiatrist and humanist author, Juan José López Ibor, is always a "vital elaboration, a catharsis, a digestion of suffering."

As he distanced himself from this holy mountain of unforgettable memories, Íñigo pressed on in his journey, a journey that had witnessed the death of the gentleman within him and the birth of another man. "Whenever a man does something heroic, or a deed of great virtue, or a performance of challenging exploit," observed his contemporary, fellow Basque, and illustrious physician, Juan Huarte de San Juan, "he is born again, and he acquires other and better parents in the process and loses the self he had previously been." Íñigo, the newly born man, now carried in his soul "a promised land," and was prepared to cover the earth in order to seek it out. It was yet a land unchartered, veiled in dense fog, a land that was unlike the promised lands of the majority of men of his times. For the moment, Íñigo was in tune with himself alone; he was out of step with his times.

24

The Times, the Lonely Hero, and the Apprentice Christian

At this juncture in the book, the indulgent reader will remind me that I have not been faithful to the promise I made earlier to study the personality of Íñigo and *his times,* and he will accuse me of being guilty of the sin of psychoanalyzing Íñigo. But really, how else could I have proceeded in giving a description of the reeling battle that took place in every nook and corner of Íñigo's psyche, the recesses of which he discovered to be deeper and deeper, until they were unreachable? Could the treaties signed between Charles I, Henry VIII of England, and Pope Leo X, or the thematic developments of the wars against France, or the conquest of Mexico by Hernán Cortés have meant anything to this man who was in the throes of an existential crisis, and who had an insatiable thirst for the Absolute? And could he have been concerned that Selim I the Grim had assured the world that his successor would be his only son, Süleyman I the Magnificent, or that the Muslims had overrun Belgrade and Rhodes? Such events meant nothing to him except for the fact that they might have an effect on his travel plans to Jerusalem. Could he, who was absorbed in crossing the meridians and parallels of the extremely vast microcosm that is man, have been outraged by the poverty of his fellow Guipúzcoan and Magellan's lieutenant, Juan Sebastián del Cano, who had recently arrived in Seville, the first man to have circumnavigated to the globe?

Because he wanted nothing from the court, he in no way anticipated the return to Spain of the Emperor Charles, and he was not at all involved in the litigations that tied up his family in the disputes between the parish priests and the Poor Clare nuns of Azpeitia. Likewise, he was indifferent to the fact that his priest brother had made trips to and from Rome in the family's interest. He did not even want to come near Pope Adrian VI's court or the papal cortege that was lumbering toward Rome, past cities like Logroño, Zaragoza, and Barcelona, the same route he was taking—alone. He never considered taking advantage of his connections with the Sovereign Pontiff or his court to beg for prebends; he would go to these men of influence only to request a license or passport to the Holy Land. At a time when different presses were printing copies of the Alcalá Polyglot Bible, Erasmus's *Colloquies,* Thomas More's *Utopia,* Ludovico Ariosto's epic verses, and Martin Luther's brutal invectives, he was satisfied with his notebook containing those excerpts that he had read with such deep emotion from the *Flos Sanctorum* and the *Vita Christi.* He made no claims to the times in which he was living. They were not his. For him, they were merely simultaneous and synchronized events that took place and were of interest only to those involved in keeping calendars or composing chronological tables for history books.

And how about Martin Luther? Luther, who was condemned and excommunicated in 1520, appeared before the Diet of Worms in April 1521, and was then walled up in Wartburg the same time that he, Íñigo, was recuperating from his wounds and reevaluating his life at Loyola—what did Íñigo think of Martin Luther? Brother Martin had been responsible for the tremendous upheaval that was devastating the European world. Did all of these polemical conflicts that he stirred up touch Íñigo in any way? No, not even Martin Luther was present in his world. Íñigo's conversion owed its origin solely from what was, and had been taking place, within Íñigo. This conversion did not mean that Íñigo was against anything or anyone, except Íñigo himself. The idea of his being the antagonist to Luther or the organizer of the anti-Protestant fighting forces throughout Europe, or of becoming the knight-errant for the Catholic Reform movement had never crossed his mind. He made a vow of chastity freely and spontaneously at the very time when Luther was mocking and attacking the tyranny of religious vows, which he considered unnatural and contrary to the Gospel. Loyola is the antithesis to Luther when he goes from shrine to shrine, leaving his ex-votos, but particularly when he believes, simplistically, that Christian life consists of *doing* great things.

An author is tempted to weave compelling and lovely literary counterpoints out of the simultaneous dreams of Luther at Wartburg and Íñigo at Loyola, and to create simple, after the fact, prophecies from them. But the truth of the matter is that Luther had less influence on Íñigo's thinking than did Amadís de Gaula. The fictional character was more real to him than the thundering, flesh-and-blood German. The only way we can compare the two is the way Plutarch compared unconnected personalities in his broad gallery of parallel figures—and by definition, parallel lines never meet. Of course, before making comparisons, we first should ask ourselves which snapshots of Martin and Íñigo we should choose from our photo album, remembering that a photograph captures only the given instant; whereas each man lives out his life within an extended time frame. When we look at the picture of the young Brother Martin with his fine figure and flashing eyes, we can ask ourselves, Is this the same person as the old Luther with the dull eyes and the heavy girth? And is this young swaggering Íñigo the same as the pilgrim who dressed himself in sackcloth and plodded along the road with one sandal on and one off? In 1522, the Loyola of historiography had not yet come to be. He was simply Íñigo, an unknown pilgrim, whereas the name of Luther was resounding throughout all of Europe. Almost ten years older than the Basque wayfarer, Luther was already well advanced along the road he had chosen to follow to the very end.

If we compare these 1522 snapshots of the two men, we will unquestionably find profound differences, the most striking of which is their respective attitudes toward the Church. Luther, the past master of the emotional outburst and the devastating word, attacks the Church head-on, lashes out mercilessly against it, separates himself from it—all in the name of the Gospel. Íñigo, whether he was a cleric or not, was likewise an anticonformist, and miles apart from his brother Pedro, the priest in the family. He does not go out to reform; he seeks to reform himself from within. He does not judge, although the transformation of his life itself stands as a judgment. It is possible that he did not even have time to think about the Church. He realized that everything could and should be good and that it is ourselves who are bad. For him, the Church was like a sheltering roof overhead, or a lap as snug as the lap of a mother, or it was like the air one breathes without asking at each moment whether it is polluted or not. Íñigo was a quiet man, the master of the soft, serious word whispered in the ear at the opportune time. Someone has written that Luther was born a petit bourgeois who did not know anything about the world, even though later in life he was forced to become thoroughly involved in its politics. Íñigo was an aristocrat who entered the world by way of privileged avenues, only to turn his back on that world at a later date.

However, I would prefer going against the conventional approach and point out the similarities between these two men. Both Brother Martin and Íñigo were reclusive heroes, each retired within himself; both were passionate men and each was seduced and conquered by an intense experience, the one in his monastery tower and the other in his Manresa cell. Their interior worlds were sufficiently seductive and obsessive to absorb all of their energies at every moment of the day and night. The personal experience of each had more power than any kind of theoretical knowledge, and it was from their experience that they hammered out their respective beliefs. Both had a certain sense of the poetic, a candor opposed to deceit, a generosity alien to any form of calculation. Each had had an experience of sin and of self-loathing that had shaken him to the core of his being, but this experience had rendered both of them more open to the long-awaited peace, the consolation that was the fruit of their convictions. At a particular time in his life, Íñigo would have understood very well these words of Luther: "My rebellious flesh burns me with a devouring fire. I, who should be the prey of the spirit, am consumed by the flesh, by lust, sloth, idleness, torpor." If Íñigo had been tempted to put his own thoughts in writing, he could have told his old hunting friends at Arévalo how the German Luther had once written, "You courtiers who make a life of hunting, your hour will come—as mine has already come—when you are hunted in paradise and kept very close to Christ, who is an excellent hunter. While you amuse yourselves by hunting, it is really you who are the hunted."

Lucien Febvre, the French biographer of Luther, observed that the solitary, lonely Luther did not so desperately stand in the need of "teaching . . . but [of a] spiritual life, inner peace, liberating certainty, and rest in the Lord." The same can be said of Íñigo. Each man transformed his way into a universal teaching, because both of them were convinced it was in the heart of man where the definitive battles were fought, and that the hearts of men, with their miseries and yearnings, are all alike. The Augustine scholar, Joseph-Marie Malègue, observed that, just as waters are drawn by a cascade, so all of Scripture's obscurities and clarities flow together at that particular point where focus depends on what we already believe. Both Martin and Íñigo will broadcast the discovery that brought them happiness; the one will rise a hue and cry and with the assistance of the printing press; the other, in quiet corners face to face with his conversation partner. In their respective orthodoxies, both will be men of certitude. Self-confident and provocative, each of them will hurl out challenges; the one will defy Rome, the other will brave various inquisitional courts. Both were passionate Christians. Luther sees in Christ the Redeemer, who gives us everything. Íñigo will not argue with this position, but he will see that Christ asks something more from us than faith alone: He asks us to follow, imitate, and serve Him so as to be able to offer Him our will, even if it is a weak will. If today Luther and Loyola were to take stock of their respective legacies, they might very well be able to ask themselves the same question, that is, "Have my work and my followers been faithful to my original generous designs, to that 'first love,' so full of illusions and sincerity, that was my first real encounter with Christ?"

But let us not lose sight of our pilgrim who has now made his way down from Montserrat. This pilgrim wanted to be nothing more than a Christian, a real apprentice Christian. He had moved far from the folk, or popular sociological style of religion that had been his, far also from the affectations of the *docta pietas* that Erasmus had proclaimed to the four winds was the sum and substance of Christian living. Íñigo was a Christian in a way that one was a knight with the purest fervor

and an ingenuousness, in a way that was totally "chivalrous."
He was impregnated to the core by Pelagianism and obsessed
with notions of *doing* great things, rather than enduring them
or experiencing them. He wanted to achieve sanctity by shortcuts. Without his being conscious of the fact, he was a "chosen
instrument," but he never suspected "how much he has to suffer" (Acts 9:15–16). His fantasies, which, in fact, were nothing
more than attempts to imitate others, dreams of following
along paths pursued by others, could never possibly have
given him the slightest inkling of the surprises that lay in store
for him. Battles there would be, but quiet battles, fought in
the front line; training workouts or "Spiritual Exercises,"
designed to conquer himself and to order his life, "so as not
to let himself be led by any inordinate attachment." At this
juncture in his life, his faith was the faith of God's knight, but
it does not, on that account, imply it was a faith that feared
life or death, weakness or timidity, nor was it a cunning,
human faith. He did not want to stand in the way of the kind
of unexpected and powerful desire that would renew his
youth like that of an eagle (Ps 102:5). There were still many
things for him to learn, but he was determined to begin the
"adventure of a poor Christian." He wanted to be so poor that
he would even renounce his own name. He would no longer
be known to others as Íñigo; much less would he be a Loyola.
He would simply be "the pilgrim," an anonymous Christian, a
Christian without a proper name, but not without identity, not
without Christian fervor.

Part II
Jerusalem

I am a pilgrim of today,
I don't care where I go;
Tomorrow? Tomorrow may never come.
Manuel Machado y Ruiz

1
A Pilgrim of Today

"I am a pilgrim of today." Manuel Machado y Ruiz's charming expression eloquently describes the mode of life Íñigo began after leaving Montserrat. An insecure life, an uncertain future, a life dependent on daily handouts—if these are not so much the companions on the road of today's pilgrims, they certainly were of the pilgrims in Íñigo's time. He left Montserrat in order to flee notoriety. Possibly someone there had directed him to the hospice at Manresa, where he would be able to spend a few days writing down the experiences he had been living through. At the same time he would be making some headway on his journey toward Jerusalem. These "few days" turned into eleven months, months that proved to be the crucial interlude that would leave an indelible mark on his life. Much more than just the sketchy outline of the little booklet that would become the *Spiritual Exercises* would see the light of day at Manresa; there are some who even maintain that the germ of the Society can be detected in his famous vision at the Cardoner. For this reason it is understandable why Jesuit historiography puts such importance on these two formative events, but it does so from what took place later on. Once again, we are faced with the illusionary process of seeing events from a chronicler's point of view, as opposed to just watching the way they took place as they were unfolding.

Let us now simply follow along with Íñigo on his long journey, keeping in mind that, ever since his adventure with the Moor, he refers to himself in the *Autobiography* by the nameless term, "the pilgrim." And "the pilgrim" is the name that will define perfectly his attitudes for a long time to come. To impress this fact on the mind of the reader, we too are going to use this term when we speak of him in many of the pages that follow. The pilgrim is one who ventures into a foreign land, who makes himself an alien, who loses contact with the familiar props of his ordinary life, and who deprives himself of all help, other than that type of charity people show to those they do not know, particularly to those who have all the obvious indications of being poor. A person could also be rich and be a pilgrim, a pilgrim accompanied by servants and escorts, or at least with some provisions and money. Even in a foreign land money opens doors, obtains service, ensures security. But our pilgrim wanted to make a profession of poverty so that he would be able to imitate the pilgrims of former ages who did penance and went along their way unnoticed by others. Without his actual choosing to do so, our pilgrim is now going to see life from a point of view beyond all his previous experience, that is, he is going to see it through the eyes of a beggar. He will no longer think about life as a beautiful adventure, but he will live it to the ultimate limits of total self-renunciation. "The greatest enemy to heroism," says Unamuno, "is the shame of seeming to be poor." Once this enemy is overcome, heroism races forward with free reins. But at what a price! And how often does it have to be paid!

His abrupt change of clothing—the symbol of social status—had not proved to be as discrete a gesture as he had desired. If the poor man disguised as a rich man had not been jailed for his presumed theft, then this rich man disguised as a poor man would never have been seen in the vicinity of Montserrat for what he really was. Pilgrims coming to Montserrat in those days, as in our own, were not used to performing such bizarre capers. Íñigo's insatiable desire for immediate anonymity, which was a compensation for his former idolatry of the Loyola name, led him to hide his identity; however, these actions of his had made him somewhat of a celebrity. His change of clothes had nothing in common with a quick-change artist's act. He wanted what he wore to be the external sign of a changed interior, a radical change of life, a complete rupture with the past, and this was certainly the way that those who saw him and heard him speak interpreted his action. Because his appearance as the elegant knight was still too fresh in the memories of so many, the change he had made could only invite an array of comments and conjectures. "For as much as he avoided the esteem of others, he was not long in Manresa before people were saying great things about him, all because of what had happened at Montserrat. His reputation started to grow and the people were saying more than what was true about him, that he had given up a large inheritance, etc." The reader should read in this laconic "etc." commentaries and conjectures of the common people. Such people are usually given to gossip, and so speculations about who he was were being exaggerated.

2

L'home sant

The pilgrim arrived in the neighborhood around Manresa before the rumors about him had followed him there. Manresa was a small industrial center of a few thousand inhabitants who were, for the most part, *cotoners*, the Catalan word for people whose lives were centered around cotton growing, manufacturing, or trading. They were used to seeing pilgrims passing through their town on their way to and from Montserrat, but they had never seen the likes of him who now made his appearance among them. He was a young man, still strong and robust. In one hand he carried a pilgrim's staff and he was dressed in a garment of sackcloth that went down to his two feet, one of which was bare and the other was slipped into a flat sandal made from esparto grass. He would have been carrying a type of knapsack filled with papers and writing materials, his inseparable book of hundreds of pages, and some items, one of which was the picture of Our Lady of Sorrows that he had brought from Loyola and would keep at his side for many years, until that day in Rome when he gave it to his nephew Antonio Araoz. Besides the stories about him that came from Montserrat, the people of Manresa could detect in his bearing, manners, and speech, a certain gentility that could not be concealed and that set him apart from a common man or a rogue outfitted in a pilgrim's guise. This gentility would have been noticed very quickly by the good people who had dealings with the pilgrim, although it would not have been perceived by those who saw him from afar, and it was a gentility that the dogs of this world, despite the reputation they enjoy for having keen instincts, would never have detected. The distinguished Viennese animal psychologist, Konrad Lorenz, is a recognized authority on the behavior of our canine friends, and it would certainly make me happy if he could tell us why it is that dogs always bark at poor beggars. This canine aversion to beggars was shared by all the artists of the baroque period because whenever they would carve a statue of the shabby pilgrim they would inevitably adorn him with coats of brilliant-colored paints and gold leaf. But the fact is that Íñigo's plain, unadorned sackcloth, like the black habit of Saint Benedict and the simple white robe of Saint Bernard, did not lend itself gracefully to such embellishments. However, to refrain from blaming anyone, let us humbly acknowledge that none of us would ever have recognized the champion and the knight we find in many pieces of triumphalistic hagiography, dressed in this guise that was at best sad and pitiful, and at worst utterly ridiculous. But it was Íñigo. Yet, even he had no way of knowing that he was beginning a crucial phase in his life; crucial, not because of the exploits he had dreamed about doing, but because of exploits he had not anticipated.

We should not hurry on ahead, leaping over the years to that moment when the Society was born, to that event that will make Íñigo an important historical personality. Let us rather accompany, day by day, step by step, the obscure pilgrim who preferred making his slow way along the road, limping and alone. If we stretch this period up to the time he embarked from Barcelona on his way to Rome and the Holy Land, these days take up twenty paragraphs of recollections in the *Autobiography*. Before dictating to Gonçalves da Câmara what had taken place during these days, he must have given his Paris companions an account of these events, because Laínez gave his own rendition of them in his letter, written in 1547, and Polanco did the same shortly afterward. With the aid of these three men we shall attempt to rediscover the "tapestries of Manresa" that Íñigo had kept hanging on the walls of his memory.

There were also many other people gifted with good memories who kept before their eyes and in their recollections vivid images of the pilgrim who stopped over at Manresa. Joan

Pascual gave a detailed account of his reminiscences that were transcribed in 1574, 1579, and 1582. He was son of Agnès in Catalan, or in Castilian, Inés Pascual, the Manresa woman who had shown exceptional kindness and charity toward the pilgrim. Then, there were the testimonials from witnesses of Montserrat, Manresa, and Barcelona, dating from 1595 to 1604, who participated in Íñigo's beatification processes. It is true that more than seventy or eighty years had passed since the events described at these respective processes had taken place, but whoever has the patience to read them attentively can almost feel the contours of the lasting mark the pilgrim left on the Catalonian landscape. In some rare cases we encounter eyewitnesses in their eighties, and even nineties, whose memories about what had happened in their childhood are sharper than what occurred subsequently in their adult life. Such was the case of Gabriel Perpinyà. He remembered having seen Íñigo at Montserrat, richly dressed, and he recalled that when he spoke it was in Castilian; and afterward, he remembered having seen him dressed in sackcloth. The nonagenarian Damiana Farbés testified how the children of Manresa sometimes followed the pilgrim, calling *l'home sant*, "the holy man." Bernat Matellà, who was over eighty, recalled that, as a child of about eight, he saw the pilgrim and that, on orders from his mother, he had brought him food on more than one occasion. There is nothing surprising about this wealth of recollected information. If I ever reach eighty-six, I shall remember the beggar covered with medals that I knew in my childhood. I shall remember how, when I was ten years old and the Spanish Civil War was at its height, I went along with him to the Frontón Moderno in San Sebastián to deliver food to Catalan refugees who had taken shelter there, and how eventually they fled Spain by crossing into France at Irún.

The majority of the witnesses at the different processes belonged to the second generation, that is, to the generation that had heard from their parents and others stories about the pilgrim who had spent some time in Manresa or Barcelona. In describing events, witnesses would occasionally confuse the time element, but among their mythologized recollections there are many bits and pieces that are valuable. Even when responding to questions within the format of the preestablished questionnaire, the number of meticulous and homely details these witnesses recall gives their testimony the unmistakable seal of popular memory, which is always characterized by recollections of the trivial and the inconsequential. Such was the case of the woman who kept the scissors she had used to adjust the length of the pilgrim's sackcloth. It seems it was longer on one side than on the other. This ocean of repetitious and concurring trivia came from men and women whose intuitive conviction told them they had been in the presence of a saint, or at least in the presence of the image of sanctity that the common people instinctly have, an instinct that is as accurate as the logical conclusions made by learned experts who hand down verdicts on the quality and quantity of a candidate's heroic virtues.

Although these testimonials show considerable variations among themselves, they all basically rely on the same source, namely, on a number of individuals who had dealings with the pilgrim in the past. There were members of the Pascual, Amigant, and Paguera families; as well as individuals like Pere Canyelles, Maurici Salas, Ramon Capdepós, Joana Dalmau, Isabel Matellà, Agnès Claverà, the Ferrera and Riudora women, and Caldoliver, the very old master of the works at Montserrat—for the most part, all were the ordinary, humble people of Manresa. Later, we shall have the opportunity to see that there were people of quality from among the Barcelona witnesses. The testimonials from both sets of witnesses will help enrich Íñigo's account found in the *Autobiography*, and most especially, it will enable us to view his narrative from a different perspective. He gave a rendition of these eleven months from the interior point of view, from the intimacy of his own spiritual development; the people of Manresa, however, considered them from the exterior aspect, and they handed down their impressions to their children. The summation of these impressions is that in a very short time the people came to recognize *l'home sant* in the traveler whom they had at first called *l'home del sac* "the sack man."

Without becoming bogged down in the fine points that professional scholars employ in their pursuit of historical facts, let us try to see how the substitution of the one nickname for the other shows us how the people went from judging him on his appearances to judging him on the basis of a deeper, interior set of criteria. What do we care here about the rigorous chronological succession of events, the location of houses in which Íñigo lived and whether or not they still exist, the exact spot on the banks of the Cardoner where he received ecstatic graces, and other such details? What we are interested in is the substantial, the significant. What we want here is to capture the course of his days. We want to see them not only in terms of mysterious and hidden graces, but also in the ordinary events that took place in the everyday life of the town and its people. We are more interested in life than in hagiography. Let us begin by stating that at the end of March 1522, something happened in Manresa that was still part of the living memory of the people in 1574. The Jesuit Father Joan Plà was astonished by the innumerable witnesses who still remembered the "sack man." There was Angela Seguí, who was still living. She had been the wife of the city controller, Amigant, who had welcomed the ailing pilgrim into his house. Joan Pascual was also yet alive, and there were people who still remembered places and things that had been associated with the pilgrim, who had died and who was now on his way to becoming a saint.

In 1522, when the townspeople first met with the pilgrim, life in Manresa ceased being dull, simple, and uneventful. Joan Pascual gave the reasons why. He had to rely on what his mother had told him for some of the details, but he himself had also experienced with "his own eyes and his own hands" what had taken place. This is the way he began his simple account. His mother, Inés Pascual, had been staying a few days in Manresa where she had come to settle the inheritance of her first husband, Joan Sagristà, who had died a year after their marriage. On one occasion, she was returning to town from a day's pilgrimage at Montserrat, accompanied by her children and three widows, Paula Amigant, Caterina Molins, and Jerònima Claverà, who was the supervisor of the hospice of Santa Liúcia. While they were "making their way home slowly, talking with one another," a poor man approached them. He was carrying a pilgrim's staff. "He was not very tall; his complexion was pale and flesh-pink; he had a handsome, grave face, and especially he had great modesty of the eyes . . . he was very tired and walked with a limp in his right leg." He asked if there was a hospice nearby where he could be lodged. The appearance of this pilgrim, who "was balding a bit" and who spoke in Castilian, touched the heart of Inés Pascual. She told him that he could find the hospice he was looking for in Manresa and invited him to join the group of these good women. They walked along slowly to enable him to keep up with them, but they were unable to persuade him to ride the little donkey they had at their disposal. They arrived late in Manresa. Now, the Catalans have the reputation of being people endowed with a generous amount of good, practical common sense—*seny*, as they call it—and the *seny* of the enterprising Inés warned her against wagging tongues, and so she did not come into town in the company of the pilgrim "because she was a widow and the man had a handsome face and was young." She sent him on ahead to the hospice of Santa Liúcia with the widow Jerònima Claverà, who worked there, and she requested that they give him every consideration. She also promised that she herself would look after him from her own house. On the first night, she sent him a dinner of good broth and some chicken because "he had been walking with pain," and on the following days she sent him more chicken and soup. Within a week, the pilgrim had attracted the attention of everyone.

3
Admiration and Slander

As the newcomer began his new life, he came to know the open-handed, good-natured people of this working-class town. He slept little and when he did it was always on the floor, and he spent his time in reflection and prayer. He girded a strong rope around his sackcloth robe, to which he attached a small dangling cord with knots of varying sizes. Dressed in this manner, he began to attract people's attention, chiefly because of his modesty of the eyes and his reserve. Sometime later, that is, after Íñigo began to have contact with the people, it was the seriousness of what he said that impressed them. Here was a poor penitent covering up some mystery, a mystery that became more and more intriguing once the news of his vigil at Montserrat and the story about how he had changed clothes with a beggar became known. Inés was won over by the pilgrim's virtues and patience, and she treated him as if he were her own son. She even did everything she could to have the Dominicans accept him as a guest in their monastery. Later on, it was the widow Joana Serra's turn to be responsible for his food and laundry. She would have gladly put him up in her own house were it not for the fact that such a move would have antagonized her relatives, with whom she was already entangled in a lawsuit. The pilgrim was lodged in other Manresan homes, and one of them, the one he names specifically, was that of the Ferrera family.

Gradually, the people got used to the pilgrim's way of doing things. Every day he begged for alms. He ate no meat and drank no wine, even when it was offered. But he did not fast on Sundays and if he was offered a little wine on that day, he would drink it. Each day he attended High Mass, during which time he would read the Passion; in the evening, he would attend sung vespers and compline, which he loved dearly because of the music. Despite the many places where he could have passed the night, he spent hours in prayer either at the hermitage of Our Lady of Viladordis, the Dominican church, the hospital chapel, or in a nearby cave that he had discovered. He would also spend time praying before the roadside crosses and would stop to pray whenever the Angelus bell rang. He relied on his Book of Hours and his rosary, as well as vocal prayers, for the source of some of his prayer. He visited the hospitals where he bathed the sick. He confessed and went to Holy Communion weekly. As far as his body was concerned, he punished it with the discipline and hairshirt, but otherwise paid absolutely no attention to its needs.

> And because he had been preoccupied with the care of his hair, which was according to the fashion of the day— and he did have nice hair—he decided to let it grow wild, without combing, or cutting it, or covering it with anything during the night or day. And for the same reason he let his toenails and fingernails grow because he had also taken excessive care of them.

This wild, nonconformist behavior, performed in imitation of the models he had discovered in the *Flos Sanctorum* and executed according to his practices of extreme poverty, was in marked contrast to the fastidiousness that so characterized him at a later date. Even more did it stand as a repudiation of chambray bed linen, silver dinner plates, and many other luxuries of the life he had recently known at Arévalo. He was an imitator of the great penitents of pious legends, but it would take him a long time to learn how important was the advice of another idealist knight-errant, especially when it came to the intense battles of the spirit. Don Quixote observed that "one does not bear the weight of arms and the sufferings they entail unless he has control over his own heart" (*Don Quixote*, I, II). Laínez would later say that "even though he was strong and had a solid constitution, his body was totally changed."

The Manresa people remembered him during this period as the man with the young, ruddy complexion who was transformed into a lean and haggard man. Íñigo had ruined his health forever with these excesses of his. We discover a trace of the hard lesson he learned as result of his misdeeds, in the kindness he showed the sick later on in life, and in the concern he would have for the health of young Jesuit students. He used to say that we render more service to God when we are in good health. But this observation came about at another period in his life, at a time when he saw things from a different point of view.

The pilgrim ate what was given to him, when it was given to him, and where it was given to him. When he was invited to eat at someone's house, he spoke little and skillfully sidestepped questions from the curious who wanted to know who he was. He was a sinner, period. He suppressed his natural fiery temperament and answered questions with studied composure. He would speak with the children in the streets, to people who were solicitous of the needs of pilgrims, and to old people who wanted to hear what he had to tell them. He was no orator, but his rhetoric had more force than all his arguments. His message was simple: one should not sin; one should examine his conscience and make an effort to do better; it is good to confess and receive Communion weekly. His advice did not fall on fallow ground, and gradually it began to transform the spiritual life of many people in Manresa, but there were only a few who really sought him out. As is always the case, the pilgrim's measured and honest speech made more of an appeal to women, who were by nature more receptive to what he had to say. He began to have some faithful followers, "honest women, married or widows," as Joan Pascual recalled,

who followed him religiously day and night, eager to hear what he had to say and to partake in the spiritual conversations he always offered, and willing to assist him in the good works he did, either at the hospice or when he went to serve the sick, to wash their hands and feet, or when he busied himself with other poor people and orphans that were in the city. He would go out begging from door to door for them and then, at set times during the day, he would distribute alms to them in a discrete

manner by setting what he had collected before the door
of the house where he was staying.

A description of this unusual behavior would not be complete if one failed to mention what Pascual called evil and
envious tongues, that is, people who publicly spoke ill of the
pilgrim, of what he was doing, and of those who were associated with him. All of this backbiting had a chilling effect on
Joana Serra, who was taking care of his lodging, but in particular, it affected Inés Pascual, who was "responsible for these
troubles and novelties, she who had introduced the pilgrim to
Manresa and continued to support him." These slanderous
stories cast a slur on the honor of the pilgrim and his followers. People tended to mythologize both the good and the bad.
These "numerous and senseless slanders" made men and
women deaf to whatever the pilgrim was saying about the salvation of their souls and the way they should take to get to
heaven. To explain the town's social psychology, Joan Pascual
declared that Manresa was "a very small town whose inhabitants were backbiters," and he added that his mother had seriously considered taking the pilgrim away and putting him up
in a house she had on the Carrer de Cotoners in Barcelona.

It is probable that the pilgrim may have gone back to
Montserrat for a few days, where he would have lived as a hermit in the area around the monastery. This hypothesis was cat-
egorically denied by Ribadeneira, although it was persistently
defended by no less a person than Íñigo's nephew, Antonio
Araoz, who was a Jesuit during his uncle's lifetime and who was
responsible for the preliminary investigation process that covered the period of time that Íñigo remained in Catalonia.
Many biographers interpret the text in the *Autobiography* literally and conclude that Íñigo left Montserrat on the very next
morning after his vigil, and they do not accept the possibility
of his making a return trip during his stay in Manresa, which
was only a few hours walk from the holy mountain. In the tradition of the monastery, which was compiled in 1595, the
memory of Íñigo's triduum before the Virgin of Montserrat
was still very much alive. But here we find witnesses who stated
that the austere Chanones introduced him to García de
Cisneros's *Exercises*, and that the pilgrim returned from time to
time to the monastery in order to give an account of how he

was putting these Exercises into practice, to the one who had so warmly welcomed him during his first and very brief stay at Montserrat. Even better is the testimony of Gabriel Perpinyà, a ninety-five-year-old priest. He had stayed eight months at Montserrat with another priest named Guiot, who was vicar of the parish church at Prats del Rey, a small mountain town some twenty-five miles west of Manresa. Gabriel remembered that while they were at the monastery, he saw a knight who was dressed in well-appointed soldier's clothes, and he recalled that he had later heard that this man had renounced his earthly possessions and made an offering of his sword and dagger to the Virgin. Gabriel further testified that afterward this same man dressed himself in a sackcloth, the clothing of a pilgrim, and that one day he heard some persons who were in Montserrat ask this pilgrim, "What would your family say if they were to see the penances you were doing? How they would reprimand you!" Perpinyà gave his account in Catalan, but he switched to Castilian when he recorded the answer he, as a very young man, had heard the pilgrim give, that is, "I would rather go to heaven with one eye than be cast into hell with two." He was most explicit when he assured those taking his testimony that after Íñigo had gone to the hospice at Manresa, he came back to Montserrat dressed in his sackcloth, and that during his stay in the monastery he had asked questions about a trip Guiot had to make to Rome on behalf of the monks, and that the three of them went together to Barcelona to embark. All of this is possible, if we do not put too much of an emphasis on the time sequences and the literalness of certain expressions.

The plain truth is that even while he was in Manresa, the pilgrim lived very much like a hermit, that is to say, that even though he lived in near proximity to other people, he did not live with them nor was his lifestyle in tune with theirs. Good people respected his being recollected and withdrawn and his uncommunicative way of proceeding; they would come to see him to draw out of him his simple and heartfelt exhortations. The pilgrim missed the isolation of the desert, but some mysterious distance kept his heart within the confines of a spiritual desert. Although not shy, he was a solitary man, immersed in his own thoughts. He knew how to break his bread with others, the poor like himself, and infrequently he would share his soft, strong, and repetitive words with them. He attracted others to himself, but his radiance sent those who heard him back into the dormant interior of their own selves. What the people found intriguing and moving about him was his penitential zeal, his radical kind of material poverty that was symbolized by his unkempt appearance, and by his spiritual poverty that was evidenced by a total abandonment to and a dependence on others for alms. The pilgrim was a man without roots, who jealously guarded the golden past that his courteous manners betrayed; he was a man with no roof to shelter him, other than that which charity alone provided. Since he was young, there was no lack of people who criticized him for being a bum. But he paid the heavy price of living a life of dependence on others in a most austere manner. He exercised the right to live that type of poverty that the great Dominican theologian, Fra Domingo de Soto, would defend with the most subtle arguments a few years afterward. This was a right that neither Erasmus nor Luis Vives would ever have understood, because they were less exposed than our pilgrim to the extremes of refinements that could be found in houses worthy of kings. They were less free than the pilgrim; they would never have been able to do without their discrete comforts, but in their own way they also begged—they obtained favors, protection, and money in exchange for the flatteries and praises they gave. "It should be noted," Polanco commented, "the liberty God gave Íñigo at that time and the little respect he had in turn for anyone." How delightfully ironic! Here he was treating all types of people—the sick at the tiny poor hospice of Santa Liúcia and the poor who ventured to accept his paltry handouts—with as much respect as he had previously reserved for members of the Castilian nobility.

4
From "Great and Constant Joy" to Crisis

The people were at a loss trying to figure out just how much money the pilgrim had given up, and they were determined to learn the mysteries that lay hidden in his heart. At least during his first few weeks among them, there was less mystery about him than later on. He remained strong and decisive, relentless in the performance of penance, which was so important to him. He had admitted that during these first months "he had no knowledge of the interior things of the soul." But with the extreme fervor characteristic of converts, a fervor whose flame burns day and night, he copied the practices and activities of the saints he had read about in his books. "Great and constant joy," was the cheerful expression he used to describe his beginner's soul. Soon, trials would come along that would be able to dash asunder this "great and constant joy." He, who one day would write wise rules about the "Three States of the Soul When a Sound and Solid Choice of a Way of Life May Be Made," was now about to learn that the prevailing atmosphere of any given time can envelop and imprison our soul without giving it the possibility of making a choice. Joan Pascual remembered that the pilgrim's wounded legs caused him great discomfort whenever it rained or whenever there was a change in the weather. Climatic conditions of the spirit also are not always untroubled, pleasant, and serene.

In the beginning, the recurring vision of something luminous and beautiful that gave him great pleasure surprised
him. It had many things within it that shone like eyes.
Hallucination or the result of physical exhaustion? Modern-
day psychology might risk giving an interpretation. Íñigo was
being tempted by thoughts of vainglory. The vision, therefore,
was a kind of mirror that reflected the alluring image that
Íñigo wanted to have of himself, even though he would have
denied ever wanting such an image. So, in looking at himself
in this vision, he saw himself. Less mysterious, and yet more
vexing, was the "disturbing thought" that began to gnaw away
at his simplistic joy. It magnified the difficulty of his being
faithful to the life he was now leading, as if someone were saying deep within his soul, How can you stand a life like this for
all of the years you have yet to live? He began to give in to
weariness from the fatigue he was feeling at the time, but even
more from the weight of the impending future. The "first
temptation" was what he called this thought, a temptation he
would conquer with willful determination: Could this interior
voice that threatened him with many years of unsupportable
sufferings promise him one day more of life? Really, this
answer was a bit weak and seems to put more store on the
brevity of the sufferings than it does on a faith capable of
bearing them over a long period of time. But this was only the
beginning of the bitter spiritual winter that fell upon the pilgrim just when he was relishing the delicious springtime of
the soul. The good women of Manresa would never have suspected as much. The pilgrim alone was able to give us an
account of what took place. Thirty years later, he would
describe it in a marvelous way, much like a physician might
give a meticulous diagnosis of the different phases of an old
disease long since cured. In a stylized manner, bereft of any
trace of the heart-rending agony that was a part of the succeeding episodes he had lived through, he described the
process in finely nuanced and suggestive terms. How much he
had lived and learned in so short a time!

In the first place, he lost that "great and undisturbed joy,"
which had enabled him to believe that his will and emotions
were once and for all anchored in that new promised land.
Suddenly "he began to experience great changes in his soul."
It is evident that the undisturbed joy could not have become

anything other than sadness, a harsh, dry desolation that was new to him, even though it is very common along the roads traveled by the spirit. "Sometimes his distaste was so great that he found no relish in any of the prayers he recited, not even in hearing mass, or in any kind of prayer he made." Had he lived today, he would have used a phrase that we hear often enough, "I couldn't care less." Dryness is what this state is called, and it had a bewildering effect on the pilgrim. Saint John of the Cross uses a graphic metaphor to describe this internal frustration; he said it was like the suffering that a child goes through when it is being weaned. A person feels so disagreeable that he can neither put his heart in what he is doing nor in what is going on around him; his will alone remains on target, but it is a will that is completely forsaken. Sometimes the lost joy can return, unexpectedly, suddenly, and at that time it seems as though sadness and desolation do not weigh us down; they are removed "just as when one snatches a cloak off from another's shoulders." The depression is as suffocating and heavy as that. Because exploits of this nature had never been a part of the adventures that had haunted his imagination, the pilgrim was taken aback by these changes and he asked himself, What kind of a new life is that we are beginning? As long as he spoke with people who appreciated him and admired his spiritual conversations, he experienced great fervor in his words and showed "a great desire to go forward in the service of God." It was his way of compensating during the moments of tepidity, an effort at autosuggestion, a way of obtaining positive feedback from his resolutions. When this change came about, he did not quit the field of battle; he overcame all by the force of sheer willpower, and against all contrary winds and tides he kept up his practice of confessing and going to Communion each week. In such moments he received some words of comfort, like those of the pious old lady of Manresa who, in a prophetic way, told him that she wished Jesus Christ would some day appear to him. It was an absurd fantasy, but it undoubtedly made him smile and perhaps even hope.

Christ he did not see, but "he had much to suffer from scruples." He had just faced the crisis of what the future would bring and now he had to face this crisis of scruples, which caused him to focus on the past, a past that he considered had been removed from his shoulders like a heavy coat and buried in oblivion. Now, it was as if some evil weed had begun to grow deep within him. It was accusing him of responsibility for whatever indiscretions lay in the back roads of his memory. In the Sixth Mansion of her *Interior Castle* (ch 7), Saint Teresa of Avila compares the favors God gives to a person to a mighty river that runs through the soul. But the person's "sins are like the river's slimy bed; they are always fresh in his memory." On the advice of a reliable spiritual man, a doctor of the *Seo* (Manresa's cathedral church), the pilgrim wrote down all that he was able to remember and then read it off in confession. But it was to no avail, because "his scruples returned even with regard to minute and piddling matters." The phenomenology of this spiritual torture is described in manuals of ascetical theology and in textbooks of psychiatric medicine, and one can find it spelled out in a condensed form in the *Autobiography*—"it still seemed to him"; "but nothing helped him"; "he was so deeply distressed"; "although he understood that these scruples were doing him much harm and it would be good to be free of them, still he could not cast them off." Through what degrees of meticulous cunning and deliberation a scrupulous person goes! He thought, and secretly desired, that his cure would come about if his confessor gave him the order in the name of Jesus Christ not to confess these things again, nor even to think of them anymore. His hope was realized when the confessor, probably a Dominican from the house where the pilgrim was lodged, gave him the desired order without his even realizing that this was precisely what his penitent wanted. He added, however, a restriction that was normal, but in this case, fatal: he was not to confess anything more from his past life "unless it was something absolutely clear." Like all scrupulous people, the pilgrim "considered everything was manifestly clear." And so, "the order benefited him not at all, and thus he continued in his anxiety." He persevered in performing his liturgical devotions and spent many hours of the day and night praying on his knees. His torment went on for months. "No remedy." A constant uniformity perdured. But this time it was the uniformity of anguish that cut to the very quick of his spirit, without respite and without leaving him any room for hope. In one of those extreme situations, the pilgrim exploded in the solitude of his small room and, in the fervor of his hopeless prayer, "he began to call out to God in a loud voice." These were real cries, shouts that could be heard, laments that enfleshed the inaudible cries of his spirit and gave a visible form to the road upon which he was traveling. At this juncture in the *Autobiography*, he abandoned the use of the third person and he inserted the words of his heart-rending prayer, "Help me, O Lord, since I find no help from men or from any creature. No trial would be too great for me to bear, if I thought there was any hope of finding that help. Show me, O Lord, where I may find it, and even though I should have to follow a little dog to help me, I would do so."

Heaven did not answer this prayer, and in the depths of his heart, powerful, repetitious temptations began to take shape, urging him to commit suicide by throwing himself into a deep hole that was close to his room. His strong superego dictated that it would be a sin to kill himself, and so the pilgrim repressed these temptations by crying out anew, "Lord, I will do nothing to offend you." He was now prey to confusion, knowing the abyss of what it means to be human, deprived of moorings, and finding no relief from anyone or anything. He did not pronounce what Jacques Rivière called the fatal words of renunciation, "My God, take away from me temptation to strive for sanctity!" He was, however, suffocated by what the prophet Isaiah called "the spirit of giddiness" (19:14). One Sunday, after he had received Holy Communion, he remembered the story of a saint he had read about who would not eat or drink anything until God gave him the grace he had been seeking. He thought about this for a long time, and even speculated about not taking any food or water until God came to his aid, or until he found himself at the point of death. For a whole week, this pilgrim with a will of iron refrained from eating or drinking anything, and all the while he continued to perform his customary spiritual exercises and to attend the divine office. On the following Sunday, he gave an exact account of what he had done to his confessor. He still had the strength to continue his fast, but he blindly obeyed the confessor's advice to desist from what he was doing. For two days he was free from scruples, but on the third day, that is, on Tuesday, while he was at prayer, the remembrance of his past sins returned, "one by one, and thinking about one led to his thinking about another and that would remind him of yet

another, until he felt bound to confess them all once again."
This new agony led logically to "a disgust for the life he was
leading and a desire to give it all up." Here he had come to
the crisis of hope, the existential void, the loss of reason, the
prelude to surrendering the citadel of his will.

It was at this very moment that he realized he was not holding the reins of his life in his own hands, that he could not
place confidence in himself. It was then that an unexpected
and hoped-for change took place; it was if he had awakened
from a bad dream. It was something that approached the
"Ah!" psychoanalysts speak about. As he recalled what he had
learned through experience about different spirits while he
was at Loyola, he saw the knot in the tangle and discovered
the key to the puzzle. Then, everything fell into place; he had
found again his sanity and security. "He therefore made a
decision and with great clarity of mind." He would not confess
any of his past sins anymore. As a result of this resolution, his
scruples disappeared immediately and he firmly believed that
God's mercy had freed him. He had rediscovered the basic
confidence to live and the proper discernment to confront
difficulties. He decided to eat meat with a willingness that surprised his confessor. He made up his mind to sleep during the
little time he allotted for sleeping, and not to think about the
great illuminations and spiritual consolations that came to
him at the moment he was dozing off. His "I" was restored
and strengthened; he decided for himself; and he rediscovered his vital energy after so many painful adventures that had
taken place "on the crossroads," rather than "in the isles."

Don Quixote had dreamed of the fair isles of Riaran, but it
was on the crossroads where "the most stupendous combat of
the valorous" actually took place (*Don Quixote*, I, 3 and 10).
For the pilgrim, the isles, or those delightful adventures of the
spirit, were to come later as mysterious lights that transformed
his soul. In the *Autobiography* there is a phrase, "from that day
forward," that is, the stitch line between suffering and joys.
These very illuminations that he experienced were able to
reveal the abysses of the spirit and therefore they could bring
on moments of great desolation. Apart from this fact, everyone seems to agree that the trials that came one after another
during the first four months of his stay in Manresa finally gave
way to a period wreathed in light that began around the

month of August. The overall impression that the pilgrim gave to this dawn that had followed the blackest of nights throws into relief his rudimentary solitude, his previous spiritual immaturity, and above all else, it focuses on the beginnings of his new course of training:

> During this time, God treated him just as a schoolmaster treats a child he is teaching. Whether this was because of his thick and dull understanding or because he had no one to teach him or because of the strong desire God himself had given him to serve Him, he clearly believed and has always believed that God treated him in this way. Indeed, if he were to doubt this, he thought he would offend his Divine Majesty. Something of this may be seen from the following five points.

The next chapter lists the five points and explains each of them.

5
Along the River

Before reviewing and commenting on these five points that he describes with great precision, we should acknowledge the fact that saints, like geniuses of another order, attain to degrees of clairvoyance that we ordinary mortals, with our limited understanding of such matters, are not able fully to comprehend. We either have to believe what the saints tell us or part company with them. We should keep in mind, too, that thirty years after the event, Íñigo's experience was still vividly present to him. The metaphor he chose to describe his experience is rather charming. When he recalled what had taken place at that time, it was not the learned masters of the University of Paris who were conjured up in his memory, but it was the figure of the way a schoolmaster treats a little boy. Perhaps the model for this schoolmaster was the one at Loyola, who taught him to read and write, and the little boy was soft wax, pure receptivity, unlimited confidence mixed with wonder. Such was the way the pilgrim saw himself. The other element in the metaphor is more problematic. God and God alone was his schoolmaster. This statement is disturbing, not only for that time in history when the *alumbrados* were affirming that they spoke with God "just like they spoke with the *corregidor* of Escalona," but it is also disturbing for any period of time. Such a direct tutorship would seem to short-circuit the teaching authority of the Church in matters of the faith, and also the role of the Church as the transmitter and interpreter of God's revealed word. Martin Luther had just radically liberated everybody from the mediation of the Church. The Manresa pilgrim did not wrestle with a similar temptation, nor did he ever contemplate taking such a step. Just the opposite: he participated in the sacraments, he immersed himself in traditional devotions, and he took his problems to his confessor, whose direction he blindly obeyed. At the same time, he clearly understood that apart from all of these matters, God and God alone taught him as a schoolmaster teaches a young boy. He had no fear of the Church, which, even though ever suspicious of possible illusions, would one day choose the following passage from the book of Deuteronomy (32:12) as the Entrance Antiphon for the Mass of Saint Thérèse of Lisieux: "The Lord nurtured and taught her. . . . The Lord alone was her leader." In this same sense, the Lord was the director and teacher of Íñigo.

God did not teach him a new lesson. This pupil that He was illuminating, however, now seemed to see new meanings in the old truths he had learned from the study of his catechism, or that he had heard while he was sitting around the kitchen table at Loyola, or what he had subsequently picked up from the books he had read. Later on, using brand-new maps of the world, his schoolmasters were going to teach him about the dimensions and configurations of the newly discovered globe. Now, with the same awe and wonder, he learned the infathomable depths of things about which we speak today in terms that have been all but worn out by overuse. The five points, or chapters, in this new science he was learning dealt with nothing other than God, the Trinity, the creation and essence of creatures, the Eucharist, and the near presence of the humanity of Christ. He had difficulty in articulating all of this, but what he did learn he described in a delightful way. He also remembers the place where this enlightenment took place: "It seemed to be on the steps of the monastery; during the elevation at Mass." But when it came to describing the experience itself, the task became much more difficult—the elevation of his spirit, seeing with the inner eye of the soul, and visual but nonaudible images were all accompanied with great joy and consolation and followed by much sobbing and uncontrollable tears. It would be impossible for us to explain the things that God had impressed upon his soul. But we can say that He branded him with a red-hot iron, because after these visions had ceased, their effects perdured. For the rest of his life he felt great devotion while praying to the Holy Trinity. Thirty years after the fact, the evidence of these illuminations had not lost one bit of its power and splendor. "All these things he saw strengthened him at the time and always gave him such conviction in his faith that he often thought to himself that if there were no Scriptures to teach us in these matters of the faith, he would be resolved to die for them, merely because of what he had seen." Seen rather than believed? As paradoxical as it may seem, this is a "belief" that came out of an experience; it was something very different indeed from Luther's faith. What a pity it is that the book he began to write on the Trinity has been lost. According to Ribadeneira, it consisted of more than eighty pages, and we can rest assured that it was not written in the style of the scholastic schoolmen!

We have not yet spoken about the fifth point, where Íñigo records the greatest of these experiences, the one that took place along the banks of the Cardoner River. Only the person who underwent such an experience could describe it to us in such terminology, depicting for us the physical setting of these riverbanks washed in spirituality and mystery.

> Once he was going, out of devotion, to a church about a mile from Manresa, and I think it was called Saint Paul's. The road ran along close to the river. As he went along, occupied with his devotions, he sat down for a moment facing the river that ran deep at that place. As he sat, the eyes of his understanding began to open and, although he saw no vision, he did see and understand many things, both spiritual things and matters of faith and learning. This took place with so great an enlightenment that *everything seemed altogether new to him.* Although there were many things, he cannot point out the particulars of what he then understood, but he can say that he received a great clarity in his understanding. This clarity was so great that in the whole course of his life, right up to his sixty-second year, even if he were to gather all the helps he had received from God and all the many things he knew, and added them all together, he does not think they would equal all that he received at that one time. And thus, his understanding became enlightened in so

great a manner that *it seemed to him that he was a different man and that he had a different intellect from the one he had had before.*

Modern-day scientists are for the first time taking note of such strange, magnetic concomitances, and they are bewildered by this transition from the rational, reflective consciousness to the field of profound intuition; by this mysterious process of visualization; by this unknown, interior sense. They refer to it as "altered states of consciousness." Such unexpected and unique, certain and indescribable experiences as the pilgrim underwent are special gifts given to the privileged persons of very different religious backgrounds and in every era of history. They are not permanent states, but passing stages. Their effects, however, are stable and long lasting, like the peace and harmony that take possession of these persons' souls. This "other understanding" points toward the heights or depths of understanding not reached through the logical processes. Therefore, what one has learned through discursive knowledge seems obscure and incomplete, compared to what one comes to through intuition. This illumination affects the deepest layers of one's being, not one's understanding alone. His revivified heart feels whatever exists in a new way, and he also becomes aware of the newness of things. From the depths of his interior he communicates with the universe and with Someone who remains outside it, yet present to him in all of his difficulties. *"Everything seemed altogether new to him"* and he had the impression of being *"a different man."* He began to see everything "with *other eyes*," wrote Laínez; "with *other eyes* than those that he had," remarked Polanco. *A different man, other eyes, altogether new things*—these are charismatic words that today stir up wistfulness and yearnings among those who seek renewal and profound transformation from the ancient springs of Eastern religions, forgetting, when they do not despise, the lost Christian tradition of their own roots.

6

Another Man with
New Eyes, New Things

But let us get back to our pilgrim. He does not use the superlative to describe this event that was the linchpin of his whole life. By using comparatives (*so great that . . . so much that*) he reveals the magnitude and depth of this experience that marked him forever. Many years later, when making decisions that affected the Institute of the Society, he was heard to make a veiled allusion to "an experience that happened to me at Manresa." This statement has caused some enthusiasts to see the seeds of the Society and its complex constitutions already planted in his mind as he sat there on the banks of the Cardoner. Those of a more judicial bent are content to see in this aside the evidence of a feeling he had then for the apostolate and service to Christ; a feeling which, with the passage of time, would take on a corporate aspect. Even many years after Íñigo's Manresa experience, one could say with Nadal "that he knew that he was being led gently toward somewhere, but he did not know where." If we use Saint Thomas Aquinas's metaphor in defining Providence, we could say that Íñigo was the arrow in flight, but only the archer knew the target.

Illuminations such as the one Íñigo experienced are never an end in themselves. Rather than being the point of arrival, they are usually the point of departure for a person's insertion into the real world, the beginnings of a new interior restructuring of the absolute and relative. The pilgrim now feels himself more free, more the creator of his self-identity, open to others in a different way. He gives up his excessive ways, trims his hair, pares his nails, and abandons the idea of becoming a Carthusian because he sees "the good effects he could have on souls through his dealings with them." He wants to give to others what he has found. An extraordinary change has come about, transforming the recluse into a missionary, an apostle. Into this potting soil of Manresa were planted the first, the primordial seeds that sprang to life in his notebook and that eventually flowered in the *Spiritual Exercises.* These *Exercises,* which are not the result of his reading, constitute a "navigation chart" for others. When dealing with the origin of the *Exercises,* the classical style of hagiography found in books and depicted in paintings and statues would have us believe that the Blessed Virgin dictated the text of the *Exercises* to an enraptured penitent. Could it possibly be that the Virgin of Nazareth, whose soul resounds to the joyful poetry of the Magnificat, dictated such dry prose, the innumerable rules, and the complicated methodology we find in the book of the *Spiritual Exercises?* The effects produced by this little notebook, or better, the application of what it proposes has been extraordinary, right from the beginning down to our day. Nadal and Ribadeneira considered the book inspired and held that it could not have been the work of an unlearned soldier, a penitent unlettered in the spiritual life. As if the intense and varied experiences of this docile student at Loyola and Manresa were not as good as a doctorate from any faculty of spirituality imaginable! After the pilgrim's enlightenment on the banks of the Cardoner, which was the crowning point of unexpected spiritual insights following his generous apprenticeship, Íñigo gained considerable experience about the problems of the human heart. He came to know something about how heavenly visitations, obstacles, ways, deceits, and discernments affected it. He gained insight into the mechanism of human freedom, and he learned about the voice of what the German poet Rainer Maria Rilke described as "the giant call," the call that only the saints hear and to which they alone are able to respond.

He knew that this call was not a rare and reserved privilege and he also knew that the obstacles that prevented one from hearing it were not exceptionable either. The pilgrim, who believed in grace and in man, observed some order in what had taken place within him and he jotted down these experiences with the notion that they could be useful in guiding others. In the encyclical *Mens Nostra* (1929), Pius XI declared that the book of the *Spiritual Exercises* contained "a very wise and most universal rule of norms for directing souls on the way to perfection." This rule appears abstract and quintessential, but when it is held up against the light, it very frequently enables us to see the soul of its author and his own lived-through experiences. In this aspect it stands in opposition to lessons learned from reading textbooks. If one looks attentively beyond the assortment of directives, what he will see is man, a respect for his freedom and interiority, and a scrupulous concern for the conditions that enhance or prevent this freedom. These are the essential components of the Exercises. Remembering his own experiences, Íñigo takes for granted that whoever decides willingly to follow along the path of the Exercises does so "with magnamity and generosity toward his Creator and Lord," and he also firmly believes that all men are illuminated and moved by divine grace.

It is possible that Íñigo borrowed themes from García de Cisneros's *Ejercitatio* to which he had been introduced while he was at Montserrat, and that perhaps he was influenced in a more subtle way by the spirit of *The Imitation of Christ*, which at that time was attributed to Jean Gerson. We know for certain that the pilgrim was well acquainted with this book which he kept ever close at hand, referring to it as "the partridge," the very best of spiritual books. He savored its pages, finding in them much food for thought, doubtless because the author believed what he wrote. Erasmus, Luther, and at a later date, Dietrich Bonhoeffer, the deputed father of the most secular kind of modern theology, were all devotees of this little book. This in itself is strange, seeing that it was recommended reading only for readers of retired age.

More than anything else, the little book of the *Spiritual Exercises* presents a stock list of methods and directions to the one giving and the one making the Exercises, that is, to those who are the participants in what takes place during the retreat. Like every book of rules, it is dry reading; the merit of its worth rests in the way the directives are put into practice. This is why it is as demanding and meticulous as performing piano finger-exercises. For one who has no desire to learn to play the piano, such lessons are boring, but for the aspiring concert pianist they are lessons that are wonderfully effective and absolutely necessary. The pilgrim's little book appears, and justifiably so, on the list of "Books That Have Changed the World," but it would not find a place in even the most unimportant paragraph in a survey of works of great literature.

For many years, this notebook-guide remained *ad usum privatissimum* ("for the exclusive use") of him who owned the book, that is, Íñigo. He continued to be led by the events that unfolded in his own life, and, on the basis of what these experiences taught him, he would one day eventually complete it. In some rare cases of absolute necessity, Íñigo was obliged to *show it* in order to get the seal of orthodoxy for it, but many years had to pass before he came *to entrust it to others* (as fathers entrust to their sons the secrets of their craft, so as to insure these crafts will survive). The first Latin edition appeared in 1548. It was published in Rome anonymously and with a printed statement that protected it from being reprinted. The first draft Íñigo made at Manresa must have included the key meditations of the four weeks, the two examinations of conscience, and the rules for the discernment of the spirits that went back to his convalescent days at Loyola. So much for the makeup of the new book itself. We know nothing for certain about how he applied its contents, other than the fact that from his Manresa days onward Íñigo began to guide others in the first steps along the path he had already traveled, in the "conquest of self and the regulation of one's life in such a way that no decision is made under the influence of any inordinate attachment."

During the final months of 1522, the pilgrim felt eager "to help other people who came looking for him to discuss the affairs of their souls." In testimonies from the beatification process we find statements collaborating this desire of his to help others. We also learn that he used to give lectures in the little chapel of Santa Liúcia to the devout women of Manresa who had become his followers. He became ill on a number of occasions in Manresa. Once, for a whole week he remained in a state of complete prostration that gravely concerned the families who cared for him. Inés Pascual blamed her own negligence for this mysterious sickness and set out to cure it with her infallible remedy for all ailments—chicken soup! In his version of these events, the pilgrim speaks of one illness that was accompanied by an exceptionally high fever that left him at the point of death. He also spoke of another grave illness he had at a later date, in the middle of winter, that won for him the hospitality of the Ferrera family and a night vigil on the part of the good women who were his followers. After this bout, he was very weak and subject to frequent stomach pains. That winter was exceptionally cold, and the solicitous women were successful in their efforts to make him dress properly. He put on shoes and covered his head "with a large bonnet of very coarse cloth shaped like a little beret." Íñigo found himself surrounded by maternal care. If the memories of Miguel Canyelles and Joan Pascual are reliable, for the first time in his life the reserved, discrete pilgrim and a woman exchanged two words—"mother, son!" As far as he was concerned, these words were both wholesome and deleted from his autobiography. The woman had a keen realization that she was sheltering a saint, and she considered herself fortunate in being able to exercise maternal protection. Her name was Inés Pascual. According to her son, Joan Pascual, she saw to it that the pilgrim had lodgings in Barcelona, where he had to go to the big city to put into effect the project that he had not forgotten.

Indeed, "the time he had set for his departure to Jerusalem was drawing near. So, at the beginning of the year 1523, Íñigo left for Barcelona in order to set sail." This was a reference to that fixed-as-a-nail desire that had come to him while he was still at Loyola. On this point there was no modification. How close, and yet how far away, were Loyola, Pamplona, Nájera, Arévalo, and even Montserrat—all replaced now by that little corner of land near "where the river ran deep"! But at this point we should ask ourselves why he had waited almost a whole year before embarking on the Jerusalem pilgrimage. There are some who conjecture that it was because of the plague that had been ravaging Barcelona and that had caused the city to close its gates to nonresidents. Perhaps the reason was that he did not have enough time to get to Rome before Easter 1521, the date the pope granted licenses to pilgrims going to the Holy Land. However, at that date Pope Adrian was still in Spain. But the pilgrim would have never considered presenting himself in person to the pope, because in doing so he risked meeting some acquaintance of importance among the members of the papal entourage.

His time spent in Manresa was not time lost. Later, he would designate this period in his life as his "primitive church" phase. Never would he forget the good people of Manresa who gave him food and lodging. The town kept remembrances of its own: his sackcloth gown and his belt were regarded as relics. There was also the hospice, the Dominican convent, the hermitage of Viladordis, the cross of Tort, a number of different rooms, and the cave by the river— all of these were places stamped by the memory of his presence. Without knowing who he had been, people followed him because they knew who he had become. The immense gratification that filled Íñigo's heart manifested itself when he was about to take his leave from Manresa and its people.

Íñigo did not enter into Barcelona in the same way that he had drifted into Manresa. After discussing the matter with her brother, who was in the service of the archbishop of Tarragona, the ever-kind Inés Pascual provided the pilgrim with a tiny room in the garret of her small apartment on the Carrer de Cotoners, which today is the Carrer de Sant Ignasi. The pilgrim had need of so few things that he was a guest who caused no inconvenience. He had a place where he could sleep and pray. That was all he needed, because he followed the same daily schedule in Barcelona that he had in Manresa.

7

"Charity, Faith, and Hope"

Cities are whatever one is looking for in them. For the pilgrim, the most important thing in Barcelona was how to go about booking passage on a ship bound for Rome, and that was not a very difficult thing to do. But over and above this, Íñigo wanted free passage and he wanted to go alone. In 1595, the very old priest Perpinyà asserted that he had accompanied his relative Guiot and the pilgrim on this voyage. From another source we are informed that George of Austria, the illegitimate son of the Emperor Maximilian, half-brother of Philip I, and bishop, first in Bressanone (Brixen) and later in Liège, met the pilgrim aboard ship and gave him food during the crossing. If we cannot be absolutely certain of these facts, what we can be sure of is the pilgrim's raw determination. Many people who held him in high regard argued with him that it was only reasonable that he team up with someone on this trip because, among other things, he spoke neither Italian nor Latin. Using another kind of logic, he said that he would not accept any company or protection, not even from Fernando, the duke of Cardona, nor his brother (the wife of his former patron, the duke of Nájera, was also a Cardona). This unrelenting stance was not because he was a loner, nor was it because of his desire for solitude; its source was of a different order. It was "because his whole purpose was to have God alone for refuge." He wanted to take on this adventure by giving up all human security and living totally dependent on Providence alone. "He wanted," he said, "to exercise the

virtues of charity, faith, and hope," naming the three theological virtues in this curious order, and he wanted to practice them
in the highest degree, unhampered by any attachments.
Reflecting on various possible scenarios, he had considered the
consequences of traveling in the company of another and concluded that "if he had a companion, he would expect help
from him when he was hungry, and if he should fall down, he
would expect him to help him get up and he would also confide in him and on this account would feel affection for him.
What he said came right from his heart. It was with such a disposition that he wanted to set sail, not merely all by himself, but
also with no provisions for the journey."

The pilgrim, a prototype of today's hitchhikers and homeless people, was a tenacious man with rare gifts for persuading
others. With no other recommendation beyond his own presence and persuasive speech, he managed to get free passage.
But the ship's master imposed one nonnegotiable condition: he could not embark unless he had the prescribed
amount of biscuit to last him on the journey. This posed a
problem of conscience for him, and he began to ask himself,
"Is this the hope and faith you have in God who would not fail
you?" There is a great deal of the radical Franciscan evange-
lism at this stage of the pilgrim's life, and he hesitated
between accepting or rejecting this imposed condition that
undermined the purity of his actions. He brought his
dilemma to a confessor who recommended that he take a
middle course. He would embark with the biscuit, but to get it
he would have to beg for it.

From his first day in Barcelona, Íñigo continued doing what
he had done in Manresa, that is, he begged from door to door
and then immediately handed out what he had collected to
other poor people, who had turned Señora Pascual's house
into a giveaway store. But now he began to beg for the sole
purpose of collecting provisions for his journey. There were
witnesses who remembered anecdotes about this obstinate
beggar of devotion. The great-granddaughter of a woman who
testified in the beatification process said her great-grand-
mother was struck by the pilgrim's fine features and delicate
hands. So she looked at him straight in the eye and lectured
him in terms that made the results of his begging uncertain
and costly. "You certainly seem to me an evil man, going

around this way as you do. You would do better to go back to your own home, instead of wandering around the world like a good-for-nothing." The pilgrim accepted the reproach calmly and humbly and he agreed that he was a good-for-nothing and a sinner. Struck by this answer, the good woman gave the pilgrim bread, wine, and other items for his voyage. Another woman was a bit more discreet. She began by asking him a question, "Where are you sailing?" Her feminine curiosity posed a real problem for the pilgrim. He did not want to say that he was going to Jerusalem for fear of "vainglory," the same reason he had kept secret his place of origin and the house from which he came. Such was this curious form of vainglory he sought to avoid; it had nothing in common with old, more obvious, pride of blood, nor with the fact that he was going to the Holy Land. But these two factors, along with his guise as a beggar, could make the people think that he was a saint. He answered the inquisitive woman's question with a half-truth, in the same way he had answered his brother when he left Loyola. He was going to Rome, he said. "So," said she, "you want to go to Rome, do you? Well, there is no telling how those who go there come back." This spirited Barcelona woman did not have a high opinion of the Renaissance Rome of Pope Leo X, where in a very short time the dour Adrian VI would die of a broken heart. Along with such exhortations and lectures, the pilgrim managed also to collect his provisions. In fact, he even counted a surplus of six coins that he scrupulously left behind on a waterfront bench.

While he was waiting for his ship to sail, the pilgrim sought out something else during the three weeks he spent in Barcelona, that is, he looked for "spiritual persons," as he called them. As opposed to experts in catechetics, these were souls who were able to sympathize with his interior state, people of a spectacular kind of sanctity, perhaps like the heroes found in the *Flos Sanctorum*. We do not know who it was that advised him to leave the city and visit the hermitages scattered along the slopes of Mount San Jerònimi de Vall d'Hevró. We know that the pilgrim conversed with some nuns and that he remained as still as a statue in prayer before the Blessed Sacrament. We also know the name of two of these nuns: Brígida Vicent and Antonia Estrada, to whom the pilgrim would bring a little box of mementos from Palestine. But he found none of the people he sought. His account does not give us much of a hint about how these "chosen affinities" were determined. From the gallery of persons he dealt with on a frequent basis in Montserrat, Manresa, and Barcelona—Chanones was a part of this group—there is only one who found favor in his eyes. This was the old Manresa woman mentioned above, who was nameless and who had asked God that Jesus appear to him. She was "a woman of many years, who for a long time had been a servant of God. She was known as such in many parts of Spain, so much so that the Catholic king had called her once to seek her advice." We do not know what the pilgrim found in her, nor do we know if her sanctity was accompanied by ecstacies, visions, and prophecies. Looking back, he noted that "she was the only one who seemed to be deeply versed in the spiritual life." Looking ahead, this frustrating quest for "chosen affinities" no longer held an interest for the pilgrim as he became more mature, less dependent, and given to greater solitude. "After leaving Barcelona, he lost for good this eagerness to seek out spiritual persons."

The crossing from Barcelona to Gaëta was made in five days, thanks to a strong aft wind. The storm-tossed sea, however, had filled the passengers with fear. When they disembarked (about March 20, 1523), the plague was ravaging Italy. The pilgrim set out immediately for Rome. He was joined by a young man and a mother accompanied by her daughter, who was dressed as a boy. All of them begged along the way. The trek was long and not without frightening moments. They intended to spend the first night in an inn, near which there were many soldiers huddled around a large fire. The soldiers gave them food to eat and were particularly generous in sharing their wine with the newcomers, "as though they wanted to warm them up," commented the pilgrim, who knew very well the ways of soldiers. Afterward, the travelers divided into pairs, the two women retiring to a room and the pilgrim and the young man to the stable. About midnight Íñigo was awakened by the shouts of the woman and her daughter, who, by the time he got to the inn, were already in the courtyard weeping and saying the soldiers had attempted to rape them. For a few moments the former bold and valiant soldier came to life again in the humble pilgrim. "So angry did he become" and so loud did he shout that all the people in the house were frightened and the soldiers gave up what they had intended to do. The young man had vanished under the protection of the darkness, but the two women and the pilgrim continued their journey even though it was still night. They arrived at Fondi, but the gates of the town were closed and so they had to sleep in a church. But even during the day they were not allowed to enter the city because of sanitary precautions, and outside the city they were not successful in collecting alms. They went to a castle that was nearby. The exhausted pilgrim, who had already been weakened by the hardships of sea journey, could go no farther. The mother and daughter continued their trip toward Rome, while he, "not being able to continue on his way, remained there." As fortune would have it, on that very day crowds of people came out of the city to receive the lady to whom Fondi belonged, Countess Beatrice Appiani, the wife of Vespasiano Colonna, duke of Traeto. In a gesture of desperation, the pilgrim literally planted himself in the middle of the road so that they would not take him for a victim of the plague because of his drawn face, but would say "that he was ill only from weakness," and was asking the favor to enter the city. Once inside, he collected a good number of small coins, recovered his health, and arrived in Rome on Palm Sunday (March 29, 1523).

Íñigo spent Holy Week there in prayer and in begging alms. He has left no account of his stay, but we now know that he received the blessing of Adrian VI. Although it was only on the twenty-ninth that he had arrived in the city, by the thirty-first he had already received the desired pontifical permission to go to the Holy Land. Prior to this date, he had to go to the Penitentiary to make the necessary arrangements for this license or passport. Someone had written out for him, in Latin, the required form petitioning the license. It has since been found in the Vatican Archives. In it, the pilgrim is identified as *Enecus de Loyola* and as a *clericus pampilonensis*, which would explain his recourse to ecclesiastical jurisdiction to solve his problems back in 1515. It was not very difficult for him to obtain such a passport. On the other hand, all of those to whom he confided his intentions tried to discourage him from carrying them through, assuring him that without money it would be absolutely impossible for him to book passage. Nothing could change his mind, because "in his soul he had great certainty, which would admit of no doubt that he would find some way of getting to Jerusalem."

About April 13, 1523, Íñigo took the road to Venice with the six or seven ducats that he had been given to defray his passage. He had accepted this money "because of the fear with which others had inspired him of not being able to get to Jerusalem otherwise." Two days after he left Rome, he repented of his lack of confidence and of his having taken the money, and so he determined to use it as alms for the poor. By the time he reached Venice, the pilgrim had only a few small coins that served him well on his first night there. The trip, which was made all the way on foot, was rich in misfortune and hardships. We know for sure only two places where he stopped, Chioggia and Padua. Probably he passed through Tivoli, Orvieto, Spoleto, Macerata, Loreto, Ancona, Senigallia, Pesaro, Rimini, Ravenna, Chioggia, Padua, and finally, Venice. It was a delightful itinerary, one that today would be an ideal "Backroads of Italy" tour, although at that time it was made difficult because of the plague. He ate as he could and slept under porticos or in the open fields. One morning, as he was awakening, he saw a man flee from him as if the devil were after him. Once daybreak revealed Íñigo's sallow, drawn face, this man, who had spent the night near him, thought for certain that he was looking at the face of a man stricken by the plague. Such was our pilgrim "of the sorry countenance." Getting into Venice presented more problems. Some of his traveling companions went off to get a health certificate at Padua. He could not keep up with them because they walked too fast, and so they left him behind "at nightfall in a vast field." It was one of his worst experiences of total abandonment, and he tells us that here "Christ appeared to him in His usual way," referring to his Manresa days. This was not an external, visible vision, but a lived experience viewed with "eyes of his understanding," a sensation of the nearness of the humanity of Christ in the form of a body vaguely white, with no distinction of members. This vision consoled him, gave him strength, and helped him to arrive in Padua where he went in and out of the city without having to show a health certificate, much to the amazement of his more prudent fellow travelers. Then, still without the required certificate, he came to Venice. The guards inspected everyone who had arrived there in a boat, allowing only him to enter the city of the canals undisturbed. It was mid-May; he still had two months to wait for passage to the Holy Land.

A tourist he was not. He supported himself by begging and he slept in the Piazza di San Marco, where he was able to learn to recognize the sounds of the Venetian bells: the *Marangona* called the people to work; the *Trottera* summoned the senators; and the *Rialtina* advised all the people that the night curfew was in effect, and warned him that the hour had come for him to look for a place to sleep in the beautiful piazza. A gondolier may well have repeated for him the words of Pope Julius II, who said, "If Venice did not exist, someone would have to invent it." The Venetians were masters of the art of staging colorful and spectacular city festivals. During his stay there, the pilgrim could have watched the Corpus Christi procession in which the doge, the ambassadors, and the municipal officials took part, each one solemnly proceeding along the designated way with a Jerusalem pilgrim at his right. He could also have admired the nautical feast during which the symbolic marriage of Venice with the sea was celebrated. In a sumptuous vessel accompanied by innumerable boats, the doge took to the high sea where he threw a golden ring into the waters, and then afterward everyone returned to sing a Te Deum in the church of San Niccolò. The pilgrim would never have wanted to go to the house of the emperor's ambassador, nor would he have been especially concerned about preparing for his trip to the Holy Land. He had blind faith, "a deep certainty in his soul," as he said, that God would give him the wherewithal to get to Jerusalem. All the reasons and fears others represented to him had no effect whatsoever on his resolve.

One day he met a rich Spaniard who was living in Venice and who asked him what he was doing there and where he was going. He invited him to come and eat in his house, and he gave him a few days' lodging. At first, the pilgrim remained silent at the table, listening, eating, and answering the questions he was asked, and then at the end of the meal, picking up bits and pieces of the table talk, he began to speak about God. The family of this unexpected host became fond of him and persuaded him to remain with them. What is more, this unknown Spanish gentleman was successful in getting him a private audience with the doge of Venice. The pilgrim took over from there. The end result was the doge ordered that he be given passage aboard a ship that was taking the Venetian governor to Cyprus. The fact that Süleyman had captured Rhodes during the previous year had dissuaded a number of pilgrims from going to Jerusalem; moreover, pilgrims who were already on their way returned home to Venice. A second ship, also known as the "pilgrim ship," set out first with thirteen pilgrims; the eight or nine that were left behind had to leave on the governor's ship. Today we know the names of these ships, thanks to Peter Füssli of Zurich, one of the pilgrims who had kept a diary. The governor's ship, the *Negrona*, was a magnificent vessel that carried nineteen cannons, thirty-two sailors, and some one hundred passengers. Four of these were Spaniards, one of whom was our pilgrim. A few days before the departure, Íñigo was stricken with untimely bouts of fever. The treatment he received was inadequate and on the very day of his departure he was given a purge. The doctor said that he could set sail, but only if his intention was to be buried en route. Íñigo, stubborn Basque that he was, boarded the ship. After a period of continuous vomiting, he began to feel better. The ships, going at a snail's pace because of the all-pervasive calm, took a whole month to arrive at Cyprus, where they finally touched shore on August 14. All of this inactivity fostered vice. The pilgrim chanced to see "some individuals engaged in openly lewd and obscene behavior," that is to say, homosexual activity. Íñigo severely upbraided the guilty individuals. The three other Spaniards aboard ship pleaded with him not to overreact because the crewmen were talking about dropping him off on some island. Fortunately, shortly after this crisis the ship arrived at Famagusta in Cyprus. Íñigo went off to a different port, which is present-day Larnaca, where he embarked on another ship, *La Peregrina*, with nothing more for sustenance than his hope in God. As a compensation, he had the vision of the nearness of Christ in the form of "a large round object, as though it were of gold," and this brought him consolation and courage. Füssli had provided himself with a large store of meat, eggs, fruit, cheeses, wine, and spirits, and we can be certain that Íñigo must have shared in these provisions. On August 19, they set sail from Cyprus and spotted Jaffa on the twenty-fifth, but a mistake made in maneuvering the ship delayed their landing until the thirty-first. They sang the *Te Deum* and the *Salve Regina* and shortly afterward, accompanied by some Franciscans and an escort of Turkish troops, they mounted small donkeys and made their way to Jerusalem.

8
Jerusalem

As the twenty-one pilgrims approached Jerusalem, one of the four Spaniards, Diego de Manes, a member of the Commander of the Order of Saint John, announced to the others that they were two miles from the holy city, and approaching the hill from where they would be able to see it for the first time. He recommended that all of them prepare their conscience for this event and that they proceed in silence. The emotion was extreme; the picture of this event remained vivid in Íñigo's memory. Just before arriving at the viewing spot, they came upon a number of Franciscans, one of whom was holding a cross on high. These had come from Jerusalem to welcome their arrival. The pilgrims dismounted their donkeys and proceeded on foot. "When the pilgrim did see the city, he experienced great consolation, and all the others affirmed that they experienced the same and they confessed that they felt a joy that did not seem natural." The pilgrim was overcome by an awe and fervor that never left him during all of the time he visited the holy places. We know in detail his Jerusalem itinerary and we will give a summary account of what he did while he was in the holy city. He and his fellow pilgrims were lodged in the hospice of Saint John, and on September 5 they visited the Upper Room, where Christ instituted the Holy Eucharist, and the Church of the Dormition of the Virgin Mary. That same evening they went to the Church of the Holy Sepulchre, where they passed the night in vigil and where each one confessed his sins in his own

language, heard Mass, and went to Holy Communion. At daybreak, they left the church that had been locked until that
hour by the Turkish guard. That afternoon they made the sta-
tions along the Via Dolorosa. During the following two days
they visited first the Mount of Olives, and then the place of
the Ascension, and then the villages of Bethphage and
Bethany. Afterward, they saw Bethlehem and its grotto, the
Valley of Josaphat and the torrent of Kidron, the Garden of
Olives, the grotto where the Agony took place, the spring of
the Virgin, the Pool of Siloam, and Mount Zion. After another
all-night vigil spent in the Holy Sepulchre and two days of
rest, they left under the escort of Turkish soldiers for Jericho,
and here they saw the Jordan River. Their last two days were
spent shut up in the Saint John hostel.

Íñigo's eyes drank in the landscape surrounding all of these
places and what he saw was engraved forever on his memory.
These days put into focus an evocative meaning to the direction he gives the retreatment, at the beginning of most of the
meditations in his Exercises about the "composition of place,"
that is, about having the retreatant place himself imaginatively
in the actual place where the mystery unfolds. After the eyes
have seen, the imagination does its work, and the spirit follows
along the footsteps of Christ into those places hallowed by
Him. "Christ's fool," as he was called at Montserrat, inscribed
on his own spirit the earthly scenes where the Word was made
flesh and where the historic flesh-and-blood Christ revealed
Himself. Íñigo's powerful "christocentrism" found a particular
spiritual nourishment in the very concrete setting where Jesus'
voice resounded and where He worked out our redemption.
This longed-for Jerusalem pilgrimage, that had been so much
a part of him ever since his Loyola days, meant more than performing a series of penitential set of devotions. It was an effort
to grasp Christ, who, although no longer present in physical
form in the places and the scenes associated with His historical, physical presence, became more ardently experienced
each day within the heart of the pilgrim, who was visiting the
holy places and scenes associated with that presence.

In the deepest part of Íñigo's being, these days in Jerusalem
were not meant to be merely a passing phase in his life. He
desired with all of his heart to remain for the rest of his days
in these holy places; moreover, he secretly believed that his

presence there could bring some help to souls. With this belief in mind, he brought some letters of recommendation to the Father Guardian of the Franciscans, indicating that he wanted to remain in Jerusalem. He had already confided his plan to a number of people, although he kept to himself the part about his being a missionary. But any missionary activity was all but impossible in this closed, hostile Muslim world. Even his plan for staying on in the Holy Land was impractical. The Franciscan house in Jerusalem was extremely poor and the friars there had even considered sending some of their own members back on the pilgrim ship. The pilgrim asked only that the friars allow him to come from time to time so that he could make his confession. The guardian did not want to make any decision without consulting the provincial, who was at the time in Bethlehem.

Íñigo believed that the problem was resolved, and even began writing letters to spiritual persons in Barcelona. The letters he would confide to the care of departing pilgrims. He recorded that he wrote one long, three-page letter. This well may have been the one we know that Inés Pascual received. It was a document that testified to Íñigo's ardent enthusiasm, and it was treasured by the Pascual family, who made it public at the time of Íñigo's beatification process. On the evening before the group's departure, Íñigo was writing a second letter when the Franciscan provincial returned, and, however kind his words, he dashed all of the pilgrim's hopes of remaining in the Holy Land. The provincial was a man who had had a great deal of experience, and he thought that Íñigo's project was preposterous. Other individuals had appeared on the scene before him and had attempted to lead the same type of life he was proposing, but, after causing all kinds of problems and complications for the Franciscan custody, they ended up either by being thrown into prison or by being put to death. Íñigo simply had to get ready to leave the following day with the other pilgrims, and that was all there was to it. In vain was he able to "stick to his resolve" and his determination not to give up under any pretext. He argued that he was able to assume responsibility for his own fate and that he feared nothing except that his determination would end up being a sin. But the Franciscan provincial was clear in making him understand that he had the exclusive jurisdiction over those who came to Jerusalem and that he could excommunicate anyone who refused to obey him. He offered to show him the pontifical bulls that gave him these powers, but the pilgrim believed him and obeyed the decision that was so painful for him to carry out. Íñigo wanted to utilize his few remaining hours, and so he returned once again to the Mount of Olives so that he could verify the position of the feet in the stone that was said to have borne the imprint of Christ's footprints at the moment of His ascension. Without saying a word to anyone and without even taking a guide, he slipped away from the others and went up to the place all by himself. He bribed the guards by giving them a pair of scissors he was carrying. Shortly afterward, the alarm spread throughout the hospice that he had disappeared. One of the servants went out to look for him and found him on the road. The servant was very angry and threatened to strike him with a huge staff he was carrying, and he grabbed him violently by the arm and brought him back to the hospice as if he were a criminal. Under these circumstances, the pilgrim felt the help and nearness of Christ in a most tangible way. Finally, after an unforgettable twenty-day stay, the pilgrims mounted their miniature donkeys and left Jerusalem on the night of September 23. Íñigo had fulfilled the greatest desire of his life, and he considered all of the inconveniences he had suffered worthwhile. For the moment, he had to give up the idea of living and dying in Palestine, accepting this as a manifestation of God's will for him. His destiny was not to be found in Jerusalem right now. Where, then, was it to be? "I am a pilgrim of today. It is not important where I go," as Manuel Machado y Ruiz was to write.

The pilgrim began his return home. After arriving in Cyprus, the group parted company and continued on in three different ships. Some of the pilgrims asked a rich Venetian, who was the owner of the largest and best-equipped ship, to allow their penniless companion to make the journey with them, free of charge. The Venetian was deaf to their entreaties and even joked with them about their request. If this man was really a saint, as those who were making intercession for him had probably described him, then, the Venetian said, let him cross the sea miraculously as Saint James did. His petitioners were more successful with the owner of the smallest ship, on which Íñigo ended up sailing. The two larger ships were overcome by a surprise storm. The third one had a hard time of it, but it alone managed to reach Italy, landing at Apulia. The pilgrim had to face this bad weather in his miserable, shabby clothes that consisted of a black jacket cut off at the shoulders; a pair of shorts made of coarse cloth that went as far as the knees, leaving the legs bare; a pair of shoes on his feet; and a short, threadbare cloak. Dressed in this fashion, he arrived in Venice in mid-January 1524 after being two months at sea. Perhaps Titian could have seen him, but the pilgrim was not a model that would have attracted the painter of Paul II, Charles V, and Venus. Some individual, who had shown him hospitality on his way to Jerusalem, gave him alms of fifteen *giulii* and a piece of cloth that he folded several times over and placed on his stomach to protect him from the intense cold.

Venice he considered nothing more than a rest stop for him. After he had gone through so many months of wandering, his future was altogether uncertain. Now that the possibility of staying on in Jerusalem was a dead issue, "he kept thinking of what he *ought to be doing*." His earlier plans for entering the Carthusians had gone by the boards, supplanted by the desire to help souls, a desire that had come out of his Manresa experience. Faced with a new goal, "he finally felt more inclined to spend some time in studies." He thought again of Barcelona. We will never know anything about the long and involved interior process that led him finally to opt for this unknown and never-traveled way. He was thirty-three years old. He began his return trip to Spain on the land route, walking all of the way. At Ferrara he tarried for awhile in the cathedral, giving himself over to his particular devotions. He gave a coin to one poor man who asked for alms and a coin of greater value to a second beggar, and to a third he gave a *giulio*. The word soon spread and more poor people came in droves. He gave away everything that he had and then he asked pardon of the late-comers "because he had nothing left to give." From that day on, he had to beg for food to eat. It is no wonder, as Ribadeneira reported, that the crowd of poor people cried out, "The saint, the saint!" whenever this bizarre-looking pilgrim walked out of the church.

He became a victim of a serious misunderstanding during his trek from Ferrara to Genoa. Lombardy was the theater in the war between Francis I and Charles V. Prospero Colonna, the commander of the Spanish troops and father of Vespasiano

Colonna, had just died, and was succeeded by Antonio de Leiva. As we have already seen, his relative, Sancho Martínez de Leiva, was captain-general in Guipúzcoa. The French were under the command of Admiral Guillaume Goufflier, lord of Bonnivet, who had captured Maya, Behovia, and Fuenterrabía during the fall of 1521. In the following year, the two armies clashed at the terrible battle of Pavia in which the flower of the French nobility perished and the French king was taken prisoner along with Andrés Asparros's brother, Thomas de Grailly de Foix-Lautrec, viscount of Lescun and field marshal of France. He was wounded twice defending the person of the king and died a week later from his wounds. At the time when the pilgrim was making his way westward (1524), the two forces had dug into their respective positions. He encountered some Spanish soldiers who put him up for the night, astonished that he had "walked that road because it passed almost in the middle of the French and combined Spanish imperial armies." They urged him to leave the main road and take a safer road, but he paid no attention to their advice and continued on the direct route. Coming across a village that had been burned, destroyed, and abandoned, he contemplated the ravages of war. Night was coming on and he had had nothing to eat all day. "At sunset he came to a walled town," he informs us in a rare adversion to the landscape. The guards seized him, taking him for a spy, and they confined him to a small shed close to the town gates. Recalling similar incidents that he had already lived through, the pilgrim noted that "they began to interrogate him, as they usually do with suspects." He answered all of their questions, saying that he knew nothing. They stripped him, inspecting his shoes and every part of his body to see if he was carrying any written messages. Not finding anything, they bound him and took him to their captain. "He would make him talk"—this, as he recalled, was the threatening and frightful expression they used. He was dressed only in his shorts and jacket; they did not even let him put on his short cloak.

At a moment of such sheer danger, only a man who was completely recollected could find a spiritual dimension in the events taking place around him, which seemed to presage execution. As he was being lead through three wide streets, he remembered how it must have been when Christ was arrested.

Thanks to this thought, he was able to walk on fearlessly and courageously, with joy and elation. During all of this time his thoughts were spinning. He had been in the habit of addressing everyone he met with the simple form "you" (*vos*) because he believed that in this way he would be imitating the simplicity of Christ in dealing with His apostles. However, as he walked through the streets, he was tempted, out of "some lurking fear of the torture they might inflict on him," to forego this habitual way of speaking and to address the captain as "Your Lordship." The old, eternal tale of wily, self-cross-examinations! But he saw in this change of attitude a temptation to lack confidence in God, and so, without any further adieu, he decided not to change his usual way of addressing people, not to perform any obeisance before the captain, and not even to doff his cap. He was led to the palace, and the guards locked him in a downstairs room. A short time later, the captain made his appearance. The pilgrim deliberately gave him no sign of courtesy, responding to his questions with few words and long pauses. The furious captain thought he was deranged and mocked him in front of his subordinates, saying, "This fellow has no brains. Give him his things and throw him out." Leaving the palace, he fell in with a Spaniard along the street. The man lived in the town and so he brought him home with him, gave him his first meal of the day and all that he needed for the night.

He left the next morning and walked until late afternoon. Two soldiers stationed in a tower spotted him and came down to question him. They brought him to another captain in the French army who asked him what country he was from. When this captain learned that he was from Guipúzcoa, he confessed that he himself was from Bayonne. Basques understand one another better when they are far from home than when they are in their own country. The Bayonne captain ordered that the pilgrim be given something to eat and be treated well. Íñigo did not comment much on other minor adventures that befell him on his way to Genoa. In this city he met another Basque named Portuondo, an important man in Genoa, the one who was responsible for the safe embarkation of all the troop ships arriving in the port. Ribadeneira assures us that Íñigo had already known this man at the court of the

Catholic monarchs. With such an influential power behind him, it was not difficult for him to find a vessel bound for Barcelona. This ship was nearly captured by the galleys of the Genoan patriot, Andrea Doria, who at the date was in the service of Francis I. After the French defeat at Pavia (1525), Doria served under Pope Clement VII. Two years later, when Francis was released from his captivity, Doria rejoined the French forces, but, disillusioned that Francis did not keep his promise to grant freedom to the city of Genoa, he transferred his services to Charles, and remained allied to the imperial forces until his death. Íñigo at last arrived in Barcelona after his Palestinian odyssey, with no other provisions than his hope in God. There was a great deal of the Franciscan bohemian spirit in his incredible undertaking, born out of obstinate stubbornness and pure hope. This last factor explains why the detailed and selected accounts of his adventures are unlike the journal of a tourist, and indeed unlike even the diary of a pious pilgrim. Íñigo's account is a simple hymn to the Providence that guided his steps.

He finished his hazardous voyage to the unknown only to return to the city where he already had a number of acquaintances and friends. February 1524 was already coming to an end. He must surely have learned then and there that Adrian VI had died and had been succeeded to the papal throne by Giulio de' Medici in November 1523, and that the new pope took the name Clement VII. But he certainly would have had no way of knowing that in Italy during this same year, the future Pope Paul IV had founded the congregation known as the Theatines. The pilgrim regularly conducted his life beyond the pale of what was taking place in Europe, and so what would he have known about the Diet of Nuremberg, or the League of Ratisbone, or the controversies with the sacramentarians, or the Peasants' War, or of Thomas Münzer and Andreas von Carlstadt, or of the debates between Luther and Erasmus? Erasmus was able to reproach his adversary, Martin Luther, by saying: "I see many Lutherans but few, if any, who are honestly evangelical." At this moment in his life, the pilgrim with good reason could have sung along with Luther the celebrated hymn that the latter had just composed, *Ein feste Burg ist unser Gott*— "A Mighty Fortress Is Our God"—but he would not have understood the debates that were taking place between the humanists and the Lutherans. Íñigo was not an intellectual; he was rather a potential student candidate, and only for apostolic reasons. Moreover, he had not even arrived at a "determination"—his favorite word for expressing a firm resolution—but only at the indecisive "inclination" to begin studies.

9

"What Should He Do?"

As a way of ridding himself of doubts, Íñigo shared the secret
that was in the back of his mind with Isabel Roser, about
whom we have more to say, and Master Ardèvol, a Barcelona
professor of grammar. Both approved of the project. Even better, the master volunteered to teach him free of charge, and
Isabel promised to take care of his needs. Their advice and
support went far beyond what the pilgrim had imagined he
would do if he did decide to take up studies. He had supposed that if he did go ahead with this plan, he would go back
to Manresa and seek out a monk he knew there who had a
reputation for great holiness. This man could teach him while
he, in turn, continued to make progress in spiritual matters
and carried on his apostolate of helping souls. However, he
accepted provisionally the generous offer of the Barcelona
woman, and then went off to Manresa with the intention of
discussing the matter with the monk. When he got there, he
learned that the man had died, and so once again events had
pointed out to him the path he was to follow. Returning to
Barcelona, "he began his studies with great diligence," and
thereby entered into a new phase in his life that was to last
more than ten years.

We already know a great deal about Master Jerònimi
Ardèvol, the humanistic climate of Barcelona, and the books
that were being read in the "City of the Counts." But we should
point out to the reader that our superannuated student stood
out as being very singular indeed, and not only so because of

his advanced age. To the ordinary anticipated difficulties that came from studying the grammar of Élio António Nebrija and memorizing Latin texts, must be added what we politely call our student's distracted or inattentive level of concentration. His attention would be drawn away from studying verb conjugations by greater delights for and new insights into spiritual matters. What else could he do?—they were so overwhelming, so powerful! He mulled over this problem and was struck by the fact that these delights never came to him when he was attending Mass or while he was praying. He finally came to recognize that they were a temptation, and he went to Santa Maria del Mar, a church that was near to where his patient teacher lived. He asked the master to come and join him there, and "while the two of them were seated together," he confided to Ardèvol the difficulties he was having and the reason why he was progressing so poorly. "'I promise you,' the pilgrim told him, 'that as long as I can find bread and water in Barcelona to support myself, I will never miss any of your classes during the next two years.' Since he made this promise with great determination, he never again had those temptations." The *oppositum per diametrum*—the opposite of any compromise—is not a popular axiom in modern-day spirituality, but it is a recurring theme in the life of Íñigo. Between these lines we have cited from this section of his *Autobiography*, we can read that he was a man of prayer who attended Mass regularly and who lived an austere life of poverty. The stomach pains he had contracted when he was first in Manresa were the reason why he modified his penances and began wearing shoes. These pains had left him as soon as he sailed for Jerusalem, and so his improved health made him think again of taking up his former penances. He bore holes in his shoes and by the time winter of 1525 arrived, these holes had widened to the extent that nothing remained of the shoes except the upper parts. It was Íñigo himself who gave us the account of these events. But we know many other details besides, thanks to the testimony of Joan Pascual; moreover, the witnesses at the beatification process that took place at the turn of the century have given us additional information about the life of this unusual student during this period of his life.

Inés Pascual—perhaps the only woman in this world whom Íñigo called mother—welcomed him once again into her home where he had spent three weeks prior to his departure for Jerusalem. The octogenarian Miguel Canyelles recalled how Inés, overwhelmed with joy, had told him the news of the pilgrim's return to Barcelona. At the instigation of Inés, Canyelles went to visit him and found him surrounded by the virtuous women of the city who had flocked to see him. Miguel's mother, who was originally from Manresa, had learned the weaver's trade in the Pascual household. When he was eight years old, Miguel had been received out of charity in the same house where Íñigo was lodged, thanks to the generosity of Inés Pascual, who had found him wandering in the streets during the ravages of the plague. He gave his protectress the highest testimonials of praise, describing her as "a woman who loved the truth and would not tell a lie for all of the gold in the world." Miguel remembered the upstairs room that the pilgrim occupied in the little house; he recalled the wooden bed that had no mattress; and he remembered how Íñigo would spend hours on his knees in prayer. He recalled that he was a silent man, unwilling to converse. In fact, Canyelles recalled, he spoke only when he was asked a question, and then it was with restraint; however, what he said "would speak to the heart." He attested that Íñigo came back from Jerusalem dressed in the same clothes he was wearing when he departed, and that he carried with him a rosary that he was usually saying continuously. The most surprising part of his testimony is about Íñigo's begging practices. Begging food seems to have been an essential feature of the pilgrim's life, for day-to-day survival was not an easy problem for him to resolve. Canyelles stated that he begged for his food during the whole of the time he remained under Inés Pascual's roof, and in addition to this fact he gives us some interesting details about how he begged. For example, he said that each week the pilgrim would go to the homes of Señora Guiomar Gralla, who was connected to the Marquis de Aytona's family, and Isabel de Requenes, the mother of the grand commander of Castile, as well as to the homes of a number of other people of rank. But he did so always accompanied by Inés, because "otherwise he was very poorly qualified to beg for whatever he needed." How do we interpret this detail, given the fact that Íñigo had already spent many months begging on his own and that he had begged all the way to Jerusalem and back? Did some personal shyness or natural timidity persuade him to ask for alms with Inés at his side? If so, his long experience as a beggar would render him even more heroic. For my part, I am inclined to believe that the devout ladies of Barcelona devised this organized begging program, persuaded that they were accommodating the wishes of the poor Íñigo. But he was against whatever deprived him from what he considered the benefits that resulted from begging, namely, an encounter with the unknown, the unpredictable; the experience of depending on pure charity that gives without question to a nameless poor person; the frequent scorn and the accompanying condescending lecture that is the price paid for begging; and finally, the feeling of total hopelessness before men, along with a complete reliance and hope in God alone.

10
Íñigo, the Poor Pilgrim

If we do not agree that there was an understanding among these women to oversee Íñigo's begging endeavors, then how do we account for the fact that each week Doña Guiomar brought him a weekly supply of flour that Inés would knead and bake for him, and that whatever he had not eaten he would then distribute to the poor? Slowly and with great precision, Miguel recounted a tender, homely anecdote that demonstrates Inés's respectful veneration for the pilgrim. It seems that Íñigo used to bring home scraps of white and dark bread and he would eat the most unsavory pieces and give away the best. On one occasion, Miguel and the other boys looked through his knapsack and said, "You've got a lot of bread down there." The pilgrim answered him gently, "Miguel, help yourself to it." In spite of Inés's disapproval, the boys accepted the invitation. "You rascals, you let him eat it," she said. The pilgrim intervened in this dispute and in a most gentle way said, "Mother Pascuala, let them alone; it gives me joy just watching them eat it all."

Inés's son, Joan, shared an upstairs room with the pilgrim. When the time came for them to retire, Íñigo would say to the young man, "Joan, you go to bed now, I have something else I want to do." The boy would get into bed and then pretend that he was asleep, but in fact he would stay awake, fascinated, watching his roommate praying on his knees for hours on end, and sighing aloud, "My God, if only men knew you!" These were words that it would be difficult for a person to forget, nor could he ever forget the threadbare clothes and the hairshirt the pilgrim used to wear.

Despite the pilgrim's desire to remain hidden and alone, he was becoming more and more well known throughout Barcelona. Jaume Cassador, the archdeacon and soon to become bishop of Barcelona, held him in the highest esteem, and so did Master Ardèvol, Isabel de Josa, a lady of recognized culture, and members of the Pujalt, Benet, and Ribelles families. People paid far more attention to him than he thought. Whenever Don Juan Boxador saw the pilgrim walking along the street, he would whisper to his companions, "Look over there. There goes the noble knight." Although he could keep hidden his interior life and how he spent his time, there were some telltale things that took place that showed who he really was. For instance, the Dominican nuns of the convent of Nostra Senyora de los Angeles had the reputation of socializing with lay people. He visited these nuns on a number of occasions and succeeded in convincing them to put an end to such habitual idle gossip sessions. He had to pay the price for what he had done in this instance when a thug, who had been hired by a nobleman, assaulted him, insulted him, thrashed him, and left him for dead in the middle of the street. Some millers picked him up and brought him to Inés's house where he remained laid up for almost two whole months. He was in such a sorry state that whenever they made his bed they had to use towels to move him. They cured him by wrapping him in sheets soaked in wine. He never indicated who might have been the perpetrator or the instigator of this act of revenge. Joan Pascual recalled that during these days, "My mother treated and coddled him as if he were her own son or an angel come to earth; she stayed by him during the night, without ever sleeping a wink. . . . The flower of Barcelona's nobility came to visit him, both ladies and gentlemen, and they all pampered him to death, Doña Isabel de Josa, more than all the others." Included in this "all" were Doña Estefania de Requenes, the daughter of the count of Palamos, Don Joan de Requenes, Doña Isabel de Boxador, and Doña Guiomar.

Íñigo's life was a mirror in which many townsmen from Barcelona contemplated themselves. His person radiated something that brought out veneration and affection in others. Many made mention of a light that lit up his face, a physical transparency of his intense interior life. The most remarkable testimony of this radiation was given by Isabel Ferrer, wife of Joan Roser (also called Rosell). She saw the pilgrim for the first time in the church of San Justo in Barcelona during those days just before his departure for Jerusalem in 1523. He was seated on the church steps surrounded by children. She was struck by a light that shone forth from the pilgrim's pallid and somewhat luminous face. She heard a voice from within say, "Call him." When she returned home and received permission from her husband, she sent for the pilgrim and invited him to dine with her family. At the dinner table she joined the others in asking him to speak to them about God, for they wanted to hear his truly efficacious words. The pilgrim was on the point of embarking on a brigantine, but the family made him change ship, and they took his books off the brigantine, which was ready to set sail. The ship departed, and, while still in sight of Barcelona, it sank. Doña Isabel would always remain fond of the pilgrim, and years later, during the time he was in Paris, she would help him defray the costs of his schooling. In 1532, he would write the following words of gratitude to her from the French capital, "I owe more to you than to any other person I know in this life."

The impression that the pilgrim made on the people of Barcelona would not be easily effaced with the passage of the years. But during all of the time he was in Barcelona, Íñigo remained a confirmed recluse. He relied on the protection of friends who, in turn, regarded him with a certain veneration. Soon he wanted to attract companions around him. Polanco alludes to these Barcelona years when he said that Íñigo "began from that time on to have the desire to gather certain persons to himself in order *to put into operation the plan he had, beginning at that time, of helping repair the defects he saw in serving God, namely, persons who might be like trumpets of Jesus Christ.*" This is the first instance that his reforming ideal begins to take shape. His first companions were named Juan de Arteaga, Lope de Cáceres, and Calixto de Sa. Their enthusiasm would dim with time. During this same period, a fellow countryman of his, a certain Lope de Celain, who enjoyed the protection of the marquis de Villena, was traveling about the Medina de Rioseco country with the idea of founding a kind of apostolic school whose purpose would be the conversion of the world.

In 1530, he ended up in the clutches of the Inquisition and was condemned in Granada as a Lutheran.

Íñigo's vague reformist plan of this period encouraged him to continue along his yet unclear path. His teacher, Ardèvol, was pressing him to begin his studies of arts at Alcalá. A doctor of theology who examined him concurred with this opinion. The only thing that remained was to follow the path blindly, to press ahead toward an uncertain future by following his shining star, which was Alcalá with its famous humanist university founded by Cisneros in 1508.

What he left behind him in Barcelona was a profound spiritual heritage—people whose lives had been touched by his unique personality; places and objects associated with his memory, where his lingering presence hovered; and that letter he sent to Inés Pascual giving the details of his Jerusalem pilgrimage whose very reading inspires devotion. He had foretold that Inés's son, Joan, would be visited by terrible misfortunes in the future, and these events did come about exactly as he had said they would. But their presence did not weaken Joan's faith nor did they lower his esteem for the pilgrim. On the contrary, after Íñigo's death, Joan's devotion for him became an even greater driving force in his life. We have the letter that the pilgrim sent to Inés Pascual at this time. It is dated December 6, 1525, and he probably wrote it while he was at Manresa. He warned her of some serious problems facing her and advised her that she should try to avoid them. This man, who was so exacting when it came to dealing with himself, showed himself lenient when it came to his adopted mother: "Our Lord does not ask you to do anything that would cause you harm or injury; on the contrary, He wants you to live joyfully in Him and give your body all that it needs. You should speak, think, and converse in Him, and, in regard to what you should give your body, you should observe the Lord's commandments before all else. The reason is that this is what He wants and this is what He asks us to do. . . . And thus, through love of our Lord, let us put all of our effort in Him, seeing we owe Him so much. . . ." "[T]hrough love," "put all of our effort," "live joyful"—such are the characteristics of the man who signed his letter, "The poor pilgrim, Íñigo." Since he was a man freed from all desire to possess, he was a man who did not for a moment hesitate before what

Erich Fromm called the existential alternative that explains reality as a basic mode of existence—that is, as the alternative between either *being* or *having*. Íñigo was truly liberated from the desire to possess and therefore from the structure of an existential mode based on *having*.

11

"To Help Souls"

"To seek means is to have an objective, whereas to find means to be free, open, not in need of any goal." This saying of the German-born poet and novelist, Hermann Hesse, can well serve as the introduction to the new life Íñigo was entering upon. Did he really have an actual objective during this period of his life? The reasonable supposition is that he went off to study, that he sought to improve his knowledge in some celebrated university, even though his ulterior objective was "to help souls." However, no one knows what this introspective Basque was seeking when "he left all alone for Alcalá," not even he himself. It was odd enough that he set out for the university somewhere around March 1526 because classes had already begun for the Saint Luke's Term on October 18. It would be rash to suppose that this late desire to take up studies was motivated by a consideration to go for the priesthood. Whatever his reason really was, he spoke very little about his studies in the *Autobiography*. Later, when he recalled this part of his life, he did so with the sole purpose of showing us the paths along which God had been leading him, and so his attention was on other events. In a very few lines he tells us about the courses he took at the university. He said that for almost a year and a half he studied the logic of Domingo de Soto, the physics of Albert the Great, and the work of the Master of the Sentences, Peter Lombard. This was a real mishmash of courses that would never have been recommended by any *ratio studiorum*. On the other hand, he devoted eight paragraphs to detailed recollections of other adventures that he had at Alcalá.

Íñigo's distant past was now interred in oblivion, and with it was buried his family. He progressed toward an uncertain future with a joy that defied description, and with the same joy he welcomed each day with all the pleasures and sufferings that that day brought. At a time when the courtiers of Charles V were introducing luxurious tastes and new lifestyles into society, and when the call from the Americas was awakening greed for quick and easy riches and the desire to break the bonds of social immobility in the hearts of men, the poor pilgrim persisted in his wish to be unknown and to live in total poverty. He had nothing of his own. When he departed from Barcelona, he once again cut the ties of support and security and left behind his reputation for being a holy man. He had freed himself from all limitations and dependencies. He was not a young man whose head was filled with woolly revolutionary ideas, nor was he one of life's dropouts, someone who was disillusioned and skeptical. If we call him independent, we would be taking into account only one—and not a very important—dimension of his personality. Although he was a rebel, he was not a fatuous rebel ranting against consumerism and the ills of society, but a rebel of the spirit who fought against himself alone. We cannot say the pilgrim possessed a rich interior life but that it was the rich interior life that possessed him. And his interior life did not consist of empty loneliness, for he was ever aware of the companionship of God, the presence of Christ who dominated his being. His existence was not defined by having, but by being. This happiness of being came not merely from repressing desires and greed, but from the joy of loving, sharing, and giving. Erich Fromm reflects on these elements and concludes his findings in this one sentence: "Interior independence alone leads to freedom." But in addition to all of this, he was not alone in Alcalá. Three young men made their appearance as his companions, and soon a fourth joined this threesome.

If we adopt the pilgrim's point of view, we might ask ourselves, Why should we distract ourselves here with the history of what the Romans called Complutum—the town later called Alcalá by the Moors—or with the university that Cardinal

Cisneros founded there? Why should we be concerned about this university's buildings, colleges, and its reputation as a center of humanism, or why should we bother ourselves with learning about its curriculum and its program of studies? It is probable that Íñigo was not a bona fide student of the university anyway. Yet, even though he was not enrolled, he did register his name on the roster of poor students as soon as he arrived in Alcalá. This roster was not a list of those starving vagabond students that are highlighted in Spanish picaresque novels, but it was a roster of the genuine poor, the beggars. "As soon as he arrived at Alcalá, he began to beg and live on alms." He already knew the scorn associated with such poverty, and for two weeks he carried on what he had already begun in Barcelona. Finally, a priest and some people walking with him came across the pilgrim begging alms in his customary way, and they began to laugh, poke fun, and insult him "as they usually do to those who are hale and hearty but who take to begging." Íñigo blocked out neither this event nor its unexpected result from his memory, for at the very moment when this humiliating drama was taking place, the man who was the superintendent of the hospice at Nuestra Señora de la Misericordia, founded by Luis de Antezana in 1483, happened to pass by. What he witnessed filled him with disgust and shame, and so he invited the pilgrim to come and stay at the hospice. "He gave him a room and all he needed," which was understood to mean he was given "food, a bed, and a candle." This compassionate host's name was Julián Martínez. On another occasion, a young Basque student by the name of Martín de Olave helped him out by giving him alms. Íñigo would meet this generous student many years later, because Olave would become a Jesuit and a professor at the Roman College, and he would die two weeks after the death of the beggar he had once assisted. Soon after he arrived in town, the pilgrim met a certain Don Diego de Eguía, whom we have already cited. He was the brother of Miguel, the famous Alcalá printer. The Eguía brothers were natives of Estella in Navarre and were relatives of Francis Xavier. They used to give help to the pilgrim so that he could distribute food to the poor, and one day, when Don Diego had no money, he gave the pilgrim bedspreads of various colors, some candlesticks, and similar items. The pilgrim wrapped all of these in a sheet, threw it over his shoulder, "and went out to assist the poor," not with the candlesticks and the other items, of course, but with the money he got from selling them. Life is wrought with mysterious coincidences. Later on, Don Diego became a Jesuit and the favorite confessor of Father Ignatius. This generous giver of cloths and candlesticks managed to maintain his open-heartedness to the end of his days, winning from his penitent the appellation, "saint." The confessor died in Rome a month and a half before his penitent.

The pilgrim, in his capacity as a secondhand goods dealer, did not have a philosophy on giving handouts, and it would never have crossed his mind to write a learned treatise on the ways to help the poor as did his contemporary, Luis Vives, the author of *De subventione pauperum* (1525). Íñigo's way of giving was the same in Ferrara, Manresa, and Alcalá: he gave to any nameless poor person who was hungry and close at hand. Hunger is not assuaged by beautiful utopias of the future nor can it wait for the implementation of the most constructive remedies of social critics. The pilgrim was a "proto-poor" man, the father of other poor people. Along with the bread he would give, he would also bequeath "the interior man he carried within himself," who, each time he gave, would want to give more than bread alone. So, provided with bed, board, and a candle, it seemed he had all he needed to concentrate on his studies, but in fact he gave other projects and preoccupations greater priority.

> During his stay in Alcalá, he was busy giving spiritual exercises and teaching Christian doctrine and in so doing brought forth fruit for the glory of God. There were many persons who came to a full knowledge and delight in spiritual things; but others had various temptations. . . .

Let us rid ourselves of all false notions about Íñigo at this time. He was no venerable Jesuit father who worked in a residence or retreat house. The Society would be established in Alcalá at a later date, but in 1526, Íñigo was a bizarre pilgrim, a layman dressed in a curious manner and surrounded by four companions. He was a student of advanced years, who had arrived at the university when the classes were about to end, and who found lodging in a hospice. Moreover, as far as studies were concerned, he showed no enthusiasm for making up lost time. Whatever he said and did "caused much talk among the people, especially because of the crowds that came wherever he taught catechism." He was a past master of the simple word directly delivered, without any padding and oratorical style.

The truth of the matter is that Íñigo was not the first to cause talk among the people and to preach in a convincing manner. According to an edict listing an inventory of beliefs peculiar to the *alumbrados*, it was exactly one year prior to his arrival in Alcalá, that is, in 1525, that the Inquisition moved in with force against the alumbrados's secret meeting places of worship that abounded in the vicinity of the city. In Castile at this particular time, these alumbrados were more akin to trendy groups than to an organized, homogeneous movement. From the sociological point of view, their most telling characteristic was meeting houses where prayer gatherings were conducted in a kind of underground manner. The affiliates would gather together in these meeting houses to read and comment on passages from the Bible and other books. Members of the sect preferred mental prayer to vocal prayer, which they held in low repute, and they distanced themselves, at least psychologically, from the customary devotions of the masses of ordinary Christians, even though they went along with the ordinary people as far as their external conduct was concerned. They claimed to be moved by intense mystical communication on the part of the Holy Spirit, especially the so-called *los dejados*, or "the perfect." They glossed over ascetical practices and aspired to the highest degrees of spiritual freedom that sometimes encouraged them to indulge in the grossest sins of the flesh. From the theological point of view, their most compromising belief was that they repudiated the mediation of the Church, specifically the hierarchy and the sacraments, while seeking direct communication with God. From the political perspective, their flight from the world was thought to lead to inaction and disinterest in civic matters, and marginalization of the conventional ideals of contemporary society.

12

"In the Manner of the Apostles"

It was no wonder that the authorities suspected that these get-togethers the pilgrim was conducting were simply repetitions of the old *alumbrados*'s meetings that the Inquisition had set out to stifle the previous year. Íñigo's meetings were giving rise to widespread rumors, and different people had various opinions on what they were all about. These rumors finally reached Toledo, and very shortly afterward two officials of the Inquisition, Miguel Carrasco and Alonso Mejía, arrived in Alcalá to do some investigating of their own. Understandably, the man who put them up told Íñigo all about them because he had heard them refer to the pilgrim and his companions as the *ensalayados*, or the "long robes," because of their attire and what was more serious, as alumbrados. All of this did not bode well for the future, for it was said the officials "were going to make mincemeat of them."

The inquisitors began their investigation by researching the life of Íñigo and his companions, but they soon had to return to Toledo and had to leave the case in the hands of the archbishop's vicar, Don Juan Rodríguez de Figueroa. A few days later on November 21, 1526, Don Juan summoned Íñigo and his companions and gave them the findings of the investigation. Íñigo summed up the admonition Figueroa gave him and assured the readers of the *Autobiography* that the judges found nothing reproachable in what he and his companions taught nor in their lives and that there was no objection to their continuing what they had been doing. At the same time, the vicar found fault with the fact that Íñigo and his companions were going about in a group dressed in habits, despite the fact that they were not religious. Did they think they were clerics? Don Juan therefore ordered that Íñigo and Arteaga dye their clothes black, and Calixto and Cáceres dye theirs yellowish-brown. Jean de Reynauld, or, as the Spaniards called him, Jeanico Reynalde, was a young page of the viceroy of Navarre whom Íñigo had met at the Antezana hospital where he had been recuperating from wounds he had received. According to Don Juan, he could continue to dress as he was. The pilgrim promised to obey all of these directives. This was the first time that he collided with the Church, and he took advantage of the situation to complain openly before Figueroa himself about such inquisitional proceedings. He told the archbishop's vicar about a recent event that pertained to the advice that he, Íñigo, was in the habit of giving others. A certain priest, he said, had refused to give one of the group Holy Communion. This priest argued that this person received the sacrament on a weekly basis, and Íñigo added that even he himself had encountered difficulties when he attempted to receive it once a week. The pilgrim showed he had the strength of his convictions by complaining to Figueroa about this matter. He who welcomed poverty, contempt, and humiliations would not tolerate anyone trifling with the correctness of his orthodoxy. This exchange with Figueroa was spirited and surprising on the part of the humble pilgrim. "We would like to know if they found any heresy in us," he said. "No," replied Figueroa. "If they had, they would have burned you." "They would likewise have burned you," retorted the pilgrim, "if they found heresy in you." The four accused dyed their clothes. Three weeks later, Figueroa ordered the pilgrim not to go barefoot, and the pilgrim "did this without any fuss in matters of this kind when he was given a command." Such a way of acting was that of a man of the Church. All of this account was Íñigo's version of what had taken place; today, we are in a position to compare it with the official report of the process that was written up.

The formal inquiries were made on November 19. Witnesses were the Franciscan Fra Hernando Rubio, the *beata* Beatriz Ramírez, and the administrator of the hospice, the man named Martínez, and his wife. The inquisitors were interested in "certain young men who went about town dressed in brown-colored habits that went down to their feet; some of these young people went about barefoot and claimed that they were living *in the manner of the apostles.*" This was a kind of composite picture of these young men; the testimony of the witnesses filled in details. In the sketchy description found in these reports, we detect certain external marks of identification—a group of young men wearing distinctive clothes—but more especially, there are internal elements in common—a desire for an apostolate or, perhaps, even a desire to imitate the apostolic college in the manner of life. The *apostolica vivendi forma* or the "living in the manner of the apostles" was a very popular movement at this period of history, and it bore obvious reformist overtones. A number of similar groups inspired by this model of living had sprung up throughout Italy. In Spain, Lope de Celain tried, with disastrous consequences, to set up such a band in Medina de Rioseco. In various kinds of utopist and messianistic literature about America, this formula was embodied in ·the famous expedition of *the twelve*—the number is evocative—Franciscans under the leadership of Fra Martín de Valencia who were reported to have converted more than a million Indians in New Spain. Erasmus was the most enthusiastic eulogizer of the theoretical *sublimitas evangelista* of the apostles in opposition to ornateness, precepts, and censures with which certain individuals presumed to employ in reforming the hierarchal authority of the decadent Church. With neither theories nor stances, our pilgrim was satisfied to live with his companions simply "in the manner of the apostles." Did such a mode of life constitute the seed of the future Society of Jesus?

Eighteen months after their arrival in Alcalá, Íñigo and his companions were known as the *Iñiguistas* throughout the region. What was the image they projected to those who saw them? There were five that made up the group. One witness, Fra Hernando Rubio, considered them teenagers and young adult men. Some of them were studying the principles of grammar and logic; they did not attend the regular classes at the university but were tutored privately. They met together at certain times at the hospital or at some fixed place. This good Franciscan was understandably surprised one day when he

went to the home of Isabel, who was called "the prioress," to
pick up a quarter bushel of grain. As he peeked through a
crack in the door, he witnessed an unexpected scene. Seated
on a chair that had been placed on a mat in the middle of the
patio was the oldest of the group, the one who used to go
through town barefoot, lecturing to the rest. Two or three
women were kneeling, "with their hands joined as if they were
in prayer," staring at the young man and listening to what he
was saying. "The prioress," who was a participant of the group,
got rid of the indiscreet visitor, saying, "Leave us alone now,
Father, we are busy." Later that same afternoon, she tried to
set right what the Franciscan had seen. "Father," she said, "do
not be scandalized by what you saw today because that man is
a saint." *Del hilo se saca el ovillo,* as the Spanish proverb has it,
"From the thread one can know the ball of yarn." The meetings, which took place in the hospice, where men and women
would congregate, certainly followed the same format. The
circumstances were unusual, particularly the matter of the
meetings. Fra Hernando considered that all of this "was something most novel."

The *beata* Beatriz Ramírez contributed new data in her testimony. She knew the man who went about barefoot. His name
was Íñigo and it was said that he was of noble lineage. The
baker Dávila had allowed one of the members of the group to
lodge with him and it was at Dávila's place that the whole
group would sometimes assemble. Beatriz had gone there on
one occasion to hear Íñigo. Also present at this gathering
were the baker and his wife, a wine maker, Isabel Sánchez,
who was the housekeeper of Fra Hernando, and a fourteen-
year-old girl. Isabel had gone there at the invitation of Íñigo
himself. He spoke to them about the primary commandments
and spoke a great deal of the love of God. The *beata* admitted
being a bit disappointed. As far as she was concerned, love of
God and neighbor were nothing new. She also knew a few
more details about the group. Cáceres and Arteaga lived in a
room in Hernando de Parra's house, Calixto and Jeanico
were at the baker's, and Íñigo had a room at the hospice
where the others would come to see him. A spiteful question
has revealed to us some other details. The *beata* was asked if
she had given them anything for their teaching. Indeed she
had. She gave them some petty alms, such as a bunch of

grapes and a little piece of lard, but she had to force them to accept these items because they did not want to take them. Moreover, the *beata*, taking advantage of the reputation she enjoyed as a holy person, prevailed upon some wealthy women in the city to give Íñigo and his companions four yards of cloth for the dress he was accustomed to wearing. These women also gave him one mattress outright and lent him two others, along with two sheets, whereas the *beata* herself gave Calixto and Jeanico two woolen pillows.

13

The Superintendent
and His Wife

The people who had the best advantage to observe Íñigo closely were the hospice superintendent and his wife, and there were very few things indeed that escaped the curiosity of the latter. The fact was that, although she did not know why the companions dressed in the way they did or who it was that made the original suggestion regarding their dress, she did know that when Jeanico first came to the hospice he was wounded and well dressed, and that after a short time he was dressed in the same manner as the others. She also knew that Cáceres was in the habit of having his main meal at the middle of the day or evening supper at the hospice before going back to his lodgings, and that when Calixto would come to the hospice, he would visit with Íñigo in his own room or in the patio; however, the two of them had carried on their conversations so quietly that the superintendent was never able to learn what they were discussing. At first, both Cáceres and Calixto would sometimes sleep at the hospice, but after they had been given clothing and lodging, they no longer did so. That is, they had not slept there in four months. It was evident that the couple who were the caretakers at the hospice had missed none of the details of meetings within the hospice's confines, particularly those that took place on feast days. Sometimes these meetings began at dawn, and at other times they occurred after the midday dinner, or in the late afternoon, and sometimes students even came after nightfall looking for Íñigo. The day before the superintendent and his wife had given this testimony, four or five women had come to the hospice seeking Íñigo. The superintendent and his wife played the role of official receptionists who discreetly oversaw the length of these visits. The husband sometimes upbraided the visitors, telling them to go away and let Íñigo study because Íñigo had told him "to stop them from coming to see him and not to open the door to them." Instinctively, the wife showed more intolerance toward the veiled women who used to come looking for him before daybreak. Five days before she gave her testimony, she reported that she had refused entrance to a number of them, despite their pleas to open the door. Today, thanks to the separate testimonies given by the man and his wife, we are able to reconstruct a composite picture of the visitors who came to see Íñigo. There were married men and women, young unmarried women, students, and monks. The superintendent and his wife have supplied us the names of some of these devotees: there was Juan the saddler; the wife of Dávila the baker, who had been a woman of loose morals before her marriage; the *beata* Ramírez; Isabel "the prioress"; one of Parra's daughters; one of the young daughters of Isidro, the tax collector; and the widow Mencía de Benavente. There were times when the number of his guests reached as high as a dozen.

When the inquisitors finished their investigation, they concluded that the case fell under ordinary pastoral surveillance and referred it to the attention of Vicar Figueroa. Two days after the testimonials had been concluded, Figueroa issued the formal order that Íñigo and his four companions should cease and desist from dressing the way they did and that they should comply with wearing what was the ordinary dress of clerics or laymen within the kingdom. At a later date, he may also have advised Íñigo orally to give up his spiritual counseling. The pilgrim was quite clever in making a clear distinction between what he had been ordered to do and what he had been advised to do.

Scarcely four months had passed when Figueroa began another inquiry. Íñigo suspected that new grievances had been added to the old. The cause for this later investigation was a certain married woman of quality who had shown a particular attachment to the pilgrim. One morning at dawn she

came to visit him, and, as was the custom in Alcalá, she veiled
her face so as not to be seen. But nothing resulted from this
investigation; Íñigo was not even summoned to appear before
Figueroa. Today, we have at our disposal the depositions made
by the widow, Doña Mencía de Benavente, her daughter Ana,
and Leonor, the very young wife of Andrés López, a girl of
only sixteen. Íñigo was not aware of the contents of any of
these documents. Even though this latest inquiry had ended
in a blind alley and had had no effect on Íñigo, the attestations are of value to the historian because they offer us the
first glimpse into the nature of these little mysterious meetings with the pilgrim, which is another way of saying they indicate to us how he adapted his Exercises to his devout
followers. Íñigo taught his followers about "the commandments, capital sins, and the five senses and powers of the soul,
and did so very well. He explained these by using the Gospels,
the writings of Saint Paul, and the examples of other saints.
And he told them that they should make an examination of
conscience twice a day by calling to mind how they have
sinned, and that they should perform this exercise before
some religious image. He advised them further to confess
every eighth day and to receive the Eucharist with the same
frequency." The list of these devotees gives us new names, all
of them women. There are a number of servants, some
weavers, and a woman who, at one time, had wanted to hang
herself. Íñigo's normal clientele was made up of the kind of
people Don Quixote said serve only "to increase the number
of the living," that is, the afflicted, the marginal, not those
who were content with themselves and their lot (*Don Quixote*,
II, 6 and 12).

Two months later, or more precisely, on May 10, more
inquiries began, and this time they were made more in
earnest. By this date, Íñigo had acquired a small house outside the hospice proper where he was probably able to carry
on his work with greater freedom. An *alguacil*, that is, a type of
constable, came there to fetch him and threw him into prison,
ordering him to remain there until further notice. As he was
making his way along the road to this prison, he came face to
face with an elegantly dressed young man who was on horseback, surrounded by friends and retainers. Everyone in his
entourage was fascinated by the prisoner's bearing and

demeanor, and all felt great compassion for him. The name of
the young man was Francisco de Borja, known to us today as
Saint Francis Borgia. One of his retainers was a Portuguese
gentleman named Dr. Manoel Miona, who held a chair at the
University of Alcalá. With the passage of time both men would
become Jesuits.

On this occasion, Íñigo was jailed for almost a month and a
half; it was the first time he had experienced any long imprisonment. More than two weeks passed before he was given any
inclination as to why he had been apprehended. The prison
regime could not have been rigorous since "many people
came to visit him"; and among those who did come most frequently was the same Dr. Miona, who became his confessor.
Doña Teresa Enríquez, wife of Gutierre de Cárdinas, the *gran
contador* of Castile, and mother of the duke of Marqueda, was
another who took great interest in Íñigo and worked hard to
have him released. There were many others who volunteered
their services as lawyers and advocates for him. But this
strange prisoner wanted no help from anyone, and his only
answer to their appeals for help was, "He, for whose love I
have come here, will set me free whenever it is to His service."
Like another Paul, Íñigo converted his prison into a theater of
operations, doing the same things he had done when he
moved about freely; namely, teaching catechism and giving
his Spiritual Exercises. His freedom knew no limits and his
mastery of these adverse circumstances was the fruit of his
interior self-assurance.

14
María de la Flor

This time, the Vicar Figueroa wanted to get to the bottom of the case once and for all, and so on May 10 he began interrogating the witnesses. This phase of the investigation began with María de la Flor, Mary of the Flower—a lovely sounding given name for the one who "once had been a woman of ill repute, who went around with many of the enrolled students, and who was lost," as she described herself. From her attestation we draw a very human and most moving history. She was the niece of Doña Mencía de Benavente and had seen the pilgrim come and visit her aunt at home on many occasions. She had become intrigued by the secret conversations that went on between Íñigo, her aunt, her aunt's daughter, and the other women who met at her aunt's house. Soon she came to realize that all these women were in the habit of telling the pilgrim about the troubles that were bothering them and that the pilgrim would console them and talk to them about serving God. Flor must have had troubles enough that came from her dissolute life, and so one day she determined to see the pilgrim herself and ask him to speak to her about "serving God." Íñigo informed her that he would have to speak with her continuously for a whole month and that during this thirty-day period she would have to go to confession and receive Holy Communion on a weekly basis. He warned her that she would experience days of great interior joy, "and that she would not know from where this joy would come," and that on other days she would experience profound sadness. It was in these ups and downs that the secret of her advancement could be found, for these were the signs of deep resonances within her spirit. Íñigo placed confidence in the success of his spiritual remedy because, he told her, if at the end of the month she felt that she was still not cured, she could go back to the life that she had been living.

María de la Flor's long, meticulous deposition is of extraordinary psychological value. Her name had not appeared in any of the earlier declarations—it was suppressed, perhaps, out of a certain sense of propriety. It would seem that she was a woman without any guile or ulterior motives beyond those of her own subconscious. The source of her exceptional self-giving nature was to be found in her very biological makeup. This was perhaps why, again, she was prodigal in offering her body and thereby became the victim of the deceptive love offered by the students. Before her interrogators she was diffuse in pouring out words and she needed no coaxing on their part to do so. She was all emotion, all sentiment. As she spoke of her sins, desires, interior struggles, and even about those dark zones of her conscience about which she was not fully aware, she remained totally transparent. Íñigo's pedagogy must have been to go slowly with her, to be patient, and, in the beginning, to stick to what was purely elementary. The regeneration of this flower that blossomed in a dunghill was not easy, for it implied the purging of her thoughts, words, and deeds. It meant that he needed to be supportive during those periods when she experienced desolation and was learning, painfully, that this desolation was the result of the first steps she was taking in the interior life. Flor must have felt a secret envy toward those who dedicated themselves to serving God. Íñigo wanted to transform that sterile envy, which was really more akin to a kind of an aesthetic attraction, into a zeal and an endeavor to excel that would be operative. He wanted to create the efficacious will and desire to reach beyond herself in the soul of that unhappy woman; he wanted her to make this choice from the depths of her own soul.

Íñigo was the first man who did not regard Flor as an object, who spoke to her about propositions different from selling her body and enjoying sexual pleasure from it. He taught her the Commandments, the reality of sin, and the lesser or greater gravity of that sin. Little by little he got her to give up her habit of swearing and substitute "yes indeed" for expressions such as "as God is my witness" and "I swear on my life"; thereby, giving her words and her person a semblance of dignity. For Flor, temptation was not limited merely to what the future would bring. Íñigo taught her to be strong during present trials, to put concrete demands on herself, to make an examination of conscience twice a day, and to keep her spirit in good condition, and all of this was to be done by the method he had taught her. He instructed her to kneel down and say this prayer, "My God, my Father, my Creator, I thank You; I praise You, for so many benefits You have bestowed upon me and I hope that You will continue to bestow them. Through the merits of Jesus' Passion, I beg You to give me the grace to know how to make a good examination of conscience." The act of giving thanks to God is a primary step in accepting a new way of life. Íñigo gave this young woman, who had been better schooled by life's misadventures than by casuistry, the most fundamental norms of morality. "He told her," she said, "that when a woman came to speak to a young girl about bad things, if the young girl did not listen to what she said, she would not sin mortally or venially, but that if, at another time, the woman came again and the young girl listened to what she said, then she would have sinned venially; and that if the woman came a third time, and the young girl did what the woman told her to do, then she would have sinned mortally." The ways of whorehouse madames were not confined solely to examples of book-learned catechism.

The obedient and generous Flor began to go to confession and to receive Communion and to take her problems to a confessor. The confessor stated that a certain thought that had come to her, which Íñigo judged not to be in any way mortally sinful, was indeed a mortal sin. Calixto confirmed the opinion given by his master and both of them went so far as to tell Flor that she was not obliged to tell the confessor about the things they had said to her. This advice could prove dangerous. It is likely that at this time Flor began working as a weaver with Leonor and that she became a group member of the *Iñiguistas*. Íñigo, meanwhile, continued to teach her her catechism and to introduce her to the methods of prayer that today we find spelled out in the *Spiritual Exercises*, namely, the measured, rhythmical recitation of a particular vocal prayer, known as "The Third Method of Prayer"; contemplation in applying the five senses (*Spiritual Exercises* 121), and meditation employing the three powers of the soul by using the memory, understanding, and the will (*Spiritual Exercises* 45). We should recognize the fact that he had confidence in his methodology, in God's grace, and in men and women. Even though more pessimistic than Erasmus about human nature, he was more optimistic about it than Luther.

A path of roses he did not promise, warning in advance against temptations that come from indecision and weariness. All of this he himself had already experienced. He was merely a guide, trustworthy, farseeing, and down-to-earth. The artifices of the psychological principles of transference, countertransference, and dependency are obvious in Flor's case. After the first fervor came days of dryness and desolation. On four occasions her soul was inundated by "a sadness that was so heavy that nothing seemed right to her and she was unable to raise her eyes to look into the face of Íñigo, but when she spoke with him or Calixto, her sadness would go away." Such was also the experience of Señora Mencía de Benavente and her daughter. When the former wanted to talk with Íñigo but had to wait for some reason, "a great weight would press upon her heart until the moment came when she was able to speak with him." Íñigo was not alarmed by these highs and lows of the spirit. He used to say that "whenever one entered the service of God, the devil intervened and that a person had to remain steadfast in the service of God and bear all of these things for the love of God." He would say the same about the raptures, ecstasies, and other such phenomena that began to manifest themselves in the other devout women, once they had taken themselves out of the world, stopped laughing and complaining, and had refrained from being concerned about dressing themselves in a vain manner.

What one senses surfacing in these statements are the deep tides of the sea of the unconscious, bearing a decided sexual undertow. How else could one account for the attraction that the chastity of Íñigo and his companions had, a chastity that was extolled and contemplated in so morbid a fashion? "Chastity," Paul Claudel once remarked to Jacques Rivière, "will make you as penetrating as the sound of a clarion." It is not easy to sort out the pure truth from the imaginary, the

libidinous, or from unconscious obsessions. With total ingenuousness María de la Flor asserted that she had heard Íñigo and
Calixto declaring that they had made a vow of chastity, and
that they were certain no evil thought could overwhelm them,
and that they would not fall into sin, even if they were to sleep
in the same bed with a young woman. (Such an excessive pre-
tention—an outrageous abuse of language—was borrowed
from the writings of the Fathers of the Desert.) Thanks to the
testimony of Ana de Benavente, we know that it was María de
la Flor who recounted this statement and that it pertained to
Calixto alone; she added that when Íñigo and Calixto talked
with them, they came very near to them "and their faces came
as close to one another as if they were newlyweds." Through a
memory transference, María de la Flor got it into her head
that she wanted to go off to the desert where she could live a
life similar to that of the saintly Mary of Egypt, and her cousin
Ana de Benavente thought that she would do the same. Flor
wanted Calixto to play an active role in this adventure. She
brought the matter to her confessor, which won for her an
admonition from Íñigo. Moreover, he told her "that when he
himself had left [to pursue a new life], he had taken counsel
from no one." In warning about the obvious difficulties—
hardly uncommon in that era—that two women might face
along the way to their projected solitary lives, Íñigo and
Calixto told them that if, en route, someone forced himself on
them against their will, they would not, on that account, lose
their virginity—an assumption that, as far as María de la Flor
was concerned, might seem—well, a bit presumptuous.

15

"Vidi Paulum in Vinculis"

What alarmed Vicar Figueroa most was the news of the strange swoonings and convulsions that were taking place among the women *Iñiguistas*. Four of the women who had manifested this kind of behavior were Leonor de Mena, Ana and Mencía Benavente, and Ana Días. On May 18, Figueroa put off his investigations temporarily so that he could pay a visit to Íñigo in prison. Once there, he reproached Íñigo for having continued meeting with different people and for persisting in giving them instructions, and he ended up by accusing Íñigo of having disobeyed the orders that he had been given. From the extant document that was read to Íñigo on the preceding November 21, it is clear that there were no such orders contained in the text. The prisoner therefore could have responded that he understood that such an order was given him as a suggestion, but not as an injunction. Figueroa's new inquiries boiled down to three specific questions, and to these he now set out to find the answers. First, he wanted an explanation for the faintings and ecstatic raptures that took place in the meetings of the Iñiguistas. Second, he wanted to know if Íñigo had ordered the women to tell him what passed between them and their confessors in the confessional, and whether or not he had presumed to advise them about what they should or should not confess. Finally, he wanted to know if Íñigo had counseled certain women to leave their homes and go as pilgrims to far off, deserted places.

Íñigo respectfully addressed Figueroa's questions. To the first question he said he believed the reason for the faintings, to which five or six of the women were prone, was clear. Since these women had changed their lives and distanced themselves from sin and from powerful temptations, which the devil or members of their families were in the habit of offering them, these swooning fits were reflections of the interior resistance and repugnance they felt taking place within them. For his part, Íñigo said that he encouraged the women to persevere and be strong, and he assured them that such temptations would disappear after a few months. He justified his predictions "because as far as the temptations are concerned, it seemed that he had experienced the same himself, even though, as far as the faintings were concerned, his case was not the same." As for Figueroa's second point, Íñigo responded that he had never asked his followers to divulge what went on between them and their confessors, but he did say that there were times when some women had confided to him their scruples and temptations and that once he had realized that such confidences were not about sinful matter at all, he had recommended that they not be brought up in confession.

It seems that he did not answer the third inquiry at this point. Figueroa did not bring up the subject of María de la Flor's projected plan, which perhaps she would never put into execution anyway. But he did broach the subject of the recent disappearance of a mother and daughter, who had recently left Alcalá, much to the consternation of their tutor and protector, who was none other than Dr. Ciruelo. These two women were Doña María del Vado and her daughter Luisa Velázquez. Íñigo supplied the details in his autobiography for this part of the account given by Figueroa's notary. The vicar must have quizzed the pilgrim on a number of points, even asking him if he observed the Sabbath. Íñigo understood the intent of this loaded question and answered that "Saturday was the day consecrated to the Blessed Virgin and that he knew of no other celebration for that day, and that *in his country there were no Jews*." The vicar then got down to the point and asked him if he knew the two women in question who had disappeared. He answered that he did, but he swore that he never knew of their plans to leave before they had already gone. Figueroa's vaguely suspicious attitude began to lift.

"The vicar, placing his hand on the pilgrim's shoulder as a sign of his satisfaction, then said: 'This was the reason why you have been imprisoned.'" The detailed version Íñigo gave thirty years later of this scene is incredible. The mother and daughter were widows, and the latter was "very young and attractive." They were aristocrats and intent on going by foot to the shrine in the city of Jaén in Andalucia where the veil of Saint Veronica was kept and venerated. They were also determined to make the pilgrimage alone, begging all of the way. Íñigo spent considerable time speaking man-to-man with the vicar about this case. The fact was that these two pious women had told Íñigo that they were determined to travel about the world, going from hospice to hospice in the service of the poor. He had always dissuaded them from such an undertaking because the daughter was "so young and so attractive." Íñigo said that he told them that they could visit the sick and poor without leaving Alcalá and they could even accompany the priest when he brought Viaticum to the dying.

Three days later, the vicar found himself in the presence of the women, who had reappeared after being a month and a half away from the city. The misplaced anxiety of the wizened Dr. Ciruelo abated. The mother and her daughter, accompanied by their servant Catalina, had made a pilgrimage to Jaén and Guadalupe, and they had done so on their own initiative, without seeking advice from anyone. The mother admitted she had spoken with Íñigo on a number of occasions and she considered him "a good person and a servant of God." The daughter had known him for six months and had spoken with him several times in different houses and at the hospice. Íñigo had lectured to them on the Commandments, told them the story of the life of Saint Anne and about Saint Joseph and some other saints, and he had recommended that they go to Holy Communion once a week, provided they were properly disposed to do so. In the *Autobiography*, Íñigo described the two as women who "had made great progress in the spiritual life, especially the daughter."

Therefore, as far as the activity of Íñigo and his friends was concerned, everything was normal, but at the same time, it was strange. No one could reproach them for their teaching nor for the type of lives they were leading; they enjoyed the respect of all. Moreover, when Calixto returned from Segovia where he had been recuperating from a severe illness, he had voluntarily gone to prison in order to accompany Íñigo. Íñigo sent him back to the vicar, who received him well enough, but who sent him back to prison until the mystery of the two women pilgrims who had gone to Jaén was unraveled. The prison did not prove to be an ideal place for someone who was supposed to be convalescing, and so Íñigo managed, thanks to the influence of a certain doctor, "a good friend of his," to have Calixto released from prison. Some think that this anonymous benefactor was Dr. Juan Jacobo de Naveros, the occupant of the chair of physics and metaphysics, a canon of Palencia, and a preacher at the court of Charles V. According to the information gathered by the Jesuit Daniello Bartoli, who published a five-volume work on the life of Saint Ignatius and the beginnings of the Society of Jesus in 1650, Naveros used to come to visit Íñigo in prison, and on one occasion he stayed for such a long time that he was late in arriving at the university for his class. On this occasion he began his lecture with these rather startling words: "*Vidi Paulum in vinculis.*" (I have seen Saint Paul in chains.)

Once the pilgrims made their return, the vicar took a few days to put a discrete finish to the Íñigo affair. A notary came to the prison to read him the sentence, a sentence that was meant to apply to each one of his companions as well as to himself. We have the complete text of the original judgment that was dictated on June 1, and this document tells us that there was no question whatsoever of any condemnation. Íñigo and his friends were given ten days to get rid of their habits and to dress either in the customary clerical or the lay attire of the kingdom, and if they failed to do this in the allotted time, they would be confined to the house where they were living. This was a reiteration of the sentence previously passed. But now another stipulation was added that proved more difficult for Íñigo. For a three-year period he and his fellow accused were absolutely forbidden to teach anyone, either publicly or privately, individually or in groups. After the three-year period had passed, he and the others could petition the vicar for permission to take up teaching again. They were bound to conform to this sentence under the pain of excommunication and banishment for life from the kingdom. The reason for this restriction was not because of any doctrinal irregularities in what they had taught, but because, as Íñigo stated, "they had no learning." He himself acknowledged that "the pilgrim was the most educated" of the group, and then added, "though his learning had little foundation, and this was the first thing he usually mentioned when anyone examined him." Íñigo was unhappy about the sentence, but he accepted it and was ready to obey it, even though it did cause him to entertain some hesitations and doubts. One thing was clear: the doors for apostolate were being closed to him. Rather than follow his university studies in peace, he made a rather audacious decision. He describes it in these few lines: "As a result of this sentence, he was somewhat doubtful what he should do, since it seemed they were closing the door to him in helping souls, without giving him any reason except that he had not studied. At last he decided to go to Alonso de Fonseca, the archbishop of Toledo, and put the case in his hands." Íñigo was not a man who was easily defeated. He did not clearly see as yet that for such spiritual ministries knowledge was "desirable and necessary, and not only infused knowledge, but acquired knowledge as well," as he would write in a 1548 letter addressed to Francis Borgia, the elegant young man who, twenty years previously, had seen Íñigo as he was being taken to prison.

Such, then, was the Íñigo of flesh and bone who spent some time in Alcalá. His name, like the names of Saint John of Avila, Diego Laínez, Archbishop Carranza, the Emperor Constantine, and Juan de Valdés will be associated with the town on the banks of the river Henares, but only as a place where he made a brief stopover, an event that had little to do with the history of the city itself. A short time after his departure, some of his followers would be embroiled in the trials against the *alumbrados*. Among those affected would be the *beata* Ramírez, Luisa Velázquez, the husband of Ana Días, and Miguel de Eguía. Even Dr. Miona would be accused of being a friend of the alumbrado Bernardino Tovar and would have to flee to Paris. There he would meet Íñigo again and even become his confessor. The fact is that Íñigo was closer in every respect to the alumbrados than he was to the enthusiastic majority who adulated Desiderius Erasmus, whose thinking was so popular at that time at the University of Alcalá.

16
Erasmus and Ignatius

At this juncture of the book we should say something about the differences between Loyola and Erasmus because we want to have a sympathetic understanding of the Íñigo who lived in Alcalá in 1527. To do so, we must be able to appreciate the sociological importance of the Erasmian movement that had such a profound influence at the university during this same period. Here, then, we are face-to-face with a series of circumstances (keeping in mind the Latin origin of that word: *circum stare*). We will look at certain facts taken together, *circum*, that stand out, *stare*, to describe the Alcalá of 1527 in order to understand the differences between Loyola and Erasmus.

The Alcalá brand of Erasmianism at that moment of history owed its origin to the Castilian edition of the *Enchiridion*, which had been published by Erasmus's friend Miguel de Eguía, to whom we have already been introduced. Eguía, acting on his own, had made quite a few significant modifications of Erasmus's original text, and therefore this Castilian text did not represent the totality of Erasmus's thinking. Íñigo glosses over everything about Erasmus and the Erasmian controversy in the *Autobiography*, a fact that gives some historical significance to a problem that has astonished a number of historians. We know that he had a copy of the *Enchiridion* in his possession and that this book by Erasmus was recommended to him by no less a person than his confessor, Dr. Miona. This bit of information comes to us from that faithful depository of Ignatian memories, Gonçalves da Câmara, who records that

Íñigo read the *Enchiridion* while he was in Alcalá. It is true that Ribadeneira, on what authority we do not know, has Íñigo reading the *Enchiridion* while he was still in Barcelona, although it seems improbable that his confessor at this time, who was a Franciscan, would have recommended it to him. It also seems improbable that Íñigo would have been able to have read the Latin text at that date. Did Ribadeneira write what he did because he wanted to free Íñigo from the slightest taint of Erasmian thought at a time when Erasmus's teaching had already been reproved? Or did he want to accentuate the glory of the future accomplishments of this uneducated man who passed his days in Barcelona wrestling with the complexities of learning Latin? Whatever the motive, the question was of no importance to Íñigo because he gave up his superficial contact with the scholar of Rotterdam for reasons that were understandable and consistent with his way of thinking. According to Ribadeneira, Íñigo stopped reading Erasmus because Erasmus dampened his fervor. Gonçalves da Câmara reported that Íñigo himself claimed the reason he veered clear of Erasmus was because preachers and men of authority criticized him and that he, Íñigo, preferred reading books "upon which there was no shadow of doubt." The reasons Ribadeneira advanced were subjective and personal; the reasons Gonçalves da Câmara attributes to Íñigo are objective, that is, based on the judgment of authority figures. Both sets give insight into two important aspects of Íñigo's personality. As far as subjective reasons are concerned, Íñigo was in agreement with Luther who had said that Erasmus's words were "colder than ice." From the objective point of view, Íñigo put infinite distance between himself and the German reformer, who completely rejected the authority of the Church and who had the habit of making himself the center of discussion in debated issues.

Íñigo preferred Thomas à Kempis's *Imitation of Christ* to Erasmus's *Enchiridion*. The soul of Erasmus's beautiful little book is the interiorization of Christianity. But was not the internalizing of the Christian Gospel the sum and substance of Íñigo's life, and was not this what his whole personality radiated? Of course. But between Íñigo and Erasmus there is a difference of stress, of temperature, and this difference can be seen straightaway. Erasmus had praised folly and passion, but he himself, personally, was a dry and rational logician who always remained outside the totality of what he so lavishly extolled. His feeble flame of Christian enthusiasm combined with a vast cultural erudition and an esteem for classical pagan values resulted in his creating an atmosphere of evangelical inspiration where Christ was a kind of master who taught a set of noble principles. Why should one go to Jerusalem if he could find Christ in the Gospels? Why should one accumulate the relics of saints if one does not imitate their spirit? Erasmus was right in a way, but his words were of more value than his deeds. After all, no one ever said of him that he was a "fool for Christ," as the people of Montserrat had said of Íñigo. Erasmus lacked that spark of madness that Íñigo had in so great an abundance, and perhaps it was that Erasmus consoled himself by thinking that being a Christian consists in appreciating the beauties of Christianity, of finding aesthetic satisfaction therein, and of mistaking deep-felt sentiments for hard realities. Erasmus had never posed to himself in as dramatic a way as Íñigo the question, What ought I do for Christ? Nor had he ever dreamed, in some surge of generosity, of cutting himself away from his attachments. In his attacks against the luxurious living habits of the bishops, who were supposed to be the successors of the apostles, he praised the poverty of Christ and His apostles; however, he himself was never tempted to strip away everything and embrace a life of radical poverty as a way of imitating Christ and identifying with Him in an existential manner. Erasmus's way of reading the Gospels was very popular at the time. One should have at hand the most authentic Greek text that had been dissected and analyzed by Lorenzo Valla and the early philologists of the Renaissance. Íñigo, on the other hand, slaked his thirst with the ingenuous waters contained in the meditations of Ludolph of Saxony, and in the models of old-time, radical Christianity incarnated in Francis of Assisi and Dominic de Guzmán, or in the dry parched places of the Holy Land, where his Master and Redeemer had walked.

Íñigo and Erasmus were on different wavelengths; their frequency modulations were not the same. They did not seek nor did they find the same thing. It was during this particular period in Íñigo's life that the great theological lights of Salamanca and Alcalá met in Valladolid to debate on whether or not Erasmus was orthodox. The atmosphere between the Erasmians and anti-Erasmians was charged. Íñigo belonged to neither one party nor the other; he was out of the game altogether. He was a satellite to no man; he was no team player. He was a prisoner of Christ, *vinctus Jesu Christi* (Eph 3:1), not blinded by books. Like Luther, he read only what he was looking for, and what he was looking for he did not find in Erasmus.

With the passing of years, Erasmus would become more circumspect, less caustic, and Íñigo would become more appreciative of the world of culture. The bases for comparing the two men will change, and the distance that once separated them will become narrower. Íñigo, who will become a promoter of personal renewal, will gradually come to appreciate the Bible and the Fathers of the Church, and, in many respects, he will even break with monastic traditions. All of these elements were dear to the heart of Erasmus. Erasmus could have taught Íñigo many things, but not depth of experience, mystical ardor, asceticism, enthusiasm for the apostolate, or an active participation in the melee that was taking shape in Europe. On the other hand, the biting public criticism, the satirical and outrageous liberties of Erasmus that made people roar with laughter—better, that made his admirers roar with laughter—would have found a gut reaction of disapproval with Loyola, who was the most successful, but also the most silent, of the reformers of that century.

Before he left Alcalá, Íñigo obeyed the first injunction of his sentence; he exchanged the clothes he had been wearing for others. Someone had to buy these new clothes for him. He was probably helped to some extent by Figueroa himself. In the later testimonies of his beatification process, we learn of another anecdote that is worth recording. It was asserted that at this time, while he was in Alcalá, a certain individual named Lucena helped him collect alms. On one occasion the two of them approached some wealthy *caballeros* who were engrossed in playing ball. One of the players, a certain Lope de Mendoza, lashed out at Íñigo saying, "I'll die burned if this one doesn't deserve to die at the stake." Íñigo responded, "Take care that what you say does not happen to you." A short time after this incident took place, Mendoza and one of his servants were handling some gunpower in preparation for the fireworks display honoring the birth of Prince Philip, who would be known in history as King Philip II. The gunpowder blew up in their faces killing both men. Word got around that Íñigo had prophesied this event.

Somewhere around the twentieth of June 1527, Íñigo and his companions took their leave from Alcalá. Íñigo left a lasting memory there, but it was nowhere as deep as the impression he had left at Manresa and Barcelona. To all appearances, he left a defeated man, a fugitive. As a matter of fact, for many years afterward he would be bedeviled by the rumor that his flight was probably occasioned by the fact that he was going to be burned at the stake. This was certainly the reason why Juan de Valdés and Dr. Miona took flight from the city shortly afterward. But Íñigo did not flee; rather, he was taking the battle to Alonso de Fonseca, the archbishop of Toledo himself. I personally believe that Íñigo learned a lesson in Alcalá that remained firmly anchored in his soul, namely, the need to have a certain reserve in dealing with women. He had come out clean from three judicial processes, but his departure was providential. Perhaps in three years his future would have been more problematic, and, given all the secret meetings of irregular or heterodox enthusiasts that were so much a part of Alcalá, who knows what may have been his destiny. One of his fellow countrymen was startled to see how much he was persecuted, and this man's son, the famous historian Esteban Garibay y Çamalloa, has left a record of that fact for us. Garibay reported that Íñigo was not allowed to call together his usual meetings where he gave spiritual advice, and that he was loathe to restrict himself to studying, which was the reasonable thing for him to do. Our knight-errant could no more accept the advice to settle down and study than Don Quixote could accept similar advice given to him. "Have pity on yourself, good Don Quixote," Sancho Panza told him, "retrieve your lost judgment, and make use of those abilities Heaven has blessed you with, applying your excellent talent to some other study" (*Don Quixote*, 1, 49). Like Cervantes's famous knight-errant, Íñigo was happy to fight for the ideal that was in his head.

"I am today's pilgrim." Today for Íñigo was Valladolid, the theater of his youthful escapades, because that is where Fonseca was at the time, having come there to baptize the newly born Prince Philip on June 5. There was a damper placed on these celebrations by the news of the sack of Rome that had occurred on May 6, 1527. The festivities were called off. Shortly thereafter, some Spanish Erasmians "theologized" on the event that had made Pope Clement VII a prisoner, and they justified it, declaring it was a punishment sent by God. Because of these events, as well as the Turkish menace, imperial messianism, which had been unleashed by Charles V's victory over Francis I at Pavia (February 24, 1525), took on added strength. Fonseca, a personal friend of Erasmus, put off his departure from Valladolid, where, on the twenty-seventh, the debates among the theologians concerning Erasmus's orthodoxy were scheduled to take place. It was while Fonseca was preoccupied by this thorny question that the pilgrim showed up before him "to put the case in his hands," which was another way of saying Íñigo was trying to exempt himself from what Figueroa had decreed. On his way to Valladolid, did Íñigo pass through Arévalo, the town of sweet memories? Fonseca, the protector in Spain of Erasmus's good name and an avid reader of everything that Erasmus wrote, graciously received the humble visitor who "gave him a faithful account of what had happened." After the archbishop had recourse to all sorts of subtle canonical subterfuges, Íñigo proceeded to give him his own reflections on the case. Íñigo said he was not bound to comply with Fonseca's decision because he was not in his jurisdiction, nevertheless he would do what his archbishop ordered him to do. He used the term *vos*, "you," rather than *vuestra merced* while addressing the archbishop. Cervantes would later consider the use of *vos*, "even among equals, as unparalleled arrogance" (*Don Quixote*, 1,51). Fonseca had received Íñigo in a friendly fashion, but he did not open up the gates of Alcalá to him by lifting the sentence. Since the archbishop understood that his interlocutor wished to go on to Salamanca, he recommended him to some of his friends there at the Colegio Mayor de Santiago, which was also called "The Archbishop's College," because the archbishop himself had founded it in 1521 for poor students. Íñigo recorded that Fonseca "offered everything to him." Finally, as he was leaving, the archbishop gave him four *escudos* or gold crowns.

17

"Either by Virtue of Learning . . . or by the Holy Spirit"

Sometime during the first two weeks of July, Íñigo came to Salamanca to start his studies anew. Hardly a propitious time of the year to begin a course of studies! His "company," as he called his four companions, had already gotten there a few days earlier. Upon arriving in the city, the first thing he did was to go and pray in a church where an unknown woman came up to him and asked him his name. When she heard it and was satisfied with who he said he was, she brought him to his companions, whom she already had met and whom she had come to admire. These young men, who had arrived in the city on the Tormes just a few days before the end of the academic year, were dressed in caps and gowns, and so there was at least something about them that indicated they were university students. This is not the place to describe the great University of Salamanca with its colleges, famous professors, and its throngs of students. After all, Íñigo and his friends only passed though Salamanca without Salamanca passing through them. As the old saying goes, *Salamantica docet*. That is, "Salamanca teaches"—a saying completed by another equally venerable maxim, *Quod natura non dat, Salamantica non praestat*, "What nature does not give, Salamanca will not provide." Of course, what the word *nature* means here is intelligence plus a serious will to learn. When he was an old man, Ignatius dedicated nine paragraphs to Salamanca in his memoirs, but what he said in them was limited to events that had very little to do with the glories of the university itself. Let us sum up, then, what he did record in his autobiography.

Once in Salamanca, Íñigo—and how differently he acted from the *alumbrados!*—continued his custom of going to confession once a week. He would go to the Dominican church of San Esteban, where it was not every day of the week that the confessional there welcomed a penitent like himself. His confessor must have said something about him to his brothers in religion because twelve days after his arrival in the city, he became one of the participants in a meeting, as the following dialogue testifies. He described the event in the *Autobiography* in a most straightforward and incisive manner, with sentences one needs to study one by one with care: "The fathers of the house would like to speak with you," his confessor said.

"In the name of God," he replied, "I shall come."

"Fine, it would be good if you were to come here to eat with us on Sunday. But let me warn you of one thing: they will want to know many things about you."

On the following Sunday, he and Calixto came to dinner. Calixto was dressed in a short gown and wore a large hat on his head and boots on his feet that reached halfway up his calves; moreover, he was carrying a long staff in his hand. Even Ignatius acknowledged that his friend offered a ridiculous sight for all to behold. Furthermore, since "he was very tall," he looked all the more hilarious. The prior, Fra Diego de San Pedro, was not home, and so in his absence, the subprior, the confessor, and another priest brought Íñigo and Calixto to a chapel after they had eaten, and here the subprior proceeded to make some favorable, friendly comments on what he had heard about the type of life his guests were leading— that "they went about preaching like the apostles." The friars expressed the wish to learn more details about their manner of life. One of them asked Calixto about the way he was dressed. Then Íñigo recounted to them how they had suffered in the prison at Alcalá, and he told them about the order the judges there had enjoined upon them to dress as students. Because of the extremely hot weather, Calixto had gotten rid of his long student gown and had given it to an impoverished priest. "At this instance the friar said, as though through clenched teeth, '*Caritas incipit a se ipso*'"—"Charity begins at home." But what intrigued these self-appointed inquisitors more than anything else was what type of studies the two had already completed. Íñigo loved the truth and so he hid nothing. He told them how little he had studied and how weak his academic foundations were, but, in spite of that, he asserted that he knew more than his companions. "Of all of us, I am the one who has studied the most," he said.

"Well, then, tell us what you preach."

"We do not preach, but we speak of the things of God in an informal manner with a few people, just as a person might do after dinner with the people who invited him."

"But what are the things of God you speak about? That is what we would like to know."

"Sometimes we talk of one virtue and sometimes we talk of another, praising it; at other times, of one vice or of another, condemning it."

"You are not educated men and yet you speak of virtues and vices! No one can speak of these things except in two ways: either by virtue of education or by virtue of the Holy Spirit. But you have had no education. *Ergo*, you speak through the power of the Holy Spirit. Now, precisely what comes to you from the Holy Spirit is what we would like to know more about."

This was not a harmless dialogue; it was a trap of most refined syllogistic inductions mined from a vein of scholastic reasoning. The divisions caused by a woman known as La Beata de Piedrahita still lingered in the convent cloisters of San Esteban. She was a famous visionary whose many ecstasies and revelations had captured the interest of Cisneros, the duke of Alba, and even Ferdinand the Catholic himself. Even if the prudence of the Dominican theologian was understandable, it is nevertheless sophistic to maintain that the only people who can speak of God are professional theologians and the illuminati. Now Íñigo was anything but naive. "The pilgrim was a bit beside himself because that kind of argument did not seem good to him. After a short silence, he said it was not necessary to speak further of these matters."

The friar pressed on: "What do you mean! There are so many errors in circulation from Erasmus and from so many others who have deceived the world today. And you do not want to explain what you tell people!"

"Father, I will not say more than what I have said, except before my superiors who can oblige me to do so."

"Very well, then stay here. We can easily make you tell us all."

With those threatening words the friars hastily left the chapel. Imperturbably, the pilgrim asked where they should stay, whether they should remain in the chapel or go to some other room. They stayed in the chapel, and the doors were bolted. They waited three days in the convent before the matter was resolved. They ate in the refectory with the friars and were put up in a room that was almost always filled with friars who would come to visit them. Íñigo spoke to them about "the things he usually talked about," and managed to gain the admiration of some without overcoming the reticence of others. There was a division of opinion among the friars who had come to talk with him.

After a period of three days, a notary appeared and took them to a common prison. They were not confined with the ordinary criminals but were housed in an old, unused upper room that was very cluttered and dirty. They were put in irons with their feet fettered to a single chain that was approximately eight feet long and which, in turn, was riveted to a post in the middle of the room. "Whenever one of us wanted to do anything, the other had to accompany him." The recollection of all these particulars, including this last painful detail, was still very much alive in the memory of Ignatius as an old man. He and Calixto remained awake the whole night. The next day, the news of their imprisonment spread throughout the town where, in view of what later transpired, we learn they must have already had some friends. People sent them mattresses on which to sleep and more than everything they needed. Many came to visit them, and Íñigo continued his practice of speaking about God.

The Bachelor Sancho Gómez de Frías held a university chair and gave evening classes. He was also vicar to the bishop of Salamanca. It was he who came to interrogate Íñigo and Calixto. Íñigo handed over to him what he most loved in this life, namely all of his papers— that is, his *Spiritual Exercises*—so that they could be examined. This is the first instance Íñigo himself alludes to the *Exercises*. Frías asked about the other companions and their whereabouts. Then, on his orders, all of them came to the prison and all, except Jeanico, were detained and billeted with the common prisoners. Even then, Íñigo would have no attorney, no advocate whatsoever.

A few days later, he had to appear before Hernán Rodríguez de San Isidoro and Francisco de Frías, two doctors of canon law who were accompanied by Dr. Alonso Gómez de Paraviñas and the above-mentioned Bachelor Sancho Gómez de Frías. All of them had already read his *Spiritual Exercises* and asked him questions about them concerning the Trinity and the Eucharist. Íñigo probably made some introductory remarks explaining his lack of formal education, and then he tried to give an account of everything that he was being asked. Bachelor Frías presented him with a point of canon law and then asked him to tell them how he usually explained the First Commandment. He went to such lengths on this point that they did not question him further. The most difficult question of this examination, an examination for which he would not be granted an academic degree, was the one that related to the annotations of his *Exercises* dealing with mortal and venial sin. How did he, not being a licensed theologian, make a judgment about which was which? Íñigo avoided the *how* and concentrated on the *what*. "You decide whether what I say is true or not, and if it is not true, condemn it." The judges did not dare condemn anything, and they made their exit.

In a few days Íñigo had won the admiration and respect of a good number of people. Many came to see him in prison, among whom was a surprising visitor, Don Francisco de Mendoza y Bobadilla, son of the count and countess of Cañete. At that time, Don Francisco was a young man of about twenty, and yet he already held the chair of Greek at the university. In time, he would become bishop of Coria, and later, in 1545, cardinal, and then finally, in 1550, bishop of Burgos. He was not the first one to visit Íñigo, nor was he the first to ask him, in a most frank manner, the question that seemed to be on everyone's mind, namely, why was he in jail and did he suffer because he was imprisoned? With unusual curtness for him, the prisoner responded, "I will answer you as I answered a woman today who spoke words of compassion at seeing me a prisoner. I told her: 'Your words show that you have no desire to be a prisoner for the love of God. Why does prison seem to be such a great evil to you? I assure you there are not enough bars and chains in Salamanca that would make me wish that there were even more so that I could endure them out of the love of God.'" Even though they did not express themselves in the same words, his companions, who had been confined with the common prisoners, put them into practice by the way they acted. Indeed, one night all of the prisoners escaped from the jailhouse, and the next morning the guards found the doors wide open with only Cáceres and Arteaga still there. This event caused a great deal of talk throughout the city, and the result was that the four of them were now jailed in a palace.

After twenty-two days of confinement, the prisoners were called to hear their sentence. Like the text of sentencing at Alcalá, the actual document of adjudication has never been found, but the substance of the sentence must have remained engraved on Íñigo's soul. The judges found no errors either in the lives of the accused or in their teachings. Even better, the judges said they could continue as they had been doing, teaching catechism and speaking of the things of God in a general way, but with the proviso that they could not definitively say, "this is a mortal sin," or "this is a venial sin." That would be something they could do only after they had completed four years of studies. These very reasonable precautions imposed by conservative Salamanca were much less harsh than those imposed by liberal, humanistic Alcalá. The manner of communicating this sentence—"the judges gave signs of much affection"—indicated that this was more of a friendly reproach than a severe judicial decision. The jury even looked for a frank and friendly acceptance from the accused. To the surprise of all, however, Íñigo, as the spokesman for the group, said that he would obey and carry out what the judges ordered, but that he would not accept the sentence because, without condemning him in any way, the judges "were closing his mouth and making it impossible for him to help his neighbor in the best way he could." Bachelor Frías, who had initiated the whole investigation and who had shown great affection for Íñigo, insisted that he accept the adjudicators' decision. Íñigo replied that as long as he was in the jurisdiction of Salamanca he would scrupulously comply with their verdict.

What a disconcerting attitude this was on his part! No one was gagging him or telling him that he could not speak about God, nor was anyone preventing him from speaking about truths and principles. But to speak about God *in order* to help his neighbor, as Íñigo practiced and understood it, meant much more than merely joining words into sentences. It meant creating an environment where God and the human person could begin to question one another; it meant setting up the stage that would enable the soul to embark on a process of making a commitment. What it *did not* mean was an involvement in a purely abstract enumeration of vices and virtues; it *did* mean coming face to face with *the actual* personal sins committed, *the real* attachments that had become obstacles to freedom, and *the here-and-now* personal invitations to accept grace, and since all of these were very concrete elements, they had to be defined in a concrete manner. It was out of the confrontation between sin, attachments, and grace that abstractions became real and personal—"Who am I and who is He?"— and from this encounter was born shame and inner confusion, magnanimity and spontaneous generosity, and the I-Thou dialogue between man and God. Íñigo was no theology professor, not even a modest instructor of Christian doctrine; rather, he was an educator, a guide who tried to get close to every person. Consequently, these professional theologians were indeed gagging him because they were forbidding him to talk about God as he was accustomed to speak. He was ready and willing to give an account of his hope to everyone who would ask him for it, according to the spirit of 1 Peter, 3:15, ". . . and always have your answer ready for people who ask you the reason for the hope that you have." But he did so in a very different way from another famous Basque, a *gamboíno*, not an *oñacino*, a man who was one of Salamanca's truly great lights of that day and a member of the San Esteban priory, the great Dominican "father of international law" and major figure in the reintroduction of Thomism into the Catholic world, Francisco de Vitoria.

Íñigo and his companions were released from prison on August 22, 1527. Once more it seemed that he had to start his life again from scratch. Our poor Christian adventurer "began to commend the matter to God and *to think of what he ought to do.*" The question was not as vague now as it had been when he first posed it to himself at Loyola or during his pilgrimage to the Holy Land. He now had some idea about what his course of action would be. He was clear and resolute about this one thing: he would help souls. But he saw insurmountable obstacles in implementing this decision. "He found great difficulty in staying at Salamanca," for the price he had to pay was giving up his vocation and ministry. During his imprisonment he had had time to think about and consider his new life. Ever since his days in Barcelona, when he toyed with the idea of pursuing a course of studies and considered the time it would take, he had been preoccupied by whether he should enter a religious order or "should continue going about the world." Deeply ingrained within his personality was the desire to perform great deeds; he would always be drawn to what was challenging and difficult. That is why, faced now with this final choice that remained as yet unresolved, there were the remnants of his desire to enter a religious order that was decadent and in need of reform so that he could suffer all the more and, perhaps, become an instrument in that order's regeneration. "God gave him great confidence that he would be able to endure all the affronts and insults they would heap upon him." A few years later, a young friar, as small of stature as he himself, would experience this same kind of temptation. This young man would want to "get as far away as possible," either by entering the Carthusians or, better, by joining an order "that seemed the most lax of all." His name was Fra Juan de Santo Matía, although today we know him better as Saint John of the Cross. Íñigo considered these same options during his meditations in Salamanca's prison. But alongside this thought was another that ultimately prevailed, even though Íñigo at the time did not see exactly how it would unfold. It was "to help souls, and, in order to accomplish this end to study and then, *to gather together* a few companions animated by the same desire, while keeping those he already had." For Íñigo, to make up his mind was to act, or, as he would say, "to determine." A word occurred to him—we do not exactly know how—as the key for him to implement his project, including the end and means he had in view. That word was *Paris*. Without making any "detours," Íñigo determined forthwith to go directly to the city by the Seine. He discussed the matter at length with his companions and it was agreed that they should remain in Salamanca while he sought ways for them to join him, so that eventually they could all pursue their studies together. Paris was the "today" of the pilgrim.

18

Alone and on Foot

Influential people tried to talk him out of leaving, but all their arguments came to naught, for "they were never able to convince" this Basque. As so often happened before, on a lovely morning in mid-September "he left by himself alone." But this time with a difference, a considerable innovation; this time, a small donkey went along with him, "carrying some books." How we would love to have in our hands today the list of books in that portable library! Most certainly it included the manuscript of his *Spiritual Exercises*, which he could now show carried a *nihil obstat* from the doctors at Salamanca. So much had changed for this traveler since the torrid month of August that he had spent in the city on the Tormes. The odds are that it would not have occurred to him, as he was about to make his way across the arid plains, to stop and address that golden city, tucked alongside the river that he was now leaving, with the eulogistic words Cervantes would employ a few years later, "Salamanca bewitches the will of those who have relished the sweetness of living with her, so that they leave with a strong desire to return to her once more." The filthy old room, uninhabitable and stifling, and the leg irons were not exactly symbols of a delightful stopover, nor were they designed to conjure up memories of a nostalgic sojourn.

Despite all the sufferings that his stay in Salamanca had caused him, his love of God, which was stronger than any iron chains, became purified. He retained pleasant memories of Don Francisco de Mendoza, Bachelor Frías, the many generous people of Salamanca, and even of a number of the friars at San Esteban. It was in Salamanca that his decision to go to Paris had its beginning, and it was here that his life acquired a fixed direction. What was to follow would not alter his decision; it would merely confirm it. Never would Íñigo return to that city, although in a relatively short while his followers would, a fact he could never possibly have imagined at that time.

Then, as now, the route from Salamanca to Paris passed through Íñigo's native land, but this was not the road he took. It had been five long years since he had left home without his family having the slightest idea of his whereabouts. An authority of religious development, Jean Séguy, described Íñigo as "a hippy before the term was invented," and if we restrict ourselves to the external appearances of his life, Séguy is perfectly correct. Íñigo did not go back home and he did not even let his family know where he was. Like every hippy, he stressed his freedom *from*; however, the difference between him and the state-of-the-art hippy lies with the *what for* of this radical freedom. He went from Salamanca across Spain to Barcelona, his second home, where his freedom and autonomy seemed guaranteed, but once there he found himself more tied down than he had anticipated. Like blood, affections create bonds, and perhaps these bonds of the heart are even stronger and less selfish. "Everyone who knew him" in Barcelona tried to dissuade him from going to France, all with very persuasive arguments, namely, that France and Spain were on the verge of going to war. This war was not formally declared until January 22, 1528, but by that date the eldest brother of his old friend Andrés of Asparros, Odet de Grailly de Foix, vicomte de Lautrec, with the support of Andrea Doria, had already conquered Genoa and Alessandria in Piedmont. The rivalry between Charles V and Francis I, who had just returned to his kingdom after being imprisoned in Spain, was fanatical, completely irrational. On December 12, 1527, the ambassadors of France and England failed to make any headway in their political negotiations with Charles V. On the following day, in accordance with the medieval custom, the two *rois d'armes*, representing each nation, appeared before the king to declare war by presenting a challenge. The emperor accepted the challenge, but then he publicly denounced Francis I by saying to the French representative,

"Tell your lord he has acted in a most wretched and villainous manner by not respecting the word he gave me when he and I spoke to one another alone, and that I hold him personally accountable for his conduct." When this imperial censure reached the ears of the king of France on June 28, 1528, he retorted by directing a personal challenge to Charles V, and for his part, Charles accepted the challenge and agreed to fight a duel in some mutually agreeable field of honor located between the French town of Hendaye and the Spanish town of Fuenterrabía. As a result of all of these events, the people Íñigo knew in Barcelona tried to dissuade him from leaving by telling him what they had heard about Frenchmen roasting Spaniards on spits. But it was useless; nothing they said could change his mind.

"But no one was ever able to frighten him with anything." There was a certain unnerving self-assurance about him. Therefore, in the beginning of January 1528, "he set out for Paris, *alone and on foot.*" Inés Pascual tried as best she could to get sufficient provisions for him for his trip. He accepted a letter of credit extended by a merchant that would enable him to cash twenty-five *écus* in Paris. This would be enough money for him to cover expenses for awhile in Paris. In addition to this, Isabel Roser, Aldonza Cardona, Isabel de Josa, and other women promised to send help to him while he was in studies. The good-byes they gave him were emotional.

After traveling through France, Íñigo arrived in Paris on February 2, 1528. One month later he wrote to Inés Pascual to tell her that the journey had gone well and to thank her for the goodwill and affection she had shown him. "I shall study until the Lord asks me to do something else," he wrote, and he did not forget to extend a grateful greeting to Inés's neighbor, who must have slipped a few little gifts in his traveling bag at the moment of his departure. He also had a very touching message for Inés Pascual's son Joan, who used to spy on him during his night prayers in the upstairs room. "Remember me affectionately to Joan," he said, "and tell him always to obey his parents and observe the feast days, and if he does so he will live not only a long time on this earth but also he will live in heaven above." Just as Íñigo had predicted, Joan's life was a saga of trials and reverses of fortune. He died, a man of great piety, during the Barcelona plague of 1589. During his lifetime he had become a veritable encyclopedia of Ignatian memories, and he bewailed the fact that he had not taken better advantage of the opportunities he had had while the saint was alive. Íñigo mentions his name and asks to be remembered to him in the letter he wrote to his mother on March 3, 1528. He signed himself off with the ambiguous formula, *De bondad pobre, Íñigo*—"poor in goodness, Íñigo."

This lame man, this greatest walker in Europe, who had been attracted by the country that enjoyed the reputation of being the cultural capital of the world, hobbled alone across France during the height of winter. With recollections of Salamanca golden and shimmering in the sun still fresh in his memory, he entered Paris on February 2, 1528. This was the great city whose cold, gray walls embraced some two-hundred thousand inhabitants (more than four thousand of whom were students), innumerable colleges, churches, and convents. Just before he arrived, the city learned of the liberation of Pope Clement VII, who had been the emperor's prisoner ever since the fatal sack of Rome. Had he arrived a year earlier, Íñigo could have witnessed the wedding of the king's sister, Marguerite, with Henry, the legitimate heir of the throne of Navarre, and he could have watched the formal entry of the royal couple into Paris. All of this may well have reminded him of why he still walked with a limp. Pamplona—how far away it all seemed now!

Íñigo found lodgings with a few Spaniards. They were the first to show him around this city that was so charged with history and where both past and present seemed to live in harmony. For the most part, the life of our elderly scholar centered around the Latin Quarter with its narrow streets and its colleges of unequaled historical importance that were piled up on top of one another. In time he would come to learn the names of each of these colleges. There was also the Sorbonne, whose faculty was comprised of doctors, and the rue Saint-Jacques, which he would soon come to know well, and the different convents of Dominicans, Franciscans, and Trinitarians. Not far away could be seen the Île de la Cité, where the heart of the city was concentrated and where he could contemplate the cathedral of Notre Dame with its forty-five chapels, and where he could visit the Palais de Justice and Sainte-Chapelle, both of which were living memories of the Crusades. Little by little he would become acquainted with the castle of the Louvre, the Grande-Châtelet, the markets, the pilgrims' hospital of Saint-Jacques, and the famous religious houses situated in the *faubourgs*—places such as the abbey of Saint-Germain-des-Prés and the Pré-aux-Clercs, which was said to have been the gift of Charlemagne; the Chartreuse or Charterhouse, which was the monastery of the Carthusians; Notre-Dame-des-Champs; the hill of Montmartre; and farther beyond, the town and cathedral of Saint-Denis.

19

A Poor and
Vagrant Student

Íñigo was no tourist in Paris. Even though he was almost forty
years of age, it seems that he had come there to study. The
first proof of his seriousness was that he came to the conclusion that he had advanced at too fast a clip in his former studies and "found his knowledge of the fundamentals very
shaky." With a sense of realism that was no greater than his
humility, he signed up to take courses in Latin at the College
of Montaigu. This was a mandatory preparatory course where
one obtained skills in grammar, rhetoric, and versification.
The pupils in this class were very young, some even as young as
ten years old. He does not exaggerate a bit in the *Autobiography*
when he says that "he attended classes with young boys and
made progress according to the prescribed curriculum of
Paris." The fact was that in Paris there was more than just one
prescribed curriculum, and that followed at Montaigu, which
was one of the most conservative, based as it was almost exclusively on the *Doctrinale* of Alexandre de Villedieu. At the same
time, it was a well-organized, sequential program that was
geared to the student's progress. Each college was a separate
star in the vast Parisian constellation and Íñigo's choice had
been the college where Erasmus had studied. The great
Dutch humanist had never forgotten the rotten eggs, lice, and
the absence of health facilities that were so much a part of the
college in his day. His lampoons about Montaigu would be

continued by more mocking satires from the pen of Rabelais. The two of them could have made more serious accusations about the lack of mental hygiene at the college and about the intellectual backwardness that prevailed there. Montaigu had been founded in the fourteenth century, and toward the end of the fifteenth it underwent a thorough reform under the direction of the Flemish scholar Johannes Standonck, whose policy was carried on by Pierre Tempête—the *horrida tempestas,* as Rabelais called him. There were a number of Spaniards whose names would go down in history that had matriculated from the Montaigu, among whom were the author Juan Prado; the physicist brothers, Luis and Pablo Coronel; the theologian Juan de Celaya, known as "*the* doctor of the Sorbonne"; the great Dominican theologian Domingo de Soto; the mathematician Gaspar Lax; and the humanist philosopher Luis Vives. A former student, the Scotsman Johnnes Mayor or John Mair, had been living at the college since 1525 and at this date was considered the most esteemed member of the faculty. As for Íñigo, the fact is that he had no scholarship, no allowance money, and no lodging in the college. He was simply a *martinet,* that is someone who lived outside the college and merely attended classes. For this reason he was not personally acquainted with the herrings, rotten eggs, and college lice, which had been so vilified by Erasmus, but he could well have had some contact with the spirit of Standonck's *devotio moderna* that he had gotten to know while he was at Montserrat.

Even though he was not a typical, run-of-the-mill student, Íñigo was able, for the first time in his life, to devote himself to his studies without worrying about money. The twenty-five *écus* he had received from the bill of exchange he had brought with him from Barcelona was enough to enable him to spend two years in Paris. But because he had some kind of instinctive horror of lucre, for safekeeping he turned over all the money he had to a Spaniard who was living in the same boarding house. Within a very short time, this Spaniard recklessly spent all that he had received, leaving Íñigo penniless, barely two months after he had arrived in Paris. He had to leave the boarding house and was forced to beg in the Paris streets—not the first student in history to do so and by no means the last to pursue this time-honored practice.

Íñigo was received at the pilgrims' hospice of Saint-Jacques, but this solution to his housing problem presented him with another problem, namely, how he would manage to continue his studies. The hospice was almost two miles from the college, and the times for opening and closing the doors at the two institutions were hardly synchronized. He could not get out of the hospice before sunrise, and he had to be back in the evening before the first stroke of the Angelus bell at eight o'clock. He needed a good half hour to get to the college, whose schedule was terribly rigorous and exacting. According to the rules laid down by Standonck, the students rose at four in the morning and had already attended their first class before Mass, which was celebrated at six o'clock. Classes resumed at eight and went until ten, after which there was an hour given to disputations. In the afternoons, there were two hours of class, between three and five. Íñigo realized that under these circumstances he would have to cut down on the time he could spend in class; moreover, in order to make ends meet, he had to put aside a certain amount of time for begging. The inevitable result was that he saw that "he was making little progress in his studies." Since he had already set his mind to study, he thought of a solution to his dilemma. Just as some other students had done, he would have to "find a master," that is, he would have to find a job where he could study and at the same time work as a domestic servant to some professor. In 1490, Standonck had envisaged the existence of a community of poor students under the aegis of one of the college licentiates, who would be called the "father of the poor." Mindful of the twelve apostles and the seventy-two disciples, Standonck intended the community would be made up of twelve students of theology and seventy-two scholars from the liberal arts program. Perhaps it was this model that Íñigo had in mind when he imagined "that the master would be Christ, that one of the students would be called Saint Peter and another Saint John, and so with each one of the apostles." But this project remained nothing more than a dream because, in spite of the fact that Íñigo spoke with the Bachelor Juan de Castro from Burgos and with a Carthusian who knew many of the professors, none or them or anyone else was able to find an employer for him. Through experience Íñigo had come to taste the despair that is so much a part of the life of the ordinary poor and vagrant student.

In the end, he took some realistic advice given to him by a Spanish friar. This man told him about the generosity of the Spanish merchants in Flanders and advised him to contact them. Íñigo at last decided that it was worth missing classes to go up to Flanders and stay there for two months every year, provided that these excursions did indeed help him to defray the cost of his studies. During Lent of 1529, he undertook his first annual trip to Bruges and Antwerp, and during the summers of 1530 and 1531, he returned to these cities. In 1531, he traveled as far as London. We know that while he was in Bruges he was the guest of Gonzalo de Aguilera, whom he had so won over that when Gonzalo came to Paris on business, he determined to remain with Íñigo in his own room. While in Antwerp, he took advantage of the hospitality of Juan de Cuéllar, whose family name reminded him of his former protector, and of Pedro Cuadrado, who, at a later date, would become the founder and benefactor of the college of the Society in Medina del Campo. His most remunerative trip was the one he made to London, and his repeated trips to Flanders eventually gained him the goodwill of protectors, who, by sending him letters of credit in Paris, saved him the pain of having to walk all the way to Flanders to beg for alms. His unfortunate experience with the Spaniard who had cheated him made him more cautious, although no less charitable on that account. He instructed the man in Paris who exchanged his bills of credit to cover his own living costs as well as the needs of other impoverished students, whom he had singled out as sharers in his good fortune.

From the historical point of view, his most important encounter, even though it was of short duration, was the one with Gonzalo de Aguilera's friend and neighbor in Bruges, Luis Vives. This famous humanist from Valencia, an admirer of Erasmus, invited Íñigo to dine with him. Since the event took place during Lent, and therefore on a day of abstinence, the main dish was a fish that had been exquisitely prepared. The fish, however, was not the real *pièce de résistance*; that was, rather, the spicy conversation at the dinner table. Vives began by making comments on the scant penitential significance of such a refined way of observing the Church's strict law on abstaining from meat. Íñigo, who as a rule spoke little while eating, took a stand contrary to his host on this occasion, and, according to Polanco, he spoke his mind with an unexpected line of reasoning. "You and others who have the means to do so can dine on deliciously prepared fish without, perhaps, profiting from the Church's purpose for abstinence, but such is not the case with the majority of people, for whom the Church cares. These people cannot be as exquisite as you; they find abstinence a means to mortify their bodies and to do penance." This contretemps has been used often enough as an example of pitting the knight-errant against the refined courtier of the Renaissance. But the fact is, Íñigo was not a knight for any cause; he was merely a poor, obscure, somewhat superannuated student, a man acquainted with difficult penances and who lived much closer to the ordinary people than Vives. Neither Erasmus nor Vives could ever understand Íñigo's attitude in respect to bodily mortification. But in Íñigo's response to Vives—a response that is more sociological than theological—there is more agreement between host and guest than would at first appear. In the last analysis, Íñigo and Vives agreed that certain customs were not authentic ways to comply with laws regarding penance; they also agreed that fulfilling these customs placed a lesser burden on people of means than on the ordinary people, and there were many other people living at that time who also realized that such was the case. This basic agreement led Vives to criticize the Church's law of abstinence while Íñigo defended the law and its general penitential value; but at the same time, he judiciously criticized those who got around its holy purpose by clever devices, and he mildly called to task those moralists who justified stretching the rules. This discrete confrontation between the two men had consequences. Vives came away from the disagreement with a very high opinion of Íñigo, and, as he confessed to his close friend Dr. Pedro de Maluenda of Burgos, he discovered in his companion at the dinner table a saint, even a founder of a future religious order. However, Íñigo, for his part, seems to have come away with a poor impression of Vives's opinions. At a later date he would forbid members of the Society to read his works, as well as the writings of Erasmus. Íñigo perhaps was ignorant of the fact that this man, whose opinions appeared to him to be suspect, had forfeited a handsome sinecure at the richly endowed Corpus Christi College, Oxford, because he had opposed the divorce of Henry VIII. Perhaps Íñigo did not realize that Vives was a man of exacting principles who would one day write a beautiful treatise, *Defensio fidei christianae*, which is a profession of faith in and fidelity to the Catholic Church, and he took the position he did in spite of the fact that he had lost his parents and grandparents in the persecution of the Jews orchestrated by the Spanish Inquisition. There are many different ways of behaving heroically besides interpreting the laws of abstinence from a laxist or rigorist point of view.

20

"I Was Held Responsible for Everything"

But let us now go back to our story and consider the person of Íñigo, now a beggar lodged in a Paris hospice for pilgrims and forced to shorten his demanding course load of studies. Even though, after his return from his first excursion to Flanders—that is, during the Lenten season of 1529—he was in a position to give up his habit of begging. However, "he began to give himself more intently than usual to spiritual conversations" as a way of compensating for his newly found free time; but these conversations were not with the boys from his humanity classes nor were they limited to in-between class time. On the contrary, during the course of May and June, that is, at the very end of the school year, he gave his Spiritual Exercises separately to Pedro de Peralta, a native of Toledo who was living at the Montaigu and was scheduled to complete his master's degree that year; Bachelor Juan de Castro from Burgos, who was a teacher at the Sorbonne; and a Guipúzcoan named Amador de Elduayen, who was a student at Sainte-Barbe. Íñigo's influence on these three men was spectacular. As a result of his conversations with them, their lives were so radically changed that their behavior became a topic of conversation throughout Paris. After completing the Exercises, these three university men began giving everything they had to the poor, including their books. They then moved into the Saint-Jacques hospice and took to begging in streets all over the city.

Every genuine conversion always ends up forcing the person who has undergone the change to justify himself and his behavior to his family, friends, and acquaintances. Íñigo's own experience had taught him that such was the case. Now, two of these three, Peralta and Castro, were very important men, celebrities in their own right. Their change caused "a great disturbance" throughout the university, particularly among the Spanish students. Peralta and Castro's friends and relatives tried to dissuade them from their bizarre ways of acting, and, because verbal persuasion had no effect on them, they dragged them physically away from the hospice. After this incident, both parties came to an agreement: first, the two men would finish their studies, and then they could go back to the way they had been living. Years later, Castro would become a Carthusian. Peralta made a pilgrimage to the Holy Land and on his trip home he met a relative of his in Italy, a captain who was serving in the army. This man whisked him off to the pope, an action that resulted in his being sent back to Spain where eventually he became a canon in Toledo's cathedral. Amador de Elduayen was the least known of the trio; however, his conversion provoked the opposition and hostility of a man who enjoyed much greater importance than the young Guipúzcoan, namely, the young man's rector at Sainte-Barbe himself, Master Diogo de Gouveia.

Íñigo was held responsible for his companions' strange decisions and he became the object of much gossip and suspicion, particularly within the circle of a group of men from Burgos, among whom were Pedro de Garay, Bernadino de Salinas, Pedro de Malvenda, and Francisco de Astudillo. Íñigo mentioned their names in a letter he wrote in 1542. He recalled the resentment they had shown toward him because of the bizarre change in the behavior of their countryman, Master Castro. "I was held responsible for everything," he wrote. Such a charge was not exactly the most positive consequence that could have been laid at his door. Moreover, how would it ever be possible for the university students to line up on Íñigo's side once the great Master de Gouveia had declared before all that he "had turned Amador into a madman"? Gouveia accused Íñigo of being a "seducer of students," and even threatened to give him *la salle*, "the hall"—that is, a public flogging—the first time he showed his face at Sainte-Barbe. The fact of the matter is that this furious Portuguese, who was ready to give a public flogging to a first-term Latin student because of his seductive spiritual qualities—an apprentice scholar, who had shaken up bachelors and masters and who had, in 1528, already planted the seeds of a *"mai parisien"*—in reality gave him one of the most beautiful compliments he had ever received. Real sanctity, like authentic poetry, is an illness not easy to eradicate. What was the secret of his sorcery? What was the source of his charming delusions? All lay in what he said and what he did; in how he said it and how he did it; in how he gave himself to others. Íñigo took seriously and loved sincerely those who listened to what he had to say: those who became his followers, those who were his persecutors, and even those who took advantage of what he said and how he loved.

Take, for example, the case of the Spaniard who went off and spent all the money Íñigo had entrusted to him—money that would have kept him living comfortably in Paris for two whole years. This fellow disappeared one day from Paris and the last thing that was heard of him was that he was on his way back to Spain. However, when he got to Rouen, where he had intended to book passage home, he fell ill. As it happens, we now know that he wrote a letter to Íñigo informing him of his situation and of his need. Íñigo, who in his youth had never hated anyone, on this occasion showed himself not only generous and forgiving, but he even conceived the notion of going off to visit and help this gay blade who had squandered all his money. He made his decision with a higher and more noble purpose. "Thinking in this circumstance, he might induce him to leave the world and give himself entirely to the service of God." It was then that a madly generous idea crossed his mind: he would walk barefoot all the way from Paris to Rouen, and he would refrain from eating or drinking anything until he got there. Was this not tempting God? He considered the question in the quiet of the chapel in the Convent of Saint-Dominique, and then in peace he made up his mind. The next morning he got up very early to put his resolution into practice, but as he was getting dressed, his feelings revolted so much against the idea that he was all but paralyzed. Still fighting this repugnance within his soul, he left the hospice at dawn, made his way down the rue Saint-Jacques, crossed the Seine, followed the Pointoise road that passed through Monceaux and Argenteuil, in whose ancient convent Héloïse, the wife of the famous philosopher and theologian Abelard, had been clothed in the habit of a nun. Perhaps Íñigo knew nothing of one or the other of these famous tragic lovers. On the other hand, he was aware of a small Romanesque church where, according to tradition, the seamless robe of Christ was kept; he knew of this church in Argenteuil because the relic it housed bore a concrete reference to Jerusalem and to Christ's passion and death. At this point of the journey, Íñigo was still prey to the "spiritual anguish," the dread and aversion that had been his ever since he left Paris, but now the recollection of this seamless robe had a purifying effect on his spirit. Like a bad dream, his anguish disappeared and a wave of consolation broke upon his soul. "So great a joy and spiritual consolation came upon him that he began to cry out and talk with God." On the first evening, he bedded down with a poor beggar in a hospice; the next night he took shelter in a barn where hay was stored; and on the third day, after "eating and drinking nothing and barefoot just as he had planned," he arrived in Rouen. Unquestionably, this man with the willpower of steel was a most austere madman; he was the incarnation of those knights, so common to the Middle Ages, who went out to assist the needy. In three days time, he had been able to cover 150 kilometers—close to 100 miles—without eating or drinking anything. This in itself is an astonishing record worthy of the best modern-day athletes. But in singling out the physical prowess achieved, we should not underestimate the moral exploit accomplished. Íñigo brought consolation to the sick man who had such a heavy heart; he booked him on a ship bound for Spain, and gave him letters of introduction to Calixto, Cáceres, and Arteaga. In all of his behavior there was nothing about demons or revelations; he offered no reasons wrapped in devious arguments, no flowery apologias. He simply acted; that is all.

21
Íñigo's Dance

Íñigo's strong will and rugged nature could also act in a way that was less physically demanding and spectacular, and it was for this reason, perhaps, that such actions seemed more spontaneous and touching. We do not know if the following incident dates back to his stay in Paris at this particular time or if it took place at a later date. Ribadeneira described it in his biographical manuscript, but out of prudishness it was deleted from the printed edition and was forgotten until the critical edition appeared in 1965. Ribadeneira's delightful style is reminiscent of one of Saint Francis of Assisi's *fioretti*.

> A grave person and former spiritual disciple of our father in Paris told me that one day when he was very sick and depressed as a result of a malady, our father paid him a visit and out of great charity asked him if there was anything that he could do in order to bring some happiness into his life and dispel the gloom and sadness that he was experiencing. And as he answered that there was no remedy for his suffering, Íñigo again asked him to reconsider the question and to think if there was not anything at all that would bring him some joy and relief. After having thought about it for some time, the sick man said something quite silly. He said that there was just one single thing that he could think of that would make him feel better, and so he said: "If you could sing a little and dance a little as they do in your country,

in Vizcaya, I think this could give me some consolation and to some extent it would dispel my depression."

Íñigo replied: "Would that make you happy?"

"Oh, yes, very happy," said the sick man.

Íñigo's charity prevailed over his own personal preference and restraint; he considered such a request could only come from a very sick man indeed, and so, in order not to increase his sickness and depression by denying the request, he did what the sick man asked him to do. When he had finished, he said: "Please do not ask me to do that again because I shall not do it." The sick man was so overjoyed by Ignatius's charity that after he left, the depression that was eating up the sick man's heart was lifted; he began to improve, and after a few days, he was cured.

With this exceedingly touching gesture, the serious-minded Íñigo, who walked with a limp and who had satisfied the request of a depressed sick man, was faithful to the promise he had made, and at the same time gave eloquent proof of belonging to that small nation of people, who, centuries later, would be described by no less a person than Voltaire, as "the people who dance at the feet of the Pyrenees."

When Íñigo got to the point in his autobiography where he described his Paris-Rouen expedition, he made a brief allusion to his Alcalá-Salamanca companions. This aside gave him the opportunity to stop and speak of them for the last time. "To avoid saying anything more about these companions," he wrote, "this is the way they ended up." Here, after almost twenty-five years, he described what happened to them and why he and they separated the way they did. While in Paris, Íñigo did to some extent keep the promise he had made to them by writing to them frequently, but he told them of "the slight chance there was of his bringing them to Paris to study." Was there a reason for all of this? Íñigo did indeed help other needy students while he was in Paris; moreover, his former companions could have begged their way there just as he had done, and he would not have been at all put out had they followed in the footsteps of Peralta, Castro, and Elduayen. Was what he wrote in his letters a pretext for brushing off men who may have been of less worth than the new people he was meeting in Paris? The fact is that Íñigo did take a great interest in

Calixto's future, and it was Calixto's fate that presented Íñigo
with his first opportunity to exercise his art of diplomacy in
obtaining favors. We do not know exactly what he meant by
the expression "he did his best," although we do know that he
strained all of his resources, and we also know for whom it was
that he went to such extremes. He wrote a letter to Doña
Leonor de Mascarenhas, a Portuguese Renaissance scholar
and one of the most important ladies-in-waiting to Charles V's
wife, the Empress Isabella, and the nurse to her newborn son,
Prince Philip. Íñigo had probably met Doña Leonor at
Valladolid during the summer of 1527, when he spoke with
Archbishop Fonseca, and he may have told her at that time of
his pilgrimage to Jerusalem. Doña Leonor always had great
esteem for Íñigo, and in the future she would be one of the
most influential protectors of the Society. On this occasion,
Íñigo asked this prestigious woman to obtain for Calixto one of
the many scholarships that the king of Portugal granted to students in Paris. Doña Leonor provided Calixto with a mule and
money, but just as when he and Íñigo were together at Alcalá
when Calixto had never shown the same firmness of purpose
as Íñigo, so too now, on this occasion, Calixto went off to
Portugal, and then, rather than continuing on to Paris, he
returned to Spain and from there he embarked for Mexico in
the company of a *beata*, a member of the Third Order of
Franciscans. In New Spain the *oidores*, that is, the judges of the
crown, forced him to separate from the lady in question, and
so he came back to Salamanca alone, although, to the astonishment of all who had known him previously, he returned as a
very wealthy man. As for Cáceres, Íñigo reported that he
returned to his home town of Segovia, and there he settled
down "and began to live in such a way that he seemed to have
forgotten his earlier resolves." The third of the trio, Arteaga,
received his degree and, thanks to the influence of the Zúñiga-
Requesens, an old, well-established family who had been protectors of Íñigo while he was at Barcelona, he became a
Commander of the Order of Santiago and the tutor of the
family's children. In 1540, he was appointed bishop of Chiapas
in New Spain, but he died a tragic death in Mexico before taking possession of his see and was succeeded by the famous Fra
Bartolomé de Las Casas, O.P. Finally, Jean de Reynaulde
(Jeanico) became a Franciscan.

Veritas temporis filia—"Truth is the daughter of time." Time clarifies and fathoms the mysteries of the human heart and the consistency of its desires. Íñigo's seductive power was no guarantee that fidelity would withstand every assault. When it was deprived of his presence, the group that constituted the Alcalá and Salamanca companions faded away. The Paris trio, "his second birth," as Polanco described them, was likewise a stillbirth. Íñigo, for all of that, did not give up his attempt to look for companions that he could gather around him, and he did not easily abandon his resolve in this regard.

After his return from Rouen, in September 1529, Íñigo finally made the decision to be serious in the pursuit of his studies in arts or philosophy. But now a new obstacle stood before him. Because of all the weird happenings surrounding Peralta, Castro, and Elduayen, "widespread rumors had been broadcast against him." Diogo de Gouveia was by now bristling because of the conversion of Elduayen, one of his students at Sainte-Barbe. No less annoyed was Dr. Pedro Ortiz, Peralta's tutor at the Montaigu, who was on the verge of returning to Spain. Before he gave up his chair at the Sorbonne to teach Scripture at Salamanca, he brought his grievance against Íñigo to Fra Valentin Liévin, O.P. Íñigo learned about the charge and did not wait until he was summoned. Rather, he showed up before the inquisitor and told him he knew that he was looking for him. Íñigo said he was eager to cooperate with the inquisitor, and, to the astonishment of the latter, he presented him with all the information and details he sought. Íñigo then asked him to deal quickly with his case because he wanted to begin the new university term on the first of October, the day classes began, in peace and free from any involvement with the Inquisition. Liévan admitted that he had indeed received a complaint, but he showed no concern about the case and allowed the intrepid student to go free.

22

At Peace with Everyone

Íñigo began his course in what was called "Arts," or the humanities, on October 1, 1529. Surprisingly, he was admitted to Sainte-Barbe, the college administered by Gouveia. Here he began four difficult years during which time he disentangled the pure logic in the *Summulae* of Petrus Hispanicus and its commentaries and Aristotle's *Organon, Physics,* and *Ethics,* and some of his other works. What a terrible struggle he waged against axioms, categories, syllogisms, universals, and the like—particularly so, given his age and his temperament was not exactly overflowing with enthusiasm for the grandiloquent rigmaroles and the interminable quarrels between the various philosophical schools of the day. Had he ever heard about it, he well may have approved of Melanchthon's invective against the "pagan scholasticism" of Paris, which this spokesman for Luther said would make the healing of the Church impossible if it continued to be tolerated. At any rate, book learning did not constitute Íñigo's preferred occupation nor was it the center of his preoccupations. Rather than having the exhilaration for some unadulterated Aristotelian passage that Thomas Stapleton, S.J., professed having, Íñigo may well have appreciated the verse that Johannes Murmellius inserted within the textual commentaries he himself wrote on Aristotle:

> Only virtue lasts.
> Power, riches, and renown

Vanish and fade away with time
And how short-lived is the bloom of youth.

How could anyone not excuse him if his mind became distracted during class and if he became embroiled with the spiritual thoughts that assailed him. He considered that these spiritual thoughts might be temptations, just as they had been in Barcelona, and so he made his will dominate his preferred inclinations. He sought out the master and promised him that he would be faithful in attending class and that he would pay attention to the lectures. However, he felt more at ease on Sundays among the Carthusians, where he managed to meet some students and excited in them the beginnings of a spiritual way of life. This is why Master Juan de la Peña, the only one of his teachers that he mentions in the *Autobiography,* saw to it that Íñigo cut down on the amount of time he gave to his Sunday meetings. Peña warned him on a number of occasions and advised him against becoming involved in other people's lives and against upsetting other students. Finally, Master Peña took his complaint about Íñigo to Rector Diogo de Gouveia. Ribadeneira learned about these details in 1542. Gouveia decided to come down hard on Íñigo for his egregious lack of discipline with a most stringent punishment, a "hall" or a public flogging, for having disturbed the college and transgressed its rules under the pretext of religion. The college was convoked to witness this deplorable spectacle, and Íñigo went to speak with the fearsome rector. He himself did not mind the personal humiliation, but as a guide and apostle, Íñigo worried that his followers would not be able to support such a trial. It took only a few minutes for his persuasive words to change the rector's mind and turn him into a friend. Many years later, it would be Gouveia who would open to the Society the doors to India. How ironic are the ways of Providence!

To the great surprise of observers, such as the Sorbonne Scripture teacher, the Aragonese Dr. Jerónimo Frago, Íñigo settled into a period of moderated zeal. One day, the doctor ventured to tell him "that he was surprised that he was getting along quietly without anyone causing him trouble." Íñigo fired back a blunt response, saying, "The reason is because I do not speak to anyone of the things of God, but once this course is over, I'll go back to my old ways." He did study during the academic year, but at his age there was no room for any youthful enthusiasm for learning, only for seriousness and stubborn adult tenacity. Philosophy and theology did stir up in him the esteem and respect that they provoke in anyone who approaches them in a methodical way; no form of unadulterated spiritualism was ever able to be a substitute for them. From his painful apprenticeship as a student of philosophy and theology, Íñigo would later be able to draw some practical consequences that would some day have profound and manifold consequences for many others. Among some of these lessons learned was that a man should appreciate academic learning; he should be convinced of the need to integrate Scripture, the teachings of the Church Fathers, and the wisdom of scholasticism; he should have a feel for pedagogical methods and appreciate the value of academic degrees in the world in which he lives; and he should understand why students must be given the minimal conditions to enable them to dedicate themselves totally to study.

Study he did, but an intellectual he was not, nor did he want to be one. Íñigo was a man of action who radiated activity. Never would he astonish his masters by the subtleties of his thought, but he would overwhelm them by the mastery and majesty he showed when speaking about theological matters. There was something about the spell of his personality that gave him a certain command over his peers, who were much younger than he, and even over his professors. He was not a glib or brilliant conversationalist who was able to win the superficial sympathies of others. He was something else altogether. Wherever he went he created a ferment, sowing restlessness; he drew the attention of others and, what was more important, he transformed the environment where he found himself and the people in it. Exteriorly, there was nothing special in the way he came across to others. He knew nothing about the skills of oratory. In initiating a conversation, he was specific and to the point, and his speech was devoid of all those precious affectations so characteristic of the world of academe. He himself was a person who had been converted; he knew that in dealing with another, the breaking-down point had to be reached before there could be a surrender, a self-giving, and so he was not afraid to get down to essentials. The past had to be liquidated, or to put it simply and provocatively, the person had to make a general confession. The break with the ambiguous or sinful present had to take place; evil companions and bad habits had to be given up; and the person had to free himself from the influences of his surroundings and take a firm stand against anything and anyone. The symbol of this break with the past, this liberation, was weekly confession and Communion, and attending the meetings at the charterhouse. The symbol was simple and yet it implied a commitment. Once the person became involved in the symbolism, other more profound changes could take place, and Íñigo stuck to the techniques of his Exercises to bring about these changes.

The secret of his attraction resided in the authenticity of what he said and how he lived, in the example he gave, and in the direct way he dealt with others. There was nothing at all deceitful or artificial about him. He was a committed man. People could always go to him when they needed material help, advice, encouragement, or support. Polanco has recreated the atmosphere surrounding Íñigo at this time of his life when he wrote that Íñigo "lived in peace with everyone, even with those who had the spirit of the world." He spoke with persons of influence in order to help students. He came to the aid of his impoverished fellow students by giving them alms or by helping to get them jobs with masters who could give a room where they could study, or by getting them "portions," that is subsidies, or just by giving them good advice. His circle of friends, made up of both benefactors and the recipients of their benefactions, was large indeed. At his advice, more than one of these entered the religious life and became a Franciscan, Dominican, or Carthusian. His spiritual influence reached out to the theologian Petrus de Valla at the College of Navarre, to Don Álvaro Moscoso, the rector of the university in 1527 and later bishop of Pamplona, and to the principal of the College of Saint-Michel, Martial de Mazurier. Mazurier, who had a doctorate in theology, was so impressed by the teachings of this strange layman that he wanted to confer the degree of doctor of theology on the student who, he said, was teaching him. Drs. François Le Picart and Jerónimo Frago were also members of his circle of friends.

Íñigo's presence, which for the most part was low key and discreet, could, at times, expand to the point where it manifested itself in a most courageous action. On one occasion, he wanted a man to leave the woman with whom he was living, and, in order to convince him to do so, Íñigo waited for him on the outskirts of Paris. Then, as the person passed by, Íñigo threw himself into an icy pond in an effort to rid the man of his passion. He also knew how to win over a bad priest. He went to confession to him and told him about his own sins stressing what steps he took to repent of them. He showed extraordinary nerve in overcoming himself.

Once, when Íñigo was with Dr. Frago, a friar came by and asked the doctor to find someplace for him to live because many people were dying in the house where he was presently lodging. He suspected it was the plague that was causing all these deaths. Frago and Íñigo went to inspect the house, and they brought along with them a woman who was skilled in diagnosing the plague, and who was therefore in a good position to confirm or deny any suspicions. The woman confirmed that indeed the house was plague-stricken. Íñigo insisted on going in to visit and console one of the lodgers there who was sick. He placed his hand on the man's sores, "and this action made him feel a bit better." Afterward, when he was all by himself, Íñigo noticed his hand began to hurt, and he became obsessed by the thought that he had contracted the disease. His imagination became so strong that he could hardly control it, and finally, in order to put an end to his apprehensions, he thrust the sore hand into his mouth. The result was he was quarantined from the college for several days. This gesture is much more than just another edifying tale from the *Flos Sanctorum*. Modern psychology recognizes in Íñigo's *agere contra* action a paradoxical intention, which, even if it does not always infallibly cure obsessive-compulsive, phobic behavior patterns, is at least an efficacious remedy against them, particularly those where an anticipative anxiety is an underlying factor.

Such were some of the activities Íñigo resorted to during his Paris days. They are described in the pages of his autobiography, which is singularly meager when it comes to giving details about what was taking place at the university and in the world at large. This fact might lead one to suggest that he lived apart from all of these happenings, immersed as he was in his world within, his immediate academic concerns, and ever eager to guide others to discover their interior worlds. Despite this impenetrable silence, one must concede that it was impossible for him to have been impervious to the events that were going on in the world about him. In the Paris of his day, the terms *Luther* and *Lutheranism* were not reserved for what was evolving in far-off Germanic lands. The *parlement* of Paris, the court of justice, and the theology faculty gradually showed themselves inflexible against this new wave from the East. In 1521, Luther was condemned; two years later, his books were burned on the square in front of Notre Dame and the sale of his writings was proscribed. In 1525, the evangelical Meaux group, led by Bishop Guillaume Briçonnet, was cut short. With the coming of 1526, the atmosphere became even more taut. Accused of being Lutherans, the licentiate Hubert, a nobleman named de La Tour, and a student identified as Master Jacques Pauvant were burned at the stake. In certain cases, suspected Lutherans died after having had their tongues cut out or pierced. This growing opposition to new ideas did not stop Erasmus, who at the time was at the zenith of his glory. In 1525, there were already fifty editions of his *Enchiridion* that had been published and twenty-five editions of his *Colloquies*; tens of thousands of copies of *The Praise of Folly*; and one hundred thousand copies of his *Novum Instrumentum* had already been sold. Paris, however, condemned the *Colloquies* in 1526 and accepted the censorship of the implacable Noël Bedier (Latin, Natalis Beda) by ratifying his condemnation of one hundred propositions against Erasmus. In their writings, the Carthusian Pierre Couturier (Latin, Petrus Sutor) and the corpulent Beda attacked Erasmus ceaselessly while Erasmus attempted to vindicate himself by employing the most acerbic criticisms and insults against them. During Íñigo's stay in Paris, the university condemned anew the *Colloquies*. How could Íñigo have possibly been unaware of the fact that in 1527 the rector of his college was invited to participate in a conference at Valladolid and that he used this occasion to take a position against Erasmus? How could he have been ignorant of the fact that Josse van Clichtove (Latin, Jodocus Clichtovaeus) and Pierre Descornes, O.F.M. (Latin, Petrus de Cornibus) were using their Parisian pulpits to condemn both Luther and Erasmus? At the time he went to Flanders, Louis de Berquin, "the Luther of France," was burned at the stake for having relapsed into Lutheranism, and in that very same year the Diet of Speyer gained notoriety for having been the place where the word *Protestant* was used for the first time. While Íñigo was struggling with Aristotle in Paris, Catholics and Protestants in Augsburg were arguing about the tenets of new Christianity condensed in the *Confessio Augustana.* These new ideas were even coming to Paris. A fanatic decapitated the head of a statue of the Virgin Mary, an incident that caused such public consternation that the king himself was moved to make solemn public reparation during the course of magnificent procession through the streets of Paris. At the time, none of these things seem to have had any effect on Íñigo, but they did indeed make his attachment to the Church more binding, secure, profound, and unqualified. Despite the diatribes that Luther and Erasmus were venting on religious vows and on the religious and monastic life, and even despite the fact that religious communities in Germany were becoming more and more depopulated, Íñigo continued to direct people to the cloister. Why did he himself not follow the same path?

True, his spirituality touched many different people and he gave himself unstintingly to everyone, but he did not sow without his eye on a particular harvest. "He won the love of many," wrote Polanco, "keeping in mind his desire of attracting for his own project some individuals who seemed to him to be more adept and qualified for the project he had in mind." This statement was no pious invention on the part of Polanco. Íñigo himself wrote that when he began his arts courses in 1529, he determined to restrict his conversations to those who were intent on serving God, "but he would not try to add to their number, as he wanted to give himself with less pressure to his studies." In both sentences the word *project* appears, although it pertains to different subjects. In the first, the reference is to persons apart from Íñigo himself; the second time he uses it, it refers to Íñigo's secret designs. What did he mean at this time "to serve God" or "serving God"? Did he have a clear and well-defined project tailored to the persons he was trying to find that would fit into this undertaking? We do not know, but what we should do is reject the false image of the brilliant strategist plotting out the organization of a grand army designed to battle the Protestants or to defend a weakened Church. There is a time for every season, and things make progress slowly. At the time of its inception, Íñigo's project was more simple, more modest.

23

It All Began in a College Room

Ínigo's life is full of unexpected encounters that have more or less long-lasting consequences. He seems to have been a man sure of the final results who cast his net in all directions without knowing the exact moment of the happy catch and, at the same time, without being daunted by any number of failures. Among his many encounters there is one that stands out because of its singular consequences. After being admitted to Sainte-Barbe, he went to live in a room situated in a high tower that everyone referred to as "the paradise." Here he met Master Peña and two students who were soon to receive their degrees, Pierre Favre and Francis Xavier. Here appeared the first fertile seed of what was to be the Society. We can describe its birth with this sentence: "Everything began with conversations that took place in this room." Can it really be possible that all the information the *Autobiography* contains on the beginning of this group is limited to these laconic words: "During this period he was carrying on conversations with Master Pierre Favre and Master Francis Xavier, both of whom he later won to God's service through the Exercises"! Favre and Xavier were not yet masters when this singular conversationalist first began talking with them, but before they had even finished his Exercises, the two had already surrendered to him. Fortunately, Favre, Xavier, Laínez, Simão Rodrigues, and all the others who joined him also had grateful memories for

Íñigo whom they considered their father in spirit. With their help, we can reconstruct a history that is as simple as it is unbelievable. We might even call it Íñigo's *Fioretti*.

Favre was a young blond man with a soul as pure as the Alpine heights of his native Savoy. Son of peasants, he himself had been a shepherd boy during his childhood days at which time he used to play at being priest and preacher with his young friends and companions in Villaret. His desire to study was supported by one of his uncles, who was a Carthusian monk. After attending a number of different schools, he came to Paris in 1525. Favre was a man gifted with a special goodness and a natural sympathy for all. He had a real charm about him. He was able to solve all the hard problems Master Peña gave him on the original Greek text of Aristotle. With how much more reason, then, could he help Íñigo, his new roommate, who was a good fifteen years his senior. An extended conversation between two honest people is much like a path leading to an unknown destination. The point of departure could be Petrus Hispanicus or Aristotle, but the point of arrival is unchartered, and this would be all the more so if the two people exchanged more than just their knowledge acquired from books. When Favre wrote his *Memorial* (1542–1546), that is to say his confessions, he praised God for having allowed him to meet Íñigo, the consequences of which, he described, took place bit by bit. They passed from small talk to a deep, spiritual conversation; from the *Perì Hermeneías* to confidences, from anecdotes to spiritual conversations. Genuine conversation is like a fishing net; it enmeshes the two people more and more. The tutor and the old student had to cut short their interminable conversations so that they could be faithful to their studies. A deep friendship was born, sustained by a common life, for they were roommates who shared their meals and money. One day, Favre, who was a shy, uncertain soul tortured by scruples, allowed Íñigo to penetrate even further into the intimate recesses of his being. Although his friend was an apprentice when it came to logic, he knew a great deal about what Favre was telling him, and Íñigo gave him peace, a gift that has no price. The older man gave his younger friend a gentle, encouraging lesson; he spoke to him about the knowledge of God and of oneself and how to understand one's conscience. From that moment on, Favre kept no secrets from him. Íñigo had put to rest in the angelic Savoyard sensual temptations that had been tormenting him. Favre knew the meaning of fornication only through his reading, others knew it through experience, like one of the professors on the college faculty who had recently died (1526) from syphilis. Besides his scruples, Favre was undecided about his future. Would he be a doctor, a lawyer, or a theologian? Should he get married, join a religious order, or be a simple parish priest? Even before making the Exercises, Favre gained self-confidence and identified completely with the ideals of his friend and counselor. After he became a Jesuit, he wrote about the sentiments he shared with Íñigo and his companions at this time of his life: "We came *to be one* in wish and will and firm purpose of embracing the kind of life we are now living." Íñigo spent four years working on the spiritual crafting of Favre. He sent him to Dr. Castro to begin a schedule of weekly confession and Communion; he had him examine his conscience each day, and Favre ended up by choosing to follow the same form of life as his friend. In time, Pierre Favre would become a valiant and tireless worker and one of the pillars of the young Society.

24

Francis Xavier: The Hardest Dough to Knead

Favre's friend, Francis Xavier, was born in the same year as he, and almost on the same day in April. Like Favre, he had been at Sainte-Barbe since October 1, 1525. The two of them had been roommates for four years. Xavier was a friendly, jovial young man; outgoing and energetic and one of the best athletes in the games that were played in the fields of the Île de la Cité. By nature a dreamer, he wanted to compensate for the rough times his family had undergone with his own personal triumphs. Like Íñigo, he was the youngest in his family. Dr. Jassu, his father, had been the president of the Council of Navarre when the events took place in that small Pyrenees kingdom already described, and these hostilities had cost him his life. Francis's brothers had fought in all of the battles against the Spaniards and were loyal to the deposed Albret dynasty. They knew what it meant to be imprisoned, to be condemned to death, and to have had the sentence reprieved. His mother, "Doña Marina, the sorrowful," as she used to sign some of her letters, had already died. Xavier had grown up in a family that had been ruined. When he was twelve years old, he watched the towers of the family castle being torn down in compliance with Cisneros's orders. Did he recognize Íñigo right from the outset as the erstwhile defender of Pamplona, an enemy of the Xavier family? He probably referred to him by the same caustic pejorative term he considered proper when speaking about anyone who hailed from Guipúzcoa.

But all of that unpleasantness—the war and its consequences—was already a thing of the past. Now the road to be taken by the Xavier castle's youngest son seemed to be clearly marked. On March 15, 1530, that is, a few months after Íñigo arrived at Sainte-Barbe, Xavier received his licentiate. Shortly afterward, he spent the little money he had to become a master. He was now entitled to wear the master's rosette on the left shoulder of his long robe, and, what was more important, he could fill a chair at the Collège de Beauvais. He was now a member of the Faculty of Arts and was authorized to take part in faculty meetings and in the election proceedings for the rector. As a finishing stroke to all of these accomplishments, he took steps to prove his nobility and thereby be appointed a canon in Pamplona. The Navarrese student Miguel de Landívar became his serving man. He must have been a bit short on money to meet all the demands of his new position because the doctorate cost him dearly and his family was in no position to assist him regularly or generously.

Íñigo assisted him with money; moreover, he went out of his way to find him pupils whom he personally introduced to him. At a time when the intellectual climate of Paris was opened to a fresh generation of humanists of doubtful orthodoxy, Íñigo kept a discrete eye on the new circle of friends Xavier was acquiring. Íñigo knew very well the attractiveness of being more, of having more, of being worth more; he knew what it meant to want honors, prestige, and glory. Just as steady drops of water eventually wear away the hardest stone, little by little he weakened that rock-like soul whose resistance is noted in some extant contemporary sources. One of the earliest compilers of the events of this period was the Jesuit Manoel Teixeira. He wrote that Master Xavier was "a somewhat harder and more difficult" challenge for Íñigo. Another contemporary, a close friend of Pierre Favre during their student days, later composed a series of fictional dialogues about the formation of the Society and its way of life. This man was Edmond Auger, who himself later became a Jesuit. In one of his vignettes he puts these revealing words in the mouth of Polanco: "I have heard Ignatius, our great molder of men, say that when he began his enterprise, the hardest dough that he ever had to knead was young Francis Xavier." Xavier, the man from Navarre, was not in the least attracted by the style of life led by Íñigo, and indeed he scoffed at and made jokes about his followers. Out of some subconscious self-defense, he kept himself at a distance from Íñigo. "What does it profit a man to gain the whole world. . . . ?" This sentence from the Gospel deflated all his ambitions and took all the importance and meaning from them; finally, like so much fog, they evaporated altogether, enabling Xavier to attach himself to Íñigo and make Íñigo's projects his own. He changed his life and dismissed his servant. To use the old description of Gouveia, Íñigo "had turned the head" of the Navarrese master, that is, he had changed him into a madman. His servant Landívar suffered as a result of being let go, and so he decided to kill the man who had thrown a spell on his master. He even went so far as to climb the stairs of the college, blinded by rage and grasping a dagger in his hand. A single word from Íñigo was enough to stop him and to cause him to fall down on his knees at his feet. Ribadeneira heard the account of this episode from the lips of Ignatius himself. Xavier had not yet made the Exercises, but, during the first half of 1533, he had already decided to follow the way of Íñigo. He was as tough as the oaks that grow in the Pyrenees, but Ignatius carved this oak-like man in a way that gave him an undying shape and grandeur. At the age of twenty-seven, these two roommates, Favre and Xavier, had already completed their apprenticeship in the spiritual life.

25

Seven Friends Called the *Iñiguistas*

The winning over of two more was easier done and faster, too. Diego Laínez and Alfonso Salmerón were both very promising young men; the first was twenty-one and the second eighteen. They were "very close friends" and eager to learn. They came from Alcalá, where they had heard about Íñigo, and they were anxious to meet him. Fate had it that the very first person Laínez met on his arrival at the place where he intended to stay in Paris was Íñigo. Íñigo's first pieces of advice about living in Paris were extremely useful to him. In no time, he became familiar with the way to get to Sainte-Barbe, and he joined the group that met each Sunday at the charterhouse. On October 23, 1532, he had received his master's degree from Alcalá. Had it not been for favoritism shown to two others, he would have been the first in his class; as it was, he was rated third. He was intuitive and intelligent; skillful in disputations and erudite. Physically, he was small and weak, and he had large expressive eyes. He was a pious, pure, and docile young man. His aquiline nose indicated that his racial origins were Jewish. His inseparable friend, Alfonso Salmerón, was a native of Toledo, a frank, jolly, and expansive young man blessed with a prodigious memory, who was in the habit of reciting by heart the works of the Greek and Latin poets he had studied at the trilingual college of Alcalá. Íñigo dealt separately with Laínez and

Salmerón, and so, without either one knowing the intentions of the other, they eventually learned both were committed to the same cause. Just at about this same time, Nicolás Alonso, who later would be known as Bobadilla, made his appearance in Paris. He hailed from Old Castile, from the small town of Bobadilla in Palencia to be exact, and he was a hothead who had a passionate, direct way of expressing himself. He held a bachelor of arts degree from Alcalá and a regent degree in logic from San Gregorio in Valladolid, and he had come to Paris both because he was attracted by the reputation of the professors at the Collège Royal and because of his desire to master the three erudite languages that would enhance his theological formation. He came to Íñigo because he had heard that Íñigo helped students, and, as a matter of fact, Íñigo did manage to get him a job in the Collège de Calvi, but at the same time he warned him about the orthodoxy of the professors he had come to Paris to find. Bobadilla changed his mind about the Collège Royal and went instead to the Dominicans and Franciscans to study theology, and he also joined Íñigo's group. The Portuguese Simão Rodrigues enjoyed one of the scholarships given by King John III of Portugal, and ever since 1526 he had been living at Sainte-Barbe. In the beginning of 1529 he moved in with Íñigo, but he had no direct dealings with him in spiritual matters until 1533. As an old man in 1577, he wrote a delightful account of his Paris days. He recalled that he himself had taken the initiative to contact Íñigo because he was attracted by the sanctity of this elderly student who was already in his forties. "He decided to share with him some of his desires and give him a part of his soul," and shortly afterward he became determined to follow a new way of life. This change caused a great surprise among his fellow Portuguese, and even surprised Favre and Xavier as well.

They now numbered six. Without knowing what the others were thinking, each of them was coming, one by one, to the same resolution, namely, to go to the Holy Land and spend his life there working for the salvation of his fellow human beings, or what Laínez would later say, and what amounts to the same thing: "to follow the institute of Íñigo." *Institute* means nothing other than the way of life or the teachings of

Íñigo, neither of which was yet clearly defined and certainly not within the confines of ordinary ecclesiastical structures. From the very beginning, Íñigo had founded no group, but, like Errazti the smith at Loyola, he forged pieces one by one that eventually would all fit perfectly together. This remarkable group, made up of men from diverse ethnic origins and having different national identities, became a homogeneous entity because its members were of the same age group, shared a similar cultural background, and, most especially, had the same ideals. It was merely enough to mount or join these different pieces together so that a compact group would come into being, a group that would identify itself with a leader who would be the guide for each one individually and for the group as a whole. But an intimate bonding also took place among the members of the group, thanks to the points they shared in common and to their mutual friendship. All of this began in a room. Later, the room of each one became the room of all. On certain afternoons they would bring food and meet together in one of the rooms to talk and dream. Íñigo was not a strategist nor was he an imposing leader; rather, he was the companion-guide who exerted a calm, strong, and trustworthy type of authority and influence. He had made it possible for each one to hear God's call to him personally. It was curious that the call they all heard was identical to that which he himself had heard many years earlier, even down to the unpredictable detail of wanting to start their new way of life by visiting the land of Jesus. We are now at the threshold of the adventure initiated by six poor Christians plus Íñigo, none of whom was a priest. They had come together, as pilgrims have a way of doing, through a mutual agreement on how they should proceed about making the actual pilgrimage; however, in this case each one had come to his own decision independently of the others. They were seven men; each one who was master of his own fate; each one who had made up his own mind freely, who was now renouncing everything because he had come to one sole decision, and that was to dedicate himself to serving his fellow man. This was a generous ideal but, up until now, it had no precise shape. For the time being, however, the important thing was for each of them to maintain an attitude that was completely open and totally ready for whatever came along. It would be the vagaries of history that would finally give direction to their resolve.

There were a number of events that transpired during the course of 1533, and, even though Íñigo did not make the slightest allusion to them in his autobiography, they most certainly should be noted because of their historical importance. The least significant of these happenings was that, on the thirteenth of March that year, Íñigo received his licentiate in arts, the *Licentia docendi, disputandi, determinandi . . . Parisiis et ubique terrarum*. This event must have given him some satisfaction, especially when he recalled the restrictions placed on him at Alcalá and Salamanca regarding conversing with others about the things of God because, it was asserted, he did not have the academic credentials to do so. Four years had passed since then, four years dedicated to study! And now he was able to teach, even though Aristotle's *Analytica* and, much less, his *De anima* would not be of much value to him in helping souls. The European event of the year was the wedding of Henry VIII and Anne Boleyn that resulted in breaking the thousand-year-old link between England and Rome. That same year saw Paris victimized once again by the plague and the very severe measures authorities took to eliminate it. The plague was difficult to stamp out, but even more difficult was the infiltration of the Protestant virus that was becoming more widespread through books and sermons. One symptom of this spreading sickness was the fact that Noël Beda and François Le Picart, who had been the most formidable adversaries against Luther and Erasmus, had been banished from the university. Meanwhile, Calvin had come back to Paris and was living near Sainte-Barbe. The tension that had previously manifested itself by a certain restraint in a number of theater productions had grown into a veritable storm by the beginning of the 1533–34 academic year. The new rector of the university, Nicolas Cop, who was a friend of John Calvin and a bachelor of medicine and philosophy, showed in his inaugural speech an unequivocal sympathy for Protestant teaching, which he ambiguously referred to as "Christ's philosophy." Cop's speech unleashed a lightning reaction. He was censured by the faculty of theology. A general assembly was then convoked, but the different faculties fought among themselves and ended up taking different stances. A hullabaloo ensued and Cop had to flee for his life at the very moment when he was about to be arrested. Calvin also disappeared during this uproar. The *parlement* of Paris, and even Francis I, who the year previously had signed the Treaty of Saalfeld with the Protestant Schmalkaldic League, reacted forcefully. Le Picart and Beda made a triumphant return to Paris and edicts were promulgated decreeing that anyone accused of Lutheranism by two witnesses would be tried, condemned, and burned at the stake. The year 1534 began under no better auspices. Humanist professors of the Collège Royal were being attacked and they were forbidden to interpret the Bible under the pretext that they were not theologians. Parlement forbade any new translations of Scripture into French. At times the agitation became even more intense, and it was fired up by a new decree promulgated to extirpate heresy and to hunt down heretics.

It was in this atmosphere that Íñigo gave Pierre Favre, the first member of the group, the Spiritual Exercises, and he did this in order to strengthen the bond between him and Favre that was already strong. A few months later, Favre received Holy Orders and he celebrated his first Mass on July 22. Later Laínez and all the others, except Xavier, made the Exercises separately; Xavier made them in September. Íñigo had them follow his method strictly and did not allow any exceptions or accommodations to his additions and annotations. He did not consider them exercises that led to conversion, but rather as exercises that led to an election or confirmation of a state in life. Even before they began the Exercises, each of his companions had already made up his mind about what he was going to be. "It will be very profitable for the one who is to go through the Exercises to enter upon them with magnanimity and generosity toward his Creator and Lord, and to offer Him his entire will and liberty, that His Divine Majesty may dispose of him and all he possesses according to His most holy will." This is the fifth annotation of Íñigo's thin book, and it is a recommendation that many people have religiously followed throughout the ages. But when has it ever been carried out with greater conscientiousness than by this group, which served as the "experimental group" for Íñigo in judging the efficiency of his technique, the purpose of which was to make the unlimited potential of every person expand in response to the invitation of God's grace?

The six companions made their retreats, one after the other. In order to do so, five of them left where they had been living and moved into a small house where together they indulged in harsh penances and long fasts. Íñigo visited them frequently and followed up on their progress. Bobadilla was the only one who made the retreat while remaining in his room at his college. The Exercises did not win new adepts on this occasion; they confirmed the six irrevocably in the decision that they had already made. On March 14, Íñigo obtained the title Master of Arts, and he did so more for reasons of social convenience than out of ambition or vanity. The biretta was bestowed on him in the Church of the Mathurins, or Trinitarians, on the rue Fouarre. He was now *Master*—not yet Father—*Ignatius.* This is how his name appeared in the official registers of the university, although no one can give a satisfactory explanation for this change of names. There are some who suggest that the name he adopted at this time— Ignatius—was more universal, and others suggest that he did so out of his devotion to the martyr, Ignatius of Antioch. It may even have been that he believed both names were really the same. He was still known as Íñigo among his close friends, and he himself would sometimes use his old name to sign his letters; yet little by little he became known as Ignatius, the name by which he is known in history.

The next year, he was inscribed in the faculty of theology as *"Dominus Ignatius de Loyola, diocesis Pampilonensis."* His anonymity was no longer necessary. Now that his position was well established and firm, he could write to to his family, which he did in June 1532. It could be that this was not the first letter he had written them. After years of silence, Íñigo— and this is the way he signed his letter to his brother Martín— attempted to explain his adventure with these precious words: "You say you are delighted because it seems I have taken to writing to you again after so long a period of silence. Don't be surprised. A man with a serious wound begins by applying one ointment, and then in the course of its healing another, and at the end still another. So, in the beginning of my own way one kind of ointment was necessary; then another, and finally, another type." He brought up the example of Saint Paul. In his younger days he lived a life much like the young Paul and now, at this present stage of his life, he aspired to be like Paul the saint. He did not use his past occupations as an excuse for not writing earlier, but rather he doubted that any of his correspondence would have been of any profit to his blood relatives. He wrote this letter as a warning to his family, which was obsessed with the affairs of his world and preoccupied by social success—that is to say to be *more*—in order to give them a savor for spiritual matters and to communicate to them the importance of doing deeds that will last for eternity. For Íñigo, blood no longer counted. He was open to all men and women. It made no difference that they were sinners, provided that they admitted they were sinners. He was interested in their immortal destiny and in the fact that they themselves were aware of their destiny.

In July of that year, there was a convocation called for the whole university in which Master Xavier participated. The winds of reform had affected all of the colleges and as a reaction a number of different policies were adopted, especially by the Faculty of Arts. On the agenda for discussion were placed such subjects as Latin and logic; the piety, morals, and conduct of the professors; policy standards against obscene literature and writings that contained Lutheran ideas; and the improvement of the physical conditions of the colleges. As a result, a number of resolutions were adopted for implementation. This convocation was an important event, considering the attacks Erasmus had launched against all professors who were not actively involved in the quarrel that was dividing Europe. None of these academicians, however, were about to follow the example of that former grand chancellor of the university who, during a similar crisis at an earlier age, stepped down from his exalted chair in order to teach catechism to children. The name of this renowned theologian was Jean de Gerson.

26

The Future, the Church, the Inquisition

That summer, the select group known as the *Iñiguistas* deliberated seriously about their future. They were in no hurry to make any decision because a number of them were about to begin their theology. They constituted a close group of intimate friends who, united among themselves, were intent on following Íñigo. Whatever the future held, they concentrated now on a few specific points. They would choose actual poverty, and this presupposed that they would give up everything to live such a lifestyle. Their university degrees would not serve as an entrée *de pane lucrando,* "as a way of making their living." They would exercise their apostolate gratuitously without aspiring for prebends or stipends. Once their studies were completed, their style of poverty would become more radical. It goes without saying that they chose to live celibate, chaste lives. In no way were they gloomy ascetics; rather, they were joyful and trusting followers of Christ, the Christ whom they had discovered and had come to know through the Spiritual Exercises and whose footsteps they wanted to follow in the Holy Land. One by one, they had committed themselves to make this pilgrimage, and this commitment was the most obvious, tangible link that joined them to one another. It was the most agreed-upon objective of all their projects, although there were some differences of opinion as to how it should be undertaken. Master Ignatius, better than all the rest, knew how much the realization of this enterprise depended on unforeseeable obstacles. For weeks, the group discussed the possibility that their projected journey might end in failure, and, if so, they talked about what other alternatives they would take. Ignatius, Laínez, and Xavier fantasized about living the rest of their lives in Palestine, giving themselves totally to the service of the Christians and infidels there. Were they not fleeing old and divided Europe that was sated with learning and deaf to the commitment of the faith? Favre and Rodrigues dreamed of returning home after their voyage. However, if circumstances prevented them from fulfilling their vow to make the journey to the Holy Land, how long would they be bound by what they had promised to do and what would they do as an alternative? Experts in the art of debating, they discussed all possibilities until they at last drew up a plan of action. They would continue to pursue their courses in theology, and then, in 1537, they would leave Paris for Venice, and there they would wait for *a whole year,* if need be, for the opportunity to board a ship for the Holy Land, but if the door to Jerusalem proved to be closed to them, they would place themselves at the disposal of the pope. If they succeeded in reaching Jesus' country, they would decide then by voice vote to remain there for good or to return. In case they opted to return, they would agree to take on whatever work the pope wanted them to do. This reference to a future undertaking was what properly constituted them as a so-called group, and, for the first time, the destiny of each individual member was left in the hands of the choice that the group as a whole would make. Jerusalem was the fixed and unchangeable objective; as an alternative, there was Rome, but Rome was only a substitute dream for Ignatius. He had no intention whatsoever of conquering the capital of Christendom. As he had done in the affair of the Moor, Ignatius let the reins go slack because he knew that Someone else was directing his steps.

They were seven men with seven different names, but their ideals were interchangeable and identical. As a way of confirming the decisions they had taken, these *Magistri Parisienses,* who were bent on serving their fellow human beings in poverty, gathered together as a group in one of the most remote churches on the outskirts of Paris. The setting and the date were doubtlessly selected with forethought. The place was the chapel crypt of Saint Denis and his martyr companions at Montmartre (*Mons Martyrum*), and the day was the feast of the Assumption of the Blessed Virgin Mary. These two circumstances tended to give an air of transcendence to this special meeting. Master Favre, the only one among them who was an ordained priest, celebrated the Mass. Just before the Communion, each one pronounced his vow one after the other, and then when they were finished, Favre pronounced his. Their collegial commitment thereby took on an aspect that was sacred. Forty years later, Simão Rodrigues, one of the surviving members of the group, still remembered with emotion that "holocaust." The recollection of it even seemed to enkindle in him that same joy of the spirit, abnegation of the will, and immense hope in the Divine Mercy that had animated the group on this special occasion. For the next two successive years on this same feast of the Assumption, they renewed the vows they had made on this occasion at Montmartre. Ignatius was absent for both meetings, but in his absence three more companions joined the group: Claude Jay, who was a Savoyard, and two Frenchmen, Paschase Broët and Jean Codure. By then, they numbered ten.

Was the Society born here at Montmartre? In the strict sense, no: it did not as yet have a rule, a hierarchical structure, or a program of action; and even the place where the members of the group were going to exercise their ministry depended on an uncertain future and was subjected to unforeseeable events. On that Assumption Day 1534, the group had merely consolidated a romantic desire, a desire that was as broad as the heavens themselves. They had put together the chrysalis out of which one day an institution would be born. Years later, Laínez would express it clearly this way: "While we were in Paris, our intention was not as yet to form a congregation, but rather to consecrate ourselves to the service of God and helping our neighbor by living in poverty, by preaching, and by serving in hospitals." Three years after the Montmartre ceremony, Ignatius, who at the time was in Venice trying to find some way to embark for Jerusalem, would himself write to a friend in Barcelona named Juan de Verdolay, saying: "I do not know what future God our Lord holds in store for me." In 1563, Nadal would write about this period of Ignatius's life describing it in this manner: "He was being guided slowly toward he knew not where, and he was not thinking of founding any religious order."

In September 1534, Master Xavier was finally able to make the Exercises and in order to do so, he retired to a small, isolated house. He attended mass in the neighboring church; Ignatius saw him quite often, and sometimes one or another of the other companions would come to visit with him. For a four-day period, he abstained completely from all food and drink. As penance for the vanity that resulted from his being a fine athlete in the games on the island in the Seine, he bound his arms and legs so tightly with cords that it was impossible for him to move a limb; finally, gangrene was on the point of developing in one arm and there was talk of his having to have it amputated. Because of, or in spite of, these excesses, the Exercises proved to be a profound and unforgettable experience for him. He came out of them with his proverbial joviality, but he was "*another man.*" He would never part from his small book of the *Spiritual Exercises,* for it was the mold in which he had been formed. His passionate affection for Ignatius, which bordered on idolatry, would never know any bonds. He was able to refer to him as his "only father in the profound love of Christ," because it was thanks to Ignatius that God had spoken to him heart to heart.

In October of that same year, all these "friends in the Lord" went back to their studies. Ignatius continued at one of the different centers of the Dominicans. He rejected nominalism, which enjoyed such popularity among the university set, and drank deep in the fountains of Thomism, for which he always had the deepest respect. He passed from the trinitarian visions of the Cardoner to the tortuous study of the *Summa Theologica,* but the inspiring richness of Thomistic sentences fed his soul ever so much better than the dialectics of Mayor or Celaya. Autumn that year in Paris was unseasonably warm. On October 18, Protestant *placards* attacking the Mass made their appearance on the walls of the capital and in other French cities, and, in reparation for these blasphemies, the *parlement* and the university sponsored processions that took place on the twenty-second and twenty-third. On November 10, the first sentences of death were handed down, and the condemned, after having their tongues pierced or their hands cut off, were burned at the stake in a number of city squares.

King Francis I returned to Paris and reinforced his decrees to ferret out the heretics. On January 21, he took the leading role in a huge procession in which the parishes, abbeys, convents, colleges, the university, prelates, ambassadors, and the whole court participated, and afterward, he gave a most uncompromising speech against the heretics. Later, six more Lutherans were burned along the rue Saint-Honoré. A few days after this event, another seventy-three people—courtiers, merchants, monks who had already escaped the city—were convoked to appear before the tribunal. Whoever attempted to hide a Lutheran would suffer the same fate as the Lutheran, and whoever turned a Lutheran over to the authorities would receive a reward. This had become a war between irreconcilable enemies, and the stakes had made the noncommittal reticence and equivocal positions assumed by the humanists impossible to defend. All positions had to be clear and precise, and under these dangerous circumstances people were forced to choose one way or another.

27

"The True Attitude of Mind We Ought to Have in the Church Militant"

Ignatius was constantly reediting his notebook that contained his Exercises and during his long stay in Paris he added a number of new pieces to it, such as the meditations on the Two Standards, the Three Modes of Humility, and a number of rules. In Paris, he may even have given a different literary structure to what he had already written. It was during this same time that he appended the well-known addition that he called the rules "For the True Sense Which We Should Have *in* the Church Militant," as the original Castilian text has it. In the definitive version of 1541, there are eighteen of these rules, but it seems that he added the last five to the original thirteen later on in Italy. Much has been written about these rules, which are considered to be the very quintessence of the Counter-Reformation, and some authors claim that they have traced their literary source to the 1529 Council of Sens. The published *Acta* of this council contain both the decrees of the council condemning current errors and Clichtove's redaction of orthodox Catholic doctrine, and it has been asserted that either one or both of these two documents is the literary source of Ignatius's *Rules for Thinking with the Church*. Other scholars stress the similarities that appear in these rules with some of the points contained in the unsolicited response

Francis I and the theology faculty of the University of Paris made to Melanchthon on August 30, 1535. However, these scholars do not take into account the fact that Ignatius had left Paris several months earlier and that the text of his *Exercises,* which at the time was in the hands of Favre and that later went into the manuscript called the Cologne Codex, already contained these rules. The fact is that Íñigo was more influenced by the atmosphere of Paris than he was by any literary influences. It was enough to live in Paris during those times and under those circumstances to realize that before putting a person face to face with Christ, he first had to give him some kind of compass to enable him to hold onto his bearings in that storm of opinions, some kind of map to enable him to plot out his way. Did he write these rules before the Montmartre event or was it perhaps when he presented his Exercises to the inquisitor Valentin Liévin, that is, in the spring of 1535?

The truth is that up until now, Íñigo had been living very much *in* the Church, not having a shadow of a doubt about her dogmas, and not having any problems whatsoever with questions of authority or the position of the hierarchy or with traditional forms of popular devotion. In his personal relations with his hierarchical superiors, he always gave proof of complete submissiveness. As we already stated, for Ignatius the Church had always been like the atmosphere that was a part of his everyday living, or like a mother's lap; living in the Church was something natural and uncomplicated, like breathing or being healthy. But now, without hedging or hiding behind palliatives, he had to explain and profess his belief in the Church, in "holy Mother Church." This profession of belief in her could not be given in a merely human way, nor would he take refuge in describing her by using some idealized description of what the primitive Church might have been. His was a statement of faith in what she really was, as history presented her, that is, as a stained Church, the Church "militant."

Ignatius believed that the Church, in spite of the weight of the centuries, continued to be "the true spouse of Christ our Lord." This belief was the living principle that animates these meticulous rules. Faced with the confusion of ideas that were circulating at the time—proponents of each one claiming infallibility to himself—Ignatius preferred to hold on with faith and trust to the Church that had endured throughout the ages. He believed a person could always find reasons to criticize the Church, but that person could also find numerous reasons to defend her, and so Ignatius believed that we must "keep the mind ever ready and prompt to obey," and reject disobedience if for no other reason than for the esprit de corps, because the Church is always faced with danger. However, we would distort Ignatian thinking if we did not consider the matter in its totality or if we reduced it to a blind discipline. Aside from the fact that the Church does not command adherence to a new belief every day, nor does she place the same weight on all matters of belief, there is that oft-quoted sentence in these rules: "What seems to me white, I will *believe* black if the hierarchical Church so defines it." This sentence must be seen in the light of belief and faith that Íñigo clearly stated when he wrote immediately afterward: "For I must be convinced that in Christ our Lord, the bridegroom, and in His spouse the Church, only one Spirit holds sway, which governs and rules for the salvation of souls. For it is by the same Spirit and Lord who gave the Ten Commandments that our holy Mother Church is ruled and governed." I dare say that it was the historic situation itself that enabled Íñigo to affirm explicitly and to deepen his faith in the Church.

Scholars have often argued whether or not these Parisian rules, that is, the first thirteen "Rules for Thinking with the Church," contain anti-Lutheran and anti-Erasmian propositions. It seems to me that when posed in this way, we set up a false disjunction. The very opposite to whatever these rules both defend and condemn is found in Luther and Erasmus. The former opposed them head on, radically; the latter opposed them with ambiguities and shades of meaning. Such things as confession, the Mass, the Office and canonical hours, the religious life, vows, celibacy, marriage, devotion to the saints and to relics of saints, pilgrimages, indulgences, fasting and external penances, customs followed during the Lenten season, vestments, and the whole notion of keeping secrets—all of these had been rejected by Luther and blithely criticized by Erasmus. Ignatius, who took all of these things very seriously and made them part of his religious practice, said simply that we must praise them and not denigrate them, much less reject them. Likewise, he insisted on respect for the precepts of the Church and its hierarchical representatives. As for the precepts, he had to find arguments in their favor— remember the conversation he had with Vives—and as for the hierarchical representatives of the Church, he was not about to defend the indefensible, but he sought ways to correct them efficaciously without completely discrediting them. Under the heading of devotions, rules ten through twelve deal with how those in authority can regulate a person's spiritual life and how situations can have an effect on it. Faced with an authority that was continuously challenged and ridiculed, Íñigo was more inclined to approve the orders, recommendations, and customs of hierarchical superiors, rather than find fault with them (Rule 10). Moreover, since it was typical of the period to pit the Bible and the Fathers of the Church against the scholastic theologians, Ignatius showed how theological knowledge and enlightened piety can be made complementary. He said it was characteristic of the Bible and the Fathers of the Church to arouse our affections so that we are moved to love and serve God, but we need scholastic theologians to define truth, to state it clearly, and to help refute error. Certainly, scholastic philosophers should never overlook the learning found in Scripture and in the writings of the Fathers of the Church. Finally, when he considered the power that contemporary masters of the spiritual life have on influencing people, Ignatius recommended prudence and discretion, particularly when such masters are compared with the great masters who have been tested by time. Always the enemy of the superlative, in this matter Ignatius becomes the enemy of the comparative. It goes without saying that within these perimeters there was no room for Luther, even though many of his own admirers compared him with Saint Paul. Ignatius, ever since his Alcalá days, had shown a preference for what was safe and proven, and so he was not now presenting this type of navigational chart merely to avoid the kinds of obvious heresy. Rather, he was drawing up a chart to save the less adept from hidden reefs that, because they were hidden, were even more dangerous. Whether such reefs were tabbed "Erasmus" or called by less famous names was of no importance.

We can ask ourselves again, To whom were these precautions directed? There are many who believe Ignatius intended them for those who would make his Exercises, a fact that leads these scholars to conclude that these rules are much like a fine net woven to protect gross heretical errors from making their presence felt. This would mean that the Exercises were the equivalent to a manifesto or a strict program of orthodoxy. It is possible that those who hold this position have not reflected sufficiently on how the Exercises developed. These "Rules for Thinking with the Church," like all of the rules contained in Íñigo's Exercises, follow a certain reasonably clear pattern of evolution. In the beginning there was simply some observational, purely personal notes that he had jotted down; later, these notes became norms that he drew up to help others who were making the Exercises under his direction, and finally, the time came when his companions would implement his special techniques for giving his Exercises. For this reason, these particular rules, like all of the rules contained in the Exercises, were meant to create a style of action, a *modus procedendi* for the directors who would adapt his Exercises in giving them to others, a further reason why there is no connection between these rules and some specific, defined heresy. Even when the Exercises were published in book form—which would not take place until 1548—it would be reserved exclusively for use within the Society. It was not meant to be a book that the retreatant would read but rather an itemized list of methods for the director. The director should know the book, but not necessarily have it with him: "Whoever gives the Exercises," we read in Íñigo's handwritten directory, "should not take the book with him in order to read it to the exercitants, but he should know very well what he is going to talk about to them." Originally, then, these famous rules were an additional proof intended to guarantee the orthodoxy of the author of the *Spiritual Exercises*, whose secret methods could have been disquieting in the opinion of a public that had become hypersensitive to heresy. Furthermore, they also served as a repertoire of criteria to guide future directors of the Exercises in their dealings with retreatants. It is true that, even though these few additional pages remain separate from the book as a whole, they do have a general, universal soundness in coming to grips with something that always has been and always will remain a problem: "The true attitude of mind we ought to have *in* the Church militant," as the original formula read. Ignatius authorized Father André des Freux, also known as Frusius, to make a Latin translation of these rules. In this 1548 version, the formulation is not as rich and is more restrictive. The Latin reads: "Some rules that should be observed for thinking *with* the Church." Although one can appreciate the subtle nuances between the preposition *in* and the preposition *with*, both have the Ignatian imprint.

In summary, the innumerable theological battles of unequal gravity and importance during Ignatius's time resulted in an equal number of bifurcations. Faced with this situation, Ignatius allowed for no option between the authority of science and the authority of religion, between the authority of the most prestigious theologians and the ordinary magisterium of the institutional, hierarchical Church (*quae romana est*—"which is the Roman Church," as he later added to the original text). His partiality here for the magisterium was not based on conservative thinking, or on rigidity, or on fear. Later on, he would show that he knew how to open up new frontiers, and at that time there would be many who would not be able to accept his innovations. He would know how to be flexible, and drawing up the Constitutions would cost him dearly. When this project was completed, he left what he had stipulated in the rules for the Society open to particular living situations and to time-tested experience. Dare we suggest timidity in a man who had a history replete with unheard-of, audacious feats? His unequivocal preference for the teaching directives of the Church was quite simply the result of his faith in Christ, in his desire to perpetuate His "true spouse," in the manifest and ever-active presence of the Holy Spirit Himself.

28
His Native Air

After spending three years studying theology, Master Ignatius's health began to show serious signs of deterioration. He reported that his stomach had been giving him many problems, and that after every fifteen days or so, he would be gripped by terrible stomach pains that would be followed by a fever. On one occasion he was overcome by a spasm that lasted sixteen hours. His autopsy revealed that he had been suffering from gallstones, which were the cause of intermittent and extremely painful attacks. The doctors had tried in vain to apply all types of remedies until there was only one left, and that one had been vouched for as far back as classical antiquity, namely, breathing the air of one's own native land. In old Castilian prose, the Spanish-born Latin epigrammatic poet Martial is made to say: "Experts tell us that people can contract maladies outside of the country where they were born and reared, and that these maladies cannot be cured unless those who are so stricken return to the country they had left. The reason is, they are conditioned by the air of that country where they were nurtured; and in other countries that have different air they may become ailing or ill. This refers not only to the living ones, but these same experts say that even bodies after death fared better in the earth of the country of their ancestors than in others." On this occasion, Ignatius "let himself be persuaded by his companions," who provided him with additional reasons besides his health for going to Spain. They told him that if he went he could visit the families of his Spanish companions and settle any business matters in their name that needed personal attention. Because of the seriousness of the commitment that he and his companions had made at Montmartre, to which he alluded at this juncture in the *Autobiography*, Íñigo had no qualms about leaving. The group would remain intact. So, in the spring of 1535, after being away from his home for thirteen years, he found himself making plans to return. Even though he had been all but forced to make his decision, he was aware that he had an additional reason, a very personal reason, to make the trip back to Azpeitia and Loyola. Once there, he would have the opportunity to make amends for his old image that had resulted from his vanity, his scandalous actions, and his pride.

Ignatius was still in Paris on March 28. On the twenty-fifth, Master Francis Xavier had signed the letter he entrusted to him to deliver to his family. Just as he was about to leave, Ignatius heard some alarming news: someone had denounced him before the inquisitor of Paris, the same man before whom so many people who were accused of conniving with Protestants had to appear. The prevailing atmosphere was so charged with mistrust and suspicion that everything had to be examined twice. This meant that even the private devotions associated with the Exercises had to be looked into and the suspicious cult-like character of this group called the *Iñiguistas* had to be investigated. Ignatius's confessor during his Alcalá days, Father Manoel Miona, was in Paris at the time and was by no means reassured by this news. The same could be said of a short man from Majorca who was teaching mathematics and studying theology. This individual had had frequent dealings with the Iñiguistas and, for its part, the group manifestly wanted him to join them. But he put them off. He was recovering from a sickness he considered very serious when Ignatius came to pay him a visit. He confided to Ignatius that he had been frightened by the prospect of death and was quite impressed by the categorical response his visitor gave him: "For the past fifteen years I have no longer been afraid of death." This response, however, was not enough to dissipate the little Majorcan's misgivings about the present orthodoxy of the Iñiguistas and about their problematic future. These suspicions did not escape the notice of Ignatius and one day, when he met this young man in the chapel of Saint-Etienne-des-Grés, he tried to dispell all suspicions by outlining for him his future plans, and he even told him about persecutions he had undegone at Alcalá and Salamanca, where his innocence had been proven. But all of Ignatius's talk was to no avail. Upon leaving the chapel, the Majorcan, who had a copy of the New Testament in his hand, said farewell to his bothersome sermonizer with these words: "This is the book I want to follow. I do not know how all of you will end up, and so leave me in peace—for good." At a later date, he returned to his native Majorca where he eventually became a canon, but he did not find peace there. Many years afterward he met Ignatius again in Rome and, in 1545, he became a Jesuit and one of Ignatius's greatest admirers. His name was Jerònimi, or in Castilian, Jerónimo Nadal.

He was not the only one to feel a certain mistrust about the Iñiguistas. Alarming news had spread even as far as Navarre about Francis Xavier's association with Íñigo and his group. It is therefore by no means strange that suspicions focusing on Íñigo should have circulated in Paris.

Íñigo went on his own to see the inquisitor, Fra Valentin Liévin. He informed him about his impending journey so that no one could interpret it as a flight, and he told him "that he had companions." I believe that it was because of his concern for his companions and because he was the leader of the group that he asked the inquisitor to hand down a decision on the case. Liévin placed no importance on the denunciation that had been formally made against him, but he did express an earnest desire to see "the manuscript of the Exercises." After he read it, he praised the Exercises highly and asked Ignatius to give him a copy, and this was easily done. Unfortunately, this copy has never been found. If it were extant, it could show us today the state of editing that Íñigo had made by this date. Íñigo was not satisfied with the inquisitor's words of praise, but insisted that a sentence on the proceedings be given in proper form. Liévin showed some disinclination to comply with this request, but Íñigo brought witnesses and a notary with him and thereby forced the court to draw up a formal attestation. Liévin's secretary, Mathieu Ory, O.P., who on May 30, 1536, would become the inquisitor for France, formalized the proceedings in 1537. When it came to his orthodoxy, Íñigo was always dead serious about his reputation.

Finally, at the end of March, after a stay of seven years in Paris, the little Basque left the city never to return. He said good-bye to his friends and promised to meet them again in Venice. The plan was that they would leave Paris for Venice on the feast of the Conversion of Saint Paul, January 25, 1537. This was still a long time off, but Íñigo had confidence that he could leave his companions in the care of Favre. Acting together, they fulfilled the definition Homer gives of freedom, namely "two people walking together." At this time, the group numbered seven but as yet no one yet knew exactly where it was going, but certainly it was headed toward something new. Once more, Íñigo set off alone, but this time not on foot. "He mounted a small horse which his companions had purchased and he started off alone for his native land, finding himself greatly improved along the way." The others remained in Paris, finishing their studies. They had all agreed that their ultimate destination was to be Jerusalem, a place that was both concrete and symbolic. They were dreaming of a utopia, just a few weeks before the death in London of Thomas More, the man who had coined this famous and seductive word, *utopia*—that is, something unattainable in itself that pushes us onward because it has the power of awakening in us insatiable desires and hopes.

By returning to Spain, Íñigo was opening a parenthesis in his life's journey, a momentary deviation from his itinerary. This master had learned to live in his Parisian college like the run-of-the-mill student; he had learned to construct syllogisms and how to distinguish a predicament from a predicable; he had added new and strange terms to his everyday speech— words like *binary*, for example, and other Latinisms. He even took to riding a horse, even though it was a gift. He was living for the future. Had he given up doing heroic deeds? Had he put behind him those endless highways that led to far-off horizons? Had he forgotten what it was like being close to ordinary people, what it meant to be poor and having to beg for one's food? No. Going home to let himself become soft by his ancestral hearth was really more of a penance for him than going back to breathe his native air.

On his way back, he had time to think about, and most especially to "determine," what he should do and how he should
act once he reached his destination. His freedom *from* was in
no danger whatsoever: he would certainly not go to live at the
manor house where his brother Martín would graciously welcome him and where his sister-in-law, Doña Magdalena, would
care for him with the same solicitude that she once had shown
him. The freedom *for* obviously demanded something from
him that the others would never understand, that is, the freedom to be who he now was, *at this time in his life*, acting with the
same nonchalant self-confidence he had felt, particularly when
dealing with the people of his own town when he was with
them before he left them thirteen years ago. Ever since his first
stay at Manresa, he had lodged in many hospitals or hospices
throughout the length and breadth of Europe. So why not go
now, like a typical beggar, to a hospice in his own town? This
thought led him to consider the Magdalena, which was one of
the two hospices in Azpeitia. In order to safeguard his freedom
and to avoid any pressure, he would arrive there incognito,
without any forewarnings.

All this scheming on his part went awry when someone recognized him near Bayonne. Eventually, his brother got wind of
the fact that he was on his way home, and wanted to intervene
in his plans. The two brothers Loyola now deployed a strategy
of moves that did honor to the wolves on their coat-of-arms,
but in the end it was Íñigo who proved to be the more astute
by checkmating Martín. Once Íñigo entered the province of
Guipúzcoa, he left the main road and sought out the most
lonely back roads that looped around "through the mountains." He passed through an inhospitable country rich in legends about robbers and murderers, and on one occasion he
came upon two armed men who passed him by and then
turned around and followed him in great haste. For once, he
confessed, "he felt a moment of fear." In such a situation there
is nothing like engaging the individuals in conversation. This is
precisely what Íñigo did, and as a result he learned that the
two men were servants of his brother who had been sent to
find him. He managed to persuade them to go on ahead of
him and when they did so, he continued on his own way. They
then returned and wanted to accompany him back to the

manor house. In 1595, Potenciana de Loyola, the illegitimate daughter of Íñigo's brother, Don Pedro the priest, would remember a highly wrought adventure that took place during this return journey through the jumbled mountain passes of Guipúzcoa, the itinerary of which we are able to reconstruct today. When nightfall came on, Íñigo took refuge at the inn in Iturriotz, which was a stopover point in this vast open country. The innkeeper did not recognize the traveler, who claimed he was from Azpeitia, but he did speak about him to another guest, a merchant who used to pass by on the same road when business took him to Behovia where he purchased meat for the town of Azpeitia. This man, whose name was Juan de Eguibar, was María Garín's son and therefore Íñigo's foster brother. He and the innkeeper peeked through the planks of the door to the room where Íñigo was spending the night and spied on the mysterious traveler. They saw him on his knees, praying in the middle of the room, and Juan then recognized him as Íñigo. Eguibar went back straightaway to Azpeitia to give the good news of his discovery to the Loyola family. Fearing that if any of them went to where Íñigo was, he would turn around and go back, the family had recourse to a priest named Baltasar de Garagarza, who would act as a go-between. It would be up to Garagarza to certify that the traveler was indeed Íñigo, and, if so, to try to bring him home. The priest did confirm the identity of the traveler, but he had to give up completing the second part of his commission because Íñigo steadfastly refused to have anything to do with him. In the morning, Íñigo was the first to leave the inn, allowing Don Baltasar to follow behind, spying all the while on his movements. At one point, Íñigo momentarily lost his way by swerving too far to the right of the road (there is a lone farmhouse in the mountains, where even to this day tradition has it that Íñigo stopped and asked for proper directions from the people who lived there). But the fact is that he mapped out his itinerary so perfectly that he arrived at Azpeitia from Lasao, that is from the east, which is the opposite side of the valley where the the manor house of Loyola was located. He was thereby able to enter Azpeitia and go directly to the hospice of the Magdalena, which was on the outskirts of the town. He was now breathing the spring air of his native land, air he had not breathed since another springtime, that of 1522, when he made his departure. As for

Azpeitia, the town would breathe in a new Íñigo, no longer the young dashing knight so full of energy, but rather, a wasted, sick, and disarmed man. His "great thoughts" of bygone times had not in any way diminished in their intensity; their focus, however, had been changed substantially.

29

The Hospice in His Native Land: A Beggar and Catechist

The very sober account that Íñigo gives us of his return in no way tells us anything about the commotion it provoked in Azpeitia. "And so, he went to the hospice and later, at a convenient time, went out begging for alms in the neighborhood. In this hospice he began to speak of the things of God with many people who came to visit him, and with God's grace he gathered much fruit. As soon as he arrived, he determined to teach Christian doctrine every day to the children, but his brother roundly objected to this idea, saying that nobody would come to listen to him. He answered that one would be enough. But after he began his catechism classes, there were many who came faithfully to listen to him, and among them was his brother." All of this is true, of course, but his account is merely a résumé of the events that transpired.

In the declarations in preparation for Ignatius's beatification, taken sixty years after these events had taken place, one can still hear the living echo of Íñigo's footsteps walking through his native land. I have studied the testimonies of twenty witnesses. All but one *saw* and *heard* Íñigo. The one exception is Catalina Eguibar, who heard from her mother what she reported. During Íñigo's stay in Azpeitia, these witnesses ranged from nine to twenty-eight years of age, but half of them were between ten and fifteen years old at the time. They were the innocent children who, with insatiable curiosity, surrounded the strange beggar about whom the adults were doing so much talking. When we put together the bits and pieces that were rescued from popular memory, we can reconstruct this chapter of Íñigo's life, right down to details that we would never expect to find. How could we ever disbelieve Domenja de Ugarte, who was twelve years old at the time and a servant in the hospice, when she stated that Íñigo first arrived at the hospice on a Friday afternoon at five o'clock, or when she tells us that one day she discovered his hairshirt and penitential waist-chains? All of these witnesses were well aware of the fact that Íñigo's brother, Martín, and other important people put pressure on him to make him move into Martín's home, or at least to take lodging in a proper inn. Some of these witnesses testified that his family brought a bed from Loyola to the hospice, but that Íñigo refused to use it. His family did not think it seemly that a Loyola should live with beggars in a hospice, and it was even less appropriate that, from the very first day he arrived in town, a Loyola should go around begging from door to door for his daily fare. This was a veritable indignity. His physical appearance was still very much alive in the memories of these witnesses. He dressed poorly in a dark brown serge and he had sandals made of hemp which he sometimes tucked into his belt.

The day after his arrival in Azpeitia (somewhere around the beginning of April 1535), he began begging. Soon, an old woman named Teresa recognized him. How much more so did Catalina de Eguibar realize who he was. After all, her mother had nursed him as a child in their home! In no time, Catalina advised Don Martín de Loyola what was happening. For Martín, this piece of news was one more cause for embarrassment, but Íñigo's action provoked admiration among other people. Given the quality of his status, his begging brought about a miraculous increase of alms and some people even began sending gifts to the hospice. Íñigo gave everything he received to the poor at whose table he ate. An old man, Andrés de Oráa, was more specific when it came to describing the meeting that took place between the two Loyola brothers. He told how Íñigo apologized for his actions to Don Martín, but told him that he had not come to Azpeitia to ask anything from the House of Loyola, nor to live in palaces, but rather to sow the Word of God. Next to begging, preaching the Word of God, he said, would be his principal activity. He told Martín that he had already conquered his fear of failure and so he was prepared to give himself unreservedly, even to one listener who might show interest. Don Martín told him that no one would come to listen to him anyway; however, this prediction merely reflected Martín's resentment and his hope, not the reality of what did take place.

We know that on the day of Saint Mark's litanies, he preached—by way of exception and perched on a plum tree—at the hermitage of Nuestra Señora de Elosiaga. In doing so, he was following the popular tradition that brought people together from the neighboring villages on this feast day (April 25) and at this particular shrine, and we also know that on this occasion he censured the yellow headgear worn by the women and the dyed blond hair of the girls. The regular place for Íñigo's meetings was the hospice church. But soon the church was too small to accommodate those who came to hear him, and so he had to preach in the open air. The people crowded in to see and hear him, and they even climbed the trees and hedges to get a better view of him. The grass and shrubbery around the hospice compound turned brown because they were trodden down by the crowds. There were some days when Íñigo preached in the parish church. According to Ribadeneira, he made a public confession to the crowd for stealing some fruit during his adolescent years, a theft that resulted in an innocent person's being heavily fined. We know that from the feast of the Ascension to Pentecost Sunday he gave an explanation of the Commandments. Every witness remembered his zeal and fervor, and some recall that, despite his reedy voice, the effectiveness and power of what he said could be heard even by those standing far away from him. People came from the nearby villages to hear Íñigo, and some even came from places as far away as Régil and Tolosa. Some of the witnesses remembered that at times he would use strange words that they, as children then, did not very well understand. Such was the case with Juan Odriozola, who remembered his mother talking about the three powers of the soul: the memory, the understanding, and the will. Domenja de Ugarte never forgot the emphasis Íñigo placed on his explanation of the Second and Sixth Commandments.

Very soon the effects of Íñigo's preaching could be seen in the moral lives of the people. Instances of using blasphemous language diminished, and people gave up playing cards and gambling. Many people who had been leading evil lives amended their ways. Íñigo openly condemned those activities and behaviors he saw as harmful to the people. For instance, he condemned concubinage because it sometimes destroyed marriages.

The conversion of three prostitutes, whose names were clearly remembered sixty years later, was a particularly important example of Íñigo's influence. One of Íñigo's cousins, a certain Ana de Anchieta, remembered the words she heard from the mouth of the most famous of these three, Magdalena de Mendiola, whose nickname was "Sendo": "Íñigo's words have rent my heart. I have been serving the world, now I want to serve God." Two of these converted women went on a pilgrimage to Rome. One of them died on the way; Magdalena came back. The third woman did not dare make the pilgrimage because of her age, and so she became a hermit at San Juan de Elormendi. Besides bringing about these conversions, Íñigo was able to help patch up broken marriages, and in some cases he summoned the errant husband back by writing him a letter. He also helped make peace between parents and children. Íñigo was a messenger of peace and concord. Speaking of him, one witness declared: "He achieved what he wanted to do with everyone." This seems to be a good description of his powers of persuasion.

Perhaps this Paris master's favorite activity—certainly the one he performed most frequently—was the most humble activity of all, that is, teaching children their catechism. What a joy it was for her, María de Ulacia confessed, that she learned her catechism from Íñigo! He taught the children how to pray, awakened in them religious sentiments, and explained the Commandments to them. His pupils were usually well-behaved while he was teaching them. The people from Azpeitia, however, could be very mocking and cruel; they could be brutally accurate when they labeled someone with a nickname, and they had a certain tendency to laugh at the expense of others. Listening to Ignatius was one thing, but listening to the one who was trying to answer his questions was something else, especially when the other person had a speech defect. Surely, this was a case when laughing seemed justified. On such an occasion, the catechist, in a friendly enough way, reprimanded a woman who was doing all the laughing, and he told her that he would like to see her in the place of the poor fellow he was quizzing. And what can we say about Martín de Errazti, who according to the witnesses, had an ugly, irregular face? People were always laughing at him in a cruel way, and their laughter hurt Íñigo deeply because Martín was one of the sons of the woman who had nursed him and, like his father before him, he was a blacksmith. Íñigo praised him before all and predicted that one day he would be a great man. Perhaps these words relieved Martín from the pressure he always felt from the people who mocked him, the kind of pressure that can prevent a person from becoming what he would like to be. At any rate, a desire to become a priest took root in the heart of this blacksmith, and in time he became an outstanding confessor. We can never predict the consequences of a word uttered in a kindly, opportune way.

The popular reaction to Íñigo gradually changed from curiosity to veneration, and this veneration in turn spread beyond the town of Azpeitia. He was able to calm an epileptic named Bastida, who lived in the hospice. People considered that what he had done was miraculous. A woman from the coastal town of Zumaya who had a lung disease also came to see him, and when she left, she said that she was feeling better. Twenty days later, this grateful woman returned, bringing gifts and a basket of freshly caught fish. Íñigo asked her to sell her fish in the market and give away the money she made to the poor. She replied that she already had money to give as alms and that he should accept the fish caught in the Bay of Biscay. Íñigo had to accept it, but he shared it with the poor. On that day he experienced the generosity and proverbial kind-heartedness of the *arrantzales*, that is, the fishermen of the Cantabrian coast.

Because of his growing reputation as a healer, one day some people brought Íñigo a young girl from the province of Biscay who was thought to be possessed. Íñigo advised these people that he did not "read the Mass," but that he would make the sign of the cross over her and that he would pray for her. This incident gives us the opportunity to recall that, even though he preached, he was not yet a priest. This fact notwithstanding, the priests and clerics of Azpeitia were the special targets in his plan to carry out a reform. The force of his personal holiness and his exemplary life, plus the fact that his brother held the patronage over the parish church of Azpeitia, made it possible that during his stay one written agreement was reached between the feudal patron, the rector, and priests of the parish. Then another one was drawn up between the *Isabelitas*, the local name for Azpeitia's Franciscan nuns at the monastery of the Immaculate Conception, and the signatories of the first document. This agreement solved once and for all an old controversy between the nuns and the leading faction at the church. In addition to solving this problem, he also tried to put some order into the manner of living of the priests who accepted his rule of life, according to one of the witnesses, "as if he had been a bishop or an appointed judge." At his suggestion, the people reintroduced the old devotion of praying for the souls in purgatory whenever the church bells rang. He even introduced the custom of having the church bells ring at noon, inviting all to pray for those who were living in mortal sin. The Loyola family perpetuated this custom and gave an annual sum of money to insure its continuance. One witness saw in this decision on the part of the Loyola family a kind of compensation for the heritage that rightfully belonged to Íñigo. He was also unquestionably influential in a decision reiterated by the town *corregidor* that reinforced an order handed down by the Catholic monarchs for the town of Azpeitia. This precept forbade the wearing of the *toca*, a kind of headdress, to all women who were not legitimately married.

Íñigo's most lasting work was his organization of public and ordinary assistance for the poor and needy. Ordinances approved by the town council on May 23, 1535, give us some notion of how this beneficent work was conceived. It was subsidized by the man who was the first to recognize Íñigo at Iturriotz, Juan de Eguibar, who donated a capital of 160 *escudos*. Eguibar, a man of means, was a supplier of the butcher shops in Azpeitia. According to the plan, Eguibar, who was childless, would eventually manage the future revenues accruing from his original endowment. These ordinances were designed to stamp out begging and, at the same time, to assist genuinely poor people who needed food but were ashamed to beg. The ordinances stipulated that two delegates from the town, who were to be chosen on a yearly basis, would be officially in charge of collecting alms on Sundays and feast days and then distributing them among those poor whose names had been previously registered on an official list. The hospice and this assistance were made available only to those who were deemed to be the truly needy. Íñigo himself certainly qualified as someone who was entitled to this assistance, because he owned absolutely nothing. But there is something altogether paradoxical here when we consider that he, who was the most confirmed beggar in all of Europe, wanted to stamp out begging. In taking this stand, he allied himself with the leaders of the fight against poverty, whom he had seen in Flanders and who were the inspiration behind the program outlined by Luis Vives in his treatise entitled *De subventione pauperum* (1526).

During the three months he spent in Azpeitia, Íñigo was much too active to have time to think a great deal about his health. We know that apart from his ordinary ailments he had some serious bouts with an illness that forced him to be bedridden for awhile. Once when he was ill, he was visited and cared for by his nieces, María Sanz de Arriola, daughter of Petronila de Loyola, and Simona de Alzaga, daughter of Juaniza de Loyola. On one particular night he told them to blow the candle out and go to bed, and there was nothing further they could say that would make him change his mind. His will was such that "others did what he said." He had already told his family that he did not come back to Azpeitia to visit the manor house and, even though they put all kind of pressure on him to compromise in this matter, he paid a visit there only once—apart from the day he left his native land for the last time. Domenja de Ugarte, who was twelve years old at the time, remembered the scene vividly. Doña Magdalena, accompanied by other members of the family, came to the hospice one day and begged Íñigo to come home for a visit. He said that he was tired, and that he would go some other day. Doña Magdalena continued her pleading and added that he should oblige her "for the sake of your parents' souls." She then threw herself on her knees and begged him "through the Passion of Christ" to comply with her request. Íñigo answered: "You speak to me of the Passion of Christ? For the Passion of Christ I will go not only to Loyola but even to Vergara." (Vergara is a township in the Basque country, about thirty miles from Loyola. To get there from Loyola one has to cross a number of difficult mountain ranges.) Probably Domenja did not hear everything that the anguished Doña Magdalena was asking of her brother-in-law. The only thing she knew was that he went to the manor house at night, but he did not sleep there, and that he was back at the hospice the next morning. We would never know what transpired at Loyola that night were it not for what Íñigo confided to the Jesuit priest Pedro de Tablares many years later. It was not out of any family pressure or because of blood ties that Íñigo made a visit to his ancestral home that night; rather, it was to accomplish a daring spiritual mission. Although the following account of this event was passed from Tablares to Father Gil González Dávila, and then from González Dávila to Father Cristóvão de Castro, it still manages to retain the freshness and vigor of the original version. "He was told that one of them [one of his relatives, probably his brother Martín] was living in concubinage and that every night the woman made her way [into the manor house] through a secret entrance. One night [Íñigo] waited for her, came face to face with her, and asked: 'What are you doing here?' She explained to him what the situation was. He took her inside the house and installed her in his room where he kept watch over her until the morning so that she would not sin. Then he put her out-side because up until that hour it was impossible to let anyone out of the house. When Íñigo said, 'I took her to my own room,' Father Tablares replied, 'I wouldn't have done that.' 'I did,' Father Ignatius responded, 'because I knew perfectly well that I could have done it.' Then, suddenly realizing what he had said, he turned around immediately and said: 'May God forgive you because you made me say something I had no intention of telling.'" Íñigo's words that had so often con-verted others had no effect on Don Martín, and so he had recourse to this desperate action in order to bring the sin of his brother into the light and also to show compassion for his beloved sister-in-law. This was the last sermon he preached, not so much in words as in action, in the manor house that he now left, presumably, never to enter again.

But when was the last time he visited the manor house? There is a document drawn before a notary that seems to confirm the fact that Íñigo was indeed present at the house in which he was born on July 23. Real or spurious, this document deals with the purchase of a chestnut horse for thirty ducats. Beltrán, the heir to the Loyola title and properties, was the buyer; the seller was Beltrán López de Gallaiztegui, the son of Magdalena de Loyola. Both men were Íñigo's nephews. The notary was Pedro García de Loyola, the illegitimate son of Íñigo's father, who had been legitimized by Charles V and appointed clerk of the local court. The document was signed at the Loyola manor house and one of the witnesses was Íñigo López de Loyola. Did Íñigo's nephew present this gift to his uncle as a going-away present for the journey upon which he was about to embark? Did Íñigo spend the night at Loyola after he signed this document? These are questions we cannot answer.

What we do know is that after spending three months in Azpeitia, Íñigo left as his legacy a halo of deeds, both praiseworthy and spiritually fruitful, that would be remembered for a long time to come. Many people begged him to remain there because he had accomplished so much good for the people. But he told them that "unless he left he could not serve God as he should and could." He was now in good health and "determined to leave" so that he could settle the business affairs of his companions in Paris. Of course, his plan was to depart on foot and without a cent. This caused his brother Martín to feel ashamed, and his shame soon turned into annoyance, just as it had thirteen years previously. As a way of compromise, Íñigo agreed that Don Martín and other members of his family should accompany him to the provincial frontier. From here, he made his way toward Pamplona, following in the opposite direction the same road he had taken many years before as a wounded casualty of a memorable war. At the Navarre border, he dismounted his horse, and getting rid of his money and all his goods, he once again took up a lifestyle of poverty and begging. So he continued on his way toward Pamplona *alone and on foot.*

30
Alone and on Foot: Azpeitia to Venice

The months that followed Íñigo's departure should not be viewed as a haphazard interlude, but rather as a prolongation of the plan that had been worked out in Paris. The *Autobiography* is extremely laconic at this point: "He headed for Pamplona; and from there to Almazán, the hometown of Father Laínez; then to Sigüenza and Toledo; and from Toledo to Valencia. In all of these hometowns of his companions he would not take anything for himself, though a great deal had been offered to him and with great insistence." This itinerary that took him four months to complete began in Navarre, the native land of Francis Xavier. Xavier's parents were already dead and his sister Magdalena, who had been a Poor Clare, had also died in 1533. Ana, another sister, had just died. His brothers, Miguel and Juan, had accepted the amnesty given by Charles I in 1524, settled down, and were now married. We do not know if Íñigo visited Miguel at Xavier castle, but certainly he met Juan, who was living in Obanos. Íñigo carried with him as a credential a precious letter from Master Francis, who had already been ten years away from home. This letter was of the greatest importance because in it Master Francis tried to counteract any and all ill feelings Juan may have entertained about Íñigo "as a result of reports given him by certain wretched and contemptuous men." The youngest of the Xavier clan claimed he was not able to identify the men who were spreading these rumors among the members of his family, since everyone in Paris treated him in such a friendly fashion: "It is difficult to know who they are and God knows how much it pains me that I have to delay punishing them as they deserve." But, he declared, the only thing that gave him consolation was *quod differtur, non aufertur* or "what is reported is not, on that account, ignored." Master Xavier balanced these threats against those unknown calumniators of Íñigo with the warmest praises of Master Íñigo, for "I will never be able as long as I live to repay him the great debt of gratitude I owe him." This was so, not only because of the "many times he has assisted me in my needs with money and friends," but also "because he has been the reason why I gave up evil companions whom I, in my lack of experience, did not recognize as such." Francis added that those evil associates appeared outwardly good but they were in fact full of heresies, "as has been proven by events." No "evildoer"—the term must give some idea of what Juan had heard—"surrenders himself into the hands of the one he has offended." The fact was that Íñigo was "such a great man of God," and his good way of life was exemplary for all to see. Francis was happy to advise Juan that "your Grace can learn more about my needs and burdens from him than from any other person in the world, since he knows better than anyone else on earth my miseries and needs." Therefore, Juan should receive Íñigo "as you would my own self." The letter says nothing about what Xavier has been doing nor does it inform Juan of his intended plans. Perhaps he had informed Íñigo to bring his brother up to date on this aspect of his life. On the other hand, the letter specifically requests that Juan send some financial help to Francis "in order to alleviate my extreme poverty," and, toward the end of this piece of correspondence, we are informed that Diego Laínez's father would be the one who would send to Paris the monies that Íñigo collected for his companions during his stay in Spain.

We do not know anything about Íñigo's stay in Almazán. Years later, when Favre visited this hometown of Laínez, he had nothing but praise to say about the Laínez family. Íñigo did not go to Bobadilla in the province of Palencia because the mother and father of his companion Nicolás Bobadilla had already died. On his way to Madrid he had to go through

Alcalá, and, although he mentioned Sigüenza as one of the cities visited, he makes no mention whatsoever of the city on the Henares where he had lived for more than one whole year. But this oversight did not imply that he had forgotten the companions of his Alcalá days. When he got to Madrid, he met Juan de Arteaga in the royal court, but Íñigo was not able to win him over to accepting his latest project. While he was visiting the court he also renewed his contacts with Doña Leonor de Mascarenhas, the governess to Prince Philip—the son and heir to Charles V. Many years later, after Prince Philip became King Philip II, he was studying Alonso Sánchez Coello's portrait of Saint Ignatius and was heard to say: "I met Father Ignatius and this is certainly his face, although when I saw him, he had more of a beard." The only possible explanation we can give for this statement is that the future Philip II and Saint Ignatius of Loyola were introduced to one another on this occasion, when Íñigo visited Doña Leonor de Mascarenhas in Madrid during his stay there in 1535. Íñigo then went on to Toledo, where he visited the family of Alfonso Salmerón and most probably Dr. Pedro de Peralta, to whom he gave the Spiritual Exercises in Paris in 1529. At this date Peralta was a canon and a preacher in the cathedral. All of his efforts to regroup the original threesome from Alcalá and the first group that he had formed in Paris were to no avail. "None of them was prepared to follow him," he noted. When he got to the kingdom of Valencia, he went to the Carthusian monastery of Vall de Cristo near Segorbe, where he visited with one of his former exercitants, Dr. Juan de Castro. He remained at the monastery for eight days and left a vivid impression during his stay with the monks. Íñigo, who deep down was a frustrated Carthusian, was able to tell his spiritual son about the future plans he and his Paris companions had made concerning the future. In later years he would keep in contact through an exchange of letters with the Carthusian doctor he had known during his Paris days.

So concluded Íñigo's Spanish journey. His immediate plan was now to go on to Italy, where he would pursue his theological studies until the arranged date arrived for his meeting with the group in Venice. Many people, even the Carthusians at Vall de Cristo, attempted to discourage him from making the trip by sea. The Turkish pirate Barbarossa (Khayr-ad-Din), who had been chased out of Tunis by Charles I two months earlier, had conquered the fortress of Mahon on the Balearic island of Minorca and was now menacing the coast of Valencia with his galleys. "Although they told him enough to frighten him, nothing they said made him hesitate." Probably he embarked from Valencia, and, although we do not know if the ship put in at Barcelona, we do know that he disembarked at Genoa. During the crossing the ship lost its rudder in a frightful storm, causing all on board to think that there was no way they were going to escape death. Íñigo did not let this opportunity pass without making a keen observation of his reaction on this particular occasion as he came face to face with death. It was a reaction that bears comparison with other reactions in similar circumstances. He told us nothing about what his thoughts were on death while he confronted it at Pamplona and Loyola. When he believed that he was dying at Manresa, he flattered himself by thinking that he was justified, a saint, but he recognized these thoughts as a temptation and begged the people who had come to see him that if, in the future, they found him in such a state, they should cry out and remind him that he was a sinner. During the crossing to Genoa, he went back over his past life carefully and had no fear because of the sins he had committed, only confusion and sorrow for not having made better use of the gifts the Lord had given him. When, in 1550, he again believed he was going to die, the very thought of death brought him so much joy and consolation that he had to put it aside as being indicative of selfishness. These three attitudes toward death reflect the successive spiritual states he had come to know.

No sooner had he arrived in Genoa than he took off not for Venice, but for Bologna. Very probably he wanted to register at Bologna's university. It was in the thick of winter and the journey was most difficult. The days were short; the roads had been turned into quagmires because of the rains; and it was bitter cold. The path he followed through the Apennines hugged a cliff along a river bank. The river was swollen and the farther he went, the higher and narrower the path became, until he had to crawl along on his hands and knees, clutching at the bushes and being unable to either turn back or make much progress in moving forward. This time, he admitted that he had "great fear." Every time he moved he thought he would fall into the river. In the large catalog of punishments he had to go through during his lifetime, this certainly was by far the greatest. "This was indeed the greatest physical strain and exertion that he had ever experienced, but in the end he made it." When he was just about to enter the city of Bologna and was crossing over a small wooden bridge, he fell into a creek and came out of it soaked to the bone and covered with sludge. "The people who were watching, and there were many there, had a good laugh." This was his introduction to some very difficult days ahead. He proceeded to go through the whole town begging, but he did not get a single *quatrino*, not even a crust of bread. At last he was welcomed into the famous College of Spain founded by Cardinal Gil de Albornoz, where he encountered some former acquaintances, and was able to dry out his clothes and refresh himself. At first, he thought he could study in Bologna and, with this plan in mind, he even went so far as to get some money from the Catalan woman, Isabel Roser. But eventually he could not take Bologna's cold, heavy fog. He was confined to bed for eight days—from December 11 to the eighteenth—with chills, fever, and his old companion, stomach cramps. By this date he had developed his Christian theory of sickness that he shared in part a letter to Isabel Roser, dated 1532. God sends us sickness and infirmities, he said, "to show us the shortness of this life." He continued: "And when I think that He visits those whom He loves through these infirmities, I can feel no sadness or pain, because I believe a servant of God who goes through a sickness comes out of it already half a doctor, because he can straighten out and order his life for the glory and service of God." Without picking up any more academic diplomas, but halfway through his coursework for a doctorate in virtue, he made his departure from Bologna toward the end of December 1535. He went on to Venice, where he soon felt much better. He still had a long year—the whole of 1536—before the arrival of the agreed-upon date when he would meet with his companions.

31
Venice, the Crossroads

Fifteen thirty-six was a relatively calm year in Íñigo's life, a year spent in Venice where his health seemed to improve. He had time to study theology on his own because there was not one single university in that extraordinary city on the Adriatic, the mother of so many skillful diplomats. A contributing factor to the peaceful quality of this year was the fact that he did not have to make so many trips and excursions; but especially it was because he had been offered accommodations by "a very good and erudite man," who was, according to some authorities, Don Martín de Zornoza, the Spanish consul in Venice, whom Íñigo described, in a letter written in 1540, as "an old friend and brother in the Lord." According to others, the man who accommodated Íñigo at this time was Andrea Lippomani, prior of the Trinità. The alms he received regularly that year from Barcelona—read Isabel Roser—and from Paris, freed him from being a burden on anyone and from having to beg for his food. Consequently, he felt no anxiety, no pressure during this year's stay in Venice. His old friend from Barcelona, the Archdeacon Jaume Cassador, who would soon be named that city's bishop, wrote inviting him to preach a series of Lenten sermons in Barcelona. In his answer, Íñigo assured Cassador that, although he desired to somehow meet the needs of the city to which he owed "more than to any other city in the world," he really preferred "to preach in a minor capacity on subjects that are more easily understood and of less importance . . . like a poor man," and most certainly not "with the embarrassing abundance I now enjoy because of my studies." He advised him that as soon as he finished his studies he was going to send Isabel Roser his books, as he promised her he would do the previous spring. Before the year was out, he would make the same promise to his protectoress in Paris, probably one of the ladies-in-waiting to Queen Leonor. "I enjoy perfect bodily health and I await the coming of Lent so that I can put aside my studies and can concentrate on the things of greater importance, duration, and value." Although he was standing fast to his commitment to his Paris companions, he told Cassador that his future was still open and uncertain. Would he be returning to Catalonia? He promised Cassador that he would not preach anywhere else in Spain until he saw him, his dear friend, once again. But such a return was conditioned by a sentiment right out of Don Quixote's mouth. The Don said that he too would return, provided "that God our Lord does not employ me outside of Spain in enterprises that are more painful and humiliating for me, and whether they will be painful or humiliating I do not know." Here, especially, one is reminded of the verses from the poet: "I am today's pilgrim. It doesn't matter where I go. Tomorrow? Tomorrow may never come." Íñigo lived in terms of the tomorrow of the still greater, the *plus ultra.*

He did not dedicate these days in Venice exclusively to quiet study. It was here in this city that the solitary Íñigo took up letter writing, and some of these Venice letters are particularly rich in doctrinal matters, such as the two he addressed to Sister Teresa Rajadell, a Benedictine nun in Barcelona. In these letters he gives very precise rules for prayer and the discernment of spirits that, when we read between the lines, teach us a great deal about his own experience. He frequently spoke in these Venice letters about the trials that affected others and he showed himself to be much more sensitive than one might suspect to the problems of those about him. There is one sentence in the letter addressed to Jaume Cassador, which we cited above, that is particularly relevant in this regard. Íñigo was commenting on the community tensions within Sister Teresa Rajadell's monastery. "I certainly could hardly consider him a true Christian," he wrote, "whose heart would not be pierced when he sees so many setbacks in the service of God our Lord." There were more examples of failure than stories of success for the Church throughout Europe during those days, and it is good to realize that this sad state of affairs did indeed affect Íñigo. He did not lend his voice publicly to the so-called critical spirits of the age, and he did not consider anyone a Christian who, in pointing out vices within the Church, caused the Church to suffer, and he did not believe the impact they had on others to be Christian. His love for the Church, "the true spouse of Jesus Christ," did not blind him or prevent him from recognizing the abuses within the Church. We should also mention here the very personal letter that he addressed from Venice to his old friend and confessor, Dr. Manoel Miona, during his stay at Alcalá and later in Paris. This letter is dated November 16, 1536. Miona still had some misgivings about Íñigo's future, and he had put off making the Exercises. It was because of his guardedness toward the Exercises that Íñigo wrote and begged him to take the step immediately and "do what I have already requested of you" because "knowing as I do that the Exercises are the best means I can think of in this life both to help a man to benefit himself and to bring help, profit, and advantage to many others. Even though you felt yourself in no special need, you will see how they will help you to serve others beyond anything you ever dreamed of." Miona eventually did what Íñigo requested, and as a result he entered the Society in 1545.

While he was in Venice, Íñigo also busied himself with organizing a program where an exchange of spiritual conversations could take place. It is easy for us to imagine that these reunions were something more than simply pious get-togethers. During his stay in Venice, the city was a very special place for feeling the pulse of Christianity. Even though its two famous bells continued to regulate daily life—the *Marangona* called the people to prayer and work at dawn, and the *Realtina* tolled at sunset indicating the end of the working day—it was really no longer the city it had been in 1522. At that time, northern Italy had been the theater of endless wars and, even though the relations with the Sublime Porte had since worsened, the Venetian doges were trying to work out trade arrangements that would be beneficial to themselves as well as to the Turks. Wealth and splendor existed side by side, but the number of orphans and widows was also great. Here in Venice, Western culture mixed with that of the East, as did the culture of the Protestant North with that of the Catholic South. The city was surrounded by a veritable mosaic of different races and peoples. All of the corruptive elements of Christianity could be found here, as well as movements for reform. Its geographic proximity to the empire placed it in an ideal position for the expansion of Protestantism. On the other hand, Íñigo could watch at close range the work of the Venetian aristocrat, Jerome Emiliani, who had gone from being an irreligious soldier to the founder of a religious order in 1528. The "Company of the Servants of the Poor" was a congregation whose purpose was to attend to the most pressing needs of the impoverished. Emiliani's group later became known as the Clerics Regular of Somascha, named after the town between Milan and Bergamo where they worked. Eventually they simply came to be called the Somaschi. This group was not a religious order, but rather an association made up of reformed priests. Jerome, who was a patrician of the Venetian republic and who is today a canonized saint, was similar to Íñigo in many respects. He dressed in rags and begged for his food; he cared for marginal people and victims of the plague; and he devoted himself to the needs of abandoned children. In 1535, both men returned to their respective homes for a visit, Íñigo to Azpeitia and Jerome to Venice, and just as Íñigo had done in Azpeitia, Jerome lived in a hospice, where his family was obliged to go whenever they wanted to see him. He was driven by a desire to teach catechism to the young. His example attracted followers, and his work extended rapidly from Venice to Milan, Paris, Bergamo, Como, and Brescia. During Íñigo's year of waiting in Venice, 1536, the Company held its third chapter meeting at Brescia. In February of the following year, Jerome Emiliani, who was a contemporary of Niccolò Machiavelli and Balthazar Castiglione, died from a disease he caught while attending the sick. At the same time, while another Venetian patrician, the humanist Cardinal Pietro Bembo, was delivering unctuous dissertations designed to prove that real love found its culmination in divine love, Jerome Emiliani was dressing the repugnant wounds of soldiers and civilians at the Hospital for the Incurables, founded by Cajetan Thiene or Gaetano da Chieti, whose motto was: "For those who love God all things are easy."

Venice had even more to recommend it as a nerve center of Europe. Its prestigious book publishers and printers had made it a very important cultural center, where diverse and conflicting ideas clashed or converged. At the time of Íñigo's stay in the city, the theological scene in Italy was teeming with controversy and turmoil. In 1530 and again in 1534, Tullio Crispoldi, a humanist and member of Cajetan's Oratory of Divine Love, had stirred up the cauldron by his sermons on predestination and faith versus works, themes that clearly resonated with Protestant ideology. The Dutch theologian and humanist, Albertus Pighius or Pigge, took to his pulpit to answer Crispoldi's assertions. At this juncture, Gasparo Contarini felt obliged to step in and clarify theological ambiguities and at the same time to set up pastoral guidelines for preaching. Besides being a renowned Venetian statesman, Contarini was also a theologian of considerable repute and, since 1535, the year he was given the red hat, one of the Church's most outstanding reform-minded cardinals. Accordingly, he requested that all preachers praise the belief in the efficacy of works and free will and that they avoid the topic of predestination because some people seemed to draw false consequences from any consideration of this subject. Venice was the city of spiritual currents promoted by Cardinals Contarini; Reginald Pole, the last Catholic archbishop of Canterbury; and Bishop Gregorio Gheri, bishop of Fano until 1524, and later bishop of Bologna. At the same time, the city was the refuge for crypto-heretics, men like the Augustinian friar named Musæus, who had taken flight from Siena, and Antonio Bruccioli, a refugee from Florence. After the sack of Rome in 1527, the Theatines, an offshoot of the Oratory of Divine Love, founded by Cajetan Thiene and Gian Pietro Carafa, had also taken refuge in Venice. Carafa at that date was the bishop of Chieti (Latin *Theatimum*), and since he considered himself a guardian of orthodoxy, he regarded the teachings of two of Venice's prominent humanists, Luigi Lippomani, and the theologian and humanist, and later cardinal, Gregorio Cortese, with great suspicion. Lippomani, as bishop of Verona, would one day preside at the Council of Trent. *Chietino*, that is a Theatine, was a pejorative term in the mouths of some religious figures and also in the writings of others, such as the Florentines Pietro Aretino and Iacopo Bonfadio, who considered the Theatines nothing more than hypocrites. At the same time, the books and sermons of

Bernadino Ochino, the general of the Capuchins who went over to the Protestant side in 1539; Cardinal Marino Grimani, another Venetian humanist bishop and afterward cardinal; and the theologian, Girolamo Seripando, who likewise would receive the crozier and cardinal's hat, had captured and were holding the attention of the well-educated citizens of Venice. A few years later, the silent battle between the intransigents and the spirituals would reach its zenith, thereby showing the internal crisis within the movement that naively had been called the *Evangelicalism* of the scholars and humanists. A Dominican theologian named Ambrogio Catharino, who would later play an important role at Trent, bears considerable responsibility for precipitating this crisis. Among other things, he criticized anyone who preached at all about such matters to the ordinary people, arguing that such sermons should be reserved for those who had reached such a degree of spiritual perfection that they would act only out of the pure love of God.

We know nothing about the theological studies Íñigo made on his own while he was in Venice. Obviously he was not insensitive to the theological trends that were whirling about Italy, and, most certainly, his reaction can be seen in the last of the four "Rules for the True Sense Which We Should Have in the Church Militant," which he composed at this time, that is, between 1538 and 1541. These four rules probably came about as a result of his Italian experience, and more exactly they are most likely due to his Venetian experience. Although he touches on some fundamental points of dogma in these four rules, his point of reference is how these dogmas should be preached to the people. It is not difficult to discern in his directives an echo of the situation in Italy that we described above: "We should not make it a habit of speaking much of predestination," most especially in a deterministic sense, because by doing so we can lead people to become indolent and indifferent about the efficacy of good works. Likewise, one should not speak of grace so highly "that the poison of doing away with liberty is engendered"; one should not praise the pure love of God excessively because we should not forget that, when a person does not have the aptitude for pure love, filial fear and servile fear of God are also "very pious and very holy." Íñigo intended all of these rules to be both practical and prudent guidelines that would enable his friends in the Lord to give direction in their pastoral apostolate. They were also designed to make explicit just exactly where he himself stood on such matters "in times as dangerous as ours."

In spite of all his intentions, however, Íñigo was not totally free from suspicion. Apart from his studies and meetings, he kept himself busy at his preferred task, that is, giving the Spiritual Exercises to others. To paraphrase 1 John 1, he was not able to keep silent about what he had seen with his own eyes and touched with his own hands, namely, the Word Incarnate. He was not selling a how-to program for self-control nor was he peddling nostrums designed to achieve equanimity. He wanted to go to the root of man's destiny; he wanted him to see what his destiny was. He wanted man to be able to approach God and the world with an attitude of gratitude and service. This was the "Principle and Foundation" upon which his Exercises were built. He gives us the names of some distinguished persons who made these Exercises. One was Master Pier Contarini, the procurator at the Hospital of the Incurables, who was a relation of Cardinal Gasparo Contarini and a friend of the promoters of the spiritual reform in Venice. A year later, Íñigo would address a beautiful letter to him from Vivarolo in which he would pay unlimited praise to the life of poverty. The letter was written in the rather tolerable Latin that he had learned after he had already passed his thirtieth birthday. "If you have possessions [his correspondent belonged to a very wealthy family], they should not possess you," he wrote, "nor should you be possessed by anything temporal." This had become Íñigo's motto. It was a motto that had grown more out of his own personal experience than from some theoretical principle he had latched onto because, he confessed to Pier, he savored more each day what Saint Paul had written in the Second Letter to the Corinthians (6:2): "Yet here we are . . . having nothing and yet owning everything." His second noteworthy exercitant was Dr. Gasparo de' Dotti or de Doctis, the vicar general of the pontifical nuncio to Venice and later *Uditore* of Cardinal Rodolfo Pio de Carpi. The third was a Spaniard, who some have identified as a certain Rodrigo de Rojas, who lived in Naples ten years later and was a friend of

Íñigo and Laínez. Others claim that he was another Rojas, the one who had accompanied the celebrated convert, Magdalena of Azpeitia, on her return trip to Guipúzcoa in 1539.

He mentioned a fourth exercitant in his autobiography, and that was Diego de Hoces, a cleric from Málaga who was both well educated and virtuous. He had known Íñigo at Alcalá and on his return trip from Jerusalem met him again in Venice. He conversed a great deal with Master Íñigo, but not less than with the bishop of Chieti, Gian Pietro Carafa, who had taken refuge in Venice after the sack of Rome in 1527 and who was living with the Theatines near the Church of San Niccolò di Tolentino. Hoces had a desire to make the Exercises, but he had never put his good intentions into execution. At last he took the big step and on the third day of his retreat, he made a surprising confession to Íñigo: he had been frightened that in making the Exercises he might be taught some wrong doctrine and had come armed with books that hopefully would guard him against eventual deceptions. This attitude came as a result of what "someone else had told him." It is all but absolutely certain that the one who had sowed this reticence in his soul was Bishop Carafa. (Carafa was destined to be named a cardinal in a short time, and a few years later would be elected Pope Paul IV.) Hoces profited to such an extent from the Exercises that, as happened with Íñigo's companions in Paris, he expressed the wish "to follow the pilgrim's manner of life."

Did Íñigo and Carafa contend with one another over which of their respective groups Hoces would belong? The quarrel between the two was probably deeper than this one issue, and it certainly had longer consequences. Carafa and Loyola present us with an example of two mutually repellant personalities. Even though the ambitions of each were basically the same, their methods in dealing with others were very different indeed. What the bishop did was insidious and, from an objective point of view, slanderous. He implanted in the mind of Hoces a deep suspicion of Íñigo's orthodoxy and he even attempted to feed these suspicions, as time went on. All of this was not simply a distant war waged behind smokescreens. Íñigo and the bishop had met face to face and their conversation had revolved around the reformed priests under Carafa's jurisdiction. They discussed the topic in depth and it would not be hazardous to suggest that Carafa gave way to a fit of anger, which as pope twenty years later, he was still not able to dissimulate. We know Íñigo's viewpoints because of a letter he sent Carafa. He did not seem concerned whether the letter was well thought out or not. With startling simplicity Íñigo requested—it was a layman standing before a bishop—that his letter be received with the same affection, goodwill, and sincerity with which it had been written. He began with an undeniable fact—the feeble growth of the Company of the Theatines that had been authorized by a brief from Pope Clement VII in 1524. And "as the little ones do ordinarily before the great," he dared to give what he thought were the ordinary reasons why the group had not increased. The first cause was the style of life of Carafa himself. Íñigo said that he personally was not scandalized that the person who was the leader of the group had better clothes because his dignity as a bishop and his advanced years demanded it. On the other hand, he believed it would have been "the part of wisdom to call to mind" the examples of the older models, like Francis of Assisi and Dominic de Guzmán (as he himself had done at Loyola), and the way that they had given example and orders to their *compañías* (note the word he used, "companies," or in Latin, *societates*, "societies"). Everything perhaps was permissible, but that did not mean that everything was necessarily good, according to what Saint Paul wrote in 1 Corinthians 6:12. Instead of indulging in weakness, the leader should give an example of "going further ahead." There is a considerable amount of autobiographical material expressed in this principle. Secondly, Íñigo examined the style of Carafa's new congregation. The members were too concentrated on the internal life of the group itself; they were addicted to the singing of the Divine Office; they depended on alms, and yet they did not go out and preach nor did they practice the corporal works of mercy or undergo the humiliation of having to beg. Íñigo did not dare put in writing other matters that were of even greater importance. It is not difficult for us to deduce from this negative description the positive ideal of a religious order that he had at this period of his life.

Íñigo's criticism of Carafa, a criticism that was as harsh as it was frank, had the effect of producing an open break between these two "leaders and chiefs," and when, in a very short time afterward, Carafa was made a cardinal and sent to Rome, Íñigo would have to suffer the consequences of the prelate's naked animosity. During the whole of his lifetime, Íñigo never revealed any of the details of his face-to-face meeting with Carafa, at which time he not only criticized the other's ideas, but he also laid bare his own most personal convictions. Only heroism—the "exploits," at first human and later divine, that the young man and subsequent convert performed—really seizes people and produces life. Íñigo's dreams were of seasoned heroes and not of monks installed in the heart of the city. Thanks to the group he had left behind in Paris, his dream would soon become a reality.

32

The Parisian Masters, "Novices at Walking"

This time, the small group of select men lived up to his expectations. Íñigo's departure had saddened them, but the group was solid enough to stick together and it could even have almost gone on without him. All of them had been dedicating themselves fullheartedly to their studies, and at the same time they continued confessing and receiving Holy Communion weekly and kept up their practice of daily meditation. Their intimate friendship with one another bound them together and proved to be a great support for each one separately. After all, what ultimately kept them together was Christ, not Íñigo. This was the reason why, despite Íñigo's absence, on August 15, 1535 and 1536, they renewed the vow they had taken together at Montmartre on August 15, 1534. They also had the satisfaction of seeing three additional companions join them. All three were students, but from separate colleges and from very different French-speaking regions. They were Claude Jay, a native of Savoy; Paschase Broët, who was from Picardy; and Jean Codure, a native of Provence. Two were priests, Jay and Broët, and the latter had been ordained more than ten years ago. They had gotten to know the original companions through Pierre Favre, who up until then had been the only ordained priest. Favre was the head of the group, not as a superior, nor as a second Íñigo, nor as a vice-Íñigo, but simply as the one who had the most seniority among the

Iñiguistas. The perfect cohesiveness of the group came about as a result of the fact that all of them lived out what was contained in the Exercises. Favre showed a great mastery in using the Ignatian method with others. He had a special grace for the ministry of the confessional and a real gift of sympathy that attracted many people to him. One of his many penitents was the young seventeen-year-old Portuguese boy named Luis Gonçalves da Câmara. Among those to whom he gave the Exercises, we should single out the English humanist and exile, John Helyar because Favre gave Helyar the early transcription of the *Exercises* Íñigo had made and left behind in Paris, and Helyar kept this manuscript.

On October 3, 1536, Pierre Favre, Simão Rodrigues, Alfonso Salmerón, Nicolás Alonso Bobadilla, Claude Jay, Jean Codure, and Paschase Broët were given their master of arts degrees. Diego Laínez and Francis Xavier had already received theirs. However, these two were not able to obtain their master of theology degree because this would take many more years and the date for their departure from Paris, January 27, 1537, was fast approaching. They even had to push up this date to the previous November 15 because of the war that had broken out between France and Spain. Before leaving, Laínez and Xavier did manage to get a parchment attesting to the fact that they had studied theology in the Theological Faculty of Paris for one and a half years. The abrupt interruption of their studies and their precipitous departure from Paris, along with the ensuing consequences of having to quit the apostolic work they were doing—all of which were the results of a capricious dream of going off to Jerusalem—did have the effect of surprising more than one person in Paris. One of the doctors of the university put a case of conscience before Favre that was certainly not altogether far-fetched. The group was unquestionably doing good in Paris, he argued. But now they were risking this undisputable good for an uncertain good, a success that was based on idle fancy. So, under these circumstances, was it possible that they were committing a mortal sin by leaving Paris? The doctor even asked Favre's permission to submit this case to the assembled theologians of all the doctors at the Theological Faculty. But the companions were firm in their decision, and they did not need the protection of a benefactress, identified as Doña María, or of Queen Leonor's confessor, Gabriel Guzmán, O.P. Íñigo had recommended both of these persons to the companions in case they needed assistance. It is nevertheless true that their sudden disappearance from Paris did indeed resemble a flight, and a few years later, while they were in Italy, the accusation was made that they hurried away from Paris in the same way that heretics are accustomed to make their departures.

Simão Rodrigues records in detail the adventurous happenings and perils that occurred to them on this journey. In order to avoid traveling through Provence and Lombardy, which were the theaters of the war, they decided on a longer and more difficult itinerary that took them through Lorraine, Germany, and then over the Alps. Some of the companions set out five or six days before the others; the rest remained behind, distributing their possessions to the poor. It is probable that this last contingent left Paris on November 15, and before daybreak, so that they would not be noticed. At the end of this first day on the march, they met with a group of peasants and soldiers who asked who they were, where were they coming from, and where were they going. The French companions did all the talking and answered, in the name of the whole group, that they were students from Paris. They were further asked if they were Carmelites, monks, or priests. At this point, a little old lady interrupted the soldiers: "Oh, leave them alone," she said, "they are going off to reform some province." With that everyone laughed heartily and the crowd let them continue on their way. From that moment on, and in spite of the fact that both Laínez and Xavier spoke excellent French, they decided that, as long as the group was still in France, it should be only the French or Savoyard companions who would answer questions; the Spaniards were to remain silent or confine their speech to saying that they were students from Paris. This unchanging and vague answer once prompted a soldier who was interrogating them to call one of the Spaniards a "dumb ox." They were, of course, dressed in long gowns that students wore; moreover, they wore broad-brimmed hats and each one carried a pilgrim's staff. All of them had leathern wallets suspended from their shoulders by leather straps and in these they carried their Bibles, breviaries, and papers, and each one had a rosary that hung openly from around his neck. To facilitate walking, they picked up their gowns and tucked them into their belts. When Rodrigues reminisced about these events forty years later, he recalled vividly the immense trust and confidence each of the companions had in God, and he remembered as well the extraordinary happiness that was theirs. They were undertaking such a joyful celebration that it seemed to them that their feet never touched the ground. Both groups rendezvoused at Meaux, which was some twenty-eight miles east of Paris, and here they determined that they would stay together until they had completed their journey. Rather than begging on the way, they also decided that they would use what money they had until they arrived in Venice, and they would not separate for any reason whatsoever. They prayed, meditated, sang hymns, and recited their breviaries along the way. If they were asked where they were going, they would answer that they were on a pilgrimage to Saint-Nicolas-du-Port in Lorraine. Rain was their constant companion in France and by the time they got to Germany, it had turned to snow. "We were novices at walking," observed Laínez. Most probably they came to have the greatest admiration for the vigor shown by Master Ignatius, who was a professional hiker.

Their itinerary took them through Meaux, Metz, Nancy, Basel, Constance, the Tyrol, and Trent to Venice. Their passage through Lorraine, which at the time was occupied by French troops, proved to be very risky indeed. At one time, Master Simão became separated from the rest, and as a result he had to put up a vigorous fight with a peasant who was intent on bringing him "to visit a very beautiful girl." It took them three days to reach Germany, which is another way of saying the domain of Charles V. To avoid arousing suspicion, the Spaniards now did the talking for the whole group, saying that they were students from Paris on their way to make a pilgrimage at Loreto. They gave this same answer to interrogators on a number of occasions, and as a result they sometimes had to swallow taunts from the Protestants. If the cold and snow were the pincers that tore at their bodies, the face-to-face contact they made with real, live Protestants racked their souls. Tired and worn out by exposure to the cold, they finally arrived in Basel, where they recuperated from their exertions for three days and where they defended the tenets of the

Catholic faith. On July 12, 1536, that is, a relatively short time before these events took place, Erasmus had died in Basel, misunderstood and tired of fighting, and he had found his last resting place in the same city where the two leaders of the Protestant cause were buried, Huldrych Zwingli and Johannes Oecalampadius, both of whom had died in 1531. After three days, the travelers started out again, this time for Constance, which was about one hundred miles from Basel; but because they knew no German, much less the local dialects, and because they were unacquainted with the local roads, they lost their way a number of times. On one such occasion, they stumbled into a Protestant village. It was nighttime, and all the people were celebrating the wedding of the local parish priest with music, eating, drinking, and dancing. They even had it worse in Weinfelden, where the married priest lost a debate with them and threatened to have them thrown into prison. After a terrifying night, during which they thought that they were surely going to die, a young man who sympathized with them managed to help them escape before daybreak and brought them to the other side of Mount Ottemberg, and from here they went on to Constance, which was a thoroughly Protestant town. However, with difficulty, they were able to celebrate Mass in a small church, *extra muros*, and before a congregation that had to pay a tax before being allowed to assist at the Holy Sacrifice. Just before they entered Lindau, an old woman approached them from a lepers' hospital, shouting with emotion and trying to kiss the rosaries that hung from around their necks. Then she showed them the heads and hands from many statues of the saints that the heretics had lopped off and which she had piously kept. Later, she accompanied them to the gates of the city, crying out over and over again in a loud voice: "See here, you cheats and frauds! Here are true Christian men. Did not all of you tell me, you lying frauds, that everyone had embraced the errors of the heretics? You lied. What you said is false and you wanted to deceive me. Now I know you for what you are, and so you will not fool me again." Neither threats nor favors had been able to tear away the ancient faith from this nonconforming old woman. In the dead of winter, the companions passed through Feldkirch, Innsbruck, and Brenner. They celebrated Christmas in the Tyrol, and then, passing through

Bolzano and Trent, they headed down past Castelfranco and Mestre. Finally, on January 8, 1537, they arrived in Venice, two and a half months before the arranged date of their rendezvous with Master Ignatius.

This meeting was the cause of tremendous joy, and they introduced Ignatius to their three new companions. He was not alone, either, for he had won over Diego de Hoces, who was now with him. Moreover, they gained two of the numerous Eguía brothers, who had just come from the Holy Land: Esteban, who was a widower, and Diego, who had been such a help to Ignatius during his Alcalá days. For the time being, both of them would return to their own country and later on would join the group. Then, there were two more that Ignatius considered part of the group: one was a priest named Antonio Arías, whom he had known as a student in Paris, and the other was Miguel de Landívar, Xavier's former servant, who had wanted to kill Master Ignatius in Paris. The whole group still had two months of waiting in Venice before going to Rome, where they would apply for the papal permission to travel to the Holy Land, and, once having obtained this necessary document, they decided they would give themselves six more months to try to find a way to get from Venice to Jerusalem. What plans did Íñigo, this man of "apostolic realism," have for this brilliant group of *Magistri Parisienses* that had opted to follow him in his way of life? It was simply to place them in the two Venetian hospitals, that of the incurables and that of San Giovanni e Paolo, and he did this in order to allow them to put their theological studies aside and direct their attention to real flesh-and-blood sick people; to have them exchange high-flown discussions for such humble chores as making beds, scouring pots, sweeping floors, washing bandages, cleaning sores, digging graves, and burying the dead. Íñigo already had ample experience in such matters as these, and, surprisingly enough, he himself retired to the home of his host where he continued to carry on his quiet life of study. His companions had to form themselves on their own; each one had to discover the proper stuff from within himself that would make him a hero.

The immersion of these university scholars into such unfamiliar spheres of activity, performing tasks that were in themselves most unpleasant, must have been indeed a brutal experience. A man needed gigantic inner resources to take it on and to rise above the repugnance of such an endeavor. Willpower, however, is what goes beyond nature, and the will is able to prevail over nature whenever such power of resolution belongs to men like Xavier and Rodrigues. In order to gain a victory over his natural repulsion to the chancres on a certain syphilitic patient, Xavier exerted a superhuman effort to force himself to lick these lesions. As for Rodrigues, when he learned that a leper had been denied a bed in the hospital of San Giovanni e Paolo, he invited the man to share his own bed. Later on, Xavier thought that he had become infected with syphilis as a result of his action, and Rodrigues was sick for a whole day out of fear that he had contracted leprosy. Today, we share a common human nature with men of such caliber, but they remain totally different from us when it comes to interpreting what is meant by the free exercise of the will and how religious sentiments should be authentically expressed.

After undergoing two months of trials in the hospitals, the companions went as a group to Rome to ask for the pope's blessing on their Jerusalem venture. However, "the pilgrim did not go with them because of Dr. Ortiz and also because of the new Theatine cardinal." Íñigo's decision was a discrete, cautionary measure. Dr. Pedro Ortiz, who had denounced Íñigo to the inquisitor in Paris, was now Charles V's special agent in Rome, and the newly created Cardinal Gian Pietro Carafa had recently become a member of the Roman curia. It is difficult to imagine that Íñigo, who was normally stimulated by persecution, entertained fears about going to Rome. It was discretion that prompted his decision. He wanted to stay clear of useless difficulties, and perhaps he also wanted his masters to suffer the trials of making a pilgrimage devoid of his company. Making a pilgrimage was an exercise in which he was already a past master. Unlike the trip that they had made from Paris to Venice, this time the companions made the journey in abject poverty, living on alms alone. We know that they arrived in Ravenna soaked to the skin, exhausted, and half dead with hunger. They were accustomed to traveling in groups of three, with a priest assigned to each group, and they followed Íñigo's example by spending the night in hospices, haylofts, and even stables. They ate whatever was given to them then

and there, keeping no provisions for the road. On one occasion they walked the whole day barefoot in the streaming rain,
praying and singing psalms, with nothing more in their stomachs than the little bread they had eaten in the early morning.
Once someone mistook them for a group of veteran participants of the sack of Rome who were on their way to ask the
pope for his forgiveness. In order to pay ship passage from
Ravenna to Ancona, they had to pawn a breviary. They ate like
the destitute. At Ancona, Master Laínez stood barefoot and
politely thanked women who were selling vegetables in a market for giving him a radish, a cabbage, and an apple. They
stayed in Loreto for three days, giving themselves over to
prayer and devotions. At Tolentino, a foreigner gave them a
dinner composed of bread, figs, and wine, which they shared
with other beggars. At last, on Palm Sunday, March 25, they
arrived in Rome, where they were received in their respective
national hospices. These past four months constituted a tough
novitiate. As Laínez later said, during this time they had
adopted "the way of life" of Íñigo, which meant leaving the
things of this world and placing their trust in God alone.
These months had been for them the most purely and brilliantly heroic period of their lives.

The situation had changed in Rome in the most unexpected way imaginable. The redoubtable Dr. Ortiz had
become their most solid defender, and he even obtained an
audience for them with Pope Paul III. And what an audience
it was! Ortiz told the pope about these nine most promising
Paris theologians who wanted to travel in total poverty to
Jerusalem. Their story was most unusual, almost miraculous.
Paul III liked to be surrounded by newcomers to Rome who
gave promise of livening up his dinner table and so invited
them to dine with him, and, during the course of the meal, he
listened to the philosophical and theological disputations they
engaged in with other invited theologians. These Paris masters, who only a few days back were sleeping in stables, had
now taken their places alongside cardinals and learned doctors at the pope's table. Paul III was charmed by them, and,
following the custom, he asked them what it was that they
desired. They said that they wanted neither prebends nor
benefices, but only his permission to go to Jerusalem. In the
rescript where this permission was formulized and bestowed

upon Pierre Favre and twelve companions, permission was granted to visit and remain in the Holy Land, to settle there and to return whenever it pleased them to do so. The specification of privileges was a calculated stratagem designed to off-set any pressure that the guardian of the Franciscans might offer, as he had done with Íñigo in the past. A door was left discreetly open so that they could return or remain in the Holy Land. The vow that they had made at Montmartre was being scrupulously followed. The group was constituted of these nine Parisian theologians, plus Íñigo, along with Hoces, Arías, and Landívar.

33

Next Year, Jerusalem

What had begun in a Paris room in 1529, and what had been adhered to sincerely and without any compromise—serving the sick, suffering the pangs of hunger, sleeping in haylofts—could have been totally undone at a single papal dinner. The pure privilege of living a life dedicated to absolute poverty and total confidence in God now risked being diluted by a number of human safeguards—protection by people of influence, help and support from the rich and powerful—all of which could mean jeopardizing the final purpose that they desired. The pope and cardinals had collected two hundred and sixty ducats as an alms to assist the companions in making their Holy Land voyage. Moreover, the pope issued a *motu proprio* that gave the priests among them the power to absolve reserved sins. Those who were not yet priests were given permission to receive holy orders, including the priesthood, from the hands of any bishop and without observing the prescribed canonical delays. The "lucky star," which is always a dangerous blessing, was beginning to shine on this group of "friends in the Lord" even before it had any canonical structure. The supreme star, nevertheless, the object of all of their desires remained the same, and that was Jerusalem.

These strange pilgrims returned to Venice begging, but in their *becaces* (shoulder bags, the hallmarks of beggars and mendicant monks) they were carrying more concessions than they could ever have dreamed possible. Of all of these various privileges, the most surprising was the open door to the priesthood.

But, looked at from the papal perspective, which rightly evaluated what a force this group could be, this concession was really not exceptional. From the group's point of view, however, the dispensation was not something that was hoped for, much less something that had been asked for in a formal petition. Assuredly, it was not the ordinary, customary course that candidates would take on their way to becoming priests, namely, without any bonds tying them to a particular diocese or without an inheritance or a benefice. According to the *motu proprio*, the companions could be ordained *ad titulum paupertatis et sufficientis litteraturae*, "under the title of voluntary poverty and sufficient learning." In July of that same year, Íñigo commented on all of these special privileges in a letter he addressed to his Barcelona friend, Juan de Verdolay. The companions, he wrote, "living in penury, without money, without recommendations . . . but putting all of their confidence in God . . . obtained, without any effort on their part, *much more than what they had sought.* . . ." Such was the experience of these "nine friends in the Lord," which was the expression Íñigo used when referring to the companions who had come from Paris, and what they had achieved pertained also to himself and Hoces. Arías and Landívar, on the other hand, did not make the trip back to Venice from Rome. Arías left the group during the return trip, and later on Landívar accused him of becoming involved in a life of serious moral turpitude. He was apparently a homosexual. As for Landívar, he had a very unstable temperament, and in his weakness he was ever seeking the compassion and affection of an Íñigo, someone who was ready to listen to him and give him time. Experience would soon make Íñigo tougher, more exacting, and less indulgent with the Landívars of this world, aspirants who failed to show sufficient tenacity and strength of character.

After their return to Venice, the members of the group went back to their regular hospital jobs, but in view of their eventual departure for the Holy Land, they decided to petition ordination. Vincenzo Nigusanti, bishop of Arbe, an island off the Dalmatian coast, gave them the sacrament of Holy Orders at a very fast pace: he conferred minor orders on Sunday, June 10, the subdiaconate on the fifteenth, the diaconate on the seventeenth, and the priesthood on the twenty-fourth, which was the feast of Saint John the Baptist.

Bobadilla, Laínez, Xavier, Codure, Rodrigues, and Ignatius of Loyola were ordained priests; because of his age, Salmerón, who was ordained a deacon, had to wait until the following June to be ordained to the priesthood. The bishop asked for no stipend from these men who had vowed to live their lives in poverty. The papal legate in Venice, Bishop Girolamo Verallo, then gave them all the faculties they needed to carry out their ministry in the territory he governed as papal legate, even without permission of the local ordinaries. At long last, Íñigo, along with the others, was empowered to determine "when it was a question of a mortal or venial sin," because now he was able to hear confessions, grant absolution in cases reserved for bishops, archbishops, and patriarchs, dispense the sacraments, preach, and give lectures on Holy Scripture, both in public and in private, and he could perform all of these functions in accord with the canonical dispensations he had been given. After fifteen years, the restrictions placed on him in Alcalá and Salamanca were no longer binding. It goes without saying that the "friends in the Lord," transformed now into "reformed priests," dreamed of saying their first Masses in the land of Jesus. Everything—and even more than everything—that they had planned in Paris in 1534 had become a reality. There was only one more thing, the most important of all, that had not yet been realized, and that was the journey to Jerusalem.

What had not happened in forty years happened that year: the pilgrim ships were not able to weigh anchor. The political tension between the Venetians and the Turks had reached a critical point. A formidable Turkish armada was threatening the Venetian fortresses and islands along the Adriatic, and, after the combined papal-imperial fleet under the command of Andrea Doria had withdrawn to Genoa, this armada even began to attack the important seaport of Otranto, a city in the province of Apulia. On June 3, 1537, the alliance between the Sublime Porte and Venice was broken. The Turks were not successful in their efforts to capture Corfu, but they did manage to seize a number of Venetian islands in the Aegean Sea. Venice would end up joining the Holy League that was supported by Pope Paul III, the emperor, and the king of the Romans. This came about on February 8, 1538, but because of a certain lack of financial committedness on the part of the members of the League, the alliance finally fell apart before the end of the year. Venice did not hesitate long before opening negotiations with the Turks for a lasting peace, and a new treaty was signed on October 2, 1540. These are historical events that we know today; in 1537, however, all the possibilities for peace seemed totally exhausted, or, as we read in the *Autobiography*, Íñigo and his companions "saw their hopes diminishing" as far as going to the Holy Land was concerned. Íñigo was used to dealing with unforeseeable situations and so, at first, he and his companions did not give up hope; rather, they determined to spend twelve whole months in Venice, that is, all the rest of 1538, up to the summer of 1539, and this would give them a double opportunity for going to the Holy Land because spring, the ordinary time for sailing, would come around twice within this time frame.

On May 31, 1537, the group participated in the Venetian Corpus Christi procession, and after the ceremonies they were introduced to the eighty-two-year-old doge Andrea Gritti, the same benefactor who had given Íñigo a free passage from Venice to Cyprus in 1523. The breakdown of the alliance with Constantinople took place three days after the Corpus Christi procession, and this fact made any kind of sailing to Palestine unthinkable for the time being. In view of these events, the group had already decided to remain in Venice until July 1538, as was mentioned above; however, they also decided that, during this time of waiting, they would spread themselves throughout the Venetian possessions. Accordingly, they drew lots to determine the makeup of teams of two or three, but before doing this they sent back to Rome two hundred ducats, the money they had not already used from the alms they had received in April. Now, toward the end of July, they were ready to give themselves unreservedly to the demanding service of hospital work, but first they would reserve a few months to living hidden, solitary lives, lives that promised to be almost eremitical and free from all commitments, during which time they could prepare themselves for the day when they would say their first Masses. With the advice of friends, the newly formed teams went off to the following places: Verona (Bobadilla and Broët), Bassano (Jay and Rodrigues), Treviso (Codure and Hoces), Monselice (Xavier and Salmerón). Ignatius, Favre, and Laínez went to Vicenza where they took lodgings on the outskirts of the town in a small house that had been let to them by the monks of Santa Maria delle Grazie. This house, which was called San Pietro in Vivarolo, had been allowed to stand vacant since the War of Cambrai (1511–12) and was now almost totally in ruins, having neither doors nor windows. They slept on the ground with a little bit of straw they used for a bed. During this time of his life, Íñigo was already accustomed to weeping easily and frequently; his eyes were sunken and he was supersensitive to both light and the wind. For this reason, it was Favre and Laínez who went into town twice a day to beg, but what they brought back was never sufficient to satisfy their hunger. Íñigo, who was the one who normally stayed at home, was the cook, although usually what he prepared was crusts of bread that he boiled in order to make them edible. Whenever they had a bit of oil or lard, it was an occasion to enjoy a veritable feast. They spent forty days living this type of penitential life, totally cut off from everyone, "intent on nothing but their prayers." The way they had opted to live in Vicenza was an obvious imitation of how Christ had prepared Himself for entering His public life, a life they themselves had dreamed of reenacting in Palestine.

The other teams went through this same forty days in prayer. It was summer, at the height of the dog days, and swarms of mosquitoes endeavored to distract their solitude and were successful in contributing to their penances. Most certainly these mosquitoes were also the cause of the fevers many of the companions suffered. Master Simão's sickness was particularly severe. Ignatius, anxious about his welfare, went to visit him, walking so fast that Favre was not able to keep up with him. Afterward, Codure joined the Vicenza team, and then he, Ignatius, Favre, and Laínez began to preach in the city squares, shouting loudly to the people and attracting them by waving their large Paris-style academic bonnets. The quality of their Italian was indisputably lower than the force of their simple words. Little by little, the whole group was reunited in Vicenza, and at this point the local people began to show more generosity toward them. In September, Salmerón was ordained a priest. At the beginning of autumn, Xavier, Laínez, Bobadilla, and Codure said their first Masses in the church of San Pietro in Vivarolo; Simão Rodrigues would say his in Ferrara. These Masses were occasions of a pure feast of the spirit without any concession whatsoever to flesh, blood, or social convenience. Íñigo put off saying his first Mass, undoubtedly because he cherished the secret hope of being able to offer it in the land of Jesus.

He was one of the companions, and then again, he was not. He was by no means the pompous leader, the authoritarian chief, the strategical administrator. He was rather the father to each of them. When broken down with weariness and fever, he was able to leave his hospital bed to go off and visit Rodrigues, who was sicker than he. Quiet and discrete, he seemed to be the trustee of the secret of the future, and yet this future was also uncertain for him. There was a personal, profound, intimate mystery about him that is not clarified when he tells us that during these months in Vicenza "he received many spiritual visions and great consolation that was almost continuous . . . and he enjoyed great supernatural visitations of the kind he used to have when he was in Manresa." We are moved by what he did, his poverty, his cooking for the others, but we know nothing about what was simmering in his own heart of hearts, and that must have been something of major importance. Apparently, he led the group democratically. At Vivarolo, he wanted all of them to decide what they were going to do once November rolled around, in order to fulfill scrupulously the vow they had made at Montmartre. They came to the decision that they would complete their three months of retreat, which had already allowed for some preaching, and afterward they would separate and go to different Italian universities to attract new students to their group. Attract them? But for what? What Íñigo had discretely put into his July 24 letter to Verdolay concerning the companions was now being put into practice: "All of them will now separate and go to different places in Italy and wait another year for an opportunity to set sail for Jerusalem. If God our Lord does not judge this voyage good for His service, they will not wait any longer, but rather they will continue to pursue what they have already begun."

Until the hour of decision arrived, they went off in groups of two or three to the university cities, Siena, Ferrara, and Padua. Xavier, accompanied by Bobadilla, went to Bologna, the city where his own father had received a doctorate in

1470. Favre, Ignatius, and Laínez traveled to Rome, encouraged by the invitation from Dr. Ortiz, who previously had been so much feared. If the doctor had quelled his suspicions about the group, new ones were hatched that year in Venice itself. Íñigo with good reason called these suspicions "persecutions." Who could ever have thought that such rumors would circulate throughout Venice—"the number who told such lies were many"—regarding Íñigo? It was said that he had been burned in effigy in Spain and in Paris. This rumor meant that he could be considered as a heretic who was on the run. Who ever could have been responsible for sowing such irresponsible rumors? This time, the matter was very serious and the process followed its course. It was at this moment that Dr. Gasparo de' Dotti, who was a friend of Íñigo's and one of his former exercitants and who was also vicar to the apostolic nuncio in Venice, published a sentence in the name of the nuncio. This document attested that accusations against "a certain priest named Ignatius of Loyola" were frivolous, vain, and false. For the fifth time, Íñigo saw his orthodoxy confirmed. After this sentence, he was at least able to leave his companions in peace and tranquility. And this is what he did in the autumn of 1537.

His separation was only temporary, because all of them had planned to meet again during the spring of 1538 in order to dispel once and for all the ambiguity of their future. They were friends, companions, and equals, cofounders of something that was still unspecified, but no one disputed Íñigo's title as father to them all. At the same time, when Don Martín was creating the Loyola patrimony by acquiring houses, ironworks, and orchards, Íñigo was creating a modest patrimony of men rich in learning, virtue, poverty, and priestly zeal. Was this patrimony of his destined to be linked to the land of Jesus, to be identified with the work of converting the Muslims, and perhaps even dying at their hands? Or would it be necessary to give up that resolute dream and then place their fortunes in the hands of the pope? For each one of them, who had to walk through winter snows in crossing the Alps or the Appenines in order to reach the sea that was espoused to Venice, those glossy smooth, tranquil waters, so lake-like in appearance, now presented the insurmountable obstacle.

34

If They Were Asked
Who They Were

There was still a very faint hope that Jerusalem would become
a reality, and all were hanging onto that thread of hope.
However, just before they began to separate, they considered
this very basic question: What were they to say if they were
asked who they were? This simple question posed the fundamental problem of their corporate identity. Monks they were
not. In a number of ways, they were similar to members of the
mendicant orders, but in other ways they were different from
friars, and above all else they were not members of a religious
order. They were no longer laymen, as most of them had been
a very short time before this date. To refer to themselves as
Parisian Masters was equivocal and not without a certain vanity. If they called themselves reformed priests or reformed
clerics, they ran the risk of confusing themselves with other
groups who bore similar names and who were canonically
approved. The fact was that they were companions, intimate
friends bonded together by an ideal rather than by some
juridical structure. They had neither an approved rule nor a
legitimate superior. Could one not find in Italy associations
such as the *Compagnia del Divino Amore,* or confraternities
founded by the Franciscan Bernadine of Feltre—one of which
was established in Vicenza—that were called the *Compagnia
del buon Gesù.* As far as Íñigo and his group were concerned,
they were friends held together by a linchpin, a raison d'être,

and that was Jesus Christ, and therefore when they were asked who they were, they should say that they belonged to the *Compagnia di Gesù*, the Company of Jesus. The name conveyed something more than a *confraternity*, in the ordinary meaning of that term, and yet it connoted something less than a full-fledged order. But the term had no connection whatsoever with a military organization, although they all felt that they were vassals and soldiers of the Eternal King. In a sense, the name came into being before the actual organization that will be known in history as the Company, or Society, of Jesus. When all was said and done, the name did nothing more than define this extraordinary group of friends that characterized their identity in relation to Christ.

They wanted to follow Jesus, but in the footsteps of Íñigo, in the same way one might do when he places his foot in the imprint left on the snow by someone who has gone ahead of him. This desire to follow Íñigo explains why the companions continued, as they had done earlier, to visit hospitals and prisons, to go from door to door begging for their food, to teach catechism to children and adults, and to practice giving what they had to the poor. Furthermore, they could officially preach, hear confessions, celebrate Mass, and administer the sacraments, and all of these activities they did do, and did them gratuitously, in accord with their vow of poverty. The companions traveled together in pairs, and the two were never of the same nationality, and they agreed to obey each other, alternating as the superior every other week. Íñigo also obeyed, although they all regarded him with reverence. Not everyone, however, was able to understand this strange type of life that they led, for example, as soon as he met two of the companions, Codure and Hoces, the vicar-general at Padua had them imprisoned and placed in chains. Hoces, who combined Ignatian asceticism with Andalucian humor, was not able to contain his inner joy, and so he laughed loudly when he found himself behind bars. Fortunately, the very next morning the prelate released them, and things seemed to change for the better between the vicar-general and themselves. Íñigo had confidence in all his companions and in their sense of personal responsibility, but it was taken for granted that each had to fend for himself. Unexpectedly, toward the end of October 1537, he himself set off for Rome, accompanied by Favre and Laínez. Favre specified that they were called to the Eternal City, although he did not say why nor by whom. Even though the purpose of this trip remains obscure, its results were decisive in focusing some light onto the obscure zones of the companions' collective future.

As they passed through Bologna, Laínez fell desperately ill and was unable to walk. Íñigo rented a horse for him while he himself walked on ahead at such a fast clip that the two younger men were astounded. He had always achieved what he wanted and what he considered was God's will for him. Now, however, a doubt began to gnaw at his soul: Was it possible that God would counteract the plan to go to Jerusalem, a plan that all of them had cherished for so many years and that each one of them saw so clearly as being what God was asking each one to do? If ever there was a man who believed completely in Divine Providence, it was Íñigo—a man, moreover, who let himself be guided by movements of the supernatural—but now he was in the throes of deep confusion, going through a dark night and seeking protection from on high, as he had done on other times of crisis. Along the way, not far from the city of Rome, he entered a tiny chapel that stood alone and abandoned. It was called La Storta. What actually happened there belongs in the category of those decisive events of his life, and, like Loyola and Manresa, it too became a watershed. Between the lines in his autobiography, which at this juncture assumes the tone he used at similar solemn moments when he was faced with similar transcendant certitudes, we hear but weak vibrations of what was a deep seismic convolution. "One day," he said, "a few miles before they reached Rome, he was praying in a church and experienced such a change in his soul and saw so clearly that God the Father had placed him with Christ His Son that his mind could not doubt that the Father had indeed placed him with His Son . . . and he heard Our Lord and Redemptor Himself say to him: 'I will be propitious to you in Rome.'"

35

"I Will Be Propitious
to You in Rome"

Íñigo must have confided some of the details of this special La Storta vision to Laínez because, many years later, when Nadal and Gonçalves da Câmara attempted to jog Ignatius's memory on this subject, they asked him to confirm the details Laínez had given them. Ignatius made an evasive response that can be interpreted as a confirmation of what they heard. "If Laínez told you that," he said, "then it is possible it is so." After Ignatius's death, those who went through his personal effects found the following key phrase among his notes: "when the Father was placing me with His Son." The reference to La Storta is clear, even though in itself the phrase is not particularly literary or enlightening. Íñigo was not the kind of mystic who tortured himself trying to express what was, by definition, inexpressible. He guarded it and kept quiet about it, but it had made a branding-iron impression on him.

The vision of La Storta was the final phase of a period that had been rich in visionary phenomena for him. This period included the long retreat that he had made at San Pietro in Vivarolo during the course of that interminable year, which had become more and more hopeless as the months crawled by. Ignatius had always been a man who regarded even the most insignificant happenings as being heaven-sent, and therefore having to forget his plan to spend the rest of his life in Jerusalem had the effect of reducing him to a state of utter bewilderment. This plan had been with him a long time; he felt keenly about it; and it was a project he held in common with his friends. The Spaniards have a proverb: "How beautiful is the fire that glows when one burns his own ships." The fire here was La Storta, with its mysterious words engraved, one after the other, in his mind, and with the image of Christ carrying His cross in the background. *Ego ero vobis Romae propitius* ("I will be propitious to you in Rome"). *Ego*, that is, Christ Himself, whom he had sought in his dreams about Jerusalem; *vobis*, the group of friends were the object of this reassuring promise; *propitius ero*, Christ would be favorably disposed, auspicious; *Romae*, the direction-sign pointed away from the Jerusalem that they had dreamed about, and toward Rome, which, ever since their Paris days, had been the group's alternative plan in the event that they were prevented from traveling to the Holy Land. Those who read in Íñigo's personality an ambition for unlimited power, sinister plans hatched in Rome for conquering worldly empires, falsify history. If the Venetian ship had weighed anchor and crossed the Mediterranean with Íñigo and the Parisian companions, the events that followed would have been very different indeed. After La Storta, Ignatius the pilgrim was convinced that he was traveling in the right direction; however, the road was replete with many uncertainties. He had a premonition that difficulties, trials, persecutions perhaps—in a word, hostility—awaited them in Rome, and he expressed this premonition with a graphic metaphor: he said he saw "closed windows and doors." Certitude and assurance did not mean for him that the road ahead was clearly visible and the horizon was cloudless. The only option he had was to go on walking. The poet Manuel Machado y Ruiz says: "The road is made by walking."

It was while walking that one afternoon in the autumn of 1537 the three companions reached Rome. The sun's light bathed the countryside in a bluish-green hue, illuminated the countless churches with splendor, and glowed softly on the city's majestic palaces and grandiose monuments as they soared over the humble dwelling places of the ordinary people. In spite of the fact that Italy was strangled by foreign powers and Protestants were waging terrible attacks against Rome, whose voice was scarcely heeded any more in many places of Europe, the city was still energized by the spirit of the

Renaissance. Arts and letters were thriving, and even the population showed signs of continued growth. Rome was indeed unique. A new nobility was challenging the power and influence of the dominant and established families like the Colonnas, Orsinis, Savellis, and Contis, and they were matching them in ostentation with their new palaces and villas. The glorious past of both pagan and Christian times was present in the ancient monuments that had been at least partially saved from complete ruin; in the innumerable churches, magnificent fountains, and in the catacombs that were just then being rediscovered. The cardinals in the Curia, with their large following of lackeys and protégés, played an important role in the battles that took place every time a conclave was called to elect a new pope, and they played a central part in the administration of the Catholic world. The ambassadors representing the most important governments brought to the city the heartbeat of the world, and here in Rome they vied to bring glory to the kings and princes they represented by making themselves ever visible and by engaging in all types of disputes. University scholars and clerics from all over Europe flocked to Rome by the hundreds looking for positions in the Curia, for living quarters in the palaces of this cardinal or that bishop, and for prebends from a benefice in any part of the world—whatever kind would do, from an archdeacon's pension to a humble annual stipend. From the days of the Avignon popes, Rome was a gigantic agency where appointments to offices were handed out, and for this reason it had become the city of intrigue, ambition, greed, and graft. Money opened doors. Everything could be bought or sold, irrespective of the fact that the real purpose of the revenue that came from an ecclesiastical office, the *beneficium*, was for the *officium*, the personal attention and pastoral services of the people. Buying and selling Church offices had become the standard practice. It had become the greatest scourge and the most nefarious evil in the Church because, among many other abuses, it was tied to such evils as special privileges exempt from episcopal authority, plurality of Church offices, absenteeism, and trading sees and parishes by bishops and priests. *Subversio ordinis*, "the subversion of order" is the way one contemporary moralist, Domingo de Soto, O.P., described the condition of the Church of that time. In vain had generation after generation of reformers called for action that would cut off these evils at the root, but their complaints either became lost in the void of outer space or were pulverized when they clashed against the gigantic centralizing, fiscal machine that was the Roman Curia. The Curia had too much of an interest in maintaining the status quo to support any kind of reform. The events that had taken place during the terrible sack of Rome in 1527, when the city was subjected to the atrocities of foreign troops and when the pope was imprisoned at Castel Sant'Angelo, were still fresh in the memory of the people, who reacted emotionally to any foreign intervention in Roman institutions. There was no dearth of preachers and prophets who saw in that dreadful time of pillage God's punishment for the many sins of the so-called Holy City. Others prophesied—or perhaps just expressed their desire— that an angelic, heaven-sent pope would come along and remedy all of the existing evils.

But things had not changed very much by 1537. The reigning pope was Paul III, a Farnese who had more of the charm of a Renaissance man about him than the attraction of an angel. He began his climb to power under the Borgia pope, Alexander VI, and managed to accumulate a number of bishoprics on the way. He had been elected pope in 1534 and consistently showed more concern for the advancement of his family in general and of his two sons in particular than he did for any effective reform of the Church. However, the renovation he made in the College of Cardinals by bestowing the red hat on such outstanding men as Gasparo Contarini, Reginald Pole, and Gian Pietro Carafa, who would become Pope Paul IV; on Jacques Sadolet, Federigo Fregoso, Giovanni Morone, Marcello Cervini, who would become Pope Marcellus II, and others of their caliber did give cause for some hope. Later on, Ignatius and his companions would have dealings with these men, and they would prove to be strong allies of the early Society. As a matter of fact, a number of these cardinals put together the famous *Consilium de emmendanda ecclesia* of 1536, which was a reform program for the Church that pointed out with great accuracy the ills that called for remedies. In this document, the cardinals expressed their concern about the exaggerated theories of pontifical authority and drew up basic guidelines for reform that dealt with, among other items, curial accountability, limitation of exemptions, the training of future priests, and the improvement of preaching. Their program was solid and intelligently set forth, but it remained a dead letter, a symbol of healthy thinking and goodwill. It is true that Paul III did order bishops living in Rome to return to their own dioceses, but he could do nothing about reforming the Datary, and so his orders were not carried out. His attempt to call a council were met with an even more conspicuous failure. No one on the Catholic side responded to his appeal, and added to this slight was the outright refusal on the part of the Protestants, who by that date (1537), had already formed the League of Schmalkalden, to attend any council whatsoever. The result was that the hoped-for council was not summoned until 1542, and even then the first session had to be postponed until the end of 1545 because of the incessant war between Francis I and Charles V. Despite all of these obstacles, the spirit of reform was not something that was restricted to the fringes of the Catholic world. It was, rather, more of a hope than the reality of things that animated Catholic thinking at the very heart of the Church. Side by side with the Rome that we may designate as the Rome of officialdom, there was another Rome, the Rome of the *popolino*, the ordinary people who took delight in celebrating the carnival and other festivities, who were despised and humiliated by the aristocrats, and who held on to their secular traditions and religious superstitions. There were also many hospitals, innumerable confraternities, and charitable organizations that existed cheek by jowl with the corrupt moral life of the city and the many *cortigiane* or women of the street. It was into this motley setting that Ignatius, Favre, and Laínez made their entrance. They were not merely passersby. They were there to stay. They were seeking their future, waiting for it to define itself more clearly. They had not come to ask for anything; they came to offer themselves.

36
"The Poor Pilgrim Priests"

Ignatius's premonition of "closed windows" did not material-
ize. Although selfishness was rampant, there were also good
people in the city. No sooner had the three pilgrim priests
arrived than a small house was placed at their disposal by a
very generous man named Quirino Garzonio. The house was
surrounded by vineyards, and the church of Trinità dei Monti
looked down upon it from the neighboring heights. Many
years later, one of Quirino's sons would remember that when
he was a small child, his father would sometimes take food to
the pilgrims, who in turn shared it with people who were even
worse off than they, and he also remembered that the pilgrims
used to sleep on the ground. He did not forget, either, how
Ignatius would often caress him. Very shortly after their
arrival, the three men most probably went ahead and put into
effect the reason why they had come to Rome. That is to say,
they placed themselves at the disposal of the pope and offered
him the unconditional use of their services. In this world
where everyone came to solicit favors and to make requests, it
must have been strange beyond words to see a handful of
Parisian masters offering themselves to work without asking
for any rewards. Soon Paul III sent Laínez and Favre to teach
at the Sapienza, or the University of Rome, founded by
Boniface VIII in 1303. During the reign of Leo X, it was
expanded and a magnificent new building, said to have been
designed by Michelangelo, was erected. After the sack of
Rome, Clement VII closed the university, and it was not

reopened again until the accession to the papal throne by
Paul III. Favre began giving lectures in positive and Biblical
theology, and Laínez attempted to lecture on the *Commentaries*
of the Tübingen nominalist Gabriel Biel, who was referred to
as the *Doctor profundissimus*. It took some time for Laínez to
get used to the art of classroom teaching, and he tells us that
even Ignatius was embarrassed as a result of his poor classroom performance. He and Favre must have spent about two
years at the Sapienza. This form of instruction must have fit in
well with their training as university men, although what they
were doing at the Sapienza was a far cry from the humble
tasks to which they had dedicated themselves and not in keeping with the type of work envisaged by the group.

Íñigo remained free and went back to his favorite activity,
which was conversing with people, and when he found some-
body ready for his Exercises, he would encourage him to
make them. The first one to do so—whoever would have
believed it!—was the corpulent Dr. Ortiz. He was in Rome,
where Charles V had sent him to defend the marriage bond
between Catherine of Aragon and Henry VIII, even though
Henry had already taken on another wife and had separated
his kingdom from the authority of Rome. Ortiz retreated to
Monte Cassino with Ignatius and spent forty days there under
Ignatius's direction. All the old suspicions of the Parisian years
disappeared, and this former professor of the University of
Salamanca became Ignatius's enthusiastic disciple and loyal
supporter. He claimed Loyola had taught him a *nueva teología*,
not one that a person learns in order to teach, but one that a
person learns in order to live. Others who made Ignatius's
Exercises with the same type of success included the distinguished ambassador of the Republic of Siena in Rome,
Lattanzio Tolomei, who was a nephew of Cardinal Girolamo
Ghinucci and an aficionado of literature and the fine arts; the
medical doctor Ignacio López, who became a close friend to
the first Jesuits; and finally, the Venetian patrician Cardinal
Gasparo Contarini, whose support would soon be of capital
importance for the companions. Meanwhile, while Ignatius
was conducting the Exercises for Dr. Ortiz, the *malagueño*
Diego de Hoces died in Padua. He was the first man in Italy
that Ignatius had recruited for the Society of Jesus through
the Exercises. Such, then, were the first beginnings of the

three companions in Rome. They had been separated from the rest of the group, and their lives bore very little likeness indeed to the lives they had dreamed they would be living in Jerusalem.

Six months after their coming to Rome and after Lent of 1539 had passed, the three were joined by the rest of the group. All of these had gone through a very rich pastoral experience in the different Italian cities where they had been, and they had left behind them the living memory of numerous friendships that they had formed, friendships that would in later days prove to be of great service. There was no room for them in the Garzonios' small house, and so they had to find accommodations for themselves in the central part of the city. They regularized their canonical situation as priests and were given the jurisdiction to hear confessions, preach, and administer the sacraments. These permissions were granted by Cardinal Gian Vincenzo Carafa, the nephew of Cardinal Gian Pietro Carafa, who had supported their applications. In no time at all, they were busy at work performing the same tasks in the city of Rome that they had done in the cities to the north. Soon people began referring to them as "the pilgrim priests" or "the poor pilgrim priests." These four words very well described their appearance, their lifestyle, and even their interior motivations. They would also be called "the reformed priests." One would have to be completely blind not to notice that they stood for something new and different compared to those ignorant and lazy priests whose zeal was no greater than their corrupt morals. "We began preaching in different churches," Laínez reported. As a matter of fact, the pulpits of San Lorenzo in Damaso, San Salvatore in Lauro, San Luigi de' Francesi, and Santa Lucia were turned over to these *preti riformati*. This fact, however, did not prevent them from preaching on occasion in the public squares. What surprised people most of all was that after giving their sermons, the Parisian masters went begging through the streets. "Dame Poverty" continued to be their life's companion. We know that Ignatius preached in Castilian in the Spanish church of Santa María de Montserrat, and we also know that Dr. Ortiz and another doctor of sacred theology named Jerónimo de Arze went assiduously to hear him preach. Arze commented that "never before had he seen such strength of conviction" in a preacher.

Ignatius was not gifted in the art of oratory, but he did possess the magic of the plain spoken word. All of this preaching through both word and way of life produced remarkable results. Such success was partially due to the fact that the companions were active after Easter Sunday and not during Lent, the customary time for such preaching, and also partially due to the fact that the preachers were priests, not friars. Ignatius, overwhelmed with joy, would tell his Barcelona friend, Isabel Roser, about the results of his activities, stressing that the harvest was not due to "the talent and elegance of the presentation," but rather to the grace of God. Laínez confessed that when they spoke, there was no eloquence or style in their delivery, but a generous portion of "exercising in mortification" on their part. Maybe it was precisely because of this feature that the power of the pure, unadorned word coming straight from the heart was more effective.

Everything they did seemed to be touched by success, when suddenly the unexpected storm that Ignatius had foreseen at La Storta hit them with all its fury. This storm had to be fierce to make Ignatius describe it as "the strongest attack and persecution" that he ever had to face in his life. It consisted of an alarming campaign of slander and calumny that slurred the honesty and orthodoxy, not only of Ignatius, but also of the whole group. There was a good explanation why it had taken place. The fact was that it began as a quarrel among Spaniards concerning a celebrated Roman preacher named Fra Agostino Mainardi di Saluzzo, an Augustinian hermit, a native of Piedmont, who had given a series of sermons in the church of Sant'Agostino during the Lenten season. Some of the companions had heard him and they were unsettled by his doctrine. Italy was not Germany, and so the cryptic followers of Luther's theology had the habit of using ambiguous terms when they changed over from conversing in a clandestine manner to speaking in public. The companions had already observed such tactics in a number of preachers in the cities of the north, and the preachers there were anything but simple or naive. Among the admirers of this Italian preacher who enjoyed the greatest prestige within his own order were Spaniards like Don Pedro de Castilla, Francisco de Mudarra, Dr. Matheo Pascual, and a certain Barrera or Barreda, all members of the Curia and all well connected with influential sources in Spain.

Ignatius warned these men to be on their guard when it came to trusting the preacher they held in such high esteem. The companions had already tried to draw the friar's attention to the errors he was expounding, but in view of the futility of their efforts at fraternal correction, they then began to clarify from the pulpit the implications of his teaching. They were unknown, foreigners, and newcomers to the city, and soon they found themselves entangled in a web of false accusations spun by these Spaniards who carried such weight among the influential people of Rome. The Spaniards were then aided by an old foe of Ignatius's, Francis Xavier's erstwhile serving-man, Miguel de Landívar. By September 1537 he was in Venice seeking his fortune and had definitively separated from the group. Afterward, he came to Rome where he again tried, without success, to be readmitted to the group. This bizarre on-again, off-again attachment to the companions soon changed into enmity and fierce resentment. He knew many things about the men who had spurned him, and his newly conceived revenge encouraged him to dress up what he knew according to his taste. Forgetting the attachment he at one time had had for the companions, and even the enthusiasm he had once shown for them, an enthusiasm expressed in a letter he had addressed to Ignatius a short time before these latest events transpired, he now began attacking Ignatius and his followers with half-truths. Ignatius, he reported, was a fugitive who had been condemned in Spain and France and had started a new religious order that was opposed to the mind of the Holy See. Was he not perhaps a crypto-Lutheran? Slander, slander—remnants of it are never effaced, as the old Spanish saying has it.

37

Lies

These lies had an immediate effect. Children no longer appeared at the sermons; Giovanni Domenico de Cupis, the cardinal of Trani and dean of the Sacred College, declared publicly that Ignatius and his followers were nothing more than wolves in sheep's clothing; some of the one-time supporters discretely created a distance between themselves and the companions. The companions were held in total disrepute and saw their hopes for the apostolate dashed to the ground, and so the question was: What could be done to remedy the situation? It is an irony of history that Ignatius, who today is considered as the champion of the most exacting type of orthodoxy, was so often brought to court on the charge of being heterodox. Previously, he had stood before the judges on charges that had been brought up against him alone, but now the whole group was the accused. As he had done on other occasions, he showed his mettle and strength of purpose, his toughness and dauntless persistence. He, who never backed down in the face of suffering and who had endured humiliations and opprobrium, would never put up with the slightest doubt cast on his faith because tolerating misunderstanding in this area could compromise his effectiveness in the apostolate and could even destroy it altogether. As he had done previously in Paris and in Venice, he paid a personal call on the governor and municipal judge of the city, Benedetto Conversini and also to Cardinal Vincenzo Carafa, who had been appointed legate by the pope as long as the latter remained in Nice. (The pope had left Rome to officiate at the marriage of his thirteen-year-old grandson, Ottavio Farnese, to the seventeen-year-old Margaret of Austria, who was the widow of the duke of Florence, Alessandro de' Medici, and the illegitimate daughter of Charles V.) Ignatius stubbornly insisted that he be allowed to present his case and that his accusers also appear in court. He finally won his point. The vague accusations against him lost all consistency; the accused appeared innocent and the matter was ended. Members of the hierarchy, his personal friends, and even his companions considered the case closed, and further legal steps were unnecessary. Ignatius alone, and against everyone else's advice, held firm in insisting on a formal juridical sentence, and to justify his position he asked for written attestations from the ecclesiastical authorities in Bologna, Siena, and Ferrara, as well as letters from Duke Ercole II d'Este of Ferrara supporting the position that the conduct of his companions was irreproachable. The governor was not willing to hand down a formal, written decision, and so Ignatius made an appeal in person to the pope. Paul III had recently returned from Nice and was at the time at Frascati, the summer resort twelve miles southeast of Rome.

The most discrete and patient Ignatius faced the problem head on, with no holds barred. In a most direct manner, he laid bare the intentions shared by his group and told the pope in great detail about the different court trials he had undergone in Alcalá, Salamanca, Paris, and Venice, and also about the sentences he had served in different prisons. He did not want anyone else to inform the pope about these matters in greater detail; he did not want anyone to make a stronger plea for a thorough investigation of the facts; he wanted no one to insist more than himself on opening such an investigation. At the same time, he wanted a judgment from the court that would clarify the situation and put matters back in order. He and his companions could not think of preaching while they were under a shadow of doubt. Ignatius asked the pope to name a judge, anyone he wanted, and if the accused were guilty, they would accept the proper punishment and correction, but if they were judged to be innocent, then they were to be given a formal, written declaration of their innocence. This unusual plea, which was nevertheless sincere and forceful, convinced the pope, who complied with his request. Paul III ordered that such a court be set up in short order. By a happy coincidence, there were men in Rome at the time who had examined Ignatius's case in Alcalá, Paris, and Venice. Their depositions, plus the testimonials from Bologna, Siena, and Ferrara, all concurred in giving a clear decision declaring the accused innocent. These depositions were supported by affidavits from Cardinal Gasparo Contarini of Venice and the bishop of Vicenza, Niccolò Ridolfi, the nephew of Leo X who had been a cardinal since the age of sixteen. Both cardinals had firsthand knowledge of the work of Ignatius and his group. The transactions of this case were recently discovered and have been published.

Veritas filia temporis, "truth is the daughter of time." Time undertook to demonstrate who was what in this case, because in 1541 Mainardi publicly apostatized with a great deal of fanfare, fled from Italy, and embraced Protestantism. Barrera repented of his evil actions and died shortly afterward in Rome. Mudarra, who was condemned as a heretic, escaped from prison and was burned in effigy before escaping to Geneva. In 1549, Pedro de Castilla was arrested for heresy but was acquitted, only to be rearrested on the same charges. He was sentenced to life imprisonment in Rome and, after being reconciled to the Church, died in 1559, assisted by the Jesuit father, Diego de Avellaneda.

Ignatius—and this time, the whole group with him—came out of this trial completely exonerated. This was the eighth time that he had passed his examination in orthodoxy, and this time he did so with a dignity that was akin to ferocity. There were some who considered that his reaction had been excessive and was lacking in Christian meekness. Even though he was used to humiliations and insults and to forgiving others, he would never give an inch when he was accused of not having doctrinal rectitude or not living honestly. He was not merely satisfied with being declared innocent, he took further steps by having a number of copies of the authentic transcripts of the decision made, and he sent one of these copies to his friend Pietro Contarini. The reason for his attitude was clearly explained in the covering letter, written in Latin, that he wrote to Contarini, from which we translate the following paragraph: "We shall never be disturbed if we are called ignorant, rude, unskilled in speaking, or even if we are called wicked, liars, and unstable men. But we were grieved that our *teaching* was considered unsound in this affair and that the *way* we have been following was thought bad. Neither the one nor the other is from us ourselves. They belong to Christ and His Church." The sense of the ecclesial was becoming more and more centralized in his thinking, and as time went on, it would become more coherent. The recent but crucial favor the pope had given the companions was reinforced toward the end of the year when Paul III, acting through his governor, ordered that the children in Rome's thirteen quarters or *rioni* be instructed in Christian doctrine by the foreign priests who were grouped around Ignatius. This was simply an official confirmation of what they had already been doing. A few days later, Ignatius celebrated his first Mass on Christmas night at Santa Maria Maggiore, beside a reliquary that, according to pious tradition, was the very manger in which the child Jesus had lain in Bethlehem. He had waited more than a whole year for this event, and now in this place, which in a sense was a symbolic substitution for the Holy Land, the place where he would have preferred to have celebrated this sacrifice, he was offering his first Mass and, at the same time, performing a gesture of definitive renunciation to the dream of Jerusalem. At that very moment when Ignatius was giving up forever his idea of going to Jerusalem, the former commander of the fortress of Pamplona, Miguel Herrera, who was at this date a very old man, was bragging in a letter he wrote to the king's secretary, Vázquez de Molina: "Praise be to God, I am in good health, with a great determination and desire to conquer the holy house of Jerusalem because I do not feel satisfied with these trifling skirmishes with Constantinople." The authentic Roman transcripts declaring that the teachings and manner of life of Ignatius and his companions were exemplary were not ends in themselves. They were not even meant to be a source of encouragement for human satisfaction; rather, they were the safeguards of an ideal, namely, of "preaching in poverty."

A few days after the whole tide of calumnies had been washed away, the Parisian priests placed themselves officially at the disposal of the pope, who by this time knew them and knew what their mode of life was. This step opened to them a horizon as large as the whole Church itself (and the generosity of their intention was no less narrow), but at the same time, it placed a restriction on their personal initiatives and bound their will to the pope's will. It was around this same period that the aging Diogo de Gouveia began advising the king of Portugal to send these valiant masters, who had given up their chairs in order to preach while living lives dedicated to poverty, to preach the Gospel in the Portuguese East Indies. We remember Gouveia: he was the principal of Sainte-Barbe in Paris, who had dubbed Ignatius "the seducer of students," and had in turn been seduced by this brave alumnus. Through Favre's pen, Ignatius and the companions replied negatively to Gouveia and the justification for their refusal gives us an excellent insight into the group's spirit. "All of us who have bound ourselves together in this Society have offered ourselves to the supreme pontiff, since he is the lord of Christ's whole harvest. When we made this offering of ourselves to him, we told him we were ready for anything that he might decide in Christ for us to do. So, should he send us where you propose we go, we will go there joyfully. Our reason for placing ourselves in this way under his will and judgment is that we know that he has a better understanding of what is best for the whole Church." A Spanish bishop, who was a legate for Charles V in Rome, had made them a similar offer about going to the Americas. But they saw that the pope's will was that they should stay where they were "because the harvest is abundant in Rome." "The distance of those far-off lands does not frighten us," continued the letter to Gouveia, "nor does the work involved in learning a language, provided only that this is what is pleasing to Christ." Then, after giving a brief account of the recent persecution, the letter concludes with an enlightening exhortation to the old professor. "Even in Rome there are many for whom the Church's light and truth are hateful. Therefore, be vigilant, and with as much effort you have labored for the defense of the faith and Church's teaching up until now, seek from this moment on to teach Christ's flock by the example of your life. For how can we believe that the good God will preserve us in the truth of His holy faith if we do not lead good lives? We must fear that the principal source of the errors of doctrine comes from errors in the way we live, and unless these are corrected, the errors of faith will not go away."

38

"Italy Is a True and Excellent Jerusalem If . . ."

A conclusion here is essential. The Romanism that is so characteristic of the Society of Jesus is not the result of carefully construed blueprint. Rather, it has come about as a result of the vagaries of history. It is not the end product of ambition but of the will to serve. It does not mean allying oneself with the power base of the Church, but it means accepting scrupulously the benefits of being directed by the head of the Church. Paul III, who would periodically invite Favre and Laínez to his dinner table, asked them one day this telltale question: "Why do you have such a great desire to go to Jerusalem?" Then he continued: "Italy is a true and excellent Jerusalem if you wish to reap a harvest in God's Church." Yes indeed, the whole world was the land of Jesus, and every corner of it was in need of His word and His redemption. It was God who was now showing the crucial turning point in the road mapped out by Ignatius. Ignatius had formed the pilgrims to be "ready for everything," to fear no distances or strange languages, and especially he had given them an eagerness to integrate the message they preached with the life they lived. Their fervent desire, however, had come about from an interior motivation rather than as a response to the great religious disaster that was taking place in Europe at that time.

There are some people who like to see Ignatius's work as a kind of bulwark standing against the onslaught of

Lutheranism—that is, when they do not regard it as a seasoned army on the attack, the quintessence of the Counter-Reformation. Oddly enough, the name Luther appears only once in all the writings of Ignatius. The terrible religious schism that was going on in Europe during Ignatius's lifetime does not seem to have found any literary echo whatsoever in what he was determined to do, nor do we find that the resolutions made by the group of his friends were affected in any way by the religious crisis. The situation was just the opposite when Saint Teresa of Avila became involved in reforming the Carmelites. In the *Spiritual Exercises*, the book that contains Ignatius's secret weapons, the adverb *against* and the adjective *opposing* appear frequently, but always without belligerence and always in context of the interior religious struggle taking place in the exercitant. The real conflict takes place in the heart of each man, in the halfhearted response he gives to the call of Christ, in his lack of freedom and generosity. Of course, sin is something *against* God; a person must fight *against* desolation; one has to take a stand *against* temptation; the devil fights *against* our joy and consolation; one must embrace contempt and humiliation *against* worldly love and pride. Every generous oblation implies a war *against* sensuality and carnal love. In short, Ignatius does not fight *against* anyone, but against that which is the worst in ourselves. Goethe's words are especially pertinent in this context: "If we take men such as they are, we make them worse than what they are. But if we treat them as they should be, we will take them to where they must be taken." Ignatius's own personal experience, as well as the experience he gained from dealing with different personalities and temperaments, underline the veracity of this principle. He was an excellent and convincing guide because, before guiding others, he let himself be completely guided.

39

"Ready for Everything"

Ignatius's companions were "ready for everything"; they were available for all. Two of them were lecturing at the Sapienza, and the others were teaching children the rudiments of Christian doctrine in the different quarters of the city. They lived together not far from the Capitoline Hill in a new house that belonged to Antonio Frangipani, a man from one of the oldest and most distinguished families in Rome. Each of them worked on his own, but they were united spiritually to face the future as a group. The immediate future was a dreadful winter following a poor harvest. Food was in short supply and prices were rising. In Rome and the neighboring area, there were months of snowstorms and endless rain, and it was intolerably cold. People from nearby villages poured into the city, increasing the number of homeless littering the streets, where some of them would die of hunger and exposure. Under those circumstances, preaching in poverty for Ignatius's companions meant going out, rounding up street people, and then bringing them back to spend the night in their own home. Our brilliant Paris masters begged for food in the streets and returned to their home carrying bread and wood on their shoulders, and they also brought straw, which they used to make beds for the sick. Ignatius's companions washed the feet of the beggars, nursed the sick, and tried to fill the stomachs of all with soup. Only after they had accomplished all of this did they try to instruct them in the rudiments of Christian doctrine and impress upon them the need for fraternal love.

Their efforts with the poor had an effect on a number of rich people and a few cardinals who began giving alms to the servants of those who had recently become impoverished. In time, the companions had to find places for all of the sick and starving in Roman hospitals because there were too many to shelter in their own home. Margaret of Austria, the newly married wife to Paul III's grandson Ottavio Farnese, was particularly generous in giving gifts of money to Ignatius. He scrupulously managed everything that he received without allowing a single *quattrino* to benefit himself or his companions, who continued to live on alms alone.

There could not possibly have been a better confirmation of the judicial opinion handed down by the Roman court regarding the companions than this unanticipated novitiate of perfect charity. The presence of these *preti pellegrini* in the city had become most effective, and, in addition to the prestige they had gained, requests for their services began to come from all sides. With great patience Ignatius had formed a group of tightly bonded friends who were united by the same fraternal love and ideals. But the task given to them by the pope was now about to split the group asunder and cause its eventual dispersion. The future had to be faced and planned for. Would all of them follow the way pointed out by the pope, keeping for themselves only the link of mutual affection that had taken such a long time to mature and the memory of the adventurous route they had traveled together? Or would they decide to form themselves into a community with a head, to whom they would give obedience in order to carry out better the commitment they had made to the pope? The fact was that Ignatius, who has been called a despotic dictator of spirits by some of our contemporary authors, was not the group's juridical head. At most, he was the one who had awakened each one of his companions and had guided their spirits, opened up limitless horizons for them, inspired them with ideals, and encouraged them to commit themselves to these ideals. Ignatius was the older brother, distinguished only by the filial deference each one had for him. How long was the road he had traveled since those disturbing days in Loyola when he had dreamed of performing spectacular feats, since that far-off pilgrimage he had made to Jerusalem, since those long months he spent trying to learn Latin in Barcelona, since his first apostolic endeavors at Alcalá and Salamanca, and since his friendship with Favre and Xavier first began to blossom! Íñigo walked with the slow, trudging steps of an ox, trying to concretize something vaguely intuitive that had been at the back of his mind since his experience at Manresa. The happenings that had occurred on the way showed him how the road was to be followed; he always waited for signs from on high to point his steps in the right direction. He was the artisan of the group, the "father of all," and everyone considered him as such. He waited for the mission or missions that it pleased the pope to give them. It was from this attitude that we get the modern use of the term *mission*. Ignatius's "road" exemplified the Franciscan spirit in his initial desire to imitate Christ, in his desire to help others, and in offering whatever he did gratuitously. There was a good reason why people referred to the group as the *Iñiguistas*, but Ignatius firmly held on to the inspired name "Company of Jesus." All of the companions had already vowed chastity and poverty and were even obeying a conventional superior, who was chosen from among their number on a provisional basis, but this was more out of their desire to resemble Christ than out of any need to put organization and cohesion in their work. From the time of their "holocaust" made to the pope, their future had taken on a clearly defined ecclesial form and in this oblation made by the group we have to see the essence and foundation of the Society. The initial group, including the three members admitted by Favre during Íñigo's absence, constituted the group of cofounders, or better, the group "cofounded" by Íñigo. Their way of life—perhaps because it was so difficult and heroic—had been attracting other men of varying tenacity. Left behind and lost for good were Calixto de Sa and Diego de Cáceres, who were in Castile; Amador de Elduayen, Diego de Peralta, and Juan de Castro, who were in Paris; Miguel de Landívar, Antonio Arías, and Lorenzo García, who were in Rome. All of these would have very different destinies. At the same time, old friends and new acquaintances were determined to become members of the group. These were men like the two Eguía brothers, Esteban and Diego, Francisco Estrada, Francisco de Rojas, who left the Society in 1556, another Spaniard named Carvajal, who left in 1542, the Italian Pietro Codacio, the Portuguese Bartolomeo Ferrão, and the Basque Antonio Araoz, who was the nephew of the wife of Ignatius's eldest brother. Oddly enough, Araoz had come to Rome representing Ignatius's family with the intention of persuading his uncle to give up his manner of life because of the rumor, spread by the prominent Spanish members in the Curia mentioned above, that the Iñiguistas were tainted by the teachings of the *alumbrados*. The nephew ended up, however, embracing his uncle's lifestyle. Many of these new followers of Ignatius took the step of joining the group after making the Exercises.

The future life experience of the companions would settle questions the group was considering at this time, but they first had to deliberate on a number of alternatives. This meant they had to reflect, to line up the different conditions alongside the objectives that they hoped to achieve. Their recent experiences in the north of Italy and in Rome showed that the harvest was indeed plentiful and that their initiatives had been effective. Their vocation, or the road they were to follow, was clear. The offering they had made of themselves to the pope had put a certain finality on who they were. Since it was the pope who would decide what each of the companions would be doing, no one needed a crystal ball to foresee the coming dispersion of the group. On the other hand, the very fact that the requests from those who came knocking at their door were even given consideration was tantamount to admitting that the group was a kind of congregation, but a congregation that did not have the official approbation of the Church. Should they face the future with its foreseeable needs by dissolving their cherished fraternal past and become permanently marginalized in some kind of ecclesiastical organization, or should they simply integrate themselves as individuals into papal or diocesan structures?

40

Our Vocation and Way of Life

Father Master Ignatius was an expert par excellence when it came to the deliberation process, and the companions were conversant with his techniques and methods. They had already chosen their permanent state of life, but the exact contours of that state had yet to be delineated. The norms set out in the Spiritual Exercises for making a determination in such cases as these are carried to their completion in the rules for the discernment of spirits. These rules are not captious psychological weapons designed to manipulate or deceive anyone, but rather they are valid instruments for seeking, with as much liberty as possible, the best choice among different options. Moreover, they take into account the different spiritual motions taking place within the individual throughout the discernment process. All of which is another way of stating that they help one become sensitive to what God is saying to the soul. This was not the first time that the group dealt seriously with the question now facing them. They had broached the problem on a number—*pluries*—of occasions, but without ever having reached perfect agreement among themselves. In spite of some differences of opinion, their vocation was the same. That was a clear, agreed-upon fact. But what were the best, the most effective *means* they should use to achieve their objective? In the past they had always approached this question in perfect freedom, and in the deliberations that followed a "plurality of opinions" was ever in evidence. The difference now, however, was that they had to go from opinions to decisions, from speculation to the definitive, unanimous choice. The method they now followed to arrive at this choice was in total accord with that prescribed elsewhere by Ignatius, that is, to pray even more fervently over the issue, to mobilize all human efforts, and then to wait on God. The human activity consisted in holding months of meetings where the pros and cons of the question were debated, during which time the options were held up and examined from both a more realistic and idealistic point of view.

The *Deliberatio primorum patrum,* "The Deliberation of the First Fathers," is a document that dates back to the period when the companions discussed the points at issue. It does not give us any detailed account of their meetings, but it does give us a clear picture of how their discussions took place. The document begins by stating a fact that demanded immediate consideration: the moment was close at hand when each one of the companions had to go his separate way. There was no one in the group who could doubt this fact. The possibilities being offered to them at the time were manifold. The pope could send them "among the Turks, the people of the Indies, the heretics, the faithful, or the infidels." Under such circumstances would it be better for them to be united in one body that no physical separation could divide? In a very short time Broët and Rodrigues were scheduled to leave for Siena. Should the group have a regard for them and they for the group? Should such a regard be mutually understood, or should they have no more regard for each other than for those who live outside their company? All of them came to a unanimous decision regarding these aspects of the question. Each one of them felt deep within himself that God had brought them together and united them, and it was not by chance that they already had a common history. In that history, their presence among and mutual help and fraternal affection for one another created a bond that united them with him who "had engendered them in Christ," as Favre expressed it, referring to Íñigo. The convergence of their mutual desires and the remembrance of the happy days they had lived together were both a great gift from God and the cause for the plentiful harvest that they had gained in their apostolic ministries. It was therefore clear to them that they should not dissolve the union that had been brought about by God. The members of the group had come together from many nations that historically had been antagonistic toward one another. The document, wherein the Portuguese are overlooked, singled out "Frenchmen, Spaniards, Savoyards, and Basques." The fact that they were men from such different national backgrounds was not the least impressive feature of their union. Moreover, they considered that their being united as a group would insure them with greater strength and endurance for carrying out the difficult tasks to which they would be assigned.

Once they had unanimously agreed to maintain the group as it was constituted, a second question logically presented itself: Should they give stability and structure to the group by giving it a head to whom they would vow obedience? On the one hand, adding this vow to the vows of poverty and chastity they had already taken would mean greater sincerity and merit in carrying out the will of God, and it would also guarantee that they could be more effective in accomplishing whatever the pope wanted them to do. On the other hand, taking a vow of obedience would mean that they would be opting once and for all toward a set of rules, something that was proper to a religious order. The obvious and inevitable question was this: Should they found a new religious order? Although this may appear strange to today's reader, the discussion on this one question went on for many days without their coming to a satisfactory conclusion. In order to extricate themselves from the impasse they had created, they decided to put a fixed order into their discussions. They meditated on all aspects of the question in detail, the background, the method, the end. They were tempted to retreat to some far-off place where they could carry on these meditations, but they soon rejected this idea altogether. After all the recent misadventures they had gone through, they felt that leaving the city at this time would give rise to false rumors, and they would again be accused of being fugitives. Moreover, leaving Rome would mean that they would have to give up their ministries, which by that time had proved to be so effective and had enhanced their reputation. Consequently, they resolved not to leave the city. They carried on their ordinary activities during the day, and every evening they gathered together for their deliberations. Each one would reflect on his own, without discussing the question with the others and without compromising the freedom of choice of anyone in the group. They would thoroughly think out their decisions about who they were, by having each one pretend he was someone new to the group, someone who had never considered joining it, but who now asked questions about what made it what it was. They prayed all the more intensely during these days of deliberation. The subject matter of their reflections would be that they might know "our vocation and way of life"—that is to say, how they would translate their state of life, which they had already determined, into a given form. The problem could not have been posed in a clearer way. There was no room for giving advice or personal reflections or showing off any kind of debating abilities; rather, it meant that each one in that small group of simple friends told that what he had heard was God's will on the matter at hand. For this reason, they believed that the eventual outcome of their deliberations should bear the characteristic stamp of the supernatural—peace, interior joy, the light of the Holy Spirit. Ignatius did not direct the group; he was not the leader who imposed his will. He was just one member of the group, hoping, listening, awaiting the sign of God's presence through the voices of his friends. In a word, all of them were trying to achieve freedom, sincerely seeking how to serve God in the best way possible, and all of this with the unmistaken presence of joy. Antoine Vergot, the Belgian religious psychologist, observed that "When the religious experience is deprived of abiding joy, there is little doubt that the person will suffer from a deep wound." Ignatius expressed this same idea more profoundly when he wrote in the *Spiritual Exercises* that it "is characteristic of the good spirit to give courage and strength, consolation, tears, inspirations, and peace" (*Spiritual Exercises*, 315).

They agreed that in the next session *each one of them* would have to present *the disadvantages* of obedience; each had to muster all the arguments and grounds against taking such a vow. They expressed the following objections, each of which weighed heavily on the conscience of one or another of the companions. The words *religious congregation* and *obedience* had a poor connotation among the ordinary Christian. "*Monachatus non est pietas*," Erasmus had written: "Monasticism is not godliness." If we become religious, suggested another, the pope might force us to adopt some given rule, which would immediately curtail the salvation of souls and defeat our own plans that seem to be pleasing to God. One suggested that the fear of the vow of obedience would be an obstacle to many wishing to join them, men who otherwise would be eager to work in the Lord's vineyard.

On another day, they would proceed with the opposite approach, that is, they would try to evaluate the *advantages* that would accrue from taking the vow of obedience, presenting these and examining them in a limited way. The vow of obedience would set up a certain structure, one argued, but if it were not there, who would want to be concerned with practical and material problems? Could the group be maintained and held together without the vow of obedience? Could they live the kind of poverty they had vowed to live or could they continue to take on difficult tasks without the vow of obedience? Obedience engenders heroic virtues; from it comes promptitude in the execution of one's duties. When duties are heroic, obedience is the antidote of pride, of sticking to one's own judgment. The obedience they had given to the pope could remain something vague and imprecise because the pope is not going to become involved in the day-to-day affairs of the group.

After spending many days thinking about these arguments and weighing the pros and cons, they came to this unanimous decision, *nullo prosus dissidente*: It was better and more expedient to give obedience *to one member* in the group in order to realize better and more accurately the original desires of the group, which consisted in doing God's will. Moreover, this action would result in keeping the group intact, enabling it to carry out the spiritual and temporal works assigned to it. Once this question was resolved—and this was the central question—they concerned themselves with minor details. After three months spent in these discussions, there came the day of final deliberation. It was around the feast of Saint John the Baptist (June 24, 1539). However, it was not until April 15, when each one of them signed his name to the document that had been drawn up, that the crucial question of obedience had been solved. They numbered eleven. There were the six of the original Paris group, and to these companions were added the members Pierre Favre had admitted—Codure, Broët, Jay—and the Spaniard, Diego de Cáceres. This man, who should not be confused with Lope de Cáceres, Íñigo's companion at Alcalá, left the group in 1541 or 1542, and according to Polanco he was never really a member of the Society in the strict sense. The signature *Ignatius* appears as the ninth name on this document. Just as they had done at Montmartre years earlier, they tried to put their agreement within a religious framework. The document in which they committed themselves to enter the Society, should the pope approve, was signed after a Mass celebrated that April 15 by Favre in which all of them participated.

This document outlining the future of the group had no sooner been completed than two of the members had to leave for Siena. The eleven founding fathers would never again be together as a group. On May 4, those who were still in Rome came to some further determinations. Seven signed this document; *Íñigo* is the fifth signature. In this document the cornerstones of the Society were laid: the members would make a special vow of obedience to the pope; each one would teach Christian doctrine to children for at least forty days each year; they would be assigned their work and their place of work by a superior; there would be a three-month period of probation for new candidates, during which time they would make the Spiritual Exercises, go on a pilgrimage, and help in hospitals. On May 23, 1539, the group agreed that the task of teaching catechism to children should be included in the vows. Bobadilla cast a dissenting vote. This was the first time there was a lack of unanimity in the voting process, and, as a result, the group agreed to make future decisions on the basis of a simple majority vote. Furthermore, the companions agreed that in order to decide matters of this nature in the future, they would spend three days discussing the question upon which they were to vote. Never during the course of history has a more democratic method been tried by the rank-and-file members of a religious order. Following this same system, on June 11 the ensuing points "were determined but not finalized." There would be one superior general for the whole body of the Society, who would be elected *ad vitam,* for life— something that was unheard-of in the tradition of canon law.

They could accept houses, but only as places to live, and also churches. No fixed revenues could be attached to these residences or churches, and the Society would not have the right of property over them. One was free to inform and advise the superior when it came to admitting to or expelling from the Society, but the superior would make the decision alone and with complete freedom. When it came to admitting a relative, a fellow countryman, or a spiritual protégé into the Society, the decision would rest with the majority of the members. In summary, there would be a general elected for life, a strict or evangelical kind of poverty, and a very precise selection process for candidates.

The decisive steps had been taken; the outlined project was still primitive, but it did have precise contours. The characteristic mark of the Society was availability, an availability that was particularly at the service of others and was spiritual; moreover, it was an availability that was clearly functional. There was only one contingency: *if the pope would accept it.*

During the companions' long wait in Italy, they lived in the hope of going to Jerusalem—a hope that had evolved into a frustrating disappointment. The companions' wait ended in their drawing up a plan they had never anticipated, but this plan did give a stable and juridical form to the group's ideal. They did not reach their conclusion easily, but only after mature consideration. However, once they came to realize this new state of affairs, Íñigo, with characteristic tenacity of purpose, began to construct concrete plans, while the others went off to different apostolates and accepted invitations to take on various missions. As we have already seen, the pope had Broët and Rodrigues sent to Siena. They were to work on the reformation of monasteries of religious women; they also began to work among the university students at the Sienese Athenaeum, or university. When Íñigo went to Monte Cassino to give the Exercises to Dr. Ortiz during Lent 1538, he met a young Spaniard named Francesco Strada, or, as he was known in his native Palencia, Francisco Estrada, whom we mentioned before. This nineteen-year-old became attracted to Íñigo and joined the companions. Then, despite his youth—he was still taking philosophy courses—he became a popular preacher and expert in giving the Exercises in Montepulciano. Later, he would enjoy the same success among the students at

Louvain, where he attracted Olivier Mannaerts or Manare and Jean Couvillon for the Society. Mannaerts eventually became the first rector of the Roman College and vicar-general of the Society, and Couvillon became a noted theologian at the Council of Trent. Favre and Laínez were working along the same lines as Estrada in Parma and Piacenza. What they were saying and how they were living was attractive to the point of being contagious, with the result that many joined the Society, some of whom became well known in later years. For instance, the canon from Valencia, Joan Jerònimi Domènech, and Pietro Achille, who were to become the cofounders of the Society in Sicily; Elpidio Ugoletti, who established the Society first at Padua and Venice, and later in Messina and Palermo; Silvestro Landini, who became a well-known preacher of missions; Giovanni Battista Viola, who introduced the Society into France; Antonio Criminali, the Society's proto-martyr, who died for the faith in Cape Camorin, the southern extremity of India; and Benedetto Palmio, destined to be one of the great popular preachers in Italy. Jay and Bobadilla were preaching at this time in Bagnoregio and in Ischia and Calabria respectively.

41

The Pilgrim Gives Up
His Walking

Íñigo, that inveterate walker, remained sequestered in Rome, a prisoner of his own work. During the rest of his life, he left the city only on rare occasions. He concentrated on the future and refused to let himself be trapped by the nostalgia of his erstwhile peregrinations. It was up to him to carry out the decisions that the companions had made. He summed up in five chapters the basic points of the new congregation (ends, means, structure) and used the good services of his former retreatant, Cardinal Gasparo Contarini, to bring the project to the attention of Pope Paul III. This was done toward the end of June 1539. After being examined and approved by the master of the Apostolic Palace, the Dominican Fra Tommaso Dalla Badia, this rough draft, to which was attached Badia's approval, was forwarded to the pope. The five-chapter draft constituted what is a kind of Magna Charta of the Society. Paul III was pleased and touched as he listened to it being read to him, and afterward he was heard to say: "The finger of God is here." Contarini hastily dispatched the good news to "Don Ignacio." So, the pope's *viva voce* approval of the Society took place on September 3, 1539. The approval by the papal Curia of the *Formula of the Institute*, as it came to be called, was all that was needed for official approbation, and such approval was considered no more than a formality.

What seemed to be a mere technicality, however, took a whole year to untangle. The cause for the delay was the objections raised by the highly esteemed curial cardinal, Girolamo Ghinucci, who had difficulties with a number of points in the five chapters. The cardinal was of the opinion that doing away with the organ, chanting the divine office in the choir, and failing to impose obligatory penances not prescribed by the Church, would give Lutherans some pretext to conclude that their criticisms of these practices in the Church were justified. He also judged that the special vow to the pope was superfluous. What the case needed now was a referee, and so the pope appointed a qualified canonist, Cardinal Bartolomeo Guidiccioni, the bishop of Teramo, as arbitrator. Guidiccioni was a blunt man, firm in his convictions, and anything but flexible. He believed, and even circulated his opinions in a book he had published anonymously, that given the medley of so many different religious orders in the Church—all of which were in need of reform and frequently quarreled among themselves—no new religious orders should be approved. Moreover, he felt that all of the existing orders should be amalgamated into four basic groups: Dominicans, Franciscans, Cistercians, and Benedictines. Guidiccioni, therefore, became a serious obstacle to the survival of an order that not only was new, but that also called for a number of innovations.

Faced with this challenge, Íñigo seemed to grow in stature, implementing a maxim he would later make famous; he put all of his hope in God and at the same time began to mobilize all the human resources he could. As far as God was concerned, he promised that he and others would offer three thousand Masses in honor of the Blessed Trinity to obtain the sought-after grace, and as far as man was concerned, he had recourse to all the political backing and influence he could muster. The Duke Ercole II d'Este, grandson of Pope Alexander VI, enthusiastically recommended the Society to his brother Cardinal Ippolito II d'Este, as well as to other members of the Roman Curia. The Council of Ancients in Parma argued in favor of the Society before the Countess of Santa Fiora, Constanza Sforza. She was the daughter of Pope Paul III and sister of Pier Luigi Farnese, duke of Parma and Piacenza, whose son Ottavio had married Margaret of Austria. Broët was successful in eliciting the support of the archbishop of Siena and Cardinal Bonifacio Ferreri, the acting papal legate in Bologna. On his own initiative, King John III of Portugal petitioned the pope to approve the Society and invited Francis I of France and Emperor Charles V to support his request by making similar petitions of their own. Guidiccioni gradually slackened his aggressive hostility, until at last he looked for some face-saving, honorable way out of the fray. The terms for a rather curious solution were these: the Society would be approved, but the number of professed members would be limited to sixty; however, at some later date, all restrictions could be lifted if this were judged to be expedient. At last, on September 27, 1540, Paul III signed the bull approving the Society and issued the same from the Palazzo San Marco on the Piazza Venezia. The text, which began with the Latin words *Regimini militantis ecclesiae*, incorporated, with only scant modifications, the five chapters. It not only contained the Society's fundamental rule, but it also defined its structure, outlined the program of life of its members, and enumerated their apostolic activities. If we consider the effects of this *Formula*, as it came to be called, and if we look at the array of possibilities it was able to offer, we must conclude that it was a very rich document indeed. The pope gave complete liberty to the members of the Society, and encouraged them to exercise that liberty in naming their own superior general and in drawing up Constitutions especially adapted to the aims and goals of the Society. The bull clearly defined the end of the Society by employing the very terms that Íñigo had used, with the result that it sounded more like an invitation, a request, than a mere abstract definition:

> Whoever desires to serve as a soldier of God beneath the banner of the cross in our Society, which we desire to be designated by the name of Jesus, should, after a solemn vow of chastity, keep what follows in mind. He is a member of a community founded chiefly for this purpose: to strive especially for the progress of souls in Christian life and doctrine and for the propagation of the faith by public preaching and the ministry of the Word, by Spiritual Exercises and by works of charity, and expressly by the education of children and unlettered persons in

Christianity. Still further, let any such person take care to keep always before his eyes first God, and then the nature of this Institute which is, so to speak, a *pathway* to God. . . .

The end and purpose of this pathway was clear enough, but Íñigo, who would learn from experience and from the demands that both the vow of obedience to the pope and the circumstances of everyday life would make on the Society, would have to map out an itinerary along that pathway. Embarking upon his journey called for an immense amount of courage and availability, as well as promptitude and generosity, because at a moment's notice one had to be ready to take on an apostolic mission in any part of the world, "among the Turks, in the New World, among the heretics, the faithful, or the infidels." This formula suggested that this was why those who wished to join the ranks of the Society should ponder long and seriously, in order to test whether they indeed possessed the wherewithal to bear "the burden of the vocation on their shoulders." Poverty, sealed with a vow, would be the distinctive feature of their lives because when a life is removed as far as possible from self-interest and becomes as similar as possible to evangelical poverty, it has more abiding joy, is purer, and is more suitable for giving edification to one's neighbor. "Our plan of life" was a program presented by the companions to the pope and "to those who will later follow us if, God willing, we shall ever have imitators along this path." At that moment in history—September 1540—there were barely a dozen committed companions, although another twenty or so had inscribed their names on the enlistment rolls. During the course of the centuries, there would be thousands and thousands of Jesuits who would commit themselves to embracing the type of life defined in this *Formula*. But for now, let us return to the original dozen. In that same September 1540, this founding group was so spread out that its members could not come together to celebrate the pontifical approbation of their Society. They considered service to others to be paramount; celebrating the birth of their Society was of secondary importance.

Under these circumstances, anyone may have expected the discrete and prudent Ignatius to have followed a very different course of action than he did. What were the circumstances?

Already in the spring of 1540 Favre and Laínez were in Rome and Piacenza; Bobadilla was in Naples; Rodrigues in Siena; the pope was talking of sending Salmerón and Codure to Scotland and Ireland; and the king of Portugal kept asking for men to be sent to the far-off Indies! The king knew the best way to get what he wanted. The Portuguese ambassador to the papal court at the time was Don Pedro Mascarenhas, and it would be through him that the king would obtain an order from the pope to accommodate his wishes. When approached, Paul III hinted that Mascarenhas ought to go and find out how the men who would be sent to the Indies felt about such an order. He replied that these men had already said they were willing to accept whatever mission the pope requested they take. Mascarenhas wanted ten of them for this mission, even though there were only six men in Rome at the time. Two of these, Salmerón and Broët, who was a recent substitute for the ailing Codure, had just been appointed papal nuncios to Ireland and were on the point of departing. "Señor Ambassador," Ignatius replied when Mascarenhas made his request, "what will Your Lordship leave for the rest of the world?" Nevertheless, he designated two for the Indies, Rodrigues, who at the time was in Siena, and Bobadilla, who was in Naples. Although suffering from fever, the former boarded a ship bound for Lisbon at Civitavecchia on March 5; the latter traveled by foot to Rome with the intention of catching a ship there. But when he arrived, he was in such a wretched state that the house physician declared his making a trip to Portugal unthinkable. Ignatius was also sick at the time, but was under pressure to find a last-minute substitute for Bobadilla. He had one candidate in Rome: Xavier. He summoned Xavier and entrusted the mission to him. "Master Francis, you already know that at the bidding of His Holiness two of ours must go to India, and that Master Bobadilla was chosen as one of these. He cannot travel because of his illness, and the ambassador cannot wait until he is well. This is a task for you!" "Good enough! I am ready," was Xavier's reply. Master Xavier hastily sewed up the tattered parts of an old pair of pants and his cassock and went off to receive the pope's blessing. He then bade farewell to his friends, leaving with them the written formula of his vows, his vote for the coming election of a general, and his approval of all the constitutions, rules, and ordinances that his confreres who remained behind would draw up. The following day he rode out with the

ambassador, past Loreto toward Lisbon. There he would have
to wait another nine months for a ship destined for the Indies.
Finally, on April 7, 1541, he set sail for Goa. Rodrigues
remained in Portugal, but an Italian Jesuit, who was simply
called Messer Paulo because he did not have a family name
embarked with Xavier. The crossing was very difficult; the ship
was obliged to spend the winter in Mozambique and did not
arrive in Goa until the spring of 1542. Thus it was that the
jovial Navarrese master began the adventure that would make
him the indisputable giant of modern missionary activity. His
was not a matter of aspiring for any particular mission, but
rather it was a firm, lived-out mind-set expressed in the formula "ready for everything." So it was that on the day of the
confirmation of the Society there were only three of the original members in the Eternal City.

The pontifical bull marked an end of one quest, but more
important, it was the beginning of another because there
were still some fundamental points that had not yet been
resolved, chief among them the election of the superior general and the drafting and promulgation of Constitutions.
After a few months, Ignatius summoned together those who
were still in Italy. Laínez, Broët, and Jay arrived in Rome at
the beginning of Lent 1541. Bobadilla was detained by the
pope in Bisignano, a city in the Kingdom of Naples.

On March 4 all six came together—Laínez, Broët, Jay,
Bobadilla, Codure, and Ignatius. The main question on the
agenda was this: Given the fact that a number of the original
companions were no longer physically present to attend meetings, and of those who were, most could not afford to be away
from their different ministries for long, how were they to implement the stipulation in the bull that required that all of them
together were to draft Constitutions? The six companions
decided that the task be handed over to Ignatius and Codure,
and, in compliance with the will of the group, these two began
their work drawing up Constitutions on March 10. They limited
themselves to making explicit a number of points reached in
the earlier deliberations and in the bull, beginning with their
way of life and their practice of poverty. This document, which
is usually referred to as the *Constitutions of the Year 1541*, is a far
cry from the definitive constitutions that Ignatius worked on up
until the year of his death. Nevertheless, in forty-nine short

paragraphs there were already a number of rules outlining the faculties of the superior, the reception of new candidates, the way Jesuits should dress, the obligation of teaching catechism to children, the experiments prior to admission into the Society, the liturgy and devotions, and the like. Two short instructions are worth our consideration: "Setting up colleges in the universities: There are neither studies nor lectures in the Society." Then there is note 38: "*Item*: We would like the bull modified, that is, we would like to suppress, confirm, and change some things contained in it and add others, as would seem best to us. Under these conditions, we want and think we can vow to respect the bull." Disobedience? Protest? Not at all. It simply indicates that the amorphous plan expressed in the bull was experimental. Living under its general provisions and profiting from the experience of the various missions given to the Society by the Holy See would in time either confirm or modify some of the vague directives contained in the bull. All changes and emendations, of course, would have to be worked out with the Holy See, but for the time, the definitive form of the Society remained open to the future and to its demands.

42

He Who Fathered Us

There was another question in addition to that of how to draft the constitutions, one for which it was easier to find a solution. It was the matter of determining who would be the head of the Society. Apart from being a necessary canonical requirement, the progress of the Society, the dispersion of its members, and the success of its operations needed a strong and steady hand at the helm. "Up until this time," Polanco would later write in his *Chronicon*, "Ignatius had steered the rudder on their little boat more like a father who had begotten them all in the Spirit, or as a friend who had gained their complete confidence by his prudence and charity, than like a superior who had been invested with legitimate powers to govern them." On April 5, 1541, after spending days of prayer and reflection, six members of the group came together to cast their votes for their superior general. To these ballots were added those already written out and sealed by Xavier, Favre, and Rodrigues. After remaining in prayer for an additional three days, they opened up the urn containing the ballots. As expected, Ignatius was elected unanimously. He himself indicated that in order not to give preference to any one of them he preferred to cast his ballot for the one who received the majority of votes, providing that person was not himself. He signed his name *Íñigo* to this ballot. Bobadilla did not send in his vote. The ballots were more than pieces of paper upon which was written a name; a number of the companions explained why they had voted as they did. Salmerón, the youngest of the Paris group, justified his choice in these words: "He fathered us in Christ and, when we were infants, he nourished us with spiritual milk; now that we have grown, he will give the more solid food of obedience." Rodrigues declared that he cast his vote for "the only one we can choose as our leader and president"; and, as if he could foresee Ignatius not accepting the post, he added: "If, unhappily, it proves impossible for him to accept, I think Pierre Favre ought to take his place." Jay's choice was also Ignatius, "whom we have had as a father for so many years." Codure describes Ignatius as "the most zealous artisan for the glory of God and for salvation of souls." Laínez and Favre were both more laconic, but Favre noted that in case Ignatius was dead when the ballots were read, his choice would fall to Xavier. As for Xavier, his choice went to *Don Ignacio*, and he expressed himself in these moving terms: "He is the one who brought us together with no little effort and who will also, not without effort, be able to preserve, rule, and make us advance from good to better, since he knows us best." He selected Pierre Favre in case Ignatius had died before the election had taken place. The choice for Ignatius, therefore, was unanimous—all had designated him by the name Ignatius— and in case he could not accept the position, two other men were proposed, Favre and Xavier, both of whom were not present. The three had been roommates at the college of Sainte-Barbe, and it was in their room where the ideas that would bring the companions together really began.

All of the men who were present when the ballots were read were overjoyed; the one exception was Ignatius. He had been putting together an account of the events that were taking place during this period in some notes entitled *Form of the Offering Society*. In these jottings he wrote that he wanted to explain, in a kind of informal, conversational way, "how he felt in his soul," the reasons why he refused to accept the election results. He confessed that he felt more of a will and desire to be governed than to govern. He did not feel capable of directing himself, much less anyone else. He spoke of his many bad habits, past and present, and of his many sins, his faults and his miseries. "He said that he would not accept this office, that he would *never* accept it *unless* it should become evident with great clarity that he ought to do so." He begged his companions to reflect for three more days on the subject "in order to find someone who could fulfill this office better for all concerned." They agreed to this proposal, "although not very willingly." At the end of four days, the vote was taken again and the results were the same as before. As long as Ignatius did not see an expression of the will of God in the election, that headstrong man with the gigantic will was obliged to hesitate, at least on one occasion before his death, uncertain of his future. "Finally, Íñigo, after having examined one alternative and then the other in order to determine which one would give greater service to God," decided he would leave the decision in the hands of his confessor, the Franciscan Theodosio da Lodi, to whom he would confess all of his sins, "since the day he was able to sin down to the present time," and to whom he would reveal all of his infirmities and bodily miseries. After that he would accept blindly whatever his confessor told him to do. Once again, "although rather unwillingly," his companions accepted his proposal. Ignatius retired to the Franciscan convent of San Pietro in Montorio in order to keep his promise and there, for a length of three days, he made his confession. On Easter Sunday, his confessor Fra Theodosio let Ignatius know in unmistakable terms his decision. Ignatius should accept the election results; not to do so was tantamount to resisting the Holy Spirit. Ignatius asked his counselor to reflect more in the Lord over what he had said, and to come to a peaceful solution. After which, he should write out his decision on a piece of paper, enclose it in a sealed envelope addressed to the Society, and send it to his companions. After that, he went back home. Three days later, Fra Theodosio sent his reply, which was read before all of the assembled companions. The decision was that "Íñigo should take in hand the affairs and direction of the Society." He had to accept and resign himself to the office. A few days later, on April 22, after visiting the traditional seven churches of Rome, the group came together in the basilica of St. Paul Outside-the-Walls, where they confessed to one another. After this, Ignatius began Mass. Just before the Communion, he made his profession in accord with the bull of Paul III; then each one of the companions repeated his profession before Ignatius. When the Mass was over, they assembled at the high altar of the Confession where they embraced one another in a brotherly fashion. Thus "they

concluded their profession and the vocation they were beginning," and returned to where they lived. Favre made his profession at Regensburg (July 1541). Bobadilla encountered a
number of difficulties but finally made his profession before
Ignatius in September 1541. Xavier made his at Goa in 1543
and Rodrigues made his at Évora, Portugal, in 1544. All of the
anxieties and uncertainties were things of the past; the way to
the future had been marked and sanctioned. *Facta est continua
et magna tranquillitas.*

Ignatius had dreamed of Jerusalem and he awakened in
Rome. He had come to the city without thinking of founding
a religious order and now he found himself a superior general. He had loved anonymity, radical poverty, naked hope in
God alone, pilgrim routes, and hospices, and from now on he
would be visited and solicited by ambassadors, bishops, hang-
ers-on and favorites of popes and cardinals, and all the while
he would be condemned to an immobile, sedentary life, a
prisoner of his own work. He had desperately wanted to live
and die in some obscure, much-cherished corner of Palestine,
but now he found himself at the very center of Christendom,
where he could feel the weary heartbeat of the Church and
realize his own impotence in the face of so many needs.
Everything had changed. Without his even realizing it, God
had taken him to this new scene. The only thing that
remained was his firm and peremptory commitment to work
for the greater glory of God, for the help of souls, and to be of
service wherever he could.

The pathway was set within the context and structure of the
hierarchical Church. From this moment on, the Society and
Father Master Ignatius would be as inseparable from one
another as the Pietà and the Sistine Chapel are from
Michelangelo. Ignatius was now the Society and the Society
was Ignatius, and both were inserted into the Church. It
would be through the Society that he would make a gift of his
life to the Church, a gift given hour after hour, day after day,
down to his last moment on the day of his death. There were
still fifteen years left for him to live, and this he did in the
poorest of health that brought him, on a number of occasions, close to death's door. It is not easy for a biographer to
separate the story of Ignatius from that of his work, to isolate
his life story from the account of the expansion of the Society

during his lifetime. The problem is dealing with these parallel histories without getting lost in an ocean of details. Decidedly we must limit ourselves to Ignatius, the helmsman of the Society, the blacksmith who forged the institution and its men, the patient, reflective Ignatius, who was ever open to the vast world and the needs of the time, and who was especially disposed to hearing the silent voice of the Spirit. His external aspect radiated a quality that defined his personality: he was a contemplative in the broadest sense of that term, someone who was always thinking in a reflective way. Even though he lived in the company of others, he was ever the solitary, pacing up and down in his own room or in the garden, stopping now and then to raise his eyes heavenward, thinking, always thinking. From this moment on, the high adventure in his life was a thing of the past; in terms of pure narrative, there is not much more to say. His life became more concentrated, as the deepest part of his personality hid itself. In order to penetrate that mystery, we must look at what he did, what he wrote, and what he planned for the future.

43

With All His Heart, Soul, and Will

Ignatius had wanted to help, to serve, but it was now his lot to direct, coordinate, and order. He believed that the distinctive qualities, the very evangelical qualities, of the one who was put in charge should be humility and charity. For this reason he, who had been forced to become the superior general of the order, immediately placed himself at the disposal of the house cook so that he could be put to work doing the most humble tasks. He was serious and scrupulous in his performance of his kitchen chores, giving himself to them with novice-like fervor. Later, he had to divide the time he spent in the kitchen with his growing administrative duties, and, finally, he would have to give up going to the kitchen altogether. He took pleasure in handing his kitchen job over to his brother Jesuits, who took up where he had left off, even though some of them were brilliant doctors. More than once he celebrated Mass in the nearby church of Santa Maria della Strada, where a small picture of the Virgin Mary under the title *Our Lady of the Way* was venerated. The officiating priest was a curial chamberlain, whom we have already mentioned. His name was Pietro Codacio. In 1539, he entered the Society, and when it came time for his final renunciation of property, he obtained permission from the pope to have his church turned over to the general of the Society. Later, Ignatius managed to acquire the garden adjacent to the church, and then, in 1544, he set out to build a suitable residence. When completed, it was able to accommodate some thirty Jesuits. The adjoining church of Gesù, where today the mortal remains of Ignatius lay, was begun in 1568 and consecrated in 1584. It owes its existence in great part to the munificence of Cardinal Alessandro Farnese, another grandson of Paul III and brother to Ottavio Farnese. In 1602, a new and larger building was begun to take the place of the 1544 residence. The four tiny rooms in the older building where Ignatius lived, worked, and died were saved, and they may be visited today. These rooms also served as the working and living space for the two men who succeeded him in the office of superior general, Diego Laínez and Saint Francis Borgia. In Ignatius's time they had already become the heart of the Society because into them poured news from every corner of the world and out of them were pumped countless administrative directives. These rooms were also the place where, for twelve years, Father Master Ignatius prayed, reflected, and made decisions. Very close by the Jesuit residence was the Palazzo San Marco, where Paul III lived, and the palazzi of the Astalli, Altieri, and other powerful families. And, of course, there was the church of Santa Maria della Strada—Our Lady of the Way. Was it possible to find a better name-patronage for men who spent their lives traveling and who were ever ready to take on the challenge of new horizons? Who could ever tally the miles traveled on land and sea by the greatest of these travelers, Francis Xavier? Who could add up all the distances covered by the other companions who had been sent to Ireland, Ethiopia, and Brazil, or who could map out all of the roads walked upon by that indefatigable traveler, Pierre Favre, who crisscrossed Italy, Germany, France, Spain, and Portugal before he died, exhausted, on his way to attend the Council of Trent?

But let us return to Ignatius and to his work and dreams. As a rule, traditional biographers give considerable space to describing the apostolic activities he personally took on. Aside from the fact that these undertakings were very successful, they represent a whole gamut of new works. First, during the summer of 1541, he set aside forty days to teach catechism to children. He deliberately chose this type of work because it was something he earnestly wanted to do, and also because it was a specific activity of the Society's apostolate. During the long process of drafting the Constitutions, he will repeat over and over again the strict obligation Jesuits have to teach catechism to children, and he will clearly legislate how this requirement should be implemented. There were some, perhaps, who may have thought it degrading for masters from the University of Paris to teach children catechism, but teaching the rudiments of Christian doctrine to children and unlettered persons was an idée fixe with Ignatius. Should we see in this high goal of his an enthusiasm for teaching and religious formation, an insight into the importance of education, a desire to do something about the all-pervasive, profound ignorance of basic Catholic beliefs, and a determination to safeguard the imperiled faith resulting from the schism that was tearing Europe apart? Perhaps. I am inclined to believe, however, that the precise reason Ignatius was attracted to this apostolate was because it seemed so insignificant and modest, especially when it was done by masters from the university. Teaching catechism to children and unlettered adults was a practical, no-nonsense way to put into practice his old desire "to preach in poverty." The setting and circumstances of teaching catechism lent themselves to this kind of preaching, but there was also a kind poverty that came from putting aside book learning and sharing the spiritual solitude of those who were being taught, of having to renounce education and identify with those who were reduced to begging for the most basic kind of knowledge. Every member of the Society would be expected to undergo, at least once in his life, this humble ministry that Ignatius experienced that summer when he taught catechism to children and unlettered adults. His language must have been frightful, a sorry mishmash of Latin, Italian, and Spanish, because the very young Pedro Ribadeneira, who had just then entered the Society, confessed that he had to blush whenever he heard Ignatius speaking. With more courage than the others, this young man confronted Ignatius and told him about the gaffes he was making whenever he spoke. As a result, Ignatius asked Ribadeneira to correct him whenever he erred, but in a very short time young Pedro gave up trying because Ignatius's grammatical mistakes were so many and so egregious. We have already stressed that neither oratory nor elegance of style was Ignatius's strong suit, but no one would question the strength and the weight that he gave to the words he spoke and wrote. Even if he slaughtered phonetics and grammar, what force there is in this last sentence composed in broken Italian, this *Itañolo*, as the Argentines call it, that he used to conclude his catechism class: "*Amare a Dios con toto el core, con toto el ánima, con tota la voluntà!*" The people who heard him realized he himself believed what he spoke.

He would never again repeat in any extended way this catechetical experience. However, during the course of the years that followed, he would sometimes stop in the middle of the street or stand in one of the public squares to address a few words to the children. Even if his words did not always have a positive effect, they did make a lasting impression on those who heard them. In 1606, during his beatification process, there were still people in Rome who recalled the little sermons he would sometimes give standing next to the della Strada church, or in the piazza Altieri, or in the Banchi, Zecca Vecchia, and Campo dei Fiori neighborhoods. One of these witnesses, Lorenzo Castellani, learned the Our Father and Hail Mary from the lips of Ignatius. The Florentine Leonardo Bini reported an unexpected anecdote. "I remember Father Ignatius preaching at La Zecca Vecchia," he said, "the boys were throwing apples at him, but he went on patiently giving his sermon, without becoming angry." Bini also remembered seeing Ignatius teaching catechism in the Campo dei Fiori. Both of these events, his preaching and teaching, took place in 1552.

44

The Days' Work

What other fields did Ignatius personally cultivate during the course of these years? Those that were the most unexpected. "To help souls" was an imprecise and vague goal, being more of a behavior style for action than anything else. Circumstances would determine how it was to be translated into projects, would suggest what particular methods should be used "to help souls." Ignatius, the apostle of Rome, confronted problems endemic to the big city, not those that affected the high and mighty, but rather those that were peculiar to the seamy side of the city and to the inhabitants there who needed help. He would not be able to do much by himself, but he would prove that he had exceptional gifts for organizing programs in a number of areas, and he would set up a network that proved to be effective for a long time after he was no longer involved. This is the way he would work: he would identify the problem, make the community aware of it, involve others in finding a solution, set up an institution to carry out the agreed-upon plan of action, and finally he would put the whole project under the patronage of the pope. He realized that preaching against vice was not enough; one had to confront the roots of evil and come up with remedies that would allow reform to take place in the atmosphere of newly found personal freedom of the people involved to guarantee its success.

The first open wound he attempted to heal was, in fact, a very old profession—prostitution. Rome was a paradise for the *cortigiane* who flocked there from every corner of Europe. It was not easy rescuing these women, and it was even more difficult to find any of them who wanted to be rescued. Moreover, what would be the future of those who did want to escape from the meshes of vice? There was a monastery in Rome that had been set up twenty years earlier by the Oratory of Divine Love, and which took in converts from prostitution who wanted to lead lives of penance. This monastery was for women who were single. What about those who were married or those who wanted to reform their lives in the married state? Ignatius respected freedom, especially when freedom was a possible alternative. Initially, he sought to place the reformed prostitutes who did not qualify for the monastery in the care of some woman of the upper classes. Afterward, he thought of an asylum or residence where prostitutes who wanted to give up their evil life could find a temporary place of refuge. He spoke of this project with a number of influential people, but they did not move from giving good advice to putting this advice into action. Then it happened that luck came to him from an unexpected corner. As the workers were digging the foundations for the new della Strada house, they came upon the remains of Pompey's famous *Hecatostylon* portico. Ignatius commissioned good Father Codace, the house treasurer, to sell these marble pieces. This sale realized one hundred crowns, a sum that was desperately needed to augment the house's meager budget. Summing up the courage he reserved for grand occasions, Ignatius credited the one hundred crowns to this project that was so dear to his heart with these words: "Since there is no one else who wants to be first, then follow me; I'll be first." The action was bold, and it marked the beginning of the house of Santa Marta all'Arco Comigliano, which was very near the present-day church of Sant'Ignazio, and which would continue in existence for centuries.

Ignatius, putting to use his characteristic thoroughness for detail, wrote the house's constitutions, the conditions for admission, and the questions that each candidate who sought admission was to be asked. Afterward, he founded a confraternity that would care for the house, and he received a commitment from fourteen cardinals and ladies recruited from the highest echelons of the nobility who would serve as trustees. He then had the pope write a bull giving official approbation to his project. A woman was appointed director of the house while the spiritual progress of the inmates was the responsibility of Ignatius. Later, Diego de Eguía would take on Ignatius's charge. By 1552, there were some three hundred women who had passed through this establishment. Not long after it was in operation, some women succeeded in having a part of the house made into a convent that was put under the rule of Saint Augustine. It was not an exceptional sight to see Ignatius walking the streets of that Rome of unbridled ambitions followed at a discreet distance by a poor woman whom he had convinced to take refuge at Santa Marta. For all their sardonic wit, the Roman populace gave respectful silence to Ignatius's activities, although there were some disappointed lovers, like Mattia Gerardo de San Cassiano, the head postmaster of the pontifical mail, who resorted to violence. His adored treasure had turned herself in to Santa Marta, where he came at night to throw stones at the house and to scream the most obscene accusations against Ignatius and his companions. His was an old story, many times repeated before and since. Ignatius stood his ground, but as he had done on many other occasions, he went to the pope and asked for a formal investigation that would clarify matters. Again, this was not a point of honor, the proverbial *puntiglio* of honor, as the Italians called what they considered a characteristic peculiar to the Spaniards who lived among them, but rather it was an action taken to safeguard the public reputation of the Society that had been compromised by such intemperate demonstrations. The accused Mattia did not make an appearance when he was called before the court, and he used all of his resources to stop publication of the judgment. Ignatius did not yield and the sentence was made public, but afterward he did intercede so that the false accuser would not be punished or in any way harmed. The honest truth was punishment enough. Ignatius has gone down in history as a man who was able to get things done, and what he did here in this slimy underworld of vicious living was unique, although the methods he used were characteristic of how he operated in other areas as well. The following incident illustrates this fact. Once someone commented that, given the proclivity of these women to return to their vice-filled lives, Ignatius's efforts to rescue them were really of no avail and doomed to failure. Ignatius answered that if, out of love of Christ, just one of these women gave up sinning for a single night, he would be satisfied and all his efforts would be rewarded. No amount of fatigue, he said, could induce him to give up in his efforts to rescue one single sinner, even though he knew that she would soon return to her former life. This is vintage Ignatius! His answer to his critic is reminiscent of the earlier response he gave his brother, who had predicted that all of Iñigo's catechetical efforts in Azpeitia would come to naught.

Just about this time, Ignatius's countryman, Esteban de Garibay y Çamalloa, got together an anthology of contemporary Basque proverbs. One of these old sayings throws some light on the fatalism that weighed heavily on the sad reality of prostitution in that era: *Bearrak berra eragiten du*, "necessity creates necessity," the meaning of which is summed up in the Irish proverb, "A blind man can see his own mouth." It did not demand much reflection on his part to make Ignatius realize that redeeming fallen women was not enough. It was necessary to address the root causes of this evil. What else were the daughters of the *cortigiane* going to do but follow the same walk of life pursued by their mothers? Was it not lived-with misery that predisposed innumerable women to sell their bodies? It would be a better thing to prevent this illness than to cure it. Ignatius gave favorable support to a recently founded group called *la compagnia delle vergini miserabili*, "The Society of Wretched Young Women." He did "no little amount of work" for this group in rescuing young girls of ten and twelve from the environment that would irremediably lead them into prostitution.

Another field to which Ignatius turned his personal attention was the problem of the Jews. His attention in this area began at the baptismal ceremony of an adult Jewish man that took place in the autumn of 1541 at the Church of Santa Maria della Strada, in the presence of Margaret of Austria, the Spanish cardinals Pedro Sarmiento and Juan Álvarez de Toledo, and the ambassadors of Spain and Portugal. Paul III was particularly sympathetic toward the Jews. Laínez preached the sermon at this particular baptismal ceremony at which the young man was also married. Ignatius found something about the circumstances and the setting that made him want to work for the conversion of Jews. Faced with a problem to which his

Spanish background had made him particularly sensitive, Ignatius would turn out to be an anticonformist when it came to the Jews. The obsession of purity of blood, which was one of the consequences of the expulsion of the Jews from Spain, permeated Spanish society and even invaded the ecclesiastical institutions of that country, but it never had any hold on Ignatius. He himself was a pure-blooded Christian—"in my country there are no Jews," meaning that during the course of history the Moors and Jews had not come to the Basque country. However, he had no difficulty in admitting people of Jewish ancestry to the Society, men like Laínez, and perhaps even Borgia, both of whom would succeed him as general. Better yet, on one occasion Ignatius astonished his guests at the table by saying in a most convincing way: "I would consider it a special grace from our Lord to come from a line of Jewish ancestors, because I would then be able to be a person related, according to the flesh, to Christ our Lord and our Lady, the glorious Virgin Mary." Such a confession was a source of scandal to more than one of the guests present, as the policy of the young Society in Spain made no demands that its candidates prove their *limpieza de sangre*, although this policy was changed at a later date (1594).

Ignatius took his apostolate among the Jews very seriously. First and foremost, he sought to remove any barriers that made their conversion to Christianity difficult. There were still some very old customs, which had been condemned to no avail by a number of popes, that forced any converted Jew to turn over all of his fortune to the tax collectors. There was also the unwritten law that those Jews who embraced Christianity (and this pertained particularly to those who did so without parental consent) would lose all their hereditary rights. Ignatius obtained a bull from Paul III, entitled *Cupientes Judaeos* and dated March 21, 1542, that abolished all such usages, he began welcoming in his own home people who wanted to be baptized, and he duly instructed them in the faith. Margaret of Austria, who one day would distinguish herself as the governor of the Low Lands, rented a house for him where catechumens could be received, and later, the pope constructed a double hospice, one for men and the other for women, for Jews and all nonbaptized people who wanted to become Christians. This hospice was later put under the protection of Cardinal Marcello Cervini, and a priest-director named Giovanni da Torano was made the director. Meanwhile, Cervini continued to consult with Ignatius on the most delicate matters regarding this ministry, a fact that provoked Torano's jealousy and even caused him to attack Ignatius and his companions. He made all kinds of accusations against them. They were heretics, he said, they violated the secrecy of the confessional, and so forth. He said Ignatius ought to be burned alive, but this time Ignatius held his peace. Afterward, it was discovered that the accuser himself was guilty of grave crimes for which he was condemned to life in prison, a sentence that was finally commuted to banishment from Rome.

Ignatius gave his support to more initiatives. We know that he made a forceful request to water down a most severe decretal, issued by Innocent III in 1215, ordering doctors to withhold all assistance to any sick person who refused the sacraments. He also promoted and supported the creation of houses for orphans and street waifs, but his involvement was not as focused as it was on other projects. On at least one occasion he was in agreement with Gian Pietro Carafa, and that was when he, too, supported setting up the Roman Inquisition in 1542.

Because he was inclined to be concerned about human suffering in a concrete, as opposed to a theoretical, way, Ignatius responded with all his heart to real situations, to hunger, and to moral decadence. He was good and compassionate toward victims of racial prejudice, a friend to children and the poor in spirit, but a rigorous opponent of heresy. His blueprint for action suggests more an attitude open to involvement and enthusiasm than some model plan outlining specific programs that should always be implemented under like circumstances. Having talked mostly about Ignatius's involvement in what may be described as social and apostolic action projects, we should point out that these activities were really sideline operations, complementary at most to the main task that he had faced since 1541, the year his companions officially and collectively entrusted him with the work of governing the Society. Meanwhile, this Society was expanding, and his task included giving it a form, creating a framework for it, endowing it with Constitutions, in short, institutionalizing it. Such an enterprise required his putting hardened shackles on his spirit. But he was no longer alone. Ignatius had at last realized his old dream of gathering around him some companions like himself.

Part III
Rome

Admirable pilgrim,
They all follow your way.
Antonio Machado y Ruiz (1875–1939)

1

"They All Follow Your Way: Agreeing to Sleep Poorly and Eat Badly"

"Admirable pilgrim, they all follow your way." Well, not exactly all, but at least many. From 1540 to 1556, the date of Ignatius's death, the number of his followers passed from a dozen to almost one thousand. What was the secret of this phenomenal growth? There were many associations or congregations of "reformed priests" founded during this same time. Specifically, there were the Theatines, Barnabites, and Somaschi in Italy, and in Spain Saint John of Avila gathered around him a group of devoted secular priests who dedicated themselves to giving spiritual direction and teaching young people. There was even some attempt, which did not get very far, of fusing the Theatines and these followers of John of Avila with Ignatius's group. The ideals of all three congregations, their manner of living, and their apostolic undertakings were very similar. Yet none of these new groups would acquire the numerical population or the historical importance of the Society. Why? Was it because of the so-called "modernity" of the Society's way of life, a manner of living that was more versatile and adaptable because of its flying squadron-like apostolates that were geared toward action and were more disciplined and generous? Did it come from the Society's rugged, even heroic, spirit, its remarkable corporate dedication to follow Christ and serve others in a countercultural manner, one that took for granted a radical rejection of the impulses that enslave men—pride, sensuality, riches (1 Jn 2:16)—or was it because the Society chose for its field of action the whole, wide world?

It is clear that the Society grew by some strange kind of osmosis or contagion. Ignatius was the one who attracted and conquered, and those who, having once been seduced, became themselves seducers—men like Laínez, Favre, and the young Estrada. Those who attached themselves to such recruiters were, at the very beginning, mature men, university professors, canons, pontifical chamberlains, all of whom changed their lives and their horizons. Young men began knocking at the door, too. Some were distinguished; others were from modest backgrounds. They found the Ignatian way an ideal, something that challenged them. Many came with minds already made up; others were goaded on by various happenings that took place in their lives. Francisco de Estrada was a young man, uncertain of the future, who had come to Italy to seek his fortune. He met Ignatius at Monte Cassino, when he went there looking for his protector, Dr. Ortiz, because he had just been let go, along with a number of other Spaniards, from the service of Cardinal Gian Pietro Carafa and he was at a loss for what to do. The meeting with Ignatius decided his future. The history of Pedro de Ribadeneira is even more colorful. On one occasion, Cardinal Alessandro Farnese passed through Toledo on a diplomatic mission, and while he was there the little thirteen-year-old Pedro joined his entourage, becoming one of his pages. Young Pedro was a lively boy with a penchant for fighting that caused him to get into fisticuffs with the Italians over questions of who was better, Spaniards or Italians. One day, right in the waiting room of the pontifical chambers, he struck one of his antagonists. Finally, after another incident similar to that one, he was forced to run away from the palace where he had been lodged. He claimed that he was also being threatened by the shadows of what he called *cathedra pestilentiae*. The reference is to Psalm 1:

> Happy indeed is the man
> who follows not the counsel of the wicked;
> nor lingers in the company of scorners,

but whose delight is the law of the Lord
and who ponders his law day and night.

The desperate young fugitive was given refuge at Santa
Maria della Strada, where in no time he became the house
mascot. Ignatius won him over forever through the Spiritual
Exercises. With a certain boyish insensitivity, however, as we
have already seen, Pedro never showed bashfulness in calling
to the attention of his venerable master the enormous mistakes he would make whenever he attempted to speak Italian.

Pedro's case, and ones like it, forced Ignatius to consider
the question of the Society's future. If, perhaps, in the beginning he had considered keeping the Society limited to a small
group of men of mature age, it would be difficult now to
answer the needs of the whole world, and especially those
pressing, day-to-day demands for men that were coming to
him regularly with greater insistency. In 1541, Ignatius analyzed the problem very realistically. The pool of men who
were good and well-educated was restricted, and most of these
looked forward to retiring from their labors and living off
church benifices, prebends, or ecclesiastical offices. Laínez
noted: "We realize that it is very difficult for the Society to
increase its numbers by means of such educated men, even if
they are learned and good, not only because great laborers
are needed in this Society, but also because each man has to
deny himself and has to be ready to go to the very ends of the
world to work among the faithful or infidels. Therefore, desiring the conservation and increase of the Society to the greater
glory and service of God, it seemed to us that it was fitting that
we adopt another way, namely the colleges." Laínez was very
important in the choice of this new direction.

It was not simply a matter of opportunism that such a policy
was enacted. It was, rather, a question of being flexible, open
to the real world. The fact of the matter is that this decision
did not disparage or compromise the raison d'être of the
Society by reducing it to the level of ordinary human aspirations. Work and mortification were still held up as the daily
bread of the members of the Society, but this decision recognized that the promising generosity for the accomplishment
of the Society's projects could be found among the young.
Ignatius could be flexible in areas where flexibility was

possible. This is why he never gave up readjusting the margins of his work. From 1541 to 1551, the Society evolved and changed much more than it would in many succeeding centuries, and it was during this decade that it acquired its particular, definitive character. It is also fascinating to see Ignatius's policy of adjustment applied to a given set of circumstances, to study his yeses and noes, and to view what was fixed and constant and what was flexible in his ever-molding spirit. We have already mentioned one innovation, the colleges. In the beginning, these were considered as houses almost exclusively for the formation of young Jesuits, but later on they became mixed, that is, institutions where those in formation were taught alongside laymen, and finally these colleges became a specific apostolate of the Society and detached altogether from the novitiates and the houses of Jesuit formation. Houses of formation had a different purpose from the colleges. The human and spiritual fiber of those in formation had to be proven by trials.

On the last point Ignatius was adamant. His policy here was determined by something more than merely the memory of his own past experiences. Each candidate had to go through a time of spiritual training that included making the Spiritual Exercises and was followed by a month of service in the hospitals "because in being berated, he will learn humility and overcome himself and he will separate himself from the world and lose respect for it." Then would come the experiment that for Ignatius was charged with memories, to wit, the pilgrimage "made on foot and without money, putting all hope in the Creator and Lord and accepting sleeping poorly and eating badly because it seems to us that the one who cannot live and walk for a day without eating or sleeping poorly cannot persevere long in our society." Neither weaklings nor romantics had a place in Ignatius's ranks. Although the Society professed a radical poverty, the colleges could look for benefactors to support them because students were expected to study and not go begging for their food in the streets as Ignatius himself had done. Ignatius explained the reason for his "great experiments" in what we might well consider modern personnel management terminology. The monk, he wrote, is protected by the religious cloister and the tranquility and peaceful atmosphere of the monastery, but the Jesuit "travels from place to place." The novice in a monastery is given a long time to correct any former bad habits and to seek perfection whereas the Jesuit has to be proven and well-tested *before* he is admitted to the Society because, in a very short time, he will be plunged into the world and therefore will have to have more strength and experience and greater gifts and graces from God. This was an ideal, although in practice concessions had to be made because of a candidate's age, health, and background and also because of the growing demands of the day. Often, men were needed in the field before their time of formation had been completed. There was a certain haste in the air, and those who obeyed the orders they were given did not lack generosity, nor did those who gave the orders lack confidence in those who obeyed them. But how, with just a handful of men, was Ignatius to respond to the countless demands that were pouring down on him, from Italy, all of Europe, and even from the newly discovered Indies in the East and West?

2

"Tailor the Clothes according to the Cloth You Have at Hand"

During the early years of the order's springtime, Ignatius asked those who wanted to follow his way to have upright, pure intentions; take their bearings from the Institute; respond generously to whatever they were asked to do; be totally available for any mission; and be detached from all things, including their own selves. He gradually showed greater flexibility when it came to what he termed "the experiments" and, perhaps toward the end of his life, he thought he had been too generous in admitting men because the Society was larger than he had initially envisaged. Even though he did not bear the title of master of novices, he personally oversaw the formation of new members, of both the mature and the younger aspirants. In his process of shaping hard men, he followed the example of the smithy of Loyola whom he used to watch as a child. First he would have the novice's soul glow as the man went through the Exercises; then he would hammer it to give it shape and resilience; and, finally, he would let an assigned ministry authenticate the measure and the quality of the man's resolution. He did not seek out geniuses as recruits, but honest, upright men, who had been conquered by an ideal. He had the habit of delegating responsibilities, and, as a consequence, he was able to transform men of middling talents into tireless and effective workers. By so acting, he created a style that became self-perpetuating, a mold that could be used anywhere that new candidates were received into the Society and where great tasks were waiting to be done.

Those who entered the Society in Rome came to know Ignatius. Even though these novices were somewhat isolated where they were lodged, they nevertheless partook of the life of the community, and they could drink in the spirit and the manner of life of the early members. Those who passed through Ignatius's hands retained an unforgettable picture of the physical and spiritual portrait of their incomparable formation director. The young Majorcan Nadal, who would have nothing to do with Ignatius in Paris, was already a priest and a doctor when he fell into his net. He was pushed into taking the steps he took because he had read a long letter from Xavier, who described his own apostolic activities. As a result of this letter, which had received wide circulation, Nadal came to Rome, made the Exercises that years earlier he had refused to make, and entered the Society. In the days that followed, Ignatius assigned this brilliant doctor as helper to both the cook and the gardener. On one occasion, as Ignatius walked about the garden in the company of Dr. Miguel Torres, this Majorcan theologian, who was an acknowledged authority on Latin and Hebrew, did the best he could to keep his mouth closed and stick to his job of shoveling the sod. His trial lasted four months, but then he was excused from making the hospital experiment, and because of his health, he did not have to make a pilgrimage. He never forgot Ignatius's "mildness and friendliness" in his dealings with him, or the visits Ignatius paid him in his cell, or the times he invited him to eat at his table and to take a walk with him. Ignatius dispensed Nadal from fasting, but when the novice protested saying that this would shock the others in the house, Ignatius responded: "You tell me who gets scandalized and I'll throw him out of the Society." Ignatius would not let Nadal perform any more penances either. "You'll do enough penance, all right," he told him, as he gave him the special food that had been prepared for himself. Contrary to the false image that makes Ignatius out to be an inflexible dictator, Nadal was persuaded that these kindly gestures were given him because he was new in the community, still frail, and in need of such concessions.

Benedetto Palmio has also left us some memories of his novitiate made under the direction of Ignatius. Palmio had known Favre and Laínez at Parma. Afterward, he went to Bologna for his studies, and while he was there made the Exercises under the direction of the Valencian Jesuit Joan Jerònimi Domènech and entered the Society at Rome in 1546. There he spent more than a year and a half making his novitiate. When he wrote his autobiography toward the end of the century, he had these years very much in mind, and he confessed then that he missed the simplicity and bonds of charity that united everyone during those earlier years. In spite of the florid Latin style in which he dresses these memories, it is not difficult to discern the unadorned reality beneath all his embellishments. He recalls with pathos the difficulties he had begging in the streets of Rome and having to put up with so many insults. The worst of these insults, the one that cost him the most, was the one that was delivered by a former companion he had known during his university days. This man was shocked when he saw Benedetto dressed in a cassock and begging, and he began upbraiding him on his lifestyle, even trying to get him to leave the Society by telling him that the Society was the joke of Rome. Serving in the kitchen cost Benedetto just as much, if not more, than that particular incident. Palmio was a very squeamish young man who had a horror of dirt and found it very difficult to overcome a certain natural repugnancy whenever he was exposed to it. On one occasion, as he emerged from a cellar covered with dust and cobwebs, he ran into Father Ignatius in the corridor. Ignatius smiled at him and said: "I like you better this way." He even had to put up with some public penances imposed by Ignatius, but he was intelligent enough to realize that these were more a way of testing him than punishing him.

Olivier Mannaerts, who was also sometimes known, incorrectly, as Manare, was attracted to the Society by Favre's zeal and Estrada's eloquence; however, at this time he was too young to enter the novitiate. After finishing his studies at Louvain, he contacted the Jesuits in Paris, where he made the Exercises under Everard Mercurian, and then entered the Society in 1551. Immediately afterward, he was sent to Rome where he met and was formed by Ignatius. Fifty years later, he wrote some reflections on his novitate days and, using some broad strokes, he painted a portrait of Ignatius that helps us recompose our image of him today. Ignatius, Mannaerts recalled, used to invite the novices, in a most gentle way, to come and sit side by side with him for a chat in the garden or elsewhere. Once when Mannaerts became ill, Ignatius came to visit him and treated him as a father would treat his son. At other times during his novitiate, Ignatius would call him to his table where he would offer him an apple or a pear that he had taken meticulous pains to peel. Mannaerts recalled that Ignatius's manner of speaking was admirable, always grave, never excited. Moreover, his words were never empty or superficial, but always powerful and efficacious. He seemed to have thought over everything he uttered, and no one ever left his presence without being consoled. What he looked for in each novice was a spirit that was both docile and unattached, but he would also respect the different temperament of each man. Above all else, he looked for cleanliness and silence in the house. He did like order and discipline, too; noise and loud voices disturbed him. He stressed obedience over and over again, and he scrupulously observed poverty. One day, Mannaerts confided in him that the old vestiges of anger and bad temper were awakening in him. Ignatius encouraged him to fight against these urges, but he also told him that curbed anger was an advantage for the man who had to carry out the office of governing others, but only when that anger was successfully controlled.

Ignatius was always turned toward God, even when many things were on his mind. Mannaerts still retained a vivid image of the founder walking in the small garden, and how he would sometimes stop to lift his gaze heavenward; he was always absorbed in thought. Above all else, Ignatius was a man who had immense trust in God, and he was capable of taking bold action in moments of crisis. He also had confidence in men. When Mannaerts was appointed rector of the Roman College, he asked Ignatius to give him precise directives for carrying out his office. "Do what you can," Ignatius answered. "Fit the rules to the circumstances. Do as you see best and the Holy Spirit will illumine you." When he inquired about which members of the community should be assigned to what jobs, Mannaerts received this curious answer from Ignatius: "Tailor the clothes to match the cloth you have at hand."

Ignatius had a very special cloth in the person of Pedro de Ribadeneira, the energetic fugitive who was admitted to the Society before he was fourteen. Pedro had to wait five years before pronouncing his first vows and thirteen years before he could be ordained a priest. He was the youngest in the house, both a joy and torment for so many of the older members of the community, but Ignatius showed a tenderness toward him that was not merely paternal. It resembled more that affective weakness so often attributed to grandparents. With rude candor and juvenile insensitivity, Perico, as he was familiarly called, was the only one who could correct the abominable Italian Ignatius spoke in the catechism classes he gave, and he was even bold enough to sum up for the class what his venerable master had intended to tell them the previous day. Who would have suspected that that vivacious little fellow would one day write the first biography of Ignatius? Ribadeneira enjoyed a number of unique privileges: he slept in the same room as Ignatius; he served his Mass each day; he frequently accompanied Ignatius whenever he left the house; he was a privileged witness to the day the Society was confirmed; and he was present when the first members made their profession in St. Paul Outside-the-Walls. During the eight years he lived with Ignatius, he never tired contemplating "as a lover," he tells us, the face of his beloved master. Everything about Ignatius—the way he looked, the way he acted, and the way he thought—Ribadeneira engraved on his own soul. Later, it would be enough for him to dip into the source of his memory in order that a biography might spring forth, a biography full of gratitude and wonder, one that is "a pious and dutiful appreciation, a delightful memorial, and a pleasant recollection of that blessed man and father of mine who begot me in Christ, who fostered and reared me, I who, through pious, devout tears and ardent prayers, confess to be the insignificant person I am." Ribadeneira was yet alive in 1610 and still had energy enough to write. On this occasion he wrote a kind of tract on Ignatius's method of governance. At this time Ribadeneira was the only surviving member of the early group, and therefore he wanted to condense in a few pages some of Ignatius's traits that had been so strongly imprinted on his soul and that he had observed seventy years earlier. In savory prose, interposed frequently with the phrase

"I saw and I heard," which he employed as a guarantee for his veracity, he revealed some remarkable pieces of information for us. For instance, he tells that in the beginning Ignatius was not too strict when it came to admitting people into the Society, but later on he became much more exacting, even going so far as to say that if there was one reason he wanted to continue living, it was to show how demanding he was in admitting people to the Society. He preferred candidates who were active and hardworking to those who were quiet and dull, and he thought that "the one who is not good for the world was not good for the Society either." He wanted—and here Ribadeneira was an exception—candidates who were "grown-up, no longer youngsters," and especially, "he paid particular attention to the character and personality of each one of them," to their good judgment, their ability to carry out a ministry, their health and physical strength. If they had many academic degrees or were exceptionally prudent, he did not pay too much attention to their health because such men, "even though they be half-dead, can still help." He did not want useless men or men who would not work to the full extent of their abilities.

His policy in dealing with the novices was "little by little." He combined gentleness with severity, being particularly gentle toward the sick and those who were in the throes of temptation. He showed incredible patience and tenderness with the latter, waiting for more auspicious times to deal with them. His dedication to the sick was sometimes uncomfortable for them because he would take it upon himself to kill lice and clean their beds. What he particularly looked for was obedience and availability in everyone. He expected everybody to have an upright, pure intention. He wanted each of them to have a good education, and, although he allowed for many points of view as far as approved doctrine was concerned, he did not like an excessive variety of opinions, and he liked even less for his men to show a preference for questionable or polemical authors. He was insistent on a strict observance of the rules, but he knew how to be flexible and he would tolerate exemptions, depending on the circumstance. He very much regretted if anyone took scandal at this because "it seemed to him not very discrete to measure unequal things with the same measure." He received people with great amiability; he showed care for all and he strove to make everyone happy. Whenever he had to be unpleasant to someone, he did so by going through that man's immediate superior. He was never known for handing out excessive penances for grave faults, rather he preferred that the guilty party would suggest a penance on his own, after which he would generally mitigate it.

As we have seen from Ribadeneira's analysis, Ignatius was unquestionably an extraordinary judge and maker of men. His principle method was "to gain the man's heart by a very supportive, gentle, fatherly love because he was, indeed, a father to all of his sons." The means Ignatius used with his own and with others "to gain their will" seem to be a bit crafty—to have a real and sincere love for the other; to express it in loving words and deeds; to trust everyone; to take into account each man's personality and situation and then be open to make any accommodation that did not contradict God's law; "to begin with them and end up with us." But his ultimate secret was love. "This love of our Father," his great admirer Ribadeneira said, "was neither weak nor forced, but was vital and efficacious, gentle and strong, as tender as that of a mother, and as virile and strong as that of a father. . . . [T]o those who were infants in the way of virtue, he gave milk; to those who were making some progress, he gave bread with crusts; and those who had reached a certain degree of advancement he treated with greater rigor so that they would run at full speed toward perfection." The widespread, stereo-typed image of Ignatius as the iron despot, the Prussian *ganz soldatisch*, is, from a historical point of view, something totally false and kept alive either out of laziness or bad will on the part of professional historians and others.

3

The Sedentary Vagabond

Father Master Ignatius, however, was not content to be a master of novices, peaceful and retired, watching over the new recruits to the Society as if they were pearls of a great price. As he explained in a letter to Francis Borgia, the viceroy of Catalonia, he knew very well that the superintendency of the Society rested upon his shoulders. And if it were only that alone! But it was not, for besides holding the reins of the Society in his hands, he also had to work to imprint upon it in a most concrete manner his way of living and acting. He had to work hard at giving it a specific spirit, Constitutions, and a set of rules, and he had to map out for it a particular field of apostolic work. In order to accomplish all of these things, the pilgrim, the vagabond of yore, was now going to become an immobile, sedentary administrator, caught in the trap of his own making. It was going to be Rome, not Jerusalem, where he would spend the rest of his days. Even though he himself would leave the city rarely, the outstanding feature of the early Society was going to be roads traveled and voyages taken. The primary result of that generous offering made to the pope, of that grand "ready for everything that he [the pope] shall ask of us in Christ," which was the way Ignatius described the essence of the Society to Gouveia, that is, to be *en route*—not a chosen, but an imposed route.

This "ready for everything" opened up the Society, from its very inception, to the highways of the wide world, and it had the effect of scattering its members to the four winds, even before the Society had been approved. Tracing Favre's itinerary, even for a few years' time, is fascinating: he went from Worms to Speyer, to Mainz, to Antwerp, to Portugal, and then from Portugal he went to Cologne and then back to Portugal, and from Évora, on his way back to Rome, he passed through Valladolid, only to die exhausted in the Eternal City in 1546, as he was making preparations to attend the Council of Trent. Jay, who took Favre's place in Germany, went to Regensburg, Ingolstadt, Salzburg, Dillingen, Trent, Ferrara, and then back to Germany. Broët and Salmerón were sent to Ireland in 1541, a mission that was as painful as it was ineffective. A short time later, Laínez went on a preaching mission to Venice, Padua, Brescia, Rome, Bassano, and then to Trent; and from the Council of Trent he went back to Florence, Sicily, and Genoa, while Salmerón went off again, this time from Naples to Rome, Trent, Ingolstadt, and then back to Naples before returning to Germany and off to Poland. Bobadilla was an extraordinary walker. He began in Ischia and Naples, and then he made his way to Innsbruck, Vienna, Passau, Prague, Worms, Brussels, Augsburg, Rome, and then back to Naples, from where he started out again, this time going to Ancona, the Valtelina district of northern Italy, and then on to Dalmatia. Rodrigues, who was chosen for India, remained in Lisbon. And who could tally the miles covered in far-off lands, on islands and over seas by that missionary chosen as a last minute substitute, Francis Xavier? All the roads began at Rome and all the roads led back to Rome, not only to the pope, but also to the tiny church of Santa Maria della Strada, Our Lady of the Way, and to the small adjoining house where Ignatius followed the steps of each one of his companions, of each member of the "least Society," as he liked to call it. There was a community at La Strada, but it was also a house of passage, where men were arriving and departing all of the time. Ignatius took great pleasure in greeting the visitors, who, during that generous and adventurous springtime of the early Society, arrived in Rome laden with all sorts of stories. He could not hide his joy at seeing them and his meetings with them could lead to those rare occasions when he seemed to lose control of himself and break out in loud laughter. He loved joyful generosity and did not hesitate to tell the ever-smiling Flemish novice Frans De Coster: "Laugh, my son, and be joyful in the Lord, for a religious has no reason to be sad and has a thousand reasons to rejoice." Indeed, those who persist in depicting Ignatius as a somber, lugubrious individual give a false interpretation to historical reality.

It also happens frequently that Ignatius is presented as a genius of military strategy who was able to identify the flash points of tension throughout the world and then devise a plan of action, send out the Society, diversify its ministries, and finally launch seasoned divisions on all fronts. Once again, let us look at the facts, facts that follow a long thread of history. Rather than planning events, these facts show us that Ignatius was towed along by what was taking place, confident that it was God who was doing the steering. It was God who was leading him through and by the events that were taking place around him. He was a captain; his sailing craft was shipshape, and the winds, billowing the sails, directing the ship's course, were the happenings that were taking place on a day-to-day basis. They were the pope's peremptory demands as well as those repeated petitions on the part of bishops, cardinals, kings, and princes. Ignatius did not choose countries or cities; he responded to requests, and then, after he had ascertained the men he had available, he made his decision in response to these requests. At times we can detect something of a personal initiative in him: he dreamed about establishing the Society in his beloved Paris and in the restored Catholic England of Mary Tudor, and he contemplated founding colleges in Constantinople and in the Jerusalem of his dreams. In all of these cases, his desires were not fulfilled. On the other hand, he did the best he could in supporting missions that had been entrusted to him in East Asia, Ireland, Sicily, northern Italy, at the Council of Trent, and in Germany, Ethiopia, and Brazil as well.

During the first years of its existence, the Society was ruled by the unforeseeable. The pope decided where the members were to go in missions among the infidels; the European theater seemed more to be under the direction of Ignatius, who was always at the mercy of those making demands on him. But there is something unmistakable in everything that he did and that was—action. But it was always an action that was enormously diversified and even disconcerting. He hardly had the time and opportunity to think about the Society itself, to allow directives for the various ministries to take root, and to enact rules. The exigencies of everyday life prevailed over everything; they compelled him to deploy men and to take on projects, to search out new canonical points of law, to be in a state of constant evolution, not to close doors but to legislate rules that would be both provisional and flexible. In this mad springtime of the first years of the Society, every year witnessed innovations. The first professed house was established in Lisbon in 1541, along with some of the earliest colleges—Padua, Goa, Louvain, and Gandía. The year 1542 saw the first group of students going to Paris, the first separate novitiate erected in Messina, the first province (Portugal) established, with the provinces of Spain and India following in quick order, and soon (1549) the Society would have its first martyr, Father Antonio Criminali.

4

Yeses and Noes

As we said above, during the first ten years (1541–1551) the Society evolved more than it would during the next four centuries. Who was able to penetrate the mind of Ignatius, a great dreamer yet a most pragmatic man? He had already embarked on a lifestyle that embraced "preaching in poverty," and therefore he stubbornly insisted that his friends, masters of the University of Paris, teach the rudiments of Christian doctrine to children and unlettered adults. However, in the directives that he drafted in 1541 and that were later made mandatory in the *Constitutions*, he preferred that aspirants to the Society be recruited from men with a solid academic background. He proposed that colleges directed by the Society be set up in the universities, although he was opposed to offering courses and lectures within the body of the Society itself. In view of the subsequent history of the Society, who would ever have thought that such had been the case? "To preach in poverty" would come to mean putting aside one's own preferences and taking on missions entrusted to the Society: going to the Indies, accompanying Dr. Ortiz to Worms, putting up with the frustrations of a useless mission to Ireland, preaching before crowds in Montepulciano, or explaining Scripture to the people in some Italian town. The colleges, which in the beginning were designed for newly received members into the Society, eventually became institutions opened to non-Jesuits as well, and they multiplied in a number of cities throughout Italy, Spain, and Germany where they became one of the characteristic works of

471

the Society. The Spiritual Exercises, particularly the key meditations of the First Week, became the stock approach for those
preaching popular missions. Giving a more serious rendition
of these Exercises in their entirety was reserved for isolated
individuals, who generally went through them in a less rigorous manner than did the *primi patres* who first made them in
Paris. Stability, which was one of the characteristic features of
the older monastic type of life, had nothing whatsoever to do
with Íñigo's followers, for their lives were patterned on mobility and total availability. They did not even form flying
squadrons; most of the time, these Jesuits were strung out far
away from one another; no community life, no regular house;
sometimes they were sent in pairs and at other times they were
all alone, and they either depended on some charitable soul to
put them up or they found lodging in a hospice, the favorite
accommodation place of their pilgrim founder.

Ignatius, who was a good judge of men and an expert when
it came to forming and managing them, ended up cutting
himself off from his men, throwing them against the hazards
of life. He had confidence in them once they were sufficiently
hardened, but most especially he had confidence in God. He
wanted his men to be "ready for everything." That *everything*
included being sent to the missions among the infidels, teaching catechism to children, helping the cook in the kitchen,
emptying bedpans in hospitals, being a cardinal's assistant,
rescuing and improving the life of a *cortigiana*, addressing the
attending fathers at the Council of Trent, or teaching Latin in
a school. He said that it was occasionally acceptable to say yes
to helping the hungry, giving instructions to Jewish converts,
bringing spiritual aid to soldiers in the different armies,
redeeming prisoners, examining candidates to the priesthood, and reforming monasteries of religious women. Besides
so many yeses, there were some noes that help us to outline
his way, but not without a certain amount of astonishment in
some cases. One of the most unexpected noes was giving
direction on an ordinary basis to religious women. Very few
saints have expressed such delicate gratitude as Ignatius when
he speaks of the assistance, sometimes maternal, that he
received from the pious women of Loyola, Manresa, Barcelona, and Alcalá. Their names would never be erased from
his memory. In his correspondence there are many letters of

high spiritual quality addressed to these women, and Father Hugo Rahner, S.J., has given us a monograph on this subject that is as prodigious as it is surprising.

In this extensive feminine panorama, however, there is one event that is little known. The results of this event shattered Ignatius to the very core of his being. It is the case of Isabel Roser, who was Ignatius's generous protectoress during his extended stay in Barcelona, and who later helped him financially while he was studying in Paris. In 1543, this faithful and audacious widow made an appearance in Rome, determined to place herself under the obedience and spiritual direction of the erstwhile destitute pilgrim. Ignatius treated her exquisitely and delegated to Esteban de Eguía the job of extending to her his continuous personal attention. Isabel persisted in her desire to become a full-fledged member of the Society and the diplomatic steps she took to do so were of such a nature that the obedient Ignatius could not resist. No less a person than Paul III himself ordered that she be admitted to the Society. She worked with Ignatius in the Casa Santa Marta, rescuing fallen women, and even came to visit him when he was sick in bed. But then she had some of her nubile nieces come and join her, and that is when the fat hit the fire. With authorization from Paul III, Nadal had to intervene, and, in the presence of a notary, he read her a declaration freeing her from all commitments to and ties with the Society.

Ignatius had preferred to think of Isabel as a mother, rather than as a daughter. The affair had caused a certain number of rumors to spread throughout the Society. The most critical of Ignatius's behavior was Father Francisco Zapata, who had entered the Society as a priest in 1546. Zapata, who was from a wealthy noble family of Toledo, went to great extremes in finding fault with the founder's conduct in this matter and stood up to Ignatius, saying: "I am a man; I have a beard; I am not a boy, and I would rather obey fifty other people before obeying you." Ignatius showed infinite patience with his accuser, but in the end he had to expel him from the Society, and Zapata joined the Franciscans in 1548. Ignatius was no less patient with the Catalan woman, who now began telling everyone that she had been victimized and even fleeced by the Society. The altercation ended up before the court, and once it became clear what the damages were, the judgment went against the woman. She had given 144 ducats to the Jesuits, but had received more than 300. This whole messy affair had besmirched Ignatius's reputation and forced him to insist that the false statements Isabel had been making be publicly adjudicated. All of this took place in 1547. Isabel had to return to Barcelona, where she too entered the Franciscans. Eventually, she ended up by being reconciled with her former guest and protégé, whom she first loved and then misused. This whole experience was not wasted on our expert psychologist. He gave a categorical no to the creation of a female branch of the Society, even though later on, as Father de Dalmases has shown, he was pressured into allowing Princess Juana, the daughter of Charles V and sister of Philip II, to take simple vows in the Society. Unhesitatingly, he also refused to become involved in the spiritual welfare of religious women. He considered it a ministry fraught with unpleasantness and distress, one that was not exempt from dangers and invited scandalmongering.

Ignatius was even more categorical, if that was possible, in pronouncing another no to requests that were becoming inevitable. No he said to ecclesiastical dignities, or more precisely to the office of bishop. It was to be expected that during a time of reform, men from the newly founded religious congregations of reformed priests like the Theatines, Barnabites, Oratorians, and Somaschi would be named to fill bishoprics. By accepting such a charge were they not helping the Church that direly and sorely needed good men? Ignatius's refusal was not merely a prudent prohibition; it was a negative response to a real threat. He very graphically described the situation as "the tribulation of the bishoprics." Within a few years (1543–1547), Rodrigues was being talked about as next bishop of Coimbra; Laínez was rumored for Ljubljana, and Favre as the patriarch of Ethiopia. The king of the Romans, Ferdinand I, was particularly eager to have Bobadilla or Jay appointed to the see of Trieste. With the greatest tenacity, Ignatius mustered up all of his resources to cut short these nominations and to fend off papal confirmation. He resisted as much as he could. He went to see the pope and cardinals, even paying them late night visits. He had recourse to the influential offices of Margaret of Austria, and he did not admit victory until the very moment the issue was decided. But he did win. It was not that he was refusing to serve the Church, but he was saying no to this particular way of serving the Church. His reasons were patently clear: to open the door to such dignities would spell the ruination of the Society, and even though some immediate good could come from making a particular Jesuit a bishop, it would ultimately be harmful for the overall good of the Church, and it would also be a source of confusion for generous young men who joined the Society because they wanted a more austere and difficult lifestyle. Such was the thinking of the man who has been accused of having an unsatiable hunger for power. A few years after this crisis had passed, he would be successful in making sure that the pope did not make Borgia and Laínez cardinals.

If his apodictic no to bishops' miters pertained to a limited number of Jesuits and could seriously affect the future of the Society, there were other noes whose range was more general and affected everyone in the order. He said no to adopting a particular habit; his men were to dress in the manner of ordinary honest priests. No also to chanting the office in choir because it affected mobility and hours given to work. No to solemn chant and to having an organ at liturgies for the same reason (Ignatius, as an older man, confessed that he would not have made this proviso if he had merely followed his own inclinations because he was exceedingly sensitive to the magic of music). No to the discipline and to other penances imposed by rule, which was the common practice in monasteries and among the mendicant orders. No to long hours of personal prayer, to the attractiveness of contemplation, which was also very common at the time, particularly in Spain. From the college at Gandía, impregnated by the aromas of Franciscan spirituality and protected by that zealous convert, Francis Borgia, came requests for longer contemplation. Ignatius always responded no, and he never obliged by rule more than one hour of prayer a day, and even this hour was to be distributed over the whole day, and it included his famous examinations of conscience. He wanted his students to study and the others to work. They could make their work a prayer, and they should spend special effort in finding God outside of their formal prayer, in their daily occupations, and in the people they dealt with. Ignatius himself was a living example of such effort. His yeses opened up wide horizons; his noes marked out frontiers. Between these yeses and noes he worked out a style of life and work, and through them he was hammering out the particular form the Society was beginning to take.

5

Esteem, Poverty, Tears: "Warm and Intense Charity"

Meanwhile, Paul III, the pope who had so willingly approved the Society, proceeded to honor it by raining down upon it a veritable torrent of protective bulls and briefs. In 1543, he gave the Society faculties, indulgences, and privileges applicable to those who had already pronounced their vows and who now wanted to be professed Jesuits. In 1544, Paul III issued the bull *Iniunctum nobis* removing the original clause that limited the number of professed fathers to sixty and opening the doors to an unrestricted number of Jesuits. The previous year, the number of the properly so-called professed was still only ten. In 1545, with the brief *Cum inter cunctas*, he granted faculties to all of the priests to preach, confess, and absolve from reserved sins. The following year, Paul III accepted Ignatius's suggestion and issued the brief *Exponi nobis*, which was to have such a great bearing on the future structure of the Society. This brief permitted the Society to accept spiritual and temporal coadjutors into the ranks of the Society. These men, both priests and lay brothers, would free the professed priests to carry out their spiritual apostolates and would relieve them from temporal domestic functions. The coadjutors pronounced the three vows of poverty, chastity, and obedience. The Society now appeared as a *corpus*, or a body at whose epicenter was the professed, the authentic pillars of the institution. The final incorporation of members into the ranks of the professed would take place only after a long testing period. After the professed were the spiritual and temporal coadjutors, and finally there were the students, who were called scholastics. After their novitiate, these young men would pronounce the simple, perpetual vows, their "first vows" in the order—a real novelty at the time—and only much later would they pronounce either the final solemn vows of the professed or the simple vows of spiritual coadjutors. Their definitive insertion into the Society rested with the Society. All groups went into forming one and the same family, and they all shared the same general mission, but individually, each one through his particular job, be it in a university chair, a pulpit, a kitchen, or answering the door of the house. Ignatius would have enthusiastically agreed with the saying of Saint Teresa of Avila: "God can be found in pots and pans." He could have even added more places than that, places he had known as a pilgrim—the banks of a river, prisons, hospitals, and talking as one walks along the road. The favor of Paul III was even more in evidence after he learned that the duke of Gandía, to whom he was so indebted, gave the Society his highest recommendations. The duke, who was the great-grandson of a pope (Alexander VI) and of a king (Ferdinand of Aragon), and the grandson of an archbishop of Zaragoza, got Paul III to grant special graces to those who made the Exercises and, in 1548, he was even instrumental in obtaining the papal approval of Ignatius's small book, the *Spiritual Exercises*. A year later, the Society was granted the benefits of the immense *Mare Magnum*, the term referring to the 1474 bull of Sixtus IV, which compiled all the different privileges that had already been granted to the Franciscans, and to which Paul III was adding more. Ignatius had thus achieved for the Society, which was not yet ten years old, what the Franciscans and Dominicans had not been able to obtain for centuries. After the old days of trusting in God and in Him alone came the era of seeking favors, protection, privileges, and in the wake of these came all the inevitable resentments attached to them.

In the very midst of this veritable spree of consideration and growing esteem for the Society, Ignatius remained obsessed by his ideals of poverty. As an individual, he had lived poverty generously and had tried to inculcate it among his followers.

Poverty was the school of learning confidence in God, the concrete way in which one could imitate Christ; it was an inseparable ornament for those who aspired to preach the Gospel to others. The days when he had a personal spontaneous effect on others had passed; now he had to think of how to transmit to an institution the spirit of living poverty in a concrete way. Ignatius, who was once a student-beggar, did not want his young men in studies to beg; he did not want them to be distracted from what they were supposed to be doing by worrying about how they were going to get their day's ration of food. He hoped that generous benefactors would come on the scene to make sure that his colleges had a fixed revenue, but he was adamant that no such endowments be established in those houses where the professed fathers lived, and he insisted that the gratuity of Jesuit ministries be maintained. A question arose about a precise point: Providing the poverty of the individual men was safeguarded, could there be some kind of income allowed for the *sacristies* of Jesuit churches, that is, for the real economic needs to provide proper worship? This question, which seems trivial today, was basic for Ignatius, and it illustrates his radical thinking when it came to poverty. Although in 1541, before Ignatius was general, the companions had voted to accept a poverty that allowed churches to have fixed revenues in order to cover the expenses of worship alone, the problem was still not solved as far as he was concerned, and he debated the question in his own conscience for years. The result of these ruminations is found in a 1544 document written in his own hand. Apart from the actual question of poverty itself, his deliberations on this point give us a clear picture of the manner he personally used to discern a question. By this thorough research technique, and by the way he weighed the pros and cons of the question before coming to a final decision, he bequeathed to the Society a certain characteristic style of acting. He began by arguing that having a fixed revenue for the maintenance of worship and the upkeep of the church did have some advantages. An endowed church would enable the Society to be better maintained; it would do away with annoying and disedifying others by having the members of the Society begging; it would do away with the temptation to be oversolicitous in seeking funds; the Society would be able to give itself greater peace of mind to worship and hold prayers at scheduled times; the time spent in begging could be devoted to preaching, hearing confessions, and other forms of worship; the church would be kept cleaner and more adapted to better devotion; the members of the Society could give themselves to study and to the ministry and thereby be of greater help to the neighbor. Against these seven reasons, he listed fifteen in favor of a radical, extreme type of poverty: the Society would have greater spiritual strength and greater devotion by resembling more Christ and the Blessed Virgin; greed would be put to flight; the members of the Society would be more closely united to the Church by looking to the poverty of Christ in the Blessed Sacrament; it would be easier to hope for everything from God; there would be a greater help in humbling the members of the Society, and therefore there would be greater union with Him who had humbled Himself for us; it would be possible to live in greater independence from worldly consolation; more opportunities to live in greater hope would result; more of a probability to give greater edification and also to speak with greater liberty of spirit and, therefore, have a greater effectiveness in dealing with others; there would be a greater incentive to help and encourage others, and likewise there would be a greater opportunity to persuade others to embrace evangelical poverty; it would result in a greater ability to be more available to travel to different missions; evangelical poverty is a more perfect way to live; Jesus taught this same poverty to His disciples when they went out to preach; and finally, this evangelical poverty was the lifestyle that the original companions chose to preach under His standard. "More," "greater": they are repeated over and over again. That is Ignatius. It is the old *más valer*, the "wanting to do more," that he had in his blood, that had grown alongside courtly ambitions and was stimulated by novels about knights-errant, a *more* and a *greater* that has now a very different orientation and horizon. It is the plus ultra of the Renaissance applied to the conquest of spiritual spaces and heights of a knight who is now a knight of the divine.

But let us not make a mistake when we confront arguments that seem both rationalistic and voluntaristic in this document, which he himself called the *Deliberations on Poverty*, wherein he reasoned and proposed the conquest of something very difficult. A contemporary document, his *Spiritual Diary*, written in his own hand, will save us from such a possible error and will open to us unexpected vistas in the soul of this Christian who knew that God is not something that is infallibly found at the end of our efforts as a reward for what we have achieved, but rather is someone who comes to us gratuitously and with open hands. Only two of his small notebooks that make up the *Diary* are extant, considerably less material than the "large ream of notes" that Gonçalves da Câmara saw Ignatius holding in his hands and from which the saint read him a few paragraphs, even though he refused to let him see it, not even allowing him "a little peek" at his manuscript. These two surviving notebooks that contain about twenty-five pages were not published before 1892, and then only partially. In 1934, the complete text was published. The first notebook covers the period from February 2 to March 12, 1544, and contains Ignatius's spiritual debate on the problem of poverty. With striking clarity, both books reveal Ignatius's greatest secret, namely, that he was a very great mystic. His deliberations on poverty represent a reasoned search for an ideal way. But it is not simply a monologue, the product of an introspective reflection. Rather, it is a dialogue between himself and the transcendent, the divine. It is a typical Ignatian search for the light and the divine confirmation of the promptings through which God speaks to us and guides us. On the fringe of this inner debate, the *Diary* reveals to us the unfathomable depths of Ignatius's high mystical experiences of great trinitarian depth that are centered about his celebration of the Mass. The words he uses are sober, even impoverished, when we compare them with the language of Saint John of the Cross or Saint Teresa of Avila. But although the wrapping is different, the "thing" itself is the same. With this *Diary*, the stereotyped image of Ignatius as a wooden ascetic, a voluntarist, even to the point of being a Pelagian, a man of action with a military panache, fades away, or at least, in order for the picture to be complete, must be seen alongside the view of Ignatius the mystic, with infused contemplation, with a total passivity of his knowledge and love; his unfathomable intuition of divine things; his familiarity with the Incarnated Word of God and His mother, the Virgin Mary, and with his unbelievable gift of tears, to which he alludes 175 times in the *Diary*. The natural modesty of this taciturn and undemonstrative Basque makes it more difficult for him to express what all mystics call indescribable and ineffable. Basically, one can say that he carried his secret with him to the grave, although these golden pages, more because of what they say than how they say it, give us some snatches of his secret and his personality and of that which better defines the totality of his way. Before anything else, he was a man infused with the gifts of the Holy Spirit, one who listened to God all of the time.

Alongside his characteristic sobriety of expression, other mystics may appear droll and loquacious. With him each word is rugged and endowed with a tremendous power of muted suggestion, like a piece of granite dug from a quarry. Who would dare deepen the evocative strength of the following phrases: "increased confidence in our Lady"; "abundance of devotion, internal and external tears," "much clarity"; "I felt within myself an impulse of approaching the Father, and in doing so my hair stood on end, with a most remarkable warmth throughout my whole body"; "I realized things in such a way they cannot be described and they cannot be explained"; "I felt a deep understanding, delightful and very spiritual"; "full of warm devotion and very sweet"; "many lights and spiritual memories concerning the most Holy Trinity, which served as a great illumination to my mind, so much so that I thought I could never learn so much by hard study, and later, as I examined the matter more closely, I felt and understood, I thought, more than if I had studied all my life."—who again could deepen the profundity of these phrases? Ignatius was not an anchorite and during this time he did not experience the same raptures and ecstacies he had known at Manresa. These experiences at Rome came to him while he was saying Mass, and also while he was walking along the city streets, while he was vesting for Mass, when he was sitting at the dinner table, while he was waiting in the antechamber of the dean of the Sacred College, Cardinal Giovanni Domenico de Cupis, when he was hearing confessions for hours, not thinking about eating, or when he was occupied giving spiritual or material assistance to the protected women of Santa Marta. His mystical experiences did in no way deter him from his normal activities nor did they induce him to seek a more isolated, retired life. Neither did these experiences take on the nuptial symbolism, characteristic of so many other mystics. In his case, mysticism is translated into service, the dynamism of a truth he loves and cherishes, which is the source of endless tears. Who would have believed it! The titan of action and of exhausting energy was a man whose eyes were ruined by mystical tears. No painter has been able to depict those eyes that once spoke and which now, lying behind his death mask, are lifeless. That possessed man in Padua has given us a portrait of Ignatius better than Titian could have painted it, when he described him as "that tiny, little Spaniard with a bit of a limp and sparkling eyes." With that kind, diminutive, *españolito pequeño*, he reminds us that Ignatius was very short. This fact might explain why, just a few years after his death, the famous Spanish Cistercian Luis Estrada, in a glowing eulogy, contrasted Ignatius's greatness with his unimpressive bodily appearance, referring to him as "a tiny grain," "so small a man," and "the little man of God."

6
The Dispersed Society

Although it may seem that at times Ignatius was immersed in the spiritual consolation of Saint Paul's third heaven, he really did live with his feet on the ground, enmeshed in thousands of prosaic duties and dull day-to-day work, giving himself to a multiplicity of ministries, particularly to what he considered was the most important task of all—forging his men and forming his "least Society" that had just seen the light of day and was already the "dispersed Society." He had to set guidelines for the order and also maintain the unity and cohesion of its members, scattered, as they were, over the face of the earth. Ignatius had a gift of and a sense for the concrete; he was not at home with either abstractions or vague ideas. That was his nature. He always infused his particular thought pattern into whatever he said, wrote, or did. Gonçalves da Câmara described this trait in a charming fashion: "He never persuades with sentiments but with things. . . . He never dresses up realities with words, but he presents all the circumstances and details, circumstances and details that are so convincing that they almost force a person to be persuaded. . . . His manner of speaking is simple, clear, and distinct. And he has such a keen memory for past events, and even the key words associated with a particular event, that he can tell what took place ten, fifteen, and even more years ago, exactly as it happened. He makes the past present, and whenever he has to speak at length about important events, he weighs every word. . . ." Gonçalves da Câmara further expounded: "When it was a question of important matters, he had them read or recounted to him three or four times, and he had such a memory that I think I can still hear him narrate incidents that had happened a long time before, sometimes in the very same order and in the exact words that he used the first time he told them." For Ignatius, as for any true Basque, the word had a tremendous importance because the word conveys the person. This is why he spoke and wrote only after having spent a long time reflecting on what he wanted to say. He would consider what he was going to say and to whom he was going to say it, to a particular person and about a concrete subject. He abhorred rhetoric, verbosity, exaggeration, and affectation.

His instructions and letters offer us a wonderful insight into his personality and way of acting. Providing we classify them broadly, there are more than two hundred manuscript examples of his instructions. They reveal the breadth and variety of the Society's early ministries, their geographical spread, their success, and, most particularly, these instructions give us examples of Ignatius's personal criteria, motives, and objectives; they show us the profound evangelical spirit that animated everything he did and they illustrate the human resources he mobilized to carry out his projects. Moreover, behind all of these directions, we divine a first-class psychologist, used to dealing with men. The instructions contain a mixture of basic principles and detailed directions, and they treat with subjects as diverse as right methods of governance within the Society, to proper dealings with women in the confessional; from how to function as a king's confessor, to how to write letters; from how to devote oneself to a particular ministry, to how to beg or the proper way to study the humanities. In these directives we find variables, the sense of adaptation existing alongside what are unchanging principles. When he sent Broët and Salmerón on the exceedingly ticklish mission to Ireland, he gave them some very provocative pieces of advice. In their dealings with every type of person, he counseled them to speak little and reluctantly, to listen long and be content in doing so. When they communicated with men of influence, he recommended that they size each one up and adapt themselves to the temperament of the person with whom they are speaking. Take on their ways, he suggested, because this is what pleases them: *I have become all things to all men.* One should not be grave and phlegmatic in dealing with a person with a choleric temperament. In a conversation between one choleric and another—and Ignatius was basically a choleric—there was always the danger of spoiling everything. One ought to be well armed through self-examination, resolved to put up with anything and not lose composure. Be guarded in speech, he told them, and remember that everything a person says in private may later become public. Be generous in giving time to everyone. If you promised to have something done for tomorrow, do it today. Make friends to make things easier. Imitate the artifices of the evil spirit when he is tempting a good man: enter the other's door and come out your own, "in order to net him for the greater service of God." Does all of this advice represent a sly combination of ethical behavior with worldly discretion, or does it merely show Ignatius's knowledge of human nature? Despite all this advice, the Irish mission was a total disaster. The insoluble problems Broët and Salmerón encountered were even worse than the rock-bound English cliffs that all but claimed their lives and shattered the ship they had boarded in Flanders. They were accompanied by Francisco Zapata, at that time a candidate to the Society, who paid all of their expenses. After landing in England, in December 1541, the three remained in hiding for some days. Later, they made their way to Edinburgh and then to Glasgow without ever getting a clear picture of the situation in Ireland. When they were in Lyons, they had met the the Scottish primate, Cardinal David Beaton, who was also an archbishop and the father of six illegitimate children, and who, four years later, would be hacked to death in his bedroom by his own countrymen. Beaton told the two nuncios that of all mankind the Irish were perhaps the wildest and the most incapable of any kind of discipline whatsoever. Perhaps his arguments had some influence on them. In any case, they spent a month in Ireland where the bishops in twenty-two of the thirty dioceses had already disavowed the pope's authority in favor of Henry VIII's. The fact that the two nuncios from Rome were able to leave Ireland alive was regarded by some as being a near miracle. On their way back to Rome, in their dirty and tattered cassocks, they were thought to be spies and thrown into prison in Lyons. Salmerón was not exaggerating when he wrote: "Ireland was not without its share of the cross of Christ our Lord, for we suffered hunger and thirst, and had no place to put our heads nor even a place to say an Our Father in peace."

Of great interest and worth are the instructions Ignatius gave to Laínez and Salmerón (Favre was already dead) on their being designated to take part in the Council of Trent. Initially they were invited more to do apostolic work in the town than to be actual participants in the Council's proceedings, and so the norms Ignatius sent them pertained more to their pastoral activities than to their involvement in theological affairs. He recommended that they pray hard and have others also pray for the success of the Council, and then he wrote: "I would try to be slow to speak, and would do so in a thoughtful, friendly fashion, especially about matters that could be dealt with in the Council. I should try to be slow to speak, and would help myself by listening quietly, so as to appreciate and understand the spirits, sentiments, and points of view of the speakers, in order to answer or to be silent, depending on what is the better thing to do." When speaking about controversial matters, Ignatius advised that they should not hold firm to any particular point of view until they made an effort to see the reasons held by both sides, and they should try not to displease anyone by becoming passionately favorable toward that person's opponent. They should not take their own personal recreation or a lack of time or comfort into consideration as long as they were at the service of the people of Trent, but they should try to accommodate themselves to the circumstances of the person they were dealing with at the time "in order to move that person to the greater glory of God." The purpose in going to Trent was *primarily* to preach, hear confessions, read, teach children, give the Exercises, visit hospitals, exhort the people to devotion and prayer, and come to a fuller knowledge of themselves and a greater love of God, encouraging everyone to renew his spiritual life by speaking "at length, in a practical way, lovingly, and with affection." Ignatius advised that his men should make it a point not to touch on or discuss those points that were matters of controversy with the Protestants, but rather they should expose their beliefs with great simplicity, exhorting the people to good habits and devotion, and adapting their message to the needs of their listeners. They should be solicitous in maintaining union among themselves, practicing fraternal correction, by revising together their daily agenda, and to help one another in greater charity. After their number increased, they should come to a decision by votes, and they should be mindful to spread "the truth everywhere" by their example and their manner of life. When Ignatius chose Laínez and Salmerón to carry out the orders of the pope by going to Trent, he had no idea that they would be involved directly in the Council. In a letter of presentation to the legate Cardinal Cervini, he told him that the fathers were going to Trent "more out of obedience than because they thought they could be of any help, even in the smallest matter pertaining to the Council." A few days after their arrival on May 18, 1546, the president of the Council had their names inscribed on the list of theologians—as secular priests, of course. Salmerón was only thirty-one at the time, but he looked much younger. Very shortly, both men were in the limelight, making interventions. In the next session of the Council (1551–1552), they would be listed as pontifical theologians, which was no obstacle to the fact that they were lodged in a cramped, dingy room with only one bed and no table at which they could read or write. A few days later, they rented the rooms where they had lived five years earlier. They again intervened in the conciliar discussions, but they did not on this account give up their preferred ministries—hearing confessions, teaching catechism, and visiting hospitals. By their appearance at the Council, they made the newly formed Society known, and so from that moment on, the number of bishops from Italy, France, and Spain, who would open the doors of their dioceses to Loyola's family, increased.

The Council became an ideal public relations platform for the Society, whose representatives were Laínez, Salmerón, and Claude Jay, who from the first days of the Council had been the deputy with the vote of Otto von Truchess von Waldburg, cardinal archbishop of Augsburg. Together they projected a certain image, and this image was that the typical Jesuit was a conciliar theologian who possessed an unsurpassed amount of theological knowledge, but what was really conspicuous about these former masters of the University of Paris was the probity of their lives and their apostolic zeal. The secret of their impact—and the impact was there whenever a Jesuit was present—lay in their priesthood. They were authentic, effective priests. They followed the traditional practice of the so-called *ministeria assueta* or *consueta*, that is, either a permanent ministry carried out from a single residence or house by two companions, or a temporary stay of two companions in a given city. The only novelty was that the companions were conscientious in performing their pastoral duties, duties that, unfortunately, the local clergy had neglected. Such duties consisted in catechizing the people, preaching, explaining the Scriptures—that is, explaining the faith and making it credible; in encouraging the people to partake in the sacramental life of the Church, particularly through confession and Holy Communion—that is, to try to get them to embark on a religious experience; and finally, in taking a strong stand against personal and social vices—blasphemy, concubinage, vengeance, feuding—while at the same time fostering permanent changes in the customs of the people, which meant revitalizing and sustaining the faith over a long period of time. Ignatius and his followers insisted on going into the very heart of men and man's culture. They encouraged those who were well disposed to high ideals, but at the same time, they did not forget the abandoned masses. They were able to pass a whole day hearing confessions, taking off barely enough time to eat. The seeds they sowed fell on multitudes of people, on monasteries that were beginning to reform, on individuals who wanted a deeper spiritual life. Their efforts changed the lives of many priests and canons; they attracted generous young men to the Society and encouraged the laity to become involved, either on an individual or on a corporate basis, in activities that they had never previously considered. Furthermore, they tried to insure that what they began would continue after they left. At Faenza, a doctor of laws decided to give his services freely in defending the rights of the poor. Another lawyer agreed to argue cases of the poor before the governor. A doctor agreed to be more generous in serving the most needy members of his neighborhood, to care for them and clothe them. Many laymen agreed to attend to the sick through the "Company of Charity," a confraternity that was founded for that apostolate. In this "service" of Ignatius's men, we cannot discern between what was planned and what was an on-the-spot, improvised response to immediate and fundamental needs. Whatever the case, they poured themselves out unsparingly, down to complete physical exhaustion. Spread out as they were from home base and from one another, the lives of these first Jesuits were lives exposed to all types of adversities and marked by personal responsibility.

7

Staying Together through Correspondence

There was a critical problem the first Jesuits now had to face. How were they going to maintain the union, cohesion, and familial spirit of this ever-growing band that was rapidly spreading out over four continents? "The more we are dispersed geographically, the deeper ought we to be rooted in what makes us who we are," commented the amiable Savoyard, Pierre Favre. Ignatius was keeping watch over the spiritual formation of the novices, but he also had to strengthen the bonds that held the Society together. The period of the small Parisian group, that brief interim with all of those hours of common life spent in forming ideals, was nothing more now than a nostalgic memory. The reality of life had imposed a forced separation. Initially, the Society had been an adventure of very closely bonded university friends. Simplicity was the keynote in their dealings with one another. When Araoz responded to his family's request and went to Rome to rescue his uncle, he knocked at the door where the companions were staying, and Master Francis Xavier let him in. Ignoring the formulas of courtesy that were so highly regarded in that age, Xavier announced the nephew's arrival by simply calling out: "Hey Íñigo, Araoz is here." The surprised visitor was favorably impressed by this example of simplicity and fraternity that existed among the companions. Under these circumstances, how difficult it must have been for Xavier to cut himself off from the master and friend whom he idolized! Francis left Rome suddenly and unexpectedly. He stopped over in Bologna en route to Lisbon and the Indies, and while he was there, he received a letter from Ignatius, "with it such joy and comfort, that only God our Lord could measure it." His soul was tormented by the thought that he and Ignatius would never meet again, except through correspondence. "During our free moments we should not think of anything else except of one another and writing to each other." The very day he turned thirty-five, April 7, 1541, his ship sailed from Lisbon. A few days before, he wrote to Ignatius: "When you write to India, write to us about everything, since this will be possible only once a year; and write in such great detail that we shall have to read the letter for eight days. We shall do the same."

That deep friendship of the original companions was impossible to sustain among men who did not know one another or who met each other only fleetingly. Only the mail, the slow mail of the sixteenth century, could keep alive affective bonds, allow for an exchange of news about different men and their apostolates, and insure that the same plan and manner of living was kept intact by all. Ignatius understood the importance of correspondence and insistently reminded his followers that they had an obligation to write, that writing letters was not something that they take up merely as a pastime or hobby. At the same time, he himself accepted the responsibility of answering letters and of carrying on a never-ending worldwide correspondence.

We still have approximately seven thousand of his letters, some long, some short. He wrote many more than these. In one of these letters he recounted that he had sent 250 letters out in one night. We have about one thousand letters dating from the year 1555. A collection of letters is always interesting, but in the case of Ignatius's letters, it is the personal factor, as opposed to any literary value, that gives them value. He was a man who took great pains at writing carefully worded letters. Like all Basques, he had a respect for the word, to the word pronounced and expressed, and a kind of veneration for the word that was written. What flowed from his pen in the solitude of his *cameretta* has the solemnity of matters declared before witnesses. He chiseled words and sentences; he corrected them and retouched them; he inked over drafts, sometimes rejecting one and beginning another. He recommended the following norm that he himself put into practice: "What one writes must be considered more carefully than what one says, because the written word remains and is a witness for all times." Such caution may have squelched spontaneity because his letters are so different from those written by Saint Teresa of Avila; however, what Ignatius wrote serves to strengthen the intention contained in every word and thereby renders each word more rich in its expressive density. Too often we come to a knowledge of Ignatius through our reading of his *Spiritual Exercises* or the *Constitutions*. There is no question that his personality emerges from these writings in an unmistakable way, but in his letters the abstract becomes more personal—both on the part of the writer and the addressee—his method and his rule take on a here-and-now meaning. Rigidity dresses itself with flexibility and adaptation. In his letters he narrates, counsels, exhorts, and gives orders; he sets out plans for unbelievable undertakings, such as a crusade against the Turks. He reaffirms principles; he directs business affairs; he solves problems; and he makes the best of given circumstances in his letters. He reveals his top priorities in these pieces of correspondence; his aspirations and his ideals, his worries, his mettle before adversity and in the face of confrontation; his sentiments of affection, gratitude, and patience, and even a certain dissimulated irony sometimes shows up. In a word the very essence of his personality is manifested in his letters. He is ever polite and measured, human, but he has no room for frivolity. He faces his correspondents squarely in all types of circumstances, that is, he remains consistent whether he is writing to Charles V, Philip II, John III of Portugal, or to members of his own family, or to Gouveia, or to one of the Barcelona women who once looked after him, or to some particular nun. An indifference to the accepted social conventions runs throughout all his letters, and, whether he is grappling with problems associated with the reform of the University of Vienna or whether he is trying to help one of his correspondents with scruples, aridity, or some other spiritual infirmity, he always comes across as serious and reserved. He is the same in addressing cardinals and bishops as he is when he writes to his first companions, to novices, high-placed ladies, or ordinary women. For each one there is the appropriate and exact word; he addresses each pleasantly and with grave courtesy, giving him or her a small light that may illuminate truth in a singular, personal way. And to all his correspondents he gives a word of parting, like a necessary *ritornello*, that comes from affection and points toward transcendence: "May it please God that we may know His most holy will and fulfill it perfectly." To know and to fulfill—in duple rhythm, as musicologists would say. Knowing God's will and fulfilling it: one element was as necessary as the other in achieving a difficult, however authentic, conversion.

But we must not forget the original reason why Ignatius undertook the arduous ministry of writing letters *inter muros*, within the Society. His letters were a means of giving an evolving form to the Society, of dealing with his men individually, and of safeguarding the union, even the uniformity of the group.

Polanco had a genius for organizing a secretariat that was accommodating and efficient. Ignatius turned over the job of answering letters to him. Sometimes Ignatius dictated letters to him, sometimes he gave him a detailed outline that Polanco would later complete, and sometimes Ignatius merely indicated to him in a general way what the answer to a particular piece of correspondence should be. A number of copyists would rewrite the rough copy in duplicate, keeping and eventually filing away the second copy. Ignatius would then reread the document and make corrections if necessary. He had acquired the type of abnegation and humility to make him confident in his own limited knowledge. Polanco deserved the confidence Ignatius placed in him, and he knew just when he should verify more thoroughly the contents of the document that was to be mailed. These two men were responsible for the miracle of maintaining the unity, despite its dispersion and growth, of what Xavier called the *societas amoris*. The letters gave the Society life, and gradually, over a period of time, they gave birth to the living entity well before the rules came into existence. Some of these letters already contained a nearly complete set of rules because they indicated the patterns that the Society was later to adopt. Ignatius did not appear to find separation from his followers very difficult, and he readily sacrificed the community spirit by sending his men off to distant places, alone and involved in risky undertakings; however, he wanted to know the news about his men and wanted them to

know the news about one another. In those few instances when
he had spare time, the recreation that gave him the greatest
pleasure was enjoying those fleeting encounters with his men
as they passed through Rome. If they were not in the area, he
looked forward with the same anticipated joy to receiving letters from them. In an uncharacteristic hyperbole, this man of
guarded language once said that he wanted to be informed
even about the lice that were biting his sons. How much more,
then, did he want to know about their labors, their successes,
and failures! Receiving news brought him the greatest joy,
especially when it was news about Xavier, who would sign his
letters "your least son in the farthest exile."

Ignatius soon came to realize that, apart from their importance for the members of the Society, these letters should be
shared with others, non-Jesuits, who were true friends of "the
least Society" and who were in some ways involved with its mission. The letters provided an insight into the lives his men
were leading and into the work they were doing, but they
were generally scribbled out quickly and at random and were
not meant to be broadcast. However, the friends of the Society
knew that Ignatius was receiving communications from this
man and from that, but he was "very much ashamed" because
he could not share these letters with them. This was the reason he imposed on all the norm that they should write a well-
structured "principal letter" that could be shown to others,
and therefore edifying in content, in addition to a second letter whose style would be less formal, and whose content could
be written out of the abundance of the heart and without
order. Before it was sent, the first letter had to be written and
rewritten, which is to say it had to be copied to avoid untidi-
ness and hurried writing. At any rate, all had to write to him
and bring him up to date about their apostolic endeavors.
They, in turn, were assured that their letters would be
answered. "With God's help," Ignatius promised Favre in
1542, "I will write you all once a month without fail, but
briefly, and more at length every three months, when I will
send you all the news and copies from the letters I receive
from all the members of the Society. Therefore, let all of us in
the Society help one another, for the love of God our Lord. In
this way you will help me and in some way lighten the heavy
burden you have placed on my shoulders. . . ." There were

some who were slow in fulfilling this sacred obligation, and there were even some who went so far as to criticize Ignatius's directive about the "principal letter." Bobadilla, who had been sent off to Germany, was a case in point. Ignatius accepted his "fraternal and loving correction," and, with infinite patience and self-control, he responded to the reticence of his recalcitrant companion and to "his ill-considered correspondence." However, Ignatius reiterated to the rebellious Bobadilla his directions on how to write letters. Perhaps what hurt Ignatius most was the cold way Bobadilla expressed his grievance. He judged that Ignatius was wasting time on details, and as for himself, he did not have the time to read the letters and news items that he had received. Ignatius answered: "You say my letters are not worth reading because of your lack of time. By God's grace I have the time and time to spare to read and reread all of yours." Ignatius promised that he would try to please him in the future, made a gentle allusion to his vow of obedience, and asked Bobadilla to let him know the best method Ignatius should use in writing to him. The saint of obedience wanted obedience to be spontaneous and generous, coming from the soul, not a mechanical response of an order given.

As far as he was able, Ignatius fulfilled scrupulously the office that had been imposed upon him, but occasionally his confidence faltered, and he would utter something that resembled a complaint, as is evident in this letter to Bobadilla, when he wrote: "And if some in the Society say they are very busy, I am convinced that, if I am not very busy, at least I am no less so than anyone in the Society, and with even less health." This was a veritable lesson, not without some irony, on how to behave. Of course others, in contrast to Bobadilla, were grateful to Ignatius for his concern, even if they had to wait two years before his letters reached them. I think of Xavier, for example, an affectionate man with an immense heart. His letters to Ignatius also took two years to arrive in Rome, but they lost none of their refreshing qualities and sensitivity on that account. It sometimes occurs in families that the child who has been most chastised is the one who shows the greatest affection for his father. Xavier, who had been Ignatius's most difficult conquest, was the one who was most eternally faithful to him. And to what an extent! We learn from his own hand that he cried like a child whenever he received a letter from Ignatius and he read his letters on his knees, and that he wore the signature from one of these letters, along with his vow formula and the signatures of his other distant companions, in something like a lover's amulet around his neck. Xavier, the incurable optimist, the jovial man with the ever-present smile on his lips, found time to write long letters and to await with impatience for the return word from his companions. The pope named him nuncio to the East and provincial with jurisdiction that extended from the Cape of Good Hope to Japan, and yet he never lost his simplicity, his great love for children and lepers. The memory of his past life as a companion increased his tenderness to unbelievable extremes. He greeted Ignatius as "my true father," "my unique father in the compassion of Christ," and he signs off his letters with the expression "your brother," or more frequently, "your son." We can see today the intense and secret love that united these two Basques, who were so reserved in the manifestation of their feelings. One cannot read without emotion the sentences Xavier addressed to Ignatius shortly before his death, which occurred on December 3, 1552. In the previous January he had written: "Among many other holy words and consolations of your letter, I read those last which said: 'Completely yours, without my ever being able to forget you at any time, Ignatius.' Just as I read those words with tears, so I am writing these with tears, thinking of the time past and of the great love which you always showed me and still show toward me. . . ." Both men missed one another, and each would have liked to have seen the other in this life. Xavier expressed his desire frankly but with a delicate touch, and he even hinted that obedience could work the miracle that would shorten the distances. In the end, Ignatius called him back to Europe so that he could learn firsthand about the problems of far-off Asia. That longed-for summons arrived two years after Xavier had died on an island off the coast of China.

Xavier's letters were a huge success. They were copied and recopied and read avidly in the courts of Spain and Portugal, at the Council of Trent, in Paris, Cologne, and Coimbra. Besides his spellbinding descriptions of an exotic world, one should add that his apostolic zeal, the immense field he was opening, the total abnegation he demanded of future missionaries, and the insistence he used to encourage them to follow along the path he had chosen were the reasons why these letters became so popular. By 1545, three of them had already been published in Paris. One of these resounded with his powerful appeal and his vibrant challenge to Europe, and more specifically the university communities: "We fail to make Christians here in these lands," he wrote, "because the people here have no one who is concerned with religious and holy matters. Many times I am seized with the thought of going to the schools of our lands, and especially to the University of Paris, where I could cry out like a man who has lost his mind, and tell those in the Sorbonne, who have a greater regard for learning than for doing, that they ought to see to it that their learning has some positive results." He further reflected that if those who were trying to obtain wisdom and knowledge were to consider that one day they were going to have to give an account to God for the talents they received, they would then offer their lives generously to bring the Gospel of Christ to people in mission countries, and as a result they would live happier lives and would have greater hope for divine mercy. But he knew that those who were presently studying in the universities—and perhaps he himself had been no different from them in days gone by—"studied more to obtain honors, benefices, or bishoprics with their learning than with the desire of conforming to the exigencies that these honors and ecclesiastical states require." Such students made their decisions "according to their inordinate affections"—that was the judgment of this former university student who had covered thousands of leagues proclaiming the Gospel and baptizing, alone and all but invisible in the huge expanse of Asia, while in Europe a swarm of clerics was discussing abstract questions and trying to climb the ladder of social success. One of Xavier's letters achieved what Ignatius was not able to do a number of years earlier, and that was to conquer the Majorcan, Jerònimi Nadal. After reading Xavier's exhortations, as we have already seen, Nadal came to Rome, sought out Ignatius, and joined the Society.

If Xavier's letters were successful and soon edited in collections, the other companions also carried out the obligation of writing that Ignatius had imposed upon them. The custom soon developed of sending a letter to Ignatius every four months. These letters have been edited today and constitute a precious source in tracing the spiritual history of Europe, although at the time they were written they were seen to be an instrument for informing their fellow Jesuits of what they were doing and of keeping the Society united. The names of the cities where the companions were sent cover the map of Europe. Then there are the letters that came from Mozambique, India, Malacca, China, and, thanks to Xavier, even from Japan. There were also letters from those who had gone to Brazil and Ethiopia. One could hear the heartbeat of the world in Ignatius's small, narrow rooms, and more than anything else, he could hear the heartbeats of each individual Jesuit who had been sent out on mission. Ignatius assumed the heavy yet consoling task of dealing with each one of them, of doctoring this one's scruples, rescuing that one from lethargy and discouragement, putting the brakes on the indiscreet zeal of another, of correcting someone's mistakes of judgment, giving direction to another's activities and initiatives, of reminding some man of unchangeable principles, and ensuring the whole way of life that was particular to the Society. Indeed, the heart of the Society was in those small Roman rooms, in the soul of Ignatius.

The Society was a living body, growing ever larger and more diversified each day, and yet it was a body in which everything and everyone was geared to the same mission, even though in different ways. In the beginning there were ten members, and soon the number would be in the hundreds. The ministries of these Jesuits were varied and life much more complex than the sketchy plans and forms of the beginning years. A division of work became necessary. Those who had academic degrees could be relieved and exempt from working in the kitchen, at the door, in the garden, or in the upkeep of the house, provided that others could be found to take their places. As we have already seen, Ignatius conceived the idea of having spiritual and temporal coadjutors to take over many tasks in the Society, but the prototype Jesuit was the religious with four solemn vows. Ignatius had been pressured to break the *numerus clausus* of sixty members that had been imposed by the first pontifical approbation of the Society of 1541, but he was in no hurry to admit everyone to the final profession of the four vows. When he died, there were only thirty-five professed out of one thousand members in the Society. At the other end of the scale were the scholastics with their perpetual but, from the Society's point of view, provisionary vows that included the promise to enter the Society either as a spiritual coadjutor or a professed father. Different classes? No, diverse functions, different degrees of incorporation. All members were useful and all served, conscious of collaborating in the same mission from different positions. "Seeking God in all things," was a motto that Ignatius repeated over and over again. One could find God in all things, brilliant or humble. The important thing was to work, to conquer oneself by forgetting oneself, and, through total abnegation, to give oneself to the task assigned.

8

A Book for "Exercising"

If we were to ask Ignatius today what the secret was of this extraordinary dynamism, which was also the hidden source of so much generosity, without hesitation he would answer that basically this strength was a grace from God. If we were to inquire further by asking how, when, and why this grace acted in this way, he would say that the grace acts whenever we take steps that allow it to permeate us; and, he would add, for it to act in this way he had a formula, borne out by his own personal experience and his dealing with others, namely, the Spiritual Exercises. Over the course of his many years and in the midst of all of his countless activities, Ignatius concentrated his efforts and expectations on the Exercises as the ordinary, specific conduit of this particular grace. He has gone down in history as the author of this special formula whose effectiveness has been incalculable, from his time right down to the present and in every part of the world. Among the "books that have changed the world," the *Spiritual Exercises* has a place of distinction. Such is not the case merely because this little volume has gone through more than forty-five hundred editions, which averages one edition per month over the course of four centuries, nor is this the fact merely because his book has been translated into so many different languages, but primarily because its message has been put into practice by millions of people. The success of the book, which was composed without any literary or aesthetic pretensions and which is meant to be lived, not read, lies exclusively in the fact that it is so effective in what it sets out to do. Centuries ago, Saint Francis de Sales used to say that this book produced more conversions than the sum total of all the letters contained in the words used in writing it. A man who was as non-Catholic as the distinguished Protestant scholar Heinrich Boehmer placed it among the books that "have marked the destiny of mankind." A dyed-in-the-wool opponent like René Fülöp-Miller, who described the *Spiritual Exercises* as a book "that brought about a complete revolution in Catholic thought," recognized the magnitude of its influence when he wrote that "indeed there is no other work of Catholic literature, which as far as its historical effects are concerned, can be compared with this little book by Ignatius. Soon the *Exercises* won recruits throughout the whole Catholic Church." Because of its transforming power, this same author saw a parallel between Lenin and Ignatius—and let us add in passing that the first man did in fact admire the second. Fülöp-Miller observed: "Both men possessed the inflexible courage to carry into effect, even to its utmost consequences, a principle that they once acknowledged to be right. . . ." From a different perspective, this book has received more than six hundred statements of high praise from one pope after another, among which was that of Pius XI who referred to it as "a very wise and universal code for directing souls." But let us forget all of these judgments on the *Exercises* and trust what Ignatius himself, who was less inclined to use exaggeration, said in a letter to his former Paris confessor, Dr. Miona. The *Spiritual Exercises*, Ignatius wrote, are "the best means that I can think, feel and understand in this life, both to help a man benefit himself and bring help, profit and advantage to many others." Indeed, it is an unbelievable book, the very best of books!

Before the Exercises were made into a book, however, they were a praxis, and before that, a personal experience. In the days when he was convalescing from his wounds at Loyola, "he paused to think and to reason within himself." This was a personal experience, the beginning of the Exercises. Ignatius himself confessed that some of his insights apropos the discernment of spirits, of the different movements and inclinations that he recorded in writing at the time, go back to those distant days. Ignatius was the first exercitant. Later at Manresa, he sketched out the bare essentials of what would become an immortal book, namely, early notes that were intended for his own personal use rather than for others. The result of what he found through his own introspective observation was vitally important. At Manresa and later at Alcalá, he began to propose to others certain fundamental truths and elementary methods for cultivating this same spirit. These points were undoubtedly contained in the notes or annotations that he gave to the examiner at Salamanca, which, unfortunately, are not extant. During the course of his Paris days, the themes and techniques characteristic of his Exercises had already become recognizable, and to these he attached some additions and modifications. At this same period there were a number of copies of his *Exercises*, both complete and partial, that were in circulation for the benefit of the first companions. Almost all of these men determined to become followers of Ignatius as a result of having first made the Exercises, and they became proponents and proselytes of Ignatius's method even before the Society was approved. After the official recognition had been given, they used the Exercises even more, either in the first houses that had been established by the Society or in the scholasticates and colleges. Provided we understand the word *country* as the real world of *the spirit* and *the spirits*, would it be proper to designate the Exercises a "country road guide"? The fact is that they were designed as a veritable navigational chart that indicated the sandbars of the human heart. Ignatius had begun his spiritual pilgrimage by standing before others, giants like Francis of Assisi and Dominic de Guzmán, and asking himself: "If they did it, why cannot I?" Afterward, he changed the question and asked: "Why just me and not others too?"

Ignatius channeled, systematized, universalized his own experience and showed men how to open themselves so that they could hear a personal invitation God was giving them. This is how the praxis and the book, the "first-born" of Ignatius came to be. This was how he conquered his first followers, who in turn worked profound changes in many other individuals. In Spain, he aroused suspicion; in Paris, his adversaries directed a storm of abuse against him; and later, as his method became better known, he was the victim of slanderous attacks. The reason was the type of life he led, added to the fact that he remained outside the mainstream of what was taking place, and there was the slight hint of occultism in what he was all about, but most especially, it was because of the radical changes that took place in the lives of the persons who became his followers. In order to quell all suspicions about him, Ignatius decided to publish these private notes and have them placed under the highest protection, namely, that of the pope. The process got under way as a result of the favorable decisions given them by Cardinal Álvarez de Toledo, or Silíceo, whom we have already seen, and Cardinal Girolamo Foscari, both Dominicans, and the prelate of the Curia, Filippo Archinto. Very influential as well were the recommendations of the duke of Gandía, Francis Borgia, who had been a Jesuit since 1546, a fact that was not known publicly "because," as Ignatius said when he told him to keep his being a Jesuit secret, "the world does not have ears to hear such an explosion." After settling his vast holdings, this grandee of Spain announced his secret to the world in 1551, and, predictably, the shock was indeed great. Paul III, the reigning pope until 1549, who owed so much to Alexander VI, could scarcely overlook the recommendations of the great-grandson of the Borgia pope. Accordingly, on July 31, 1548, Paul III issued the bull *Pastoralis officii* approving the book of the *Spiritual Exercises* and exhorting the faithful to practice the same. "*Mira approbatio,*" commented one of the more ferocious adversaries of the book—an astonishing approbation! Indeed, it was a singular approval and for more than one reason. The book that pretended to be the spiritual basis of the Society was approved even before the definitive redaction of the Constitutions of the Society had been submitted for approbation. The whole business seems less strange when we consider Ignatius's way of proceeding. He loved papers and documents that provided him with protection. The book was published without the name of the author. The famous typographer, Antonio Blado, was given the job of printing a few hundred copies that were to remain in the hands of the Society and could not be sold or reprinted. The book was no longer a secret, but it was not altogether public, either. We know that Borgia ordered six copies because he had financed the printing costs, and that Ignatius sent as many to friends and benefactors. Some copies ended up in other hands, or they were distributed one by one to those Jesuits who regularly gave Ignatius's Exercises to others. In 1546–1547 Father

André des Freux came out with an elegant Latin version, which was called the Vulgate and which superseded the older, 1541 version, which was more literal. We have a copy of the original Spanish text (1539–1540) with later additions written by Ignatius in his own hand. We can read all of these texts published by the *Monumenta Historica Societatis Iesu* in a 1969 critical edition that contains a splendid introduction giving the history of the various codices, redactional steps, sources, vocabulary, and so forth.

The official publication of the *Spiritual Exercises* was clear, precise, and without mysteries, and it could have helped solve misunderstandings that perdured, in spite of the papal approbation, particularly in Spain. In the years that followed this official approval, there were some uncontrollable rumors in the form of pulpit denunciations and unfavorably written opinions that were rife "in certain corners." Well known was the hostility of the Dominicans Melchor or Melchior Cano, Tomás Pedroche, and Silíceo, the cardinal archbishop of Toledo. However, the critics were not all of the same mind. In conversations, sermons, lectures, and even before the president of the *Consejo Real*, Cano criticized "the Society's way of proceeding." He went so far as to add his own marginal notes to the *Spiritual Exercises* in a most hostile fashion. In one of these observations, he called the annotation in which Ignatius admonishes the exercitant not to be hasty in making any vow, a *pestilantissima regula*. In another observation he considered Ignatius's ideas concerning indifference as being no different from the teachings of the *alumbrados* on the same subject. More serious were the criticisms made by Pedroche, who was a member of a team selected by Cardinal Silíceo to examine the *Spiritual Exercises*. He detected traces of *alumbradismo* in Ignatius's precept that the director should not lean one way or the other while the exercitant was considering a life's vocation, but that he should permit God to deal directly with him. This criticism, which was venomous and geared to disseminate false impressions, unwillingly took on the trappings of praise in a sentence where he personally attacked Ignatius.

This Ignatius or Íñigo of Loyola, as it was well known, was brought before the Inquisition as a heretic, a *dejado* and an *alumbrado*. The said Ignatius then fled to Rome to escape the Inquisition and the inquisitors . . . and was a man of so little education that he was incapable of writing these documents in Latin, but [he had them published] in roman type and in Spanish. *Item.* It should be noted and taken under consideration that the aforementioned Ignatius or Íñigo declared that he composed these exercises and spiritual writings more from his own personal experience and the internal gifts of the Holy Spirit than from books. In this respect he very much resembles the *dejados* and *alumbrados*.

The Salamancan professor Fra Pedro de Sotomayor considered the methods Ignatius proposed for the examination of conscience to be "calculations" while his fellow Dominican, Fra Luis de Granada, interpreted the rules for mental prayer found in the Exercises as "a modern invention to drive men mad and to do away with the copious psalmody that the Church uses." Finally, there were the ever-present rumors that persisted against the secret aura and unknown practices prescribed by the Exercises and against the visible changes they brought about in the lives of those who had made them. There were stories about former exercitants having visions or great expectations of gifts from the Spirit and being guilty of holding suspected beliefs. The most balanced and considered judgment was that these Exercises were "a new thing." All the favorable expressions on the part of the pope served to change matters not one bit.

Today, when one looks at the *Spiritual Exercises,* all of these former cautionary considerations fade. It is a mature book, the fruit of experience and reflection, considered as a practical guide, not so much for the retreatant as for the one who has assumed the role of director. The pages are written to be lived and *practiced,* like the pages in manuals that teach one to play the piano or perform gymnastics. Before all else the Exercises are designed for exercising, "a way of preparing and disposing the soul to . . . find the will of God." They can be judged only by those who have submitted themselves to their discipline. From the very outset, Ignatius presupposed that the retreatant would have an open, generous, and confident disposition. He asks him to try to withdraw from people and worldly cares; to keep silent; to concentrate; to maintain a tension between body and soul, memory and imagination, understanding and reasoning; and to maintain goodwill throughout the whole retreat. He submits the retreatant first to a gradual and progressive process of considerations, and then to an initial *rhythm* of purification and liberation from obstacles that hinder him from being receptive to God's call; then to a flowing tempo, when the retreatant opens himself and gives himself to the inspirations that come from God. The director points out the steps and discerns their effect; however, he must not be a manipulator of conscience, but rather a simple Simon of Cyrene. He helps the retreatant to confront himself and respond to God's calling. Both in substance and form, the doctrine Ignatius proposes is completely traditional but the Exercises are not learned conferences, they are the personal expression of the person making the retreat to God's revelation. The retreatant's interior monologue—analysis, reflection, illuminations, "feeling"—concludes in a colloquy, a conversation with God. This "I" and "Thou" are the protagonists in the colloquy and they lead, on the part of the retreatant, to the final offering of himself: "Take and receive, O Lord, all my liberty, my understanding, all my will." The God of Ignatius is not an abstract, distant being, but the trinitarian God revealed in Christ, who works now through the Spirit. The trinitarian and Christological horizon in the Exercises is evident.

What is the objective or end of this effort? Is it the luminous seeking of the divine will, of what one should be or do in life? Is it to make a choice of a state of life? Is it sanctification or union with God, the synthesis of which is the contemplation for attaining divine love? If any one or all of these purposes constitute the finality and objective of the Exercises, the road to them is marked by the constant effort, the insight that prevents one's being led astray by possible deceptions such as apathy, contrary inclinations, and a lack of determination in carrying out one's resolves. Indeed, the number of cautions and rules is impressive. Still, Ignatius shows himself immensely flexible. For example, he gives no specific rules for the place of prayer, bodily positions that should be taken during prayer, for penances, or different methods of praying, and he is silent about the spontaneity of colloquies made during the period of prayer. In some matters, however, he is not flexible at all because he thinks these are spiritual laws, as unchangeable as physical laws. "To exercise oneself" means to bind one's soul, to be in tension. It means "to look for what I want," "to find what I desire"—phrases he repeats over and over again. To see and feel and then to decide and act is another one of his constant rules. He looks for motion and emotion, but he does not accept the decisions that result from purely emotional states, from joy or sadness. Contrary to the opinion of those who accuse the Exercises of having a tendency to be instruments of manipulation, some people, notably the French theologian, Gaston Fessard, S.J., have interpreted them in an existential framework, and have shown that they insure the maximum of authentic freedom, valid not only for choosing a particular state in life, but also for making any choice whatsoever. Ignatius is no less demanding than any psychoanalyst in establishing the a priori conditions for freedom, and he is implacable when it comes to detecting the conditioning factors that go into making a choice, what he calls the "inordinate affections." According to Fessard, Ignatius confronts his "extremely concrete reflection on the act of liberty" with his vital understanding of sin and the great condition of an authentic existence.

The steps in the First Week of the Exercises show dialectically the moments and the essential elements in the human-divine drama of liberty. It is only in recognizing one's own sin, the authenticity of one's existence, and by making a firm resolve to purify oneself that it is possible for one to appropriate the truth—Christ is the truth—to pass to an existential structure of faith, to the unity of one's own being, to liberty in a concrete historical commitment, to a life that makes sense. The modern psychiatrist, who is the substitute, the *ersatz* for the old "spiritual director," suddenly loses the dialectic tools of his trade when confronted with a total lack of meaning. In love he sees only a sublimation and as an end in itself whereas love is really the precondition for all else. Standing before Christ, Ignatius stresses the *pro me*, so dear to Luther—that is, the conviction that all Christ did was "for me" personally; and, while invoking traditional Christology, Ignatius provokes in the Christian a personal awakening with drastic consequences. This is why the *Spiritual Exercises* is a closed book for unbelievers.

Many will ponder the structure of the different steps of the Ignatian way, its unquestionable psychological merits, its subtle unmasking of our different resistances or vain illusions, the engaging energy and the integrality of its approaches. Yes, Ignatius knew men. He unmasks and at the same time encourages; he makes true freedom possible for man by an authentic liberation from his previous operant conditionings. He is an expert at discerning the spiritual ebbs and flows and contradictions within the heart of man, of cutting hidden knots of intention and behavior. But we would not be faithful to his fundamental intention were we to reduce his Exercises to the merely psychological level—even while praising them as a work of consummate wisdom—and were we to forget that what he believed and affirmed, what he felt and experienced himself and for others was impregnated by his conviction of the efficacious and active presence of God in all creation and, most particularly, in the soul of each man "living, feeling, reflecting," and deciding. Ignatius had confidence in man because he had confidence in the power of Christ's grace. He had hope in the power of "shame," a very rich sentiment for him, one that stops us from sinking forever and is the starting point of unforeseeable recoveries; he had faith in the innate tendency that spurs us on to fidelity and high ideals. What a difference there is between *exercere*, the term Erasmus used all his life in the rather scornful sense, without any personal commitment, and the *se ejercitar* of Ignatius, immensely serious and authentic, transforming and operational. Ignatius did not look for aesthetic complaisance in beautiful theories, but for efficacious conversion. He pressed for commitment—"What should I do?"—convinced that it is in commitment that one finds God.

Of course, everything that we have been saying pertains to the Exercises in the broadest meaning of the term, integrally and religiously lived in all their annotations and rules, where all four weeks are real weeks spent in complete retirement from friends, acquaintances, and worldly cares. But Ignatius and his companions *adapted* the Exercises with great flexibility by truncating directions and making them more elementary and thereby limiting the number of days, shortening the hours of prayer, and gearing the meditation topics to basic themes designed to lead the exercitant to make a good confession.

Here, too, "they tailored the clothes to fit the cloth." However, so that we may get some idea how the more exacting and full form of the Exercises spread, we should consult the figures found by Father Ignacio Iparraguirre, who is the expert on the history of the Spiritual Exercises. According to Iparraguirre, during Ignatius's life the full four-week schema of the Exercises was given to approximately 7,500 persons, of whom about 1,500 were women, including religious, and about 6,000 men, of which number only approximately 1,000 were either already members of a religious order when they made the Exercises or became religious afterward. The large majority were laymen who continued on in their chosen state of life. Among all the total number of retreatants, we find some cardinals, a good number of bishops, many religious and priests, and a large number of lay people. For all of these people, the Exercises meant an increase in religious fervor, a learning experience in personal prayer, a more significant and frequent reception of the sacraments, a radical spiritual conversion, a lasting reform of life, both personal and social. Many of these people described their personal experience in a most graphic sentence: they were born again, born again in the Spirit; they became "new men." Ignatius was right when, toward the end of his life, he said that in addition to the papal approval, the Exercises were blessed with a second convalidation that was no less important: the practical effects brought about to people all over the world who made them, "men coming from all kinds of backgrounds and states of life." Iparraguirre counted almost one hundred directors of the Exercises and more than over a hundred European towns where they were given during the short space of time between 1540 and 1556. Among the places that were known as centers for the Exercises were Alcalá de Henares, Barcelona, Bologna, Coimbra, Gandía, Granada, Lisbon, Louvain, Messina, Naples, Paris, Parma, Rome, Salamanca, and Valencia, and the cities that followed these centers in number of retreatants were Córdoba, Cuenca, Ferrara, Florence, Oñate, Padua, Palermo, Venice, and Zaragoza. In this tally, we should not overlook the central European cities of Vienna, Augsburg, Speyer, Ingolstadt, Mainz, and Ottobeuren, nor should we omit the far-off cities of Goa, Cochin, Hormuz, Malacca, Funaio, present-day Oita in Japan, and São Salvador (Bahía) in Brazil. Unbelievable but true. Ignatius came to the fore against contemporary and future attacks with an observation full of self-assurance: "And no man of good will and free of passion will be able to read them and feel the same."

Despite their transitory, fleeting appearance, the Exercises constitute something more than simply a decisive historic event—so many days spent on retreat—because for many people they are a rich and extraordinary experience. They are a method and a scheme, a tightly constructed body of doctrine, a school of prayer, a way of guaranteeing and exercising freedom and the fundamental option, an instrument of spiritual conversion, reform, and regeneration. In a word, they are a well of spirituality valid for every age of man, for Jesuits and non-Jesuits alike. The discipline, learning, and experiences that they inculcate and that result from them are not a momentary burst of religious enthusiasm but a method in one's continuous quest for God in regenerated freedom, a way in which one can give himself to the Absolute, an attitude that can be applied in the making of fundamental choices as well as making minimal decisions of everyday life. On the theoretical plan, we can verify such options by analyzing the text of the *Spiritual Exercises*, but most especially we can experience this verification in practice. Xavier, Favre, Nadal, and Borgia were the sons of the Exercises, living examples of the efficacy of their spirit. And what indeed could one say about Ignatius himself! His letters, the advice he gave, the Constitutions, his way of making decisions, his entire life—all of these are the constant living incarnation of the very heart of this book. Ignatius was the autopraxis of the Exercises, and someone who knew him well could say, without exaggeration, that "he seemed to have planted them first in his own soul" before he gave them to others.

9

How to Define
His Charisma and Life

Only nine years had passed since the day Ignatius, filled with uncertainty, had arrived in Rome, nine short years since those decisive deliberations of 1539. Since then, how packed was the history of this "least Society," already scattered throughout the world! How concentrated also was the history of Europe during this decade. The on-again-off-again war and peace between Francis I and Charles V; the threat of Süleyman the Magnificent, who had already conquered the plains of Hungary; the strengthening of the Schmalkaldic League; the Council which finally met at Trent in 1545, only to have the sessions momentarily suspended until 1548; and the 1547 victory of the emperor over the Protestants at Mühlberg. Outright war had superseded the sterile colloquies on religious questions held first at Worms and then at Regensburg and Hagenau. Juan de Valdés and Luther were dead, and dead too were Henry VIII and Francis I. The Roman Inquisition had come on the scene along with the Sistine Chapel; the New Laws of the Indies of 1542–43, which prohibited Indian slavery and suppressed the encomienda system; the poetry of the Catalan Joan Boscà Almuhàver and his Castilian friend Garcilaso de la Vega; the anti-Lutheran satires by the Franciscan Thomas Murner; the *De revolutionibus* of Nicolaus Copernicus; Calvin's catechism; the theory of algebraic equations of Girolamo Cardano; the silver mines of Potosí; the

chambre ardente in France. In 1548 the transactional formula of
the Interim of Augsburg was reached as a possible solution to
the terrible religious division in the Empire. Soon Paul III
would die and be succeeded by Julius III. Xavier arrived in
Japan. The *Book of Common Prayer* was published in England.
The Council reconvened at Trent in 1550. Fra Bartolomé de
Las Casas, O.P., published his *Historia general de las Indias*.
Universities were established in Mexico City and Lima, and
Pierre de Ronsard published his sonnets. The antitrinitarian
theologian Michael Servetus died screaming at the stake in
Calvin's Geneva. Protestants acquired their freedom, and the
princes gained their ascendancy in the empire through the
Treaty of Passau in 1552. Everything was seething, changing,
fighting, conquering, and new.

Ignatius realized that he had a task yet to complete: Constitutions for the Society that Paul III had ordered the group to
draw up. First of all, they had to define their way of life, spirit,
and work; afterward, there would be the rules that would
encapsulate their experiences and better define the mission
they were to achieve. "In the meanwhile" was the expression
describing the confused religious state of affairs that existed in
the Society. Ad hoc solutions always had to be found for immediate problems. For the moment, everything was watch and
see, giving things time to clarify themselves, trying, experi-
menting, and, all the while, not becoming frightened by the
unexpected. "In the meanwhile" was also Ignatius's solution
during the slow elaboration of the rules of the Society. The
changing scene was opening ways to him that he had never
before considered. He did not want to shut off such openings
by being too hasty, nor did he want to narrow them by an
excessive number of rules. Furthermore, the task of drafting
Constitutions was his alone. Although it was the pope's directive that the cofounders were to give the Society its own laws,
these companions soon scattered abroad leaving the responsibility to Ignatius and Codure. Codure died shortly afterward,
in 1541, and so from that moment on, the whole burden of
fashioning the Constitutions rested on the shoulders of
Ignatius, who had been the father and guide to the group and
who was now its superior general. How was he to incorporate
the charisma of the group in rules while the vagaries of history
were ever at work, fashioning a program they were to follow?

That was the question. He was not in a hurry to find the answer, but he never stopped working to find it.

Ignatius responded to the realities of life by offering to serve in the most realistic way. We have already seen how he was constantly forming his men, challenging them, keeping them as one, watching over their individual apostolates, and in the meanwhile, little by little, he began to plan out the broad framework of the Institute, its general directives and rules. All of this activity gives us an insight into his immense talent as an organizer. He was doing everything at the same time, giving himself completely at each moment to all of these projects. As deliberate as a sculptor, he slowly chiseled the cornerstones upon which at a later date he would erect the cathedral of the Constitutions. Bit by bit he added fundamental yet partially hewn pieces to the group's initial 1539–40 deliberations and resolutions. Here are some examples of his elaborations: the rules concerning the foundation of houses and colleges that underwent two separate redactions, one in 1541 and the other in 1544; the rules regarding the missions and commissions entrusted by the pope (1544–45); the directives regarding poverty (1544); the decisions against aspiring to dignities and being appointed to bishoprics (1544–45); the rules regarding students or scholastics; the norms fixing the impediments to admission to the Society; and the ministries that were to be avoided, among which was taking on the spiritual direction of women religious. These adjustments as well as other touches and retouches were gradually giving a profile to the juridical status of the Society.

After Codure's death, Father Joan Jerònimi Domènech helped Ignatius for a short while, and he was followed by the Portuguese Bartolomeo Ferrão, who served for a while as secretary of the Society; but of capital importance was the arrival, in 1547, of Juan Alfonso de Polanco, a native of Burgos. His contribution, silent and efficient, was critical. He understood the mind of Ignatius perfectly and helped him in the governance of the Society by drafting and writing many letters at the general's behest. Polanco never got lost in the forest of regulations as he sorted out and managed the materials at hand. He served Ignatius well by going and studying the rules of different religious orders. Afterward, he would intelligently call to Ignatius's attention points that had to be clarified, presenting them as the *dubia* (problems), and finally, he drew up indices that proved to be practical indeed. Although the substance and the core of the directives represented Ignatius's contribution, Polanco's collaboration was fundamental. The steps already taken in regard to drafting the Constitutions were ratified by Laínez, Salmerón, Broët, and Jay in 1548, a step that opened the doors of profession to another ten members. The years 1547–1549 were decisive for clearing up a number of points and for organizing the materials that had to be dealt with. Shortly before his death (November 10, 1549), Paul III gave the final testimony of his benevolence toward the Society by issuing *Licet debitum* (October 18, 1549). It was the fourth time he had issued a solemn bull in favor of the Society, and once again it was accorded more privileges. Six months later, July 21, 1550, Paul III's successor, Julius III, satisfied an old wish of the cofounders with a new bull, *Exposcit debitum*, in which he summed up and confirmed what his predecessor had granted in a number of different documents. The new bull also clarified a number of points and sanctioned the accommodations experience had imposed on the earlier documents. By this date, the maturation of the Society had reached its term, and these modifications of 1550 were made to fit the same framework and spirit of *Regimini militantis Ecclesiae* of September 27, 1540. The molds were now set that would last for centuries. Several paragraphs from the original *Summa instituti* of 1539 and *Reginimi militantis Ecclesiae* were repeated in Julius's bull, but there were also some significant touches added. Before, the purpose of the Society had been described as the propagation of the faith, but now it was spelled out as the *defense* and the propagation of the faith. This change shows the difference between the pilgrim and the general leading the Society, between the *preti reformati* and the spirit of the Counter-Reformation, and it bespoke of a Church that had been attacked and had lost hope in reaching a reconciliation with those who had separated from her. Only ten years had intervened. But what years they were! After this intense amount of work, everything was, at last, ready for the final and definitive steps in drafting the Constitutions.

The first overall compilation was called "text *a*" and it was polished and retouched into a final form by the fall of 1550. Today, this rendition is referred to as "text *A*." In conformity with the wishes of Paul III, Ignatius wanted to submit this text to the *primi patres* for their revisions, corrections, and approval, and with this purpose in mind, he took advantage of the Holy Year and summoned them to Rome. His ensuing meeting with them was something like a general congregation, a collegial assembly of the surviving members of the original group, to which some later professed Jesuits were added. Obviously, Xavier was not able to be present, and there were also others who were not able to meet jointly in Rome, but these did make their appearance in the city whenever their activities freed them to do so. Borgia, who had already made his profession at this time, came to Rome during the final months of 1550; Laínez, Salmerón, and Araoz would pass through the city in the following January; in February, Simão Rodrigues came from Portugal and Bobadilla arrived from Germany. Their observations are carefully kept to this day in a dossier entitled *Observata Patrum*. In their suggested redactions, these early Jesuits covered the smallest details of the rules. Salmerón, however, was in favor of shorter, more abbreviated constitutions that would be expanded by separate declarations, and Bobadilla criticized some repetitious parts and stressed the need to sum up in an abridgement the substance of so many regulations. Ignatius and Polanco took all the observations into consideration when they drafted a new, definitive redaction, "text *B*," which is also called the "autograph text" of 1552. This was the text that was approved, after Ignatius had died, at the First General Congregation in 1558.

After a long time and many efforts, there was at last a fundamental, organic body of detailed rules that dealt with diverse problems. The moment now had come to promulgate these rules, and above all it was the time to make them living norms and to make certain that they would become the marrow of the whole Society. Ignatius had recourse to a faithful follower to carry out this project. Jerónimo Nadal was an intelligent, well-balanced man who had penetrated, as few men had, the spirit of Ignatius. After he made his profession on March 25, 1552, Ignatius entrusted him with the task of explaining the Constitutions to the Jesuits in Sicily. Afterward he was to carry on this same assignment in Spain, Portugal, northern Italy, Austria, and Germany. Broët was given the same task for France while Ribadeneira was assigned to cover

Flanders where he met a certain amount of resistance. In all other places the acceptance was enthusiastic and joyful, even in Brazil. The Society was adapting to its mold in a very practical way because Ignatius, who always allowed himself to be taught by life, now allowed life to impose itself on the inflexible laws of the Society. The good judgment of each superior was to take care in applying the laws *in situ*, in his particular situation, and under the circumstances that prevailed there. Meanwhile, Ignatius himself remained open to the demands of experience. In a letter addressed to Xavier, dated February 11, 1552, Polanco revealed Ignatius's fundamental intention: "Our Father Master Ignatius, by the grace of God, is enjoying moderately good health and I hope that he keeps it until the Constitutions and Declarations of the Society are determined; and we are convinced that, by the special providence of our Lord, these should not be finished as long as experience continues to teach us many things and until the Society has struck stronger roots in many parts of the world." At the death of Ignatius, the Constitutions were still open to modifications.

The Constitutions are a legislative, social, and juridical code. They depend in a very special way on the spirit of the Exercises in one concrete operational aspect, namely, the creation of the Society of Jesus. Even though one can find influences of older religious traditions in these Constitutions, they are the personal work of Ignatius and reflect his ideals. He was no canonist. His directives seem to be written much more in the spirit of a man of action, rather than precepts elaborated in an erudite laboratory. They are the consequence of much prayer, a great deal of reflection, and lessons learned from life and from the dictates of daily experience. Noble principles, grand ideals and high objectives, explicit intentions and purposes, and a very exacting asceticism cement them together, and yet, just like the one who drew them up— he who was never content with vague, abstract formulations, but who always went down to the small print—they, too, go into unbelievably minute details. When we read them, we can sometimes get the impression that we are standing before a confused labyrinth, a forest of rules impossible to comprehend much less to observe, as Bobadilla observed in one of his typical moments of bold frankness. But Ignatius realized that an insignificant leak could destroy a roof, that very often it is through the tiniest apertures that the most precious liquid is lost, and, as the Spanish proverb has it, gigantic mud pits are made from specks of dust. When it came to watching over the darkest recesses of the spirit, he was unquestionably a specialist, and now he translates this very same attention and style to organizing his corporation. He is no admirer of the illusive or the more-or-less. He either focuses all his attention on the smallest details of life—trivial matters like food or dress, writing letters or caring for the sick—or he altogether skips over what seems necessary. This is why one finds in his rules, which from the literary point of view are so impersonal, so many obvious traces of his personality, ideals, and convictions, of his deepest dreams, and, at the same time, his sense of the real. That explosive, scattered, almost zany early Society needed the reins of a series of demanding rules, but, even more than external regulations, it needed the personification of a style in which interior demands would be in accord with the given directives. In these Constitutions, Ignatius collects and synthesizes either his own former experiences—pilgrimages, visiting the sick in hospitals, catechizing the young—or experiences that were later rectified and improved—taking care of one's health, complete dedication to study for the scholastics—and he gives evidence of his sense of accommodation to the needs of the group or a family that was already very numerous; his response to fulfill incredible tasks imposed on the Society by circumstances or entrusted to it by the pope; his cautiousness when faced by the large number of new candidates to the Society; and the meticulous trials he imposed on them to test their vocation as well as the level of their adaptability to the rules of the Institute. One must read between the lines of the published *Constitutions* to discover there, as in a watermark, the image of Ignatius's plan of action, his ways, the heart of the Exercises—in short, the most profound part of his personality. The *Spiritual Exercises* and the *Constitutions*—parallel works intimately entwined—coming into being under different circumstances, treating different subjects and having different objectives, are both the work that comes from the heart of the same man.

The very structure of the *Constitutions* is rather surprising. It shows how Ignatius built them up from the foundations to the superstructure, and how he transformed into law and paradigms what at first had been life lived and history experienced. In fact, before the Prologue and the ten parts of the Constitutions properly so-called, there is "The First and General Examen Which Should Be Proposed To All Who Request Admission Into the Society of Jesus." The purpose of this Preamble is to give the interested candidate a brief overview of the raison d'être of the Society of Jesus and of its field of action. What he does in fact here is to repeat the original statements of purpose of the Paris companions. The end and purpose of the Society, the meaning of a vocation to the Society, the manner of life in the Society, the experiments—all clearly stated. These elements are the foundation upon which everything else is based, the point of departure for the Constitutions, which are then set forth in the following manner: (1) The admission of candidates to probation, their aptitude, and the manner of dealing with them; (2) The dismissal of those who were first admitted (no one here is excluded, not even the superior general); (3) the formation of novices (under the anvil of the type of asceticism that is typically Ignatian); (4) the instruction of those in formation; (5) grades of insertion into the Society (from the scholastic to the professed father); (6) the meaning of the vows in the practical order (obedience, chastity, and poverty) and the manner of life in the Society; (7) the fields of activity entrusted by the pope or the superior general; (8) union between the members and the head of the Society, and among the members themselves; (9) the superior general of the Society; (10) résumé of the principles and means to achieve them in the Society. Ignatius wrote a great part of these Constitutions seated at a small table in the garden. Here he listened to the voice from within, reflected on his own ideals and personal experience, and emphasized what he deemed essential, while at the same time attending to details. The Constitutions are more a mold than a cold law. As a matter of fact, Ignatius did not want the Constitutions to oblige under pain of sin, and, before listing innumerable rules, he stressed what he considered was the essential: "More than any exterior constitution, it is *the interior law of charity and love* that the Holy Spirit writes and engraves upon hearts that should help us."

10
Ars Gubernandi:
"The Interior Law of Charity and Love"

It is almost impossible to sum up the near one thousand paragraphs contained in the *Constitutions.* The text is far from typical dry legalese; the rules incorporate profound motivations. Our spirit becomes lost in this living cathedral and in all of its archways, and at every step we take we detect that difficult *ars gubernandi,* the art of governing that is so characteristic of Ignatius's style. The former harsh penitent who ruined his good health now becomes the solicitous guardian of health and the body: "Just as it is unwise to assign so much physical labor that the spirit should be oppressed and the body be harmed, so too some bodily exercise to help both the body and the spirit is ordinarily expedient for all, even for those who must apply themselves to mental labors." He who at one time combined studies, begging, and spiritual direction now wants his own students "to keep their resolution firm to be thoroughly genuine and earnest students, by persuading themselves that while they are in the colleges they cannot do anything more pleasing to God our Lord than to study with the intention mentioned above (i.e. 'seeking in their studies nothing except the glory of God and the good of souls')."

He began the study of Latin at a late age, but in the *Constitutions* he wants to see his studying men master "humane letters, different languages, logic, natural and moral philosophy, metaphysics, scholastic and positive theology, and Sacred Scripture"; and he wants them to be placed in the universities "according to the age, ability, inclination, and basic knowledge" of each man and "in accordance with the common good that is hoped for." He conscientiously took the greatest interest in the colleges and warned those in studies about "the obstacles that distract from study, both those that arise from devotions and mortifications, which may be too numerous or without proper order, and exterior occupations, whether in duties inside the house or outside it, in conversations, confessions, and other activities with one's fellow men." Learning from his own experience, he wrote that "there should be order in taking academic courses. The scholastics should acquire a good foundation in Latin before they take up studying the arts, and they should be well grounded in the arts before they go on for scholastic theology, and they should be proficient in scholastic theology before they try positive theology." He wanted the colleges to have libraries, and he was insistent that the scholastics be present for class; that they repeat lectures after attending their classes; that they ask about anything they did not understand in class; that they take notes; have repetitions and disputations; and that they be successful in passing their examinations "without considering spending money inappropriate for poor men when they receive their diplomas, which they should receive without detriment to humility, for the sole purpose of being better able to help one's fellow man for the glory of God." The same one who, a few years earlier, had excluded "schools and lectures" from the Society now wants the Society to "extend itself to undertaking the work of the universities, that through them the effects sought in the colleges may be spread more universally," and he puts into his rules norms for the studies of the humanities and erudite languages, philosophy and theology, and he leaves the door open even for the study of law and medicine. His old devotion to strict poverty persists throughout the *Constitutions*. Poverty is that "firm wall of religion," and everyone must be ready to beg from door to door whenever obedience or necessity shall require it.

The chapter about the occupations that those in the Society should undertake and those that they should avoid (part VI, 3) is a good example of the difficult balance that must be achieved in plotting out the itinerary—the means and ends—of the Society's way. In the seventh part, he describes the Society's fields of action. These are assigned directly by the pope or indirectly by the superior general, and despite the fact that there are a great variety of them, they all are entrusted to the Society under the seal of docility and total availability. One can hear very clearly in this section the echo of that first offering the Companions made to the pope, and he can distinctly perceive the typically Ignatian characteristic of the *more* and the *greater*: the desire to succeed better; "the *greater* service of God and the good of souls"; "that part of the vineyard ought to be chosen which has *greater* need or is in *more* danger"; "consideration should also be given to where the *greater* fruit will probably be gathered through the means that the Society uses, for example, where one sees the door *more* widely open and the people show *better* dispositions and *greater* aptitude." To win over important and prestigious persons (princes, lords, magistrates, or men of letters) "ought to be considered *more* important for the reason that the universal good derived from them is *greater*." His directives for the missions, that is, anywhere the Jesuit is assigned by his superior, is to look for the greater universal good; to those options that are more perfect; to the better and the most urgent place; to those missions that help people the most; to those effects that are the most lasting. All of this has to be translated into the choice of the best qualified persons to fulfill specific tasks. The instructions of Ignatius, that great leader of men, reflect his experience and tact in this regard. He decreed that those Jesuits in whom the Society placed greater confidence were to be sent to fulfill the missions entrusted by the pope or "by superiors of the Society, according to the faculty granted them by the sovereign pontiff." "In matters that involve greater physical work, persons who are more strong and healthy" should be considered as apt candidates. Only those Jesuits "more approved in virtue and who are more reliable" ought to be assigned to "those missions where there are greater spiritual dangers." On the other hand, only "those who have a special gift of ability and learning should be considered for assignments to places where they would be expected "to deal with cultivated persons of talent and learning." Those men "who are less gifted" for the world of ideas "and who do not have any special gifts for learning" are the best candidates for a mission to people who are "less gifted or poorly educated." Some men have "a talent for preaching, hearing confessions and the like." In general, they "should be assigned to care for the ordinary people." As we read Ignatius's job profile qualifications today, the question that occurs to us might well be: Is this a guideline for success or is it an up-to-date modern system of personnel management efficiency?

How can one fail to see in the eighth and ninth parts of the *Constitutions* anything less than the epitome of what experience and history taught him? It is here that he treats such topics as "Help toward uniting the distinct members with their head and among themselves" and "the Society's head and the government descending from him." When he composed these parts, the members of the Society were scattered throughout the world, and this was a subject upon which Ignatius meditated at great lengths. He concluded that the Society could not survive or be united "if the members were not united to the head and among themselves." A union of minds was essential, and fundamental to achieving this union was obedience and giving commands, "after having well considered and ordered them." It is conducive to union that the one in command does so "with all kindness, modesty, and charity," and the one who obeys should have more love than fear toward his superior. Another great help to this union of hearts and minds is found "in uniformity, both interior uniformity of doctrine, judgments, and wills, as far as that is possible, and also exterior uniformity in respect to clothing, the manner of celebrating Mass and other ceremonies, to the extent that the different qualities of persons and places permit." It is useful for the internal unity of the Society that the general live in Rome, "where communications with all regions can more easily be maintained," and provincials should reside in places where they can easily communicate with their subordinates and the superior general. Meetings between superiors and subordinates should be fostered as a help of maintaining this union and still another help would be keeping up a correspondence by writing letters faithfully "through which subjects and superiors learn about one another frequently and hear the news and reports that come from different regions."

At the head of the whole body and as the first servant of the universal good stands the superior general. The fact that he is elected for life was a novelty in the canonical tradition of modern religious orders. Ignatius lets us speculate, up to a point, on the reasons that moved the newly formed Society to make this decision at a time when he himself had not as yet been elected general. The argument went like the following: the general who was elected for life would have experience and would be used to governing; he would have a knowledge of his men; a life-term appointment would do away with "thoughts and occasions of ambition, which is the pestilence in such offices," and are liable to come about whenever elections take place periodically. Other reasons are "the facility of finding one capable person rather than many; the example of common practice in most Church and civil governments (pope, bishops, princes, lords); the greater consolidation of authority." And—he twice repeats this reason—the Society, which is "ordinarily busy with important matters in serving God," will not be distracted so much by the preoccupations that come from periodic general congregations. In all of these explanations, there is no personal self-defense. Everything is objective, timeless, the result of experimentation.

11
A Self-Portrait

How could one fail to see some kind of self-portrait—of his intentions and the way he really was—in the detailed description Ignatius gives us in chapter 2 of the ninth part of the *Constitutions* entitled "The Kind of a Person the Superior General Should Be"? Ignatius's authority was manifold, even though it was tempered by certain checks and balances. This fact leads one to think of some historical despot, a tyrant who had absolute domination over his men. But how far is this caricature-image from the description of the man responsible for ruling the destiny of the widely dispersed Society that Ignatius so lovingly fashioned in this section of the published version of the *Constitutions*! The first quality of the general, he wrote, was that "he should be closely united with God our Lord and intimate with Him in prayer and in all he does," so as to become the source of inspiration for the whole body of the Society. He ought to be a person whose example in the practice of all the virtues is a help to others. He ought to be a person who loves others, especially other members of the Society, and he should be resplendent in genuine humility so as to make him more loving in the eyes of God and men. He ought to be free from passion, or better, be the master of his passions; he should be a man of serene judgment, measured in acting, prudent in speaking. In a word, he should be the mirror and model for all. Specifically, he should know how to combine rectitude and severity, be inflexible in what he judges to be more pleasing to God, and at the same time compassionate with his sons, so that even those who have been punished recognize that what he does comes from the Lord. Magnanimity and fortitude are necessary for him, so that he can bear the weaknesses of many; so that he can take on great projects and persevere in them without losing courage in the face of contradictions, without letting himself become proud in successes nor cast down in adversities, and ready to die for the Society in the service of Jesus Christ. "He ought" to be gifted with great mind and judgment for speculative as well as practical matters, but, although learning is most necessary for one who has so many learned men in his charge, it is even more necessary that he have prudence along with experience, spiritual maturity, discernment, the ability to give counsel; that he have discretion in dealing with so many different matters; and that he be able to converse with people within and outside the Society. "He ought to be" vigilant and prudent in undertaking projects and decisive in carrying them through to their completion and perfection, as opposed to leaving things half done and being slipshod. "He ought to have" physical strength to carry out his job and also have the good health, appearance, and age that are in harmony with his dignity and authority. He has to have a good reputation and high esteem. Nobility, wealth, which he may have possessed in the world, honor and other endowments of this nature are worth consideration, but even if these are lacking, there are other things that are more important and would suffice for his election. "Finally," Ignatius concludes, "he ought to be one of those who are most outstanding in every virtue, most deserving in the Society, and known as such for a considerable time. If any of the aforementioned qualities should be wanting, there should be at least no lack of great probity and of love for the Society, nor of good judgment accompanied by sound learning. . . ." Ribadeneira was right when he considered that in these paragraphs from the *Constitutions*, Ignatius, "without thinking of himself, drew a sketch of himself and has left us a perfectly finished portrait of himself."

When he seems to have said everything there is to say, Ignatius formulates in the tenth part of the *Constitutions* "[h]ow the whole body of the Society can be preserved and developed in its well-being." In all the preceding texts the catchword is *ought*, but now, in these last pages, where he sums up the points he has already made, he writes in the future tense. Someone has called them Ignatius's "spiritual last will and testament." Here, as in a final symphony, the already-known melodies are repeated; here, once again, the cornerstones and foundations of the building are strengthened, and here natural and supernatural means, rules and liberty, are put in equilibrium. The text opens with a paragraph expressing Ignatius's most intimate and deepest conviction, the staunch belief of the one-time pilgrim who would place his hope in God alone: "Because the Society was not instituted by human means, it is not through them that it can be preserved and developed, but rather through the omnipotent hand of Christ, our God and our Lord. Therefore, in Him alone must be placed the hope that He will preserve and carry forward what He deigned to begin for His service and praise and for the aid of souls . . ." That text that opens with this profound conviction, an assuredness born from a deeply living sentiment of poverty and need, ends with a concern for the health and welfare of the members of the Society and an interest that the houses and colleges of the Society be built in healthy locations where the air is pure. In the center of this great divine-human arch, there is this basic law: "Live always in love and with charity for all . . . a universal love that embraces everyone."

Yes, there are quite a few rules in this wonderful Ignatian code. But in his mind, the Society is designed as a legion, ready to take on the most risky missions; disciplined, heroic, in which everyone from the general to the cook should do what he is supposed to do and do it with scrupulous attention. But Ignatius is no egoist, bloated with a desire to possess and dominate by any type of manipulative ambitions and military prowess. Unfortunately, this is the image of him that has become widespread, and it is broadcast by those who have projected on him the passion for later battles, in which the Society is purported to have been one of the protagonists. But this image is a totally distorted image. Ignatius's personality, ambitions, motivations, his style, and the way he acted—all of these come across clearly in the ever-temperate prose of his *Constitutions*. It is a prose that is lucid, spiritual, and very human for those who want to read them and who know how to read them. He formed a community whose destiny was to realize an ideal. He broke with the historic culture of his time by turning his back on wealth, by introducing a fraternal spirit between people whose countries were at war with one another, by encouraging persons to make a gift of themselves for the service of God and the peoples of five different continents, by making courage a bonus and hard work a premium, by encouraging each one of his sons to accept the fact that he will be the object of unproductive criticism and sterile whimperings, by waging battle in the heart of all men, and by winning them over one by one. *Utopia*, as we mentioned above, is the title of a very famous work written during this period by the English statesman, who later became a saint, Thomas More, but More's book was purely a literary success that could be savored only by the learned. The work of the pragmatic Loyola, the man whose action was energizing precisely because it was not self-centered, because it left aside the how-can-I-be-self-fulfilled attitude, and shunned the personality cult mentality, was a kind of micro-utopia or a partial realization of More's *Utopia*. Action was Ignatius's form of hope in a society that was living without hope, a society that was being crushed by black forebodings and fatalism. But Ignatius was not the ordinary man of action, trusting in his own resources and leadership. Rather than being an actor, he felt acted upon and he did not give way to the temptation of believing in his own self-sufficiency. "I am a total obstacle" was the expression that he used to express his boundless spiritual nakedness. Is this the pious exaggeration of a saint? Such an interpretation is most comfortable for us to accept. For my part, I believe it corresponds to something very deeply rooted in his spirit, and it underlines the tremendous distance that he saw between his own self and the extraordinary fruitfulness of what he was able to achieve.

12

"Another One Better or Not So Poorly As Myself"

In 1551 at the precise time that he was crowning his work on the Constitutions and meeting with the *primi patres*, Ignatius tried to resign from the generalship. The episode appears in a passing, short-lived episode by his biographers who, given the facts that his efforts were not successful, do not place much importance on it. Nevertheless, this action on his part probably is very important in a biographical study of Ignatius. We learn about it from a document signed by Ignatius in Rome, dated January 30, 1551. He gave this document, closed and sealed, to his first companions when they came to Rome at the time to study and ratify the Constitutions. His resolution to resign his position as general was not a decision he came to at the last minute, nor was it the result of some momentary discouragement.

Perhaps he felt he was too old for the job because he was almost sixty and during the previous year had suffered serious health problems. Two years later, he was reported as "rapidly declining." It is probable that his decision to step down was inspired by the realization that he had accomplished what he set out to do. The Society and the *Spiritual Exercises* had been approved, and he was putting the finishing touches on the Constitutions. As he looked back over his life at this stage, he saw that these accomplishments were his three greatest goals, the basic reasons for his existence. There was no doubt about the fact that his companions could not honor his request, and perhaps they did not attach to it the seriousness that it merited, or perhaps they did not realize the intensity that Ignatius had put into some of the sentences and that he had meditated on them at length in silence. Even to this day these sentences cannot be read without emotion. "After having thought about and considered it for months and years without any intrinsic or extrinsic disturbance that I could feel," he wrote, "I shall say before my Creator and Lord, Who is to judge me for all eternity, what I feel and understand is to be to the greater praise and glory of His divine Majesty. Looking realistically and without any passion in myself, and taking into account my many sins, my many imperfections, and my numerous illnesses, both interior as well as exterior, I have come to the conclusion, many times and on different occasions, that I do not have by any means all the qualities required to take charge of the Society with which I am now endowed by the Society's will and order. I wish that this be carefully considered in the Lord and that another be elected, who could do the job that I have of governing the Society better or not so poorly as myself . . . I renounce this post and I simply and absolutely give up the charge I now have, asking and praying with all my soul, in the Lord, that the professed, as well as those who will join them in deciding upon it, may accept this which I, justified before His divine Majesty, request. . . ."

These were sincere words. They were circumspect, long-considered wishes. His conviction was that God was inspiring them. There is the same wish for solitude and retreat from the world that he had known after his conversion at Loyola. Ignatius is not his own master and does not determine his own life. Through the mouth of others, God spoke to him and opposed his most fervent desire. There was only one man who hesitated before that simply stated request, and that was Father Andreas de Oviedo, who later became famous for his work in Ethiopia. He alone trusted the reasons Ignatius gave, both those he had expressed and those he kept within his heart. All the biographers of Ignatius blame Oviedo for his naïveté, but perhaps he alone was sensitive to the imploring request of his indisputable leader, who was condemned to follow his route to the very end, aided by the tireless Polanco and, beginning in

1554, by Nadal, who was named vicar-general. Ignatius therefore continued on, not completely resigned, but giving himself, body and soul, to his work and energetically undertaking new, important enterprises.

13

"The Treasure of the Hopes We Have"

During these final five years of his life, Ignatius consolidated the activities he had already taken on, and he initiated new ones. As the days wore on, the Jesuits' "method of proceeding" became larger and more voluminous. The colleges were multiplying, especially in Italy (Bologna, Florence, Naples, Perugia, Gubbio, Modena, Monreale, Syracuse, Catania, Genoa, Siena), and these institutions were no longer restricted to Jesuit scholastics, as had been the case at the beginning. For the first time lay students would attend Jesuit schools, and, equally important, the education was free of charge. Jesuit pedagogy perpetuated the *modus parisiensis*, the method of the University of Paris, in these academic centers, and the Jesuit style of teaching gradually forged methods that were later enveloped in that pedagogical monument called the *Ratio Studiorum*. Ignatius was convinced that with just a little bit of Cicero and a lot of spirit he could carry out his fundamental mission. He proceeded with his feet solidly planted on the ground, aware of the historic situation in which he was living, and, as matters developed, he eventually opened the doors of culture to his Society, and that culture, taking on the Society's patina, would in turn shine in all fields of knowledge. This opening up to the whole world came about as a result of unintended circumstances that developed during the early years, and it gradually took on new dimensions with projects and undertakings on a grand scale. "In the light of the treasure of the hopes we have, all is small." These hopes meant the various projects that were taking shape, but especially it meant confidence in God.

Ignatius had no modern organizational charts to rely on, nor did he have the means of communication that are at our disposal today, but the absence of such advantages in no way prevented him from responding to the heartbeat of the whole world. He oversaw all of these projects, down to the last detail. His creativity was channeled by ambitious plans that he undertook after consideration and prudent advisement. He was very much the realist in every one of his endeavors. In 1551 and 1552 Ignatius began two undertakings that were destined to make their presence felt down through the centuries: the Roman College, the immediate predecessor to the present-day Gregorian University, and the German College, founded for the purpose of forming future priests for Central Europe. Both would become famous training centers, and both were realistic answers to the needs of the day. The historian must take account of their subsequent successes. But in the beginning Ignatius entertained doubts about these ventures, and he anguished over promises for their endowment that were partially kept or not kept at all. History gives Borgia credit for getting the Roman College off to a start because he contributed the largest amount of money for its endowment, but it was Ignatius, in spite of the fact that he would slough aside all intellectual questions and would never have any other precious books in his life—and in his cell—other than the Gospels of the New Testament and the *Imitation of Christ*, who was the founder of the most prestigious university in the very heart of Christendom. Shortly after his involvement with the Roman College, he drew up a plan to reform the University of Vienna, and he saw his men teaching in the universities of Ingolstadt and Dillingen. He was never able to establish them in *his own* Paris, but he was successful in placing them at Salamanca, Alcalá, Coimbra, and Louvain.

Although he realized that every important battle takes place in the heart of man, he was also aware that men are carried along by the flow of the tide and subject to the actual *zeitgeist* in which they live. This was the reason he tried to promote the faith in those places where Christianity had never been introduced, that is, "among the infidels," or in places that had been compromised by the religious divisions of his contemporary Europe, or in places infected by the spirit of decadence. He did not complain about the darkness of the age, but he lit small lights everywhere. The province of Portugal was responsible for the missionary activities in the East Indies, and over the course of the years, he entrusted to this province other projects in the Congo, Ethiopia, and Brazil, and, at the end of his life, his great desire was to found colleges in Cyprus, Constantinople, and—oh yes, in his beloved Jerusalem, too. Xavier had made names like Goa, Cochin, Malacca, Ternate, Amboina, the isle of Morotai, and Yamaguchi familiar words in Europe, and he asked continuously that more men, real men seasoned and proven, be sent to the east. He wanted no rejects from Europe. For the Japan mission, he wanted men imbued with wisdom; for India, men steeped in humility and gentleness. The Middle East was a hermetic and hostile world, continuously threatened by the raiders along the Mediterranean coasts. Ignatius obtained indulgences for the army of Charles V, who conquered Algiers in 1551. Laínez had served as a chaplain to this army, and during his free moments Ignatius drew up a fantastic plan that envisaged a Christian fleet that would dominate the Mediterranean and would insure peace. Like the greatest of harebrained dreamers (*arbitristas*), he even had a project for financing this fleet. With the same concern for details, he likewise drew up a set of instructions for Father João Nunes Barreto, who was wrongly called Prester John, with the aim of subjecting the kingdom of the Negus of Ethiopia to the authority of the Catholic Church. In a letter he wrote in his own hand to the king of Portugal, he proposed that he himself personally participate in this mission.

Finally, and not from the very beginning as it is wrongly thought, Ignatius could not be blind to the chaotic spiritual situation in Europe, to the defense of faith in those areas where faith was torn, threatened, decadent, and in danger. I allude to the Protestant schism. It is true that at a very early date Favre, Bobadilla, Jay, and the newly recruited Canisius worked courageously in the Germanic world. They hoped against all hope and tried to stop what seemed irreversible, namely, the total loss of Germany to the Catholic Church. Ignatius, who remained very well informed of the situation in Germany, knew that the Church there had to be raised from the ruins; the masses had to be reclaimed; the Church had to be present in the universities, where the debate was the most strident; and most especially, priests and apostles had to be trained, a situation that meant starting practically from zero, that is, teaching the very basics of the faith. He had only a handful of men for this mission, but he counted on the favor of Maximilian, the king of the Romans, and William IV, duke of Bavaria. In the rear guard, that is, in Rome, there was the German College he founded, and only he knew the headaches that financing it cost him. In the vanguard, the Germanic world, Ignatius moved his men to Cologne, Ingolstadt, Dillingen, and Vienna, and he drew up the blueprints of reform for the university in this last-named city. His instructions to the men in the field were clear. The first objective was to regain Germany for the Catholic Church and the second was to establish the Society in the German-speaking world. In 1549 he gave the Jesuits working on this mission precise and prudent instructions. They were to have complete confidence in God; they were to pray, give example by their lives, show sincere love to all, and adapt themselves totally to all; they had to accommodate themselves to the customs of the different nations, gain credit through what they taught and preached, and win the friendship of those who governed, as well as the teachers at the universities and influential persons in the communities; they must not only think and speak alike, but dress alike, too, and have an exact knowledge of the people they would be dealing with, and work in teams. They were expected to teach in public lectures, instruct and exhort, to render men not only more knowledgeable, but also better; they were to hear confessions, attract young men who could be co-workers with them in the future, give the full thirty days' Exercises, visit prisoners, the sick, and the poor. They were advised to become friendly with the leaders of the heretics, making headway "step by step," dexterously, showing them friendship in order to elucidate controversial dogmatic points, combating heresy but, at the same time, treating all persons "with love, desire for their well-being, and more than anything else, compassion," so as to gain them to the obedience of Rome. They were to avoid, however, all imprudent defenses of the faith that would make them pass for "papists, and thereby render them less credible."

Matters did not change overnight and the Protestant infiltration could be felt in Catholic Austria. The perspective was desperate. In ten years, the colloquies and dialogues of 1540 had been relegated to oblivion, and war had come in their place. Charles V did not have time to relish his Mühlberg victory. He had learned firsthand what treason and failure were, and he was on the brink of being made a prisoner. France supported the Protestant League, and the emperor was forced to give religious freedom to the Lutherans in accord with the Treaty of Passau of 1552. That very year Ignatius was sending extensive instructions to Peter Canisius. Protestant authors consider these the "Manual of the Persecutor." These instructions reflect how Ignatius judged political responsibilities. In them he asks the king of the Romans, who was to be the next emperor, to take a resolute stance in favor of Catholicism and against heresy. History had already demonstrated that the attitude of kings and princes was crucial when it came to determining the spiritual future of their dominions. Ignatius proposed that the king of the Romans declare himself an effective enemy of heresy by not admitting heretics to his council or allowing them to take positions in any branch of his government; that he should purge the university of suspected heretics; control the printing of books; and decree that the Protestants could not call themselves "Evangelicals." In contrast to these purely repressive measures, he recommended a number of affirmative policies; for example, the king should be solicitous about choosing good bishops and good preachers; he should exercise a control over the selection of the clergy and educators of the young; he should see to it that the people were properly catechized; and he should provide adequate preparation to insure the presence of honest priests. All of this is the Counter-Reformation, the "declared and non-dissimulated war" against heretical error. Could anything else be expected during the reign of Edward VI, Calvin, the Scandinavian kings, and the German princes who were partisans of the Lutheran Reformation? The Society took on a warlike attitude during this era of pitched battles, and it would go on the offensive boldly and be defensive against onslaughts. Apart from the fact that it was unquestionably successful in these enterprises, it ended up having to pay a heavy tribute of hate and animosity, and had to suffer the sobriquet, *papistissimi.*

The mentor of these grandiose plans, however, lost none of his sense for detail, his feeling for the concrete. During these same months and years, Ignatius's correspondence was divided between these long, highly strategic pieces of correspondence and his personal letters in which he comes down to the transient events of everyday life. For example, he wrote a letter of condolence to his generous benefactor, Don Juan de Vega, the viceroy of Sicily, on the occasion of his wife's death, another to the duchess of Parma, Margaret of Austria, encouraging her in her adversity, and another to King John of Portugal, consoling him on the death of his only son. Ignatius's correspondence tells of his concern for the health of Father Gaspar Berze or Barzaeus, who was in India, or Father Araoz in Spain, and Father Giovanni Battista Viola at Modena. He had to show the very spiritual-minded Father Manoel Godinho that one also serves God in attending to financial matters and temporal affairs. He had to write to Father Miguel da Nóbrega, who was taken captive and enslaved by the Turks, offering him only a slim hope of being redeemed because the price demanded was too high, and he had to write to the duke of Nájera, assuring him of his everlasting gratitude. He fought, by means of more correspondence, to make sure that cardinals' hats would not be placed on the heads of Borgia and Laínez. He had to write to the provincial, Father Jaume Miró, restraining his interventionist tendencies and rigidity; to Father Philippe Faber or Filippo Leerno reprehending him for his spiritual greed, to Father Nicolaas Florisz or Niccolò Goudanus reproving him for his immoderate desire for the gift of tears, and to Father Domènech, censoring him for his insatiable desire manifested by wanting everyone in the Society assigned to his province of Sicily, where he was stationed at the time. He sketched out a plan of reform for a monastery of nuns and sent it to Father Ponce Cogordan, and he warned Francis Borgia, who showed a fondness for prophecies, of the dangers of pseudo-mysticism as a means to reform the Church and even the Society itself. Ignatius, who no one ever heard speak of mysticism or revelations, advised Francis that "one should not pay any attention to all those who *say* that they are prophets." His heart bled not only for the fate of Germany but also for England where, unexpectedly during the reign of Mary Tudor, there had seemed to be some hope. He asked everyone to say fervent prayers for these countries that were in danger, but he did not give in to the pressure of those who wanted him to issue a rule legislating that there be more than just one hour a day for prayer. He was especially adamant in this regard, as far as the scholastics were concerned. "The scholastic's objective is to study in a college," he wrote, "to acquire knowledge so that he may serve God for His greater glory, and to help his neighbor; this *requires the whole man*. The scholastic could not give himself wholeheartedly to his studies if he gave long periods to prayer."

Once Ignatius had decided that a particular project was worthwhile, nothing or no one could deter him from carrying it through. He gave himself to it completely, right to the very end. This is the way he was and just one anecdote is enough to show that such was the case. On November 2, 1552, Ignatius was on the point of leaving Rome; it was the fifth and last time in eighteen years that he had ventured forth from the city. His intention on this occasion was to pay a visit to Giovanna d'Aragona, the wife of the powerful Duke Ascanio Colonna, in one of the family's Neopolitan fiefs at Alvito. Ignatius was trying to save the couple's marriage that was floundering, and he was determined to use all of his persuasive powers to salvage it. According to Ribadeneira, just as Ignatius was about to leave the house, the rain came down in torrential buckets. Everyone in the house wanted him to put off the excursion, or at least delay it a bit. His answer was a veritable self-portrait. "We are leaving right now," he said to Polanco his companion, "because in thirty years I have never altered the time I had fixed to do something in God's service because of rain, wind, or any other weather problem." He was already sixty-one years old, and just a few months previously he had undergone a serious health crisis. He went to see the duchess but failed to achieve what he had set out to do; however, on his way there, he had stopped and spoken to the people in the village of Alvito, and on his return trip he addressed the people in the village of Ceprano. In both places he organized the practice of monthly Communion for the total population. He never took a step without leaving the trace of his footprint behind.

14

"The Sad Misery of This Life"

Such activity, however, did not stem from some natural enthusiasm or rare biological energy in an old man. Just a few months before this particular journey to Alvito, he wrote a short letter in his own hand to Xavier in which he described what life was like for him, confessing that it was more something he had to put up with than anything like what he experienced in the energy of youth. His fine script was a way in which he could show his distant brother and friend that he could still move his hand and control his pen "to let you know that I am still alive amidst the sad misery of this life." But the sad misery of life was not the same thing as lack of spirit, indolence, an excuse to neglect work, or being forlorn because right beside Ignatius's brief note, Polanco, following Ignatius's instructions, wrote a long letter in which he included information on a number of things. It was indeed a kind of map of the mind and heart of the general. He spoke to his far-off companion, whose desire to hear any piece of news was accentuated by loneliness and distance, of what life was like at Santa Maria della Strada and the Roman College, where more than five hundred students were working on Latin, Greek, and Hebrew. He also brought Xavier up to date on the teaching and apostolic work that was going on in the colleges of Tivoli, Naples, Ferrara, Bologna, Venice, Padua, Messina, Palermo, Trent, Ingolstadt, Vienna, Cologne, and Louvain and what was taking place in Paris, Portugal, and Spain. All of these cares fell in some way on the shoulders of Ignatius. Their pressure seems to render the complaint he let escape in this handwritten note—"the sad misery of life"—more human.

Curiously, on the very same day that Ignatius was writing his letter from Rome, January 31, 1552, Xavier was writing from Cochin a long account of his own adventures that were also rich in worries and filled with the sadness of life. "I am covered with gray hair . . . and on this I finish, although I cannot finish writing this letter that I address to my very beloved fathers and brothers." To this report he added an even more personal letter to Ignatius, whom he addresses as "My true father." In this letter he expressed his wish to see Ignatius again in this life, and he even suggested very plainly the way to realize this miraculous encounter: obedience could bring about this miracle, or, to put it more bluntly, an opportune order from the idolized Ignatius could bring the two together again. Xavier also was suffering from a *taedium vitae*, although he, too, kept on working, and just as hard as ever. This fact was seen in a letter he wrote—his last—just a few days before he died. "If it is God's will, I shall not die, although in times past I have had a greater desire to live than I do now. . . ." At the same time, he spoke with unrestrained passion of Japan, China, and India, and he asked that men, solid in virtue and learning, be sent to these places, but only men who were ready to take on great trials and persecutions. His Navarrese temperament, generous, unabridged, self-giving, clashed with a number of the Jesuits who had come to the East Indies from Portugal. He asked one man to be "long-suffering, mild, patient, and humble," and encouraged others to love the people to whom they were sent. He preferred that the Society would remain small and that it be made up of men who were well-trained in abnegation, "persons who have the courage to do much and in many places," and he wanted to close the door to those who were weak, "weak even for the slightest reason." Life had taught him a great deal, as is evident when he wrote: "Look at all the scandals that have come about by imperfect and ignorant men who have become priests. . . . Do not be mistaken by apparent devotion in anyone because in the end each one shows who he is. Look more to the interior of people than what appears on the exterior. Do not pay too much attention to sobs and sighs, which are external things; inform yourself about the interior of

these persons." Xavier, who in the beginning was a very difficult pupil to form, became the best finished product from
Ignatius's forge. Ignatius finally ordered him back to Europe.
The anxiously awaited summons, however, arrived after
Xavier's death, a death Ignatius did not learn about until two
years afterward. The news caused him great pain, one that was
added to many other sufferings and tribulations. Ignatius's life
was no *vie en rose*.

15

Dashed Hopes

Ignatius knew frustrations during the later years of his life, but he bore them peacefully and in silence. Disputes with a number of powerful families whose sons had joined the Society without the expressed consent of their parents were certainly predicaments that gave him a certain amount of concern, although these were by no means at the top of his list of disappointments. Two cases gained considerable notoriety during these years, that of Octaviano Cesari and that of Tarquinio Rinaldi. The former entered the Society in 1552 and was dismissed in 1558, and the latter entered in 1553 and persevered. Disputes with both of these families had to be resolved in civil court proceedings. Always a learner from experience, Ignatius resolved that in the future he would never admit any young person without expressed paternal consent. More troublesome were the problems that resulted from distrust of the local Jesuit college by the Republic of Venice. The cause of this distrust was the jealous hostility on the part of teachers from other institutions, who were suddenly faced with the unexpected competition from the new college. These professional academicians resorted to spreading lies, throwing stones, and causing violent interruptions in the classes of the Jesuit school. But bad feelings were not limited to Venice, and the most serious demonstrations against the Jesuit schools took place in Rome itself. What occasioned these clashes was a sign announcing the opening day of the Roman College. This sign read: *"Schola de Grammatica, d'Umanità e Dottrina cristiana.*

Gratis." Even though on the surface the basis for disagreement
was concern about the college's academic credentials, in reality it was the last word on this sign—"free of charge"—that was
the cause of opposition. The quality of teaching was guaranteed by the *ordo parisiensis* that the Jesuits implemented, an academic plan that soon caused a revolution in teaching methods
throughout Italy. The Roman College met with overnight success for a number of reasons. Among them was the addition of
classes in rhetoric, philosophy, and theology. Then there were
the public disputations to which cardinals came to witness.
The pope was quick in giving the college the right to grant
diplomas while more and more well-selected masters began to
appear in the college's lecture halls. Finally, thanks to ever-
increasing enrollments, the college had to move to a new and
more functional building.

But these advantages did not exempt the prestigious college from giving Ignatius any number of nightmares. This
free-tuition institution was founded without a single cent of
endowment, but, thanks to the generosity of the duke of
Gandía, Francis Borgia, and the alms given by Pope Julius III,
it did manage to stay afloat. Julius's successor had made great
promises to give financial support to the college, but these
promises were as short term as was his own tenure on the
papal throne, for Marcellus II reigned but three weeks. The
pope who followed, Paul IV, did not give one *scudo* to this
important work, although he elevated the college's status by
giving it the right to confer degrees. Ignatius always had to
find strength in his own weakness in order to take on difficult
and heroic undertakings, and he had to rely more on God
than on man. In this case, his debt was in excess of seventy
thousand ducats, and he was not able even to pay the interest
on the loans received. There were times when the days for the
Roman College seemed to be numbered, when it seemed that
Ignatius would end up in prison; yet such dire consequences
never came about. But the Roman Jesuits had to tighten their
belts and be content with seeing their daily ration of meat cut
in half and with having one egg apiece on Fridays and
Saturdays. Ignatius wrote to Francis Borgia, advising him of
the situation, and he sent the faithful Nadal to Spain on a
fund-raising mission. Shortly afterward, he received the first
banker's drafts from Burgos. The famous Roman College,
however, would not know economic stability until Gregory

XIII , who began his reign in 1572, endowed it. Gregory's generous support is the reason why the college has come down to us in history as the Gregorian University. But that did not happen until 1581, twenty-five years after the death of Ignatius. It goes without saying that chronic economic crisis was the same tune, even though played on a different instrument, for the German College that was so vital for the Catholic reform in Central Europe. But even though the leitmotiv for both institutions was the same, the specter of bankruptcy at the Roman College was always more urgent.

A lack of money can present a challenge to fight harder, and the harm it brings to one's reputation is relative. There are other problems, however, that go straight to the heart. For Ignatius, one such problem must have been the behavior of Simão Rodrigues, the frustrated missionary to the Indies who remained in Lisbon where he was kept and pampered by King John III of Portugal. He was one of the *primi patres* for whom Ignatius always had special consideration. He did not go to Rome when he was called there in 1545 because the king would not allow it. But he did make the trip in 1551, in order to revise the Constitutions. He was the head of the first province in the Society, the province of Portugal, in which vocations abounded. These vocations supplied men for the missions in India and the Far East, areas toward which the province was oriented. Ignatius, however, had received alarming news about the atmosphere that prevailed in the Portuguese houses. Alongside a visible show of external mortifications, there was a lack of fraternal charity and no respect for superiors; men sought out privileged positions and the comforts of life. There was a certain anarchy that reigned throughout the province. Rodrigues, who had a mercurial temperament and was impulsive, extremely independent, very much attached to his native land and to the pleasant company of its nobles and men and women of the court, was relieved of his office in 1552, and appointed the provincial of the province of Aragon. His reaction was not the one Ignatius would have wished for. He looked for excuses not to obey; he flaunted his bad health; he tried to get the king to veto his removal; and he spoke ill of Ignatius. For his part, Ignatius had to resort to an order of strict obedience to make him leave Portugal. Rodrigues complied but immediately asked for permission to return, and return to Lisbon he did, on his own, at the end of the year. Ignatius had to act firmly and he did so by forbidding anyone to admit Rodrigues into a house of the Society and thereby forcing him to have recourse to the hospitality of the duke of Aveiro. Ignatius was compelled to give him an order that he had to obey within eight days. Contrary to what some may believe, these were not the preferred and usual methods of governance Ignatius employed. His real feelings are expressed in a personal letter he addressed to Rodrigues, encouraging him to come to Rome.

> And as for your reputation, I tell you that I will take care of it, the same care you would take of it yourself because I understand what you feel . . . Please trust me with this, for the love of Christ our Lord, and take lovingly the road I ask because, if it pleased His divine Majesty, I would be very happy if, before leaving this world, I could see you and leave you in a different state of affairs. If I have to have similar wishes for all my brothers, how much more so for the first ones that God our Lord deigned to assemble in our Society, and especially with you because, as you know, I have always had a special love in the Lord for you. . . . I ask you again to trust me because, in spite of what might have been said, I shall take care, as I should for the divine glory, of your consolation and your reputation.

The recalcitrant Portuguese arrived in Rome at the end of 1553. Hurt and wounded, he asked that a commission be set up to review his administration. Four judges listened to the charges made against him by his fellow countrymen, Gonçalves da Câmara and Melchior Carneiro, who became, in name, the patriarch of Ethiopia after the death of Oviedo. After a few weeks, the members of this special commission rendered their verdict. They acknowledged Simão's services and exonerated him from some of the charges made against him, but they sustained others, among which were disorder in governance, disobedience, immoderate attachment to his native land, pleasure seeking, and hardheadedness. They ordered him to leave Portugal and never to return, and they also imposed upon him some other penances. Ignatius alleviated the penances, but he did sustain the order forbidding him to return to Portugal.

Rodrigues showed no submission and carried on his intrigues, and so he finally had to leave Santa Maria della Strada. He wanted to go on a pilgrimage to the Holy Land and got a license, the necessary money, and a companion for the journey, but shortly afterward he gave up this project. Nadal visited him in Bassano on Ignatius's behest. Lacking the resolute strength of his other companions and dominated by what the Portuguese call *saudade*, a special type of nostalgia that is brought about by homesickness, a typically Portugese and Galician ailment from which the more austere-minded Spaniards seemed to be immune, Rodrigues made an attempt to return to his fatherland during the generalates of Laínez and Borgia, but he was rebuffed until after the election of Everard Mercurian in 1573. Again, he asked for permission to die in Portugal, and this time it was granted. He returned home in 1574 and died there five years later.

Whether his conduct was excusable or not, it was the very denial of the style Ignatius expected of the members of the Society. It is in this context that we must place the famous letter that he wrote to the Fathers and Brothers in Portugal in March 1553, the single theme of which is obedience. It is a letter that Ignatius's detractors cite and so often misinterpret. Ignatius insisted in this letter on the fundamental characteristic of obedience; on its inspiration, which is more profoundly religious than disciplinary; on its degrees and levels; on the ways to obtain it; and on the necessity of dialoguing with the superior in a spirit of indifference and freedom. It is not enough to execute externally what one has been ordered to do; one has to adhere to it with his will, even to submit his understanding and judgment "to the extent that a devout will can bend the understanding." Only in this way can obedience be lived "cheerfully and lovingly," with promptitude and humility, with a tranquil spirit and in peace. Obedience is the participation in the mystery of Jesus' obedience; it is also a victory over oneself, "over the highest and most difficult" part of oneself, which is the will and the judgment. These are words that deal with concrete situations, but they are repeated in other pieces of Ignatius's writings and they fit perfectly in a long monastic spiritual tradition. For Ignatius, obedience is the capstone of the Society. He gives a lengthy enumeration of the consequences of failing to maintain obedience: pain, discontent, weariness, complaints, excuses, and other faults, "which are far from trivial and completely strip obedience of its value and merit." Ignatius wanted a prompt and spontaneous obedience that came from the interior and that made an appeal to an expressed order unnecessary. He recognized the fact that the older religious orders surpassed the Society in the matter of performing penances, in a life ordered around the liturgy of the hours and consecrated to singing the office in choir, but he wanted no other religious order to surpass the Society in the matter of obedience. He accepted the fact that some of the members of his order might be less intelligent or less educated and were suffering from various illnesses, but he did not want a single disobedient man in the Society. Only the man who could observe perfect obedience could enter the Society "on two feet." For this reason, Rodrigues made him suffer.

Ignatius also had worries that came from outside the Society. Over a period of time, his relations with the archbishop of Lisbon and the king of Portugal had deteriorated. News that came from Spain caused him even greater headaches. The archbishop of Toledo, Martínez de Silíceo, was his avowed enemy; the archbishop of Valencia, Thomas of Villanova, who was subsequently canonized a saint, harbored some misgivings about him. But the most damaging shots fired at him came from incessant attacks, both overt and furtive, that were carried on by some Dominicans, and the worst of these were the strafings directed by the prominent theologian, Fra Melchior Cano. Not far behind him was Tomás Pedroche, who had not only written that severe criticism of the *Spiritual Exercises*, but who also wrote attacks against Ignatius himself and the Society. He accused Ignatius of being a heretic, a member of the *alumbrados* and *dejados*, who, in order to escape the Inquisition, went to Rome, and he confessed that he did not even like the name of the Society of Jesus, saying that it was "a proud and schismatic name." It is clear that the detractors were not intimidated by the papal approval given to the Society. Nadal had to write a reply to these accusations in the form of an apologia. But the fact was that such attacks were often invalidated by the very weight of their own exaggerations.

The battle that was waged in Paris was more ferocious by far. The charter issued by Francis I's son, Henry II, authorizing the

Society to exist in France and to establish a college in Paris was contested by the *parlement* of Paris under the pretext that the privileges granted to the Society by Paul III were in contradiction to Gallican privileges, the sovereignty of the State, and the French hierarchy. The king reexamined the papal bulls regarding the Society and then, in 1553, reiterated his concession, only to have the parlement bring the affair before the archbishop of Paris and the faculty of theology at the university. The archbishop, Eustache du Bellay, showed his disfavor toward the Society, despite the fact that it had received the support of the king and Charles, cardinal of Lorraine. The theology faculty went even further. Its deliberations, preceded by a Mass of the Holy Spirit, issued a remarkable decree that attacked the Society head-on. The Society was castigated for its name; for the fact that some of its members were illegitimately born and others criminals; for the fact that Jesuits wore no religious habit; and because the Society had accumulated privileges to the detriment of episcopal authority, ecclesiastical discipline, lay princes, universities, and nations. According to these theologians of the Sorbonne, the Society harmed other religious orders because, by its customs, it weakened the practice of abstinences, liturgical ceremonies, and bodily austerities; it also fostered apostasy among cloistered monks; it refused to submit to bishops; it had contempt for the rights of the Church and state, and it disturbed the concord that reigned between Church and state by fomenting quarrels, jealousies, and dissidence, which is the mother of schism. Finally, the members of the theology faculty of the Sorbonne declared the Society posed a danger to the faith; it disturbed peace within the Church; it was baneful to religious orders; and was composed of individuals who were born to destroy rather than build. Voltaire could not possibly have used coarser language with greater pomposity.

The terrible tempest of *l'affaire lutécienne* did not cause Ignatius to lose his peace and tranquility. He was spurred on by controversy; it gave him strength in his weakness. He respected this negative decision and he did not allow anyone to contest or contradict it. He wanted to reply only to the suspicions and false facts leveled against the Society, to its history, and this was the reason that prompted him to ask for a qualified testimony from those who knew the Society. This attitude was an excellent example of his style of acting. This same style was recorded in some of the notes taken by Gonçalves da Câmara. "Write to all of ours throughout the whole Society *today straight away*," he said, "and tell them that they should begin sending testimonies from princes, governors, universities, from wherever the college is, from every province." An impressive harvest of praises was collected. They were of no avail, however, nor were the dialogues that went on in Rome between the four doctors from the Sorbonne who had come there in the company of the Cardinal of Lorraine. There were some who even thought of drafting a pontifical bull of excommunication directed at these inconsiderate enemies of the Society, but Ignatius refused to listen to such a solution, out of respect and love for the University of Paris, "which was the mother of the first members of the Society."

Ignatius would die with this thorn in his heart. He lived through the first of many furious attacks leveled against the Society that would continue throughout the centuries. He was still alive to appreciate the support given to the Society by the Cologne Carthusian, Bruno Loher, whose esteem for the Jesuits was written in a letter and published in 1555. However, he was already dead when a similar piece of testimony, published in 1566, was published by Loher's fellow Carthusian, Laurentius Surius of Cologne, who was also a dear friend of Peter Canisius. There were more works about the Jesuits published after Ignatius's death that achieved some notoriety, such as the 1556 *Apologia* by the Spanish Dominican, Diego de Valantas, which was a strong testimony in favor of the Society and its teachings. In 1556 there was a fourteen-page letter praising the Jesuits, addressed to the Austrian Islamic scholar, Johann Albrecht Widmanstetter, from his father Philip, who was at Ingolstadt. The following year, Nadal's *Apologia* made its appearance, along with a favorable tract written by the popular Spanish Carthusian, Luis Estrada. In 1560, the eulogies to the Society by the somewhat bizarre one-time Jesuit, Guillaume de Postel, made their appearance, and in 1565, Etienne Pasquier, who was the council for the University of Paris, delivered his masterful *plaidoyer* against the Society and its intention to open the Collège de Clermont. In 1564, a defense of the Society appeared in Latin and French by Diogo de Paiva de Andrade that was widely read.

16

"What Could Make Me Sad"

The most painful trial of all for Ignatius, who was a most faithful servant of the papacy, was one that was in a totally different category altogether. He had enjoyed the protection and esteem of Paul III and Julius III, and he was even more delighted when he saw his friend Cardinal Cervini exalted to the tiara. The new pope, Marcellus II, received Ignatius shortly after his election, embraced him, and asked him to give him two of the Society's theologians to remain with him, assisting him in the reform of the Church. The new pope also promised Ignatius generous economic support for the Roman College. Ignatius immediately assigned two theologians, Laínez and Martín de Olave, to be at Marcellus's service. The pope's desire to protect the Society was unequivocal, as were his words of encouragement. "You gather together soldiers," he told Ignatius, "and train them to be fighting men. We shall make use of them." A heart attack cut these beautiful promises in the bud and put a pall of uncertainty over the new conclave.

Ignatius was, as we have said before, a providentialist, but this fact did not stop him from paying attention to human affairs. A few years earlier, perhaps during some health crisis, the doctor ordered him to avoid anything that could cause melancholy, or depression, as we would name it today. We do not know if or how he answered the doctor, but we do know that he referred to the incident during one of his conversations with Gonçalves da Câmara. There was only one thing that could sadden that robust man who was never discouraged. "I have been thinking," he told Gonçalves da Câmara, "about what could cause me to become melancholy, and I found there was only one thing—if the pope were completely to disband the Society. And even in this case I think that if I were to recollect myself in prayer for a quarter of an hour, I would be as happy as before." Was this just a hypothetical consideration; was it the unconsciousness speaking; or was it the realization of a possible threat? His fear had a name that Ignatius did not utter: Gian Pietro Carafa, who was, as we have seen above, the cofounder with Saint Cajetan of Thiene of a group of reformed priests. Ignatius stoutly resisted the idea that his Society merge with the Theatines to form one and the same group. This was also the same Carafa who had spread rumors about Ignatius throughout Venice and had brought him to the attention of the Inquisition; the same man who had lived in Rome for ten years without having his name appear on the long list of cardinals who supported Ignatius's initiatives in founding Santa Marta and the German College; the same man who, in his capacity as inquisitor general, sent Ignatius a monitory letter, which was subsequently vetoed by the pope, ordering Ignatius to send back the young novice Octaviano Cesari to his family; and he was the same man who did not agree that the Society should be exempt from choir. Once again the notes of Gonçalves da Câmara speak volumes. He wrote that Loyola "fears the Theatine because of chanting in choir." This is a clear allusion to Carafa and to the imposition of choir in the Society. When the conclave was called together, Ignatius asked his men to pray "that if it be to the equal service of God, there will not be elected a pope who will make changes in what pertains to the Society, for there are some among the candidates for the papacy about whom there is fear that they would make such changes." Despite the opposition of Spain, Carafa stepped out of the conclave as pope, having been elected on May 5, 1554. The news surprised Ignatius, who was sitting near a window alongside Gonçalves da Câmara. For once, Ignatius could not hold back the tide of feeling that ebbed within him. According to his companion, his face was visibly changed and his body trembled. He got up from his seat and went to pray in the chapel. A few minutes later, he returned, his face transformed and serene, accepting superlatively what could not be changed.

It is not at all surprising that these two men, Carafa and Loyola, could not get along well together. Both had choleric temperaments; the Basque was a suppressed choleric; the Neopolitan an irrepressible choleric. Sometime before, the Florentine ambassador wrote to Cosimo de' Medici about Carafa. "He is a man of steel and whenever he wants something that is not done, the stones he touches give off sparks that cause fires." Ignatius and Carafa had avoided one another up until that time, but now it was impossible for Ignatius to ignore him. Moreover, he was not Cardinal Carafa any more; he was Pope Paul IV. Would the pope give way to the hidden desires of the cardinal? Ignatius addressed the whole Society through Polanco, asking all to pray for the new pope about whom he perhaps too generously said: "He has always been a friend of the Society." However, all of this was not simply a question of mutual dislike; it went much further than that. Ignatius had a foreboding of the ominous threat that lay ahead, the dark shadow that would fall not only before himself, but would affect the whole Society, threatening not so much its work as its "way." This way, as far as could be judged, was mapped out by Divine Providence and had been approved by popes. The axis of the unconditional self-surrender to the pope, around which the whole Society revolved, was grinding under the possible changes that the iron, rigoristic will of Paul IV could set into motion. For Ignatius, this was the dark night of faith, the purification of hope, the total abandonment to the designs of Almighty God. In reality, he was always listening for what God was asking him to do, and now there were new ways that had opened up for him to seek the assurance of what God was asking—the guarantee that came from hierarchial approval. Would he now put into practice the obedience of judgment that he had recommended? He simply waited until the horizon became clear, and possibly he even prepared himself to carry out a formal order, but that order never arrived. He maintained his fidelity, dryly, without the recompense of favors that he had known in the past. He was living the "feeling with the Church" in a tense, naked, uncomfortable, painful way, without precipitous action, but with patience. He was being taught the tension between the institution and the charisma, between the voice of authority and the strength of the voice of God. Such tension is obscurity and confusion; it was the time of the *noche oscura* of action, the time of pure faith and confidence without any support, what one scholar had called the "dramatic understanding of the Church."

In reality, all of this was an intimate, hidden drama as opposed to an open confrontation, because things were not as bad as he had feared they might be. Carafa, now Paul IV, first received Bobadilla, and then, after many days of waiting, he received Ignatius, who knelt before him. The pope, however, raised him up and walked with him. He showed favor to Laínez and wanted to make him a cardinal. He appointed him to a number of congregations in the Curia, and he even went so far as to reserve a room for him in the papal palace, a room that Laínez never used. He took notice of Salmerón and Olave. Instinctively he had respect for Ignatius, the "Biscayan general" as he called him, but he never accorded him the favors his predecessor, Pope Marcellus II, had granted him verbally, despite the favorable recommendations from the emperor, the king of the Romans, and the king of Portugal. He did not give Ignatius a single cent to relieve his desperate situation. Ignatius continued to hope in God, to hope against hope itself. The Carafa pope was an upright man, even rigorous in his personal life, but he put himself into the hands of his scheming nephew, Cardinal Carlo Carafa. Deceived by this debauched military adventurer and blinded by his own anti-Spanish prejudice, Paul IV, reminiscent of the military alliances pursued by Julius II, embarked on a policy of making pacts with France and became involved in an absurd war against Spain. When matters had reached this state of affairs, he could not control his fits of rage, and his violent verbal attacks against Charles V and his son Prince Philip were notorious, as were his threats of excommunication. His suspicions led him to order a humiliating search of Santa Maria della Strada, the house in which Ignatius lived. The purpose of the search was to uncover hidden arms, which, as a matter of fact, never existed. Also, he forced some Jesuits to work in reinforcing the defenses of Rome. It was at this juncture that the anti-Jesuit theologian Melchior Cano respectfully wrote a justification of the war waged against the pope, arguing that it was an activity not unlike the filial gesture of a son who ties the hands of his enraged father.

Ignatius never spoke a word against the pope. One day, however, a revealing sentence escaped his lips. The pope, he said, could reform the world if he would first change himself, his household, his Curia, and the city of Rome. The sentence was full of futures and conditionals, all of which were deliberately used. But Ignatius would die soon, asking for the blessing of Paul IV. The pope revealed his hidden feelings about Ignatius shortly after that event had taken place. In the presence of Laínez, he pronounced a terrible verdict on what he claimed was the tyrannical domination of Ignatius over the Society. It was finally at this point that he was able to impose on the Society by force the obligation to chant the office in choir and the rule that the general would not serve for life, but only for three years. This irreverent victory lasted only as long as his own pontificate. Frustrated by the failure of his political policies, his war losses, and his nephew's manipulation, he turned against his family. He then went through a fury of orthodoxy, extending his suspicions as far as Cardinals Morone and Pole. Next, he initiated draconian reforms in Rome, but of course he was not able to witness the popular uproar in the city that broke out as a result, because he died in 1559. So ended the era of Paul IV and Ignatius of Loyola, a period that was not without lasting importance. It was during this glacial and stormy atmosphere that the life of the papacy's most faithful servant of all times came to an end. Added to his "every day concerns," to the weariness that came from his never-ending correspondence, the worries about mounting debts, the fatigue that ensued from the prospect of dealing with budding rancors and new enterprises, the distress caused by seeing his men threatened with expulsion in some places, the apprehensiveness of the rising cost of living—to all of these was added his deepest and all-preoccupying suffering, that which followed the election of Paul IV.

Ignatius continued his hands-on policy in all administrative affairs, but he did not have the strength he once had. He spent most of 1554 in bed. The following year he felt better and put his signature on more than one thousand letters. He was now able to rely on the assistance of a vicar-general. After consulting with a number of possible candidates, Nadal was chosen to fill this post and soon he would have assistants himself to help him carry out his job. Meanwhile, Ignatius did not give up supervising all business, from the greatest projects to the most minute details. Accompanied by Cardinal de la Cueva he was able to lay the cornerstone for the new church of Santa Maria della Strada, with no one less than Michelangelo himself offering to oversee the work. But the inflationary prices that resulted from the first rumors of war made Ignatius table this project, and it would not be until the end of the century that the present church of the Gesù was built. The stones of the Society were its men. Ignatius was generous in granting profession to those who went to far-off places, for example to Ethiopia, but he was more cautious and demanding when it came to granting the four vows to those who remained in Europe. He had been in a great hurry to undo the *numerus clausus* of sixty professed members that had been imposed by *Regimini militantis ecclesiae* of 1540; however, as we have already stated, the Society, which counted almost one thousand members, had only forty professed fathers. In the summer of 1555, Ignatius expelled a number of aspirants; he was disturbed by an easy admission policy. He also decided "to clamp down on" the students in the German College, who were showing a certain lack of discipline, although he did not abandon the idea of colleges. At that time, he was dreaming of founding one college in Prague and another in Mexico, of establishing an Arab college in Palermo, and others in Cyprus, Constantinople, and Jerusalem. He was tireless, incurable.

17

The Physical Decline of the Biscayan General

Without Ignatius being aware of it, his men tried to free him from his labors. They limited the number of visitors he received; they filtered out the news and matters that would worry him; and they isolated, protected, and surrounded him with the care befitting a man suffering from persistent fatigue. The doctor prescribed a diet of nutritious food for his chronic cold and for the pains that he thought came from stomach problems. He further recommended that the patient take more exercise and counseled him against the pernicious consequences of "deep thinking and especially vivid spiritual or temporal imaginings," which was perfectly useless advice. In fact, the doctor's suggested remedy bordered on the sarcastic. Ignatius was always most austere when it came to eating. He never asked for anything nor did he complain about the food he was given; he seemed to be insensible to the pleasures of the table, and he did not like it when people complained about the mistakes cooks made in the kitchen. Occasionally someone would prepare a small glass of sweet wine and a special treat for him. Out of courtesy he would taste them and then give them to someone else, such as Ribadeneira, and say something like: "Here, you are in poorer shape than I." He also liked to offer Ribadeneira a pear peeled with painstaking precision, and sometimes at table he would eat bread crumbs just to show that he was eating. He slept little; he would pace up and down in his cell, thinking and praying. He would work; he was always working whenever he was not sleeping. As a remedy for his worries, he would sometimes get away from his workplace. Laínez noticed this habit, and with the finesse of an artist, Ribadeneira tells us about it: "He would go to the terrace or to a place where all the heavens were visible. There he would stand, take off his cap, and remain still a short while with his eyes lifted toward the sky. Then he would kneel and bow down before God; afterward he would sit down on a low bench because the weakness of his body did not permit him to do anything else. There he would sit with his head uncovered and with tears streaming ever so gently and silently that one heard not a single sigh nor any rustling whatsoever." There was another remedy that soothed his cares, but he used it only rarely. That was music, the magic balm for the afflictions of body and soul. Father André des Freux would come from the German College and play on the clavichord for him. And—why hide it?—on that short repertory of pleasantries, there was one more human pleasure, unbelievable, humble, and touching: "Sometimes the greatest thing that we could do for him was to give him four roasted chestnuts, which, because they were a fruit of his native land, seemed to give him pleasure." Who could ever guess the nature of the Proustian sensation that came from tasting these four chestnuts, the imaginative feast of Father Ignatius that, for a few moments, evoked for him the image of Íñigo and shadowy memories of a kitchen scene back at Loyola.

The essential was now completed, his fundamental aspirations—the approbation of the Society, the *Spiritual Exercises,* and the *Constitutions*—were capped with the crown of success. Once these objectives that he had lived with for such a long time had been achieved, Íñigo satisfied a number of his companions by revealing the intimacy of his soul in the autobiographical account that he dictated to Gonçalves da Câmara. Only one stone was lacking to complete the arch of his life. Nadal had a premonition of the nearness of Ignatius's death. As he was leaving Rome in 1555 for a long stay abroad, he recommended that people should not tire Ignatius; that they should screen the news, bringing to his attention only those things that were of the utmost urgency. "The thing that we must be most concerned with is that our father have rest," enjoying himself in the vineyard or in some other place. Nadal realized that this leisure was not laziness nor an adventure in woolgathering, but that it was something active and effective: "His leisure moments (since he is so familiar and united to God) nourishes and supports the whole Society." Old Father Diego de Eguía, who was Ignatius's confessor, was more effusive than Nadal, and he never stopped telling all who would listen to him that his penitent was a "saint and more than a saint." Because of these indiscretions, Don Diego very shortly lost his position as Ignatius's confessor.

At this moment of his declining years, this soft twilight of Ignatius's life, his companions had to give up their desire to have his portrait painted. The celebrated Iacopone del Conte would try to do one immediately after his death, but Ribadeneira would not accept the result as a valid likeness. "This is not our Father Ignatius," he said. "This looks like a pampered, fat priest." Lacking a portrait painting of him, which would always be a lifeless image anyway, each of his followers engraved with a red-hot branding iron on their souls a spiritual portrait of Ignatius. Gonçalves da Câmara's sporadic notes, duly censored, help reconstruct for us Ignatius's human characteristics and thereby give us somewhat of a picture of him. This Portuguese scribe copied down what Ignatius said and the way he spoke; he collected memories and attitudes of the present moment, and he gives us insights into the way the saint thought and acted. All of these characteristics are reflected in the strokes of his brush, which, when put together, give us a very personal and unmistakable portrait of Ignatius.

Viewed from the outside, Ignatius's life at this point seems to have been simple, monotonous, and retiring. Over a period of fifteen years he left Rome only five times, and yet the whole world came to his cell in the form of letters, news items, and projects planned. His early Roman apostolic activities soon gave way to the business of administration and to the direction of souls. His daily sedentary life was interrupted only by sporadic exits from the city. He lived a life hidden behind his correspondence and papers, retired within himself, but ever active. He was taken out of his solitude by traveling Jesuits who would come and go; for hours and hours his faithful secretary Polanco worked alongside him. We can still see the rooms where he spent this phase of his life. He slept in the cell, worked in one room, and in an adjacent room he ate, joined by Jesuits who were passing through Rome, superiors of the Society, or guests "who wanted to do penance" at his table. He loved poverty in everything, but he also loved order and cleanliness. There was something courtly and noble about the way he received his guests, but it was more in his manners than in the fare he offered. He wore a simple, austere cassock and fought off the cold with a large coat. When he left the house he wore a voluminous cape and a broad-brimmed hat with attached cords that he tied beneath his chin. He walked with his arms crossed beneath his cape. In the house, he used a cane. It was impressive to see him walking in the house or on the street. He was always going, because of some business, to some specific place, or to see some particular person. At this period in his life, the fair hair of his youth had long since disappeared; he was bald and wore a short beard from which loomed an aquiline nose and high cheekbones. His complexion had become darker. Perhaps even yellowish because of his liver ailment? His countenance, serious and peaceful, was the image of circumspection and of a life lived interiorly. Some found it particularly luminous and expressive. His eyes, which at one time had been sparkling bright, were now blurred by work, old age, and copious tears. They had lost their gaiety but not their penetrating force. He seldom looked at people straight-on. When he did, however, people said he took in the person from head to toe. If his gaze was not bathed in benignity, at least it seemed to have the power of seeing straight through a person, right to his heart. Sometimes he would look at the faces of his questioners to study the changes in their expressions.

18
Word, Action, Will

Ignatius was not a bookish man, but there was always one volume that he kept close at hand: Thomas à Kempis's *Imitation of Christ*, the first spiritual book to which he had been introduced, the book he referred to as the "partridge," that is, the most savory of all spiritual books. He was not an intellectual, not even a serious scholar. He was not the slightest bit interested in speculation about religious matters, nor did the fiery disputations of the period demand his attention. He did not like controversy. He preferred to affirm; he did not like to discuss or to wrangle. His strength was in word and action. What interested him was individual human beings, personal problems, concrete things. He relied more on experience than on books. The naked, clear word, endowed with an enormous strength, was his greatest weapon. He spoke little, but always after much reflection. He exaggerated not at all, used adjectives and superlatives rarely, and he never uttered a gratuitous, unessential, meaningless word. The word for him meant commitment. This is why he recounted events simply, without ornamentation, suggesting directly, never obliquely. He always kept his word, and he was always in command of what he said. From the day of his conversion, he never uttered an injurious word about or scornful word to anyone. His control over his tongue was absolute. He paid a great deal of attention to what he said and to whom he said it, how he said it and when he said it. This was why his words "were like rules." He was never a great preacher or a professor, but it was with his words that he made all of his decisive conquests. He made conversation an art, not a human-istic, artificial thing, or a show, or a delight, but an art in com-munication and a profound dialogue in which there was always a challenge present. He did not carry on a monologue; he dia-logued. Above all else, he listened with all his being, sometimes asking questions. He would make his conversationalist speak; he knew how to analyze the content of what the person was say-ing and even what he was not saying, as well as when he was holding something back. He would never bully, but he would persuade the other person and slowly but definitively convince him. He would lay siege, corner the other, and for the most part he would beat back all resistance, not by imposing himself, but, by drawing out from the other the answer he was awaiting, he would help that person get a hold of his own freedom. This he would do by divesting himself of any semblance of artificial hypocrisy and by inviting the other to do the same. He would establish a total transparency between himself and the other. For this reason, braggarts instinctively disliked him, as did peo-ple who were insolent or garrulous, people who were flighty, affected, and pretentious, those who went back on their word, and those who were complainers. Such people were his exact opposite because they misjudged the weight of words. He was direct and simple, he said *things* without any embroidery; with the exact word. He was grave, never reckless in speech, but he was not solemn, either, and he did not listen to himself speak-ing, to how he expressed himself. He did not care for people who spoke assertively, nor did he like those who pontificated; these he called "decreers." He considered the word a gift that should be offered with humility, and when written, it was a twice-said word. He wrote with the same kind of seriousness that he used when he spoke, as if he were a secretary to himself. He chiseled each word with care, continuously correcting what he had written, and it made no difference to him if he was writ-ing the *Constitutions*, a letter to a king, a woman, or a fellow Jesuit. He has to be read slowly, calmly, aloud, with the same tempo he gave to the idea and its expression, to the details of each sentence. He will never appear in any anthology or history of literature, and yet the distinguished French scholar and lin-guistic structuralist, Roland Barthes, analyzed the Ignatian use of the structures of articulation and disarticulation, of synthesis and choice, and concluded that he deserves the title of a true writer, a master of communicating his message. Ignatius put himself completely into whatever he said or wrote. This cult of the word is typically Basque. The word is the substance of the person; in a way, it is the person himself facing a "thou," who is also a person.

We have no examples of his oratorical style, not even notes from his catechism classes. The form he used when speaking in public must have been very elementary; the extraordinary power that came from his words must have been due to the personal conviction he put in them. He was a master when it came to interpersonal, intimate conversations, to a deep communication between two individuals, and he left an indelible mark on people who conversed with him in those situations where there was a mutual consensus of authentic communication. These situations were very important and they may have played a definitive role in the lives of people whose biographies do no more than register the consequences of such an encounter. Life's prose is made up of everyday words. For Ignatius, this meant giving orders, praying, counseling, exhorting, reprimanding. He was not a witty man, but he knew how to laugh when, at the very end of a frugal meal, someone asked the brother who was waiting table, "Brother, are you bringing in the toothpicks when we haven't even yet soiled our teeth?" But what he did not at all like was shouting, loud laughter, any kind of excessive conduct and criticism. He himself never criticized anyone. He excused the faults of others, and he refused to believe evil gossip about others. He was remembered as "the most courteous and naturally polite" man. He never forgot the good manners he learned at Arévalo. He was equally respectful and refined when dealing with people of humble origins or novices or with persons of influence. But this courtesy was empty of any kind of insincerity, totally unlike the hypocrisy of those social customs that were becoming more intricate during the reign of Charles V. His was a courtesy that resembled more the manners of Ferdinand and Isabella's time. He tried to inculcate in his Jesuits a polite way of dealing with others, a courtesy that was deeply grounded in simplicity and kindness, and he would gradually take away from them all of their worldly titles. For instance, Lord Doctor de Olave, the young man who gave alms to Íñigo in Alcalá, at first became Dr. Olave and ended up being simply Olave, despite the fact that he was a Jesuit of great talent and was entrusted with many important missions. Even when he addressed the high and mighty, Ignatius never adopted a servile manner. Almost immediately after his conversion he adopted the habit of addressing everyone as *vos*, that uniquely Spanish form of the personal pronoun *you* that showed both respect to persons of dignity and confidence among equals. In 1549, he addressed a letter to the Spanish prince, the future Philip II, with a salutation of respectful simplicity: "My Lord in our Lord."

The word and the action, and as an engine for the action— the will: here we have the most characteristic features of Ignatius's profile. This typical Basque was more interested in being there than in just being, in knowing how to be. But he understood that being there was not an apathetic abandon. Rather, it was as a response to his environment and to life, as acting, as a will to action. To be is to will, to decide, to act. For Ignatius, the mechanisms of coming to a decision were very complex. Even actions that were seemingly improvised were preceded by a mature reflection that would lead to his decision. He would always thoroughly think out a problem before he made up his mind, and whether it took him a short while or a long while to do so was not important. It was said of him that he gave others the impression "of acting from reason." This explains why once he made up his mind about something—a promise or a decision—he would follow up on it irrespective of the consequences. His bulldog tenacity in matters small and great was legendary. On one occasion, Cardinal Carpi used a phrase that subsequently became a kind of descriptive definition of Ignatius: "He has nailed the nail." It was not easy to pull out a nail so firmly riveted. But Ignatius was nothing if not a realist and he was no fool either, but once he made up his mind, he would deal with the future as if it were already present. "Whenever the Father makes up his mind that something is to be done, he has so much faith in it that he acts as if it were already done." He had faith in action, in commitment. He was both patient and active; he was able to wait in a cardinal's antechamber a whole day without thinking of eating. He was a believer in Providence, almost to the point of being ingenious, and at the same time he was thoroughly rational. His deep-seated attitude is summed up in a sentence, formulated in different ways, but basically having the same meaning: "Trust in God as though the entire success of your affairs depended on you and not at all on God, and at the same time give yourself completely to work as if you were not able to do anything yourself and God alone could do everything."

His will had always been great; the difficult or the impossible never frightened him. In him the old principle "more is greater," which was ingrained in his marrow and in the soul of his progeny, changed its focus as it became progressively purified. At first, "more" was honor and renown, then it was the great deeds of the newly converted convalescent, and finally it became the greater glory of God. He did not know fear, but he was not foolish or imprudent. Mature consideration and tenacity of purpose were his secret weapons. First, he was successful in the battle over himself, and afterward he was successful with others: "He never undertook a thing he did not finish," and "He never asked anything from the popes that he did not get." This exaggeration contains a great truth that is perhaps expressed with greater clarity in this sentence: "He did not allow himself to be easily defeated." Fighting battles and facing adversaries fortified him, reinvigorated his precarious and failing health. Better, and from a different point of view, he firmly believed that where there are many contradictions, one should expect a great spiritual harvest. He bore his trials without a single complaint. At Loyola he endured the surgeon's "butchery" for a whole day; during a great part of his life he put up with gallstone attacks; and then there was the time when one of the brothers, who was intent on sewing a piece of cloth around his neck, put a needle through his ear. He also supported, without ever complaining, his spiritual sufferings that came about as a result of the moral decadence of the Church during the time in which he lived.

Those who were around him most frequently admired his radiant serenity, his equanimity. Although a choleric by nature, he seemed to be imperturbable. It was not that he was insensible, but he was "master of his interior passions," as Gonçalves da Câmara wrote. Ribadeneira stressed this same feature of his personality but in a more expressive fashion. "He was always even-tempered," he wrote, "with a perpetual and unchanging uniformity." The ups and downs of his health did not affect the serenity that prevailed within him, no matter what the circumstances were. "In order to obtain something from our Father," observed the picaresque Ribadeneira, who demonstrated that he was no amateur in home psychology himself, "it was the same thing to approach him after he had finished saying his Mass or when he was eating, when he got up from his bed or came from prayer, or after he had learned good or bad news, and it made no difference if the world was at peace or if it was consigned to destruction. And so no one needed to take his pulse to find out what his bearings were, or to consult some navigational chart to guess what he was thinking, as one must usually do when dealing with those who govern, because he was always imperturbable and the master of himself. Thus it was that, when at table or recreation, someone allowed a word less than honest or not circumspect to fall from his lips, those present could read it immediately in Father's studied expression, even though often enough the one guilty of the gaffe himself missed seeing it, and therefore did not realize what he had said or done."

19

"A Source of Healing Balm and Kindness"

Peace and quiet do not mean coldness and inflexibility. The lugubrious, dominating, and despotic Ignatius has been invented by those who dislike him. Dr. Gaspar de Loarte had been a disciple of Saint John of Avila and later became a Jesuit. When he met Ignatius the first time, he described him as "a fountain of oil," meaning a source of healing balm and kindness. Ignatius himself used this same metaphor when he said that in matters of domestic discipline, the Father Minister ought to apply the vinegar and he himself should apply the oil. Gonçalves da Câmara corrected the false but widespread image of Saint Ignatius by giving us some additional on-target observations. "He seemed to be all love. . . . He is universally loved by everyone. I know no one in the Society who does not have a great love for him and does not think that he is very greatly loved by the Father." Ignatius was respected, venerated, but most especially, he was loved. He inspired trust, confidence, and freedom. All who left his little room left comforted and smiling. He was very exacting, beginning with himself, but he was infinitely more flexible than what is usually believed. He was like a spiritual tower of strength presenting and giving security, strength, and fervor. "In his conversations he is in full command of himself and the one with whom he is speaking; even Polanco looks as if he is a small child who is dominated by a mature man." He was supremely competent in how he dealt with each person, and he was particularly thorough with the wayward. With a very skillful hand, Gonçalves da Câmara paints for us a picture of Ignatius in action: "And so when the Father began speaking with some-one, at first he would let the man speak as much as he wanted, and then he would speak to him in such a way that, even if the person were very imperfect, he would not be scandalized. When he would get to know the person better and the person felt more at ease, the Father would slowly proceed and, with-out any violence, change the whole game." This is the art of creating in each person increasingly larger spaces of freedom. Ignatius loved order and respected rules, but he was liberal in dispensing whenever there was a reason to do so, and he showed a solicitation toward the sick that was almost motherly. In the beginning, he would ask for a total abnegation of the will from each of his men, and then he would examine the natural inclinations and strong points of each man and then accommodate himself to them. In March 1555, while he was telling Gonçalves da Câmara how at one time he would pray long hours and perform terrible penances, he added this small gloss, a comment from someone who had learned a great deal from life, "It seemed to him that there was no greater mistake in spiritual matters than wishing to govern others as one rules himself." He did not make the mistake of believing that everyone was a spiritual giant, but he did train some to become just that, and he gave to all the desire to strive and to surpass what they thought was their capacity.

How do we reconcile this flexibility with his rigidity in the matter of obedience? We know to what extent he was uncom-promising on this point. The "yes, but" had no place in the Society, and the only man who had *both feet* in the Society was the man who practiced obedience of the will and the under-standing, that is, the full and willing acceptance of the order given. In spite of everything, those who lived under obedience had to allow themselves to be *perinde ac cadaver*, "as if they were a dead body," or like "an old man's staff that serves the one who holds it in his hand." But this type of obedience that frightens people so much does not mean carrying out orders in a mechanistic or militaristic fashion. There is always the right to dialogue, to present one's side of the story. Every man has to assume personal responsibility and, even if one considers the superior to be a saint, canonizing him does not mean making him infallible. But the final word does indeed lie with the superior, and even the cook is the superior over his temporarily assigned helpers. His word has to be accepted—not only accepted but joyfully embraced. There was no distinction between superior and superior; one should not consider who was the major superior, the mediate superior, or the lowest superior who commanded him. God should be recognized in each of them. Ignatius preferred to suggest, rather than to order; he wanted everything done generously and with gladness of heart, without obedience explicitly being invoked. Gonçalves da Câmara recorded that when Ignatius had to turn down a permission, he preferred someone else carry out the order, but if he had to do it himself, he liked to explain the reasons why the request was denied, "and universally he gives everyone so many good words and shows so much love that all who leave him with a 'no' are quite happy, and all the things that he says are well-grounded so that the person accepts fully what he says." It was inconceivable that the harsh *"this is an order"* could come from the mouth of Ignatius. He possessed the inimitable secret of the art of commanding. He was a man who commanded and obeyed; he commanded his men and he obeyed the pope. He realized that it was as difficult to form men capable of commanding as it was to form men capable of obeying, men who would have the same secret as himself toward commanding and obeying. He seemed to control everything, and yet he gave provincials and those he sent on special missions all the personal responsibility possible, and he wanted them to use it, keeping in mind this principle: "Show love and consider the universal good."

In some situations he could show himself to be severe. The secret behind his expelling some early members from the Society died with him. At times he imposed penances that seemed disproportionate to the infraction committed. His *capelos* or reprimands, which always ended with the same formula, "that is enough for you," had certain external characteristics that did not seem to be the by-products of excitement, bad humor, or anything similar. Ribadeneira, as always the keen observer, gives a most insightful interpretation of

Ignatius's way of acting on these occasions. He wrote that, although Ignatius had a choleric temperament, the medical doctors considered him phlegmatic, because that is just what he appeared to be, since he had all his passions under perfect control. However, even though his choleric nature did not prevail, at times he showed that he was cross, "and that was frightening." It is impossible to sum up Ribadeneira's descriptions of his way of acting without recounting the following event: "We often saw our Father, who would be very calmly engaged in the most holy and pleasant conversation that one could imagine, call for someone to give him a capelo. As soon as the person entered the room, our father would change his demeanor and flare up, but once he had finished speaking with the other, and that person had left the room, the same serenity and gladness would appear on his face that had been there in the beginning, just as if nothing had ever happened." The conclusion Ribadeneira drew from such a scene shows how psychologically insightful he was. "Consequently, one saw clearly that in his soul [Ignatius] was not disturbed and that he assumed this face using it as a mask that he could put on and take off as he wanted." Of course, not everyone understood this game of masks that he would play. As a result, one might question the veracity of the judgment that all—even those who were the recipients of Ignatius's capelos—who "left his little room, left comforted and smiling." Moreover, the upright Laínez suffered greatly as a result of the exceedingly rough treatment he received from Ignatius, and he often asked God what sins he had committed that such a saint would treat him in such a manner. This last sentence shows us that Ignatius's sanctity was a given fact in the eyes of Laínez, and no less was poor Laínez seen in the eyes of Ignatius, who was not scant in praising the virtue of his companion. On one occasion, when Laínez was quite insistent on a particular point, Ignatius cut him short: "Fine, you take the Society and govern it." Laínez would be—and Ignatius was preparing him for it—his successor as general of the Society. Gonçalves da Câmara noticed that the usual gentility Ignatius showed toward everyone, particularly those who were weak, became harshness toward a few. It was the designed purpose of the one who hammered the iron to forge it into something of his own design. "To the strong he gives hard bread and the food of grown men." The strong ones were Laínez, Polanco, and Nadal, all of whom he treated "without any consideration and sometimes harshly." Nadal, however, will be the one who will give us the most marvelous description of how Ignatius dealt with individuals on a person-to-person level. He said Ignatius was "like the one who embraces your soul and insinuates himself into it softly and quietly."

Was there some hidden shyness in the soul of Ignatius that would explain all of these things? Shyness is common among the Basques, and let us not forget that the timid person often hides strong feelings, that his timidity or shyness masks his vulnerability under an opposite appearances. There is a mystery that is hidden under this particular brush-stroke of Gonçalves da Câmara when he wrote that Ignatius was "affable toward all, intimate with none." Was this the loneliness of the man on top? During the whole course of Ignatius's life, two opposite tendencies seemed to coexist and clash in the intimacy of his soul. He was affable, communicative; he could talk about his personal experiences; he sought out help and persons to guide him, but he was undemonstrative and he manifested his feelings rarely and then only in the strictest confidence. Aside from these special moments, he controlled his inner world, his feelings, and he repressed their spontaneous manifestation. For those who did not know him, he seemed to be even more of a private person, someone who hid behind a mask. He himself tells us that "the one who would measure his love by what he shows greatly fools himself, and the same thing goes for familiarity and harsh treatments." Such is the secret pleasure of the shy, the timid: to play the game of the mask, the game between the persona and the real person. This is something that is altogether different, however, from the show put on by a play-actor. At any event, this observation of his reveals an immense, hidden inner world, impregnable, jealously guarded, and not only because showing favoritism or personal preference for anyone is highly improper for a spiritual guide. One must not confound Ignatian serenity with imperturbability. Ignatius was supersensitive. He had what psychologists call a secondary-type temperament—a passionate temperament in which impressions, thoughts, and facts vehemently affected him and stayed with him for a long time, ever producing further excitement—as opposed to a primary temperament in which the stimuli, however strong, do not cause long-lasting reverberations. Having this secondary type of temperament meant that reactions to past experiences resonated within him, leaving their deep impression. Ignatius's prodigious memory, his ability to conjure up the past again and again, without additions or embellishments, recalling the precise order of events, the exact words spoken, his magic-like ability to resuscitate and set before the eyes a past that one could almost see—all of this betrays the imprint made on him by the past he had experienced. This was his natural *humus*. His will, self-control, and action-orientation would compensate for this tendency in his personality. In studying Ignatius, we must distinguish these two superimposed layers: first, his nature, and then, what he made out of it, or better, how he chiseled it, conquered it.

20

Nature and Conquest

Nature and bending; iron and forging. A genetic code. Tendencies checked, channeled, sublimated. A synthesis of the conscious and subconscious; a personal history with imposed or willed changes. Ideals and achievements. All of these are elements that form the background to what we have been studying, to what Ignatius said and did, to what others said about him, to what we know about him. They constitute the elements in our effort to penetrate into the deep caverns of his personality. The graphologist Carmen M. Affholder explained how we can also get some insight into his personality through the secret gallery of his handwriting. He had a neat, strong, down-to-earth hand that wrote with the precision of a sculptor. He adapted his system of writing and the pressure of the pen to the paper, and his organization of the sheet itself, with the varied spaces between the words, manifested a mind that was methodical, orderly, and clear. All of this gives a clear insight into the understanding of the integral personality of Ignatius, the fiber and tissue of his concrete being. His writings, of course, extended over a period of many years, and in analyzing them, we can see how much he had declined during the last years of his life. What is striking about the collection as a whole is the fact that he was true to himself, to who and what he was, from the very beginning to the end of his life. For example, the rough, sharp rigorism that he manifested in the early days, a rigorism exacerbated by certain guilt feelings that disappeared in time and gave way to that long period of time that was so definitive and that proved to be the modeling force in his later days. By then, his aggressiveness had been channeled. This was a decisive conquest in which he was aided by his ability to withdraw into himself, to contemplate, and to listen attentively and carefully to an inner Presence deep within his being. His writing denotes greatness and nobility of soul; an interior resonance accompanied by irradiating warmth; a confident progression toward the future that was troubled neither by fear nor illness; the realization of an inner harmony, and an interaction between the conscious and subconscious. At the root of all this correspondence there is an attachment to the personal and familial past; a tendency that some saw in him that enabled him to become receptive to telluric themes; a facility of being in contact with things and nature; a natural need to communicate; a very keen sensitivity to all the subterranean and sensorial wealth in the storehouses of his memory; and a sure control over all his personal feelings. Ignatius lived very close to his subconsciousness; he perceived its images, and then assimilated them and sublimated them. Conscious and subconscious activity interpenetrate all his writings; their interaction has the result of projecting great security. Open to pleasure, to the enjoyment of the senses, he dominated and orientated his libido and showed an extraordinary aptitude for sublimation. The largeness of the field of his consciousness and his openness to the whole world propelled him to take on great undertakings. He had tremendous power of concentration; he would accept no half-measures; work energized him, all the difficulties that accrue from it notwithstanding; his judgment was always nuanced; his discernment sure and the strength of his tenacity and self-discipline was extraordinary. The heart of Ignatius—a heart so enigmatic and controlled—sang in his writings and here he wore no protecting mask. Everything had a profound affect on him, and the reverberations within him to stimuli would lead him to suffering, to painful interior crises. He was a well of goodness, understanding, affectivity, compassion; he was a source of courteous respect, solicitude, and tender love for others. Such is the clear and luminous lesson we learn from those who are experts in graphologic studies. The conclusion is that Ignatius was vital dynamism—with reins attached.

Psychology can help us understand Ignatius, but his total personality would be unintelligible if reduced to sheer psychological analysis. Genuine sincerity, about which Jacques Rivière speaks, defining it as "a perpetual effort to create one's own soul, such as it is," without giving up on oneself, without succumbing to mere emotions or following the inclination of a complacent access to interior facility, is one of the dominant characteristics of the way of Ignatius, who always wanted to be authentic, who was not content in being as he was, and who never gave in to a sterile and inactive introspection. His sincerity goes hand in hand with the will to transform; however, in the words of Louis Lavelle, it is more "a need to entrust oneself to impulses in which the 'I' is forgotten and letting himself be guided by forces that are superior," with a discipline in his attention that not only acknowledges and is in touch with abstract superior values, but also recognizes and feels the presence of an all-surrounding, fundamental reality, which is God, manifested in Christ. Ignatius was an introvert, but he found in himself something that went beyond himself. His authenticity was found in an act of subordination. His freedom—or his liberation—made him the captive of truth, captive in mind and heart, as John Henry Cardinal Newman wanted. He was a mystic, a saint, always attentive to the "rumors of angels" that he perceived in the very depths of his soul. He passionately sought what the Augustinian scholar Erich Przywara called the ultimate transparency, the unconditional flexibility in the hands of a superior agent that pushed him on not by words but by actions toward a future that remained for a long time uncertain. He was a perpetual, sensitive listener to the word of God, to an internal Word strengthened by joy and peace, more than by the written word found in the Bible. An attitude of supernatural empiricism that is as concise and clear as his can be found in very few of the saints.

21
"Finding God in All Things"

The people around Ignatius detected a profound mystery in his soul. From time to time, he let some intimate detail of this mystery escape either in the pages of that which was known only after his death as his *Spiritual Journal*, or in the biographical account of his life he dictated to Gonçalves da Câmara. Ignatius, a reserved, discrete man, spoke with greater ease about his old sins than he did about his interior illuminations. He died without revealing the secret of "a certain thing that happened in Manresa," and without really telling us about his visions, his mystical conversations, and the ultimate reason for all of those tears that ruined his eyes, tears that he shed while at prayer or saying Mass. *De rebus suis taciturnus.* He did not even attempt to describe what all the mystics define as indescribable, ineffable. He gave witness to the *ante paginam* of the Austrian philosopher, Ludwig Wittgenstein, who after spending a lifetime studying the essence of language, gave the following skeptical piece of advice: "It is better to be silent about the things one cannot speak about." And silent he remained. But silence could not dissimulate the excessive interior tension. It was a spectacular sight watching him say grace before meals, and everyone knew that celebrating Mass was an experience for him that tested his physical strength and health. The Mass, which for so many is a simple rite, a routine religious function, was a very singular event for Ignatius, the privileged moment for his intimate mystical experiences. We get a glimpse of these, no more than a peek, when reading his

Spiritual Journal, which he wrote in his desperately laconic style. He did not have the physical strength to offer Mass each day. Because of what was described as the "vehement commotion" that took place within him, he became ill whenever he said Mass. The author of this phrase, who is none other than Nadal, was held in awe by two things about him: the continuous and uninterrupted activity of his spirit, praying and reposing in contemplation of the Most Holy Trinity and the ease with which he found God in all things. He found God not only in quiet prayer, but also in the confused messiness of his daily work, with all of its problems and concerns, as well as in his ordinary conversations with others. So it happens that the ideal and final objective Ignatius proposed to his followers, "finding God in all things," constituted his own inner attitude. Referring to this inner attitude, Nadal got to the essential idea when he summed it up this way: *ducentem Spiritum sequebatur, non praeibat.* "He followed the Spirit who led him, he did not go before it." Rather than being a leader, Ignatius was basically, as we have stated so often before, someone who was always being led. In this autumn of his life, a secret escaped his lips, a confidence that is typical of mystics: he said that his way was more *passive* than *active.* The proverbial man of action, therefore, was a man acted upon, more receptive than active, although without doubt he appeared to those who saw him to be more active than passive. In his notes of 1555, Gonçalves da Câmara insists on this same notion, even though in a far more imaginative and elementary way. "Whatever thing the Father does for God," he wrote, "he does it with wonderful recollection and promptitude, and it seems that not only does he imagine he has God before him, it seems that he sees God with his eyes, and one can notice this in the way he says grace at table. This is why people think that his body is racked whenever he hears or says Mass. When he is not in good health—and even when he is in good health—we have very often become sick the day he says Mass." How many light years do we find ourselves from Fülöp-Miller's definition of Ignatius as "a will to power"!

Such is the way that those who lived with him and venerated him thought of him. Certainly, during those long hours of reflective meditation, and during those moments of retrospection that his quiet, hidden life fostered, Ignatius must have reflected upon the curve of his life's arch and on his work in much the same way, that is, as one who was led. No longer would he refer to himself as an ulcer, as he had done during the early days of his first fervor. Rather, he now expressed great conviction, which is also an autobiographical reflection, when, in the tranquil peace of his maturity, he wrote the sentence that has the sound of a master's axiom, "The one who thinks he is something is not worth much; he who thinks he is much is worth nothing." Perhaps more than a theoretical thesis, this reflection is an intimate and autobiographical balance sheet in which astonishment is infinitely greater than complaisance. As he looked back from this date, 1556, the weary general of the Society could contemplate a solid realistic fact, the fruit of only fifteen years. From the nine original companions, the Society now numbered almost one thousand; of this number there were about 300 priests, some 500 scholastics, and 150 coadjutor or lay brothers. They were spread out in some eighty houses throughout the whole world. Provinces had sprung up in the following order: Portugal, Spain, India, Aragon; Castille and Andalucía after the division of the Province of Spain; Italy, Sicily, France, Brazil, Ethiopia, Upper and Lower Germany, and also Rome. All of these Jesuits were working in the most varied types of ministries, many of them in the educational apostolate, or to be more precise, 8 percent of the priests and 25 percent of the scholastics were involved in the colleges. There was a total of 113 novices. Had he been a prophet of the future and if he had had the statistical tables, Ignatius could have contemplated the following graph that modern technology offers us:

	Jesuits	Priests	Scholastics	Brothers
1556	938	271	499	168
1574	4,088	1,226	1,676	1,186
1600	8,272	3,146	2,449	2,677

22

"If I Followed My Own Taste and Inclination"

The future, however, was unknown, uncertain, but Ignatius was not without confidence. At this particular time in his life, he was besieged by debts, the anxiety about Paul IV, and a number of problems that demanded great tact. Perhaps he was also concerned that there were too many Jesuits and, most certainly, that the later generation of Jesuits were not as heroic as the early Jesuits had been. On one occasion, as he was thinking about the Paris days—something he did quite often—he remembered how rigorously the companions as a group had made the Exercises for the first time. It was rigorous in terms of being shut off from everything and everyone, fasting, putting up with the severe cold, and performing a number of other penances. He was prompted to make this rather excessive judgment: "Now, all of that means nothing." But he did appreciate what had been achieved and what was being done at the present time. He found encouragement in the generosity of the young, and he recognized the extent to which the improvisation and gropings of the past had influenced the present: "The ones who will come will be better and will do more because of our stumbling along." This was quite a judgment on the romantic spring and on the summer that now bore a well-attended ripened harvest. But as he looked toward the future, Ignatius had something more than just reasonable confidence; he had something that was profoundly

Christian, "a treasury of hopes," that was greater than the realities themselves. Such a treasury came from his deep conviction that God was leading the Society "as if it were a thing of His own." The contemplation of the past supported the certitude he had for the future because, when he looked at things realistically and from the summit of his life, his own past as well as that of his "least Society" was disconcerting, paradoxical, contradictory. But this was like someone looking at the reverse side of a tapestry and seeing only a mass of threads and knots mingled together. *Ducet te quo tu non vis.* "Someone will lead you where you have no wish to go" (Jn 21:18).

As a symbol of this strange destiny of his life, of the paradoxical side of his history, we shall single out one aspect—music. Gonçalves da Câmara presents one aspect of the subject in a telegraphic, stylized fashion: "On how our Father loves music and how he feared the Theatines because of the singing of the office in choir." We already know the story about the second part of that sentence. Ignatius eliminated choir from his order, thereby rejecting an element of the religious life that had more than one thousand years of tradition behind it, and he was worried that Paul IV would not accept this change. Nevertheless, Ignatius was, to an uncommon degree, an enthusiastic lover of music. He did not forget the songs and dances of his native country, and, as we have already seen, because he had talked about these dances, was pressured into performing one of them as a remedy for the depression from which one of his friends was suffering. We have also seen that when he was in Arévalo, he lived with his fellow-countryman, the Master Ancheta, who was the court musician to the Catholic monarchs. Ignatius relished the fine music of the Renaissance, and he even learned to play this music. This fact alone explains the categorical affirmation of his relative, Araoz: "[Ignatius was] a musician, but he never played on Fridays or Saturdays." Gonçalves da Câmara is less cryptic when he describes the sensitivity Ignatius showed toward music during the last years of his life, and he added some precise details that are important for the modern devotees of the very old art of musical therapy. "If there was one thing that transported him in prayer, it was the music and chant of religious ceremonies such as Mass and Vespers and other ceremonies of this nature; and so much so that, as he told me himself, if he came into a church where they were singing the office, he was completely transported out of himself. And this was not only for the good of his soul, but also for his bodily health, and therefore when he was in bad health or when he was very weary, nothing was better for him than to hear a brother sing some religious hymn." Gonçalves da Câmara was astonished that Ignatius did not soothe himself more frequently with the balm of music. In the two and one half years that he lived in Rome, he called only five or six times for Father des Freux to come and play the clavichord, without singing, while Ignatius remained ill in bed. Sometimes he would listen to a coadjutor brother singing "many religious songs so similar in music and voice to the songs the blind sing, that he seemed to have been one of those little children who accompany the blind." Between Arévalo and Rome there was Manresa, where the pilgrim attended sung Masses and Vespers assiduously. Could it have been that these services reminded him of childhood days in Azpeitia? We do not know, of course, but the debate between taste and feeling, on the one hand, and choices determined by the mind and will appears clearly exposed—and explained—by Ignatius himself in a very carefully dated note made by Ribadeneira: "Monday of Holy Week of the year 1554. I accompanied our Father, and, as he entered the church of Saint Joseph (it was the feast of Saint Joseph), he felt a great consolation in hearing the music there, and he added these words: 'If I had followed my own taste and inclinations, I would have introduced choir and chant in the Society, but I did not do so because God our Lord let me understand that it was not His will, and He does not want us to serve Him in choir but by doing other things in His service.'"

Music was joined to the word, forming a kind of silent choir during the most intense part of Ignatius's mystical experiences. In his *Spiritual Diary* he tells us that the summit of divine consolation for him took the form of a vibration, a sonority, a "heavenly music" that was perceived both interiorly and exteriorly, which he called the *loquela*. The most vivid impression of the presence of the Lord in the heart of Ignatius's being was modulated in a sound. It was so beautiful that he had some doubts, not about the loquela itself but about the "relish and sweetness" of the excessive delight "in the tone of the loquela, attending to the sound without paying so much attention to the meaning of the words and the loquela." For this reason, although never denying the existence of the loquela, he did not stress its importance and, we might say, remained suspicious of it.

"If I followed my taste and inclination. . . ." Here is a key, a dramatic confession that can pertain to many other things beyond the subject of music. Ignatius's whole life was like a ceaseless conversation, and his entire part in this conversation was an act of subordination. Aside from the period in Manresa, Ignatius, the man of obedience, stood alone. To all appearances he was completely free, in no way under the obedience of anyone, born to be a leader and guide of others. It is true that he played at being obedient during the days of his all but hermetic life in northern Italy. It is also true that sometime afterward he accepted as an order—coming from God—the decision that the first companions had made as a body, namely, that he follow the dictate of his old Franciscan confessor and accept the office of general. But for his spirit, "the Lord was his only guide" (Dt 32:12). His whole life was an act of heroic submission to the Divine Will that at times seemed so disconcerting. Ignatius becomes understandable only in the light of this fact. The master of his life was not himself; it was Another. This is why his personal history is a chaplet of unfulfilled desires, of unexpected results, a surprising mixture of death and life, a succession of "burned ships" and circuitous meanderings. Snatched away from the Loyolas, who never accepted his transformation, the story of his life is a denial of any kind of fatalism—not everything was written in the genes of someone who could rebel against the "I, or we-are-like-this," attitude. The pride, lust, and desire for power of his lineage had died in him many years before. The lady of his thoughts, his desire to go back to the world, the plans to enter the Carthusians and lead a hidden life—all of these too had long since been buried. He was no longer tempted to perform extreme penances nor did he continue to harbor the desire to emulate Amadís or the saints in performing brave or spiritual deeds.

Later, there were more subtle forms of renunciation, frustration of noble and legitimate desires, dreams, and projects. For a long time he did not think of founding an order in the strict sense, but, lo and behold, he became the head of the most organized and modern order of all. He had thought of

surrounding himself with a handful of men, but these multiplied like grass on the plains. He had wanted a hidden, anonymous life, but he became prestigious, well known, and he saw
his company of companions spread throughout the whole
world. He had liked dusty roads, hospices that catered to travelers, simple people, and he ended up visiting palaces, surrounded by academicians, and corresponding with cardinals
and kings. The resolute pilgrim had become the most immobile and sedentary of men. The pilgrim's spirit had become
an organizational spirit. He had wanted to obey, but he was
saddled with giving orders and directions. He was a most sub-
missive man to the hierarchial Church, but he appeared to be
a silent, effective rebel against many of the Church's laws and
regulations. He had been a kind of free-spirited spiritual
vagabond, and he finished up dictating the *Constitutions* and
interminable rules. His simplicity and spiritual spontaneity
appeared to have been transformed into a complicated system
of organizational norms. What for others was complicated and
difficult was for him natural and possible. Everyone thought
that he was a masterful planner, but only he knew to what
extent he had listened to and was at the mercy of the Holy
Spirit, the signs of the times, and diverse circumstances. He
was a man whose roots were burrowed deep in the soil of the
Middle Ages, and yet he was the very incarnation of innovation and modernity. Driven by the desire to catechize children
and illiterate people, he founded and supported colleges and
universities for the educated elite. There were some who
thought him totally immersed in his own egocentricity, while
he handed over his soul to Another: "Take, Lord, and receive
all my liberty, my memory, my understanding, and my entire
will, all that I have and possess." And, as we have stressed
often before, to top off all of these contradictions, Ignatius
was tenacious in believing that God was calling him to
Jerusalem; yet God led him to Rome. Georges Bernanos
observed that the exterior life of very few people reflects the
changes that are going on within. Loyola was certainly not
one of them.

23
An Itinerary Drawn Up
by Another

Better yet, his history, which was so often conditioned by events, could have had a different set of endings. What if he had died at Pamplona or at Loyola, or what if his wound had been totally healed in the first place? What if there had been books on knight-errantry at Loyola during his convalescence? What if he had killed the Moor along the barren Aragonese plain or had drowned in the Mediterranean during his trip to Palestine? What would it have been like had he been killed at the hands of the French on his way through Lombardy, after he had returned from the Holy Land? Or, what if he had decided against going to Paris or if he had fallen over a cliff while crossing the Apennines on his way to Bologna? If the pilgrim ship had been available to take him and his companions to Jerusalem, what then? And what if they had decided not to go to the Rome that he knew was hostile and where he saw its "closed doors," and what if Paul III had not invited the companions to his dinner table or if he had denied their first requests? Abnegation was the stuff of Ignatius's life, and it was the motto engraved on the standard he held high as he entered the spiritual arena of combat. He would subscribe with pleasure to the radical words written in later years by another man who, like himself, was small in body and gigantic in spirit.

In order for you to arrive at that which you do not know,
You must go by a way you do not know . . .
In order to arrive at that which you are not,
You must go through that which you are not . . .
For in order to pass from the all to the All,
You must deny yourself "all-ly" (totally) in all.

So wrote Saint John of the Cross in Book 1, Chapter 13, of his *Ascent of Mount Carmel.* With this *quid agendum,* "what must be done," of each moment that spurred him on toward the future, Ignatius finished his route with the sentiment of having followed an itinerary programmed by another, driving forward, again in the words of Saint John of the Cross, "without any other light or guide save that which was burning in his heart."

Ignatius of Loyola was a profound believer, a Christian, not a stoic, and let us never forget it. The distinguished French scientist and medical doctor, Paul Chauchard, observed that "believing is enthusiasm at the service of truth. It is not possible to be enthusiastic about truth if truth is not lovable. Our desire to believe is a desire to love." It is here that Ignatius's availability and desire to serve are rooted. He was an integrated man at peace with himself, and therefore he was able to accept whatever came along and to irradiate what he had within. Throughout all his travelings and in the various events that took place during the course of his days, he put together a wise program that was later spelled out by one of his future sons, Teilhard de Chardin, as fundamental for the ascent of man. First, there should be self-centralization (belief); second, self-decentralization, giving oneself to the other (love); and finally, over-centralization of oneself in the One who is greater than the self (adoration). Loyola, the indefatigable man of action, was an indefatigable man of prayer, a man who adored at all times.

24

Questions for an Interview

I have walked beside Ignatius and followed him, step by step, along the path of his way, lovingly and comprehensively, shining the light of my interpretation on his imploring face and on his soul, covered, as they have been, by the cumulation of thick layers of the paint of baroque exaltation and by insult born of ignorance and hate. Have I succeeded in explaining how *he* was, and have I peeled away the dead weight of the different historic and literary images of him? I have not availed myself of any preconceived scheme, of drawing parallels with other historical or literary figures, of employing sonorous and conventional rhetoric. What I have attempted to do is to study him from within, to allow him to speak and act within the parameters of his actions and according to the hierarchy of his values. But it is legitimate—obligatory even—to pose a number of big questions. Could we line up these questions for an imaginary interview with him in the small garden of the Roman church of Santa Maria della Strada, sometime during the month of July 1556, the month that the pilgrim arrived at his final port of refuge? Shall we ask these questions like some up-to-date reporter intent on controlling the interview to the extent that the questions asked will produce the answers that he, the interviewer, wants to hear? Or shall we act with the respect that comes from our being together for a long time, a respect inspired by his old age, his inflamed eyes, his gentleness of manner, his unthreatening serenity, and the assurance that comes to one who thinks he has been faithful in following *his* way? We cannot lose sight of the advantage that we have, but at the same time we must realize that such an advantage is a heavy weight, a prism that can distort the things we see. What we do see is the backside of the events, that is, we see the events not immediately, as if we were immersed in them, but from the perspective of a different time frame; we see past events and their consequences from where we stand at the present. Four centuries of European history and the history of the Society have intervened between Ignatius and ourselves; we cannot forget Pascal, Voltaire, Castelar, and so many others.

What is the greeting we should use to begin our dialogue? Shall we call him Saint Ignatius, Patriarch, Father Master Ignatius, Íñigo—or shall we speak to him in his native tongue, referring to him as his wet-nurse, María Garín, might have done: *Loyolako seme txikiye?* Were we to use this Basque greeting, meaning "the youngest son of Loyola," would we awaken in his heart sweet memories and thereby break down his defenses and inhibitions? Perhaps, as he looks at us, our solemn prefabricated questions might seem out of place, artificial, unsavory. But let us go ahead and ask them anyway, so that we may get some answers.

Would you consider yourself a medieval or a Renaissance man? Within the long gallery of Renaissance figures, were you one of those who looked for your own system that would bring together the medieval tradition and representations of the modern age? Were you a man of your times? Why was it that in the things that demanded your interest and in the subjects you dealt with in your letters, we find only a very distant echo of the intellectual quarrels that were taking place all around you? Were you not involved? Do you remember your contemporaries, Castiglione, Ronsard, Cardano, Tartaglia, Copernicus? What does the name Erasmus mean to you? Were you a crypto-Erasmian who thought that faith did not consist in going to church all of the time, in venerating images of the saints and lighting candles before them, in repeating innumerable prayers; that it is not worth making a bodily pilgrimage to Jerusalem if the spirit remains in Sodom or in Babylon; that "the habit does not make the monk"; or that "monasticism is not godliness"? Why did you forbid Jesuits to read Erasmus? Was it merely because he was a controversial author like Savonarola and Vives, and you preferred that your men should confine their reading to what was sure and uncontroverted, or did you think reading Erasmus would only lead to sterile polemics? Was it possible that in this matter you were looking for security at the price of dependence and submission? Why did you pass over in silence the name of Luther, and in such an obstinately conservative manner? Did you consider yourself Luther's adversary and antithesis? What does the term Counter-Reformation, a term you never heard, mean to you now? Were your preferences more in line with an administrative reform in the Church or with a doctrinal reform or did you prefer a reform in the practice of the faith? Did you pretend to reform the Church according to Scripture alone, that is, according to Luther's program, or to restore and reinstate the Church of the Scriptures, which was the idea of the Antibaptists, or to reestablish true Christianity, which was the plan of Servetus, or to reform yourself within the structure of the Church? Were you not in favor of setting up vital influences and conditions that would purify the preestablished order without overthrowing it? You presumed to harmonize initiative and obedience, charisma and institutions, mortification and an integration of human values, rules and freedom, prayer and action, rationalism and mysticism—was not all of this terribly presumptuous? Were you an engaging conversationalist, for instance, like Juan de Valdés? Where along the graph between Renaissance optimism and Lutheran pessimism do you place your anthropology? Did you not go from someone who was marginal to being a highly placed man of influence; from a hippie-type vagabond to being a pillar of the establishment, and from a layman to a religious? Which do you prefer: affirming or fighting, persuading or imposing? What did you expect to be the more profitable, personal experience or books, life or the world of ideas? Do you really believe in the freedom of man or do you think that "all is grace"? Were you not tempted to pride, knowing you were able to exert more weight throughout Europe and the world than Francis I of France, Henry VIII of England, and your friends Pope Paul III and Pope Julius III? Do you think that all questions can be resolved by scientific knowledge and that in the last analysis it is education that will solve the world's problems, or do you think that man has need of a cure that is radical and that being cured means more than having knowledge? You were so silent about such questions; you refused to become involved in critical debate. Why? Was it that you expected so little from culture? Why did you think less about biblical philology and the sweet quest for manuscripts and their different versions than you did about the internal dispositions of the one who read the Bible and about seeking out people to catechize along the roadsides and streets? Do you honestly think that culture and education are necessary shortcuts for arriving at the *philosophia Christi?* Under the pretext of "helping souls," did you not attempt to dominate the consciences of others? And your desire to serve, is this not a mask for ambition and power? Are you not a man of enslaving authority? What were you really—a *ganz soldatisch* person or an unsparing, sensitive companion-guide? Did you seek to liberate the individual by giving up the idea of transforming structures, or did you seek to change the structures and sacrifice the individual in the process? Were you drawn toward the *elite* or toward society? Did you put too much of a premium on success and efficiency? Do you ever think the end justifies the means? Was and is your work essentially bourgeois?

25

"The Adventure of
a Poor Christian"

Questions, judgments, questions. Words, words, words. Forms, questionnaires, graphs, polls, and projections. All for the satisfaction of our complacent rationalizations . . . It could well be that the bewildered interviewee would not answer any of our questions. Perhaps the only thing he would give us would be cold silence; not the silence of someone who did not want to answer, but the silence of one who felt dismayed by so much complex artificiality, by so many trick questions or questions asked from such a strange point of view. Medieval? He had never heard that word; it had not been invented during his lifetime. He was simply someone who was born in 1491, on the eve of the discovery of America, and who died at the time Charles V was renouncing his imperial crown and his vast dominions. He was simply a man who cared not the slightest bit about quarrels and the manners of the times, at least not those that had nothing to do with the faith. He was a man like so many other of his contemporaries who lived during a muddled period of history that was so passionate, so heroic, so torn apart, so rich in the names of men and women who have left their imprints on the subsequent history of Western civilization. In his youth, he had been indistinguishable from millions of other Europeans; he only became different, original, and even singular after "he stopped to think," and this led him to cross an invisible frontier that the majority of the human race never crosses. Then, he started on his way; in part, it was a very old way, but in part it was also a personal and new way, like those small, all but imperceptible paths that the beasts and other animals create along the mountain sides in his native land, paths his people name with the sweet-sounding word, *bidaxka* (little trail). With a blind faith in the future, the faith of another Abraham, he left his own country and followed this little pathway, uncertain but determined, not knowing where it would lead him. He was *obstinate*, as Herman Hesse defines the term, that is, obedient only to the law of one's inner calling, but Ignatius never understood that sentiment as something that he possessed, rather, as something that possessed him, or more exactly, as that Someone who leads us we know not where.

At heart, he was perhaps a lonely, solitary man, even though he was always surrounded by a constellation of friends, followers, and people sympathetic to what he said and did. And he had his share of enemies, too, but he never let his heart be invaded by hatred toward those Christians, false and official, who persecuted him. His basic impulse was not against anyone or anything. Rather, he had an obsession to help, awaken, and liberate people, not with beautiful theories, fine-sounding ideas, or seductive schemes, but with the simple, down-to-earth, demanding-a-commitment *quid agendum*, "what ought I to do." He had no time to think about questions we find important or diverting. He had enough to keep himself busy at each moment. He had questions he posed to himself in all types of situations and events, at the intersection of mighty highways, or where humble footpaths crossed. They were questions about coming to a decision, after having long thought out the pros and cons, when the Spirit did not speak with sufficient clarity, that same spirit who had once guided him through the capricious steps of a mule, through the will of a group, or through the episodic misadventures aboard Venetian ships. Initially, he had only the force of his poor and unpolished word, and this he did not proclaim in either a stentorian voice or in the harsh accents of a commander, but he whispered it to each soul, as all of his true followers testified. He conquered for the good through his quiet contagious influence. Lucretius had already said it: "One torch lights another." During the course of the year 1521–1522, Ignatius was dreaming in Loyola at the same time Luther was dreaming in Wartburg and Erasmus in Louvain. Each one of these three knew what it meant to be marginal among those close to him, and each one of them fostered a distinct type of rebellion. All three fought against the emptiness of the Christianity of their day. "The only thing that remains Christian today is the name." Loyola said this, but it could also have been said by either Erasmus or Luther. All three felt deeply about the shambles into which the Church had fallen, but Ignatius reacted with neither criticism nor whimpering, and this he did out of a sense of decency and out of what he considered manliness. Decency, because one did not display the family's dirty laundry from the balcony, neither the dirty linen of his Loyola family nor his larger family, the Church. Manliness, because a real man should not cry over dirty laundry, nor should he cast it aside. What he should do is clean it. In other words, Ignatius believed he should *act* to remedy the situation in the Church. He began by acting on himself; next, he would act on the flesh and blood men and women he came in contact with; and finally, he would act in the temporal and geographical space that our activities can reach, and this space is always much larger than we think or can see.

Everything else was purely consequential, bends along the road. We are asked no more than to know how to stand face to face before every individual person, before the ever-growing circumstances of life, and we must accept the fact that whatever we encounter is impregnated with an inevitable historical dimension, and we even have to learn to accept that the impossible desire for absolute purity degenerates to some extent. In other words, we must be realists: we must work with what we have and work for what we can do. The important thing is to work. Even as he worked in view of eternity, Ignatius gave to his work the obvious signs of his time, the limitations and the stamp of all historicity, this feature for whose discovery and evaluation one needs a larger perspective than the one allowed by the brief span of the life of one man. The most authentic of all utopias has to be a micro-utopia, a germ or miniature utopia, if it really intends to go beyond the confines of a purely sterile dream. Life is a modest arrow in the space of history. The tip of the arrow is more important than the space it travels through because it is the tip that makes the arrow a vector, giving it a precise direction, shooting it upward or downward, at a closed or open angle.

The fact of the matter is that Ignatius did not close himself up within himself, nor did he seek anything for himself. Finishing his program, he sought everything for his work because the things we would never wish for ourselves we wish for what we love. Humbly, Ignatius continued the journey along his way, without undue plans, pledges, or methods—"we have stumbled along." By this time, he was followed by many who were "ready for everything," even persecution. Six months after his death, the Cistercian monk Luis Estrada, one of his most enthusiastic admirers, made an inventory of the first attacks launched against the members of the Society. "Some," he said, "persecute them because they say they are introducing innovations; others say that they very arrogantly attribute to themselves the name of Jesus; still others grieve because they do not dress like friars. There are also those who find fault in them because they do not sing the canonical hours in choir. There are still others who criticize them because they are too much involved with the people, while others complain that they have grown too fast in a very short time." Then, referring to Ignatius, he concluded: "That little man of God (*aquel hombrecito de Dios*) had the patience to suffer all of these things." A beautiful, concise definition of what was coming to an end, the closing of "the adventure of a poor Christian." The pathway, trod now by so many feet, had been mapped out: *Via quaedam*, as the papal bull that had approved the Society expressed it, "A particular way." It was one way among many others, a way that passed through Ethiopia, Brazil, Japan, Germany; a way that made its inroads through the ducal palace of Gandía, the court of John III of Portugal, penetrating the lecture halls or porters' lodges of any number of colleges, and through the kitchen of Santa Maria della Strada, Our Lady of the Way, in Rome.

26

The Final Stage

This way was now to be the way for others, no longer for Ignatius because his own personal way was coming to an end. By the beginning of 1556, his health had shown considerable decline. He made a real effort not to show that he was suffering from pain and poor health, but perhaps old Father Diego de Eguía, who was to die very shortly thereafter, was right when he said that it was a miracle that Ignatius was still alive. He had no reason to keep on living if we understand by this a reason for accomplishing a particular goal, finishing some basic personal task. His gallstone attacks became more persistent and to these were added constant low-grade fevers. By January, he could no longer say Mass. His few hours of sleep were interrupted by a whole variety of physical ailments, and he took his meals in bed. He would spend a few hours working in the late afternoons of those days when the pain subsided, preoccupied by a whole raft of problems, among which were the apostasy of Ceylon, the Turkish menace, the Protestant world, some touchings-up on the Constitutions, and problems that resulted from implementing the Constitutions, the economic problems of a number of houses, the sick throughout the Society, setting up the German Province and the College of Ingolstadt, England's return to the Catholic Church, a college of Jerusalem, the purchase of good sets of type so that a printing press could be installed in the Roman house (this press would soon publish an Ethiopian edition of the New Testament), the purchase of a number of houses around the Roman College so that an expansion program could get under way, collecting testimonies favorable to the Society in order to counterattack the bitter decrees published by the Theology Faculty of the University of Paris, the advisability of having the language of each house the same as the language of the country, the problem of two of his *primi patres*: Bobadilla's lack of interest in matters of the Society and Rodrigues's recalcitrancy. Ignatius was involved in all these matters, and he continued to dictate letters—some seven hundred during these last few months of his life—addressed to such diverse places as Ferrara, Cologne, Clermont, Naples, Sicily, Spain, Trieste, England, Ethiopia. In one of these missives, addressed to the secretary of the imperial chancellery, Alejo Fontana, he commented soberly on Charles V's recent abdication of the imperial crown and on his renunciation of all his political power, a piece of news that had shaken up the whole of Europe. Charles, he wrote, "courageously divested himself of such great estates because he was not able to support their weight, and he was not able to hold onto the dignity and the office as monarch without holding the responsibility. This is a rare example that few will imitate, although many should." Was this a veiled allusion to the octogenarian Paul IV? No one can say, of course. At any rate, Ignatius continued to support weight, dignity, and responsibility, his last letter being dated July 23, eight days before his death.

At the beginning of July he decided to leave Santa Maria della Strada, which was situated in the middle of the city. He turned over the governance of the Society to Fathers Cristóbal de Madrid and Juan de Polanco. He wanted to face the dog days of the Roman summer in the small country house, informally called "The Vineyard," that belonged to the Roman College and was situated near the Antonine baths. The country air and the green surroundings seemed to improve his health, although that improvement proved to be illusory. After Saint James's Day, July 25, he returned to his old place of residence and it was here that he would end his long earthly journey. Perhaps he had a presentiment of his oncoming death at this time. At any rate, something was beginning to fail in that solid oak of a man because on the twenty-ninth, he asked to see the doctor, who was more worried about Laínez and some of the other sick ones in the house. But from that moment on, the state of his health took an unexpected and precipitous turn, and one can read in the letters that came out of Rome that announced the news of his death an unmistaken sense of surprise, shock, and even a certain hint of deception. Deprived of the "loving presence" of the one who could have successors but no substitutes, his followers were possessed by a strange sensation of sadness without pain, and they shed tears mixed with devotion, hope, and serene joy. But the "old saint," as he was referred to in one of these letters, left them without their realizing he was going. Such is the fate of those who are always sick—it seems that they will ever be so because they are shameless in the way they always seem to overcome their illnesses with a great surge of strength.

Rome was under the sway of the *ferragosto*, the deadly, suffocating heat of August. To add to this torment, one medical man prescribed for his illness the customary remedy that was in vogue during that period. All the windows in his rooms were closed tight, and mountains of blankets were piled on top of him. The effect was that he perspired even more than he ordinarily would have and was thereby weakened even further. By the time another doctor changed this treatment, took away some of the blankets, and ventilated the room, it was too late. Ignatius, who was a very gentle nurse while caring for the sick, was also a most obedient patient who submitted himself, *perinde ac cadaver*, "as a dead body," to medical prescriptions. Silent and discrete right up until his death, he asked the infirmarian if he could speak with Polanco in private. It was about four o'clock on the afternoon of July 30 when Polanco responded to his call; Ignatius gave him an alarming mission. He wanted Polanco to go to Paul IV and tell him that he, Ignatius, "was near the end and almost without hope of temporal life," and he asked for the pope's blessing for himself and for Father Laínez, who was also in danger of death. It was a grand gesture. At that very time, the Romans were bustling about in preparation for the most absurd war that was ever conjured up by any pope, for it was a war against no less a person than Philip II. The duke of Alba was poised at Naples, ready to attack, while in the Eternal City the people relived the memories of the dreadful sack of Rome that had taken place in 1527. Now, at the present date, Paul IV was pope, the same man who had ordered Santa Maria della Strada searched in a vain attempt to discover nonexistent arms to supply Philip's troops. This papal gesture may not have been designed to awaken the hope of men who lived there and inspire them with a tender love for the pope, but in no way did it affect the deep faith of Ignatius in him who was the vicar of Christ. Ignatius's last request was a kind of official statement of his affirmation to "the true spouse of Christ our Lord, our holy Mother, the hierarchial Church," and to the one who, in spite his cold treatment and reserve toward Ignatius, represented the Church.

For once in his life, Ignatius was now in a hurry, and he stressed his request with words that were frightening for a man who was accustomed to weigh every word he said, never saying a needless syllable: "I am in such a bad way that the only thing I can do is die." Unbelievably, the faithful Polanco did not take these words very seriously, thinking that Ignatius was exaggerating his state of health. Moreover, the mail courier was leaving for Spain that very day and Polanco had to get a large packet of correspondence ready for the trip. He therefore told Ignatius that he would take care of the matter the next day, and he was not impressed by the strange insistence of the sick man. "I would prefer today, rather than tomorrow," Ignatius replied, "or at least as soon as possible, but do what you think best. I place myself entirely in your hands." Polanco consulted with the doctor, was reassured that there was no reason to fear, and so he decided to put off fulfilling Ignatius's request until the next day. Thus, without anyone else realizing what was taking place, Ignatius remained alone before death, silent and resigned. We have already mentioned that he himself left us an account of his feelings on the three other occasions when he thought he was facing death. At Manresa in 1522, he had been bothered by thoughts of vainglory as he considered the eremetical life that he had been leading. In 1535, when he felt in danger of drowning during the perilous crossing from Valencia to Genoa, he experienced a great peace of soul combined with considerable confusion because of his poor use of the gifts he had been given. And finally, in Rome in 1550, he told us that the prospect of facing death had brought him immense joy and spiritual consolation. Now, as death really stood before him, he covered his feelings with silence. He simply put himself in the hands of God, the pope, and the will of others. He renounced his own will and desires.

That same evening, favored by those hours of mysterious improvement that sometimes come just before death, Ignatius seemed to have a better appetite and spoke with his companions. He then retired for the night. Brother Giovanni Tommaso Cannizzaro, the fifteen-year-old infirmarian whose bed was next to Ignatius's, noticed he was a bit agitated and then he became quiet. The brother heard him groaning occasionally. Like some people who are on the point of death, did Ignatius repeat the first words he had learned in Basque? Did he anxiously call out for his mother, whose face had remained so vague? In his delirium did he say the word of his dreams, Jerusalem? We know one expression he repeated, the most universal, potentially personal, and untransferable of all: *"Ay, Dios! Jesús."* It was a groaning, a supplication; an expression of abandonment, supreme surrender, and hope.

During the first visit after dawn, the fathers found Ignatius at the point of death. Polanco rushed off immediately to the Vatican to accomplish what he had been asked to do the previous afternoon. He returned with the papal blessing, but Ignatius had died about seven o'clock in the morning with the same sentiments as those expressed by Saint Teresa of Avila, who said on her deathbed: "At last, I die as a daughter of the Church." Dying is something as easy as living, as natural as the daily spectacle that men present and that Ignatius described to us in so peaceful a way in the "Contemplation on the Incarnation" in the *Spiritual Exercises*. He asks the retreatant to picture the great diversity of men on earth: "some are white, some are black; some at peace, some at war; some weeping, some laughing; some well, some sick; *some coming into the world, and some dying.*" Ignatius died a death stripped of all its trappings. He died alone, without theater, without the tears of companions at his bedside, without naming a vicar, without putting the definitive finish on the *Constitutions*, without bestowing blessings or final bits of advice, without transports or miracles, without sacraments, without the papal blessing, without having the final ritual prayers said for his soul. He died "in the common way," as one witness noted with consternation.

An autopsy was made on his corpse. Stones and more stones were found; these mute witnesses to his hidden sufferings appeared in the liver, kidneys, lungs, and even in one of the main arteries. After four centuries, the autopsy on his soul is not yet finished. Oh, and his feet! If the feet of Goethe were as delicate and beautiful as those of a maiden, the feet of Ignatius were covered with callouses hardened by so many European roads that took him "to help souls." This was a pilgrim who walked his way "alone and on foot."

The death mask, the hastily made postmortem portrait, the burial of his small corpse, the General Congregation and its problems that followed on the heels of his death, the scant number of professed fathers, the nomination of his successor, the future beatification and canonization processes, the splendid altar in the grandiose Roman church of the Gesù, Bernini's sculpture, the grand church of Sant'Ignazio, the development of colleges and missions, the plans of Paul IV, and those of kings and princes, the magnificent basilica at Loyola, the praises, attacks, and tremendous trials of the Society—all of these were things for those he left behind. As he arrived at the end of his way, Ignatius was leaving behind in his wake a contagious enthusiasm, a pattern of life, a treasury of hopes, the certainty that God had guided him and had accomplished all. In other words, Ignatius was leaving behind him the Society of Jesus.

Christianity, recovered and bled white,
learned from you the strength of forgetting lamentation.
A. Hernández Carratalà

Index